July 2008

If you read The first three
chapters — This is what I
experienced as a boy & young man.

Recollections in
Tranquility

— gone with The wind
& good riddance!

Recollections in Tranquility

A Sequel to Immigrants' Son

Richard Joseph O'Prey

To order additional copies of this book, contact:
Xlibris Corporation
1-888-795-4274
www.Xlibris.com
Orders@Xlibris.com
42097

Contents

Dedication

I dedicate this book and the concomitant efforts of writing, editing, proofreading to my patient wife Mary; to my understanding children, Brendan, his wife Christine Jolly and their two children Michael Thomas and Megan Andrea; to Katherine and her husband Kaih Fuller and their daughter Shannon Helen; and to Maureen and her husband Nick Daily and their son Seamus Patrick. I do so in the hope that they and any future progeny may know their roots, heritage, and cultural influences more intimately through the written word since this is my major motivation for undertaking the task of creating *Recollections in Tranquility*. I also dedicate this book to the great men of the Brothers of the Christian Schools who forged my character, influenced my judgment, and led me to an appreciation of God, country and my fellow man. For this cadre of extraordinary men, especially Brother Bertrand Leo Kirby, FSC, I am especially in eternal debt for playing a significant role second only to my biological parents in nurturing me through my formative years.

Acknowledgement

To those who shared my religious formation in triumph and trial and always maintained a sense of humor; to the extraordinary educators who taught with me and lived with me in community sharing my convictions or tolerating my eccentricities; to the parishioners, parents and students who influenced my social and racial attitudes, teaching me far more than I instructed them; to the associates in BOCES whose example of dedication in the face of opposition I respected and admired; to the support and love of my wife and children who made my family a joy and cherished replacement for my loss of community in religious life; and to all those lifelong friends I made along the way, I avidly acknowledge their contributions to a life that has been reflectively joyful. Each, wittingly or not, played a substantial role in making it easy to reflect in tranquility and realize that I led a life of contentment through the blessings of God. To all through this acknowledgement, I express my deepest gratitude.

Introduction

Perhaps the greatest distinction I had from my peers from the Irish American enclave in Washington Heights was my experiences in the Brothers of the Christian Schools. Certainly those who grew up with me on Haven Avenue in that neighborhood in upper Manhattan generally took a different direction from the one I chose. My recollections of my life in religious training in high school, the Novitiate, and four years of the Scholasticate have left me with fond memories. Many humorous events crowd the conversation when my group mates and I get together. To assess what effects my formative years have had is a more difficult task. While I can readily recognize the influences that made me the individual seeking a life in a religious community, I have a more complicated task determining the degree my religious formation may have had in how I approach people, problems, events, circumstances, family, religion and a host of other variables. In the coming chapters, I shall try to be as honest as my memory permits. For the sake of objectivity, while maintaining the integrity of what I write, I have altered the names and descriptions of some of the individuals I cite. If I upset anyone for any reason, I apologize, but insist that my recollections are essentially my own and not necessarily shared by any who viewed the same circumstances.

I do know that when I started teaching as a Christian Brother, I had absorbed many of the LaSallian traditions and techniques, honed and refined over three hundred years on many continents and adapted to many cultures. I also know that in my last assignment as a teacher, I had to challenge much of what I had to that point believed. I am especially grateful to the students and families of that parish, St. Augustine's on Franklin Avenue in the Bronx, for making me, for better or worse, the person I am today. They were as much a formative force to me as my religious community.

Some persons create monuments in steel or stone. Some dedicate their lives and fortunes to science or to technology to improve society or even promote crime. Some become artists or sculptors, ceramics designers, or even environmental manipulators. Some pursue the stage or movies, television, or the recording industry as entertainers. History and law attract their own audience as well as those whose avid reading marks them as virtual addicts. Others dedicate their talents to amass wealth, status symbols, or fame, prestige, or material goods. While I share some trace of all these ambitions, my personal compulsion is to write.

Like the artist with no sense of color or composition, or the musician with a tin ear and no talent, I may be the writer who has little concept of style, and my ideas may be banal. As the artist or poet usually doesn't design his work for any particular audience, but defines his creativity as a response to an internal drive, so too do I. If questioned about the individuals or targeted readers for my work, I am in a quandary to identify any specific group. I would like to think that my family, friends, and associates might find my thoughts interesting, but I do not expect many others to share their enthusiasm. Even among my intended readers, I might find disinterest or even criticism. Nonetheless, I have an internalized drive that urges me to define my thoughts and impressions, my opinions and judgments in a printed format. In the response to this urge and at the suggestion of many who have read my memoir and essay entitled **Immigrants' Son,** I begin this task without any hesitation.

As most of you may recognize, **Recollections in Tranquility** is borrowed from the poet William Wordsworth who defined poetic emotion in those terms. The primary focus of this volume is the recollection of my training in the religious life and the experiences I had as a member of the Brothers of the Christian Schools. I lived with these men in religious community life and began my professional teaching career among them as well. The humor, dedication, and creativity of my fellow religious sparkled with the joy of consequential achievement in those early years as a neophyte teacher. Many mistakes in procedure and in performance evoked the sympathetic advice of my fellow teachers. Those years contrast with the twenty-nine years I spent in public education as well as the opportunities I had to teach in community colleges. Furthermore, my reflections of my life as a husband and a father to three children are also germane to the text. Incidental memories about my travel adventures are also considered.

The subjects of this book represent my past, distant and recent. My ruminations or recollections are more of a compendium of the thoughts of Richard O'Prey. The author has distinguished himself

for paltry achievements during his three score years and som..
point to no major success, outstanding accomplishment, or fame
along the path of life. Neither can I find any major catastrophic
failures in the typical pursuits of mankind. I paid my bills and earned
money to feed, house, and educate my family. No institution or
charity knows me as a major contributor. No police records note
indiscretions or felonies, misdemeanors or indictments. My only
scrape with the law occurred in a speed trap in central Florida when
an Officer Brady cited me for driving ten miles above the limit in
Citrus at 6:00am.

Although I spent fifteen years among the Brothers of the
Christian Schools, I can recall with pride some of my contributions
to that religious order, to the students I taught, and to the confreres
who shared our training and our work. If I had remained among
them, perhaps I might have done something in the academic world
or missionary life to make differences to the people with whom I
had contact. Instead, I chose to leave for very personal reasons at
a very trying time in my life and search for a lifelong partner in a
quest for happiness. I did achieve that when I married my wife. Our
love produced three wonderful offspring who became the focus of
our lives. In order to care for them, I taught under very difficult
circumstances for an additional thirty years. My professional teaching
career in the public sector brought no sterling recognition or for
that matter, many pleasant memories.

Within BOCES our admission standards accepted those students
whose sponsoring districts chose not to deal with them for one
reason or another. Some had behavioral issues that threatened the
peaceful progress of education. Among these might be numbered
pyromaniacs and those who carried dangerous weapons, or
threatened specific students or faculty members. Others suffered
from an aversion to discipline or daily attendance in standard classes,
often accompanied by substance abuse issues. Among some districts
interested in maintaining high standards or outstanding achievement
levels, administrators shuttled off those whose poor performance
dragged down test averages or college admissions and warehoused
them in BOCES. In truth, many of our students benefited from the
administrative change or needed the special adaptations permitted
within special education. This was particularly evident among the
physically handicapped or the mentally challenged.

Without any accolades or acclaim, I performed my tasks of supervising and instructing children with special needs. Little encouragement, or for that matter, little criticism dogged my steps in the classroom. I perceived very minor appreciation or achievement, yet I have no regrets for my actions. My family has more than compensated me for any personal sacrifice I made on their behalf. For that reason, I follow their encouragement and begin this labor of love.

Encouraged by the modest success of my first literary attempt, **Immigrants' Son**, I attempt to supplement this essential prequel with a work that I initially hesitated to undertake. For a number of reasons, I dreaded doing a disservice to some of the people who have meant so much to me. Advised by friends to write from my heart and from my mind, I dare undertake this task at the risk of offending some unintentionally. Aware that my assessments and conclusions are the product of my own experience, I am fully conscious that few began where I did and even fewer ended up with my experience. With that in mind, I offer my commentary as an individual's conclusions and are in no way meant to serve as generalizations. If my thoughts appear unique only in their application to myself, I make no apology for that. My confreres may differ with my interpretations, with my portrayals, or with my deductions. That is the prerogative of the critical reader, a role I insist I adopted for myself in my lifetime.

Within my personality I acknowledge a propensity for criticism which I identify as synonymous with intelligent analysis. Trained as a historian and personally nurtured through religious exercises like examination of conscience, my impulse is generally to identify what is wrong rather than what is right, regardless whether that is part of my life or aspects of the program for which I work. The general impression may be interpreted as negativism, but I believe it results from an honest, objective investigation of circumstances. Others may predicate 'sour grapes' as my operative principle, but I vehemently reject that description too. 'Sour grapes' is more an overlying emotional expression that eschews an intellectual basis. For that I totally plead innocent. Religious life, family life, and professional life are not compartmentalized, but complementary to my human condition. Each has influenced my character and evoked the joys and compunction of my existence.

Young men, it is said, dream dreams and they are heroes. Older men relive dreams and realize that they are heroic in some and their human foibles are exposed in others. The assurance of youth, the conviction of right and understanding, the explanation of one's motives are clear in the youthful reveries. Older men may be wiser and more skeptical of their motives, their implementations, and their assessments. Their reveries combine images of halos and clay feet as a general rule. So it is with **Recollections in Tranquility.**

Pundits and literary critics praise the terse, staccato prose of experts like Hemingway and Steinbeck. They like their direct, declarative sentences which narrate a tale in an economic efficiency of word. I am afraid my style is at variance with that preference. When I write, I respond to an internal cadence that compels me to add another word, another phrase, another clause that will satisfy my sense of rhythm, or inspirational absurdity, or humorously incongruous description. Of such is the writing of Cicero, perhaps, but not our modernists. Perhaps I never got over the classical essays of antiquity, and I unconsciously duplicate the convolutions of clauses that challenged the budding Latin scholar. In composition, however, I do not attempt to imitate anyone. Instead, I respond to that internal compulsion that seems to permeate my being when confronted by a keyboard. Let each reader be the judge of my response.

Chapter One

Barrytown

When I was fifteen in September, 1955 I made a significant lifetime adjustment entering my third year in high school. The following chapter may hold some clues as to how I ended up making that decision and the adventures that enrolling in St. Joseph's Normal Institute in Barrytown, New York provided. My overall recollection is one of joy and contentment despite whatever negative or contradictory things I may write. I can only conclude that my entrance into Barrytown was one of the most outstanding influences upon my character, but it also presented many disparate images and conclusions. Although the concept of entering a religious atmosphere at such an early age may be questioned by pundits and psychologists today, I believe they overlook some of the factors that made such a move feasible in 1955, and perhaps even advisable for some individuals. In retrospect, I would do it all over again.

When I was in the eighth grade at Incarnation School in Washington Heights, I was very interested in becoming a member of the religious order that had educated me for the previous three years. As teachers, my instructors had demonstrated an enormous interest in their students, and as advisors, had offered some valuable counsel for the future. As coaches and intramural supervisors, they offered a glimpse into their humanity and personalities that contrasted with the businesslike approach they exhibited in the classroom. Ever since I had the honor of sitting in the classroom of Brother Christopher Lucian, FSC, now Bill Callahan, I had wanted to join the organization that produced such impressive men. One of the ironies I discovered after the publication of my first book was the fact that Bill Callahan and I were actually distantly related. His great grandfather, Anthony McGurrin, and my great grandmother, Anna McGurrin, were brother and sister in Kilcummin, Mayo.

I had also been interested in offering my life in service to God somehow. Such a commitment was not unusual in the mid years of the twentieth century. Although I was attracted to the Maryknoll priests, I wasn't particularly interested in some aspects of the sacerdotal vocation. The prospect of comforting the grieving and consoling the ill made me quite uneasy with feelings of personal inadequacy. Nonetheless, when I responded to a mailing from the Friars of the Atonement at Graymore Garrison in New York, I continued to receive information from them for a number of years. The only one to take note of this correspondence was my mother. I believe she was pleased that one of her sons might enter the service of the church. I never visited Garrison, but I did visit Barrytown on Ascension Thursday when I was in the seventh grade. The grammar schools of New York City used to generate a collection of interested candidates into a bus or two for the ninety mile trip up the Hudson Valley to Red Hook, just north of Rhinebeck and south of Clavarack, New York on the eastern shore of the Hudson River. During my tenure at Barrytown, a bridge between Kingston and Rhinebeck was completed, making access via the New York State Thruway an alternative to the northbound Taconic State Parkway.

Barrytown, called St. Joseph's Normal Institute, was the religious training center for the Lasallian Christian Brothers of the New York District. The vast majority of candidates came from the grammar schools of "the City," but there were also boys from the tri-city area of Albany, Schenectady and Troy, Syracuse, Buffalo, Detroit, Newburgh, and at that time from Long Island and New England, especially Providence, Newport, and Pawtucket. Prior to buying the four hundred acre lot in Barrytown, the Brothers had training facilities at Amawalk and Pocantico Hills in Westchester. When John D. Rockefeller made a bid to buy out the Brothers to extend his land at Pocantico Hills, he made a generous offer but insisted the Brothers' graves be moved too. To facilitate that move, he provided some financial incentives.

Around 1930, the Brothers moved, lock, stock, and stiffs to the site overlooking the Hudson with Hunter Mountain in the distance. There was a late nineteenth century mansion on the property, but it had seen better days, as did some of the other buildings on the four hundred farmed acres accompanying the estate. Beyond the barns, pig sties, and chicken coops to the north was a three story wood frame house that bespoke better times in the past. It hadn't been occupied in years and showed the ravages of neglect. A more picturesque structure lay in the northeast extremity of the property. It was a solid fieldstone house, small, compact and virtually indestructible. It too was unoccupied, but it had some historical significance, at least in oral tradition. The solitary structure was said to have been a station in the Underground Railroad System prior to the Civil War. Fugitive slaves sought refuge, safety, nourishment, rest and guidance on their surreptitious trek northward to Canada.

The Brothers built a large three story red brick complex. With all due respect to Long Kesh in Northern Ireland, it had an H-Block configuration. Without any connection to men who took to the blanket in protest for their imprisonment and the nature of the institution, the only comparison in my mind is the physical structure. Barrytown's occupants were present voluntarily and most were free to leave from the Juniorate and Novitiate when they wished. Those who were compelled to stay were the Brothers who had vowed stability in the society.

On the eastern side of the complex, the Junior Novitiate was built. It housed three large dormitories: the north, the middle, and the south. Each dormitory offered modest space for approximately forty occupants, with every boy rating a bed, a wooden chair and access to what looked like school lockers. With large bathrooms, extensive sinks and drying racks, each dormitory was a self-contained living area designed specifically for sleeping and hygiene. With at least a score of shower stalls, a laundry distribution center, prefect rooms and a few minor storage areas, the top floor was primarily reserved for sleeping. Silence was indeed platinum in this area for speaking in the dorms or showers invited serious retribution.

On the second floor, a large chapel with seating capacity for one hundred fifty and a common room or study hall for the same number occupied most of the central space. The rest was devoted to a library, director's office, and a reading room, a barber shop, several academic classrooms, two additional bathrooms, and a music appreciation center. A convenient commissary where one could purchase on personal account toothpaste, shoe laces, and minor items or toiletries was located across from coat racks for suit coats, sweaters, or indoor wear. I suppose it would be accurate to describe this level of the Juniorate as predominately designed for prayer and study, two major components of our training. Separated by smoked glass doors on the South Side of the second floor, duplicate facilities for the faculty lay, but was generally off limits to the Junior Novices except for maintenance and cleaning.

The bottom floor had additional classrooms or science labs, an athletic equipment room, and utility wash rooms accurately termed 'Slop Rooms,' just as the other floors had. From these utility rooms, mops, brooms, dust rags, pails, specialized brushes, and cleaning implements emerged during manual labor periods. Our chief detergent was termed 'atomic soap,' a cleanser so powerful that it eroded several layers of the dermis upon contact with skin. Another room was specifically dedicated to an area for shining shoes. At the extremity of the easternmost structure of the entire complex at the north and south ends, two gyms equipped with full court basketball facilities occupied two and a half stories.

On the west side of the complex stood another huge central wing. At the northern end, the Novices had their dormitory rooms. Instead of a huge open dorm as in the Juniorate, each novice had what was called a cell. Each cell was actually a curtained area containing a bed, a chair, and a bureau. At the back of the dormitory, just like the Juniorate, about two dozen sinks, cabinets and mirrors as well as drying racks offered the prospect of cleaning, shaving, and brushing one's teeth. Like the Juniorate, bathrooms and showers were present on the two upper floors as well as a special room for the Brother assigned to waken the community. Since the entire community relied on him to waken them at 5:00am, he had a separate room and even a clock with an alarm. This responsibility was imposed on a single Novice for a single week on a rotating basis. Only once or twice do I recall the 'bell ringer' failing in his duties.

On the lower floors, two large auditoria occupied most of the available space. At the back of one, the Novice Director had his office with a sub-director's and a theologian's offices nearby. In this common room the Director gave spiritual conferences and conducted other such general meetings. A room where toiletries and other sundries could be purchased also was present. Since Novices had not yet taken any vows, they had to purchase items which would later be offered free as part of their vow of poverty. A few classrooms where French was taught or could be used by the Novices for recreation completed the space in the second floor.

On the bottom floor of the Novitiate, another huge auditorium stood. It was used for more ephemeral activities like assignments for daily manual labor or occasional skits or productions organized for periodic entertainment, such as St. Patrick's Day or Christmas. It was also used for choir practice and preparation for the Gregorian chant in the liturgy. As the lowest, closest to the ground position, the bottom floor also housed coats, boots and other accoutrements for outdoor work. Since a sizable number of the Novices worked among the cows, chickens, and pigs on the farm, these coat racks and boot racks took on an aroma of its own. There was also a tailor shop where Novices mended or created robes and rabattas, the ten commandment-like white plastic or vinyl collar of the Brothers' habit.

At the southern end of the building stood a section reserved for the "Ancients," or those elderly retired Brothers. Each of the Ancients had a separate room on the third floor of the Southwest wing. On the second floor, there was a section reserved for an infirmary and a common room for the Ancients' religious studies or spiritual reading. On the bottom floor of that wing, a huge laundry system with mangles, ironers and designated baskets for distribution took up the west end while the boiler for the entire complex was on the eastern side of the wing. Several storage rooms contained the soaps, toilet paper, mops, cleaning materials, and other tools of the maintenance trade. Set apart from the building was a garage that housed several cars, trucks, tractors and other vehicles associated with the institution. On the bottom level a corridor connected the Novitiate and the Ancients while another link called a cloister permitted passage between the two sections on the second or main floor.

Like a crossbar between the east and west blocks of the H shape was a central connecting unit for a hive of other activities. On the bottom floor, stood a commercial kitchen with cauldrons, pots, stoves, sinks, refrigerators, freezers, food storage rooms, wooden tables for peeling potatoes or preparing vegetables, as well as a huge vat essential for the milk pasteurizing system. On the east side of the kitchen, the Juniorate refectory or cafeteria held tables for one hundred and fifty boys and a 'High Table' for the faculty of the high school. Between kitchen and refectory functioned an efficient scullery with a huge dishwasher, deep sinks, drying tables, and the trays that entered the machine on a timed conveyor belt. Most of the sinks and tables were stainless steel and impeccably clean. On the West side of the kitchen a similar arrangement served the dining and cleaning service for the Novitiate. Between the Novitiate refectory and reserved dining area for the Ancients and several guest dining rooms, a corridor connected the east and west blocks.

Above the refectory was a huge chapel for the entire community. Its high vaults and stain glass images from the life of St. La Salle were the primary decorative touches. Although the chapel was used for the religious activities of the Novices and the Ancients, it also served as venue for the daily Mass, Sunday Vespers and Compline, or the prayer hours of the church, and occasional Benediction. The chapel soared above the space reserved for the second and third floors of the central complex. The front façade offered an elevated statue of St. La Salle. There were also statues of the Blessed Mother and St. Joseph. Within the chapel walls, the entire community was served by a priest whose best description must encompass the word 'curmudgeon.'

Pop Carroll, as we called him, was a retired military chaplain who had served at West Point for a number of years. His military experience affected his mode of shepherding the flock of religious within the confines of his parish. He was rather elderly, somewhat infirm, and definitely deaf. Going to confession to him was an ordeal that only the saintly could describe with equanimity. Pop would slide open the door to the penitent and shove his hearing aid into the penitent's mouth. Unfortunately, Pop couldn't distinguish between the words charity and chastity, nor could he speak in a tone that didn't go beyond a few dozen pews. Many a red-faced individual left the confessional, shriven for transgressions he hadn't committed. Pop also verbalized an injunction against those who sought spiritual counsel but claimed no mortal sin on their immortal souls. Evidently only potential damnation qualified the penitent to disrupt Pop for confession before daily Mass. I suppose that left his clientele to the scrupulous and the self-confessed evil. During Mass, Pop was accustomed to whipping the altar linens at stray insects that he identified as "Protestant flies." His military experience also dictated that he summarily dismiss any altar boys whose shoes were not shined to his specifications.

Apparently, the administrators were well aware of Pop's outrageous standards and demands. A tall, thin 'Ancient' by the name of Brother Adrien Ephraim was the head sacristan, and he always maintained a staff whose primary responsibility seemed to placate the irascible cleric. A virtual 'Pop Chamberlain' was nominated to satisfy his requirements or instantaneously replace any miscreants who did not rise to Pop's standards or had unconsciously violated one of his liturgical precepts which were known only to himself. In the group ahead of us, Brother Stephen Olert was always prepared to jump into the fray and replace any altar server who might have offended our celebrant. I remember one particular occasion when a Novice who was especially noted for his piety and deep recollection accidentally picked up the table linen cloth along with the mantle used to hold the monstrance during Benediction. As he tried to wrap the errant cloth around Pop Carroll's shoulders, our officiator noticed the *faux pas,* and exiled the perpetrator to wherever those sacrilegious offenders are banished. Brother Steve Olert rushed to the rescue both of Pop and the offender within seconds and had one sedated and the other assured of a place in heaven for the savagely misjudged. In my group, I think Brother Vincent Smith inherited this role requiring tact, diplomacy, liturgical knowledge, and imagination. Those serving Pop must have achieved a level of sanctity they weren't aiming for.

Perhaps Pop Carroll's finest hour was the occasional funeral for one of the departed Ancients. As the deceased was wheeled on a catafalque into the chapel for The Mass for the Dead, he used to brace the six Brothers selected to serve as pallbearers. Pop would review the pallbearers as a general might inspect his prize brigade. After having us snap to attention and then coordinate our inexperienced martial skills, he would lead us into the chapel with his cadence of "left, left, left." After the funeral Pop would lead the procession to one of the most beautiful spots in all Barrytown, if not the upper Hudson Valley. There the Brothers would be laid to rest with their "heads to the hills." Part of Pop's graveside homilies used to be quite amusing although we dared not smile at his prayers. He usually began the obsequies with "In the Name of . . . ." and he would pause dramatically as each listener began the Sign of the Cross. Then he would complete his introductory sentence with "Brother Leo" and the mourners would scratch noses, or pluck their hair or do something to abort the Sign of the Cross. On one occasion when a relatively young Brother who had a number of relatives in attendance died, Pop Carroll chose to deliver a homily that rivaled Jonathan Edward's sermon on a sinner in the hands of an angry God. Pop chose as his theme the lukewarm or tepid religious. I often wondered what that poor Brother's siblings and their children made of Pop's outrageous remarks.

On the whole, the physical plant and the huge buildings of the central complex reminded my seventh grade imagination of the Police Recreation Center in Tannersville, New York where my family went on vacation a few times. Like many other resorts in the Borscht circuit or hotels in the Jewish Alps across the Hudson, what was inside was far from the evident. To the émigrés from urban congestion, the bucolic scene and components offered a splendid view that was hardly a deterrent for entering religious life.

The grounds surrounding the main building were diverse and attractive to the visitor too. Outside the Juniorate section extended two complete baseball fields which morphed into a football field or soccer or Gaelic Football pitch. For those from the asphalt streets of New York and the concrete housing on all sides, the athletic fields appeared like the Elysian Fields. We had exchanged dodging automobiles, clanging fire escapes and glass strewn lots for genuine playing surfaces. To the south of the building, lay four outdoor basketball courts with metal nets. In the center of the courts, two potential tennis courts were also occasionally used. Beyond the paved courts and down a small hill, several handball courts also offered recreational options. Many times at that location Sam Schaefer and I used to play fastball with a tennis ball and broomstick with a target box for strikes. At the northern edge of the playing fields, a picnic grove with tables and tall pines to provide shelter and shade offered the prospect of a pleasant visit on those few days when our families were invited to visit us.

In the spring and fall, we also had a cross country course that took us past the fields above the pond where we played hockey in the winter. The track followed the path where the barns and pig sties were. It circled around the chicken coop and looped past what would later be a swimming pool. The track crossed alongside the entrance to the beautiful cemetery with the huge RIP cross. On the back side of the track, a runner would pass the root cellar, Strawberry Walt's rows of luscious fruit, and Ollie Joe's vegetable garden. Brother Walter cultivated huge rows of strawberries and cantaloupes which we occasionally plucked before their projected harvest in the time honored tradition of feeding the hungry. Brother Oliver Joseph was noted for his sanctity, prayer life, and silence. His reveries with God and his labor in the fields recalled a different kind of monasticism than we envisioned. Ollie Joe had emigrated from France and in his retirement years, he worked harder than anyone else tending a garden that served the community. I don't think anyone attempted to harvest what he hadn't sowed in Ollie Joe's garden, for we all counted on his testimony on our personal judgment day.

On the west side of the building beyond the Novitiate and the Ancients and the mansion which was also reserved for family visits in inclement weather, another series of ball fields and basketball courts were reserved for the cloistered Novices. Nearby was another complex for chickens that provided poultry and eggs for the community. On the northern side of the buildings stood a grove of tall pine trees with picnic benches, outdoor grotto and Stations of the Cross, and statues of St. Michael the Archangel and St. Patrick. Two enormous copper beech trees introduced the Novices to an area where contemplation and communion with nature were quite accessible, especially in June when cultivated roses entwined among the stone Stations of the Cross.

My first impression of Barrytown when I saw it in 1952 was very awesome. Not only did the buildings remind me of vacation hotels in the Catskills, but the athletic facilities were far more appealing than any I knew in Washington Heights. Having a farm with huge boars, sows, piglets, dairy cows and calves, an enormous bull, countless chickens, and barnyard denizens from the farm impressed the "gossoon" who had spent some time on an Irish farm. Spacious pastures, hillside vineyards, vegetable gardens, fodder for silage and nearby orchards were far from the typical environment I recognized on the urban streets like Haven Avenue.

In comparing the Barrytown compound to the vacation resorts in the Borscht circuit, I apparently overlooked the significant distinctions between the two. The famed Jewish comedians and performers in the Jewish Alps had their counterparts in the cards, the wits, and the wags from the streets and parishes of New York City. Barrytown offered its own brand of humor. Some called it "local' humor, which demanded insider knowledge and associations among the people who lived there. Perhaps, some disgruntled individuals would cite cuisine as a contrast between the two groups. Although Barrytown didn't keep kosher, as they did in the Catskills, the meals also served some contrast. It did take some experimentation and adaptation to grow accustomed to the institutional foods served on the tables. Nobody starved in Barrytown, nor did individuals grow fat. In my own case, in my first six months at Barryburg, I burned off fifty to sixty pounds of baby fat. To describe myself as 'pudgy plus' upon arrival may have been an understatement, but hunger wasn't so much a factor as a controlled diet with little access to candy, ice cream, and soda was.

The major contrast between the Borscht Circuit and Barrytown was very obvious. One was a resort where pleasure and entertainment were imperatives. The other was essentially a religious environment where concepts like "mortification, self-denial, and personal sacrifice," replaced sybaritic indulgence. Indulgence in Barrytown concerned an acquisition of grace and insurance against eternal punishment, not personal pleasure.

Another self-evident contrast between the Jewish resorts and Barrytown immediately comes to mind. While the Jewish resorts in the Catskills had a mixture of male and female clientele, Barrytown was almost totally male. The absence of females was certainly in keeping with the monastic tradition of celibacy and vows of chastity. Perhaps what may be startling is how thoroughly the complex was male oriented. On the grounds, a few young females lived. The chef named Bob and his wife had a daughter who lived in a beautiful stone carriage house down by the Barrytown train station. The picturesque setting and the distance from the main building insured their privacy and that they would seldom be seen. In fact, in my three years on the property, I can't recall ever seeing either Bob's wife or his daughter. The head of the farm, Ed Klum also had a wife and daughter who lived in a wood frame house above the pond where we played hockey. The poor young lass was baptized Clementine Klum. Rarely, she might be seen walking off the grounds by the road toward Red Hook. Whenever we were playing on the ball fields, she never appeared. For all practical purposes, the families of the chef and the farm man weren't calculated as denizens of Barrytown. Only one female had a daily presence. She was Josie Pender, a registered nurse who took care of the elderly Brothers, coordinated periodic visits from the "third best horse doctor in all Dutchess County," and assessed the minor ailments of the other Brothers who sought some relief in the Infirmary in the Holy Family wing, as the Ancients' community was termed.

The void of girls and women in the daily life at Barrytown is what might be expected in a male monastery. Their absence, however, left a lacuna or a gap in the social development, especially of the high school students who lived there. Sensitivity, social graces, *savoir faire,* and just the ordinary evolution of relating to the opposite sex were never addressed. For those who might leave, they would have to develop these skills and techniques using whatever devices they might discover through their families or friends. In my opinion anyway, having no sisters or entering the community before I had any serious relationship with a female, I tended to place the fair sex on a pedestal and was oblivious to some of the standard ploys or wiles they might employ. I only started this stage of my maturation when I entered my thirtieth year and had left religious life.

Of course, another distinction between the Borscht Circuit and Barrytown was the role of religion. We were in Barrytown to hone our characters according to Christian principles. We were supposed to develop a close relationship with almighty God through prayer, mortification, meditation, the Mass, sacraments, spiritual reading, and counsel. Such exercises called for discipline and mental acumen as well as physical self-denial. While the resorts offered pleasure as their chief commodity, Barrytown offered character and spiritual values.

The tenure in Barrytown varied according to the individual. Many came and left after a short period of adjustment. Some stayed on the property for five years, having persevered for four high school years and the single fifteen months of Postulancy and Novitiate. Memories and recollections are as disparate as the individuals who arrived at the monastery steps. Some found the discipline too demanding, the schedule too stifling; the cuisine too inedible; the peer relationships too unrewarding. Their memories may not be as pleasant as mine. I have heard two individuals describe their Barrytown experience in comparison to their careers in the United States Marine Corps. Both were at the Juniorate at the same time and in fact in the same class. One claimed that it was the worst experience he had undergone except for boot camp at Parris Island. The other argued that his four years at Barrytown enabled him to judge the rigors of boot camp in the marines as less challenging than his time in Barrytown. He believed his time in preparing for the religious life was instrumental in making his transition to the military easier. Another friend of mine who spent five years at Barrytown described it as the most anti-intellectual environment he had known and although he served the New York District as Vocation Coordinator, he refused to allow any of his candidates to attend the Juniorate. I can only attest to my own love of the place, the fond memories I have of my time there, the friendships I forged for life among my peers and an educational training I found very rewarding as well as fruitful. My religious development and character honing suited me well enough too.

I can't speak for others who shared my time in Barrytown, but I recognize that some may take exception to my opinions. Each individual who went to Barrytown has his own recollections and images. For some, no doubt, there are pleasant as well as painful memories. For me, however, my overwhelming recollection is one of joyful gratification.

My memories of Barrytown are associated with the four seasons. Without doubt, the bleakest season at Barrytown was winter time. With trees stripped of their foliage except for the evergreens, the fields barren of green and more likely white with snow or brown with mud, the days were shorter and darkness longer. The northern latitude and open countryside permitted the mercury to dip deeper than I was accustomed to in New York City. The frozen landscape was for the most part silent since the animals were housed in the dairy barn, the chicken houses, or pig sties. Unpredictably, my clearest recollection of winter in Barrytown is a sound rather than an image. On those nights when the thermometer hovered near zero degrees Fahrenheit, rifle shots echoed in the darkness. No ammunition was used nor firearms employed. The sharp reports, rather, were the cracks created in the frozen ice upon our skating pond. Bitter cold caused the ice to expand and contract thus causing ear-piercing shots. On some evenings when there was a full moon, our directors permitted us to go ice skating, share hot cocoa, and savor the beauty of the frigid landscape, warmed only by a huge fire. I also remember those occasions when blizzards reduced the lands to depths of several feet of snow. The accumulation had little effect on us for our classrooms, faculty, dining facilities, and religious exercises were all confined within the building complex.

Nonetheless, one item was missing. We needed the services of Pop Carroll to conduct Daily Mass. To resolve this gap, two of our farm workers were delegated to bring Pop to the chapel by driving the farm tractor to his rectory and collecting the prelate. Ed Klum was the farm factotum, and he was abetted by a man named Kurt.

Kurt generally was well insulated from the cold by his own brand of rotgut or anti-freeze. Once, as Ed drove the tractor to the chapel, as he dodged howling winds and swirling snow drifts, he never checked on his passengers. Kurt and Pop Carroll were inexplicably missing upon arrival. Backtracking his path, Ed Klum found Kurt peacefully content in his stupor, but Pop Carroll, lying atop a mound of accumulated snow, was nearly frozen to death. After retrieving the pair and Pop was thawed out, we had Mass as usual. Another sound I associate with cold nights in the Hudson Valley is the whistle of the New York Central Railroad plying its shoreline route between the City and Albany. Its plaintive wail penetrated the countryside, but bore a reminder that our homes for the most part were ninety miles directly south.

Spring was a much more cheerful time in Barrytown. Some would indulge in identifying migratory birds, but most of us enjoyed the outdoor sports that the ameliorated weather permitted. The pungent smell of onion grass was inescapable for a few weeks, and it also permeated the milk that the cows produced during this time. Spring brought baseball, softball, and track onto our recreation schedule. As the days grew longer and temperatures rose, it was tempting to reflect upon the joys of country living. My deepest recollection of the glories of spring revolves around the extensive rose bushes that adorned the grotto and outdoor Stations of the Cross. I don't remember any other decorative shrubs, but the crimson roses are clear in mind. Petty thievery of the delicious products of Strawberry Walt's rows of fruit is also another image I cherish. Sometimes we would be requested to help harvest the tomatoes or weed the vegetable gardens.

Summertime in Barrytown was a period when the trees were in total foliage and the athletic fields were in their prime. An inescapable sensory recollection of that season had to be the odor of the water fountain gushing near the tennis courts. The water pumped from beneath the surface had the smell of rotten eggs and the taste of total minerals. Perhaps in today's designer world of bottled water, it might be desirable, but then it was barely potable, and then only for those whose thirst exceeded their repugnance at the offensive olfactory experience. We had to compete with the groundhogs to maintain some personal gardens of vegetables, and each of us was asked to contribute to the mowing of the extensive fields. My most vivid and pleasant image, however, is the picture of the massive copper beech trees that led to the grotto. The trees were ideal examples of their species. In fact, it was said that representatives of the World Fair of 1939 wanted to dig up the trees and exhibit them in Flushing Meadows. Fortunately, whatever honors or contributions they offered did not move the administrators to part with the enormous, colorful trees. Summertime in Barrytown at first meant swimming in the Hudson, a mixed blessing at best. The bottom of the river felt slimy, slippery, and treacherous. Whether the water was refreshing or threatening was a choice individuals had to make. Personally, I was delighted when a pool was constructed at the northern extremity of the property near a cove where we skated in winter. Summertime also meant haying, one of the farm chores I especially enjoyed. Although the bales would scratch our forearms and challenge our muscles, the exercise and sweat were great rewards.

Autumn may have been the most rewarding of the seasons along the Hudson. The deciduous trees formed a backdrop of myriad colors during the cool evenings. One scenario I cherish in my imagination is the golden glow on a field of ripened wheat between the chicken houses and the Hudson. With a sinking sun igniting the golden grain, the rays crossing the Hudson in a radiating design, and a multi-colored Hunter Mountain in the distance, the scene is one of the prettiest I retain of my days in Barrytown. On colder nights, we could often observe the night lights of the *aurora borealis*. The beauty of the Hudson Valley at this season has been captured in an Alfred Hitchcock movie. In his presentation of **North by Northwest** starring Cary Grant and Eva Marie Saint, there is a scene of sunset along the New York Central Railroad that is a sterling example of what this time of year can offer. In my mind autumn colors, apple harvesting, and football offer a splendid example of the beauty of the setting. It was my favorite season in Barrytown.

Quite a few years ago, a number of my classmates and I were gathered in the home of the parents of one of us. Most of our parents had gone to their eternal reward by then, but this couple still enjoyed good health and vitality. As the evening wore on, our laughter grew repetitious and our stories of our time in Barrytown frequent. My friend's mother humorously interjected, "Sure, all of you had a great time, and not one of you has a job to write home about." That comment evoked laughter too, but it also stimulated some reflection. Each of us had married a remarkable woman. Each of us had children we were very proud of. Each of us might not write home about it, but we were still in related La Sallian business, as teachers, guidance counselors or school administrators. Each of us had a sense of joy and no regrets for having invested our youth in a religious formation that bore blessings beyond our anticipation. The laughter was not like the maniacal reaction of the combat officer from **Apocalypse Now** who proclaimed, "O God, I love the smell of napalm in the morning!" Rather, it was the comfort and contentment of having pursued a dream and then aligned our objectives along the path where life took us. The time invested in Barrytown seemed quite rewarding in some way while it also demanded adjustments to our customs when each of us left the religious life. If entering monastery during our high school years was deleterious to our psyches, we managed to appear quite normal and basically content with the assertion that those years were time well spent.

Chapter Two

St Joseph's Normal Institute

The Juniorate High School Years
September, 1955 to June, 1957

In trying to capture the essence of St. Joseph's Normal Institute, I pondered what rationale I might employ to justify encouraging youths from their families and home environments and training them for the religious life. After some thought, I was reminded of a comparable example from the world of sports. In 1999 the United States Soccer Association determined that they would create a special class of under seventeen years of age soccer players. The talented chosen would have regular academic classes at the Nick Bolletieri Academy in Bradenton, Florida. They would also concentrate on the skills required to be competitive among the world powers of soccer. As the opening rounds of the World cup began, the experiment seemed to have been moderately successful. Like the professional tennis players who have attended the academy, or the swimmers, golfers, gymnasts, divers, and others interested in a professional athletic career, the soccer players were willing to leave home and friends and concentrate on an intense sports curriculum in the hope that they could find a lucrative career in the sport of their choosing. Their families and the general public apparently agreed with the curriculum, concentration, and intensity of athletic instruction and practice. The reward for such concentration was the prospect of profitable bonuses or endorsement contracts that would justify the familial sacrifice. The absence of a traditional high school experience was something worth sacrificing for individual and family if the fame and/or money justified it. Few criticized the psychological or social deprivations the system imposed on its volunteers.

In a similar vein, the Junior Novitiate was designed to produce professional religious vocations. Instead of cash and public acclaim, the Junior Novice invested in his future as a teacher in the religious order of The Brothers of the Christian Schools. Of primary concern of course was the prospect of earning a respectable reward in the life hereafter rather than any notoriety here on earth. I submit that there are a number of factors that made the Junior Novitiate in Barrytown a reasonable choice between the end of World War II and the tail end of the 1960 decade. Most psychologists today would probably argue that sending teenagers off to the monastery for religious formation is stultifying and repressive. After the decade of revolution that was the sixties, I probably would agree with them. In the decade of the fifties, Catholics still enjoyed a sense of faith in God, in Church and in its representatives. Their faith in these led to approval and even encouragement for those interested in pursuing religious perfection. That enthusiasm and endorsement would soon evaporate during the cataclysmic changes to individuals, to society, to religious faith, and to the church after Vatican II.

One of the major factors that changed a reasonable alternative into a poor choice was the trends that matured in the sixties. Undoubtedly, there is a clear distinction between the sexual customs of the two periods. Prior to the sexual revolution, teenagers were generally more naive and somewhat sheltered from the changes engendered by the popular acceptance of birth control, pre-marital sex, sexual experimentation, alternate life styles, and even illegitimacy. Most of these lifestyles are more common and socially acceptable today than they were just forty years ago. That is not to allege that the modern teenager is a sexual animal with a libido run berserk. He is, however, exposed to an attitude that depicts sexual activity as the norm rather than the aberration. Those of us who grew up in the fifties recognize the challenges that face the celibate in the modern world. They contrast so intensively with the attitudes that marked our own personal teenage years. Our decision to enter religious life did not mark us as "weirdoes" or single us out in any special way. There was no stigma in entering Barrytown as a teenager, or for that matter, returning home to resume the more traditional lifestyle of the time.

In conjunction with the changes in sexual morality in more recent times, one has to acknowledge the accompanying adjustments in the position or status of the Catholic Church. The 1950's and early 60's were a period when the Catholic Church in America was at the apex of its respect and enjoying what appeared to be unlimited growth. The laity had a trust and confidence in the clergy and in the representatives of the church that bordered on personality cult or worship. The typical Catholic believed that the members of the church demanded respect and obedience according to the laws of God, church, and man. Many of the potential candidates for the Juniorate counted immigrants as parents who entered America with a disproportionate adulation for religious, a remnant of old world attitudes. Parish priests and the teachers in the Catholic schools definitely attained status as *in loco parentis* and were left to their own devices in dealing with their young charges. Naturally, parents were more likely to support whatever teachers and clerics did regardless of the wisdom of their decisions. This respect and admiration translated into acceptance of junior family members' decision to join the religious life. Oftentimes such a decision was seen as an enhancement for family tradition. Sometimes too, it might alleviate the expense and cramped quarters typified by the families of immigrants. Today prospective religious from the very young might be viewed with greater skepticism and doubt.

Another factor in readily accepting a young man's decision to enter the religious life during his high school years was the nature and cultural heritage of the entrants, at least as far as the Christian Brothers were concerned. In reading Luke Salm's **Concise History of the Brothers of the New York District**, the progression of schools and parishes cited therein reflects the evolution of the Brothers and the schools they served. Together the Brothers and the Irish immigrant class seemed to march in step from the lower parishes of Manhattan to the Westside and upper reaches of the borough and the adjacent Bronx. Somewhat familiar with the northern migration of the Catholic population of New York, I recognized the pattern established by the expansion of some, the dissolution of other no longer viable parishes, and relocation of the Brothers to the new growth of schools. From educating the likes of Al Smith, the former Democratic candidate for the Presidency, who attended a Brothers' school called St. James, near the Brooklyn Bridge, the Brothers moved northward as the former residential housing became more mercantile or commercial in nature. From that same neighborhood arose the story from the mother of my high school principal, Brother Arnold Joseph Doyle. According to Brother Joseph, his mother, when she lived near the Brooklyn Bridge, used to baby-sit for Eamon De Valera, the Irish revolutionary and first President of the Irish Free State.

The list of elementary schools where the Brothers taught moved northward with the migration of the predominantly Irish Catholic population. More so than other Orders who staffed elementary or parish schools in New York City, the Christian Brothers seem to parallel the movement of the Irish. The fate of the two seemed inextricably entwined. Perhaps the only contradiction to this generality might emerge from the role the Brothers played in welfare institutions like the Catholic Protectory, later to become Lincoln Hall, and La Salle School in Albany. I have no idea of the ethnicity of those who populated Hillside Catholic Male Orphanage in Troy, but I suspect that they were generally Irish too. Once the Brothers staffed high schools, their constituency became more diversified, but these schools were not major contributors to the Junior Novitiate. Rather ironically, other religious orders addressed the needs of other immigrant groups but the Irish seemed to receive the attention of the Christian Brothers. Concentrations of German, Italian, or Polish parishioners attracted other congregations, but the Christian Brothers focused primarily on the Irish. I only recall a single parish, Immaculate Conception in the Hub of the Bronx that seemed to have a concentration of another nationality. This school staffed by the Brothers was called "The Old Dutch Prison" because of its predominately German students and formidable appearance. It also catered to an Italian clientele unlike most of the other elementary schools taught by the Brothers.

By the 1950's, parishes, noted for their Irish populations, became fruitful recruiting centers. While the Irish were evidently happy to send their boys off to places like Barrytown, the Brothers were delighted to have such recruits. Perhaps two classmates' background may illustrate the Hibernian presence in Barrytown. Jim Costello was an affable kid from St. John's in Kingsbridge. He was a respectable athlete, and my memory of him is a boy who could run forever, but his signature style was wearing a Pioneer of Mary sweatshirt with sleeves falling below his hands. Cos had a fine sense of humor that he displayed often in the classroom, more in response than stimulation. I was impressed that he was the nephew of the President of Ireland. After leaving Barrytown, Cos was to earn great acclaim as an administrator in a challenging special education program for students with emotional difficulties. Perhaps that ready smile provided the essence of patience he required during his career. Another evident Irish cultural representative was Sean O'Keefe. Sean came from Good Shepherd in Inwood, and his mother was related to the O'Donnells who managed Croke Park on 238th Street and Broadway. At Croke Park, Sean learned all the Irish sports that weren't played too often elsewhere. He was a devotee of Gaelic football, hurling, and even soccer. Perhaps the one boy in the class who would as soon kick the ball as throw it, Sean specialized in kick-offs and punting during the football season. After teaching in Holy Name, Immaculate, and St. Augustine, Sean left and had a distinguished career as our group representative in the insurance business.

Many a candidate came from the Upper Westside parishes of Holy Name and Ascension. In Harlem, St. Thomas the Apostle sent additional volunteers for training. Comparably in the Bronx enclaves like St. Jerome's where High Mass or Benediction often closed to the strains of *O'Donnell Abu*, Sacred Heart and St. Augustine sent their predominantly Irish American boys to join the Brothers at Barrytown. To this number in the late forties could be added Incarnation and Good Shepherd in Manhattan and St. John's in Kingsbridge. These parishes sent multitudes of candidates until another phenomenon arose. As the Irish moved out of these parishes to swell the ranks of suburban churches, the flight of the Whites presaged the diminishing numbers of candidates for Brother Tom Jenkins, known far and wide as the 'cradle snatcher.'

As more and more Blacks and Hispanics moved into Holy Name, Ascension, St. Thomas the Apostle, Incarnation, and most especially St. Jerome's, St. Augustine's, and Sacred Heart in the Bronx, the change in cultural identities erased many potential candidates or parents willing to send their sons off to the monastery. What was a positive to the Irish often was a negative to the Blacks and Hispanics who witnessed little welcome among the retreating Irish. The demographics of New York added to the demise of Barrytown and the Juniorate. What Brother Luke Salm describes as the glory years from 1946 to 1967 came to an abrupt end. Unfortunately, after an ambitious building expansion in the houses of formation in Washington and Barrytown, within a very brief period, the programs contracted and soon withered from the dearth of candidates. What were once active monastic communities of formation soon became white elephants that had to be sold off. Given the socio-economic realities of the period, it was a buyer's market, and the Brothers were content to sell Barrytown to the followers of Reverend Moon while the Bureau of Mines bought the newly expanded campus at De La Salle College in Washington, DC.

In 1952 with the capacity of the Junior Novitiate reaching beyond its limits, the Brothers determined to have freshman recruits remain at home with their families for an additional year. While some argued that this arrangement was motivated by the hope of the aspirant maturing, others maintained that the plan resulted from the overcrowding of the Juniorate facilities. After a freshman year at St. Bernard's, an annex of Cardinal Hayes High School, aspirants would enter the Juniorate as sophomores when there would be ample space and supposedly a more mature clientele. Beginning in September, 1953 Juniorate candidates from New York City formed a separate class among the usual enrollees at St. Bernard's on 14th Street. That initial class, calling itself the Pioneers of Mary, began their training for the Brotherhood in New York City and spent a number of weekends at Barrytown. In my class at Incarnation only one boy, Joe Emmer, was interested in following this procedure. For my part, I decided to attend Manhattan Prep and then transfer at a later date to Barrytown. In September, 1954 when the Pioneers of Mary entered the Juniorate, Emmer was joined by five other Incarnation lads. Charlie Owens became the most notorious, for he left in such a brief time that hardly any one knew him. Some left after a year or two, but a number of us from Incarnation considered Barrytown and its commitment to the Christian Brothers' vocation a viable alternative for a high school education.

When I decided to join the class in September, 1955 Joe Emmer and Tom Sloan were still there, although they left before their senior year. Dermot O'Sullivan who had been in my class until the sixth grade, enrolled from St. Patrick's in Newburgh increasing the vocations from Incarnation sources. After leaving Barrytown in his senior year, Joe enrolled at Cardinal Hayes, completed his high school education, but no one knows what career he chose to follow thereafter.

Among the vocations from the Heights, Paddy Joe Murphy, Dermot O'Sullivan, and I completed our training and taught for an average of four years before leaving the Christian Brothers. Pat Murphy became a maven in special education and even introduced me to the field. Not only was he recognized as an outstanding educator, but he also was a very competent administrator for the BOCES adult education facility. For his part, Dermot continued in education, but also attempted to create some fame that utilized his excellent voice in singing Irish songs.

One of the entrants from Cardinal Hayes was Brother Dominic Jordan who joined the program after his freshman year at St. Bernard's. Dominic, or Jimmy, as he was known in the neighborhood, has persevered to this date and is currently headmaster in a missionary school in Kenya. Between stateside assignments, for most of his years in the apostolate, Jimmy has served the people of Kenya and Ethiopia in many capacities, all related to education.

The fact that students could enter and leave Barrytown without any stigma made both procedures easy. When I left my neighborhood, a Jewish grocer merely thought I had been sent away to reform school. He questioned me extensively after I returned for a brief visit to the neighborhood in 1956. Apparently prison was more comprehensible to this man than religious commitment was. This ebb and flow of vocations was evident also in Manhattan Prep. During my tenure at the Juniorate, there was always a considerable number of candidates who claimed Incarnation as their home. The same could be said of Good Shepherd and Sacred Heart.

In my homeroom of about forty-five students at Manhattan Prep, eight of us spent some time in Barrytown. At the end of our freshman year, three boys went to Barrytown and returned to the Prep for their junior year. Beginning in my junior year, three of us transferred to the Juniorate. Although we acted independently and didn't know each of us planned to enter the Brothers, two close friends of mine and I made the transition easily. Bob Stosser from St. Jude's spent a year and a half in Barrytown and then returned to Manhattan Prep shortly before graduation. In time Bob became a successful entrepreneur and founder of his own consultant firm. His experience in the army that actually sent him to Columbia University School of Journalism prepared him for his future in communication skills. Joe Troy and I remained through formation and both of us taught for a few years before we left the order completely. Joe carved a career as a much sought after administrator both in public education and in Catholic secondary schools.

After our original class graduated from the Prep, Joe Troy and I were joined by two additional vocations from our homeroom. Ed Raff, from Yonkers, remained in what we called our Postulancy for about a month and then left to join many of his former classmates at Manhattan College. Like so many from our Barrytown days, Ed continued in education as a special educator and gym teacher in the Yonkers School System. Joe O'Brien, however, persevered through formation with Joe Troy and me and taught a couple of years at La Salle Second Street before leaving. O'Brien had become one of the major contributors to my class since his humor was contagious as well as outrageous. Unfortunately, Joe O'Brien had also developed a severe case of diabetes in his mid twenties and died of diabetic shock within months of leaving the Institute.

My decision to leave Manhattan Prep and enter Barrytown was more a deferred decision than dissatisfaction with the Prep. I truly enjoyed my time there, but I resolved to act upon what I considered a divine calling before I ignored it. While at the Prep, I liked my classmates, my teachers, the atmosphere, and playing for the JV baseball team. Since I had severely injured my leg in February of my freshman year, I was unable to try out for the varsity. When the JV dug a little deeper for pitchers and catchers, I decided to employ the tools of ignorance. Joe Troy was the varsity catcher and far superior to me in defensive skills. Another classmate, Nat Racine, was the best varsity pitcher and he used to boast about Joe as his catcher. During tryouts for the JV in early spring, 1955 I hit the baseball into next week, but my defensive skills were erratic at best. Another candidate, Tom O'Leary, and I had done pretty well during tryouts, but I was named the starting catcher, probably for my less than stellar performance in patrolling the outfield grass.

If the defensive catching left something to be desired, the pitching staff was very questionable. Our best pitcher was Mike Bernard from Highbridge. He had a ball that moved a bit, and he also had good control. The rest of the staff had difficulty finding home plate. A number of years later, I met our JV coach, Brother Francis Ralston at some function in St. Patrick's Cathedral. He remembered me but shattered my ego when he described how. He claimed I was the back up catcher on the team. I didn't have the heart to set him straight. I started every game, played every inning, and led the team in hits as well as errors and strike outs. Perhaps the record is skewered by our best defensive play. If the backstop was close to the plate, I would let the ball get by me and then try to throw out any runner trying to steal the base. This ploy worked as often as not.

A number of my JV team mates had played for Incarnation or for Good Shepherd. Ironically, our mortal enemies from elementary school generally turned into our closest friends in high school. The paths of the elementary school baseball rivals crossed in the play I remember most from my days at Manhattan Prep. Toddy Roach, who played in elementary school with our starters, Joe O'Brien and Danny Sheehan from Good Shepherd, was on third base for Mount St. Michael's Academy. With one out the batter hit a fly ball to center field, and it was caught by Tom O'Leary whose perfect peg to the plate had Roach out by five feet. Despite Roach's warm friendship with O'Brien and Sheehan, he launched a flying attack feet first upon my chest while I held the ball in my glove. His impact upon my body was strong enough to knock me backward and possibly through the backstop if I were somewhat smaller. I held onto the ball for the third out. Thankfully it was so, for my entire internal organs were scattered hither and yon by the impact. Since it was the third out of the inning, I stumbled to the dugout and took inventory and reclaimed my composure before we had to begin the next inning in the field.

The players on the Prep JV seemed to enjoy each others company quite a bit. The major glue in the adhesion was the popular, funny, witty, and perceptive Joe O'Brien who joined us in Barrytown after his senior year. Joe could recite verbatim any song he heard but once. He could also master the most arcane lyrics that made no sense to others. On a trip on the long now defunct Third Avenue El on the way to St. Mary's Park to play either Hayes or All Hallows, Joe observed the change in complexion of the passengers. Soon he began singing and leading us in "Skokian," a current popular tune. The lyrics contained his description of our ride on the rickety, rackety El. *"Far away in Africa, Happy, Happy Africa."* Our all White team was pushing propriety and good citizenship under the aegis of O'Brien's songfest. Fortunately none of our fellow passengers seemed distraught or distracted by our rendition.

During my time at the Prep, I was honored with election as sophomore class vice president. Tom Wynne from Incarnation was President. Perhaps the combined numbers of Incarnation and

Good Shepherd alliances with some from Sacred Heart led to my selection, for I cannot pinpoint any other explanation. After school and weekend activities often found us traveling the subways together to hockey and basketball games in the old Madison Square Garden or at the Manhattan College gym. Despite my comfort at Manhattan Prep, I felt it was time to fulfill my wish of entering Barrytown in the beginning of September, 1955.

In retrospect, I should have prepared my parents more for my decision. They discovered my intention when I brought a number of papers home to be signed by doctors, dentists, priests, and parents. My father was beside himself, but my mother sent me off to the dentist to have some form filled out, and by the time I returned my mother had sedated my father enough to re-enter the rational world. One of my unpleasant recollections in garnering the appropriate paper work centered on my visit to the Incarnation rectory for sacerdotal approval. I didn't know what negativism awaited me. In February of my freshman year, I injured my leg severely while sleigh riding in Riverside Park. Although I was immobilized for at least six weeks, I had broken no bones, but the extensive bruising had clotted around the muscles in my right leg. I couldn't walk and thereby couldn't serve Mass. I didn't envision that as a problem until I spoke with Father Ferarius, an Augustinian adjunct in Incarnation. He described me as unreliable and of course, hardly interested in serving the Lord, if I couldn't serve his representatives on earth. I didn't even think of explaining why I skipped my altar assignments, so I listened to his tirade and dire predictions about my perseverance. He guaranteed that I would be back in the city within two weeks. His prognostication only reinforced my determination to remain in Barrytown at least until Thanksgiving. When I had all the paperwork prepared, my family was scoped by Brother Thomas Jenkins, the alleged 'cradle snatcher.' We passed muster. Later when my sophomore year ended, I entered St. Elizabeth's hospital and had two cysts and a tumor removed from my right thigh. The surgeon described them as "big as two softballs and a football." The procedure left an ugly fourteen inch scar that looked like a fish's skeleton.

In my freshman year, I had won a scholarship that paid for most of Manhattan's tuition. In my sophomore year, I had worked enough to give my parents $150 to pay for that year. Now I was asking them to pay $30 a month for my tuition at Barrytown. While that may appear like a trivial sum today, at the time it was quite an increase in the cost of education. Actually, it was a great bargain. As we used to say, for $30, we received board, laundry, education, athletic fees, practically individual tutoring by outstanding educators, and the company of companions of approved virtue. During the summer before heading to Barrytown, my father appointed himself devil's advocate to present all the arguments why I shouldn't go. Nonetheless, he reluctantly gave permission. My mother seemed happy with my decision, at least in my presence, although my brother Ray claims she was really pretty distraught.

On the night before I was to take the train from Grand Central to the Barrytown station, my brother Bernard organized an impromptu songfest of Irish music. I'm not exactly sure who was there, but I do remember his friends, Al Diaz and Moe Friedman, two less than notable Irish tenors. Actually, the songfest helped the time go quickly and peacefully. We drove to Grand Central and I was pretty oblivious to the consequences upon my family. I suppose I was so intent on myself and the beginning of a new life that I overlooked its effects on my family. Later, Ray was to tell me that my father especially was quite upset, even broaching the irrational again. Fueled by some Seagrams Seven and a sense of loss, my father mourned my departure almost as if I had died. My mother also suffered my departure as if it were an Irish wake. While I felt on the verge of a great adventure, my parents had endured what they considered a significant loss. All the time I assessed my situation from only my perspective.

Frankly, I don't remember the train ride north along the Hudson Shore Line. I have an enduring image of dim lights and little conversation during the trip. Most of the passengers seemed lost in a mental reverie of their own. While I had reason for apprehension about a new adventure in a new environment among new classmates, I certainly knew enough of them to feel somewhat comfortable. I also detected what I could describe as a subdued attitude among the veterans returning for another year at Barrytown. My wife Mary and I once gave a lift to a West Point Cadet who got stranded at White Plains Airport where Mary worked for United Airlines. The distraught Cadet had no money, no ticket, and no composure as she realized that West Point was a distance from White Plains. Calming her down and speaking reassuringly with her mother in San Diego, Mary assisted this young woman to the extent that she invited us to her graduation and has sent a Christmas card every year. As we drove to the citadel on the Hudson, the young lady was extremely polite and informative, responding to our sundry questions. She said she was returning to the academy for her third year and members of that class were called "cows." The name arose from the solemnity of the third year cadets who now had a commitment to the military for at least five years. Their subdued trek from the train station along the banks of the Hudson to the barracks above engendered a mood of reflection since the cadets now contemplated the next five years of their lives. I had a sense that something similar permeated the returning Junior Novices who probably would have enjoyed an extension to their brief summer respite.

When we debarked from the train at the miniscule Barrytown station, a truck awaited the baggage, and the students trudged, some with leaden steps to the main building about a quarter of a mile distant. In my own mind, I pondered what awaited me without fear, but definitely with some apprehension. I wondered whether I would fit in or find the transition from Manhattan Prep to Barrytown a greater challenge than I anticipated. There was little animated conversation, joking, or commentary or reflections on what took place during the vacation period in New York. Once we arrived at the Juniorate building, the pace quickened. I was assigned to the middle or junior dorm, given a locker, and started to unpack. An afternoon snack of Department of Agriculture grape jelly and peanut butter sandwiches provided some distraction, but most of the time was consumed in settling in. A few prayers added the religious flavor to the transition too. Even veterans seemed consumed in their own thoughts and by the time for lights out, everyone seemed exhausted enough to sleep contentedly. Unknown to me, my family back in Washington Heights was not faring as well as I was. Later I was told that my mother became very introspective believing that I had left her life forever. My father had decided that John Barleycorn could help him cope with my departure, and my younger brother Ray immediately recognized the change in his own life as a result of my departure. To say the least, my adaptation to Barrytown was less painful for me than it was for my family.

As I surveyed my new classmates, I was happy to recognize Dermot O'Sullivan and Joe Emmer, both of whom had written to me frequently. They were more or less caught up in their own thoughts.

had a rocky sophomore year and had been threatened to shape up or ship out. Joe was seriously considering not returning at all, but he did so because of my arrival. Several other friends from Incarnation were available also for morale boosters. As time passed, I learned to assess my new classmates from the self-satisfied smugness of the Heights.

One characteristic stood out among all the Pioneers of Mary, or class of 1957. There seemed to be a competitiveness that permeated the relationships among the students. That competitiveness was based on neighborhood, school, parish, and culture. Bill Mueller and Ed Schwall lauded the German heritage they cherished. They might as well have been singing *Horst Wessell* or *Deutschland Uber Alles* in the Warsaw Ghetto at a *Bund* rally in 1940 for all the success they had. Bill continued on the fringes of education in one form or another and despite his lofty achievements academically, he seldom was recognized for his modest achievements. His sudden, unexpected death in Denver was a surprise as well as a wake up call to the rest of the group when we learned of it. For his part, after trying to sustain a business in printing, Eddie Schwall reverted to his first love and became an outstanding educator, administrator, and track coach at Bishop Mullin in Denver.

One of the newly arrived with me was a lad from Rhode Island. John Kullberg preached the virtues of Cranston, Rhode Island and life in the Red Sox Nation. John not only had an accent strange to Washington Heights, but he also employed an unusual vocabulary. Arriving with matched luggage, he wore jeans and tennis shoes, and a toque, alien terms to the city boys in Barrytown who called such apparel dungarees, sneakers and a hat. He spoke of gyros and submarines while we only knew of heroes. He described his thirst for a frappe, and no one knew what he was talking about. From the perspective of many years, it is possible to assess John as a one man cultural and vocabulary enrichment influence upon the narrow-minded influences of my youth.

Most considered John's apostolic zeal as the ravings of a borderline lunatic in the Red Sox Nation, for when he wasn't wearing a 'toque' he displayed his Red Sox allegiance on the top of his head. For all his proselytizing, John barely managed to escape the fate of Jean De Breboeuf and the Jesuit martyrs who tried to convince the Iroquois of the divinity of Jesus and the efficacy of the Catholic Church in attaining eternal salvation. Undeterred by the tepid interest in his crusade for Rhode Island, he displayed determination and courage in his lonely zeal. John did have one very irritating trait, however. Whenever we were engaged in a spirited hockey game, he took great delight in knocking the puck into a snow bank that generally delineated our rink and then jumping on top of the puck. Of course this stopped the flow of the game and earned him the sobriquet 'Snowberg.' In later years I reflected upon the self confidence and self assurance that possessed John. The qualities that I was unable to decipher in my youth, later served John well when he became President of several organizations like the SPCA and Lighthouse, addressing congress, and appearing often on television. My arrogant, uninformed dismissal of this talented son of New England underscored the parochialism of some of us who enlisted in Barrytown.

There were a few other Rhode Islanders who claimed citizenship in the Red Sox Nation, but they didn't promulgate their allegiance so ostentatiously. 'Easy Ed' Lewis from De La Salle Newport was exactly as his nickname indicated. If anything, he looked like a magazine ad for expensive Ray Ban sun glasses since his dark, curly hair and tanned skin and good looks served him well. Most of the time, 'Easy Ed' took it "Easy." He was friendly but quiet and reserved, and in no way exhorted us to appreciate life in New England. He was joined by a tall, lanky lad from Providence, Rhode Island named Jim McKenery. Jim warranted no nickname, and he kept a low profile despite his height. Now I am told he has served the Brothers magnificently as a gifted administrator at Oakdale and La Salle Providence. He was elected Visitor of the LINE district too for a period. During Jim's time in the Juniorate, he perceived wisdom in silence and rarely uttered any provocative statements, perhaps some attributes that led to his success as an administrator in the Brothers' schools. Another lad from the Ocean State was Donald Theroux who was called T-Rocks as a corruption of his name. Donald had a good sense of humor and seemed to fit in quite well, but at the end of his senior year he departed, never to be heard from again.

The kids from New York were confirmed believers that there was little value in any place beyond the streets of Gotham. Tom Mamara, who was called 'Louie' because someone thought he looked like a 'Louie,' extolled the Italian contributions to western civilization. The achievements of Petrarch, Dante, and Machiavelli, the Renaissance artists Raphael, Giotto, Bernini, Michelangelo, Da Vinci, and Botticelli, the music of Verdi and Puccini, were dismissed out of hand, and for all his best intentions seeking recognition of Italian culture, Louie won jocose disdain and mockery. With few fellow Juniors with Italian heritage, Louie had to wait for reinforcements during his Novitiate year. In the meantime, he was relentless in his pride and obstinate in the face of derision undeservedly presented to him.

Almost invariably, my fellow Pioneers were narrowback sons of Greenhorns off the boat only recently. Sure, there were some whose Irish ancestors arrived a few generations back. Joe Troy's father, for instance, had been bat boy for the Giants during the McGraw era. He probably was the only individual who had any job involving management or supervision. He worked in the hotels. Jim Marrin's family had been citizens of Highbridge for some time too. But the parents of most of my compatriots came from the Irish ghettos of the Westside or South Bronx, or northern Manhattan. We had a pretentious pride that was built precariously on comfort in numbers and scorn for others. Barney Quigley might boast of the scones from his mother's native Scotland, but the pronounced patois of the Kerry man who was his father was almost indecipherable to us narrowbacks. Mr. Quigley could easily converse with the fathers of Dermot O'Sullivan, Pat Murphy and Sean O'Keefe. There were a number of classmates whose parents shared the accents of Connemara or Connaught too. Without a doubt, Irish heritage was an asset in assimilating into Barrytown. Far from humility and charity, most of the Juniors were smug and haughty in their similarities. Deviations from that norm were assessed as inferior and often verbally mocked.

Like my own parents, few of my classmates' folks had graduated from high school. As far as I know, none had ever attended college. Most believed that in the pantheon of Irish saints, the highest rank was reserved for St. Patrick with Sts. Bridget, Brendan the Navigator, and Kevin of Glendalough just about even in the second tier. From amateur observations, there did not appear to be many advocates for sanctity for Matt Talbott, but an article of faith, however, saved a treasured spot for St. Michael Quill of Kenmore, Kerry. Many of the fathers worked as bus drivers, trolley, and train men and were ardent supporters of the head of the Transport Workers Union, Mike Quill. My father was the only policeman in the group, and I don't recall any fireman. Ed Schwall's father, however, was a court officer who recognized my father and my brother for their appearances in his courtroom while serving as policemen. A significant number also worked for Con Ed. Although I can't remember every parent's job, it is safe to say that most worked in civil service or union protected roles, and earned a modest salary that permitted them to raise their family in decent circumstances. Beyond blue collar and Civil Service, few parents would claim membership in other groups. Banking, finance, law, education, the arts, professional tradesmen or merchants sent very few candidates to Barrytown. Also, very few, if any, mothers were among the work force. Upon this base of solid, but in no way substantial income, many of us would boast of our Irish heritage.

On visiting Sundays, our parents would arrive either by car or bus. For many the first stop was an inspection of the dairy barns, the hen houses, and of course an interview with the pigs, especially the giant boars. While the intent was to visit the Junior Novices, no one complained if the fathers especially took a mini-economical trip back to the Auld Sod in the form of inspection of the farm life they knew on the other side. With no evidence to support my contention, I suspect some fathers were envious that their city bred sons had the opportunity to learn about life on a farm too.

Perhaps I underscore the role of the Irish too much among the Brothers, but I don't think so. Every St. Patrick's Day, the Juniorate would celebrate with an Irish assembly that demonstrated the roots of the students. No other ethnic group had such an event. The assembly would often consist of the songs, speeches, and dances learned in our even younger years. I for example was given the task of reciting an oration made by Owen Roe to his troops of Ulster during the struggle against Elizabethan invaders. Others quoted the famed speech of Robert Emmett from the docket of the trial in which he was condemned to death. Pat Daly, a graduate of St. Jerome's in the South Bronx, could be counted upon to do a few steps of an Irish jig and reel. Barney Quigley, the espouser of Scottish scones, would saw out a few bars on his fiddle. Barney had such huge shoulders and arms that the violin looked like a ukulele when he tucked it under his chin and into the crook of his arm.

Kevin Burns from Incarnation would be called upon to sing some traditional songs that evoked nostalgia for 'home' or stirred the blood for insurrection. Several sang, despite poor voices, songs that were part and parcel of the Irish parties from the old neighborhoods. Dermot, Pat Murphy, Bill Simon and I called ourselves the **Four Tinkers** and sang a medley of songs like *The Wearing of the Green, Kelly, the Boy from Killan, The Dying Irish Soldier Boy, and The Minstrel Boy*. One of the highlights in my memory is the dilemma I presented Brother Peter Mannion our director who tried to describe my voice and still remain polite and tactful. In his unique way, Brother Peter assessed my singing talent in short order, then making his signature right hand movement that conveyed a sense of deep thought or possibly the threat of psychological evisceration, except for the benign, bemused expression on his face, uttered the unforgettable words, "O'Prey, you're sort of a . . . . baritone." "Please take a step or two backwards and sing more softly." He, like my wife, had a nice way of telling me to stifle my volume and cancel my off-key renditions. As my wife Mary often said, "He who sings, prays twice, but in your case silence may indicate praying thrice!"

My introduction to life in Barrytown went quite smoothly. Having attended Incarnation and having lived in Washington Heights, I found many *compadres* who assisted in my adjustment. One of the original adaptations was in speech. Barrytown had its own lingual nomenclature which wasn't the language of angels to say the least. Bathrooms were 'castles' and candy was called 'bait.' Newcomers were called 'babies' in contrast to 'originals' for those who began their freshman year as a group. The sluggish at manual labor were 'racketeers,' and those who ate more than their allotment earned the title of 'slashers.' Unfamiliar words like 'tureen, ladle, refectory, scullery, bug juice, mucker, flookie, and the world' all had definitions peculiar to Barrytown. 'Bug juice' was a fruity concoction made from the grapes from the vineyards. Sometimes it even fermented and had a 'heady' flavor. A 'mucker' was the term for a muscular, huge body like Barney, or Dermot, but most especially Joe Emmer. A 'flookie' was an individual who left Barrytown to return to the 'world,' usually a neighborhood in New York City. Sometimes the peculiar argot or expressions that filtered into conversation were deemed inappropriate for proper society. One such expression of unknown origin, nebulous meaning, but prolific in conversation was 'monster faggy savage.' In all probability the phrase was an alternate for the adjective 'big' or adverb 'very.' It was common enough that Brother Peter advocated its extirpation in one of his occasional politeness lessons. Usually such convocations were reserved for table manners, correct silverware usage, or in one outstanding case, the proper procedure for peeling an orange using a table knife for an initial incision, inserting a tablespoon and pushing it along the contour of the orange. It actually worked very effectively.

In the lexicon of the Juniorate, the AD or Athletic Director dispersed necessary athletic equipment from his room adjoining the 'shoe' room and 'slop' room. Shoddy work or infractions of a minor order like talking excessively during manual labor could rate extra assignments for cleaning details after the afternoon and evening meals. These assignments emanating from the PB or Punitive Board were made by the 'Czar,' or the current president of the senior class. PB should not be confused with PD which represented the first letters of Peeling Detail, or the group assigned to shuck corn (in reality, separate the bugs from the kernels), peel potatoes, or prepare fresh vegetables for the dinner table. Among the myriad collection of letters, one also had to consider PF, or 'Particular Friendship." As a religious community, we were always advised to avoid any PF that might alienate fellow community members because of its exclusivity, or perhaps, might endanger one's vow of chastity. While individuals formed friendships and cabals, the specter of PF or the allegation thereof, often inhibited the natural association with friends. In some ways we knew each other very well, and at the same time, we hardly knew each other at all.

At the time I arrived, the Czar was Joe McGowan from Incarnation, and he was replaced by Pat Daly who shared my table in the refectory. Being friendly with both was helpful. The Czar was a prestigious position since it reflected the popular election of your senior classmates as well as the recognition of the responsibilities the role entailed. Each class generally elected an individual for each quarter of the school year. After McGowan and Daly in my first year, the seniors selected Mickey Bukowski (how did this Polish kid from Greenpoint in Brooklyn smash the strangle hold on elections?) and Tom Reilly from Tolentine.

As I discovered early in my introduction to Juniorate life, competition was ubiquitous and sometimes in the strangest places. Each evening as the junior class prepared for lights out, an unusual competition surfaced. Rich McKay and Jim Marrin vied for the title of who could stay up the latest. The consequences of failing to comply with the lights out procedure were relatively dire. As the bewitching hour approached, Brother Austin Gerald, the dorm moderator whom we named 'Merry Gerry' would circle the dorm and finally press the buzzer which meant all should be in bed and lights were turned out. Marrin and McKay tried to time their ablutions, and rituals so that each would be the final boy standing just before the buzzer rang. To increase the odds of success, each attempted to win by giving the other a French sheet or in someway preventing the other from a victorious, penalty-free retirement. My bed was directly behind Marrin's, so I witnessed the contest on a nightly basis. On one night, just as Jim Marrin evidently won the long standing contest, he jumped into his bed precisely as the buzzer rang. I heard a gasp, a gulp, a stifled moan and observed Jim's rigid body under the covers in the nick of time. Rich McKay however had planted an everted fur glove at the bottom of the sheets. Marrin believed he was sharing his bed with a rat, a mouse, a squirrel, a chipmunk, or some such furry creature, but he dared not move or Merry Gerry would catch him. In this immobile, breathless state, he waited for the prefect to close the door to his room. As soon as that happened, Jim jumped up and started beating the bottom of his bed with his shoes. Finally, he extracted the furry glove and acknowledged defeat.

When my class became seniors, we elected for our first Czar, Barney Quigley from Ascension on the Upper Westside. Barney was one of the most impressive of the classmates I met in September, 1955. With broad shoulders and excessively long arms, he was admirably called "Barney Big Arms." Aside from his taciturn nature and devotion to hard work, Barney was the kind of student who engendered a great deal of respect without much verbalization. He was exceptionally bright and multi-talented. A strong basketball player and powerful runner in football, Barney also had a flair for writing. He was one of the editors of the Juniorate newspaper, **The Beacon.** Barney chose to major in Physics at Catholic University where Dr. Herzfeld, a noted assassin of academic honors, taught as chairman in the physics department. When I lived in Stony Point, one of my neighbors, now a doctor, cited Barney, at that time a professor of math and computer science at Manhattan College, as the most lucid, patient teacher he ever had in those sciences.

As long as I knew him, Barney used to regulate his stomach by ingesting a Doctor's prescription, a vile concoction that could have passed for hydrochloric acid. Unfortunately, he developed stomach cancer and had an operation that guaranteed him a ninety-five per cent success rate. Ever laconic, Barney said to me, "Frankly, I have never worried so much about a five per cent chance before this." True to his fears, his cancer returned with a vengeance, and he had to retire while still in his forties. Barney went to Lincroft where Pat Murphy and I visited him during his fading life span. No other human impressed me with heroic resignation greater than Barney. While he awaited death with holy acquiescence to the inevitable will of God, he helped with the sick and infirmed older Brothers. During our visit we got to admire his patience and availability to those who needed some help. In unusual candor, I never felt so much in the presence of sanctity than I did in observing Barney during this period. With his premature death, he added to the suspicion that those who worked in the paint shop in formation were exposed to leaded paints, solvents, and other possible carcinogens that led to the deaths of Tom Reilly, John Kissan, and Bill Barron.

While Barney was Czar, I was given the responsibility of supervising the cleanliness of the bottom floor. This entailed not only checking on the "castle" keepers, the athletic room, the stair wells, and the shoe racks, but it also introduced me to proper care of the American flag. I had the responsibility of raising the American flag on the pole at the north side of the building every day. In the evening, I also hauled it down and folded it according to regulations and stored it for the following day. Supervision of the first floor also entailed a weekly scrubbing and waxing of the refectory floor after lights out. I actually enjoyed the extra task since any alteration to schedule was appreciated. My daily chores ended with the closing of the front doors for the night at about 9:00pm. Many an early summer's evening I mused wistfully about the premature shut down when I could hear some children's voices in the distance, but the 6:00am rising was often incentive enough to catch some sleep.

During my Juniorate years I became a member of the Benilde Club. It was a club intended to spread knowledge about the works of the Brothers throughout the world. Special emphasis seemed placed on the missions of Aruba and Nicaragua. I imagine a few years later the focus would be on Eritrea, Ethiopia and Kenya, but in the mid fifties, they weren't part of the apostolate of the future. The Benilde Club also sponsored speakers and lectures on catechetics and class room procedure. I actually enjoyed what was achieved and was pleased when I was elected President replacing Pat Daly when he went to the Novitiate.

My class honored me in September, 1956 by selecting me for our second Czar. I was surprised at the honor and not at all disappointed to be among a group of extraordinary individuals. Barney Quigley had done an admirable job, and I suspect I left the position no better or worse than it had been. I enjoyed the prestige of the job and found that supervising manual labor and assessing reasonable punishments for minor infractions had its rewards too. The elected officers would scan the rolls of students and try to match the personalities, skills, and interests according to their judgment. The recalcitrants or noted 'racketeers' demanded strong supervision, and some avid workers also merited easier assignments. Many jobs entailed greater visibility and managerial skills as in the refectory or supervising each of the three floors. From my experience, serious thought went into the assignments with only an occasional overture toward irony or humor.

Perhaps the most unusual experience I had during that tenure had nothing to do with manual labor. Early in my office, I was asked to accompany Brother Peter to Rhinebeck hospital under peculiar circumstances. Joe Emmer had been experiencing some problems with narcolepsy. He would actually fall asleep while participating in sports. The hospital aides asked me to slap Joe around in an attempt to awaken him from what seemed to be a coma of sorts. At the hospital, the staff also directed me to press my thumb under the upper orb of his eye socket. Joe only moaned, but he didn't wake up. They said that if that didn't work, he wasn't going to be roused by anything for awhile. He remained in the hospital for a few days and then was sent home. Rumors asserted that Joe had some rare disease, that he used to leave the grounds at night to visit Red Hook, or that he was on some kind of pills. I don't know what the ultimate diagnosis was, but we never saw Joe again. He enrolled at Hayes where he starred on their football team, and we always expected him to return. For whatever reason, he didn't, nor did we ever see him in the subsequent fifty years.

Part of the responsibility of the job of Czar entailed ordering the soaps, cleaning equipment, toilet paper and other items from a general storeroom presided over by a man called Brother Ambrose

Austin. He didn't particularly like or trust me. Jim Jordan, who worked in the 'bait' room, and I would go to the storeroom with a wish list and try to lure Ambrose into relinquishing whatever items we could. With the dedication of the determined, Jordan would insist that we needed all on the list. I was behind him for moral support, but Ambrose interpreted my participation as "the one who made the snowballs but insisted someone else throw them because I was too timid to do so myself." Maybe he was right, but Jordan did an effective job regardless. When my tenure was up around December, Jordan was elected my replacement.

Jordan was a Czar of another kind. While I confess I treated my tenure as a politico might, Jim was definitely a reformer. He believed in leadership from the trenches, and as such he devoted himself to the humblest, most menial tasks. Typically, Jim was a rigorist in interpreting the rules and regulations of a Junior Novice while Barney and I were more the loose constructionists or devotees of the elastic clause. This same disparity would display itself when Jim entered the Novitiate and Scholasticate where some might be tempted to describe his behavior as scrupulous or "up the wall." Perhaps, the future might be illustrative of Jim's behavior. For many decades of devoted service to the Brothers in the African missions and more competence as an administrator in high schools in New York City, Jimmy brought great honor to the community, to Washington Heights, and to his groupies. At the moment he is headmaster of St. Mary's School in Kyeri, Kenya.

For our fourth term and Czar, my class had an election or choice among Barney, Jim, and myself. It is no embarrassment to me to confess that the wisdom of my peers selected Barney again. My only question was why there were no other candidates considered for the position. When I contemplate the three czars, I consider myself to be honored as a member of that triumvirate. Certainly the Institute benefited from the contributions of Barney and Jim, even if circumstances led to my personal withdrawal from the Brothers. If one chose an apex of that triangle, be certain that either Jim or Barney deserve top billing. After my encounter with Barney near his death, I personally place him at the highest level if one keeps score about those kinds of things.

When I entered Barrytown, I didn't know what to expect from my peers. With a schedule that demanded early rising, morning prayer, a dabble in mental prayer before Mass, one should expect a number of youthful Dominic Savios with the reverence and determination of a St. Tarcisius who was martyred protecting the *viaticum* or Holy Eucharist from a pagan mob. Factor in the noon time prayers, the angelus three times a day, the rosary, multiple litanies, an examination of conscience, some liturgical offices, evening and night prayer, and one might wonder why sanctity was so elusive. That is not to say that my peers and I were sinners, but perfection was an objective not an achievement. Most, if not all of us, had the personal peccadilloes or peculiarities that mark humanity rather than angels. Some of the qualities we exhibited were more human than angelic. No one trod the halls of Barrytown with modest eyes cast downward in silent prayer or mentally communed ecstatically with the Trinity.

Perhaps one recollection of the spiritual climate of Barrytown Juniorate may be indicative of more than what it actually represents. Every year the high school department used to have a retreat in early October. One stands out in my mind for not only what it entailed, but also what repercussions it caused. A very funny retreat master named Father Dismas regaled us with jokes about a beautiful young damsel "in her high heel sneakers and looking like ten miles of bad road." It wasn't his humor that was most impelling however. He introduced every meditation, every conference, every exercise with an invitation to say a prayer for that young boy "who would make a bad confession and spend an eternity writhing in the pains of hell." Most teenage boys wouldn't take his comments too seriously, but in the religious atmosphere of Barrytown, a number of us took him very seriously and developed scruples about the sincerity and honesty about the state of our immortal souls. Actually, I believe Brother Peter advised him to back off on his theme. For the coming year, Father Paul, a Blessed Sacrament priest and our usual weekly confessor, spent the better part of his time unraveling the ravages of the inadvisable approach by assuring some that they should move on and stop reexamining their conscience and dissecting their performance in the confessional. Without the gullibility and naiveté of the Juniorate, the legacy of Father Dismas would probably have had little effect.

According to the rules and regulations of the Juniorate Novitiate, the spirit of a Junior Novice should be that of generosity. Each of us was generous in so far as each intended to dedicate his life to teaching the poor gratuitously according to the vows pronounced by the Christian Brothers. Each anticipated a celibate life within a religious community dedicated primarily to education. That spirit of generosity didn't extend, however, to people who appeared different, or spoke with an accent unfamiliar to the streets of New York, or who had interests beyond the sports arena. If I had to characterize the pervading spirit of the Junior Novitiate, I would select a spirit of competition without denigrating the spirit of generosity. There was competition among parishes, neighborhoods, personalities, sports, classes, and for some, delectable meals. One notable area where I found an absence of competition for the most part was in academics. Although manual labor groups might attempt to set speed records in cleaning up after meals, academics just didn't generate the same sense. After each meal, dishes were cleared and the tempo of the labor was determined by the adroitness of the first packer who stacked the dishes in trays. The tray would then be accelerated through a large washing machine and the unpacker would stack the hot dishes for replacement for dryers who forwarded the clean dishes to the individuals who were in charge of setting the tables. The whole operation was inhibited when an automatic belt was installed in the washing machine to allow sufficient time for the sterilization of the plates. Nonetheless, each manual labor struggled to complete the task in record time and thereby provide a little recreation moment before class resumed. Any individual who goldbricked during the manual labor would suffer sufficient opprobrium to discourage a repetition of his 'racketeering.'

When I was at Manhattan Prep, the curriculum was quite demanding and the homework assignments time consuming. At the Juniorate, I found the curriculum less challenging and less time consuming. What I also discovered rather quickly was that my fellow Pioneers of Mary came in two categories—intellectual 'Cruisers and Pluggers.' The 'Pluggers,' a term I believe was specific to Barrytown, were those who struggled with the academic demands by expending a great deal of time, energy, and dedication to succeed with the assigned classes. Schoolwork was a chore and demanded a lot of attention. The 'Cruisers,' a term I coined, were those who found the curriculum rather easy and chose to glide rather than grind. The Pioneers of Mary seemed to be divided evenly between the two generalized categories.

Perhaps the epitome of 'Cruisers' was a fellow who entered Barrytown at the same time I did. Coming from the weed strewn streets of the rather small metropolis of Troy, New York, William James Burns, commonly known as JB, seemed to get the most academically with the least effort. Over the course of our formation, JB seemed never to sweat, but did extremely well in chemistry, a difficult major. This disparity dawned on me, especially when I was overwhelmed by the subject in my freshman year in Hillside while JB had overelected to study Livy and Seneca in advanced Latin, and he aced all subjects. JB also had a talent for music and consumed more energy in that direction than he did in study. From time to time, he would direct our group in liturgical music.

Another entrant simultaneous to me, was Jim Aubuchon from Providence, Rhode Island. Jim, however, seemed more likely to combine the traits of 'plugger and cruiser' on his way to graduating with a *Summa cum Laude* from Catholic University. Aubie was definitely more scholar than athlete despite his size. Nonetheless, his remote interest in athletics did not excuse him from participating in the intramurals at Barrytown. Only an official medical excuse would allow an individual to retire from the sports activity. Ironically, for one year, Jimmy Jordan was excused for our junior year, but returned in his senior year to excel in any sport that called for running, wind, agility, and determination.

Many of my classmates were gifted intellectually but seemed content with modest efforts rather than conscientious study. Bill Mueller was the acknowledged academic leader of the class who would also graduate with a *Summa*. Those who were runners up academically seemed to change positions with each testing period or trimesters in the Juniorate. No one else seemed dedicated to replacing our number one scholar. Like others in my group, Bill had many hobbies and distractions that precluded an all out assault on school subjects. He was, for example, the Editor-in-Chief of our school newspaper, **The Beacon.** Under his guidance, the paper won many awards from the Columbia School of Journalism. He, too, had an interest in music and enjoyed sports. To us his fellow groupies, Bill appeared destined for major roles in the future of the Christian Brothers. If one were to isolate an individual who might be called upon to be a major administrator in our districts, Bill appeared to be a natural. His early promise and the prognostications of his peers didn't pan out however. His premature shocking death was almost anticlimactic to a lifetime of 'Great Expectations.' When Bill failed to appear for his high school English classes at a Jesuit school in Denver, a faculty friend went to check on him and found his lifeless body, a victim of a single, huge heart attack.

Other editors of the paper, like Barney Quigley and Eddie Schwall were typical also. They excelled in school without much effort. 'Speedy Ed' had many interests not found in the rules and regulations of the Junior Novices. The sobriquet came not only from his expertise as the class sprinter, but also for his penchant for imaginative, creative diversions "outside the envelope," so to speak. A simple illustration was an occasion when the director of our Scholasticate interrupted one of our 'pluggers' descending from a ladder in a stairwell from the roof of the building. After a brief interrogation, Brother Leo Kirby asked the miscreant, "You didn't think of this yourself. Who gave you the idea to sunbathe on the roof?" The reluctant admission involved the example of 'Speedy Ed.' Now an avid fisherman and outdoors type, Ed, or Brian as he is sometimes called, recently retired from his administration and coaching obligations from Bishop Mullen School in Denver.

Dermot O'Sullivan was another of the intellectually gifted but not particularly motivated scholars in my group. While Dermot would acquire good grades, his interests throughout his educational development focused more on his independent study of Sartre, Gibran, Teihard des Chardin, and philosophers and theologians who were re-examining the nature of truth and man. An intense interest in Irish culture, particularly music, would mark his post Christian Brother career while he earned his livelihood as a special education teacher in New Jersey.

Jim Marrin was also a quick study, and he got involved in such pursuits to the point where he graduated from the Harvard School of Divinity. After leaving the Brothers, Jim, like so many others in my group, remained close to education as either a teacher or some associated activity. Jim also offered his skills to his local public school board and served as a member for a number of years. Finally, he tapped his expertise in communication skills by running workshops for businessmen during the past thirty years.

Rich McKay combined the elements of 'Cruiser and Plugger.' No individual in my group was more organized, more systematic, more disciplined or more productive, than this emissary from St. Jerome's. He had a system of personally developed index cards that outlined everything from his academic preoccupations to the timeline he needed for the various activities of his fecund mind. Rich was also a gifted writer. In our junior year he won first place over Jim (Scotty) Curwood, another St. Jerome's product, in an original writing contest. I had to settle for third place behind these intellectuals. One of Rich's hobbies was the production of stage presentations. He wrote, produced, and directed an original variation of *Shane* and the *Caine Mutiny Court Martial.* Typically, he selected me for secondary roles in each. I played the role of the cowpoke beaten up by Shane in a bar, but I was elevated to the defense attorney Greenwald in the *Court Martial.* Rich insisted on a rigid schedule, frequent rehearsals, and total dedication to his productions. I used to argue fruitlessly with him for fewer rehearsals and less time in preparation, but I also have to confess that the end result was proportionate to his endeavors and to those who participated.

Rich also devoted a good deal of time and his competitive juices to our sports. Without doubt, he was the best basketball player in our class. As a graduate gym rat out of St. Mary's Park in the South Bronx, Rich had been coached by an avid enthusiast named Brother James Delaney. At Barrytown, he took on the task of adjusting my less than adequate basketball skills in our intramural leagues. Since most of my prior basketball playing occurred employing the fire escape ladders in Washington Heights, my touch was far from simple and soft, but Rich determined to use my bulk to his advantage.

Employing a 1-3-1 zone, Rich McKay stuck me in the middle more or less to block traffic and to be available for boxing out and rebounding. Rugged may have been a better descriptive rather than talented. As for himself, he excelled with the jump shot and his ability to drive to the basket. On one occasion, Dan Buckley, a legendary coach from La Salle Academy on Second Street, came to give a workshop to the Junior Novices. After observing McKay take his unorthodox jump shot, he made some professional adjustments. When they didn't prove too effective, he suggested Rich show him his form again. As he sank about a dozen consecutive swishes, Coach Buckley announced, "The form is unorthodox, but you can't argue with success. Don't change a thing."

After a number of years teaching and serving high schools and in the welfare institutions of the Brothers, Rich applied his talents to business. Using the characteristics he exhibited from his youth, he founded a corporation that taught his organizational, writing skills, and communication techniques to major companies. After many years as a successful entrepreneur, he has retired as a genuine mogul among his peers.

From the perspective of half a century with no notes, pictures or documents to spur the memory, I still have images in my mind of some who were only in Barrytown for a brief time concomitant with me. Joe Maguire from Staten Island remains a pleasant, funny individual with a great sense of humor. Perhaps we shared two months of mutual company. Another character evokes some serious images, however. Practically a caricature or at least a volunteer sent from central casting for a movie about the Dead End Kids, Danny Cavalluzzi from Brooklyn made a great legacy while he spent about two months as a Pioneer of Mary. Danny spoke in an accent one might recognize in B movies about gangsters or soldiers from Brooklyn. He definitely mastered the "youse guys, dese, and dose," familiar to the genre. His pronunciation of the French words he was learning was a study in hilarity too. He also had the wit and humor of a stand up comic who could do justice to Seinfeld. Combining these traits with outstanding athletic ability, especially football, Danny's future in Barrytown appeared on the fast track to most popular boy in the class. Like the excellent running back he was, Danny would wait for blocking to form and then follow his escort until he scooted for long yardage. I suppose his longest run was the dash to the railroad station early in his career leaving our class wondering where he had gone.

One of the sons of Highbridge had the dark, good looks of the Irish, like Pierce Brosnahan. Terry Heslin was probably the most handsome youth in the class, but his quiet, shy, demeanor and relaxed personality seldom placed him in the limelight. Like Joe Troy, he plied the scissors and razors in the barber shop, but I didn't get to know him very well at all. Many times when I have had the opportunity to recollect in tranquility, I savor the pleasant reminiscence of his contribution, albeit too short, to his class. Like some others from my class, their future is lost to speculation and musing. One of the gaps in my mind is the absence of information from some who shared my experience in Barrytown. Whatever happened to them remains an unsolved mystery among those of us who remain even in intermittent communication.

When my first football season at Barrytown opened, I had proved effective as a passer in our intramural Association football league, but my captain had less glorious plans for my talents. While I envisioned a role as prime passer or even receiver, given my substantial bulk at the time, Joe McGowan decided that I would be an excellent choice for offensive center and defensive nose guard. As a newly arrived, I didn't argue with his objectives. Soon, however, I discovered that several years of playing two handed touch tackle on asphalt was no match for two years of varsity football as played in Detroit. Michael Casper Klusman was a Clark Kent clone out of the Midwest. This mild manner, Midwesterner with his "Ah Shucks" personality was an illusion. At the magic incantation of "Hike," Big Klu's six foot three frame and taut muscles morphed into an amalgam of Sam Huff, Chuck Bednarik, and Dick Butkus. At the sound of the triggering word, Klu began knocking me up and down, backward and forward, to and fro, until the whistle blew the play dead. This whirling dervish of muscle and fury treated me like a rag doll in the mouth of a playful puppy. I could claim accurately as my later students did, that he hit me upside my head. It didn't matter whether a pass had been thrown or that an end sweep had gone the other way, as a middle linebacker, Klu never relented in his assault at the action through me. For my part, I was neither clever enough to get out of his way or coward enough to fall down. I took my lumps and registered them to the style of intramural football as played on the fields of Barrytown.

My other recollection of that first season was the impact of another defensive linebacker, John Regan, demolishing our halfback, 'Plugger Bill' McManus. Bill had frozen just before the ferocious hit and ended up with a fractured spine. The last time I saw him he was removed from the field on a rigid door. As he recuperated in Good Shepherd, he decided that the US Marine Corps was a better option than Barrytown. This young man who opted for the Marines over a return to the ball fields of Barrytown, died quite young of a cerebral hemorrhage a number of years ago.

In my senior year at Barrytown, I was the captain of my own team and consequently upgraded my position. I played fullback where I claimed to be "deceptively swift and strong and fleet of foot" and patrolled the middle linebacker position on defense. My position may have changed, and I was in better condition to withstand the punishing runs of Barney Quigley and his sharp elbows and knees, Dermot O'Sullivan and his low to the ground power, and Eddie Schwall and his elusive speed. Competition had not abated either.

As an example, let me cite the opening game recollection for the season. As Dermot's team got ready for the kick off, Brother Amian Bernard called time out and demanded to know whether any of the football players was not wearing an athletic supporter. Don Thoreau, or T-Rox tried to raise his hand, but Dermot stifled his gesture. Apparently, Dermot knew that Don would be sent to the dorm to put on a jock and the team would have to play with ten men without him. T-Rox would play jeopardizing his family jewels rather than be excused until he could don the appropriate gear. Competition defeated compliance.

In the beginning of the season, my team lost our first two games until some sophomores commented that we were overrated and underachieving. Those comments, made in passing, sparked a rejuvenation born of self respect. In the closing seconds of a game, we were tied, but perched on the one yard line with four downs to score. Barrytown's games were usually played on Saturday, but we also had a half day of classes on Thursday, and games were scheduled on that day too. As the game clock neared end, another factor came into play. The games ended when the whistle blew ending recreation even if that occurred before the completion of the game.

As we lined up for the first of our attempts to punch the ball into the end zone, there was a lot of trash talk and threats coming from both sides of the scrimmage. The competitive juices of Bob Stosser boiled the blood of my offensive line, and several epithets may have been uttered. Brother Amian Bernard Caulfield was the referee, and he blew the whistle decreeing official's time out to allow tempers to cool down. After a decent amount of delay, we lined up again for our initial onslaught of the nearby goal line. As I called the cadence for the play, the recreation whistle blew and ended the game before we could get the play started. I went ballistic, claiming that the referee had robbed us of the opportunity to score, and that additional time should be reinstated. Brother Bernard knew better than argue, so he just left the field to a steaming, stewing team that denied conspiracy theories but recognized the cost of undue anger and uncontrolled mayhem after some time. The rage and irrational atmosphere merely underscore the competitiveness we all shared on the playing field.

While football might epitomize the spirit of athletic competition in the Juniorate, other sports were just as illustrative. Baseball, softball, track and minor sports like soccer or Irish football were just as challenging. Aside from intramural competition, the classes also competed against each other, and special opportunities to play against the Novices or Scholastics were especially appreciated. At one time, we were playing the recent graduating class from the Scholasticate. One of their outfielders, a Big Klu type out of Detroit whom we named 'Lil Abner' because of his broad shoulders and out of town accent threatened my life as I played third base. Our pitcher, Mike Schaeffer, for some obscure reason called Sammy, had an effective curve ball. 'Lil Abner' proved totally inept in swinging at the ball. I offered the less than flattering comment that "he couldn't hit a watermelon with a banjo." Like a glib nuisance, my verbal barb reminded him about his lack of skill, so 'Lil Abner' strolled down to third base after striking out and told me to shut my mouth or he'd kick my ass. I took his advice. In another example of competition against this class of formed Christian Brothers, I asked an individual if we were going to play "against youse guys" in the afternoon. This affected Gaelic speaking fugitive from Inwood, politely admonished me with, "Youse guys! Youse guys! The last person who used those terms has been sucking his meals through a straw ever since!" As I learned later, intimidation had been a substitute for his skills for years.

Sport competition was also very evident in Ice Hockey. Given the weather at Barrytown in the winter, ice hockey was a major preoccupation. Since most of the Junior Novices hadn't skated in Gotham, they would be at a disadvantage for at least one season. After learning to adjust the skills of roller hockey in the Heights, I learned to play ice hockey pretty quickly. The time honored procedure for learning to ice skate was sticking the immobile player in front of the goal. Attacking players had the choice of either going around the defensive player with turned in ankles, or skating through them. Sooner or later, the defensive neophyte either learned to skate or get back on his feet after collisions. I really enjoyed hockey very much for it contained many of the elements I enjoyed in sports-action, contact, skill and coordination. After my junior year, I developed into a respectable forward who combined with Pat Murphy and Rich McKay, accounting for a number of goals when we played the Novices or Scholastics. Leaving fancy skating skills to Sean O'Keefe and Tom Smith, we may not have been the smoothest skaters on the ice, but we did the rugged stick work in front of the net.

With only shin guards and a hockey stick most skaters featured a layered look for mobility as we chased the puck across frozen expanse. If we had a deep freeze we could play on the cove next to the Hudson where a puck could travel half a mile if errant. Sometimes it was so cold that our injured couldn't even bleed. Tom Lynch had fallen on the ice and opened up a huge gash above his eyebrow. While a golf-ball sized swelling developed immediately, it was too cold to bleed. As soon as he got indoors, I was told, his gash began to bleed profusely. Hockey proved to be a dangerous, albeit popular sport. Some faculty members, especially Merry Gerry, Amian Bernard, and Pal Baz joined in the chaos on the rink. Brother Leo Chorman, our English teacher had someone inadvertently skate over the bridge of his nose, but another Brother suffered a concussion, and he developed a brain clot that was almost terminal. We used to pray for his miraculous recovery from his coma. Whether it was prayers or medical intervention, he survived without any negative repercussions. His example, however, inspired our Director of Novices, to insist that I wear at least a hat to supplement my shin guards as some kind of protective device. Someone, perhaps Churchill, indicated that the victories of the British Empire were derivatives of lessons learned on the playing fields of Eton. I surmise that the ethos of the Brothers may have evolved from the competition on the fields and skating rinks of Barrytown.

After we had played on the area of the pond reserved for each class, we had to form a circle and shovel the surface until the shavings were removed. Sometimes the competition of the moment led to shenanigans. Joe Emmer, as big and muscular a classmate as I had and quintessential embodiment of 'mucker,' decided to trip fellow Incarnation lad, Pat Murphy. Pat sprawled on the ice when Joe successfully stuck his shovel between Pat's skates. What happened next forced me to check my eyes, for Pat threw down his shovel and assailed Joe with his fists. I thought Pat had lost his mind for no one messed with Joe Emmer. Pat thereby proved that his anger arose from his Irish heritage, for he violated the first basic rule of survival in Barrytown—never get involved in a brawl with an individual forty pounds heavier, several inches taller, and overtly stronger than oneself. That very action proved that Pat's Irish temper was a viable defense in a temporary insanity plea. Joe in the meantime for all his size, was not mean or aggressive. He was merely playing with

Pat, albeit inappropriately. The incipient brawl came to an instant end before Joe decided to actually defend himself with the myriad weapons and strength he had at his disposal. Pat also recognized the impetuous behavior and reverted to the pleasant personality he generally exhibited.

Sometimes our spirit of competition seeped into conversation. Many times wit and humor were almost cruel in the face of some minor or major achievement. One did not acquire a huge ego under the circumstances. Each of us was conditioned to expect little encouragement or positive reinforcement from his peers. Actually, any significant achievement was more likely to inspire mockery or negative putdowns. Since it was distributed evenly and often, few took offense at the practice and grew accustomed to the procedure. It was far wiser to parry commentary with humor than complaints.

Part of the Barrytown culture seemed to be the prolific growth of nicknames. Some were derived from an individual's name or personal quirks. Others were arbitrarily selected as in the case of Tom Mamara who was said to look like a 'Louie.' Still more followed the path of alliteration or rhyme. Physical characteristics led to the names of Tilty Dowd and Pogo Murphy. A fellow inclined to operate at a snail's pace was called 'Flash' Creegan who had a younger brother in the class behind us who earned the name 'Sparky.' Alliteration produced 'Sloppy' Sloan and 'Hoppy' Haubrich and rhyme played a role in naming 'Fluffy' Duffy. Dermot became 'Chooch' for awhile when he insisted on calling others by the name he picked up by observing a movie. One fellow with a penchant for identifying the faults of others with less than tactful terms during advertisements of defects earned the name 'the Cannon Kike,' because he had a name that might have sounded Jewish. John Lennon from St. Raymond's was awarded the name 'Nick' in honor of the similarity to the last name of the famed Bolshevik leader in Russia. Perhaps in the post Beatles era he might have been called 'Bugs,' although that name was reserved for a fellow in the class behind us. The habitual use of the handkerchief and dueling with what probably was a postnasal drip earned Jim Kavanagh of Sacred Heart the name 'TB' which actually stood for tuberculosis.

'TB' had severely broken his ankle while tobogganing between the road and the bottom of the cow fields. After some rehabilitation at home, he returned to Barrytown although he still had a pronounced limp. His example on the toboggan run led me to reinforce my resolution to avoid sleds of all kinds since my encounter with a tree sturdier than I, had immobilized me two years earlier. Nonetheless, many enjoyed the toboggan run, but a few years later another kid from Sacred Heart ended up in traction for a year from a crash on the very slope. Some nicknames stuck and others were ephemeral, but the custom seemed illogical and inexplicable. Maybe one had to be there and recognize the tenor of the times.

Just in my class alone initials were identified with 'TB' Kavanagh, 'TJ' Lynch, and 'JB' Burns. Aside from those already mentioned, our class also had 'Boots,' 'Jimmy Jewels," and yes, even a 'Yerpo.' Not everyone rated a nickname, but they certainly were common. At least two-thirds of the individuals probably were known by nicknames issued without any real comprehensible reason.

Some might argue that competition was the generative force for our growing appetites. No one starved at Barrytown. Nor did many suffer hunger pangs. Some endured an assault upon their taste buds or their sense of propriety. After a period of adjustment, our palates were satisfied with most of the kitchen products. Without a doubt, the hungriest member of our class was also the skinniest. Rich McKay could put to shame any one of us with his appetite and ability to stow away food. If we had tablecloths, Rich could eat them too. Yet, he wasn't a 'Slasher.' He just ate a lot of everything.

Presentation was seldom the concern of the waiters who served the food. Each table in the refectory sat eight students. As a rule, meals were eaten in silence while a Junior read a selection from the New Testament, the Maxims of John Baptist De La Salle, and the Life of the Saint for the Day. After the religious readings, we might listen to a novel, a magazine article, or some such general information medium. Seldom did we hear any articles from newspapers or current event issues. While meals were eaten in silence, one was also required to master the various hand signals indicating a desire for meat platter, deep dish, condiments, or milk.

Only on rare occasions did the kitchen offer some inedible, unidentifiable viand. One was a greasy glob called a 'sinker,' and generally the platters returned untouched. Our palates were challenged one evening when hairy pigs' feet were served. I believe most of the entrée returned intact to the kitchen. Perhaps they were served in another disguise at a later date. Despite healthy portions of toast, every now and then unboiled eggs found their way to the table. In the tradition of poverty, we were expected to consume these runny concoctions. Brother Basilian John used to walk around the refectory examining plates to see residue on individuals' dishes. The Juniors solved the investigation by opening one raw egg and spreading its gooey mess among all the plates on the table. Sometimes one man's poison was another's treat. For example, although Kadota figs were particularly despised, I liked them and when they were served, I could have as many portions as I wished.

The faculty ate the same food at the same time as the students. Their fare was slightly upgraded only with real butter instead of margarine and cream instead of milk. Their coffee was black and intended to be enhanced according to the whim of the consumer as far as sugar and cream were concerned. The Junior Novices had pre-made concoctions of coffee or hot cocoa or even tea. Those who had been in Barrytown for a while knew that sooner or later a good meal would be served, most likely at breakfast. When the cook offered pancakes, or French toast, or corn fritters with maple syrup, appetites swelled and consumption increased notably. There seemed to be an inexhaustible supply of syrup and very few leftovers characterized these meals.

On feast days like November 21, the Feast of the Small, as it was known, or religious holidays like the Immaculate Conception, Ascension Thursday, or the Assumption, the menu generally reflected the importance of the liturgical celebration. Most often chicken *a la king* was the serving of choice and a dessert of brick ice cream was offered. On these opportunities, the rule for silence during meals would be suspended, and we would get a "*Benni*," or more precisely, a "*Benedicamus*" which might be translated as "Let us Bless," the first words of what would be a grace before meals.

The refectory was usually an equal opportunity presenter. Eggs or other portions were counted out for the eight boys with a possibility for one additional serving. If one took more than one's share, the spirit of generosity was severely challenged, unless the platter, deep dish, or dessert contained an undesirable item. Those that quickly demolished their share and then went looking for more were termed 'Slashers.' One individual was such a blatant 'Slasher' that he earned the name 'Frankie Food.' The worst case of table manners I observed occurred when one of my fellow Incarnation lads spotted an extra frankfurter on the platter, licked it, and then offered the tainted goods to everyone else at the table. Naturally, no one would accept his offer, and he contentedly consumed his hard won morsel.

One table was reserved for individuals with special dietary needs. Usually, the reason was a rampant case of teenage acne. The boys on this table didn't get alternatives, but were deprived of some of the condiments, desserts, or entrees that the rest of us received. Some looked upon assignment to the "pimple table" as a sentence rather than a medicinal solution.

Each meal was served by about a half dozen waiters. Most of us looked forward to this weeklong assignment about once a month for it entitled us to leave chapel early and eat after everyone else was finished. Any butter or cream and coffee left on the high table, as the faculty table was known, was fair game. Any left over food could also be consumed. A problem arose when the waiters attempted to spirit some delectable for later consumption while the demand was still evident. A supervising Brother generally made sure that any extra savories were distributed rather than hidden. Often the cooks would make additional food for the waiters anyway. With the exception of the head chef, most of the kitchen staff were fugitives from one part of society or another. They rarely stayed very long and sometimes proved why they were termed 'Knights of the Road.'

Despite its reputation for poor food, many pubescent boys grew strong and tall. Especially evident to me was the evolution of two groupies. Tom Lynch and Jim Marrin shed their short, pudgy bodies and became strong physical specimens. As for me, Jenny Craig or Weight Watchers wasn't necessary for the food was healthful, and plentiful enough to enable me to shed considerable weight and yet develop a strong physique.

When I first arrived in Barrytown, Joe McGowan told me how he retained his six foot six physique, slim but powerful. Joe argued that every lunch snack served at 3:00pm was a 'shouldn't miss' opportunity. He also maintained that on those days when sinkers, mystery meat, 'Malachy's Miracle' (an unidentifiable substance), or uncooked eggs were served, one should stock up on the unlimited supply of bread smothered in any kind of gravy. Before I entered Barrytown I heard a neighbor describe his eating there. The director of the Juniorate at the time was a heroic survivor of World War II. Brother Raymond was in Manila when it was captured by the Japanese. When MacArthur landed and started to expel the occupying Japanese, they bayoneted all the people in the Brothers' college in Manila. Brother Raymond had been stabbed in the leg, but left for dead. He managed to crawl to relative safety when the Japanese returned to make sure there were no survivors. After the war, Brother Raymond healed, but walked with a pronounced limp. In Barrytown, the bread served was Tip Top Bread, a brand that sponsored Hopalong Cassidy on the radio and TV. Instead of admiring the courage of Brother Raymond, the Junior Novices called him 'Hoppy' and said that they lived on Tip Top Bread because it was 'Hoppy's Favorite.' Those sandwiches at 3:00 seldom lasted beyond 3:10, but then again everything in the Juniorate seemed to operate on a frenetic schedule.

I have argued that the curriculum demands at St. Joseph's Normal Institute or the Juniorate, as it was more commonly called, were not challenging for many of the students. Perhaps the explanation lies in the existence of organized scheduled study periods and the requirement to balance academic work with the introduction to the religious exercises of the Christian Brothers. One should also calculate that no time was lost in commuting to and from school. Living in the same building as our classrooms, we had merely to move from the common room to the classroom, a two minute excursion. No time was wasted in waiting for buses or trains, or subways, or on highways. I certainly would not fault the faculty who introduced us to many of the subjects. Most were master teachers sincerely interested in our progress and the integrity of their subjects. Part of the explanation may also lie in the state of education in the United States in the middle fifties. When I was a senior in the fall of 1956, I recall seeing Sputnik in the cold sky overhead. The world was also in crisis mode because the French and British paratroopers had seized the Suez Canal. Talk of war made me contemplate joining the Marines as part of my responsibilities. War talk evaporated, but the influence of the Russian spacecraft was felt throughout the land. Demands for math and science courses grew exponentially. My Latin, French, English, and history subjects dwarfed my mathematical expertise and interest in physics and biology. I had minor courses in general science and health at Manhattan and senior chemistry. My math knowledge peaked with Intermediate Algebra.

In Barrytown, my class had a very effective Latin teacher, Brother Peter Mannion who practically conducted class without any words.

'Big Beve,' or the 'Big One' was the master of the gesture and doled out words with the precision and care of a miser. When he entered the classroom, he would signal with his fingers, how wide open the windows should be. Some of us predicated preternatural talents for him. We believed, unlike most mortals, he was gifted with the ability to travel noiselessly on foot, communicate wordlessly, and even osmose through solid walls. Most of his class discipline was controlled by a gamut of gesticulations and grimaces that conveyed his wishes. He was also the Sub-Director of the Juniorate, and reputed to glide soundlessly around the corridors and nooks and crannies, until he uncovered some recalcitrant cabal or some such malfeasance. He could appear like Jacob Marley in **A Christmas Carol.** Once he zeroed in on the noise producers, he could exact compliance without a word. With a facial message of compassion, pain, benign compassion or just incredulity, Brother Peter would correct the situation and move on to his next discovery. Once, Eddie Schwall and I were singing *"Black Denim Trousers"* quite lustfully in the shoe room. Brother Peter materialized, we thought perhaps through the solid wall of the 'slop room,' gave us his best, bemused, disappointing expression and moved on wordlessly while Eddie and I instantaneously corrected our behavior and laughed at how easily the 'Big One' had confronted us.

In my senior year I studied the *Aeneid* under Brother Leo Chorman, also called 'Casual Connie.' His class was a very small class and a virtual college level seminar without the terminology. 'Casual Connie,' had mastered the art of teaching junior English and birdwatching simultaneously. Memory places him, his anthology, and has binoculars draped around his neck in the classroom. He was more attentive in our *Aeneid* class, introducing us to the mythology of the subject as well as the arcane grammar in Virgil's epic. Our French teacher was Brother Amian Bernard Caulfield who came across as a blue-eyed mystic with unpredictable fury beneath a placid exterior. He was, actually, quite friendly and an excellent teacher of French. I believe much of his classroom conduct was dramatics and posturing that precluded the New York City urchins from challenging his authority. Under his tutelage we covered three years of regents French in two. Brother Julian Mawn, however, suffered the indignity of hostile students when he taught us **The Life of Christ.** Ironically termed 'Jolly Jules,' his classroom style was confrontational and counterproductive. Every class seemed to be a contest between irreconcilable forces. Primarily a master of liturgical music, he encountered all kinds of resistance and mockery. Unfortunately, he uttered threats that only bred contempt and scorn. Many times during the course of the year he would threaten Dermot with a "big bounce to Newburgh," or he would issue a universal statement like, "When the tree shakes, hang on." This would generally raise a howl of laughter from Jim Costello and Nick Lennon. At the end of the junior year, however, some of his greatest critics were awarded train tickets to the big city and seldom if ever seen again.

In the summer of my senior year, I recall mostly the baseball games we played on the senior diamond. Occasionally, we went swimming in the Hudson River, but that didn't appeal to me no matter how hot it was. The waters of the Hudson might be cool and refreshing this distance from metropolises like New York and Albany, but the river bed was soft and mushy, giving me the sense of plodding through cow flops. The sensation was far from either refreshing or recreational. The previous summer one of the boys from the Juniorate had drowned on an outing to Taconic Lake, so there were no trips plotted there again. We did get to participate in two picnics at Baird State Park about thirty miles south of Barrytown. When I entered the Novitiate, the Brothers had built a fine swimming pool overlooking the cove where we sometimes played ice hockey so tip toeing through the flops was not an issue anymore.

One of the summertime replacements in Barrytown was the legendary Brother Cassian Gregory Hunt, better known universally as 'Harpo' for reasons unknown to me. The boys whom he had taught at Good Shepherd idolized this man, and the attitude was contagious. I don't recall his teaching me anything, but he made me feel good when his humor and wit were directed toward me. So many thought I was from Good Shepherd in Inwood, but Harpo always made a note of referring to me as coming from the Heights and Incarnation. For some obscure reason, I particularly enjoyed his style of referring to one and all by the name 'Clyde.' We invited him to return during the regular school year to address the Benilde Club on the subject of extra curricular activities. We also had a Brother Robert from Detroit who was named "Typing Bob," for he gave me my only course in typing, a skill that I have used extensively throughout my life. We also hosted a Brother from Syracuse who we called "Clumping Cleo," for I believe his actual name was Cleophas and he had a serious limp.

In my senior year, our English teacher was a soft-spoken young Brother who offered his British heritage and impeccable diction for our enhancement. Moreover, he had an excellent knowledge of literature and exhibited an intense admiration for the subject. His devotion to the literary world was matched by his extraordinary love and interpretation of Gregorian chant. Perhaps even more astounding was his ability to inspire us to adopt his dual interests, and his incredible capacity to generate passion in transmitting it to his students. From the depths of his soul to the minds and hearts of his students, Brother Benilde James Loxham convinced even the most skeptical of the beauty, the magnificence, and the importance of chant and literature. Under his direction and inspiration the Masses and musical contributions to our religious training improved manifold. Brother Benilde had been born in England, and his family moved to the United States, while he was in the Juniorate in Great Britain. This youthful proselytizer, whom we named 'Spencer,' popularized the Gregorian style of the monks of Solesme. Rather than merely chanting the parts of the Mass or the Latin aspects of the Liturgy, Brother Benilde impressed us with his artistry and the beauty and cadence of Gregorian chant when performed properly. To him I owe a lifelong admiration for Literature and Gregorian chant. In retrospect, I have to admire his patience, for Bill Simon and I used to sing at the top of our lungs and neither one of us had a concept of tone. As a matter of variety, we used to switch jackets too. Since I was twice the size of Bill, our appearance may have been more comical than reverential.

Aside from his magnificent contribution to the singing, he also made us memorize and recite sonnets, soliloquies, odes, and passages from outstanding masters of the English language. Rather than take advantage of his youth, he took advantage of our enthusiasm under his direction and instruction. For my love of Gregorian chant and for his insistence on our memorizing significant poetry, I have felt a life long debt to 'Spencer,' a name assigned to him when one of his initial reading assignments was a passage from the works of Winston Spencer Churchill, the master of English prose. As indicated throughout, one never knew when or where a nickname might be adopted.

Brother James Hogan, an institution for a score of years in the Juniorate, and known as 'BJ,' taught physics. Since I had taken Latin,

I didn't have the honor of participating in his class, but I used to hear tales of his classroom humor and quick wit. In my senior year he was given the responsibility of turning us into incipient chemists. The students who had him in physics told us about his classroom style. After about twenty years in Barrytown, he was like a predictable institution. During one of his classes, I pulled the chair from beneath Eddie Schwall as he went to sit down. When he crashed on the floor, 'BJ' simply said, "Minus ten, O'Prey. You could have broke his ass!" To reclaim my ten points, I merely had to read an illustrated comic book which explained the process for refining galena into lead. That punitive assignment, by the way, led to my acing a question of the chemistry regents exam when that very topic was a ten point question.

One other incident sticks in my mind from senior chemistry. The class was assigned to create chlorine gas in the laboratory. Rich McKay was so impressed with his success that he invited Joe Troy to sniff the end product. Coughing, sputtering, slobbering, sniveling, gagging, gasping, choking,and throat clutching permeated the lab as Joe recoiled in pain. As the rest of the created gas escaped, we were ordered out of the room through ground floor windows if necessary, and told to walk the road while the room was aired out. We did so as Joe was taken to the hospital where he spent several hours inhaling oxygen. Joe wasn't permanently injured, but I used to wonder how many comic books Rich McKay had to read to compensate for his practical joke.

The Brother who taught us senior religion and American history was another Barrytown fixture. Brother Chrysostom Basil, 'Pal Baz,' was a superlative athlete, but a rather pedestrian teacher. Since I was always reading fact or fiction about American history, I had myriad questions to ask him. To his credit, 'Pal Baz' never answered any of my queries. I would put my head on the desk, drape my arms over the sides and when the spirit moved me, I would raise my hand from this posture. He would always acknowledge my interruption. Then he would listen to my question, ask my opinion about the answer, and then thank me, and move on without transmitting any information. For the entire year, 'Pal Baz' never once gave me any answer to my questions. When I was a teacher myself, I think I would have gone ballistic in the face of such posture and behavior.

During the course of the school year, the Juniorate paid special attention to some holidays. St. Patrick's Day of course was special, but Halloween had a unique place in tradition too. The senior class was allowed to decorate the refectory and create a tunnel of horrors which was supposed to intimidate the underclassmen. The poets in the class would create a list of victims for Igor, a monster dressed like Frankenstein. As the list was read and the individuals hustled off to an unknown fate, the rest of the underclassmen were supposed to be kept on edge. When my class had the opportunity to run Halloween, Barney was Igor and I was one of his six assistants. As one of the victims was ushered roughly into the scullery, I assisted in his persecution in what I thought was a minor shove. From out of nowhere came 'Pal Baz' who slammed me violently and said, "How do you like some of your own medicine?" Frankly, I was taken aback and later decided that 'Pal Baz' was just retaliating for some of my evident disrespect in the classroom.

Known widely among the Brothers of the New York District as 'Little Shroob,' Brother Austin Gerald was another significant addition to the Brothers who resided on the south side of the second floor. His nickname derived from his relationship with his older brother who was called 'Big Shroob.' We simply called him 'Merry Gerry the Workhorse.' One of his responsibilities besides instructing us in math was routine house maintenance. With his ever present laugh and joking manner, he involved us in some of his tasks. After thirty years the wooden chairs in the refectory had amassed a patina of decayed food, grime, grease, and whatever else teenagers might have added to the chair. Some were rickety and loose. The Russian Communists may have had five year economic plans, but Merry Gerry had his "Honor to Work Program." Some of us read the inscription on the Nazi gates to concentration camps and thought the slogan, if not the reality, reflected Merry Gerry's zeal. Above the entrance to most camps was a metal sign that said, *"Arbeit Macht Frei!" or "Work will make you free!"* Merry Gerry assigned a chair to each individual, outfitted him with abrasive steel wool and what we called Atomic Soap for its cleansing power. Each chair was taken apart, and stripped of the dirt and whatever finish was left upon the solid wood. Then the parts were left on a table for Merry Gerry's inspection. If he accepted the job performed, he then put the chairs back together, varnished them and created a sturdy, durable chair for another thirty years. Perhaps he will return from his hallowed position at Manhattan College today and supervise his honor to work program again.

On another occasion, Merry Gerry drafted Joe Emmer and me to help him drain and reconnect the huge radiators in the dormitories. Joe and I were expected to balance the unwieldy, heavy, leaden heaters while our supervisor deftly connected them to another pipe. Joe and I struggled with the weight of the huge radiators and to steady them. Gerry grabbed our burden in one hand and screwed the connection with the other. Impressed with his strength, Joe and I resolved not to test this man's potency under any circumstances, especially when he chose to join in our intramural basketball games and ice hockey bouts. Of course, Merry Gerry's "Honor to Work" exercises always took place in what was supposed to be our free recreation time. His zeal for hard work earned him the respect and name we cherished for him. We didn't recognize that we were also in the presence of a major Hibernophile who would concentrate on spreading Irish culture among the collegians at Manhattan.

In my junior year the Director of the Junior Novices was Brother Basilian John Veale. I honestly thought he was a rather inappropriate selection. He was from Rhode Island, and his sense of drollery and confusing facial expressions confounded the young teenagers in his care. His alleged sanctity did not include a warm personality or commendable social graces. To most of the kids he was an individual to be avoided whenever possible. Yet, part of our training involved a weekly meeting with him. It was called reddition of conduct and was supposed to be like conferring with a confessor or mentor. In my experience, reddition with Brother John was like sitting in front of an art work and trying to interpret its meaning or what it is trying to say to you. My time with him passed very slowly and usually fruitlessly. Sometimes I felt talking to the wallpaper might be more emotionally rewarding. At the end of the year, he was sent to the Second Novitiate in Rome. Our paths crossed again when he became our Director during our freshman year in Troy. His exposure to Dale Carnegie's, **How to Win Friends and Influence People** upgraded his personality and our appreciation of his finer points. After our round two, he became the Director of Novices at Narragansett, and his disciples always spoke highly of him.

Brother John was replaced the following year by Brother Peter Mannion, our former Latin teacher. He was much attuned to youth, ˻ ˻ also had the respect and admiration of the students. His sense ˻or became more evident, and the mystery behind his general silence gradually unfolded leaving most of us with a gratitude ....u respect for a man who helped us face the responsibilities of entering the religious life. As evidence of his impact, now almost fifty years later, many of the boys he dealt with in the Juniorate still remain in touch with him and enjoy the camaraderie of old times and memories from different sides of the coin.

Life in the Juniorate was semi-unreal in many ways. We had little contact with the outside world since radio, television and even newspapers were unavailable. When a friend of mine was released from a correctional institution upstate for his conviction of mugging a homosexual in Riverside Park, he and I compared our mutual schedules. The Juniorate seemed more punitive than the reform school. He had more free time, TV privileges, pool tables, smoking opportunities, and sleeping or recreational options. He found the regimen repressive while I thought of Barrytown as a wonderful adventure. I suppose the major difference emanated from being incarcerated voluntarily or compulsorily. Our sole entertainment was an occasional movie that had been carefully selected for our edification. At intermission we were permitted to munch on a candy bar, generally a delicious Powerhouse. The rock and roll revolution went along very nicely without our participation or knowledge. One of the last songs I remember before heading to Barrytown was *"Earth Angel,"* the forerunner of many hits. Little did I know that in a few years I would be teaching the nephew of Tony Williams of the Platters. For the most part we had little knowledge of the emergence of Elvis Presley or other stars. Somehow, that didn't seem to be a deprivation. On the other hand, I remember thinking how foolish it was when we had a conference shortly before heading home for a month in August, 1956. We had been urged to avoid reading even one edition of the **New York Daily News,** for it could destroy a month's worth of spiritual reading.

Home visits were usually a three or four day sojourn in December and in April, corresponding with Christmas and Easter. There were also two or three visiting Sundays when families were welcome to visit Barrytown. Many rented a communal bus for the trip, but by that time my family had a car. In April of 1956 while at home, I got my learner's permit to drive, took the test, and managed to secure a driver's license which enriched my opportunities later in my formation.

Almost all my memories are soft and palpable after fifty years. A few practices still rasp against my personality. Perhaps the majority of memories are gilted by time and selection but I don't think so. I don't consider myself an apologist for the Juniorate, but I have no difficulty in confessing my joyous recollections. Time and maturity should have abraded some reminders of the era, but that doesn't seem to have happened to all. One of the unusual customs of the Junior Novitiate was a religious exercise more attuned perhaps to the personality of the French than to the Americans. Once a week, we conducted an exercise called the Advertisement of Defects. In this program each candidate would invite the rest of the student body to alert him to any observable flaws or imperfections that impeded his progress to sanctity. For most of the students, it was a perfunctory exercise that evoked little response. For some, it was an invitation to tragedy. One boy from Detroit was pilloried on a weekly basis. As he stood up, seventy-five per cent of the students would stand and wait their turn to inform Charley about his defects. I thought it was far from religious, and if anything, a tribute to his ability to survive. While Charley had his quirks, these advertisements which we more accurately termed 'shots,' were a demonstration of persecution and lack of charity. It is one of the religious exercises that I believed poorly suited the maturity level of high school kids and of dubious value to those in college. I do remember only two of the 'shots' I received. One is the initial information I received on my path to sainthood. I got shot for reading novels during study periods. Actually, I thought it was a veiled compliment rather than a correction. I disregarded the correction and continued to plumb the shelves of the library, especially in the fiction and biographical sections. After two years of such intense reading, I had acquired an extensive knowledge of literature of all sorts. Perhaps since it was evident I had some spare time, Brother Peter assigned me to compile a daily record of events in the Juniorate. I was asked to maintain a log or journal that summarized the day's events. Every now and then Brother Peter would check on my work to guarantee my conscientious attention to contemporary history.

The other advertisement I remember from my seven years of experience is the comment in the Scholasticate that my conversation centered on personalities rather than other subjects. Its accuracy and authenticity may be demonstrated by the existence of this writing. I guess I really haven't changed much over the years.

I also never quite appreciated the role of one of the Broth
whose responsibility as Visitor General was to assure that the houses of
formation were following the traditions of St. La Salle and his Christian
Brothers. Brother Cornelius Luke was American born, but reputed
to have been brainwashed by the French during his tenure on the
continent. At least once a year, each student was scheduled to meet
with 'Flookie Luke,' as he was termed. During this forced reddition
of conduct with a peculiar man whose idiosyncrasies could challenge
the vocabulary of a doctorate in English, he would advise the student
about his progress in the religious life. This was accompanied by a dose
of scripture which Brother Luke personalized for the individual. He
typed this citation on what we termed toilet paper, for it resembled
onion skin rather than traditional paper. For some, Brother Luke
might offer encouragement to continue praying for one's vocation.
For others, he would suggest that the boy would "make a good Holy
Name man." Brother Luke examined our schedule, prayer life,
customs, and extirpated any abuses or relaxations he might discover.
He did so in an inimitable, almost cartoon like voice. Naturally, he
was the target of a number of imitations and amateur impersonations.
One of his particular targets of potential abuse centered on the dining
room. Brother Luke frowned upon the custom of speaking during
meals. Most of our meals were taken in silence while a lector read
from some book. As mentioned before, indications for desired food
were made by a variety of established hand signals. When we were
permitted to speak during meals, the privilege was called a "Benny,"
short for the Latin verb "Benedicamus." When Luke arrived, Bennies
grew scarce, just as when another important administrator named
Brother Charles Henry who would later be elected Superior General
arrived in Barrytown. Some wag described the reforming pair as "One
Benny Henny and Less Than That Luke." A boast of the guys from New
York centered on the largesse of the New York District Visitor, Brother
Anthony John Halpin who provided many more opportunities to
speak during our meals. Maybe he was less ascetic than Luke or Henry,
or then again, he may just have been more gregarious. Nonetheless,
I am afraid that the irrepressible personalities of the kids trespassed
into mockery whenever the Visitor General arrived.

Perhaps a contrast upon our graduation celebration might
illustrate the insular world in which we dwelt. Unlike a typical senior

prom where tuxedoes, limousines, fashionably gowned dates and a possible night club visit thereafter with a commemoration with alcohol that might challenge the contemporary rules, our senior trip was quite different. We boarded a bus to that fabulous metropolis known to some as the Tri-City area. There in sports coats and ties, we had a luncheon in Troy or in Albany. That was followed by a visit to a genuine cinema in downtown Albany where we watched a first run film. If my faltering memory is accurate, the movie was *Gunfight at the O.K. Corral* starring Kirk Douglas and Burt Lancaster. This depiction of the gunslinger's duel between the Clantons and the Earps abetted by Doc Holliday was the highlight of our senior trip. After the film we had a dinner in one of the Brothers' schools in the area and then boarded the school bus for the ride back to Barrytown. While it was a great break away from our usual routine, it contrasts immensely with the activities our peers experienced in celebration of their graduations.

I have offered these recollections in tranquility without benefit of notes, documents, pictures, or other devices that may have turned me in different directions. These thoughts are honest commentary upon my point of view. If my affection and even admiration for my classmates and experiences in the Juniorate do not permeate this narrative, then I have not done them justice. If that is the case, then I apologize for any misdemeanors committed in the transition. As a general rule, the personalities and contributions of those whom I met in Barrytown leave me with the total impression that I had the joy of knowing them and sharing a wonderful experience. When I examine their lives, or at least the lives of those with whom I am familiar, I conclude that almost everyone of us was the better for the experience.

One of the books for which I was 'shot' while reading during study period, was a fictional biography of James Michael Curley, the raffish mayor of Boston who was elected while serving a jail term for taking a civil service exam for one of his constituents. **The Last Hurrah** by Frank O'Connor was made into a movie featuring Spencer Tracy playing Frank Skeffington, the mayor. As he lay dying surrounded by politicos, friendly and hostile, one muttered, "There's the scoundrel, the mountebank, the charlatan, the blackguard on his death bed. I'll bet that rascal has many regrets and would change many things if he could." Tracy barely had the strength to open one eye, but he whispers, 'like hell I would." I can find no better symbolic ending to my chapter on the Juniorate than the dying expression of a character from one of the books I surreptitiously read against the rules. Like Skeffington, I have no regrets nor desire to change what I experienced in the Juniorate.

Chapter Three

The Novitiate—1957-1958

According to Canon Law, the Catholic Church requires a period of testing before one is allowed to wear the habit of a religious Order. This period is called Postulancy and for the Christian Brother lasts approximately three months. For the Juniorate graduates of June, 1957 our postulancy began almost immediately after our graduation ceremony. The trip from Juniorate to Novitiate was greater than a mere relocation although we would remain in Barrytown. It was an introduction to an ostensibly stricter, more mature, more self-sacrificing, more cerebral approach to mastering concupiscence and self-indulgence. Unfortunately, few of us were really mature enough to take full advantage of this phase of religious training. Body and soul may have been ready for the challenges, but mentally most of us were still seventeen or eighteen and mired in our frivolity and youthful complacency.

Upon admission to the Postulancy, each of us was assigned a 'guardian angel' to assist in the transition from Juniorate to Novitiate. This person was a Novice who was in the group ahead of us and most likely well known to the Postulant. In truth, I don't have a clear memory to whom I was assigned, but I faintly remember that Hubie Reynolds from Highbridge, now Brother Timothy, was given the task of helping in my assimilation. Whether he had some regrets over the assignment or had any misgivings over the responsibility, I do not recollect. I do more vividly remember the person who was assigned to me a year later. Bernie O'Neill was chosen for me, and I recall more about him than I did about Brother Timothy. Perhaps Tim had more to remind him about me than I had about any intervention he provided. Since I was quite familiar with the procedure and practices of Barrytown, there really wasn't much that Tim had to do anyway.

His function was to provide guidance and what the superiors cal ~ edification, and I can't fault him about either.

In the Novitiate, our morning schedule began at 5:00am with forty clangs of a bell. Within fifteen minutes we were supposed to wash, shave or whatever and then we assembled in the chapel for a brief pious reading after which we were dismissed for an additional ten minutes. The hand bell summoned us back to the chapel for Morning Prayer at 5:30. Traditional Morning Prayer incorporated some oral prayers that were part scriptural, part institutional, and part liturgical. Then the Sub-Director read from a text that was intended to assist us in mental prayer. I always found mental prayer to be problematic, for the ecstasy or illumination that was targeted eluded my mind. Frankly my efforts to commune with the Creator for half an hour were generally one way silent conversations. As intently as I tried, I seldom reached a point where I developed spiritual insight into anything other than the reality that mental prayer and I were probably not intended for each other. I reminded myself that the Christian Brothers were an active, not a contemplative, apostolate. My quest for a perception of God that transcended human knowledge eluded me. Despite my fervent attempts, I never acquired a facility for mental prayer, or for that matter, a taste for understanding the incomprehensible. I blindly accepted theology, assured that Catholic Church teaching was infallible. I never chose to plumb the depths of arcane mysteries like the Trinity or Transubstantiation. Church teaching was sufficient for me, so I never experienced the dark night of the soul as described by some mystics. I accepted the Pauline summary about fighting the good fight and winning the race, or a place in heaven. My faith was actually rather puerile and facile, leading to no crisis of the soul.

St. La Salle had created a formulaic outline for mental prayer, and we had a card that presented an outline of what thoughts we were to entertain and a sequence of prayerful acts that were supposed to occupy at least half an hour. After a while, the formula was supposed to be unnecessary and could be discarded. I never reached that stage of contemplation or asceticism. While my efforts were consistent and earnest, I wouldn't want my spiritual life evaluated on my success in this aspect of my relationship with God. My quest for intimacy, contemplation, and mysticism with the deity seemed mired in the daily distractions associated with the practical and mundane preoccupations of youth.

Immediately after the allotted time for mental prayer, daily Mass began. When the celebration of the Eucharist concluded, we had a brief additional prayer period before a five minute intermission for free time. Then we were summoned, again by hand bell, for breakfast in the Novitiate refectory. During breakfast, as at other meals in the Novitiate refectory, we listened to readers who droned excerpts from pious literature similar to the texts used in the Juniorate. Thus we ate in total silence disrupted only by the sounds of dishes, silverware, and pitchers. Platters, beverages, condiments and the paraphernalia of the dining room were summoned or passed along to the intended consumer without a word.

After breakfast, we had assigned manual labors which involved general housekeeping or cleaning up after meals. Corridors mopped, stairs swept, bathrooms cleaned, sinks and racks spiffed up, kitchen policed, and dishes washed and dried and tables reset occupied the bulk of the Novice work force during this manual labor period. Although I can't remember the exact horarium, I recall that we had several more conferences, and prayer sessions with the primary expression being six decades of the rosary. The additional decade, reflecting the French foundation, was for those Brothers who were drafted into compulsory French military service. The rosary was usually recited in Latin in keeping with the then universally approved rubrics for church prayer and services.

We also had a 'recreational' study of the French language since canon law forbade any academic classes during the Novitiate year. Because French was the official language of the Institute and its general governing body conducted business in that language despite its location in Rome, everyone in the Order was expected to have some fluency or comprehension of the language. Very few of the Brothers would ultimately end up in the Mother House in Rome where French was the first language, or would make what was termed a Second Novitiate. Therefore, the association with the language wasn't stressed too intensely. Some of us merely mastered the French words that were intended to begin any conversation among members of the Order: *"Vive Jesu dans nos coeurs"* and its response, *"A jamais."* The first segment was an invocation, "Live Jesus in our hearts" and the response meant "Forever." This ejaculation was supposed to be a prelude to any vocal communication while we were in the Novitiate. Some were more conscientious about following this by-law than others.

The **Rules and Regulations of the Brothers of the Christian Schools** insisted we use a Francophile's stilted language which reminded me of the literary *Preciosite* to which we had been introduced in French class with Brother Amian Bernard in the Juniorate. We were instructed to address each other as 'My Dear Brother Such and Such,' or as the French expressed it, '*Mon Cher Frere* . . . .' Most recognized the convolution and ignored the directive, as we did the same about not crossing one's legs. Nonetheless, as each of us tried to adopt a *modus vivendi* for living according to our rule, rigorists insisted on following the letter of the law. I confess I wasn't among them.

Many of the group sessions incorporated a study of the **Rules** which were examined and explained in great detail. Generally speaking, most of the **Rules** made good sense for peaceful co-existence in a religious community of men. We also were introduced to some of the regulations that concerned membership in a Papal Order. The Brothers transcended diocesan control since they were a pontifical institute with districts dispersed generously throughout the entire world. Brothers teaching in a specific diocese were under the direction of its bishop, but they could move in protest, or appeal to Rome if something untoward was demanded. When I had the opportunity in later years to see how bishops misused and abused diocesan Orders, especially nuns, I could appreciate the status of a Papal Institute.

Scenarios about inheritance and the meaning of the five vows were examined too. While most religious professed vows of poverty, chastity, and obedience, the Christian Brothers added two more: that of teaching the poor gratuitously and stability in the said society. The latter two were designed to address the need to remain in communities and to preclude any aspirations to the priesthood which was an alternative in many other male religious Orders. At the foundation of the Christian Brothers in 1682, St. La Salle was determined to have an egalitarian community without any distinctions in names, titles, or functions. There were Directors and Sub-Directors in each community, and each district had of necessity a group of central administrators. None of these had any outer marks of distinctions that set them apart from the community members.

An early candidate for the priesthood, following the directives of the founder, had traveled to Rome for ordination. Before this man could reach the Eternal City, he entered eternal life unexpectedly and prematurely. When La Salle heard about the man's untimely death en route, he interpreted it as a message from God to exclude any members of the new found Order from ordination. In order to preclude any sacerdotal aspirations or pressures from bishops, La Salle insisted that the Brothers omit Latin and teach in the vernacular. Since those who didn't know Latin were considered vulgar or common and uneducated, the Brothers warranted the appellation '*Les Ignorants*,' or "the ignoramuses" by no less a notary than Voltaire himself. The famous skeptic applied his acid wit in ridicule against the humble sons of John Baptist De La Salle. I doubt any felt embarrassed by his verbal assaults since the Brothers seldom associated with the salon patrons of Louis XIV's nobility.

We learned about patrimony, canonical warnings, exclaustration, financial inheritances, and so forth. With the vow of poverty, each Brother renounced possession of worldly goods and inheritances. All material goods were held in common, and like the socialists of Jeremy Bentham, "To each according to his need," was the operative principle of material goods. One could lay claim to a robe, underwear, a crucifix, a New Testament/prayer book, and a small pen knife which was used to sharpen pencils or styluses of the pupils. To the credit of the Institute, few episodes of money grabbing were ever recorded or told in myth or legend.

If for some egregious offense, a Brother warranted expulsion from the Order, a legal procedure was described in detail. The offender had to receive three official or canonical warnings related to the same offense. A canonical warning was far from casual, for it involved acolytes and witnesses in a formalized ceremony. I have no idea how often this process may have occurred, for I can only think of one affair while I was in the Novitiate. Most of that episode is shrouded in secrecy, including the alleged offense. Since Novices had no vows, or Scholastics had temporary commitments, canonicals were replaced by chapters that voted not to allow an individual to renew his vows, so canonical warnings were exclusively the domain of Brothers who had professed final vows.

One of the traditional exercises in the Novitiate was the composition of a personal mental prayer written out and read to our peers. The result was intended to reflect the formulaic approach we were to master. After we had completed the reading of our prayer, we were critiqued by our peers in a conference later in the day. I think few of us felt any great need to correct the mental prayers of our peers, for I suspect all had difficulty with the cerebral exercise. I must confess that in my pseudo-intellectual conviction of that period, I tried to utilize whatever fancy vocabulary words I had encountered in recent time. The high-blown purple prose left many scratching their heads and my self-indulgence unaddressed. There are many today that believe I never quite conquered my assault upon the arcane vocabulary I had learned somewhere or other.

In the afternoon we generally had a major portion of time devoted to manual labor. On Thursday and Saturday, we had recreation for the afternoon, and sometimes we also had some recreation time on Sundays before Vespers and Compline. The basketball courts and handball fields as well as the baseball field that doubled for football were well used when we didn't have ice for hockey. At noontime we said the Angelus, examined our conscience, and had additional prayers before lunch. Our evening prayers were quite the same with litanies to St. Joseph and the Blessed Mother and to Jesus Suffering also recited. We moreover had at least a half hour of spiritual reading from a book designated for our consumption by the Director of Novices. After lunch and supper those Brothers not assigned to clean up went on section walks which were appointed groups of about a half dozen that strolled after meals keeping a distance of about ten yards apart from any other group. Our conversation was supposed to be on religious, pious topics, or the readings we had heard at meals. Few actually followed that advice, finding other items of interest to discuss.

In the evening, we studied more about the religious life or had instruction in theology, scripture, Lives of the Saints, biographies of outstanding Brothers like Benilde, Miguel, or Mutien Marie, or some other topic of an edifying nature. Night prayer provided an introduction to the 'great silence,' a very strictly enforced custom of never speaking for whatever reason after night prayer. By 9:30pm, a bell tolled for lights out and we retired to our individual cells in large dormitories on two floors. Each cell was a curtained square approximately sixty-four sq. feet in area. The curtains hung on metal bars and only one side opened onto an aisle. There were no lights in the individual cells so no one could read after lights out. In the back of the dorm were a number of sinks and a rack for drying towels or socks. The showers were in another part of the second floor. For travel between shower and cell, a bathrobe and slippers were essential. Each cell also contained a chair and a small bureau. Heavy outdoor coats were hung separately downstairs above cubbyholes for footwear. A cell was never intended as a lounging area and we never had the opportunity to rest during the day. The confined space was merely a utilitarian area for sleeping during the 'great silence.'

Every day was pretty much the same, and the toll of concentrated prayer, disciplined silence, and organized manual labor exacted a price from the candidates, especially those who had arrived in Barrytown a matter of days or weeks earlier. The Pioneers of Mary from the Juniorate were deeply enriched by other talented candidates who aspired to membership in the Brothers of the Christian Schools. For the most part, they differed from those with Juniorate experience in that they generally did not come from the Irish American parishes that fostered vocations to the high school. Many of the new members of the group, in fact, came from farther away from the City. Although our group was named The Pioneers of Mary since we began as the first day Juniorate class, the appellation continued to have some other significance. For the first time, the New York District had divided and a new district was created. The Long Island-New England District (LINE) had been formed with Brother Charles Henry as the first Visitor. The first Novices of that district were the members of our group.

We also were pioneers in a more practical if not cerebral way. For the first time, Novices were permitted to dispose of the medieval calotte or beanie that one used to wear in drafty churches of old. To some from New York City, it was a replica of the Jewish Yarmulke. It apparently symbolized humility and obedience in its day, but we were allowed to develop those virtues without such a reminder. Naturally, it was a suggestion and not an imperative, so some chose to continue to wear the calotte. Those that did were generally thought to have their thoughts focused on heaven rather than on earth. Often with eyes cast heavenward, their ethereal attitude and posture made them perfect targets for cynics and students of human behavior rather than the aesthetics of sanctity. Some continued to wear the beanie and accrue graces reserved for those who eschewed human respect and mockery. For the most part, the rest of the Novices declared them 'up the wall' and temporarily not of this planet. The term had little to do with 'off the wall,' a phrase denoting insanity. 'Up the wall' described an intense interpretation of the rule and the consequent behavior therefrom. Those whose scrupulous interpretation of the need to shun conversation inspired some recalcitrants to play dumb so that the reticent contemplative was almost forced to speak to convey his message. In truth, I sometimes found the emphasis on silence may have been ascetic, but it seemed impolite to me.

Aside from the calotte, we also were the first group to benefit from modern plastics and tailoring techniques. A few were selected to master the molding and riveting of the white rabatta secured to a white plastic collar we wore around our necks. This accoutrement of our habit symbolized the Ten Commandments and used to be a nuisance to maintain when it required frequent washing, starching and ironing, and still looked askew. Our plastic neck pieces and rabattas gave others at The Catholic University of America the inspiration for the nickname they thrust upon us. We were known as 'The Bib and Sack Boys.' At least it sounded a step above the Salesians who we termed 'Gypsies' for their customary dirty, disheveled habits.

As pioneers in these minor areas, we continued also in another more significant realm. When we entered our postulancy, the new Director of the entire plant at Barrytown was appointed. Brother Concordius Leo, better known to us as Conky, was named to head the entire institution. Conky either wheedled a great deal more money out of the New York and LINE District Councils or else he knew how to spend his money wisely and effectively. Immediately, the change was evident in the menu. The quality and quantity of the food improved dramatically. For assistance, Conky called upon a thin, tall, taciturn man named Brother Robert. Of course, we baptized him 'Budget Bob.' Whenever anyone requested something, 'Budget Bob' always claimed he had to consult the budget. We never got a straight answer, only a promise of a consultation with the number cruncher. 'Budget Bob,' however, was actually a man with a hidden sense of humor and a wry presentation. He did a magnificent job, especially evident to those who had been in the Juniorate. In fact, grousing about food all but ceased with his achievements, and he set an excellent example for those who followed in our formation. In Troy, Brother Eulogius Austin O'Malley did a great job, even employing a pastry chef who mastered a dessert I haven't tasted since my days in Troy. Ray, the chef, prepared Nesserode pie to perfection. In Washington, Brother Brice Patrick Brown followed the examples of 'Budget Bob' and Eulogius Austin and offered meals and confections for about two hundred voracious appetites. In another area my group became the pioneers too. For the first time, Brothers received names that didn't begin with A, B, or C. Prior to my class, every Brother in the New York District had a first name that began with one of the first three letters of the alphabet. My group would introduce another centralizing policy that provided a list of second names that would be reserved for the New York District Brothers and another different list of second names for those who were members of the LINE District.

Apparently, geographical reference was not so important as school of origin. For example, Brother James Celestine Nerney lived within the boundaries of the LINE District, but he had attended La Salle Academy on Second Street on the Bowery in New York City. As the original foundation of the New York District, La Salle sent its candidate to be a member of the New York District rather than the LINE. Simply by reading each Brother's name one could ascertain what district held his allegiance. Many of the assigned names were popular, even pedestrian. For example, I chose Kevin and was given the second name Patrick, a selection I liked. Paul Murphy, from Loughlin chose Paul and his LINE name added Patric without a K. As the time for our investiture approached, we were given the chance to select our first name.

Some chose their given baptismal name. For example, Joe Troy became Brother Joseph Christopher, John Hannaway became John Stephen, Barney Quigley became Bernard Aquinas, and Tom Lynch became Brother Thomas Gordian. Others decided to branch out and were assigned names that were more unusual. Bill Simon became Brother Gregory Rowland; Tom Mamara became Brother Andrew Urban; Ed Schwall became Brian Cyril; Sean O'Keefe became Brother Patrick Omar; Jim Marrin assumed the identity of Augustine Stephen; and Dermot O'Sullivan assumed the name Cassian Christopher. Those from the New York District had about twelve common names and twelve unique ones. In the LINE District, some received the last name of Callixtus, Donald, Ralph, and James. If nothing else, some savored the new name, others tried to forget it, and still more enjoyed the singular nomenclature it conferred.

To assist in our transition from Postulant to Novice, we had the example of four Brothers who would spend the majority of their Novitiate as our confreres. They were members of the May group who took their first vows in May of our Novitiate year. Their wisdom, personalities and talents made our own Novitiate a richer experience. Perhaps the most outstanding was also the largest. Brother Aquinas Daniel Goeddeke was a huge man of immense strength and athletic ability. Dan came from the University of Detroit where he was awarded a basketball scholarship which seemed appropriate given his size and strength. As the oldest of a dozen children, Dan set a substantial pace. One of his younger brothers attended The University of Notre Dame on a football scholarship. He played offensive guard on a team that won the national title. Later, he would play professional football for the Denver Broncos—and he was a wee tyke compared to Dan. Another candidate from Detroit remained a stalwart defender of the Motor City, even if he were not of the stature of 'Whispering Dan.' Brother Louis Earnest Montpetit entered our group in September and brought a zest for information that earned him the appellation 'Louie News.' He always took special delight in being among the first to know any news item and savored relating his discovery to the rest of us unenlightened.

Brother Andrew Raymond Buck was one of the final candidates from a Brother's school which would close its doors and head for the suburbs. De La Salle High School in the seventies on the Westside of Manhattan was sacrificed to the grand scheme of shifting Brothers from New York City to what was perceived as the rich vocational fields of suburban New Jersey. Ray had come from Inwood and graduated from Good Shepherd, but entered the Novitiate after high school. He had a unique vision or interpretation on life. His version of affairs led us to create an 'Up the Creek without a paddle contest.' Someone described Bucky as '*sui generis*,' in a class by himself. He seemed adept at moving along like a ship in the water that left no wake. Later, I would share two communities with him, Sacred Heart in Highbridge and St. Augustine in Morrisania. Community members credited Ray with being a phantom who moved silently and surreptitiously wherever he chose.

Brother August Stephen Rusyn came from Bishop Loughlin in Brooklyn. That school, culling only the brightest from the elementary schools of Brooklyn, provided many vocations to the Brothers. Steve would become the master tailor of our group and supervise a large segment of the Brothers who manned the tailor shop, making robes, rabattas, collars, and a unique fashion statement. They used to cut off the bottoms off regular trousers and sew on a six or twelve inch hem of black material. Worn under the robe, the pants looked like the clerical black they were supposed to be. That alteration enabled many to keep the clothes they wore to the Novitiate until they were worn out. It wasn't unusual to observe a number of Novices decked out in these unique fashion statements when they doffed their robes for working after meals in the refectory. One of our new recruits from Loughlin, Brother Lawrence Cormac Mattson also became a stalwart of the tailor shop. Larry would become one of the significant achievers in Latin and currently enjoys a lucrative career as one of the few Latin teachers in existence on Long Island. When he retired from teaching, his former public school district made him a financial offer he couldn't refuse as an inducement to continue teaching the classical language and root of sixty-five percent of our contemporary English.

Brother Cassian Kevin Martin was the fourth member of this May group. He was probably the most quiet and unobtrusive, and therefore I remember least about him. One of his contributions to our group later was his work in the garage during our Scholasticate years. He used to maintain the fleet of vehicles, provide routine checks and repairs, and coordinate the chauffeuring schedule. While those responsibilities may sound miniscule, his power over the scheduling of cars and chauffeurs gave him a cooperative respect reserved for few.

These four Brothers, each in a Special way, added a blend of talent and perspective that made our Novitiate year operate smoothly. Of all, I had the most contact with Dan as this narrative may indicate as it unravels. When I tried to determine what the spirit of the Novitiate was, I had a harder time than I did in describing the Juniorate. Clearly, at least in my mind, the spirit of the Juniorate was one of competition. With the addition of new personnel from many different geographical as well as ethnic backgrounds, the provincialism of the Juniorate was altered in a significant way. Searching for a collective sense of what replaced competition, I can only identify consensus and tolerance. As our original group doubled in size, so too did our knowledge of different styles and values that weren't derivatives of street ethics in New York. Our new members provided a dose of maturity, cosmopolitan interests beyond sports, and a treasury of recollections and perceptions that broadened the parochial minds of the Pioneers of Mary. What the new members of the Novitiate added was a broader perception of the Brothers' role, a notion that the United States expanded beyond the Hudson River and northward above the Bronx. The new Postulants added a mix of spice and diversity that was refreshing for our entire group.

Convinced of our athletic prowess, the Pioneers of Mary from the Juniorate had to make room for an all state football player from New Hampshire. A quiet, reserved, almost caricature personality from the Granite State was Joe Horace Vaillancourt. The fact that he could divulge his middle name without suffering any repercussions or ridicule speaks volumes about the respect and admiration we had for this candidate who only stayed a brief period with us. His impressive, compact body and taciturn personality that precluded any boasting or recitation of his achievements endeared Joe to the entire group. When he left after about a month, I am sure most were unhappy to learn that Joe determined that the religious life was not in his future.

Although not quite All State Football caliber, Brother Francis Arthur Brown also provided an image that enhanced the New England persona. David Stinchcombe Brown, as he was named by his family, arrived from Wellesley, Massachusetts. His story is a vignette in the confusing recruiting wars for religious candidates. Dave wanted to join a religious order after high school and had written several Institutes requesting information. All replied with a letter to Mr. Brown, except for the Christian Brothers who addressed him by his first name. Consequently, Dave decided to join the LINE District and provided many years of talent, humor, and contribution to the La Sallian cause. One of Stinchcombe's subtle contributions was his knack for increasing the travail of minor punishments, like kneeling out for night prayer. Often a minor infraction of a rule led to a penance like standing up for a meal or kneeling in the aisle with arms extended during night prayers. If a Brother knelt in an aisle near Stinchcombe and extended his arms, Dave enjoyed pulling down on the Brother's sleeve so that he had to exert greater pressure to maintain his arm parallel to the floor. Then Dave would release his hold on the penitent's sleeve causing the arm to rise suddenly in the air. Dave's explanation was at least he didn't do what he had observed on one of his first days in the Postulancy. The previous group had a very heavy Novice named Bartholomew Gerard who was known for his Homeric appetite and lateness to prayers. When a Brother was late for a spiritual exercise, he was expected to kiss the floor as some sign of penance for tardiness. Bart had mastered the procedure, but one of his groupies added a note of hilarity to the penance by tossing a number of silverware items onto the floor as if they had fallen from Bart's pockets. Apparently not everyone's mind in prayer was on the worship of the Almighty. We all searched for humor and amusement whenever we could.

Dave Brown, AKA Brother Francis Arthur, AKA Stinchcombe, but more notoriously designated 'Sapsucker Brown,' was a master of the unexpected. Somehow, 'Sapsucker' convinced Brother Conall Andrew, the Director of Novices, that he had the knowledge, expertise, and equipment to harvest maple syrup from a stand of sugar maples at the south side of the main Barrytown building near the Ancients' section. Dave devised spouts and buckets which could catch the sap from the trees once a spring thaw came. Everything was in place, and the proverbial "sap was running." 'Sapsucker' must have harvested hundreds of gallons of the substance as it literally flowed out the spouts and into a multitude of buckets. I'm not sure who, if anyone, helped him, but then the master mixer boiled down the watery sap until he had several gallons of syrup. Thanks to the emissary from Massachusetts, we had freshly harvested maple syrup to enhance our pancakes, French toast, and corn fritters.

A cadre of athletic candidates also impressed the original Pioneers. From Tolentine in the Bronx, three young men with immense sense of humor and unusual perspective joined us as Postulants. The most athletic was a gym rat named Joe Hanrahan. He smoked many of the basketball players on the courts by the chicken coops. He was accompanied by Ross Youngs who may have left before our whole group assembled. Louis Nagy was a thin, rangy character with a story for every occasion. One of his narratives, which usually made him a foil, still sticks in my mind. Like many a Tolentine student, Louis was very familiar with the bars of Rockaway, the Irish Riviera. Like many a visitor too, Louis found himself homeless in Rockaway and filled with sand. His sensible solution was to enter a bar, change into clean, dry clothes, and return to the Bronx. Unfortunately, someone stopped him from the illegal use of the barroom bathroom, and he was arrested. Louis enjoyed telling us how he laughed as he was dragged off to the police station and was laughing until the time came for booking him. He was charged with indecent exposure and lewd behavior. That sobered him up immediately. As he relived the experience in recounting his tale and his fear of being convicted as a pervert, he had all of us laughing in a far from religious atmosphere.

Six foot five inch Joe O'Brien was also a catalyst for respect. He had played varsity basketball at Manhattan Prep and had been an outstanding first baseman on the baseball team. Among his myriad talents, Joe was particularly noted for regaling those in the group who had little exposure to the hit songs of the past few years. Since Joe had a flair for memorizing lyrics of songs after hearing them once, he could reproduce many of the songs the graduates of the Juniorate never heard. He comprehended and committed to memory the most unusual words and phrases that eluded the normal ear. As an individual who couldn't distinguish a piano concerto from a violin concerto, I was very impressed at Joe's talent. Later, on long bus rides his loud voice might not have been melodic, but it was an ideal example for those of us trying to sing along. Aside from his Good Shepherd roots, Joe knew me from our JV days together at Manhattan Prep. He had arrived with a former class comedian of ours from the Prep. Ed 'The Bed' Raff was another fine athlete with a consummate taste for good jokes. He earned his nickname by disappearing into his cell for power naps that could only last a matter of seconds since he had so little free time. Ed decided that God didn't want his services in the Christian Brothers, since the Almighty did not inspire the Brothers to adjust his rising hour.

From St.Peter's on Staten Island another kind of athlete appeared among our ranks. Brother Vincent Christopher Callahan was a gifted long distance runner and miler who set a few records as a harrier from the outer borough. Unfortunately for Vinny, the recreation opportunities at Barrytown didn't lend themselves to the maintenance of the highly trained and conditioned endurance runner. Whenever he had the chance to traverse the hills and paths, byways and open fields of the grounds, there was none that could maintain the pace Vinny set. After a St. Patrick's Day meal of green substances, Vinnie would confess that the food coloring was notoriously deleterious to his condition when he tried to run off the extra calories. Later, when the Brothers were introduced to beer, Vinny would garner the sobriquet, 'One Can Callahan,' for his notoriously poor consumption of even a modest dose of the beverage.

Joining a few veterans in the group from St. Jerome's, John Hannaway, given the name Brother John Stephen, added a cerebral contribution to our class as well as an interest in sports. As an eighth grader, he won a scholarship to Regis High School, the prestigious school for especially talented youth in New York, and he decided to accept the opportunity. While not attributing all his success to the Jesuits, John graduated from Catholic University with a Summa, taught at Manhattan Prep, instructed our Scholastics in Washington, earned a Ph D in French *Ancien Regime* history from Johns Hopkins, and upon leaving the Brothers, graduated from Columbia Law School. Like many in the class, he injected a serious attitude toward academics and hard work.

In a similar vein Larry Bruckner entered our group as a prelude to a distinguished academic career. Larry, who took the name Brother Michael Donald, graduated with the highest honors, won a National Defense Fellowship for Math, and ultimately worked at the research labs of Los Alamos, New Mexico. Larry had come from St. Augustine Diocesan High School in Brooklyn, another school that attracted super bright individuals. One of his fellow graduates was John Fenton who would join us after a freshman year at St. John's University. As a member of the LINE District, he was named Brother Patrick Callixtus. After a number of years in the classroom, he had merited a doctorate in chemistry from the University of Minnesota and taught at the college level for many years.

The intellectual acumen of our group was also enhanced by the return of a man who had left Barrytown the previous year. Dick Fagan, Brother Gabriel Alben, had spent a year at Manhattan College before resuming his formation as a Christian Brother. He would bring his considerable intellect, personal intelligence, and unusual perspective and ability to cut to the essence of humor as a contribution to our group. After graduating from Catholic University and teaching in De La Salle Collegiate High School in Detroit, Gabe pursued a doctorate in English Literature from the University of Notre Dame. Like the Goliardic poets of the Middle Ages who were known as the 'wandering scholars,' his talents took him to St. Mary's College in Winona, Wisconsin. After a number of years teaching a plethora of English courses, he joined the faculty of La Salle University in Philadelphia where he continues to offer a gamut of English classes that would challenge Carl Van Doren. This émigré from the streets of

Inwood has become an adopted Midwesterner and serious advocate for a lifestyle that precludes the provincialism of New York. His flair for the comedic side of life added a spice to our daily exercises in the Novitiate, but it was always balanced by the cerebral pursuit of such luminaries as Thomas Stearns Eliot.

Like Gabe, another member of his Juniorate class returned to Barrytown to make the Novitiate with my class. I had known Mike Schaeffer from Highbridge when he was a senior in the Juniorate. He had left Barrytown, but he returned in July of 1957 to become a member of our Postulant group. Probably for the same reason Tom Mamara was called 'Louie,' Mike was always known as 'Sam or Sammy,' although his religious name was Brother Michael Bernardine. I guess he looked like a Sam. 'Sam' was the best pitcher in our group. He had excellent control and a decent fastball and curve. During our formation together we spent many hours playing fastball with a stickball bat and tennis ball. I am not embarrassed to confess that he won most of our games. As well as an outstanding pitcher and good hitter, 'Sam' also had the habit of becoming involved in an activity until he mastered its arcane points. During our Novitiate 'Sam' decided to become a world class chess master. At one point, our saintly Director of Novices brusquely told him, "Lose that game." So 'Sam' took up pool. He dedicated his energies to mastering the felt top thereafter. It is rumored that in later years he took that same obsessive compulsion and applied it to the Racing Form. He also adopted the profession of basketball refereeing at some time. The last I heard about 'Sam' was that he applied his obsessions to flight and had become an airline pilot living in south Florida. Perhaps he is living evidence that God invites all types to follow His footsteps.

From Good Shepherd originally and ultimately from De La Salle High School came another very positive contributor to our group. Clayton David Hollinger had a fancy name, Hollywood good looks, and a generous soul, when he joined us and assumed the name of Brother Peter John. Clay looked so much like Harry Belafonte that we called him 'Harry.' Sometimes Clay questioned his ancestry for he had the close cropped hair and facial features of the calypso star. Once he pondered whether he was part Negro, and I as an expert in racial matters, told him that he should check his fingernails. If they appeared purple, Clay had Negro blood. I left him examining his hands very carefully. Clay played many practical jokes on me, but I always enjoyed his company.

He was a major asset during our tenure on the farm crew together. In fact, one could always ascertain whether Clay was in or out of the house by merely sniffing the area around the coat racks. Clay's De La Salle jacket had visited the silo so often that it had adopted the aroma peculiar to the silage. Among all my groupies, Clay was also one of the most generous. If one had a challenging manual labor after meals, like working in the sinks or pot walloping, it might be hard to locate a replacement, except for Clay. He readily volunteered to do the most menial or dirty jobs without a second thought. In 2005, I inadvertently discovered that he was very ill and suffering intensely from rheumatoid arthritis. He was confined to bed, but I had the opportunity to speak with him several times on the telephone before he died. He began every conversation with "Live, Jesus, in our hearts, or Vive Jesu dans nos coeurs, or Vivat Jesus in cordibus nostris," expecting the appropriate response from whatever language he had selected, once he knew it was someone associated with the Brothers. Our conversations indicated how much Clay loved his time in the monks and how much he appreciated their contact after forty years. Typically, he underestimated what a fine legacy he had left upon his peers.

A candidate probably twice our age came from the LINE District. Paul LaBerge added a mature presence, a cultural affinity unfamiliar to most of us, and a composure that was almost a sedative to our hyperactive imaginations and physical pursuits. Paul played the piano, for instance, instead of basketball or other sports. He must have felt quite isolated for he rarely spoke of his background or life experiences. His contribution to our group was one of respect for intellectual affairs, liturgy, and sobriety.

Like a fugitive from another planet, we also welcomed a candidate from Syracuse who seemed befuddled by our terrestrial societies. Ed Ewald appeared more comfortable among the scientific giants of electricity. A confidant of Tom Edison, Nicola Tesla, Georg Ohm, Alessandro Volta, and Andre Ampere, our fellow Novice traveled in a parallel universe so much that he earned the name "Electrical Ed" for his wizardry and knowledge in a field none of us could fathom. In most other pursuits, 'Electrical Ed' appeared disinterested and indifferent. Since he was our only candidate from Syracuse, most of the group seems to have lost contact with our own wizard.

Finally, some Italian recruits arrived to buttress the heroic efforts of Brother Andrew Urban Mamara to assert Italy's rightful place among the family of nations and contributions of immigrants. Like Jim Nerney, Brother Vincent Benildus Tannacore was a native of Long Island, but since he enlisted via De La Salle Academy in Manhattan, he was a member of the New York District. Vinny's sense of humor and good nature, his interest in sports, and his generous disposition made him a popular member among the Postulants. His support was also beneficial to Brother Anthony Ralph Tufano in promoting Italian ethnic pride. Aware of his Italian heritage, I used to call him 'Tough Tony' because it was such a contrast to his warm personality. Tony De Mento from Albany lent his assistance to the advocates of Italian equality in the brief period he shared in our Postulancy.

To support that minority voice of advocates for the Red Sox Nation, more representatives of New England were added to our group. Brother Raphael Patric Eades of Newport, Rhode Island arrived in conjunction with Brother Thomas Ralph McConaghy from Pawtucket. Over the years I have lost contact with Raphael, but only recently I have related with Tom McConaghy. Tom decided to leave the Christian Brothers to enter the priesthood. At one of our reunions at which he said Mass, Tom offered to help my daughter and her fiancé arrange for a wedding in his parish church in Norwichtown, Connecticut. Not only did he conduct the pre-marital instruction period, but he expedited the appeal process for their wedding. They were impressed with his zeal, and he presided over their nuptials. Moreover, he added a great dimension to the wedding reception where he got to rendezvous with some present and former monks.

In a short time, like De La Salle in New York, St. Augustine's Diocesan High School would close its doors after providing a substantial number of candidates to the Christian Brothers. A notable member of our group from this school was Brother Brian Donald Cleary. Brian had a magnificent singing voice—soft, ethereal, and ideal for Gregorian chant. He became one of the chanters in our class. Brian often appeared lost in a brown study and mentally preoccupied, but his contributions to conversations were witty and insightful. Although he rigorously interpreted our rules and regulations, he provided keen perceptions when he thought the time was appropriate.

While the rest of the world was adjusting to the chords of *Hound Dog, Heartbreak Hotel,* or even the melodies of the Kingston Trio, the developing audience for folk music and hootenannies, we had our own top ten music favorites too. Excluding the sentimental favorites of Christmas time, even those sung in French or German, most of us would number among our all time favorites some hymns and compositions that became memorable under the direction of Brothers Benilde James Loxham and Aelred Dowd during our formation years. There were so many funeral masses when we were Novices that two selections from the Mass for the Dead would be on most lists. *Dies Irae* and the recessional *In Paradiso* added solemnity to the already somber proceedings. In a more joyous vein, the jubilant strains of the traditional *Te Deum* and the Pentecostal sequence *Veni Creator Spiritus* always evoked a special effort. Some polyphonic compositions were also avidly anticipated. Of special note should be the paean to the Eucharist, *Panis Angelicus.* In a specific psalm with overtures toward the nature of the mission of the Christian Brothers, we also reveled in singing, *Qui ad justitiam erudiunt multos quasi stellas in aeternum.* The translation of "They that instruct others unto justice shall shine as stars for all eternity," meant something extra to a group of educators. The same may be said of *Ecce quam bonum et quam jucundum habitare in unum,* "How good and sweet it is to live in unity," for a group of men whose essential lifestyle incorporated community living. One of my favorite recollections of a hymn sung in a spectacular setting was the image of sunset on Hampton Beach. Every Wednesday or Thursday during our summers at Oakdale, we used to travel to the untrammeled dunes of East Hampton Beach before it became an enclave for the spoiled rich. After a day body surfing, playing whiffle ball, sun tanning, picnicking or whatever, the entire group would gather by the crashing waves, recite night prayer as the sun set to the strains of *Salve Regina.* Later I read that the Spanish sailors always concluded their day's work at sea by honoring the Queen Mother of Mercy. Perhaps the all time favorite song for most of us, and a hymn we sing lustfully at reunions or other opportunities, was the French hymn to John Baptist De La Salle, *Honneur a Toi.* With the shift to English language hymns and songs at Church, seldom does anyone of them approach the joy and enthusiasm each of these top hits evoked during our formation. Led by good singers like Brian Cleary and under the talented directorship we had, our massive choir left a very positive impression in my memory. Unfortunately, my warbled contributions were seldom met with acclaim or even encouragement. It would take several more years before I would realize that my singing might only have the attribute of off key volume and nothing else.

I have selected a few members of our Postulancy who seemed to make a very large impact upon the original class of Pioneers. Someone decided that we should change the name of the group and in an open election, we became the Group of the Divine Child. The Brothers had encouraged a devotion to the child Jesus as an example of what an educator should be striving to mold. Every month in grade school, students and faculty held an Archconfraternity of the Divine Child assembly and once a year we retreated to St. Patrick's Cathedral where all representatives from the Brothers' schools gathered for benediction and a blessing. The new name of our group seemed to signify a greater diversity of talent, a broader geographical and ethnic composition to our group. In my mind at least it indicated a greater maturity and flexibility that led to less competition and greater cooperation among the class membership.

Living and sharing our lives in such proximity gave a sense of community that may not have been as strong as we thought. Each seemed to withhold some intimate thoughts and information that they chose not to share. This contradiction became apparent to me when I consider the person of Brother Anthony Basilian Riordan. 'Tony Bas' was a quiet somewhat enigmatic personality who joined our group from CBA Albany. Popular, funny, entertaining and typically witty, 'Tony Bas' also was a silent, almost sphinx-like withdrawn presence at some times. He seemed to enjoy the role of observer rather than participant in conversation or casual activities. In recent years I learned more about him through exchanging e-mails than I did by living with him for five years of formation. Our exchanges had more to do with family background and history than anything else. I discovered that he was born and raised for the most part in Massachusetts west of Boston near Leominster where my daughter Kathy currently resides. Tony commissioned a professional genealogist to investigate his past. That study produced some fascinating details about an ancestor who was asked to assassinate an informer in Kerry during the 'Troubles' on the eve of his emigration to Boston. Tony also wrote of the family circumstances in Massachusetts and how he ended up in Albany. His tale is one of endurance, courage, and determination, but to me in formation he was merely a puzzling presence. With frequent warnings about particular friendships, we sometimes created a distance between each other that was unnecessary. If I had known Tony's story, I would have thought of him in less eccentric terms. The same may be true of another groupie who suffered a series of family disasters while we were in formation. While he was courageously bearing these burdens, he was often the butt of uncharitable jests and teasing. When we learned why he may have appeared preoccupied, some of us, myself especially, were ashamed of our glib treatment. We knew everything about each other, and yet we actually knew nothing!

To mold this disparate group, a few Brothers were selected by agreement between both Districts. They were assigned the task of introducing us to meditation, contemplation, prayer, sacrifice, mortification, and knowledge in the ways of the Christian Brothers. If that task sounds easy, then I haven't been careful enough in describing it. The three individual Brothers who confronted this challenge were as diversified a group as the persons entrusted to their tutelage. Our Director of Novices was a veteran in the post. He was known for his sanctity, simplicity, cleverness, and his ability to relate to young men. Brother Conall Andrew Lennon was quite elderly in a way that was ascertainable. As Winston Churchill once described Russia as an "enigma wrapped in a mystery," Conall Andrew would personify such a description too. He was by no means aloof or unapproachable, but he sauntered about in an absentminded sort of way. Many of us thought of him as having the gift of bi-location for he often appeared out of nowhere, or so it seemed. None of us had any clue whether he enjoyed good health or suffered some of the ravages of age.

Conall Andrew had an amazing sense of humor and timing. His conferences, however, were often dry and tiring, but he was at his finest in one on one situations. After experiencing the styles of Brother Basilian John and Benezet Peter, our Director from the Juniorate, Conall Andrew demonstrated a unique approach. He seldom sat in a chair, preferring to stride in the cloister approaching the chapel or even better outside. In attempting to describe his special style, I am tempted to compare him to La Rochefoucauld, Jean De La Fontaine, or even the ancient moral fabulist Aesop. Brother Andrew spoke in simplistic, yet profound allegories, riddles, or fables. The fact that they are fresh in mind not only underscores their simplicity, but it accentuates the lessons that he taught in his unique style. For example, I'll cite an instance of one of my redditions with him. As we slowly strolled back in forth in the cloister, he spotted one of my groupies outside in the cold. Andy indicated Brother Bernard Quigley, as he was wont to do, wearing neither coat nor hat. Barney was one of the few Novices, Dermot and I being the other two, who wasn't stricken with the Asian flu epidemic that fall. Brother Andrew's lesson followed. "All the bugs look for someone who isn't wearing a hat. Then they check to see whether he is wearing a coat. If he is wearing neither, then they attack him and try to make him sick. Now don't you think it would be wise to wear a hat and coat in this cold weather?" Who could disagree with his logic if not his presentation. His instruction was didactic upon reflection. In another reddition with the Director of Novices in the same location, Brother Andrew began musing about the abominable rainstorm we were witnessing. After some thought he said to me, "Well now, this is the best weather we could have wanted. It has been specially ordained by God, so it is the finest weather we could ever have. God's will is always for what is best for us." While I contemplated whether a violent rainstorm was in my best interest, I couldn't argue with his statement that God had personally sent this phenomenon for our benefit.

Brother Andrew had many such lessons to impart in an unthreatening manner that shielded truth and principles under the guise of simplicity. The only time he ever raised his voice would happen during one of his conferences when he felt that his audience had begun to doze. The point he might be making, or the principle he was explaining didn't necessarily receive any accentuation, so his increase in volume might take place at any inexplicable time. I thought Brother Andrew lived a life of understated sanctity. His preaching was through example and clever allegories. His holiness and spirit of faith were neatly packaged in a personality that enjoyed whimsy and incongruity. Among ourselves and meaning no disrespect at all, we were at once bemused and reverential to this man to whom we referred to in pre-Vatican II terms as 'The Holy Ghost.' Brother Andrew enjoyed our total respect and admiration, although it must have been difficult for him to lead us along the path of contemplation and perfection. At the end of our Novitiate year, we discovered that we were the last group to boast of his unique guidance and spirituality. The genuine love, respect, and appreciation each of us felt for this extraordinary man remained deep within our being for the rest of our lives. Although we held him in great affection and admiration, I am not sure whether he was totally successful in nudging us along the path to sanctity and perfection. It was no fault of his own, for seventeen and eighteen year olds are poorly prepared for the mature decisions that religious life demands. As for myself, I readily confess that I advanced very minutely toward the ideal religious.

Frivolity and distraction interfered with progress. I also know Brother Andrew was well aware of my shortcomings. As part of his guidance and directorship, he issued spiritual reading books for our edification. Each of us was supposed to read the three tomes of Rodriquez. The first and introductory volume was called **The Purgative Way.** After mastery of that, we were selected to read the second book called **The Illuminative Way.** Finally, the capstone of the trilogy was titled **The Unitive Way.** After examining our faults, we were supposed to read how we could achieve illumination about the path to oneness with the creator. Finally, we could secure that knowledge by discovering how our will and God's could become one. After I had been assigned **The Purgative Way,** without any evidence of comprehending its more subtle messages, I approached the Director and asked for the next volume. With that elfin smile he reserved for most occasions, Brother Andrew handed me back the original volume and said, "Well now, you might be better off rereading this book." His corrections and suggestions were couched in such kind, gentle, simple language and manner that one could only accept his judgments and follow his advice.

When my group began our scholasticate, we were reunited with Brother Basilian John, and Conall Andrew may have retreated to a less arduous task at the new Novitiate for the LINE District in Narragansett, Rhode Island. I am sure each member of my group missed him in some special way. He was replaced by Brother Albinus Gabriel Dougherty, and I for one was relieved that we had the pleasure of the unusual direction of such a gentle, spiritual man as Conall Andrew Lennon. Our group of the Divine Child felt in some way that we had been exposed to the childlike simplicity that Jesus advocated when he uttered, "Suffer the little children to come unto me," or witnessed the Christ like irony that we should become little children to enter the kingdom of heaven.

Assisting the 'Holy Ghost' in our spiritual odyssey was a Sub-Director who had many different qualities other than those exhibited by our Director. Brother Celestine Philip Milligan offered a different perspective upon our religious development. There appeared to be three primary objectives in Brother Philip's approach to the Novitiate. First and probably foremost, he was determined to follow the military aphorism that if it didn't move, paint it. Our Sub-Director Philip was resolved to paint the entire Novitiate area while we were pursuing religious perfection from the bottom rungs of the spiritual ladder. Secondly, Brother Philip also was very proud of his singing voice. Every assembly, every occasion for celebration was an opportunity to sing "Bless This House," in a voice that could be heard down by the train station. His encore was usually, "The Lost Chord" or "Jerusalem." He assumed his talent was God given and should be demonstrated whenever entertainment offered itself. Brother Philip's third objective seemed to be access to local humor and whatever gossip could grab his attention. He relished the company of the young, seemed to enjoy their creativity, but he wanted to be informed of almost every notion or plot we might conceive. Once he was aware of what was going on, everything seemed acceptable.

More a peer, it seemed, than an administrator of instruction and direction, Brother Philip was involved in the interpersonal relationships within our group. He seemed genuinely interested, and no rumor was too outlandish for his credibility. We were aware of this attribute and often planted rumors and hyperbolic stories to catch his attention. At one point, I recall Brother Richard Albeus McKay approaching the Sub-Director with the remark, "Did you hear the latest rumor about Kevin Patrick?" His ears perked up and his voice said, "No! No! Tell me." Rich then remarked, "On second thought, you're too anxious," and then he walked away. The episode seemed to epitomize our relationship with the Sub-Director. He was fair game for our teasing and camaraderie.

When Brother Philip gave a conference, he was like a chatty late night guest on Jay Leno or David Letterman. One of our group would ask a leading question, and Brother Philip would take it from there. His stories were generally entertaining and informative in an ephemeral sort of way. Perhaps his background had something to do with it. Brother Philip had spent some years teaching in Bayonne, France prior to the Blitzkrieg of Hitler's forces. When the Germans overran France and a complicit Vichy government was established, evidently it had some repercussions in the Brothers' small school in Bayonne. Some of the Brothers were German but the majority of the community was French, with Brother Philip being a neutral, the same as the United States at the time. Among the French Brothers there was no unanimity of opinion about the Vichy government or the free French forces of Charles De Gaulle. Brother Philip would tell tales about how the community's allegiance to national causes interrupted the peace and tranquility the community had known before the war. In fact, that disruption led the Director to issue canonical warnings to all parties. He ordained that the topics of the German invasion, the Vichy government, and the progress of the Blitzkrieg, Dunkirk, and so forth were not to be discussed at all since the feelings were so detrimental to community life. While his story illustrated the feelings of the religious, it also educated us to the procedures of canonical warnings. Brother Philip related these stories with all the subplots of a major novel in a style that indicated he savored the drama and emotional controversies of the community in turmoil.

After returning to the United States prior to our country's entrance into World War II, Brother Philip ended up in our Scholasticate, De La Salle College, in Washington, DC. At some point, he was appointed Director of the Scholasticate, and that gave him fresh material for his conferences. Someone in the group would ask him a leading question, and his narrative would generally begin, 'I remember this bird . . . . " Then Brother Philip would describe how some Scholastic wanted to escape temporarily from the community for some reason or other. When he was denied permission, Brother Philip explained that the individual would demand to consult privately with his confessor. With a cursory but convenient knowledge of canon law, the young Scholastic knew a religious had the right to consultation with a confessor of his choice. Given that ultimatum, Brother Philip had to relent and allow the young Brother to leave. In one story, Brother Philip mentioned that he insisted on accompanying the Brother on his trip to visit the confessor. He described how both boarded a trolley in the District of Columbia and as Brother Philip paid both fares, the young 'recalcitrant,' one of his favorite expressions, exited via the back door and then waved goodbye to his Director. He told these stories more as encomia to the imagination of the young than the fall guy routine it put him in. Brother Philip recounted how he ordered an unruly group of Brothers to leave the refectory, as they violated the silence of the meal. Brother Philip uttered the ambiguous demand, "Table Twelve, leave the refectory at once." He laughed as he recalled the group picking up the table, taking it out of the refectory

104

and then returning to finish their meals as guests of nearby tables. Although most of his stories had him playing the role of a dupe or pawn, he seemed to appreciate the creativity of the young Brothers who utilized all kinds of ploys to outwit him.

At another session, Brother Philip was delighted to repeat how he had been tricked by the intelligent ruses of the Scholastics. He advised us if we wanted to sneak out of the Scholasticate at night to walk down the stairs backwards, as he had witnessed several enterprising Brothers do. Brother Philip explained that when he encountered the escapees coming down the stairs backwards, they proceeded to head up the stairs as if they had been climbing all the time. In speaking with Brother Christopher Lucian Callahan, he recounted to me a nightly practical joke he played on Brother Philip. After night prayer, Bill Callahan would take a small glass of water and spill its contents next to a plaster dog statue that Brother Philip used as a doorstop. One's first impression of course would be that the dog had urinated on the floor. Bill said he did this almost every night for an entire year, and Brother Philip's quest for the perpetrator was fruitless.

Part of Brother Philip's responsibilities in dealing with us was to officiate over politeness lessons or a question and answer session about any topics that occurred to the Novices. Questions were inserted into a box and naturally this arrangement encouraged many to exercise their wit, or sarcasm, or just their playfulness in dealing with this authority figure who was more peer than supervisor. Brother Philip would empty the questions on his desk and then read them without any preparation. One comment in particular stands out in my memory. Someone had written, "Would the Brother who pushed the Director down the stairs please identify himself? He chipped the paint on the stairwell as the director fell." Brother Philip laughed more heartily than any of us, for the note underscored the fragility of Brother Andrew and the preoccupation of Brother Philip with painting. Marring a paint job was a more grievous offense than mugging the Director.

Brother Philip's contributions to the enjoyment of our Novitiate contrasted greatly with the image bequeathed to us from his predecessor. Brother Vincent had been the Novitiate Sub-Director for more years than we could guess. During that time, he supposedly subscribed to the theory that the deprivations, mortifications, self-denial, penances, and religious convictions of the legendary

Vaugirard of the early days of the Institute's foundation were the substantial basis of a good religious. Trained in the school that insisted that blind obedience was an essential component of our vows, he allegedly gave Novices incredibly contradictory tasks for manual labor. He reputedly assigned some Brothers to dig a deep trench and then another group to fill it in. He tested obedience by directing individuals to plant dead trees and shrubs. The objective was creating obedience rather than any utilitarian end. It is impossible to imagine our treatment and relationship with Brother Philip having any tolerance with Brother Vincent. In fact, no other individual in our formation could be treated the same way we treated Brother Philip. I stress that we were not being disrespectful at all, but we were treating him with the humor and style we directed toward each other. The result was laughter and lightheartedness that perhaps didn't reflect the somber, sobriety of a Novitiate. Whether Brother Philip was guilty of creating a frivolous tone or whether we did so on our own, I suppose is a matter of opinion or point of view. He certainly injected humor, laughter, and often hilarity into a situation that may have been too somber for the young men undergoing spiritual transformation.

The third member of the trinity responsible for our maturation in the religious life was Brother Albinus of Mary, our Catechist. Unlike our Director and Sub-Director, Albinus Heffernan never seemed to understand the nature of our group. Frankly, I believe he thought merriment reigned over a serious business, and it was his challenge to salvage the integrity of the formative process. Brother Albinus may have felt like the Dutch boy of myth sticking his finger in the dike to prevent the destruction of the fields of Holland. Perhaps my interpretation is entirely wrong, but I cite one episode that leaves me with this analysis. During the Christmas season, the area around Barrytown experienced a premature thaw compounded by heavy rains. Since the Juniorate gyms were being resealed, they were off limits to us while the Junior Novices were away on vacation. Our own playing fields were quagmires and the inclement weather precluded any outdoor games. Our hockey rink was more suitable for swimming than skating.

To amuse ourselves a group decided to create a spoof of our environment based on Dicken's **A Christmas Carol.** With a tape recorder and imagination but no written script, we undertook our version of the classic tale. Instead of the traditional cast of characters, however, we developed parallel personalities to our formation administration. Tiny Tim, for example, was replaced by Brother Philip, and the Director may have been cast as The Ghost of Christmas present. Brother Basilian John rated a role as the Jacob Marley, but the most savage satirical role was reserved for Brother Cornelius Luke, the Ghost of Christmas Past. From the perspective of some years, I realize the Visitor General was mocked and lampooned beyond appropriate measures. It did seem like a good idea at the time however. According to our unscripted play, Luke's somewhat bizarre table manners including his soup slurping and belching were underscored along with his virtuoso display of sniffs, snorts, and snuffs that punctuated his conversation and participation in our community meals. When he spoke, his voice was an amalgam of the peculiarities of Quick Draw Magraw, Deputy Dawg, and Mr. Magoo. Perhaps some of us would learn later how quickly a class can detect mannerisms and personality quirks that characterized our future lesson presentations. If so, we might have been more tolerant of 'Flookie Luke's' mannerisms. Without any doubt, he should have been offended by our presentation.

Over the course of two days when heavy rains pelted the outdoors, we recorded our production. I was sound effects man so my voice didn't appear on tape. During the course of the day, some Brothers would enter the classroom and play the tape for their amusement. Enough of them did to arouse the suspicion of Brother Albinus, although there was no attempt to keep our play a secret. In fact, we avoided assigning a role to Brother Albinus since we felt he had no sense of humor. Anyway, at manual labor after supper he circulated among us determined to discover the cast members who had ridiculed the administrators. He would approach an individual and inquire whether he was involved or not. I remember him asking Joe O'Brien who replied, "Yeah sure. I was Tiny Tim." When he thought he had identified all the Brothers involved in this travesty, he approached the Brother Director and played the tape. Expecting some kind of retribution for our misbehavior, he seemed disappointed at the response of the 'Holy Ghost' and Brother Philip.

Brother Andrew asked all those involved in the play to see him in his office whenever they could. I identified myself as a participant who arranged the sound effects. The Director of Novices had a few comments which he expressed in his characteristically soft, philosophical manner. He thought the tape was entertaining, but he iterated that our rule book had something in it about raillery and mockery. He then assigned a modest punishment like taking three meals standing up or kneeling out for night prayer for the same amount of days. No one to my knowledge received any threat of getting 'shipped' (the term we had for being sent home), nor any more severe penalty. I believe Albinus wanted the bunch of us which would have amounted to about a dozen, 'shipped' so that the holy, hallowed halls of the Novitiate wouldn't reverberate with the laughter and frivolity so familiar to my group.

In fairness to Brother Albinus, he probably was right that a solemn religious tone was absent from our Novitiate. I suppose he even felt Brother Andrew and Brother Philip should have been more severe on us. I would even credit him with love for the Institute by expecting a more somber atmosphere. Instead, we continued our trek through religious development with the seriousness of a camping expedition. Despite this set back, Brother Albinus continued to deliver interesting conferences and topics in our study of theology and scripture. He introduced us to some of the contemporary thought of pre-Vatican II theologians. He also supervised our sample lessons. I remember offering my thoughts on Thomas Aquinas' levels of being as related to angels. I don't think it would get great play after Vatican II, but at the time, I was busy distinguishing between angels and archangels, seraphim and cherubim, etc.

One of Brother Albinus' repetitive themes was on the topic of 'morose delectation.' I loved the phrase which seemed so oxymoronic or at least contradictory. I never did quite understand what he meant. To this day, I wonder whether he was accusing us of reveling in the misery of others or wallowing in self-pity for the sake of the pleasure it gave us. I also speculate whether he was actually describing himself and his assessment as assignment as Catechist in the Novitiate. Without an ability to determine whether he indeed was projecting his feelings upon us, I am left with one of the mysteries of the Novitiate year that occasionally surfaces when I believe I am in the company of an individual who apparently is miserable but somehow enjoys his state of depression more than he attempts to escape it. The group enjoyed referring to itself as 'Ali Binus and his Forty Thieves' when he led the bunch of us on section walks after meals. I don't know whether he recognized our delight in calling him 'Ali Binus' and then associating as his underlings with a term that may have identified us more than we suggested. Perhaps we were not thieves, but clowns.

When I ponder how I recall my Novitiate days, I am struck by the absence of serious religious thought. While we were supposedly learning the arcane mysteries of mental prayer and plumbing the depths of our souls in a daily examination of conscience, those psychological explorations play very minor roles in my consciousness. Instead, I recreate the fun we had, especially during manual labor. I dwell upon the influence of some of the men who shared Barrytown, but were not in my group. Although we were supposedly separated from the world and worldly influences, I resurrect images of the people I encountered in my Novitiate year. Many were peripheral contacts, but nonetheless they remain in my memory.

One of the areas where we came into contact with laymen was in the kitchen. Barrytown and in fact the Hudson Valley seemed a conduit for 'Knights of the Road,' people passing through from somewhere to somewhere else, often one step in front of the law. They would work for a few months, settle into the mansion, and then move on. We were fortunate to have stabile kitchen cooks, but their assistants often left something to be desired. Perhaps my most vivid recollection concerns a man who we called 'Circumference' or 'Herbie Horn.' Circumference was so named for he was rotund to the point where he had to enter the refrigerator facing the side he wanted to select from. If he was mistaken, he had to exit the refrigerator and turn around outside before re-entering. We also called him "You're burning my ass," because he would hit the hot stove if he bent over the counter. More appropriately, we called him 'Herbie Horn' because he seemed to enjoy bothering us. His specialty was throwing dirty, hot, greasy, pans or trays into the sinks we had filled to clean other items. The result was a splash in our faces as well as a mixture of clean and dirty water. He also enjoyed emptying cauldrons upon our feet while we were preoccupied elsewhere.

Herbie became such a nuisance that we instituted an award in his name. We developed the 'Herbie Horn' Medal of Commendation for those who managed to upset the behemoth and extract vile language for our contribution. He stood quizzically by as we presented the honoree with an index card with a shoe horn attached by string. I doubt he understood that the award was in his name or why the individual was being so honored. Herbie was later to stir the wrath of 'Budget Bob' when Brother Robert told Herbie to stay away from the Novices and Junior Novices. Herbie's urbane response was to intimate that 'Budget Bob' didn't want anyone interfering with his sexual interest in the young. Soon thereafter, Herbie moved on, but not before leaving some indelible memories with us. Later we discovered that he left his last job when he impregnated the sheriff's daughter and had a warrant out for his arrest.

Most of the other individuals who worked at Barrytown were more mainstream in behavior if not language. The man in charge of the dairy was a Scotsman called Hugh Begg whose speech was pretty much indecipherable to us. Hugh with his expertise in artificial insemination, made the bull extraneous. I don't know whether the bull was retained for his semen or Brother Fat Leo's sentiment. Hugh didn't say much, but he took pride in some of his artificial offspring. The hard working Scotsman seemed to enjoy the company of bovines more than humans.

Another person who was difficult to understand was a gnome-like German who was in charge of the boiler and the plumbing in the entire plant. Since I can't recall his name, I'll call him 'Heinzelmenschen' since he looked, acted, and spoke like an elf. One day when Barrytown was experiencing problems with its well, Dan Goeddeke and I were sent with him to the pump house which was in an outer field closer to Red Hook. Dan and I were to be the labor staff for 'Heinzelmenschen.' At one point, he said to me, "Go down into the *pumphaus* and get me a rake." After searching this narrow sector for five minutes, I reported that I couldn't find a rake anywhere. Whispering Dan shouted down to me, "He wants a rag, dummy!" Maybe Dan's familiarity with the Teutonic influence in the Detroit area made it easier to understand our friend, or maybe Dan had been working with him longer than I. In any case, I brought up the rag and 'Heinzelmenschen' was happy.

The novices also had a greater interaction with the Brothers from the Holy Family Community on the grounds. Most were retired and called Ancients, but there were some others who were assigned to Barrytown for reasons unknown or talents that could be used for the good of the Institute. Such a man was a Brother Cletus. Brother Cletus had a terrible malocclusion. His lower jaw protruded beyond his upper jaw. The man seldom spoke, but worked like a slave in the community laundry. In all kinds of weather, he processed the laundry in several industrial sized machines. I never recall any snafus in the laundry distribution or process. For his hard, tireless labors, we named the man with the serious overbite, 'Don't Eat us Cletus.' Certainly charity and forbearance were not two attributes of these youthful seekers of the unitive way.

Several of the Ancients stand out in memory also. 'Irish Eddie' was a bald man with a round Hibernian face that could make him a double for Barry Fitzgerald. Another Brother we called 'Senator Paul,' had the custom of addressing individuals with some honorary title or other. 'Senator Paul' might call you general or colonel one day, captain another, or major. He specialized in military ranks that seemed to have no specific bearing other than it occurred to him at the time. Another Ancient was a man we called 'Pilot Bob.' When he was in charge of the infirmary, Brother Robert was called 'Iodine Bob,' a tribute to the panacea he prescribed for all ailments from broken limbs to pneumonia. After he was relieved of that responsibility, he assumed the task of pushing the wheelchair of a Brother suffering from severe Parkinson's disease. Brother Clem Fehrenbach, a man who had a stellar career among various elementary schools in New York City, was confined to a wheelchair and had to have his head tied back against a headrest. He was at the mercy of 'Pilot Bob' who pushed him down the aisle to communion or brought him to meals and so forth. 'Pilot Bob' also had a peculiarity that remains in my recollections. The Ancients recited the rosary daily in Latin. While most of the Brothers were on the same words, Pilot Bob used to raise his voice blatantly for two words, "mulieribus," and "peccatoribus." I guess he liked the sound of those words more than the rest of the "Ave Maria."

A pleasant, round faced Brother Amian whose circular face and hair style might have been a model for the cartoon character Brother Juniper was also a constant presence in the kitchen. Brother Amian was in charge of pasteurizing the milk from our productive dairy. In a corner of the kitchen apart from the bustling preparation of food, a huge vat of stainless steel with a maze of pipes stood ready for its daily job. Brother Amian had a system which entailed heating the milk to above 140 degrees, and then cooling it rapidly down below 90 degrees within thirty minutes. When Brother Amian left for a retreat and vacation, he taught me how to replace him in the indispensable job. He was a fine teacher, but he insisted that every move be synchronized and orchestrated to save time and energy. If I enumerated the compulsory steps, I probably would reach several hundred movements, many of which were to be performed simultaneously. I did my best, and the electronic monitor of the measurements proved I succeeded with every batch. In spring the fresh milk assumed an onion taste, since the cows came off the winter fodder in the barns and grazed in the open fields where onion grass proliferated. As far as I know, the only solution to the onion taste was to outlast the onion grass after a few weeks. Although it tainted the taste of the milk, it didn't shrink consumption.

Another Brother whom we called 'PO Paul' was also occasionally around the kitchen area. Without any specifics, rumor recommended distance from him. He never said or did anything untoward, but we were wary of him referring to him as 'PO Paul' as in 'Pissed Off Paul.' I believe he used to disappear on a bender from time to time, but we never knew for sure. He was there but not part of our lives. Search parties from the administrators and occasionally the State Police would scour the local area until he was found and brought back in a car. While we were Novices, it was rumored that he had received several canonical warnings and had been officially expelled. He could just as readily been reassigned to another complex like Lincoln Hall or La Salle School in Albany. I believe no one ever crossed paths with 'Pissed Off' Paul again. He evidently had himself declared *persona non grata* and wouldn't be assigned to any educational institution again. Imagination may play a greater role in comprehending his fate than reality does.

Several Brothers came into contact with us during our manual labor periods in the afternoon. The Director left our assignments to Brother Philip for the most part, and he designated certain people for certain jobs. I felt honored to be assigned mostly to the farm crew. There, under the general supervision of a Brother we called 'Fat Leo' we savored the outside work and the new adventures such an assignment brought. 'Fat Leo' had a distinctive voice, part bass and part patois of central New York. He also was occasionally assisted by man, almost as rotund, but not quite so loquacious. 'Just Plain' Justin also worked on the farm, but he was more aloof and taciturn. About the only words, he uttered to the Novices were, "Nice Day." 'Fat Leo's' ample body invited the description, but his respect for certain workers made him popular and even admired. Brother Leo seemed partial to strength and naturally his favorite was Dan Goeddeke.

Dan was almost his second in command, sharing responsibility and drawing the most difficult, taxing chores. Dan drove vehicles of all sorts, a skill that Stinchcombe Brown also brought to the crew. I still recall Dave driving the truck, coming to an abrupt stop, throwing the gears into reverse and stepping out on the running board to direct the vehicle into a narrow space. When I inquired how the car operated without maneuvering the clutch, Dave informed me that most reverse gears could operate at a higher rate and didn't need the clutch and gas to move on flat ground. Although I had a driver's license, I was never called upon to drive in Barrytown, nor were the half dozen others so certified.

In the group before us, Brother Leo found a mature man who was another of his favorites. Unlike the rest of us, Harvey Turnure was a child of high society. It was said that his father was a major honcho in the Ford Company and that his son Harvey was born with the proverbial silver spoon in his mouth. Harvey was very unassuming and presented absolutely no airs or attitude that might mark him as one of the beautiful people. When he entered the religious life, the gossip columns had him partying at St. Tropez or Cannes, or Monte Carlo. Brother Philip used Harvey's 'savoir faire' to explain the intricacies of etiquette and social politeness. I especially remember his dissertation on the propriety of eating fried chicken with one's fingers. Ironically, Harvey had attempted to join the Jesuit Brothers at St. Andrew's which is now the grounds for the Culinary Institute of America. A Jesuit priest advised Harvey not to waste his time as a Jesuit Brother, but to join a productive teaching Order like the Christian Brothers. Following such advice, Harvey moved north about twenty miles and entered the Novitiate about a year ahead of me. One would never take him for a dilettante when he was one of the most effective farm members among us. By the way, when Harvey began his teaching career, a Jewish friend of the family observed, "Harvey had spent enough time as a Brother. Now he would talk to his friend, the Cardinal Archbishop of New York, Spellman, about making him a monsignor." Harvey passed on the honor without explaining that he wasn't on track to be a clergyman. The man who was from the flower of American society was definitely one of Fat Leo's favorites and most trusted workers.

On the farm crew a cadre of us worked in the dairy, or mended fences, or other such chores. The cardinal sin was squeamishness or

get one's hands dirty. When 'Fat Leo' observed anyone
at fashion, he was summarily fired from the farm crew
and returned to the Sub-Director in disgrace for reassignment. 'Fat
Leo' would dismiss the Brother who didn't meet his expectations
by saying, "You're useless, Brother. Get Brother Philip to send you
somewhere else!"

Brother Leo had an unusual manner of expressing himself too.
He urged each of us to "Pet the bull every day. Keep him tame." On
one occasion I was asked to assist Ed Klum, the hired civilian hand
who mostly handled the tractor and other equipment. Ed asked me
to catch small pigs within their pen and hold them while he wielded
his castrating knife. As I slogged around the filthy sty competing with
huge tape worms that seemed of the horror movie size and presence,
I captured the piglets with whatever athletic prowess I could muster.
Then I held the struggling future boar by the hind legs while Ed
performed the surgery. There was no antiseptic used nor anesthetic
and the pigs generally were very vocal about the intrusion, but as
soon as I completed one, I was sent in pursuit of another. I mused
that few of my fellow friends from Washington Heights had ever
developed any expertise in this area.

According to season, we had certain jobs to do. A wealthy
neighbor named Delafield allowed us to harvest any apples that had
fallen down from the trees during autumnal hurricanes. We were
authorized to select barrels or baskets of such apples which would
be used for pies or applesauce, or even snacks to supplement the
jelly sandwiches occasionally offered during long recreation periods.
Another neighbor was Bard College who advertised "We want people
who are different!" In our opinion, they got them. We were never
welcome on that college grounds, and the Bard students seldom
ventured near the monastery lands.

When we weren't involved in haying or other specifically
agricultural activities, we cleared trees and underbrush. On the last
day before we would begin the ten day prayer period and retreat in
preparation for first vows, Ed Klum assigned the bunch of us to clear
the undergrowth that beset the stand of trees lining the road into
the full grounds. As the retreat progressed, we discovered that Ed
had us pulling down huge, thick vines of poison ivy. Almost all of us
came down with severe cases of the allergy and had to get whatever
relief we could find from frequent showers. I suppose Ed realized that

we wouldn't work during our retreat, and that he might as well get the unpleasant job done so we could convalesce without interfering with his work plans.

In the summer a favorite activity was harvesting hay. A huge, flat wagon, drawn by a tractor, most likely driven by Ed Klum or a Brother Joseph who had been assigned to assist Brother Leo, would reap the bales that lay in the open field. In front of the tractor a baling machine had followed the furrows of mowed hay and spit out bales every ten yards. Our job was to hoist the bales onto the wagon and stack them for maximum volume. If the hay were dry, the bales weren't too heavy, but if the hay were still wet, the bales weighed a considerable amount and couldn't be stored in the loft. We learned about the danger of spontaneous combustion if the baled hay were drying out and releasing heat. When we got back to the barn with the hay, it generally was dry and therefore stackable in the loft. We would heave the bales to someone on the upper loft and he would carefully stack the hay for future use. The work was relatively hard; the hay cut one's forearms; and the sweat and mixture of plant life irritated the back. Nonetheless we thoroughly enjoyed the activity and looked forward to doing it as often as possible.

In early July after a complete year in the Novitiate, we got involved in an activity that almost ended my days in Barrytown. The new Postulants had just arrived and many of them were assigned to another crew that was harvesting tomatoes from a field near the barn. When we returned from haying, Brother Joseph urged us to cool off by giving Joe O'Brien a bath in the water hydrant close to the barn. Joe O'Brien noticed the conspiratorial whispers, deduced that something was up and took off running in my direction. I tackled him nicely while the 'Holy Ghost' was observing the activities from the tomato fields. O'Brien was then dragged through the water, and we all enjoyed a good laugh until the Director of Novices appeared and invited each of us for an interview before spiritual reading. Brother Andrew was particularly incensed, if one can predicate such a weakness of him, because of the bad example to the newcomers. When I spoke to him before spiritual reading, he was interested in where the idea for mugging O'Brien arose. Not wishing to involve the Brother Joseph who was supposed to be monitoring us in the fields, I claimed that the idea arose spontaneously. Brother Andrew again gave me a modest penance of kneeling out for night prayer for a week. He also invited me back in a week to tell him when I intended to start my Novitiate. Actually, I didn't think much of it until I discovered that only Bill Simon and I were invited back for an additional session. For that week, I watched my P's and Q's conscientiously, but I dreaded the weekend coming, for my family was driving to Barrytown for a periodic quarterly visit.

When my father or mother innocently inquired how I was doing, I braced myself for the shocking revelation that I could be heading home with them. Instead, Brother Andrew offered one of his pious, simplistic responses we had grown to love. Brother Andrew said, "How can anyone say anything wrong about the young Brothers? Sure, their guardian angels would come to their defense, and then I would be in big trouble." I don't know if my sigh of relief was audible, but it was heartfelt. Perhaps the Director was right on one point, however. I hadn't even begun to acquire the virtues that a Novitiate year was designed to impart. When I returned to the follow up session where I was supposed to describe my week, Andy said I was doing fine and forget the whole adventure. I immediately ran out to tell Bill Simon to go in while Andy was in a good mood. Naturally, the 'Holy Ghost' appeared and overheard my comment. Typically, his reaction was that angelic smile and kindly glowing facial expression.

While I was usually assigned to the farm crew for the extended afternoon manual labor session, I generally got the task of pot walloping after breakfast. Again, my partner was Big Dan. Our job was far from glamorous, but we set an esprit that set us apart. Our task was to steam clean all the cauldrons, vats, cooking trays, and industrial strength kitchen items. To do so, we labored over huge sinks and had a minor source of steam. In order to perform this pedestrian task, Dan and I decided to wear uniforms. The costumes for the activity were ripped T shirts, the more threadbare the better, and black suit vests from common stock. These were offset by old baseball uniform pants. No one ever commented upon our outfits. I guess as long as the pots and pans and kitchen equipment were clean, no one worried about the propriety of the clothes we wore in pursuit of cleanliness. In reality, the job was so dirty and hard on clothes that the almost inexhaustible supply of shirts, pants and vests from common stock was a practical solution rather than an irreligious expression of individuality.

As a professional pot walloper in the morning manual labor, I worked hard but made a game of the dirty exercise. Our uniform exemplified the pride we took in the necessary job, and we could always take comfort in knowing that someone else had a far less desirable job. Jim Nerney, who could conduct a dialogue with a dummy for half an hour before he recognized the figure in wood, seemed singled out for a reprehensible task. His socialization skills were severely challenged since he always had to work alone in a job that taxed the olfactory nerves extensively. Jim was placed in solo charge of fly traps and swill pails. Every day, he had to empty the fetid traps with their daily catch secured by a series of occult passages into a bottle baited with rancid meat. The flies would ultimately die in a water solution and Jim had the job of disposing of them with appropriate solemnity. Even in winter he had little relief for he also was assigned the task of scrubbing those swill pails destined for the pig pens on the farm. Remarkably, I never heard him complain about his assignment, and if he shirked his duty, it couldn't go unnoticed. He persevered in this thankless task for the entire year.

Some novices had routine assignments that required special talent or expertise. Ed Schwall and Vinny Callahan comprised an all Staten Island staff that served as handymen, carpenters, repairmen or general Mr. Fix-its. Most recently, Ed and Vinnie confessed that they used the skills and tools at their disposal to construct a still which incidentally blew up before completing its job. When these two creative individuals weren't working on some repair, they would be assigned to the farm crew. Barney Quigley, given the Sub-directors predilection for painting, was one of the most valuable laborers in the Novitiate. He was the professional painter and always had some job to do. In later years, Barney's stomach cancer raised speculation that his job had some hazards that we were not aware of at the time. Barney, as well as former painters, Kevin Kissan, Tom Reilly, and Bill Barron, died prematurely. In a safer profession as borne out by longevity, Joe Troy and John Hannaway were barbers. Although there was a ukase against crew cuts, I would ask Joe for a "short, legitimate haircut" that somehow ultimately looked like a crew cut. When they had no haircuts to give, they too would join us on the farm crew.

A number of Brothers were trained in the fine art of tailoring. They made robes, rabattas, collars, and repaired items entrusted to their skill. They were noted to some degree as great conversationalists and rumormongers, but they seldom escaped the pins and needles and rarely worked on the farm. In hindsight, it might appear that their early training was the best preparation for perseverance to this day. Of all the various manual labors we had, the tailor shop workers seemed to occupy the greatest number who remain committed to the Brothers today.

I can't underscore enough how much I enjoyed working on the farm crew. The fresh air, the physical labor, the diversity of tasks and the friendship of my peers made the work seem more like play. Sometimes it evidently wasn't. Among our responsibilities was clearing out the chicken houses from time to time. Given the freedom to range about the coop, the foul fowl dropped their droppings everywhere, and we had to clean up the mess from time to time. The dung would harden, and we would have to use a hoe or ice scraper, a shovel or some sharp edged tool to loosen the deposits which could measure an inch or two in depth. As we scraped, the hardened, calcified dung would vaporize and enter the atmosphere we breathed. Sometimes we protected ourselves fruitlessly by tying handkerchiefs around our mouths, but nothing was really adequate to filter the offensive dust. It entered the lungs and nostrils and caused what we termed 'dung on the lung.'

The chief symptom of this affliction was evidenced not only by the dirty sputum we expelled, but by the effect it had on the vocal cords. During our Novitiate year, nine Brothers died and were buried in the cemetery overlooking the Hudson River with Hunter Mountain in the background. When each Brother passed to his eternal reward for faithful service, it was a community responsibility to chant the Office of the Dead, a series of prayers and psalms that usually took about an hour to complete. The psalms were sung in Latin and those afflicted with dung on the lung often found their larynxes vacillating all over the musical scales. The Brothers on the farm crew sounded like a group of adolescent teens vocally challenged to remain on the right pitch. Screeches, sudden jumps in timbre, or even the inability to make any sound characterized our chanting. The gravity of the Office of the Dead thereby led to levity upon the execution.

I mentioned that a number of older Brothers died while we were Novices. A few even suggested that Brother Concordius Leo was killing them with kindness. Some of us, notably the less endowed with singing voices, were selected to be members of an elite group which we termed the 'assorted six.' David Brown had mastered the dedicated, mournful stare, and Barney Quigley was quite adroit at it also. Dan Goeddeke and Joe O'Brien formed a tall portion of six, and Pat Murphy and I were also part of the team. Occasionally, Dermot O'Sullivan would serve as a back up member. On one occasion the assorted six were directed to a room in the Holy Family Community of Ancients where Brother Paul had died. He was a big man with broad shoulders and a muscular body. When he died at an advanced age, he was still quite heavy. When we went to the room to bring his body down to the common room for the Ancients, we were told to wait for the undertaker's assistant, whom we labeled 'Foster the Ghoul,' while he was draining Brother's blood into large glass bottles. He was then going to replace the blood with embalming fluid. As we waited, Joe O'Brien decided to tell us some jokes from a genre that had eluded our knowledge. Like lyrics in a song, jokes remained in Joe's repertoire upon a single recitation. Now he was prepared to introduce us to 'Blasphemy' jokes. As the blood drained from the deceased Brother's arteries, Joe was telling us about that new singing group called "Pontius Pilot and the Nail Drivers, singing Rock around the Cross." We laughed heartily until the 'Holy Ghost' materialized from nowhere. I supposed we were nonplussed to describe why we were laughing at such a solemn moment. Brother Andrew sensed the less he knew the better.

In another symptom of our adventure with the chickens that would ultimately serve as our entrees, Tony Basilian Riordan was speaking with Brother Andrew. Tony related how he felt lousy. The 'Holy Ghost' assured him that he was a very worthy person and advised him to elevate his personal self-esteem. Tony corrected the Director of Novices by announcing that he was speaking in a literal sense, not a figurative sense. While working in the chicken coop, Tony played host to a number of lice which decided his body was a better treat than the fowl. They could be spotted on the white camouflage coats some of us wore during the winter months. Poor Brother Andrew must have questioned the wisdom of his role as Director of teenage aspirants! On the other hand, perhaps our unexpected behaviors helped keep him young. Certainly, his sense of humor never seemed to vanish.

The chickens also presented a periodic task for almost the entire group of Novices. The chickens were slaughtered, plucked, eviscerated, cleaned and frozen for future use. Pat Murphy was an adept executioner as he wielded a mean axe. For my part, I was relegated to the mundane task of plucking the corpses. Pat would place the chicken with its head confined between two nails. A swift chop usually did the job and then he tossed the body into a fifty-five gallon drum. The headless chicken would flop around for as long as a minute and then finally be still. Pluckers, like myself, would extract a still chicken and dip it into a vat of boiling water. The water usually softened the feathers and by sliding one's hand over the breast and legs, a chicken could be plucked in a matter of twenty seconds. Then the clean chicken would be presented to Ed Klum or Curt who would eviscerate the bird and dissect it into appropriate portions. They were then washed and placed into containers for freezing. It was messy work, but we made it a game. The problem arose when one encountered a pin feather chicken. On these birds, one had to pluck each feather individually, and it could take a great deal more time than the ordinary birds. Since we had a race to determine who could pluck the most chickens in the shortest time, the selection of the subject bird was very important. Again, we typically took a chore and turned it into a game.

During our Novitiate year, the United States was besieged by the Asian Flu. Like most of the country, many caught the flu before an adequate vaccination had been discovered. Almost all the Novices suffered the symptoms to a greater or larger extent. In my recollection only Barney, Dermot and I didn't succumb to the illness. The ailing Brothers were stacked up in the infirmary spilling out into the corridors. After Mass, 'Pop' Carroll would bring them *Viaticum* or Holy Communion. As he approached the infirmary escorted by two Brothers holding candles like Acolytes, 'Pop' would utter his blessing, "Peace be to this house, and all who dwell therein." Tending the sick, the nurse, Josie Pender insisted 'Pop' Carroll be checked for symptoms too. As she stood holding a rectal thermometer that had just been extracted from a patient, she insisted 'Pop' have his temperature taken too. The cantankerous prelate snatched the used thermometer from her hand and quickly inserted it into his mouth. No one, including Josie, had the courage to tell him its previous location as he insisted, "No one takes my temperature."

I had the good fortune to enjoy excellent health while I was at Barrytown. My experience in the infirmary was brief and entirely caused by my own stupidity. When I was in the Juniorate, I marked my laundry with PN42. Entering the Novitiate I was given another laundry identification number Δ141. Soon thereafter each of us was issued a large safety pin with our number embossed on it. The pin closed a mesh-like sack where we placed our dirty laundry. The process eliminated sorting and expedited distribution. My problem arose when I had a pimple on my knee and decided to operate with the pin that had come from the laundry. I burst the pimple and created a staph infection that had me laid up in the infirmary for two days. I suppose nobody had to tell me that such an incision was unsanitary, but my knee swelled up as the infection reached critical proportions. I had no defense for my behavior other than temporary insanity.

One of the legitimate distractions of the Novitiate was the periodic athletic competition between the Scholastics in Troy or the high school Juniorate boys on the other side of the building. These baseball and ice hockey games were spirited contests that carried boasting rights for an entire year. I had played baseball for the Juniorate for two years and in my senior year I developed some skill in ice hockey. By the time I was a Novice, I had translated the bloodlust of roller hockey in the Heights onto the rinks of Barrytown. I lacked the finesse and fine skating skills of Sean O'Keefe or Tom Smith, but I had a nose for the puck and the willingness to fight for it, as I learned in intramurals on 175th Street in front of Incarnation, or on our local rinks near the George Washington Bridge. These traits brought me personal instruction from the Director of Novices. One of the Brothers on the Juniorate staff had suffered a severe concussion while playing hockey, and we prayed for his recovery from a coma for a number of weeks. Fortunately, he completely recovered. Perhaps with that in mind, Brother Andrew summoned me to him and ordered me to play ice hockey with a hat on in the future. From that point forward I had to have some kind of naval watch hat on my head while I played that rough and tumble kind of game. Dermot got the same personal instruction when the 'Holy Ghost' descended upon him with a message about driving to the basket for a lay up.

We had been invested with the robes of the Christian Brothers on September 7, 1957. At that time we were presented with three items that we could legitimately own, despite our commitment to community property according to our vow of poverty. Each Brother was given a pocket prayer book which contained the text for the community prayers, a copy of the **New Testament** and the **Imitation of Christ** by Thomas a Kempis. Supplementing this book which would be carried in an interior pocket of the robe was a six decade rosary and a crucifix that would be worn around the neck beneath our garments. Even the clothes we wore were not really our own, but reserved for our personal use. A full year later we were to take our first vows on September 8, 1958 and then move to Troy to begin our Scholasticate training. Each ceremony was preceded by a ten day retreat involving prayer, meditation and introspection. The rites weren't interrupted by manual labor or recreation, and the silence for ten days was quite oppressive. On both occasions, I can't say I really acquired any great spiritual insights. In fact, my most mature thought was simply that after September 8, 1958, I couldn't leave when or if I wanted to, since vows were imposed from one year to the next retreat. I also had the thought that for the first time, I was undergoing a commitment that was my personal conviction and not a group activity. In all that time, I never once contemplated leaving the Brothers and had done little soul searching. My pursuit of perfection was hampered by my predilection for enjoying the moment. In truth, the serious objectives of the novitiate were pretty much wasted upon an immature youth. Many of my peers may have felt the same way. Some, no doubt, made good use of the opportunities presented by our exclusive investigation of the religious life. I am afraid I didn't make much use of those chances to draw closer to God. My prayer life remained primarily an avid recitation of formulaic, oral prayers, like the rosary, night prayer, litanies, and so forth. Sharing in the joy and ecstasy of the unitive way remained a very remote, and I dare say impossible objective, given my personality. Yet, the Novitiate year was incongruously a pleasant memory. It conjured up images of contradictions, an array of superficial impressions, a collection of episodes more notable for their humor than their introspection. Perhaps, that might all change in my freshman year in the Scholasticate.

Chapter Four

Scholasticate at Troy New York

September 1958-June 1959

Immediately after taking first vows on September 8, 1958, we packed for the trip to Troy, New York. Our first glimpse of Hillside Hall brought to mind the image of Dickensian orphanages, and in truth, there was more than a passing resemblance. Leaving the bucolic countryside around Barrytown and approaching Troy from the south across the Menands Bridge, one might experience a variation on time travel. We had left the beautiful banks of the Hudson to approach a nineteenth century city about fifty miles north. The topography of the city is obvious to the most untrained eye. The east shore of the Hudson River at this point remains level for approximately five or six city blocks. Steep hills abruptly disrupt this comfortable area, and their summits may be reached only by strong automobiles during dry weather unless one chooses to stumble along the steep streets.

As the motorist transits the Menands Bridge which leads from Albany, the boast of Troy comes into view. The sign welcomes the traveler into the home of Uncle Sam. As the sign indicates, Sam Wilson was a purveyor of beef to the American army during the War of 1812. He stamped the sealed kegs with US, meaning it was property of the United States. Soldiers took to referring to the provisions as gifts of Uncle Sam Wilson. Soon he became a symbol of America when newspapers recounted the tale and spread the story throughout the infant country. With such fame, Sam Wilson came to represent the United States in the same way that John Bull epitomized the British Empire.

Troy is also proud to assert itself as the seed and origin of feminine education in the early nineteenth century. Emma Willard had founded a female academy on the summit of the hill overlooking the South End Tavern. One of Emma's protégés became the second wife of Russell Sage, no fan of female education by the way, and she used his wealth to create the college for women that bears his name. Russell Sage College is located a few blocks northwest of where we were to begin our collegiate career and recommence the Novitiate training we evidently missed in Barrytown.

In mentioning the South End Tavern, one may use it as illustrative of the condition of the city of Troy in 1958. Like the tavern that only the familiar might enter, the city had seen better days. Everything looked like a vestige of nineteenth century industrial living. The streets were lined with two story wooden contiguous buildings that left no room for front yards, lawns, or any kind of decorative approaches. Each house was not decrepit, but it looked neglected and poorly maintained, at least begging for a fresh paint job. The tourist board of Troy encourages those who visit to take special notice of whatever wrought iron works can be found throughout the city. Apparently, during the Civil War era, Troy was home to extensive iron foundries that had huge contracts for cannons and weapons for the Union army. I recall reading in **North and South** by John Jakes that one of the characters traveled to Troy to inspect some advanced weaponry that would replace the shoddy work speculators foisted upon the army. At the end of the war, someone must have turned out the lights and shut down the factories for there were few signs of any kind of industry in the dying city.

Once noted also for its extensive fabric plants and shirt making capacity, the haberdashery industry must have fled the 'Collar City' before we got there. Perhaps the sole financially sound institution still operating in 1958 Troy was the Fitzgerald Brewery. Like the cigarette packages of Pall Mall that featured a Latin inscription of *In hoc signo vinces* (in this sign you will conquer), the Fitzgerald bottles and cans boasted an inscription from two outstanding literary works in Western Civilization. The tobacco merchants chose to compare the alleged conversion of Constantine the Great to Christianity with the more pedestrian attempt to sell cigarettes using the slogan if not the symbolic cross. The Sudsmeisters of Fitzgerald either displayed their classical education or assumed the consumers of their brew were well versed in the works of antiquity. Each container offered a reminder to the consumer that *Ilium fuit Troia est,* which translates as "The town of Ilium is past, but Troy exists." According to my consultant in Latin antiquities, Aaron Lipka advised me that the expression is taken from two separate sections of the **Aeneid**, connected in theme perhaps, but not in proximity. I can't vouch whether the beer was as classy as its motto, nor can I attest that those who drank Fitzgerald's knew they were reading the quotes of Virgil's *Aeneid* or its derivative use in Dante's *Inferno*.

Troy looked like a city that died but remained unburied. With the bland house fronts, the virtually empty streets, the steeply escalating roads, the city seemed to stifle whatever economic influence had made it a vibrant metropolis during the Erie Canal era until the Civil War. Someone explained to me that the tax circumstances for the homeowners of Troy encouraged no development or beautification of the exterior. Tax rates were reputedly based on the exterior of the building rather than such items as the number of bedrooms or baths, or square footage. Within the plain houses of South Troy most of the homes were neat, well decorated, and properly maintained.

Perhaps I do a great injustice to the citizens of Troy, for as a general rule they were solicitous for the Brothers, friendly whenever encountered, and in fact, quite generous and loyal to the Brothers who conducted La Salle Academy for some time. After a summer of teaching in the old building on Fourth Street, La Salle Academy migrated, perhaps like most of the inhabitants of the forlorn city, to the heights alongside the Community College above the river. Generations of grateful alumni and friends of the Brothers had contributed enough to build a modern school with the requisite science and computer laboratories. That of itself indicates the kindness and respect the Brothers earned while serving the citizens of the 'Collar City.'

Since we had little opportunity to meet with the people or visit their homes, or inspect whether they had back yards, or examine their bank accounts, my impressions remain just that. I can only describe what I saw and how I felt we had somehow been transported back in time to a place where the customs of the nineteenth century were more prevalent than the age to which we were accustomed.

As I consider my impressions, I am left with the image of the movie sets from *The Gangs of New York*. My first glimpse of Hillside Hall CMO (Catholic Male Orphanage) was mirrored in the movie lots representing the Five Points in nineteenth century New York City. Shortly after entering South Troy on Fourth Street, we turned right onto Hanover Street, a one way access road to the massive wooden structure that soon loomed directly overhead. The former Catholic Male Orphanage could have sheltered Oliver Twist or other victims of the industrialization in the nineteenth century. Hillside Hall was a five story, wooden structure with beams that bespoke the virgin forests of the time rather than the steel girders that would soon replace them. It was built into the sharp incline of the hill around 1865. I suppose there was a surplus of orphans at the time, given the casualties of the Civil War, rampant disease among the working classes, and periodic plagues.

My information about emigrant societies that flourished in the trade of orphans and ragamuffins westward to work on prairie farms demanded a response from the Catholic Church. It was evident that these children were being hired out as forced labor and most would ultimately lose the Catholic faith into which they had been born. Bishops decided that appropriate reaction was the creation of orphanages, even if the children were not literally orphans since many were the sons and daughters of indigent immigrants who couldn't care for their offspring. My imagination swapped places with the poor urchins as they gazed at the massive structure on the hill. On the other hand, perhaps I can only surmise how terrible their destitution may have been and that any kind of domicile might have been a welcomed refuge.

The roadway up to the lowest level of Hillside Hall was comprised of Belgian Blocks that made transit in winter time wearing on car tires in rain, sleet or snow which Troy seems to have in great supply. I also wondered if the horse and carriage transports of the original period may have been more effective than gas driven vehicles. Unfamiliar with the perils of horse drawn carriages, I can only believe the original streets presented the same obstacles that they did to automobile traffic. Maybe the location of Hillside was determined by the economics of an undesirable location that wasn't suitable for commercial use, or perhaps its height made it healthier above the banks of the fetid Hudson and its crowded shoreline.

The front façade of Hillside Hall presented an insipid, unadorned building that rose dramatically for five stories. At some time in the past, a level surface had been dredged about half way down the hill and a modest clay tennis court with a suitable tall fence was available for our use. I don't remember anyone ever using it. An outdoor circular wooden stairway characteristic of Charleston architecture led to the second floor where some parlors and small offices functioned. Despite the feature of Southern mansions, Hillside Hall offered few decorative amenities. Beneath the staircase was an entranceway to the lowest floor where a refectory and recreation hall surrounded a large industrial kitchen. Much of the building was more pragmatic or functional rather than beautiful. The front façade was an excellent preparation for what lay within. The second floor held a modest, barely decorated chapel near the offices. On the third floor, a large common room with about fifty desks was on the east side of the structure and the west side had been divided into dormitory facilities similar to the drapes and cells of the Novitiate. On the fourth floor, there were more dormitory accommodations and classrooms. The faculty shared a section of the second floor as well. Each cell was a ten foot square with a single sliding curtain entrance from an aisle. Within the sleeping quarters were a simple wooden chair and a small bureau. Sinks and showers were also nearby. The shower facilities were metal divisions that accentuated the heat or frigidity of the water. Each floor had a tin plated, high ceiling, perhaps ten or twelve feet in elevation. That height didn't provide an inducement for comfort or coziness to the accommodations.

Beyond the dorms leading to the back of the house were porches that looked like the housing I have seen in scenes from movies filmed in Chicago. The huge beams were exposed and the landings were connected by brief staircases. The porches offered about ten foot walkways outdoors, and were suitable for strolling in any kind of weather. The back end of the building had a concrete yard about twenty-feet wide, but running the length of the structure. At one end of the yard was a wall where we could play handball or fastball. At the other end of the yard was a building sheltering our chemistry lab that retained some of my most frustrating memories of life at Hillside Hall.

The interior of the building was linked by staircases at either end. Their age and decrepit state indicated that they had begun to fall away from the wall and actually listed about ten degrees off center. They creaked and groaned upon multiple footsteps, lending that sense of impending disaster that a dilapidated house might collapse at anytime. While we were in Troy for the ten months, there was a catastrophic fire in a Catholic elementary School named Holy

Angels somewhere in Chicago. According to newspaper accounts, the stairwells had been painted with flammable paint, and when the fire erupted, the exits were impassable. About eighty students were burned to death. That debacle led many civic entities to examine old buildings for fire traps. Hillside Hall was among the inspected. In order to satisfy more stringent safety requirements, firewalls were then erected on each landing of the interior fire escapes. That was the most modern concession to architecture that the building had.

The recreation room downstairs did have a radio which specialized in Tri-City music, and it also featured a pool table and ping pong games. This was something new for our group, but few had the spare time to indulge in such activities. In the backyard where the concrete covered the ground, we hosed it down during the winter and were able to play hockey from December 8 until St. Patrick's Day since the frigid temperatures assisted us. Each evening some volunteers would brave the cold and spray another coat of water over the rink. We were informed that a hot spray would be faster than cold because once water started to freeze, momentum increased the rate, and therefore hot water froze faster than cold. No one took the time to test the hypothesis scientifically. The major deterrent to our own hockey rink was the time and opportunity to use it. Most of those who played regularly did so at the risk of failing chemistry, but that's another story.

To the north side of our building several small wooden sheds stood. One was rectangular with the broad side extending perhaps fifty yards. In it were housed the heating units for the entire plant as well as a storeroom where textbooks and printed prayer books were contained. One of my jobs while I was at Hillside was responding to requests from Brothers' communities for the various prayer books and some texts that the Brothers had printed at a prior date. Separated by an alley wide enough for a small truck to pass was another taller building which housed a full court gymnasium. All the buildings were wood and apparently approximately one hundred years old. Behind all structures was a two car garage, quite essential in combating the frosts of winter. One of the dicta imposed upon those of us who drove the house vehicles was never to put on the emergency brake in the passenger cars or four wheel drive pick up truck since they would routinely freeze, even in the garage. Trojan weather offered healthy doses of cold, wind, and snow with few breaks for sunshine.

The complex was built into the hill, but the area behind the garage had been leveled to some degree. On the east side of the concrete yard, however, the cliff continued upward for about fifty yards. At the summit of the hill the terrain leveled off sufficiently for a small baseball field and a panoramic view of South Troy. In the spring we had a chance to practice for our away baseball games against the Novices or Juniors in Barrytown. There seemed little time for such exercises given the academic demands heaped upon us. Our academic curriculum seemed to vacillate between the insurmountable and the impenetrable. Most of difficulties centered around our five credit course in Quantitative Chemistry. That course alone changed the future of many in the group.

If the building complex seemed forbidding and evocative of a fire trap, the interior was simpler and in some ways relatively comfortable. The chapel was adorned in a simplistic style that complemented the exterior façade and the dining rooms. Recreational facilities were commodious enough, just underutilized because of the academic demands. The classroom windows, exposed to the harsh, cold winds off the Hudson River, often rattled and offered drafts that were unstoppable. I suppose any individuals sensitive to cold might find the facility in keeping with the image of an orphanage.

To assist in our transition into college studies, we had a fine array of talent. Our Director was Brother Basilian John Veale, fresh from the Second Novitiate in Rome. I don't know whether he had instructions to do so, but he seemed intent on turning our academic year into a spiritual reformation too. I can't remember too much frivolity and laughter during our ten month tenure in Hillside Hall. I do recall being introduced to petty punishments, abnegations, mortifications, and penances that were a daily occurrence. Although the experience in Rome seemed to have injected Brother John with some personable skills, he still was far from the exemplars we knew in our other administrative positions. Brother Pete Mannion embodied a warm, friendly, youthful authority figure who still maintained a distance from his young charges, but exuded an approachable personality who wanted to help with any adjustments to Barrytown. Of course we loved Brother Andrew Lennon, the Novice Master with the peculiar approach and twinkle in his eye. Our parents recognized this difference from Brother John, and many of them looked on him with suspicion. Brother Leo Kirby also had the gift of relating well with our parents so Brother John was outstanding as a remote, baffling personality. In the Juniorate we called him Black Jack because of his heavy five o'clock shadow. Some referred to him as Jack the Sack because of his extensive double chin. During our year in Hillside, some of us grew to understand him better and appreciate his dry humor and aloofness. For me, he remained a formative influence who emphasized abnegation and mortification more so than interpersonal relationships. After our year, he became the Novice Master at Narragansett, a position that I understand he fulfilled with great competence. I am pleased, however, that we had the opportunity to adapt to the religious life under Brother Andrew rather than John.

In all honesty, Jack had improved, but his dealings with the Scholastics took on the dimension of sobering us up after a year of frivolity and merriment in the Novitiate. We were issued minor punishments, most of which were invitations to kiss the floor, on a daily basis. The majority of the penances were so minor as to be dismissed except for their persistence. Kissing the floor became a joke as we would imitate him during our conversations. Jim Nerney's parents even invited Jack to do so when they were introduced to him. Each evening we would make a self accusation for some minor failing we had committed during the day. It might entail talking during manual labor or wasting time or some such peccadillo. Like a priest in confession, Jack would give us a penance to perform. Some were traditional, but all were designed to carry some form of embarrassment. During all my years in the Brothers, I only witnessed one uncharitable, unreasonable, downright outrageous public humiliation. That it occurred under the aegis of Brother John should be no surprise.

Two of my confreres evidently had stayed up past night prayer to do some extra studying. That was a serious offense in the eyes of the Director. We had often listened to tales from Brother Celestine Philip when he was Sub-Director in the novitiate. He regaled us with imaginative ways the Scholastics in Washington found in order to study beyond the bewitching hour. Perhaps, the most creative was the Brother he found hiding with a flashlight in a laundry chute. In any case, the severity of the offense was more in the Director's mind than in our own. Brother John had a phobia about what was termed 'PF's' or particular friendships. These apparently were exclusive friendships which sometimes led to sexual relationships. When my confreres were caught studying with a flashlight in a cell, the Director insisted that they accuse themselves in front of the entire class of "endangering their vow of celibacy," not studying after lights out. I thought the punishment far surpassed the severity of the offense and thought little of the wisdom and understanding of my Director. Even if they were guilty of some sexual offense, that would be all the more reason to avoid such public pillorying. A sad by-product of this Draconian imposition was the fact that many in my group shunned the individuals thereafter for some time.

With that note in mind, I would like to underscore that there was a concern about particular friendships that often played a role in interrelating with each other. Groups were assigned by the Director to sections for exercise walks after meals. Correspondence was monitored and clandestine messages strictly forbidden. If some individuals seemed to get too close or exclude others from their company, they were publicly advertised for this indiscretion. Most of the time, each of us had close friends within the group, but superiors were wary of individuals who spent too much time together. Usually our activities were geared for groups rather than cabals, so it never became a problem. I do suppose the focus may have inhibited some from forming very close relationships with one's peers, but the friendships have endured over fifty years. In view of the scandals now confronting the clergy and the church, I can only say that any indication of those kinds of problems was dealt with immediately and severely among the Christian Brothers. I can cite no scandalous relationships or behaviors ever surfaced in my association with the Institute.

Brother John, himself, seemed more ascetic, than most of the Brothers I had met. He seemed genuinely an individual who was prayerful and perhaps hard on himself. His difficulty in relating to others was more a personality trait than a conviction. He actually had a sense of humor if one delved deeply enough. On one occasion during Holy Week, he sent me to pick up a first run movie. One of the advantages of life in Hillside Hall was access to current movies, sometimes before they were even publicly released. I think this was a generous contribution of one of our alumni who owned a movie distribution system. In any case, on Good Friday, Brother John called me into his office and directed me to collect the multiple reels for the epic movie, "*Raintree County*," with Elizabeth Taylor and Montgomery Cliff. He ordered me not to tell anyone about the Easter treat to follow. I said, "It's Good Friday. Who's going to talk to me?" Jack's response was, "Then don't rattle the cans as you climb the stairs!" I resisted the impulse to notch my desk at this first sign of humor in the man.

I also recall a field trip he authorized for us. A French chorister group called "*Les Petits Chanteurs*" was touring the United States. One of their designated concerts was scheduled at Auriesville on the banks of the Mohawk River. We enjoyed the opportunity to get away from our daily routine as much as the music. Guys like Sammy Schaeffer even tested their linguistic skills with the youthful singers. Auriesville had been the site of an Iroquois Indian encampment in the seventeenth century. It was there that the Black robes, the Jesuit missionaries, Jean De Brebeuf, Rene Goupil, and several others were martyred by the tribe that favored the English, never having forgiven Samuel De Champlain for assisting the Algonquians in a battle near Lake Champlain. Apparently, the Iroquois were terrorized by Champlain's firearms and ran from the field. They recovered their courage but never their embarrassment, so they always supported the British in the 'Great War for Empire' in the New World. As Scholastics we also enjoyed a few picnic trips to a State Park close to the state capitol at the end of New Scotland Road. Thatcher State Park was one of the richest fossil deposits in New York, and it was easy to study the strata of rocks in the gorges and cliffs of the scenic center. These excursions were cherished opportunities to escape the pressure of study and the pursuit of asceticism.

Among the memories of a Troy isolated on the steep hillside, I do recall a very pleasant Christmas visit to the nuns who staffed the local elementary school at the base of Hanover Street. The bells of St. Joseph's Church rang throughout South Troy every day. On the quarter hour, they played an incremental arrangement increasing as the hour approached. The sound was neither joyful nor doleful. When the hour struck, the reverberation was unlike the tintinnabulation of Poe's "*Bells,*" nor did the echoes of John Donne's "*No Man Is An Island,*" peal through the streets. Rather, the sound was what it actually was—a metronomically neutral recording of passing time signifying a community we seldom saw. Near Christmas, however, we were invited down to the local convent to share a 'wassail' with the Sisters who taught in that school. After a pleasant hour of socializing with these women whom we hardly knew, the Scholastics were invited to sing a Christmas carol. Our choice of expression contained the words, "Now feed us some figgy pudding . . . . and we won't go until we get some," which evoked laughter among the performers and the audience. That is the only time we ever met these fellow teachers.

Along with Brother John's interest in converting us into budding ascetics, he also was intent on our mastering the silence of the Cistercians and Trappists. One of his consistent themes was the need for silence, recollection, and modesty of the eyes. To a great extent he succeeded in his quest, making our adaptation and assimilation into the larger Scholasticate in the months after his training an unpopular, negative experience for many. What Brother John had instilled in Troy seemed to be interpreted as a 'holier than thou' attitude to the older classes from Washington.

Our Sub-director in Troy was an energetic, enthusiastic man whose joy for life was evident. Brother Cecelian Streebling was born in Detroit and matured in a polyglot environment before entering the Brothers. 'Ce Ce,' as we called him, evidently was fluent in English, German, and French, but we could never ascertain what his best language was. He shifted from one to another in mid sentence on some occasions. When he was teaching, he often would let his enthusiasm run ahead of his tongue to the point where he would have to stop and ask, "How you say it in English?" He was in fine mettle when he would read about Ma Chimene and the Cid in French. We also had him for English composition where his favorite maxim was "writing maketh the exact man." He had a great opportunity attempting to rein in my verbosity and Ciceronian prose. I think one could say that his favorite sentence was a simple declarative statement with very few adjectives and adverbs, and of course a style devoid of dependent clauses. As the casual reader may note, I never mastered his proffered style, but I did learn some hints about brevity being the soul of wit. Another year of 'Ce Ce's instruction and I may have been writing competitively with the likes of Hemingway and Steinbeck. As it is, I muddle along with my own preferences.

As Sub-Director 'Ce Ce' assumed command when Brother John had to travel for meetings or conferences, a situation we found too seldom for our liking. When he was acting Director, Brother Cecilian would announce at night prayer, "There will be an extra sleep-in tomorrow. The rising bell will ring at 6:25am. Rise, make your ablutions, and say your morning prayers before Mass begins at 6:30." Time for ablutions was preliminary to Morning Prayer. Extra sleeping time was always appreciated since our standard rising time was 5:00am with Mass an hour and a half later. Since 'Ce Ce' taught most of us English as well as French, we had a special debt for his understanding. Our balanced study hours had little time for his subjects while we focused almost exclusively on Chemistry. 'Ce Ce' seemed to recognize the disparity of attention, but he generally sacrificed his demands to our exorbitant hours addressing the arcane points of chemistry.

The man who guaranteed that our meals were plentiful and sumptuous was Brother Eulogius Austin O'Malley. Our Latin and history teacher was a short, rather compactly well-built man with an excellent sense of humor and a sharp wit. He also sported a very close cut hairstyle like that of Roger Maris that gave him the appearance of an athlete, although I never saw him engage in any sport. Eulogius peppered his World history class with puns and humorous anecdotes, some of which I repeated in my own career. When speaking of the Greeks, he told us about the tonsorial retort, "Euripides? Eumenides!" His commentary on Nero and his doting mother, 'fair Agrippina' whom the insane emperor beat over the head with oars to make sure she drowned, was part of his repartee. We heard tales also of Theodora and her dancing 'bare' act.

Under his approval, I wrote a term paper about Goliardic Poets, the disciples of Golias, often referred to as the Wandering Scholars of the Middle Ages. To quote Brother Eulogius, "The Wandering Scholars believed in a life of wine, women, and song," and in the stutter that plagued him significantly, he added, "and they didn't do much singing." My first choice for a research paper was an investigation into the reality of the 'Black Mass.' I think my more experienced mentor realized the naiveté of my research talents and the extent of pornographic material a serious study would demand, so my request was parried politely.

Since I was one of the few Scholastics who possessed a driver's license, I had many opportunities to drive and escape the monastery momentarily. In a capacity of driver, Brother Eulogius also deputized me to go to many of the stores from Albany to downtown Troy on missions for provisions for the house. I learned where we purchased bottled soda at a nondescript factory where the carbonation was capped right before my eyes. I was given the location of the dry ice factory where they packed and preserved the gallons of ice cream for our consumption. I even discovered what maraschino cherries were when I was sent on a secret mission to resupply the faculty for their Sunday drinks. From produce markets to dry goods stores, from shoe stores to haberdasheries, I got to know the merchants of the Tri-City area under the guidance of Eulogius Austin. I usually needed no money for Hillside Hall either had accounts or generous donors. The opportunity to run errands in a car or pick up truck made my days in Hillside more tolerable, for the other demands were demoralizing after the joys of my Novitiate year.

In speaking with my favorite World history teacher in college, I mentioned that I sometimes thought of the joys of taking a cross country exploration trip, stopping for occasional work to supply funds for fuel or food and lodging. I was surprised at Brother Eulogius's considered advice. "Skip it," he said, "you have no idea how sheltered your life has been." He then launched into a description of a history convention he had attended in Montreal. Never one to shun a party or celebration of any sort, he said he left the hotel and dropped into a few bars. At one, he said that the crowd was friendly, convivial, and enjoying the beers or whatever. He felt right at home until he discovered that he had inadvertently entered a gay bar and was now the target of amorous suggestions from his fellow revelers. His advice noted that we had little idea what circumstances we could innocently encounter. I think if he had planned such a story and moralizing at the end, it could not have been more effective. Frankly, I have never pursued my initial idea of bounding around the country, and in fact I feel generally askance about unknown adventures, as my children will readily lament.

As a man whose very name seemed an ironic joke, Brother Eulogius had a wonderful, imaginative sense of humor. Aware that the etymology of his name led one to think of 'well spoken,' he was shy about his constant distracting stutter. Many times he had taken speech classes in the hopes of overcoming the disability, but they were not successful. Sometimes he would attempt to write the stubborn word on the blackboard as a means of expressing it verbally. He would especially falter over BC, and some nasty student once asked him, "How many B's are there in BC?" Eulogius also taught a select few of us who had had Virgil in our senior year of high school.

Most of us had a good command of Latin grammar, but one of our number had been victimized by a kind nun who thought she was doing Stinchcombe a favor when she graciously padded his Latin marks since she knew he intended to join the religious life. Dave had little comprehension of the sophisticated grammar and vocabulary demanded of a reading of Livy's history or of Seneca's Essays on life in Ancient Rome. Our astute teacher generally saved the standard texts or easiest translations for Dave for he knew he was really out of his element. For his part, I think Dave appreciated the latitude and then terminated his future in the study of the Latin classics. The other students in the class were quite well versed in Latin, and in fact two of them, Larry Mattson and Jim Aubuchon, ending up majoring in the subject and garnering high honors in the process. One of the class members was JB Burns who seemed to read Latin as if it were English, and he was the only member of our class who was over electing, choosing to take advanced calculus too. Ed Schwall and I enjoyed the style of Eulogius and his stories of the *pilicrepus* or artisan who plucked armpit hairs in the baths of Caracalla. We learned that *meretrix* was a fancy name for a prostitute that evolved into English as meretricious. I thought the expression, '*flos aetatis,*' or flower of one's youth was an excellent description until I was informed that it was associated with the ancient penchant for pederasty. Brother Eulogius' comment about sheltered lives and naiveté seemed more on target as I waxed wiser in age and grace. Teaching many of us two subjects, he must be commended for his patience in abiding with the exorbitant demands of chemistry made upon our abbreviated study time.

Brother Eugene Miller was attending Rensselaer Polytechnic Institute on the summit above downtown Troy while pursuing a doctorate in Mathematics. Although I didn't have him as a teacher, those that did enjoyed his style, humor, and presentation. I can vouch for those attributes beyond the classroom so his reputation is quite valid all around. His students had a significant advantage over those of us who had selected majors in the liberal arts field. All the mathematics and science majors were equipped with the learning device that identified nerds or grinds. Unfortunately, the rest of us didn't have slide rules or the knowledge of how to use them. Before the calculator, but after the abacus, and considerably older than the computer, the slide rule was the ultimate device for solving basic functions in multiplication and division. With a few adjustments and alignments the complex calculations diminished to comprehensible form in a very reasonable amount of time. This gave the math and science majors a considerable edge on those even less sophisticated for the time. This gap was most evident in the chemistry course each of us was destined to take. In hindsight, I can't justify the omission of such an essential calculating device on the grounds of poverty. Without a slide rule I spent reams of paper and multiple hours trying to solve lengthy multiplication or division problems. Their solutions were readily available to those who used the device, but the rest of us ran the risk of a simple mistake in calculation, and the consequent error skewered our conclusions.

Brother Bernardine Kevin Hargadon was the chemistry teacher. He was extremely popular among my classmates and that probably saved him from the fate that had awaited Saint Cassian, the teacher assassinated by the stylus wielding students in his class. Along with popularity, Brother Kevin also had the advantage of enjoying and excelling in ice hockey. His interest and encouragement in freezing the backyard for a rink led to many spirited games, just as his participation in basketball games set him apart from the rest of the faculty. Like Gene Miller, 'BBK' as he signed his returned assignments, was a doctoral student in Chemistry at RPI also. Since I was one of the few chauffeurs licensed to drive, I often gave him a lift to or from his classes. I enjoyed these opportunities to chat and exchange witticisms with him very much. He was quicker than I, and I was at the disadvantage of youth and telegraphing my mental assaults. 'BBK' finally told me that my body language always indicated when I intended to send a barb in his direction. Apparently, before I said anything, I would touch my mouth with my fingers as a prelude to a verbal riposte. Forewarned, he was ready to parry any of my comments.

Brother Kevin's classes were classics insofar as they contained very simple, clear directions and instructions. The problem that made chemistry my most miserable college experience was in the homework he assigned. After explaining that "hydrogen liked oxygen," he would assign multiple quantitative problems from a book written by the two dirtiest words in the lexicon of Hillside Hall—Baber and Shaum. Their textbook, or rather workbook contained exercises in balancing equations, or dealing with molar and molal solutions.

Success depended on huge multiplication and division computations. Why we weren't equipped with slide rules is a puzzle to me to this day. Fully ninety per cent of my study time was devoted to the solving of pages of a single multiplication or long division problem. This attention to chemistry precluded time and thought that should have been devoted to our other main subjects.

Despite my investment in chemistry, I managed to eke out a D in my first semester. While I was unaccustomed to this kind of result, I could take some solace in the fact that I was still allowed to proceed with the second semester. Thirteen members of my group were compelled to drop the course. The salutary effect of this negative eventuality was the happy consequence that many of the failures went on to major in biology, or take courses that kept the districts rich in biology, earth science, and geology teachers for the near future. Many of those who failed were companions of 'BBK' on the ice hockey rink. I guess he felt they were going to fail anyway, so they might as well enjoy the exercise along the way. By the second semester final, I had managed to raise my grade to a C, but in a five credit course, such grades wreaked havoc on my index. I resolved not to make high grades a priority in my college education, but I did intend to approach each course with the attitude that it should be enjoyed, and the results were in the knowledge not the evaluation.

One of my frustration memories of that chemistry course conducted or 'misconducted' by 'BBK,' was an experience in the three hour lab. I kept getting contrary data, and he kept insisting I keep trying. Despite my care, I wasted the entire afternoon getting contradictory data. Finally, he invited me back for another three hour session on a Saturday, and this time he added, "And I might suggest that you balance your beam balance this time." He had watched me make the error time and again and decided to teach me the lesson I wouldn't forget since it now cut further in my study or recreation time.

Despite the trials of the chemistry course and laboratory, 'BBK' became one of my favorite Brothers. I carefully avoid the use of teacher, here, but he did demonstrate some of the cautions I have tried to avoid in my own teaching career. In one of our conversations together, 'BBK' playfully called me an 'amadan.' That name made me feel so much at home for my mother was partial to that Irish expression when she wasn't calling my brothers and me 'hooples' or "'ungrateful whelps.' I thanked him for providing a nostalgic opportunity instead of an insolvable challenge. If we had spent as much time studying the concepts of valances, bonding, electrons, protons, the atomic chart, equilibrium, molal and molar solutions, we might have been better chemists than calculators.

During our time together on the way to or from RPI, I thoroughly enjoyed the banter and the judgments 'BBK' delivered. One of his positive contributions to my teaching style was a simple body pose in which the arms are folded upon one's chest with the back of both hands exposed. He claimed it was a position of power while the more common pose of one hand under the other arm indicated less potency in the situation. He often discussed the body language of position and exposure. Sometimes he alerted me about Vance Packard's, **Hidden Persuaders** and other pop psychological books, like **Games People Play**. I wasn't surprised when he joined us in September, not to earn his doctorate in Chemistry, but to work in clinical psychology at Catholic University. His interest in the field was evident to me. He managed to enlighten me again when he suggested I read **Kristen Lavransdatter** by the Nobel Prize winner Sigrid Unsted. I struggled through that psychological exploration of a medieval Norse woman, but I can't say it became one of my favorite books. In fact, I wonder if he made the suggestion just to joke with me. The book reminded me of another tome I received as a gift from my daughter Katherine, a graduate of the Notre Dame Program of Liberal Studies. She told me about this great book by Umberto Eco called **The Island of the Day Before.** It may have been a darling of the intelligentsia, but give me a good historical read any day.

I am also happy to say that I enjoyed meeting up with 'BBK' again when my son Brendan attended Manhattan College. I believe a motorcycle accident had literally cut short his athletic career, but he was still a prolific traveler and devotee of the arts. 'BBK' taught me more about many other things, once I exclude his primary responsibility of teaching chemistry to me. His image and my memories are fond recollections despite the toll his class took on my psyche.

Hillside Hall also was the community of another Brother who had spent years in the orphanage. At the time, he was retired and the unofficial oral historian of the institution. Brother Barnabas Hillary had an affable personality toward the Scholastics, but his relationship with us was more as an observer than a participant. Unconsciously, however, he imparted a sense of history and contribution that the Brothers had made to a neglected population of the Tri-City area.

Rumored to have been an alumnus of the orphanage, Brother Athanasius had more contact with the Scholastics. His great joy in life seemed to occur when he took us on section walks throughout South Troy. We would be gathered in assigned groups, and he would join one and begin the jog or trot through the lower city. Rain or shine, sun, sleet, freezing weather or broiling sun, Brother Athanasius would lead us on his epic jaunts. Because of his receding brow and jutting chin, some felt he looked like the missing link and merited the nickname 'Piltie' in honor of the nineteenth century scam about the body of a caveman uncovered in Piltdown, England. Of course, no one dared call him by that name, but in conversation he would be called either 'Piltie' or 'Athy.'

On one of his fast paced walks on First Street, a lady stopped my section on a bitter cold day. Our rapid pace usually kept us warm enough that few wore the old, discarded overcoats or hats of yesteryear. She chided us for not dressing appropriately for the biting cold and frigid blasts from the Hudson. She said, "I know none of you have mothers nearby to tell you what to wear, so I am taking over that responsibility. If your mothers could see you without proper clothing, they would be appalled. In the future, please wear heavy coats during this kind of weather." I suppose we were secretly delighted to have someone notice us and approach us with a kind word which was actually a reprimand for our stupidity. On the other hand, our pace was like jogging for the athlete, and one wouldn't expect to see a person exercising in an overcoat.

On one of the exploratory trips Brother Athanasius took us, he led us to the top of a hill toward the entrance to South Troy. At the crest of the hill, lay a small cemetery containing the permanent history of the city. I remember noticing how he pointed out on the small tombstones the cluster of dates indicating plagues or influenza sieges that killed several youngsters in the past. Between the clusters of tiny tombstones there would be gaps of several years. Some of the graves contained the remains of children from the orphanage as our guide indicated. Somehow, visiting the remote cemetery made the fragility of life among the orphans at Hillside Hall more tangible, especially among the clusters of stones dedicated to those who died in a cholera, small pox, or diphtheria epidemic.

There were also two laymen who lived in Hillside Hall. One was an excellent pastry chef who gave a sense of class to the simplest dessert. His name was Ray and some of his presentations showed evidence of professional work. Not all meals were sumptuous feasts. In fact, one of my clear recollections is about a Lenten meal that defies description or explanation. In the quest for originality during the stringent times of fast and abstinence during Lent according to the old calendar, we were served an item that actually sounds impossible. Tuna fish tube steaks were fish frankfurters, for lack of a better term. The irony was that they tasted good to my undeveloped palate. Not only was I unable to distinguish a violin concerto from a piano concerto, but I evidently didn't have the discrimination taste buds to find distinctions between fish and beef. Perhaps our usual hot dog fare wasn't so memorable.

The other individual who shared the residence of the Brothers was a man who allegedly graduated from the orphanage, but stayed on as a handyman. His name was Joe Gadek, but given his career, we called him Joe Gadget. He kept everything working and in good condition, not a mean achievement given the age of our house. Joe didn't have much to say to the Scholastics, and no one worked with him. He plied his trade quietly and unobtrusively. Occasionally in the morning before Mass when some walked on the back porch facing the hill, we might spot an individual who was sitting on the hillside just meditating about the building. These folks were supposedly men who had spent some of their youth in the institution and perhaps yearned for another look at the place. They didn't impose any kind of threat nor make any effort to speak with anyone. We hoped their reminiscences were pleasant and nostalgic.

One lesson from our first year in the Scholasticate was quite evident. The Brothers chosen to teach us and live in the community of formation were very instrumental in forming our education and training. For the most part, their contributions were offered in non verbal ways, but for some of us, their influence was a paramount impression we had of what it took to be a Brother of the Christian Schools. I doubt our faculty members credit themselves on what they did for us, but in retrospect, I can only admire them for what they offered us. Perhaps targeted by us for mockery or ridicule, they nonetheless performed an excellent role in dispensing advice, or offering anecdotes, or simply reflecting the image of what a

Brother ought to be. I am sure that the district administrators were quite careful about the appointments to the Scholasticate since it also entailed a major commitment to the future education of the assigned individual.

Contrary to our predictions, Brother Basilian John provided some games and replicas of the experiences he had undergone during his time in the Second Novitiate. He introduced us to memory mnemonics to help us recall a series of composed names or nonsensical data. The purpose of the game was to teach us tricks in retaining significantly more important information. He occasionally lectured us on the principles of **How to Win Friends and Influence People.** He surprised us all by introducing an imaginative game of horror through tactile senses during Halloween. John Hannaway reminded me of the time Brother John without any fanfare or explanation, played a LP record of laughter for about a thirty minute period. He neither provided rationale nor purpose in playing the long display of laughter. Hannaway mentioned that as the record played on, the laughter became contagious and the Scholastics found mirth in the recording. These behaviors on the part of Brother John seemed at variance with the kind of convictions he generally espoused. Maybe he projected such a defense shield that we never really got to know the real man.

One of the main contributions Brother John made to our group was an exposure to a personality test. By selecting or sequencing preferences, a profile was determined to be Passionate, Choleric, Sanguine, or Amorphous. If my memory is faithful, I believe I fell into the category of Choleric. The personality traits were relatively positive, but the real leadership personnel were Passionate. The Choleric personality was a good follower or implementer of another's ideas or program. Over the years, I have found that to be an accurate description of my ambitions. I rarely wanted to bear the responsibility of a project, but I was quite talented in executing the ideals of another. In administration, I dreaded the job of correcting anyone or having to fire an individual. My ambition remained to take care of myself and let another make the major decisions. Only one individual scored Amorphous, earning a derogatory nickname as was the custom among us. Amorphous meant that the person had little or no direction, no burning desires, and no crusading interests—a rather bland summary for anyone.

When one sits down to enumerate the blandishments of Troy, the exercise is very brief. With the exception of some excellent movies, popular music, dances, magazines, and the typical entertainments of our peers played a miniscule role in our collegiate years since these amusements were deemed 'worldly influences.' Exploring museums or art galleries in Troy also left quite a vacuum although some of us discovered the museums in the State Education building in Albany. When we first arrived in Troy, someone learned that a New York Yankee farm team played in Albany in the PONY league. A number went to one of the fall games. Upon their return, almost as if it were a causal relationship, our homework and studies escalated out of sight. One could make an argument that whenever we sought outside entertainment, our class work increase exponentially. After a while, we more or less were reconciled to the notion that recreation was incompatible with our academic demands. All work and no play would make us feel greater pressure than ever before.

At one time, however, we were outfitted by professional tailors who came to Hillside and measured us for clerical suits. Their efforts were quite impressive as each of us received a black herringbone suit which was virtually indestructible. The garb would wear forever and probably was rather expensive. In a sense that was a waste for as we waxed in wisdom, age and girth, the suits usually became too tight. Although the suits were fashionable, they were accompanied by movie prop hats—large black, broad brimmed fedoras. They bring to mind an image of a George Raft gangster movie, a *Mafioso* hit man, or the hat worn by Charles Durning in *The Sting*. Like the American Express Card, we were not supposed to leave home without it. I think I may have worn it only two or three times, preferring a bare head to ridicule. The broad brim and black color also mirrored the typical hat that one sees on Hasidim adherents in the New York area.

Our families were encouraged to visit us about every two or three months. When they came, they would be served a meal in the visitor's dining room with their son. On a visit from my family, my older brother Bernard had invited his current girlfriend who would also ultimately become his wife. Evelyn O'Dwyer was from Queen of Martyrs in Inwood and knew several people familiar to some of my groupies. Clay Hollinger was assigned to wait on our table and as he delivered the deep dishes and platters to our table, Evelyn recognized him and called him by name. She then inquired whether Clay knew a certain young lady. Evidently, Clay did, for he dropped all the food and it splattered all over the place. Clay was embarrassed and so too was Evelyn. At the end of our junior year in the Scholasticate, Clay finally left to seek the hand of the young lady whose name stirred such a response from him two years earlier.

Usually when someone's family came up to Troy, the family would have a meal, compliments of the community and then search for a restaurant on the second day. I believe the restaurant of popular choice was an emporium called Callahan's in downtown Albany. When my family as well as the family of Pat Murphy came, we ended up at Callahan's Steak house. As we were starting our meal, a swab jockey passed by the table with bucket and mop. My brother Ray immediately jumped up, hugged and greeted the man as if he were the governor. He invited him to join our families for the meal, but the man was too embarrassed and shy to participate in the repast laid out in the place where he worked. The man was a fugitive from the Police Recreation Center where both my brothers worked as waiters during the summers. He had performed similar duties there as well as other establishments in the Irish Alps. I think the Murphy's believed Ray knew every derelict in the vicinity, and I believe my parents were relieved that the individual elected to stay on his job.

Since I was one of the few chauffeurs available in Troy and was probably the most avid to escape, I had many opportunities to collect families at the bus station or train station in downtown Albany. On a bitter cold day, I misunderstood the directions on where to meet the Murphy family. After circling the train station several times, I decided to park several blocks away and walk to the depot. My choice was either to promenade in my habit or doff it, and stroll in my tee shirt. I chose the latter, sensing that an insane individual walking in an undershirt in single digit temperatures would attract less attention than a devoted religious in his monastery garb. I garnered enough attention, as most people were bundled up against the cold. Mrs. Murphy chided me upon my choice when we finally met up inside the station.

Since the Christian Brothers had no priests in the order, they had to contract with other orders for confessors and daily Mass. In Troy, the community worked with the Black Franciscans who had a monastery about half way down the back road to Albany. On one morning, I had Father Austin Carr for my passenger. Generally he read his breviary as I drove in the wee hours of the morning. Since Mass was at 6:30, I would collect him about 5:45 when virtually no traffic was on the roads. Father Carr was the editor of **The Pastoral and Homiletic Review** as well as a nationally known moral theologian. As I slowed down to stop at a traffic light with no cars moving in any direction, Father Carr raised his eyes from his breviary and announced that I had no moral obligation to stop for the light if there were no evident reason to do so. I decided that argument would not be effective if I were stopped by a bored policeman at that time of the morning, so I continued to obey the lights despite the lesson in moral obligations from the eminent theologian.

In my role as chauffeur, I received an assignment that focused my attention on one of my group mates. I concluded that not all of us had the same interpretation of the vow of poverty when I drove five Brothers into Albany to buy personal shoes. Brother John appointed me treasurer of the group and gave me about $120 for the purchase of shoes for the individuals. When we entered a shoe store in the downtown shopping area, one of the Brothers selected a pair of shoes that cost about $60, in essence spending half our budget on himself. When I informed him that at least two of the group couldn't now afford shoes, he told me that he was accustomed to expensive shoes and had no intention of reducing his expenditure. I was flabbergasted at the insensitivity toward the unshod confreres, but he was adamant. We returned to Troy with his expensive shoes, and I let the Director sort out the thought process. Later, the following week, I took the unshod Brothers back to Albany where they bought new reasonable shoes. I suppose a charitable Brother might surmise that the extravagant purchase was necessitated by physical health problems, but I hadn't reached that level of charity. Perhaps I remembered his arrival in Barrytown with matching luggage when the rest of us had steamer trunks or cheap suitcases.

It is difficult to recall any outstanding frivolity in Troy. Our humor and hilarity had been stifled by the ascetic training. My most pleasant memory entails the reading of a book during meals in the refectory. John Kullberg, a man whose eloquence and elocution would later lead him to winning the speech contest at Catholic University, was reading a selection from a magazine describing the incredible enthusiasm for basketball in the Hoosier State. John in his carefully enunciated New England accent, read a passage in which a

John Kielley

little old lady expressed her contempt for her team's rivals, "You no good son of a bitch. You dirty bastard," John articulated with all the solemnity of a reading of an estate will. Brother John was incensed and banged the bell reserved for ending meals or interrupting the reader. He insisted John move on and skip the foul language. I thought the performance was extraordinary in that John read the text with such panache that matched the director's panicky response. Later, after he left the Brothers, John would use his speaking skills to great advantage. He was asked to make a presentation before Congress on the rights of animals and access to public television coverage. That led to his selection as President of the Society for the Prevention of Cruelty to Animals and a career that often placed him on my television screen. Every time I saw him, I would harken back to his reading so professionally in the refectory in Troy and the instant stifling of his performance. John later suffered from a serious liver ailment and unfortunately died young leaving a wife and several children.

As our second semester in Troy drew to a conclusion, we also had the prospect of a retreat and the pronunciation of vows. According to one's age, an individual would be offered the privilege to take annual vows as we did after our Novitiate, or Triennials. The distinction lay in the age of the Brother. It was calculated that the individual Brother would reach the age of twenty-five while covered by his five vows. Most of my class required two years of annuals, supplemented by a single three year triennial period. A fair number of my confreres, however, had been skipped a year to eliminate February enrollments. We had the option of taking two sets of triennials since we were only nineteen years old while the others were twenty. Despite my assessment as Hillside being the most difficult year in my formation, I didn't hesitate to pronounce triennials at the end of the term.

My assessment of Troy may be too harsh, for I don't think I was aware of its intensity at the time. Upon reflection, however, I found it very challenging, perhaps even personality altering. The emphasis on silence, recollection, modesty of the eyes, spirit of reflection, and dissociation from one's peers carried an onus that was hard to describe. Extrapolated from the year seemed to be any notion of community life and mutual relationships. Each of us spent time in introspection and personal quest for sanctity. We did not focus too much on the aspect of community life and mutual interdependence.

For a society espousing communal living, we seemed to ignore that aspect during the training we received at Troy.

When I compound the intensity of our religious experience with the demands of academia, I deduce that the pressure surfaced in my speech. By the end of Troy, my glib, carefree conversation was constrained now by a repetitive stutter, slight but noticeable to me since my father had a lifelong disability in that realm. My speech was affected externally and God knows what other symptoms I may have detected upon closer inspection. I must confess that I noticed no overt changes in the mannerisms of my classmates, but I did observe a clear extirpation of the frivolity and *joie de vive* many exhibited in the Novitiate. We evidently underwent the self-examination, ascetic development, and divorce from worldly ideas while we were pursuing the joys of knowledge rather than meditation. After our year under his direction, Brother John became the director of novices in Narragansett, a job he performed with great distinction. He no doubt was a very holy, even ascetic man intent on serving God in the best way he knew how with the gifts he had received. I am grateful for his assistance in Troy, but I have a different perspective now that I am older and perhaps even wiser. I should also recall that despite my opinion about rigorous indoctrination, only two of our group decided to leave at the expiration of their vowed commitment. Tony Tufaro left and became a pharmacist on Long Island and has joined an occasional reunion with the Brothers. Eddie Ewald has never been heard from again.

Despite its antiquity and its seedy appearance, the city of Troy remains a pleasant memory. The few lay people we met, the local Catholic school nuns who taught in the school on Fourth Street, the liturgy of the Eastern rite which we observed one Sunday, and the stories the faculty recited about the friendliness of the people of the 'Collar City' remind me that in our relic on the hill we were apart from the real experience of the neighborhood. Barrytown may have been in the boondocks, but isolation amid a city environment seemed more apparent in Troy. When we departed the city after our ten month sojourn, it was with evident joy we looked forward to our time vacationing at Oakdale with the rest of the scholastics. For my part, while I grew to understand Brother Basilian John, he remained more enigmatic than charismatic. Among all the Brothers who provided my training, he remains the most puzzling and least inspirational.

Chapter Five

Summers at Oakdale

1959-60-61

After the intense freshman experience at Hillside Hall, the prospect of a vacation resort on the shores of the Great South Bay on Long Island appealed to the veterans of the long, hard climate of the Tri-City area. Soon pasty complexions might be replaced or enhanced by the healthful tans of the relaxed vacationers we hoped to be. From early July to middle August, the Scholastics from Washington and the incoming class from Troy would have moderately pressured summer classes as well the opportunity to test their recreational skills on the grounds of La Salle Military Academy. The Academy was a boarding school, generally occupied by rich Americans and some foreign students from Latin America or the Philippines. The school facilities on the well tended one hundred seventy-five acres of the former estate of one of America's industrial giants were at our disposal.

Elias Singer and his heirs had constructed a mansion on the shores of the Great South Bay between Bayshore and Patchogue, Long Island. The estate offered a generous array of distractions for those with athletic interests. First and foremost, there was a huge esplanade and marching field that appeared larger than the one at West Point. On this field there were several baseball and softball diamonds as well as places to play less popular sports like volleyball, badminton, croquet, soccer, or virtually any sport that required a flat surface. There were also ample tennis courts that provided Jimmy Jordan the opportunity to develop his tennis skills far beyond any of the rest of us. For swimming, one could select a fresh water pond with a diving board and gliding swans for atmosphere. If one preferred salt water, one could contest with the occasional jellyfish

148

or horseshoe crab in the Bay. A boathouse was home to a fleet of rowboats for exercise or exploring the waterways and streams fed by the bay. Perhaps the *piece de resistance*, however, was a nine hole golf course and a practice putting green. Whatever equipment required for any sport was available also. A huge field house displayed a beautiful full court basketball venue with glass backboards. Some chose to immerse themselves in water while others pursued the sport of their choice. We even developed some sun worshipers who searched for the George Hamilton perfect tan.

With about one hundred thirty-five student Brothers, we fit comfortably into the vacant barracks rooms where groups of us were housed in segments of four or five. One recollection of the barracks was the perpetual presence of moisture on the walls. A major drawback to the accommodations was the dampness and humidity of the shoreline estate. Condensation seemed to cover every article, every inch of space, every particle of clothes or construction material that might otherwise be frigid in cold weather. Perhaps an even greater negative was the presence of mosquitoes "as big as eagles," according to a senior class member named Louie Jaeger. We also joked about feeding the bloodthirsty fiends on Saturday evenings in an attempt to quench their insatiable appetite for human blood so that visitors on Sunday would not be plagued beyond their endurance or plasma by the pests. A special truck used to spray the marching field and picnic grove on Saturdays in the hopes of keeping down the number of bites on the following day.

There was an imposing mansion on the grounds also. It had glass doors connecting to the outdoors from what used to be the main ballroom. That was deemed large enough to serve as our chapel. There was also an indoor pool that had seen more magnificent days, but we seldom got near that and when we did, it was devoid of water and eye appeal. In another part of the mansion there were several offices and in the upper reaches of the third floor a number of civilian workers resided. These workers were primarily Hispanics who worked in the kitchen. The kitchen was in a separate building that housed the cafeteria which of course we called the refectory. The food fare was not on a par with what we were used to in Barrytown, Troy, or Washington.

The caterer was a company called Crotty and so we christened his product the Cruddy System. Generally characterized by miniscule portions of even the most basic staples, the Cruddy System provided little nourishment and if the cadets had any complaints about institutional food, they were well warranted. I specifically remember what they served for roast beef. If one went to a typical delicatessen and ordered a roast beef sandwich, it would contain more than was served for a table of eight. Each allotted serving for our ravenous appetites was a translucent slice of roast beef about a sixteenth of an inch thick and four inches long. I can't remember any other servings, but that one sticks in my memory. Three Cruddy meals a day for six days merited a visit from one's relatives on Sunday. Then there would be plenty to eat for all and leftovers for during the week. The weight of the portions didn't tax the sturdiness of the tables upon which they were served. Unlike our refectories before, I believe even milk and other beverages were also rationed. Those seeking bread and water could only count on water. Few were sad to bid farewell to the Cruddy System when the group departed for richer fare and broader cuisine in De La Salle College. The Scholastics and cadets could certainly agree that the food on the recreational oasis left a great deal to be desired.

When my class first arrived in Oakdale, we met a welcome that was less than warm. As the clashing convictions of the upper classmen jarred with the recently imbedded values of the sophomores, a number of disparities was indicated. Brother Basilian John had nurtured my class in an austere, rigorous interpretation of the rules and regulations. That interpretation stressed the silence, recollection, and asceticism of a more traditional monastery such as the Cistercians. The prevailing ideology of the upper classmen was much more casual, more humanitarian, more practical, and more suitable for the kind of religious life that a community of teaching monks might expect rather than a contemplative emphasis on the individual. Most of my class resisted what appeared to be a downgrade in religious fervor and were determined to maintain the lessons imparted in Troy. Barney Quigley and I were very fortunate insofar as we were assigned to work rather than attend classes. Besides the opportunity to relax academically, I also felt exposed to a litany of commentary about how 'far out of it,' the sophomore class was. Generally speaking, we were consigned to another planet where ethereal life forms functioned better than humanoids.

The Brothers who were assigned to work rather than take classes were an eclectic lot. Some may have been chosen for their expertise with paint and brush and others had carpentry or handyman qualities. I had neither, but I wasn't adverse to either learning or sweating. While Barney and I represented the sophomore class, there were no appointees from the junior year. From the senior class, the gamut of personalities, religious convictions, interpretations of the rule and academic performance was clearly in evidence. The leader of the group was Brother Kevin Kissan, a chemistry major, who had been a painter for years in the Juniorate, the Novitiate and the Scholasticate. He was knowledgeable about the requisite cleaning of brushes, trays and other accoutrements of the equipment as well as the techniques in redecorating rooms. He also was turned off by the behavior and standards my class not only imposed on themselves, but expected others to adopt. Another of our workers was a tall, easy going chemistry major from Inwood by way of the Juniorate. TA Murphy, Brother Benedict Faber, iterated the commentary of Kissan in his humorous, playful style. He too was appalled that my class should set itself up as paradigms of what a good religious ought to be. TA argued that such an attitude as we projected was inhumane, rather than reflective of community spirit. Along with those two fine Brothers, we also had the advice of Brother James Cusick and Andrew Cordell, more serious individuals in themselves, but just as convinced of the inappropriate reaction of my class. Barney and I had the good fortune to hear the other side of the arguments and thereby could assess the intensity of alienation that my group had injected into a pleasantly operating community. Many of our groupies lacked that education or insight and consequently perpetuated some harsh feelings among classes for some time. Assured they were right, many of my groupies were inflexible, obstinate, and resolute in maintaining the principles engendered during our sojourn in Troy. Some felt that the divinity had blessed them and given them the mission of converting the lax among the Scholastics.

Two seniors in particular seemed targeted by the Savonarola disciples within my class. That my confreres were misguided seems evident. That they understood the misplaced zeal wasn't so clear. In essence, they interpreted their crusade as in the spirit of St. La Salle and the Christian Brothers. Their ardor and criticism led to an ambitious effort to correct the older classes which only induced further indignation. One of the prime targets of my misguided brethren was a senior who appeared to be a vivid approximation of what a hippie might be had he joined the Brothers. Brother Matthew McAteer was a talented musician who listened to the music in his head. Consequently, his head motions and external signs of the internal symphony he heard contrasted with the notions of recollection and contemplation. To exacerbate the difference, Matt also sported a few tattoos that he had acquired under unexplained circumstances. Told to wash them off by the director, Matt announced that they were not washable, so I understood he was scheduled to have them removed surgically at a future date.

During Advertisements of Defects, he was notified of his violations of the spirit of the rule *ad nauseam.* The criticism didn't seem to bother him as much as it bothered his fellow classmates. Matt's personality and eccentricities were well known by his fellow seniors, and they accepted him as a popular contributor to their peculiar '*joie de vive.*' Another object of my class's corrective zeal was a Brother called Bitter Jack. Jack Farrell boasted of his ability to find fault and legitimate criticism about almost everything. He seemed to savor his reputation for excelling in criticism and carping. He too heard about his lack of faith and understanding, but he didn't take it as comfortably as Matt. It took most of the individuals in my class a few months to come around to the general attitude that characterized the mainstream of the scholasticate. During my years in formation with my groupies, I have very little criticism to offer on our general attitude or performance, but having the insight of my fellow senior workers, I identified our narrow-mindedness and recognized our refusal to accept the attitude that we had been trained in Troy to shun. Without the extra commentary from the painters that summer I am sure I would have been just as benighted as the rest of my class. Barney and I did not become apologists for our class' evaluations for we could see the wisdom and accuracy of the allegations directed against our peers.

For three summers I enjoyed some wonderful perks during the manual labor period after breakfast. Of course the work that replaced the summer courses the first semester had dividends beyond a break from studies. In my second and third summers, however, I was assigned a sinecure that I found inexplicable. Apparently, Brother Concordius Leo, generally called 'Conkie,' was so impressed with the manner in which I performed my manual labor in Washington that he presented me with some patronage I recognized as special treatment. He gave me a set of keys to the air force surplus truck at Oakdale and told me I was to drive to the various golf holes to check the greens every morning. If there any papers present I was supposed to dispose of them. I could also use the truck during the course of the afternoon if I saw the need. The truck had no license plate so it couldn't leave the grounds, but it provided me with plenty of luxury beyond what most others had. I didn't want to rock the boat, but Conkie simply advised me that the work I did maintaining the cleanliness of De La Salle College floors was sufficient evidence that I should enjoy compensatory time off during the summer. In a society where equality was jealously advocated, I felt like royalty, but I also experienced no pangs of conscience over my choice manual labor.

During the mornings after manual labor, summer school classes were held. Generally these classes satisfied certification credits for teaching in the multiple states to which we might be assigned upon graduation. There must have been plenty of room for credits, for I missed two entire sessions in following the directives of my superiors. Our paint responsibilities were a pleasant contrast to the stifling atmosphere of hot classrooms. On the other hand, Kissan's crew did more than paint. We were given sledge hammers and wire brushes one day with the orders to ream the hot water boiler holes. There were about two dozen circular holes extending about four feet into the boiler. Most were heavily encrusted with lime deposits. With one of us holding the steel brush and the other swinging the sledge hammer, we intended to clean out the stone deposits. The deposits were less than avidly interested in cooperating. After about six hours of hammering and cleaning, the boiler was shiny, but the workers were filthy, sweaty and exuding body fluids that were untraditional. My tee shirt became so yellow from the sweat that it had to be thrown away, unsuitable for further use. When we finished we also had to scrub the grime off each others back in the communal showers. I suppose the closest analogy I can think of would be the scrubbing one witnesses in the movies after exposure to nuclear radiation. Thank God we were in pretty good physical condition, for I believe that day's work was probably the hardest I ever did.

My other assignment that precluded participation in the educational and religious classes was far less taxing. One of the sophomores had not made it successfully out of Eulogius Austin's

World history course in Troy. He was expected to make up the course during the summer, and I was appointed his special tutor. I enjoyed the responsibility very much for my student was not only very personable, but hard working and his success was virtually guaranteed. In an essay I assigned him about contributions of North Africa to Medieval Europe, he wrote of medicine, mathematics, alchemy, astronomy and "I suppose, a few grains of sand." I found that addendum just delightful evidencing some wit and appreciation for my style of instruction. While I escaped the class the rest of my group was taking, the switch was fortuitous in unforeseen ways. Brother Cecilian, who had taught us English and French in Hillside, was teaching a course in Catechetics. Most of my group, now that they were blasé seniors accustomed to the esoterica of theology classes taught in Washington by some of the finest teachers in the New York and LINE Districts, dismissed Ce Ce's efforts as unworthy of any special concentration. Ce Ce of course recognized the disdain and retaliated by offering arcane tests in minutiae cached within hundreds of pages of assigned reading. In truth the test was unfair, and in fact, Ce Ce was determined to educate the group beyond Catechetics. When the test results were available, the disgruntled professor had issued index shattering grades, especially for the intelligentsia that were heading toward honors like *summa cum laude*. Brought to the attention of the Brother who was in charge of course selection, the problem presented a major dilemma. Does one change grades to safeguard honors? Does one designate grades based on an irrational test? Are there greater integrity and honesty in negotiating some kind of compromise? I don't know how the issue was resolved, but some kind of arrangement was provided that satisfied the demands of Ce Ce as well as the expectations of some of his students. I had escaped the controversy in Catechetics, but I would not be so successful in two other classes. A very interesting class from Scripture about Genesis was taught by a very serious scholar from Washington named Brother Aloysius Fitzgerald. Allie was about as conscientious a scholar ever produced by De La Salle College. In a few years he would be in Israel and Egypt studying the Dead Sea Scrolls. His proficiency in Aramaic and Semitic languages also led to his appointment as head of that department at The Catholic University of America. His course introduced us to *Heilsgeschichte* and *Formgeschichte,* two concepts essential for interpreting the bible accurately. He was a fascinating lecturer and excellent explicator in this unusual field. He also was determined that every Scholastic should be the kind of scholar he envisioned. I jarred his concept of dedication to knowledge. Allie determined that I spent too much time playing ball in the afternoons and therefore was neglecting the demands of his subject. I tried to assure him that was untrue. He promised that I would fail. After the test in which I thought I had performed quite well, I received a D in the course. I guess he felt I didn't warrant his predicted F, but was eligible for his scorn.

When I was a senior, he also confronted me in the halls of De La Salle College. He explained to me that I had the obligation to myself and to the Christian Brothers to get selected to *Phi Beta Kappa*. If that didn't happen, he promised to be quite angry with me. Actually, I appreciated his urging, but I had enjoyed my academic life and always entered my exams in the belief that I might get an A in the course. I wasn't presumptuous as much as comfortable. The problem became moot when I did get selected for the honor which I have been proud of ever since. His was the only D besides the grade given to me in Chemistry in my collegiate career. I figured I was ineligible from my freshman year because of that difficulty in Chemistry.

In another educational course, I also ran into some incompatible observations. Brother Clement Patrick Gardner was teaching a course in Secondary Methods. I thought most of the course was common sense and believed I had mastered whatever content he offered. That conclusion was borne out when I achieved a grade of 99 per cent on the written exam. Half of the course, however, was determined by a written paper. Brother Patrick pulled me aside one afternoon and complimented me on my submission. He said my paper was outstanding for its lucidity, organization, presentation, and comprehensive coverage of my topic. Before I had the opportunity to savor the compliments, he then added, "Where did you copy it from?" I assured him that it had been written by me and that I had not copied it from any source. He didn't argue with me, but when my final grade was posted, I got a B in the course. I don't know whether everyone else enrolled in the class got a higher grade, but I suspect not. In essence, I felt he called me a liar and didn't believe my protestations of authorship. I didn't get too excited about the put down, for I felt there was nothing I could do. Neither course would propel me upward into the composite index worthy of a *Summa* however.

Many of the other summer courses were delightful and even informative. In a class held in the boat house adjacent to the basin, I listened intently to the acerbic language of an intelligent wit. Brother Justin expounded daily in his subject matter entitled Catholic Social Principles. I savored his skepticism about 'your cardinal,' and his parsimonious way with Labor. Brother Justin was a labor arbitrator who mediated disputes among unions and employers. One of the biggest villains toward unions was none other than the Archdiocese of New York under the control of his eminence, Francis Cardinal Spellman. Although Justin's humor and anecdotes made his class entertaining as well as informative, in later years I thought that perhaps Catholic social principles could have transcended unions and employers. Ideals like racial tolerance, financial equity, and ethnic appreciation might have found their way into the curriculum during these years prior to the civil rights movement or Black power figures. To be critical of such gaps in the curriculum at this time in the history of America might also be anachronistic.

One of the most popular of the summer time professors was a pleasant man with a round red face named Brother Martin. Known to all as Uncle Marty, he taught a required course for educational certification. His expertise was in Biology for Educators. The course was more educational in content than scientific, but it was ideal for those of us who had a bad taste after our experience in chemistry. Uncle Marty had been an institution among the Scholastics for many years. His style of teaching and his manner and deportment in the classroom were worthy of emulation among the untrained teachers. There was also another teacher who taught a subject called Art for Educators. Brother Clarence William's instructions come to mind whenever I print something. One of his points of emphasis was in decorative calligraphy and printing signs for posters. I also remember his lectures on complementary colors and design.

One of my favorite courses was entitled Methodology for Secondary Education. The class was taught by a man whose dry humor and sense of comedic timing were superb. Brother Augustine Crawford had plenty of educational experience and he culled those memories to illustrate the principles he espoused. One of his points of advice concerned the need not to judge a book by its cover, or more specifically, don't be misled by a student's angelic looks. He had a regular litany of praise for some students punctuated by a contrary conclusion. One of his commentaries was about the innocent, harmless looking kid who masked a diabolical mind. He would start his description almost verbatim time and time again. "Nice kid. Blond hair, blue eyes, perfect teeth," and then he would utter the conclusion, "Vicious!" Gus Crawford epitomized so many of our summertime teachers at Oakdale. They were experienced, knowledgeable, and sensible as well as balanced. Like the faculty in the Scholasticate, they served as paragons of what kind of teachers we should aspire to be. Sometimes I conclude that they were selected more for their personalities than for the expertise in the field they represented. One example that led me to this judgment was an inimitable character named Brother Jake Leonard. Jake was teaching a class in statistics, but I wasn't enrolled as one of his students. Nonetheless, Jake was noted for outlandish commentary or conclusions, and each day those of us not in his class waited to hear his latest. I don't know whether he deliberately used malapropisms, but his conversation was peppered with all kinds of illogical contradictions. His commentary generally contained hilarious misnomers, deliberate or not. Appreciation of what he said and how he said it was an acquired taste, like the shtick of Don Rickles or Jonathan Winters. As an instructor in statistics, Jake was quoted as saying, "Half you guys are going to pass this class, half of you will fail, and half will drop the course." He could say all these things with a straight face and evidently mean exactly what he thought he was saying. His agility with numbers was also displayed to me when we were invited to his community in St. Patrick's Newburgh. Jake suggested a bowling game. After throwing two consecutive gutter balls, Jake turned to the score keeper and announced, "I'll take a nine for this frame." I understand he also worked wonders with his golf score using his unique computational skills. Despite these evident miscalculations, Jake's popularity and notoriety remained top of the line.

While at Oakdale, we seldom left the military school grounds. One obvious exception occurred every Wednesday. On that day, immediately after class we would sign up for one of three buses. Earlier a truck laden with soda, frankfurters, rolls, ice cream on frozen carbon dioxide, cakes, condiments of all sorts, cooking equipment, as well as tools for entrenching an army on a beach, would head out to the Hamptons which were about an hour's ride east along route 25A. The road took us through potato fields and duck farms rather than the estates of the wealthy. The Hamptons of the sixties was a far cry from the privacy, exclusive estates of the glitterati and literati of the present. In fact, the major sensory recollection of the bus ride was the stench that emanated from the many duck farms along the way. Whenever the bus would approach a town, the boisterous singing would turn to a melodic whisper of, "Hamlet, hamlet, shh, shh, shh!" Once through the town the selections of lung bursting melodies from Broadway or Irish songs would commence again.

Between the nearest town and Montauk Point, the buses would disgorge their passengers in a spot selected by the advanced invasion party. Like the Underwater Demolition Crews of World War II or the hallowed Navy Seals, this advance party would select a stretch of ocean beach devoid of humanity for a mile in either direction. After an appropriate beach head was established, the Scholastics would assume the role of bearers on a safari. The burdens of food, shelter, athletic gear, and tools would be trekked a distance from the impromptu parking lot. After building a garbage pit and an area for cooking, a schedule of life guards would be established and flags set up delineating the legal area for swimming. Although not a particularly good swimmer, I served as vigilant life guard several times. I never had to try to save anyone, but I cautioned those swimmers who were drifting beyond our designated area. I only saw one person pulled out by a life guard. I forget who was rescued, perhaps Jerry Buckley from the class behind us, but the rescuer was Joe O'Brien who warmed up his tonsils and muscles while singing on the bus ride out from Oakdale.

I almost became a victim myself when I was guilty of horseplay in the surf. A group of us were wrestling in the crashing waters and in an attempt to escape, Hank McNally kicked me in the head. I immediately went underwater, but the instant pain in my right ear revived me. I staggered out of the water and fell asleep for about an hour on the beach. When I awoke, I felt better and charged into the breakers again. As soon as I dove under a wave, the sharp pain in my ear returned and I retreated to the beach for some more snoozing. Later, that night, I bled from the ear and in the following morning, I felt quite woozy at mental prayer. I couldn't hear too well either. I bore those ailments heroically and silently, possibly embarrassed by the stupidity of my actions. When I left mental prayer the day after returning to Washington, I was confronted by Brother Leo.

He asked me why I had left the chapel, and I told him I wasn't feeling too good. He said that one hundred and twenty-five others weren't feeling so good either so what made me different? I found it impossible to articulate a defense, so Kirby sent me to the doctor. The doctor discovered that I had punctured an ear drum and that I had a concussion. My recovery program consisted of taking it easy for a few days. I didn't bother to inform the Brother Director about the diagnosis, believing that the less said the better.

The waters at the Hamptons were very cold and quite rough. The beach seemed endless and apparently empty of human habitation. On one occasion, however, a trio of young lasses sashayed past and tested the recollection of one hundred and twenty five Scholastics. The following weekend, the sister of Mickey Bukowski from St. Cecilia's in Greenpoint was explaining to her brother about the observation of some of her friends who had been at the beach the previous Wednesday. The pretty young things believed that the denizens of Fire Island, noted for their homosexuality had begun to frequent the Hamptons, or so they thought. They recounted how apparently red blooded young males had entirely ignored their sortie in front of them on the beach. Mickey explained who the several score individuals were, and I suppose the director was pleased that no one acted inappropriately for individuals vowed to celibacy. Can it be ascertained that among the dear Brothers there was a greater appeal to volleyball and wiffle ball than there might be to the opposite sex? Actually, the event demonstrated that the modesty of the eyes advocated by our superiors had been put to the test and success followed.

One of the seniors used to make a satire of Brother Leo Kirby's commentaries along these lines. Whenever the bus would come along side a convertible with a male and female passenger, this commentator would begin his spiel using the speech inflections and mannerisms of the Director. "Look at them. Beautiful car! Beautiful girl! But do you think they're happy?" He would answer his rhetorical question himself by exclaiming, "You bet your ass they're happy!"

The picnics at Hampton were great contrasts to the paucity of food we had under the Cruddy System at the military academy. Once, just prior to our trip, Brother Leo Kirby organized a clam hunt and competition among the three classes at Oakdale. Several hundred clams surrendered their lives in the shallow shores off the esplanade. These were sacrificed to the refined palettes of those who favored

. Frankly, they were not much of a seller in Washington ...eights so I sampled one, decided the only taste was in the sauce, and opted for alternative hamburgers. The Hampton picnics were always replete with foods of all kinds. Desserts competed with burgers, and the making of sandwiches was an alternative. Snacks formed diversions for those who were interested in a between meal serving. Some believed that this would be the last decent meal afforded by the Cruddy System until our visitors came on Sunday.

Brother Leo Kirby was also known by alternate names. Some referred to him as 'Uncle Bob,' as his many nephews and nieces did when they came to visit him at Oakdale. We could hear the youngsters shouting his name while they engaged in games in the picnic grove or near the boathouse. Others called him 'SOB' as in 'Sweet Old Bob,' but he was also identified by his signature on notes he sent as "BL.' He was often called by his family name Kirby as well. I suppose his address might depend on the current relationship between the Scholastic and his Director. As a sophomore, I found Kirby a refreshing change after Brother Basilian John. Kirby seemed to have a vivid imagination and a sense of humor. That became evident when the decision to head to the Hamptons or not was impacted by the weather. Kirby presented a virtuoso account of the factors that influenced the weather at Oakdale. He advised us to check out the number of Sea Gulls on the lawn. If an even number, we were to check the amount standing on a left leg. If it was a majority of gulls, that meant that the weather would clear up. On the other hand, if an odd number of sea gulls were on the lawn, then one was to count the amount resting on a right leg. Again if a majority were doing so, then the weather would clear up during the day, and our trip to the Hamptons would go on. Sea gulls standing on both legs were to be discounted from the computations, however. After listening to the solemnities of Basilian John, this kind of nonsense was a delightful distraction. By the way, we never found the correlation of gulls on right or left legs to indicate anything other than what was evident. Sometimes we headed to the icy reaches of the wild Atlantic only to dig into the dunes to seek some shelter from winds and rains. With pits dug for shelter and holes covered by whatever means, the beach assumed some semblance to Normandy on June 6, 1944. On a few occasions, our picnic was also postponed for a day in the hope of more clement weather conditions.

Since the Hamptons were virtually empty, the Brothers would change in and out of their bathing suits without benefit of cabana or modesty. In fact, one of the practical jokes played on incoming sophomores was to swap something of value for a pass to the locker rooms. When one observed the locker rooms, he could choose between the dunes to the left or the dunes to the right. A very moving ceremony marked the end of our day at the beach. With the sun setting westward and the light of a summer's gloaming, we would recite some night prayers and culminate the joy of the day with the hymn to Mary, *Salve Regina*. That may sound corny, but it was a memorable scene etched into my mind just as soundly as the sight of fishermen pushing their boats into the surf and spreading their nets. None tried to walk on water, but when they hauled in the nets, I was startled to witness all manner of sea robins, sea bass, and sand sharks thrashing in the sand. Sometimes I wonder whether the fishermen had as many questions about us as we had about them and their chores.

Escaping the confines of La Salle Military Academy was a rare occasion. When presented with the opportunity, we all welcomed the change even though the grounds had excellent facilities and diversions. I suppose the human soul seeks variation, even from pleasant pastimes. Every summer, the entire group would board buses and head to New York, specifically, Manhattan College in the Bronx. Brother Basil Robert Daschiewicz from the group ahead of me used to coordinate a blood drive that earned him the reputation of Dracula and garnered us a trip from Oakdale to the Bronx. A very talented violinist, Daschiewicz came from the Ocean State a virtuoso soloist on the violin, but he developed his talent for organization in the traffic for human blood upon his arrival in the Scholasticate. His sense of humor enabled him to endure all the jokes about bloodletting, but thanks to his organization and arrangements, we enjoyed the trip, even if it cost each of us a pint of blood. In the course of the summers and at Catholic University I managed to have donated a gallon of this essence of life and gathered in some interesting adventures in the process.

Our parents were apprised of the date of the blood donations, and those who could get to Manhattan held an impromptu reunion. My family was always anxious to visit with me so I could count on their attendance. Some were not so fortunate. I vividly recall driving along the Major Deegan Highway in the convoy of blue school buses from De La Salle and observing some women waving frantically to us from the windows along 138th Street near the Willis Avenue Bridge. One name I remember in particular, for she seemed to catch us coming and going. Pat Daley's mother had a commanding view of the Deegan as it approached or left the Triborough Bridge toward the Bronx. She was one of the last vestiges of the Irish bastion of St. Jerome's Parish which had sent her son as well as so many others to join the Christian Brothers. For my part, I would meet my parents and my brother Ray in person after I paid my dues for the ride in by donating my pint.

On one occasion Ray was particularly insistent that I go to visit my 'Uncle Tim.' Tim Riordan owned The Green Leaf, one of the two emporia that unsuccessfully slaked the insatiable thirsts of the college students at Manhattan. The Green Leaf was almost at the bottom of the stairs descending from Manhattan. Tim was known to my family slightly, and I even remember his non-attendance at his wedding to a very dear friend of my aunt Helen. It was the only wedding I attended that had no groom. Ray argued that he was an uncle for he devoted more time with Tim and in the other bar called the Pinewood than he spent in the classrooms. With my parents and me in tow, he entered the Green Leaf and in deference to my presence, didn't sit at the bar but at a table toward the rear. I enjoyed my coke, but I was anxious to depart. Before that happened, however, three figures strode in and took stools at the bar. I recognized them immediately. One was Brother August Thomas who was teaching a theology course at Oakdale, and the second was Brother Timothy Balfe who had taught me theology in Washington one semester. The third individual escapes my memory. After a few beers the trio looked around and spotted me. All parties were somewhat taken aback. Later, Brother August Thomas approached me before our return to Oakdale and said, "I think it is in the best interest of us all if nothing is said by anyone about our meeting." I assured him that his advice was sound, and I followed it religiously, never mentioning the encounter to anyone. I suppose they would have been in as much hot water as I was if the news reached Kirby.

During the week, we seldom had visitors, but my Aunt Helen and Uncle Joe Clancy with their four children drove out to visit me in mid-week. I asked permission to leave the grounds, but was advised to report back in before retiring for the night. Joe decided that we should take a trip to Fire Island. Now everyone from New York was well aware of the reputation of Fire Island as a haven for gays, just as Greenwich Village was. When we arrived at the ferry pier in Bayshore, we had several choices offered for the destination on the island. Since none of us knew one from another, Joe said Cherry Grove sounded as good as any. The ferry was very small, and the only other passenger was a young woman. As we debarked the ferry, she took one look at my uncle and aunt with their four little children and exclaimed, "I think you're in the wrong place." How right she seemed when we tip-toed past the open windows of the gay bar where the male partners were dancing cheek to cheek. A sneak preview of the beach exposed more than the surf and sand since few had donned any bathing suits. As my aunt sheltered her kids and practically lassoed them to keep them close we retreated to the ferry, believing that it was wiser to leave Cherry Grove than continue the exploration. Joe's brief inquiry earned the information that the next ferry left in two hours. For two hours we huddled on the pier hoping no other apparitions might shock us. That evening when I went to report to Kirby, he asked where I had gone. When I replied, "Cherry Grove," all he could utter was his trade mark, "Ah say, Brother," and I tried to explain our ignorance in plausible terms and how we decided that it was a mistake. I guess Kirby didn't know what else to say for he said nothing, but I imagine he kept a closer eye on me in the future.

In my third summer at Oakdale, I was driving the trucks and buses and I was given the assignment of bringing Brother Eugene Lappin and his baggage into the Bronx to St. Augustine's in Morrisania. Gene was a few years older than I and had distinguished himself for the solicitude he directed toward the Hispanics who worked in the kitchen at Oakdale. He and Brother Augustine Dominic Militich used to translate for the staff and generally looked after the interests of the young Latinos. This fine work of charity and exemplary tolerance earned them little more than mockery and derision from their peers. Racial and ethnic appreciation were not readily on hand for the Scholastics who had grown up for the most part in bigoted neighborhoods.

Gus Militich and I had a conversation in which he claimed I was an inveterate bigot and would rot in hell because of my prejudice. I suppose he said it with such vehemence and exhortation that I didn't take any offense at either the accusation or the condemnation. Gus was a multi-lingual immigrant from Canada who had been raised in Eastern Europe. I knew his father was an unlettered shoemaker, but Gus was brilliant and destined for a doctorate in Comparative Linguistics from The University of Chicago. While I could appreciate his academic prowess, I thought his ideas on race and ethnicity were 'off the walls.' Most likely, it would have taken a lynching to convince me that racism or prejudice was not the standard in American society, and therefore I was no different from mainstream. In any case, I remember Gus' prediction, but I always admired his zeal and enthusiasm in whatever project he undertook. Only later after some experience in racial and ethnic diversity, did I grow to analyze Gus' predictions with any clarity.

I didn't know Gene as well, but my passenger was on his way to several years' service in the missions of Ethiopia. An exemplary student and deeply religious man, Gene was sometimes referred to in conversation as "The Boy Christ." Most of that derogatory designation designed as a euphemism derived from his zeal in assisting and advocating for the Latinos at Oakdale. At St. Augustine's we met up with Brother John Devaney and Brother Louie Ruch who were packing and preparing for the same trip to Africa. Kirby always alleged that the District sent its best men to the missions. If this trio is any example, there was a great deal of truth in his statement.

Driving in the southeast Bronx was more than the challenge I expected as I maneuvered the large truck beneath the pillars of the Third Avenue El amid the aggressive drivers of other trucks, cars, and buses in the congested area. For some reason unknown to me, I had been told not to let Gene drive at all, but when he insisted and pulled rank on the way back to Oakdale, I thought it better to humor him than obey the directive. That trip to Augustine marked my first observation of what would later become my home for seven years.

Usually, the Scholastics were not permitted home for four years unless for a family emergency. We had the unexpected bonus of an unpredicted visit. A concatenation of circumstances led to a trip off the grounds of Oakdale in my senior year. This one entailed a few days at home. With De La Salle College in Washington getting overcrowded and the single year at Troy not alleviating the shortage of space, the District councils urged expanding the Scholasticate. A professional fund raising company was hired, and we received instructions in our role in the project. We were advised to reject paltry dollar donations and insist on shaking down our relatives and friends, not for cash, but for pledges. The approach sounded too mercenary for us, but no one asked our opinion. A major roadblock arose, however, in the process when someone questioned whether we could legitimately go begging without being appropriately dressed. We had our clerical suits, but the thirties stylish fedoras were deemed unseemly for summertime wear. After all, we were not embarking on a Halloween Trick or Treat excursion. Joe Troy's father had a contact in the Panama hat business, so with little more instruction, but now topped with a nice gray colored summer hat, we were sent to extort pledges from friends, family and relatives. Actually the project wasn't so bad as the anticipation, and we collected a large number of cash pledges or monument sponsoring gifts. In fact the new Chapel would be covered with the names of those who contributed to its creation and short lived existence.

I always associate the trip home with the movie *The Snake Pit*. On Saturday evenings a rented movie would be showed in the boathouse on the basin. I recall only two of these presentations. One was the classic *Citizen Kane*, Orson Welles' *tour de force* which some believe is the finest movie of all time. The other was *The Snake Pit*, a film about the incarceration of a woman in an insane asylum. One of the scenes from that movie depicted a busload of inmates returning from a picnic. They mournfully sang, '*Going Home,*' more a dirge than anything else. As we traveled by bus into New York, someone started up the dirge and the rest of the passengers joined in. I don't know whether we felt we were inmates returning to our natural home or simply sad at the prospect of what we were asked to do. That nostalgic song, the subdued bus ride into New York, the apprehension over the embarrassment of begging seemed to stifle the joy we would ordinarily feel about an unexpected trip home. Naturally, when I arrived at an apartment on Wadsworth Avenue where my family was forced to relocate on account of the expansion of the George Washington Bridge, I felt little connection or appreciation for the new lodging. In typical New York fashion, however, the family retreated to the roof top where pictures were taken with the scenic cloisters in the background. As part of my fundraising activity, my family drove to Syracuse where I shook down some relatives. My own close family didn't mind the begging, but I resented the task a great deal. Maybe my parents were happy to see me home whatever the price.

During the summers at Oakdale we also had several band recitals. Thanks to the talent of Frank Stephan, known as Brother Berard Richard, an impromptu band gave several recitals during the summer. In my first year, I decided to resume my music career terminated in elementary school. Since I had played clarinet very quietly in the Police Honor Legion Band, I determined that my future lay with the tenor saxophone. Brother Jimmy Zmich, a very talented sax player accustomed to the polkas of Detroit, was my tutor. All I could wrestle from a tenor sax was an approximation of a note. Jimmy, meanwhile, could caress a note, give it a seductive overtone, and entice a dreamy state of euphoria among his audience. Like my singing, which I decided was some note indecipherable on the standard music scale, my performance on the tenor sax was a monotone presentation that confused crescendo with higher notes. I apparently played the same note or its facsimile, only changing volume instead of scale. My saxophone career remained somewhat the same. My major contribution to the band under the direction of Brother Berard Richard Stephen was suggesting selections.

In one summer there were two major hits that featured the trumpet that Frank Stephan played so well. One was the theme from *The Man with the Golden Arm*, a plot entailing a drug addict seeking a fix. Another was the hypnotic, *Cherry Pink and Apple Blossom White*, a big hit by Perez Prado. For Jimmy Zmich, his seductive tones were perfect for *Night Train*. For O'Prey, discreet silence was in order. I also remember the alto sax playing of Brother Matthew McAteer who seemed to play music even without an instrument. The band was very good despite my participation and a gifted artist sometimes provided sets that were quite artistic. Brother Louis Lestingi was more artist in several media than most were in a single concentration. His drawings, cartoons, sets, and even his piano playing were outstanding. One of his productions concerned a spoof of Gunsmoke. A pair of rosary beads strung over the piano wires produced the perfect tinny sound of the B western bar scenes.

The nadir of my saxophone playing occurred in Washington after we had left Oakdale. I had retreated to the basement laundry and was trying to master *The Rose of Tralee*, a piece that had many flats in its score. After honking out my efforts for half an hour, Kirby appeared and asked me to move away from the laundry chute. Evidently, every squeal, squeak, and unsettling note traveled up the chute and was disturbing too many people. I took the negative review as a sign from the Lord that I wasn't destined to master the saxophone and retired soon from trying.

Every Sunday during our six week stay at La Salle Military Academy, families were invited to visit. Most fought off the beach traffic on the parkways heading to Robert Moses State Park, Fire Island, Long Beach, Atlantic Beach, Jones Beach, the Rockaways, Breezy Point, or myriad other spots along the south shore. Sundays in the summer, especially on hot, sunny days enticed thousands out of the broiling streets of New York so the families had many contestants for the marginal space on the highways eastward. Of course, those families that had no car often united to hire a bus and driver. Under these circumstances, I first witnessed a very strange vehicle approaching Oakdale. Tom Reilly's brother known as the legendary Duke, had bought a new Volkswagen Beetle and the first time I saw the car I was surprised at how much it looked like a toy rather than the chrome and fin mobiles that were popular at the time. Once at Oakdale, the grove became a major picnic area. Brothers who had no family visiting and those whose relatives lived beyond the metropolitan area would have a modest Cruddy meal, but they often visited adopted families and feasted sumptuously. At the end of the day, the orphans, as they were termed, also helped empty the trash cans and collect the leftovers which were deposited in the bowels of the kitchen unless they were consumed in transit. On these visits many of the families from different parishes got to know each other better also. Sometimes the fathers of the Brothers worked together on fund raisers after Sunday Masses in different parishes. Apparently, the parents were bonded closer by their zeal in helping the Brothers, but that bond was also greased by an occasional flute which bolstered the solicitors, especially in cold weather.

After the six weeks in Oakdale, the convoy of blue buses would head south again to continue summer classes in the confines of Washington, D.C. Kirby believed in early starts so we would often be awakened at 2:00am or 3:00am to begin the trek. He also gave each Brother two dollars and good luck in their hunt for something to eat at that price. On a few occasions, I got to drive either the bus or a truck in this caravan. One perk to that responsibility was additional funds for eating. I guess he didn't want any of the drivers to suffer hunger pangs behind the wheel. I was traveling with Dan Goeddeke on one of these extra funded sorties. He selected some diner in Atlantic City and ordered the truck driver special, only tripled. How he consumed such Homeric portions is the stuff of which legends are made.

During this period the New Jersey Turnpike terminated at a single span of the Delaware Memorial Bridge, and after that the convoy headed south on route 40 where the observant might note signs indicating 'Colored only', or even "no Colored.' When we arrived in the summer of 1959, Washington, DC was definitely still a creature of the 1950's and so were we. The Supreme Court had ruled that separate but equal facilities were inherently unconstitutional and decreed that segregation must be eliminated with 'deliberate speed.' Vestiges of segregation and discrimination were all over the District of Columbia, and the Scholastics at that time were as interested in 'deliberate speed' as any of the local racists. While the demonstrations in Birmingham, Alabama and the bus boycotts were occurring, Washington was very complacent and so too were the newest occupants. It wasn't so much that we were convinced racists as much as we were totally devoid of any interest in civil rights. In that sense, we were still more involved in the complacency era characteristic of the Eisenhower presidency than the surging movement for Black equality. In the course of our time in the Capital that acknowledgement would dawn slowly upon us, but the actual Brothers who got involved in the movement were at least two years behind us. When we entered the Scholasticate in Washington, our attitude in general toward Civil Rights was more akin to the Spanish concept of "*manana*" than it was to the Puritanical notion that "time is money."

I do recall some of the White teenagers who used our athletic facilities discussing their version of Black demonstrations. One in particular wanted to enroll in the University of Mississippi because of the adamant stance on prohibiting Blacks from enrolling in the University. The segregationist governors, like Orville Faubus, defying the integration at Little Rock, Alabama; George Wallace, insisting that Alabama would remain white; and Ross Barnett of Mississippi, as well as Lester Maddox of Georgia who defended white supremacy with his ax handle were heroes to these lads. We were south of the Mason-Dixon line, but we weren't jarred by the inequities we witnessed.

In a few years that would change, but not during our tenure in the Scholasticate. I describe this situation not so much as a boast, but as an explanation about the oblivion we possessed about this situation. Perhaps our attitude may best be summarized by a quotation uttered by Brother Black Bart Clarke, the catechist from Barrytown who preceded Albinus. Black Bart was fond of the aphorism, "If you don't know you don't know, you don't even know you don't know!" Such ignorance is not an alibi but an explanation of why it took several more years before the Scholastics under the leadership of Brian Guidera and Hank McNally began to agitate for Civil Rights. When I first heard about the activities of these two intelligent, forward thinking Brothers, I was mystified and perhaps hostile. Later, my admiration for them would know no bounds.

The Civil Rights Movement beckoned, but most Scholastics were indifferent at best. The Scholastics headed south of the Mason-Dixon Line, but we remained blissfully ignorant of the cruelties and subtle offenses segregation offered. Like myopic folk, we couldn't see the forest for the trees. We readily accepted Washington's inertia and its segregation long delayed from the changes 'with all due haste' demanded by Brown v. The Board of Education of Topeka, Kansas. Christ's injunction to love all mankind was still confined by a color barrier that remained unperceived and irrelevant.

If my memory is correct, we might have had some classes to complete in the mornings at De La Salle, but the afternoons were devoted to exploring the monuments and buildings in downtown Washington. A bus would drive to a central location, park and expel the volunteers into a specific building. A sign up sheet would indicate the destination for that day. Among the more popular visits was a trip to the FBI Building. Not only did it have rigid, pictorial displays, but one could observe the forensic scientists in the lab analyzing God knows what. Then an agent would lead the tour to the firing line where another would demonstrate the use of a machine gun. The noise was very impressive, more so than the accuracy of the bullets. Another popular destination was the Smithsonian Institute. I liked the building that contained so many exhibits from American history. It also had a pendulum suspended from the tall ceiling. As the earth rotated on its axis, the pendulum would gradually knock off the series of blocks erected in its path. The fallen blocks represented a kind of planetarium clock. The gowns from all the first ladies up to 1960 were also on display in another room, but I was more interested in the salvaged gunboat used by Benedict Arnold during the battle of Valcour Island in Lake Champlain in the early years of the revolution.

Some were fascinated by the aberrations exhibited in the medical museum. Unique 'treasures' like the section of brain excised during Lincoln's autopsy, or the sample of elephantiasis of a diseased limb, or world record organs, or some such grotesquerie drew huge numbers of curiosity seekers. One of the locations I particularly enjoyed was the National Art Gallery or Freer Collection. As I wandered among the noted works of art or relics of antiquity I came upon some fascinating works by Salvador Dali. I saw his *Last Supper* featuring a blond Jesus and all kinds of background objects. Perhaps, his *Crucifixion* was also on display there, only I believe he titled it *Study of Neck Muscles*. Since I am far from a connoisseur of contemporary or for that matter any period art, the less I say the wiser. In the interest of communication, however, I have to confess that I spent many hours absorbed in the displays, and I also became a life long devotee of Salvador Dali.

Investigations of the Congressional Library and the Capitol were very interesting also, but I never quite got to the White House. I was particularly impressed with the acoustical phenomenon within the dome that represented the House of Representatives. It was said that John Quincy Adams could overhear even whispers from across the room. The sound would be channeled up onto the dome and directed downward to the opposing party who could eavesdrop on plans or strategies of the rivals in Congress. Apparently, few knew the secret, but it was the eighteenth and nineteenth century bugging device that was purely natural. An unofficial tour of Union Station or Lee's old estate at Arlington was on the agenda also. The National Cemetery with the monuments to so many fallen heroes, the Tomb of the Unknown Soldier, the mast from the USS Maine, Lee's mansion, and the occasional discovery of a notable from our earlier history made the exploration interesting and often unpredictable. The view across the river offered an unparalleled vista of our nation's capitol. The vengeful Federal troops who wanted to punish Robert E. Lee by turning his plantation into a cemetery actually led to one of the Civil War's most visited and revered sites.

Many also wanted a personal view of the Lincoln Monument, Jefferson's Monument by the Tidal Basin, and Washington's Monument near the Arlington Bridge. It is safe to conclude that there was more to see than time allowed. Of these three monuments, I was particularly taken by the statue of Abraham Lincoln, sculpted by Daniel Chester French. Sometimes when light fell upon the statue an almost diabolical Lincoln seem to emerge from the placid, contemplative features of the martyred president. The classical dome and statue of Thomas Jefferson also impressed me so much deeper than the classic simplicity of the tall obelisk dedicated to our first president. I think if I knew more about architecture and the symbolism of the Washington Monument, I might have been more impressed. One of my early learning experiences in Washington was provided with compliments from my older brother Bernard. He had traveled up from Texas after one of his first assignments in the Air Force. He had invited me to share a dinner at the Officer's Club at Bolling Air Force Base. Envisioning a barroom, beer and pretzel environment, I questioned whether my clerical suit would be appropriate attire. When I arrived at the Club, I soon learned about an entirely different world. As Bernard made a reservation with the *Maitre D'*, I overheard the conversation that was taking place at the station. The *Maitre D'* spoke to one couple referring to the male as Admiral and his wife was bedecked in an evening gown. Right after the Admiral, came a general and his wife. Second Lieutenant Bernard O'Prey seemed so anti-climactic, but we were in the upper echelon of military Washington and the clientele were dressed accordingly. That same evening a delegation from the Turkish Air Force was also in attendance, and I witnessed tuxedo clad waiters bearing fiery Shish Kabobs between tables of formal dressed guests or military personnel in dress uniforms. I guess I looked more like an Amish plain person than anything else. I don't remember much about the meal, but I do recall the décor with vivid detail.

On another occasion when Bernard treated me to a steak at Domino's, a steak house near the motel most frequented by families visiting the Scholasticate, the staff refused to take his personal check drawn on a bank account from the First Bank of San Antonio. Despite his protestations of honesty and appeals to patriotism in accepting the very money our country was paying him to protect them, the restaurateur was insistent that the Lieutenant make the check out for an exact amount, not even allowing for a tip. Bernard's plan to acquire cash for gas to New York wouldn't work, and the fact that the owner was a foreigner made the experience more bitter.

De La Salle College property lay within two jurisdictions. A part of the property was situated in the District of Columbia, and therefore we had a mailing address using Washington since mail delivery was said to be more expeditious via that channel. Since the college grounds also were partially in Maryland, we were able to vote in national elections and our drivers' licenses were issued by the state of Maryland. At the time, Maryland drivers' licenses were black photocopies that contained no expiration date. I often wondered if I tried to use one today, if it would still be valid. In a way, the location of De La Salle College enabled the Brothers to pick and choose the better of the two options offered by its location. At that time, no one within the District of Columbia could vote in Presidential elections, but we could. Most of the Scholastics, however, hadn't reached the requisite age of twenty-one yet. Most of my class would participate in the fabled election of 1960 when the country decided between John F. Kennedy and Richard Milhous Nixon. As for me, I would still be ineligible to vote because of my age.

De La Salle College stood on an elevated knoll that offered cool breezes from the oppressive heat along the Potomac. Our building offered air conditioning only in the chapel so perhaps it was an inducement for prayer and meditation. The outdoor basketball courts and handball courts were the only facilities on ground other than the spacious ball field. Unlike Oakdale, or even Barrytown and Troy, there was no gym. For many it made little difference for most got seriously involved in studies, but I didn't. For my use of the athletic fields on a daily basis, I was ceremoniously appointed the President of the Jock and Sneaker Club by its reigning executive, Brother Bertram Patrick Kelly, known to most as 'Sweetfeet' for the pungency of his pegs. I retained that title for three years and was very proud to say I enjoyed my years of college experience. Over the course of pursuit of an undergraduate degree, I took classes seriously, but not in a life or death sense. I was determined to enjoy the great outdoors as well as the interior of the library and common rooms. Life in Washington would not be so different from my adventures in Oakdale. I suppose 'Carpe Diem' was as appropriate a motto as I can summon to explain my attitude toward both. I resolved to enjoy my collegiate career at all costs.

Chapter Six

Scholasticate Years in Washington

August 1959-August 1962

The education of the young Brothers was of paramount concern to the leaders of the New York and the Long Island-New England (LINE) District. Fearful of training the future teachers without a sense of objective, professional discernment, the New York and Baltimore Districts determined to send their young Scholastics to The Catholic University of America in Washington, D.C. Unlike the Irish Christian Brothers who were educated at Iona, a college that their order conducted in New Rochelle, New York, the Christian Brothers wanted an outside influence that wouldn't be tempted to allow any student to receive preferential treatment simply because he was a member of the same Order. Obviously, the plan was more expensive than educating one's own, but the rewards or safeguards were apparently worth the additional cost and objectivity. True, the Scholastics would receive their early training by the Brothers in Hillside Hall, Troy, as well as their second year classes in De La Salle College in Washington, an affiliate of Catholic University. Every student would have to be accepted by Catholic University and abide by their standards for courses, credits, and sequences for graduation. Upper level seminars, required reading lists, and concentration for majors became the responsibility of Catholic University. Part of that demand included an undergraduate comprehensive examination that was designed to coordinate all the courses in one major into a cohesive, integral entity. Nine hours of examinations were required for acquiring the undergraduate baccalaureate degree. I found this requirement a demand that didn't appear in too many other colleges at the time, but it filled its intention very thoroughly.

Although the purpose of the Institute was essentially conducting schools for the poor, very few Brothers were allowed to major in education. According to the demands of Catholic University, each Scholastic could choose a major from among those offered on the main campus. Generally, these majors were intended to provide a strong academic grasp of a specific field, and the educational courses would be strictly extras provided during summer sessions. Modern languages like French, German, and Spanish were offered, but Scholastics found disciplines in physics, chemistry, biology, mathematics and related fields. Latin majors were relatively common, but the number of English and history majors led the choices of most classes.

When I entered the Scholasticate, I intended to be an English major, and I followed that intention until the end of my sophomore year. At that time, my observance of the seniors satisfying one of the most difficult demands of Catholic University tempted me to change my mind. Before graduation, every student had to pass three days of comprehensive examinations in their field of concentration and in their minor. When I witnessed the minutiae of the English majors in preparing for these exams, I decided that I wanted to concentrate on American history. It seemed to me that the English majors certainly had a broad education in English and American literature, but it was the minor concentration that disconcerted me. Every English major not only had to have the panoramic view of literature, but he had to have a miniscule, microscopic view of a particular author and a thorough knowledge of theories of literary criticism. I had thought of majoring in Keats or John Donne up to that time, but many Brothers were drawn to the minor in T.S. Eliot. A Father Rooney was evidently a mesmerizing professor who analyzed not only the words of Eliot, but he specialized and demanded a structural analysis that required noting syllables and some esoteric, arcane imagery that elude my memory. Noting especially Tom Haughey, one of the most intense scholars in the senior class, and the scrutiny demanded from John O'Brien, I benefited from their example and bailed out.

Among the Brothers, the easiest major over the four year curriculum was deemed history. I avoided choosing history more from pride than lack of interest. All my life I had had a powerful interest in the field, no doubt nurtured at an early age by my father and the example of my older brother Bernard. Both read incessantly and conversed knowledgeably about myriad topics in the field. Despite its reputation as *Refugium Peccatorum,* or 'refuge of sinners,' I swallowed my pride, and asked the Brother who was in charge of academic tracts if I could switch from English to American history. Brother Amian Bernard listened intently to my request and agreed on one salient condition. If I changed my major, I would have to agree to take two years of German language as my admission fee. Unknown to me, the same deal was offered to Brother John Hannaway who dropped his major in math to concentrate in European history.

Supposedly, the additional language requirement would satisfy any graduate prerequisite if John or I were to pursue a doctorate in history. That eventuality became a reality for John, for he was asked to teach our Scholastics while he earned a doctorate from Johns Hopkins University in Baltimore. Later, John journeyed to France to study the "Influence of the Canal System in the Ancien Regime." When John left for France, I was asked to replace him in teaching the Scholastics. Brother Augustine Loes, the District Visitor of New York, offered me the opportunity to replace John and incidentally earn my doctorate from any university in the Capital area. First, I had to convince the chairman of the history department at Manhattan College that I was worthy of the investment.

Brother Pat McGarry was the chairman and a formidable intellectual. As a high school student at La Salle, he had won a national honor in history and that was just the first step in his intellectual rise. His doctorate from Columbia indicated the kind of student he was. His conversation was indicative of the cerebral heights to which he was accustomed. He is the only individual that made me uneasy in his casual conversation. His wit was sharp and his incisive mind even keener. I always felt on high alert when speaking with him, even about the most trivial of matters. Pat told me that I had the intelligence and capability of doing well in a doctoral program, but he questioned whether I had the personal interest and dedication demanded for completion. In retrospect, I suppose he was correct, but the evolution of that discovery is a story in itself. I applied and was accepted to the University of Maryland where I intended to work for my doctorate and teach history to the Scholastics. That intention was radically altered by a conversation I had with Brother Kevin Gilhooley while we were at the Juniorate on its feast day. Kevin remarked that he thought I thoroughly enjoyed teaching in elementary school, and if I pursued my plan, I would be qualified to teach at Manhattan for the rest of my days. He wondered whether my zeal in elementary school education had peaked, or did I still have the resolution to continue there. His doubt made my doubt grow and finally, I requested Brother Augustine Loes to relieve me of my graduate assignment. A factor in that request was the imminent illness that unexpectedly struck my mother at about the same time. She had a stroke, and the doctors told us to be grateful for any additional days we might have her. Proximity in New York seemed more important to me at the time than a graduate opportunity.

Sometimes I wonder what might have been, but my decision at the time was rational and well thought out. Although it would entail a slower approach to a doctorate consuming more time and involving only part time attention, I considered my future very carefully. Instead of enrolling in Maryland, I decided to pursue a doctorate in American Social History at New York University. I remember Gus Loes inviting me to accept all kinds of variations on assignments which would have enabled me to teach in Washington, but the overriding consideration was my interest in my current role at St. Augustine and the proximity to my dying mother. Both factors would play roles that eventually undermined my plan and evidenced that God works in strange ways.

In any case, John Hannaway and I took two years of German language. John used his to satisfy the demands of Johns Hopkins and amazed the faculty there when he proved sufficiently fluent in French and German before he had taken a single course. My study of German proved academic, for in satisfying NYU's requirements, I was able to use French and Latin, both of which I decided I knew better than the German I had learned at Catholic University. One of the reasons for that judgment was the style of language learning prevalent for German. I had mastered Latin and French through thorough knowledge of grammar, but in German, we had to listen to audio-lingual tapes that were designed to teach us to converse in the language. After my study of Latin and French, I think I could translate sufficiently if I had to. After listening to the German tapes, I must confess that most of the playbacks I heard contained snores rather than attempts to master specific conversation topics. Taking the German courses had some positive results, however, but they demanded additional laboratory time. If I am correct, I had German classes three times a week and an hour long audio-lingual laboratory twice each week.

Upon arrival in Washington in August, 1959 I was assigned to work in the garage under the direction of Brothers Christian William Martin, John O'Brien, Alfred Bernardine Walsh, Adrian Roland Tobin, and Cassian Kevin Martin who had been in the May group immediately prior to my Novitiate year. The work was interesting, but I found the smell of gasoline and cleanser too obnoxious to want to continue. Our responsibilities were small but vital. We kept the fleet of buses, trucks, cars, and tractor filled with gas and in top running condition. Topping off gas tanks was easy. I recall the cold temperature of the fluid as it was pumped from beneath the insulating ground on even the hottest days of August and September. Aside from minor tune ups involving changing spark plugs, one of our frequent tasks was packing the bearings in the wheels. We seemed to do this more often than might have been necessary. It wasn't my favorite activity. Working in the garage involved additional time during the day. The crew seemed dedicated to their jobs and were more mechanically inclined than I was.

One of the special perks of working in the garage, however, was the training on driving the buses and trucks. The tractor had only a few forward gears and once set in a particular gear there was no shifting until one came to a full stop and reset the gear with a clutch. The buses were quite different. I recall that there must have been three buses, but I can only name vehicles which were termed a B40, an older model, and a brand new B36. In order to switch gears while moving forward, the clutch had to be compressed twice or what was called double-clutched. Obviously, forward momentum was essential to moving into a higher gear for faster travel. One of the drawbacks to that was the sound. The roar of the engine as it inched forward in first gear initially intimidated me, but after a while, one could get accustomed to the noise as necessary for acceleration. It didn't take too long to accommodate the longer, wider turns required of the vehicle nor to adjust to the large turning radius. What did cause some passengers shortness of breath was getting the hang of assessing space and pace for entering traffic. In my early moments of bus driving, I remember a few close calls as the bus pulled out of Catholic University onto Michigan Avenue. There was a viaduct that traversed a railroad track and successfully hid oncoming traffic before the crest of the hill. If one started to pull out for a left hand turn, a rapid car coming over the crest could challenge the tardy, initial move unless one gunned the motor. I learned that it took longer and more effort to stop a heavy vehicle with brakes. To this day, I realize how difficult it may be for a truck to stop, so I try not to tempt them by pulling in front of them. We were trained in some roadway etiquette. For example, when passing a slower vehicle and signaling a return to the right, one would acknowledge the flashing of headlights indicating a safe distance for the shift by flicking the running lights on and off. When I have been driving on highways today, I notice that that courtesy is losing its popularity. Driving the truck entailed much the same courtesies, but fewer challenges. Soon, as a result of my garage experience, I was operating many of the vehicles that kept the Scholasticate and its members mobile. I was pleased that I seemed to be assigned trips with regularity and frequency that few others in my group enjoyed. I attributed that not so much to my driving prowess, but to the experience in the garage.

At the next shift of manual labors, I requested a transfer from the garage to another responsibility. Few people made such a request, but mine was honored graciously. Most Scholastics envied a manual labor to the garage, but it didn't suit my temperament or personality. Perhaps if I had spent more time in the garage, I might not be the mechanical klutz or inept handyman that symbolized my future endeavors with vehicles or home maintenance.

My next assignment would remain mine for the following years. I became a member of the floor waxing crew. In essence, we were responsible for keeping the terrazzo floors spotless and gleaming. We were supposed to strip, clean, and wax the three floors of linoleum coverings. A special assignment entailed a weekly Saturday night stripping, cleaning, waxing, and polishing the refectory floors. During a time when the rest of the Brothers were rehearsing the Gregorian chant for the Sunday Mass or the Latin text of the upcoming liturgy, a group of us were working on the floor. Some said we were selected for our lack of musical talent. Others flattered themselves into believing it was our love of manual labor that enticed us. I suppose a compromise between the two might hold the truth. After Saturday's supper the Brothers would remove all the refectory chairs placing them in an auditorium on the lower floor. About a half dozen of us then would strip the floor with a soap solution swirled about with buffers. Others would squeegee the dirty water into buckets, and finally a new clean mopping would leave the floor spotless, but unshined. A coat of wax was applied and when it dried, it would be buffed. The Brothers entering the refectory for breakfast in the morning would return the chairs. After applying the wax we were entitled to celebrate the drying period by sipping as many sodas as we deemed necessary. The commander-in-chief of this elite squad was a Brother with military experience from CBA Albany. Brother Columban John Farrar blended humor, cajolery, praise, and encouragement to plumb whatever talent he had on the team. After his graduation, I was honored to replace him. For at least two years, I had the pleasure of working with Pat Murphy and Brother Patrick Pius who we named 'PP' and by extension, 'Leaky.' We worked quite conscientiously but joyfully at this task for the next two years. Leaky thought I was crazy because of my insistence on polishing floors that may not have needed that extra portion of wax or the Shine-all substance that was a cleanser as well as a polishing agent. His secretive comments to Pat Murphy were usually funny and hysterical only in so far he was positive his diagnosis of my mental imbalance was accurate.

De La Salle College was a long four story rectangle surmounted by a peak with a ten foot cement cross atop. I know this only too well, for I was drafted to carry on a Yuletide tradition involving that cross. Joe McGowan explained to me that traditionally, guys from Incarnation were selected to attach a ten foot lighted cross to the cement figure for the Christmas season. I was a trainee in this department for the first two years in Washington. When Joe graduated and I got the chance to scale the ladder tipped against the suspiciously granular base of the cross, I debated whether Incarnation had been selected as an honor or because of their evident lack of IQ. As I leaned against the insecure, allegedly cemented cross already showing signs of mealy consistency, I could sense the increased gravitational pull in my drawers, lately increased by unexpected weight. One had to hug the statue at least seventy feet above the ground and use a ratchet to tighten several U-bolts into place. I confess from the safety of the ground and distance of many years that I was terrified in doing this. Heights aren't my thing, and leaning against wobbly structures only increased my anxiety. I recently read a description of the beehive structures off the coast of Kerry on Skellig Michael and the secondary pinnacle which was the object of pilgrimage for over more than a thousand years. The trepidation of the pilgrims upon the precipitous climb six hundred feet above the surging surf below and ultimate kissing of an embedded cross made them no more fainthearted than I was. Embarrassed to admit it, I performed the task and tried to forget that we had to repeat the process at the end of the Christmas season.

My misgivings didn't prevent me from passing the tradition along to Brother Fidelis Christopher (or Mike Keegan.) The lights shined from on high if the bulbs didn't burn out and require changing. I think our prayers prevented too many encore performances. When we went to erect the symbol of Christianity, Brother Leo told us to lock the front doors in case we fell or dropped a tool from on high. He completed his advice by adding, "I don't want anyone hit by a body falling from the roof or for that matter by a metal tool." No words of caution, just prevention of injury to others. I guess one could justifiably conclude that the men of Incarnation were expendable.

Mike Keegan was the honoree of another tradition supposedly reserved for candidates from the Heights. Gerry Fulcher warranted the name Brother Angelus for he was in charge of ringing the angelus bell three times a day while he was at Barrytown. He gave Joe McGowan the honorary title when he entered the Novitiate and Joe passed it along to Dermot O'Sullivan who seemed to perform this service for only a brief period for he then drafted Mike Keegan. I don't know whether Mike continued this hand-me-down program, but he may have selected his younger brother Kevin to perform the honors when he entered the Novitiate. Unlike Barrytown and its bells, De La Salle College began the day with an electronic alarm that some swore was army surplus from a navy submarine diving to ocean depths. The shrill sound bore little resemblance to the euphony of cloister bells.

The Scholasticate had begun as the house of studies for the Brothers of the New York and Baltimore districts. The affiliation with Catholic University was in place from the beginning. After a while, Baltimore decided to enroll its scholars at La Salle College in Philadelphia, but New York, now buttressed by the newly created LINE District, continued despite crowded conditions. The building contained an ample refectory at one end with an industrial kitchen extending almost half the length of the edifice. With storage and refrigeration the space was needed. There was a cook called Flossie who watched the pots and ordered the kitchen appointed Brothers to peel the potatoes, move the pots around, put baking trays into the oven, remove them in a timely fashion, and prepare vegetables, poultry and meat according to a menu designed by Brother Brice Patrick. Brothers Joe Troy, John Hannaway and Pat Murphy were among the top echelon of kitchen assistants. They apportioned the meals into serving dishes and distributed whatever the menu demanded. They served this cause admirably and without complaint either among themselves or among their diners.

Of course, not every meal was an unalloyed success. Perhaps the greatest critic of the cuisine was also the greatest gustatory consumer. Tom Ladley, an immensely powerful Brother with broad shoulders and insatiable appetite, had earned the nickname 'Moose' for his prodigious ability to consume epic portions of whatever was put in front of him. His capacity was so notorious that the garbage disposal unit in the kitchen was named in his honor. We called it 'a mechanical Tom.' Moose didn't hesitate to editorialize about the food either. When some roast beef was serve rather rare for human consumption, he began an incessant mooing that brought howls of laughter to the assembled hungry monks. Reminiscent of a "lowing herd o'er the lea," the mournful sound captured the disappointment so eloquently displayed when the anticipated roast beef, a rare treat, was actually too 'rare.'

On another occasion after hearing the Director of Troy rave about the excellent desserts served after their meals at Hillside, we retreated to our refectory for our own repast. Unfortunately, on that day, some kind of chocolate bread pudding was served. The contrast from the verbal description of culinary delights in Troy evinced the notion that our meal looked like cow flops. Spontaneous laughter burst out again as one wag commented about how our dessert was special for it was "shot from buffaloes." Humor during meals sometimes arose from unexpected quarters too. Once, while Brian Cleary was distributing quarts of milk to the tables, he carried a case of the bottles out of the kitchen, caught his foot on a rubber mat that protected the floor, and began to stumble. As he gained momentum in his effort to save his balance and the bottles, he began to run and finally fell, diving beneath the high table at the end of the refectory. Instead of sympathy, the diners referred to his performance as a 'milk crate throwing contest' as if it were Olympic competition. Clearly, a hallmark of our formation was the ability to find humor in unexpected places and events.

The lower floor contained a chemistry lab which was virtually abandoned in my sophomore year. There were open spaces where plays or shows could be presented. At the back of this large hall was an area where one could find the **New York Times** and a very seldom used television. That television was permissible only according to the Director's whim and his whim didn't stray too far from the essential news and documentary, although we did have limited access to football games. There was also a reading and leisure area that paralleled the television vicinity.

On the second floor a chapel that barely held the entire population at one time lay above the refectory. It was the only air conditioned room in the Scholasticate. Simple in design and decoration, there we said our community prayers and attended daily Mass. Our chaplains were from the nearby Benedictine monastery. There were two blood brothers among the chaplains. One, named Dave, was called 'Sneakers' because of his celerity in distributing Communion and saying Mass. His brother Pat was efficient, but not quite so expeditious in performing his role. Other Benedictines occasionally came, and they proved that a good singing voice was not a prerequisite for entrance into the liturgical minded Benedictines. I suppose the same could be said that the Dominicans, the Order of Preachers, did not necessarily imbue its candidates with eloquence.

At the opposite end of the building from the chapel lay a room called the common room. Every Scholastic had his own desk and chair within the confines of this room. It was not only used for study, but conferences and talks were scheduled, especially on Sunday. I used to marvel at what I considered the eloquence of Brother Leo Kirby when he gave these conferences, masterpieces of logic and interesting presentation. Some of the faculty gave us lectures or conferences from time to time. One stands out in my mind. Brother Gabriel Moran from New Hampshire used to walk around the building from one place to another with an absentminded aura that ignored anyone in his path. Occasionally, he might smile a vacant expression or acknowledgement of your presence, but he rarely spoke. When he gave us a lecture, it was absolutely enthralling. I couldn't believe that this 'spectral presence' was the presenter of a brilliant conference.

That brilliance would later come to the fore when he became a guru on community life among many of the religious throughout metropolitan New York. From a virtual mute, the academic stage seemed to transform him into a fantastic speaker.

In this common room a small stationery store was located in the front toward the left. From common stock we could take pens, pencils, paper and other paraphernalia of academia. The common room was lined with book cases containing many volumes of research material, as well as books and novels that were essential for courses. I remember that there was a Latin Interlinear or Trot section. Unfortunately, by the time I discovered it, some future Latin majors had swiped the books and kept them secreted from the rest of the class. Only after a while was I able to deduce that they had access to more erudite sources than their own knowledge when their class translations defied the credulity of those without access to the books.

In the center of the building was an exterior concrete staircase on a more grandiose scale than the one in Hillside Hall in Troy. The staircase was circular and broke off into two wings that met at the top. The front doors that we were ordered to lock during our Christmas Cross exercise led to a common foyer off which was located an office for the 'Econome' or chief purchasing agent of the community. There was a beautiful wooden map of the United States which had lights inserted in the cities where Christian Brothers taught. I think this masterpiece may have been constructed by my buddy, Brother Brian Cyril or Eddie Schwall.

Once past the foyer, another staircase beckoned to the third floor, but before ascending that, I should point out that every available space around the walls was occupied by additional bookcases. Each Brother was assigned a section to dust and keep neat. Brother Anthony Riordan was in charge of the neatness and cleanliness of the library and its books. He developed a fine tuned sense of responsibility when he customarily advertised delinquents of their failure to meet minimum standards. That zeal led to the nickname for Tony, 'Dusty and Disorderly,' a reference to the terminology employed in his shots.

The Director's office was between the common room and the staircase. It was far from impressive in any way other than the personages that inhabited it. Brother Bertrand Leo Kirby was never too far afield from the youthful charges who challenged his imagination and zeal in making us into productive members of the Order. In my calculated judgment, I thought he did a magnificent job balancing the dicta of the Institute with the individuals who came under his supervision. He had a knack of relating well with our parents. We often deemed it unwise to complain about him to our families for he was known well by them and admired in a special way. He seemed to savor referring to my father as 'Sergeant,' his rank in the New York Police Department. At the same time he was the brother-in-law of New York City Police Commissioner Murphy.

Among all the magnificent men who fostered my early growth in the religious life and had a significant influence upon my personal life, I consider Brother Bertrand Leo Kirby to be in a class by himself. Aside from my family, I count him as the most influential person in developing my character and values in life. Like us all, Brother Leo Kirby had flaws and personality foibles that marked him among human beings. Nonetheless, I rated him as the most human of saints. His moods could swing from the ebullient to the discouraged. He might be brusque and almost dismissive at times, but I recall the enormity of the task he had undertaken. Brother Leo was in charge of at least one hundred and twenty young college men whose visions of the future ran the gamut from savior to incompetent. To each, he tried to be a cheerleader and offer encouragement, according to what he perceived to be the need of the moment. When I was a senior, my father had committed a major *faux pas* while he was assigned to supervise some policemen at the Russian embassy. Unfortunately, at the same time, he was suffering from the ravages of Demon Rum. After punching a particularly obnoxious demonstrator for Jewish emigration from Russia, the offended party reported my father to a supervisor who immediately suspended him on the spot. Brother Leo knew about the problem. At one time shortly after, I was talking and fooling around while working on cleanup after meals. Although it was Holy Week and a serious time for all, Leo approached me, and I thought I was in for a severe reprimand. Instead of reaming me, he softly said that he knew this was a trying time for me and urged me to try to be more silent. I was overwhelmed by his compassion and flabbergasted that he was worried over my morale. On another occasion when I had received a nasty letter from some malcontent complaining about something my brothers had done in New York, he demonstrated that same concern.

Brother Leo could vacillate between the roles of a Director and confidante with great aplomb and ease according to the situation as he judged it. Some have said that the greatest Brother during our era was Brother Charles Henry Butterman who later became Superior General. With no aspersions on Charles Henry, I reserve that status for Brother Leo Kirby. Charles Henry didn't even know me and actually confused me with another individual when I left the community in 1970. Brother Leo, on the other hand, invited me to think of myself always as a Brother and remain close to the Institute. I respected his invitation immensely. In later years, I submitted something I wrote to him and solicited his opinion. After reading my text, his summary was, "When sitting down to eat an elephant, it is wise to take small bites." He neither praised nor condemned my essay, but his advice remains vividly in my mind.

One of the reasons I have so much respect for Brother Leo is the conviction that he suffered a great deal from the mass defections of those whom he had supervised. I often wondered whether he blamed himself, but I doubt he did. I think he knew he had done the best job he could. Some of his conferences remain cherished in my mind while some of his cheerleading exposes him to comic analysis. I am sure some of my confreres don't share my hyperbolic esteem for Brother Leo, but I am convinced that most of them have him on some pedestal reserved for major influences in one's life. I had the good fortune of having him as my Director when he was in his prime of life and good health. As he aged, his arthritic limbs brought great grief and pain. When his term as Assistant to the Superior General ended, he humbly served in a capacity as counselor to the troubled and visitor to jails. From the halls of the powerful to the cells of the powerless is a journey few of us could make. Brother Leo Kirby did that, and for that alone, he is worthy of great respect. I am grateful that Pat Murphy and I had the opportunity to visit him at Lincroft. On my last visit, I attended his wake and was sorrowful that I found no one to whom I could relate my tale of admiration for the man. Let these words be his epitaph from me now.

On the third floor each faculty member had a sizeable room with a desk and book shelves that betokened their scholarship. Brother Paul Wilson seemed to have a larger room for he used it as a counseling room. Paul was studying for his doctorate in Clinical Psychology and doing an internship at St. Elizabeth's hospital when we were in asticate. Somehow, he unnerved me and I never wanted close to him. Perhaps I suspected him of psychoanalyzing me without my awareness. I doubt that now since he had greater topics to deal with. Nonetheless, a number of Scholastics did take advantage of his expertise, but as I say, I was wary of him. Once I went to his room following a rumor that he had some very good spiritual reading books available. When I knocked on his door, he was meeting with another Brother and asked me to return in fifteen minutes. After that interval, I did return, and when I mentioned the intent of my meeting, he seemed to judge that I had chickened out at the last minute. He was quite taken aback by my mere mention of spiritual reading book, but he had one that he lent to me and then he prolonged the conversation waiting for me to disclose some profound secret or other. My only ambition was to escape as soon as possible, and he honored that quest without any pressure.

Not all rooms on the third floor were reserved for faculty members for there were a number of accommodations for Scholastics too. These rooms, however, offered space from a minimum of three Brothers to a maximum of five who shared the floor space and a modest closet. At the end of the building above the chapel, there was a minor wing that offered the coolest rooms during the summer heat. I had the good fortune of sharing one with three or four others. Generally speaking, I slept soundly each night attested by the experience of sleeping through a few harrowing shrieks in the middle of the night. Two Brothers, Gregory Hilldebrand and Gus Stapleton, caught almost everyone's attention when each had a nightmare session that induced frayed nerves upon most. As I mentioned, I slept through those episodes, but the morning buzz was fascinating because of the response of some. The prelude to each incident, evidently, was a horrifying scream followed by a dash throughout the corridors where the rooms were. Some of the Brothers themselves panicked when they were abruptly awakened. A few, believing they were fleeing into the corridors, fled instead into their closets where they believed they were being assaulted by their own garments. One fellow was confident that Brother John Regan, a stout hearted, strong man from Highbridge, would save him, but John had disappeared into the closet and was adding his dismay to the din. After the peace was restored, I was awakened by Brother Leo shining a flashlight into my face to check if I were all right. I had no idea what had happened, and neither did either protagonist of the nightmare adventures.

On the fourth floor more rooms served the Brothers and a large chamber was set aside for an infirmary. Generally, one could help himself to the non-prescription drugs available, or to the band aids and gauze pads one might require for minor cuts. This arrangement led to another of my poor judgments. I had a minor chest cold and decided that if a spoonful of medicine was good, a glassful had to be much better. I poured myself a pretty large dose of turpenhydrate, a non prescription cough medicine at the time. With a tumbler full of the heavy codeine laced medicine, I retired to a night of Technicolor dreams and weird visions. In the morning my head was spinning, and I resolved not to follow my personal medical dosages again. Perhaps I balanced that overindulgence with the only other time I helped myself to some medicine. I had a rather upset stomach and sought refuge in bringing up whatever ailed me. I induced my buddy Brian Schwall to accompany me to the bathrooms where I entered a stall and asked him to just turn a bottle of Pepto-Bismol upside down with the cap on. As the pink liquid oozed down the inner part of the bottle, the sight was sufficient to turn my stomach, and I soon had the relief I sought. I remain grateful to Brian to this day for his complicity in resolving one of the longest sieges I had ever had with stomach ailments.

The infirmary was also the scene of a rather comedic performance each evening. Brother John Ferrar had accepted the challenge of weighing in Brother Bartholomew Gerard Gabrieli. Bart weighed over four hundred pounds, and the infirmary scale was inadequate unless adjusted by John. With a counter-balance of adhesive tape rolls, scissors and other gear associated with the medical profession, John was able to escalate the amount that the scale would record. Bart willingly participated in this phase of his quest to lose weight, but he presented an inordinate challenge to John who was designated to keep Bart out of the refrigerator and away from some foods. Bart was more devious than John and his quest for food was omnipresent. I remember seeing Bart in the refrigerator where several hams had been stripped of their fat before cooking. Bart started to wolf down the straight fat until John found him. The tragic irony of the Bart saga ended when he did leave and began a diet. He lost one hundred pounds and then his heart gave out from the success of his starvation.

Each floor of course had bathrooms and showers to accommodate the Brothers. Generally, these were always available since the individuals were on different academic schedules. There was a shoe shining station with foot rests and the necessary polish and brushes on the top floor. Each floor contained cleaning closets for mops and brushes, brooms and other tools required for cleanliness of the facilities. There was also access to the laundry chute where one's dirty clothes and linens were deposited. As I remember, we were allotted one clean sheet a week. This would be added to the top sheet which was then rotated to the bottom while the bottom one was laundered. Our personal items were put into a mesh bag and sealed with a laundry pin similar to the one with which I infected my knee in the Novitiate. These bags of laundry were processed and then returned in a timely fashion. The laundry was down in the basement next to a large boiler room where I can't recall ever entering.

To say the least, the Scholasticate was bulging with vocations in the late fifties and early sixties. So crowded was it and the future so optimistic that expansion seemed imperative. With that in mind we were commissioned from Oakdale to become fundraisers in a major undertaking to add more rooms in a wing attached to the end of the current building. Moreover, our modest chapel was designed to expand into a liturgically correct and modern version of a house of worship. "Honest Bob' Rambusch became the architect and frequent orator who introduced us to the arcane intricacies of liturgical art. 'Honest Bob' rated that appellation for he insisted that all materials had to be honest, or what they purported to be. No simulated stone or wood, no plastic or vinyl, just plain ordinary daily compounds found in nature were to be used. He raved about the shape of refectory tables, although he seemed to talk out two sides of his mouth. Tables could be square because that would symbolize equality and commonality, but then again circular tables were symbolic of eternal perfection, the alleged goal of heaven via the monastery. Actually, the poor man couldn't say much without encountering the skeptics and critics among the Scholastics. Brother Leo expounded on the wonders of the improvements. He boasted that the building would be constructed with a devotion to silence and respect for the meditative reflection of its inhabitants. Therefore, Leo advised us, the light switches would not make any sound when they were turned off or on. That was impressive until they installed paper towel dispensers in the bathrooms that defied the volume of the guillotines of the French Revolution. Instead of tearing off a segment of paper towel, a blade descended with a crescendo of noise severing the paper from the roll. Between silent switches and guillotine paper towel dispensers, the critics had fresh ammunition for discussion.

Throughout our senior year the building took shape with steel girders and brickwork fleshing out the new wing. A committee of advisers was formed, and the Scholastics were represented by Bill Mueller. Brother Austin Gerald who was reassigned from Barrytown was the general overseer and daily inspector of the construction. The chapel seemed to progress faster than the new dorm wing which apparently hadn't lined up perfectly with the older building. A plaque of names honoring those who contributed specific items to the chapel was erected. Into the brick design was etched some modern sculptures and in truth 'Honest Bob's' stained glass windows and chapel benches provided a prayerful atmosphere. Since we were seniors, my group didn't have the opportunity too long to experience the air conditioned chapel nor the new rooms. Like the rest of the Districts, we anticipated that more Scholastics would be accommodated more comfortably for quite a while. Unfortunately, the fate of the Christian Brothers and the repercussions of the Second Vatican Council and its aftermath erased the procession of vocations that characterized the fifties and early sixties. Shortly after the new facilities were opened, the Brothers had to abandoned this 'honest' structure and send the Scholastics far and wide to different colleges, usually in the cities closest to their origin. The Bureau of Mines bought the building and then abused it, leaving it a derelict of what it had been. Recently, it was purchased by a Catholic group who are reinstating it to its original purpose.

Like the Brothers who taught us in Barrytown and Troy, those who were entrusted with our education in Washington seemed an elite breed. As potential teachers we could learn much by emulating their preparation, dedication, and concern for the students. I used to assess their teaching styles and determine what could be used by me and what I might not want to imitate myself. The former far outweighed the latter among the men who taught us. Most of the classes were interesting and the lecturers well informed. Naturally some appealed to me more than others.

Many in my class became devotees of theology thanks to the inspiration and example of our professors. All were studying for some doctoral degree in Sacred Scripture, Sacred Theology, or some such esoteric discipline. Each was an excellent student who mastered his subject matter and presented the information in a concise, clear, consistent manner. Perhaps the greatest of these role models in my opinion was Brother Aloysius Fitzgerald, often called 'The Chink' because of facial features that didn't reflect his origins in the Emerald Isle. Ally Fitz taught us a course in Sacramental Theology implementing the Aristotelian notions of matter and form, essence and existence, popularized in the Middle Ages by Thomas Aquinas. So great was the esteem heaped upon this figurative and literal giant in his *Summa Theologica* that his primary disparagers, chiefly Franciscan followers of Duns Scotus, gave us the English term 'dunce' for those not too heavily endowed intellectually.

Allie often raised the windows in the classroom during the winter with his first principle of education—Keep them cold; keep them awake. While many shivered as a result of his insistence on fresh air during his 8:00am classes, most usually learned to wear a sweater under their robes as protection against old man winter. Allie was a major advocate that every one of his students should study conscientiously, assiduously, and if necessarily, long after lights out. He spoke to me several times for my insistence on taking recreation at every opportunity and lectured me on my duty to perform better academically. I thought I was doing all right, but that didn't stop him from butchering my index rightfully or not. A tribute to my respect for the man, I didn't resent that, but attributed his zeal to my best interest according to his mind. Later Aloysius took his love for Scriptural studies and Semitic languages to the Middle East where he studied in Jerusalem. Caught up in the turmoil and aftermath of the Six Day War, he was so wrapped up in his academic world that when he returned to the United States, he found little comprehension in what had evolved after Vatican II. In my last conversation with him shortly before I left the Brothers in 1970, he was assigned to Manhattan College and asked me to explain what happened to the Order while he was in Jerusalem. I was saddened at his response for despite praising me for being a dedicated Brother during my time, he felt isolated. He exclaimed that as long he had St. Paul as his '*vade mecum*' or constant companion, he would persevere in his vocation no matter what. At his recent death, I mourned the loss of a man who probably was the most serious, dedicated student and scholar I had ever known.

Another very popular theologian who taught us was Brother Timothy Balfe. Tim was quite laid back, athletically inert, but intellectually sharp and sometimes acerbic. Tim taught us a course in Grace and another in Marriage. While the former could be a challenge to lesser minds, Tim enriched his lectures with witticisms and comparisons that kept the students alert and anxious to hear what he might utter next. In the course on Marriage, the content was far more Dennziger than it was practical. I remember hearing about terms like valid and illicit and thought some of the canon laws codified by Dennziger were contradictory if not absolutely irrational. In particular I recall that if one baptized a future spouse, the marriage would be not only illicit but invalid. Marooned on an island, one should find another human being to baptize an intended bride, or so I surmised. After Tim was awarded his honors and advanced degrees, he unfortunately suffered a very debilitating stroke, and I understand he spent many years in a virtual vegetative state, a devastating loss to the individual and to the Institute who encouraged his scholarship. Unlike Allie, Tim could rarely be found taking any form of physical exercise. His famous remark was, "Once I was tempted to exercise, but I went to bed until the temptation passed!" Within the past few months, I have been requested to honor Tim by contributing to a special library within the complex at Narragansett. My modest contribution may help, but it requires many wealthier donors, I think.

During our time in Washington, there were others studying theology, but they didn't teach my class. One of these men was Brother August Thomas. Although he didn't teach us, I remember one of his remarks very plainly. As we were riding the bus over to Catholic University, some of the Brothers were discussing the development of contraception through pills. The Pope had clearly denounced this development, and Tom claimed that the best thing he could have done was shut his mouth for Catholics would ignore his teaching and practice birth control no matter what he said. I suppose history has proven that Tom had the insight and theological knowledge to be aware that no other response was legitimate, but maybe silence might be justified. I hope I do him justice in recalling my version of what he said.

Another theologian who arrived in our senior year was a former track star from Bishop Loughlin. His name was Brother John Greevey. He had a distracting laugh which was supplemented by one of the quickest minds in the Scholasticate, thus meriting the name 'Johnny Ha Ha.' Brother John was especially dangerous while another was reading during meals. His raucous laugh made others stop and take notice of what had just been said. Often the double entendre or some other incongruity had escaped the notice of those eating, but John's suggestive outburst brought attention to the item. If anyone else ever caught a joke faster than 'Johnny Ha Ha,' I couldn't say who. When my class was graduating, I was asked to address the community with a few remarks at a dinner in the refectory. In the course of my thanking the faculty, I referred to their number as, "twenty some odd men." His "Ha Ha" brought attention to my idiom, and the whole refectory then responded with appropriate guffaws.

Brother James Hogan from the Juniorate had a blood brother named William who was working for his doctorate in physics while we were in Washington. Brother William seemed too busy trying to placate the implacable Dr. Herzfeld in winning his PhD to have much time for interaction with the Scholastics. His was a presence, but his academic responsibilities seemed to demand his time more than our attention. Another Brother came from the New Orleans District and studied chemistry at the University of Maryland. His presence, although not so frequent, bore testimony to the broad influence of the Christian Brothers in North America. His daily worship in our chapel reflected the religious aspect of community life among the Brothers.

While the theologians seem to make converts of many in pursuing additional students in the field in later years, I never found the subject matter or the philosophical implications to my taste. I could enjoy the classes, but felt no great attachment to the field. My interest peaked during my undergraduate years, but some in my class determined to pursue graduate work in theology. Dermot O'Sullivan, Brother Cassian Christopher, was particularly bitten by this theological bug. Dermot had settled on a major in biology, but even as an undergraduate, he spent most of his time studying theology instead of botany, anatomy or whatever. As soon as possible, he enrolled in the Theology graduate program at Manhattan College. I never had that interest at all. Perhaps I demanded more active rather than cerebral pursuits.

I have had the excellent fortune of exposure to outstanding history teachers dating back to my elementary days at Incarnation, my time at Manhattan Prep, and of course at Troy. Washington was no different. The American history professor was Brother Raymond Weitekamp. 'Bonnie Ray' presented an outstanding course replete with exemplary notes in a logical sequence. I enjoyed his classes immensely and appreciated his zeal at perpetuating the skills that made him a successful student and teacher. Perhaps a symptom of the organizational, systematic skills associated with the German people, Ray exemplified these attributes a great deal. Those skills fell upon the stubborn ears of one of my classmates. For whatever reason, Tom Smith refused to take notes in class stirring the wrath of Brother Raymond. When he insisted Tom take down certain notes, Tom's stubborn streak emerged. I think none of us was ready for this kind of classroom insubordination, most particularly Brother Raymond. I don't know how the crisis was averted, but I suspect it was through Ray's abandoning his Germanic sense of order and tolerating the minor insurrection. While Tom may not have enjoyed taking notes, I found those notes extremely helpful in preparing for my comprehensives. One of our survey course requirements was a research paper. I chose to write on Al Smith and the Election of 1928. I concluded that the anti-Catholicism of that election would not be a factor in the election of 1960. Technically I was prescient, but I was really surprised by the extent of prejudice that faced John F. Kennedy.

Brother Raymond outlined a system for preparing a term paper that I subsequently used on my projects no matter what level. He advised a central listing of our sources containing all the requisite information for footnotes and bibliography. Then the source would be assigned a number. Anytime I cited that source, I could write on a piece of loose leaf torn in quarters, just the corresponding number, the appropriate page and the quotation. When I had completed my research, I could organize each note into the sequence I wanted and then write the text and complete the footnotes as required.

Brother Raymond offered me an enticement I couldn't refuse. He asked me to accompany him to Philadelphia to help him do some doctoral thesis research on Charles Francis Adams. Of course I readily agreed. I didn't care where we were supposed to go as long as there was a change in schedule. I was disappointed when Ray was able to acquire the necessary information without going to Philadelphia, but I certainly felt flattered by the invitation. After Ray left the Order, he remained teaching at Manhattan College. When he went on his honeymoon, he asked me to replace him for two or three lectures at Manhattan. Again I was flattered to be remembered, and I also enjoyed the opportunity to teach on the college level. Ray died when he was still quite young, but my admiration for his skill and his zeal remain strong.

Another of our professors impressed me with a sense of humor hidden behind his frail body but incisive mind. Brother Joseph Wiesenfarth taught a survey course in British Literature. Together he led us into the works of Keats, some Shakespeare, Pope, Donne, Wordsworth, Byron, Coleridge and Hopkins, and many of the notable authors who used the English language or came from the British Isles. From *Beowulf* to the *Tales of the Green Knight,* the restoration poets, the metaphysical poets, the romantics, and modernists, Brother Joseph's lectures were full of humorous incongruities. The secret to their enjoyment, however, lay in staying awake for his occasional zinger. His monotonous intonations and delivery disguised a very perceptive portrayal of each author's contributions and Joe Wiesenfarth's commentaries. So many times only a few of us captured the allusions he made so frequently, but with so little fanfare that they often fell on distracted ears. I was able to stay awake and interpret his dry paradoxes and satirical analysis to the point where I found him one of the most entertaining teachers in Washington. Most of my peers may not agree with that, however. I still recall the comment he made upon one of my test essays. I had been referring to some epithalamium as a 'bridle' poem so Joe drew a figure on a horse with a noose around his neck. He made his point clearly, effectively, and without any words. I never made that mistake again. Because of his prowess in teaching literature, I was initially happy I had decided to become a major in that discipline until I encountered the dry, insipid preparation required for the comprehensives in that field.

Another admirable teacher from the past was on the staff now in Washington. Brother Amian Bernard Caulfield who taught us French in the Juniorate had been reassigned to the Scholasticate. I forget whether he was getting his doctorate in French or beginning graduate studies in clinical psychology. He was equipped with the title of Pro-Director which placed him somewhere beneath the Sub-Director in the realm of responsibility for the Scholastics. He was entrusted with the job of assuring that each individual was on track for a graduation according to the demands of Catholic University. It was he who permitted me to change my major to American history as long as I also took twelve credits in Modern German. Brother Bernard was a particularly shy individual who usually was reticent to offer any commentary or judgment upon issues that didn't demand his involvement. I was especially aware of his great respect for honesty, integrity, and objectivity. I appreciated these qualities which I had identified in the two years I had the honor to learn under him at Barrytown. After I had left the Brothers as had he, I had crossed paths with him as a consulting psychologist for Westchester Jewish Social Services. Bernard and I had a telephone conference about one of my students. I often wished our paths intersected more often, but he remained the shy, aloof individual he always was. He did enjoy humorous repartee, however, and occasionally joked with those whom he knew could enjoy his verbal sparring. Particularly friendly with Pat Murphy, he used to claim that Pat would be "combing his luxuriant, black hair" with a fork. He often accused Joe O'Brien who probably was the outstanding humorist of our group of being "dumb, but happy." None of these remarks contained any hint of nastiness, for there wasn't an unbecoming bone in his body. After we graduated, Bernard became even more involved in the training of the young Scholastics.

Two former influences were now assigned to Washington. Brother Austin Gerald Fitzgerald, 'Merry Gerry,' math instructor from the Juniorate, was pursuing his doctorate at Catholic University in mathematics. Since I hadn't any math classes, I did not have any opportunity to sample his expertise in higher math. As in Barrytown, he continued to employ his maintenance skills in the building at large. Joining the faculty at De La Salle was Brother Bernardine Kevin Hargadan, the nemesis of our class in Hillside Hall. As far as I can determine, BBK was always unique in his scholarship. I believe he might have been the only young Scholastic permitted to major in Philosophy as an undergraduate. He had eclectic interests and apparently chemistry was no longer among his ambitious plans. Now he was enrolled in a doctoral program in Clinical Psychology. He was often in contact with his battle weary veterans from Troy, and when I was in charge of the waxing crew, I even enticed him on a few occasions to join us in cleaning the refectory floor on Saturday evenings. As usual, he was an exemplary worker and a fascinating conversationalist. His sense of the finer arts of music and art led to his assuming a decorator's role in the painting of the refectory. The end product reflected his tastes more so than most of the Brothers. He chose an alternating color scheme of Evergreen and Watermelon red. On one of the walls he hung an avant-garde, abstract sculpture. Many of us were accustomed to a room being painted in a single color, but we learned something new under the creative genius of BBK.

From my days playing baseball for Incarnation's team, another friend from the past emerged. Brother Robert Laube was enrolled in a doctoral theology program too. The soft-spoken coach we respected from the days on the diamond taught us the intricacies of the Horatian Odes and Epodes. A second course examining the essay of Cicero's *De Amicitia* was not so fascinating a topic but just as challenging because of the sentence structure and classical convoluted grammar. Brother Robert was a thoughtful teacher and a man who recognized the efforts we put into translating and interpreting these works. Horace was particularly interesting to me, but providing a fluid translation was one of the major challenges presented by his style. Trying to maintain the literal sense of the language while rephrasing its essence into English was the burden of our translations. Our sometimes comical efforts offered an insight into the perplexities of those who translate classical works into respectable English. The task is greater than any description I can offer.

Brother Aelred Dowd was in charge of liturgy and music while we were Scholastics. Many of his own hymns had been notated into music published under his *nom de plume*, Brother Chrisbro. Aelred was getting his doctorate in sacred music and like Brother James from Barrytown, he loved the strains of Gregorian chant and the interpretation of the monks of Solesme. The melodic chant and its sophisticated rising and falling metric systems created a hypnotic beauty that enhanced all the singing. Polyphonic Masses were generally reserved for special Christmas or Easter celebrations. The hymns were sung with an avid attention to diction and rhythms. Traditional music associated with the Institute was a hallmark of 'Chrisbro.' Aelred was also in charge of the meager resources of the library books. Although he may have been among the older members of the faculty, he was one of the consistent basketball players on our recreation field. He had more than adequate athleticism to supplement his musical talents. Neither asking no quarter nor yielding any, he performed rather well in the combat sessions down on the college basketball or handball courts.

The youngest faculty member as far as I could judge was a Brother a few years older than us. Brother Brice Patrick Brown was assigned to the Scholasticate as Econome, or the individual responsible for planning menus and purchasing food and household goods. Pat also held the enviable position of organizing and distributing assignments of automobiles, buses and trucks. Most of the Brothers who wanted driving assignments had to appease his sense of competence as well assurance of academic eligibility. Many of the contestants for driving opportunities monitored his selections very scrupulously in the fear that somehow they weren't getting their share of trips. This was particularly true for driving the bus. Often the chauffeurs of the buses were limited by their academic schedules more than anything. Some trips to the university had numerous eligible drivers while others had few or none. Pat's job was to be fair as well as reasonably judicious. Sometimes the driver would take a round trip, or the bus might be parked in a huge lot near the history office. Perhaps the kind of job Pat performed is in an evaluation of his ability to plan and guarantee meals that appealed to the multitudes and satisfied the minorities. I believe he was so successful doing that so that I don't recall any real griping about either the meals or their service.

In my senior year the faculty welcomed another individual who had entered the Brothers after teaching at Manhattan College. Brother Pat McGarry was about as intellectual as anyone I met. His interests were broad and his knowledge profound. Unlike most of the Scholastics, he had an intense love of music, art, the performing arts, and other pursuits sometimes deemed effete by the less informed. Whenever I had reason to converse with him, I recognized his unique gifts and felt somewhat awed in his presence. He had an uncanny gift of cutting to the essence of an argument and the instinct to point out untenable positions. One didn't make any rash statements or draw inane conclusions without expecting a reply that incorporated remedial logic or advanced data processing. Unfortunately this very talented historian who taught me in the graduate school at Manhattan in an excellent class in Modern European history died much too young. I had decided to write a term paper on *The Burschnshaften Conference in 1817—An Evolutionary Stage in German Nationalism*. Even though he praised my intelligence and authorized my pursuing a doctorate in American history, my essay didn't escape his honest appraisal. I remember his written comments, "I had missed the forest because of the trees." Many times I think of that assessment and recognize its candor and unadorned criticism. Pat was like that, but no one can claim they were pilloried without cause. At one point under his chairmanship of the history department at Manhattan, he had changed the requirements for a master's degree. Instead of comprehensives and thesis, Manhattan retained the comprehensives, but it permitted a substitution of three major papers for the thesis. When I submitted my three papers, Pat analyzed them and pronounced them fit. Nonetheless, he had an accurate criticism to make. Pat declared that the papers I wrote earlier in my education were better than those I had written later. Perhaps I might have explained that in my earlier days I had more time and opportunity for research and composition, but no doubt Pat would have remarked that I was using an unwarranted alibi. My admiration for his intellect is limitless, but my wariness of his honesty and appraisal evoked a sense of intimidation in me.

Completing the faculty were two elder Brothers who comprised the remainder of the permanent Scholasticate staff. Brother Azarias Gabriel Maher, called the 'Dean,' was an elderly icon who seemed to enjoy virtual adoration from Brother Leo. Originally from Chicopee, Massachusetts, he represented a time and place long abandoned by the Brothers. The Dean had been associated with the Scholasticate for more years than one can predicate with any degree of accuracy. He was a devoted Brother with a kind word for all and an almost childlike trust of all. The Dean was very small and fragile and two hearing aids led to a less than imposing aura. Perhaps it was his devotion to the Institute or his long standing experience within the order, but Brother Leo always treated him with a deference seldom presented to others. The Director always spoke of the Dean in reverential terms reserved for the already canonized. The Dean seemed to enjoy contact with the younger Brothers, especially when groups were assigned to what was called section walk after meals. Unfortunately, his hearing was severely limited and practically the only thing I recall his uttering was, "What's that you say Brother?" I suspect he may also have had an ill-fitting set of dentures because he spoke softly between clenched teeth. I do remember another aphorism offered by this paradigm of religious perseverance and humility. When the faculty enjoyed a pre-dinner libation on Sundays, the Dean always muttered that "It made a man walk with conscious dignity!" I thought that an apt description of the minor influence of alcohol and have taken it as my own on those occasions when I am particularly concerned that my imbibing may have transcended my ability to absorb the dynamic fluid. The Dean's quiet gait to and from the chapel, the dining room, or to his room was an ideal for those heavy of foot.

There was another elderly Brother who had a long term association with the Scholasticate, but his status seemed less revered. Brother Claudius James was a man who had the deadpan presentation of Jack Benny and an exquisite sense of timing in the delivery of his remarks. 'Jimmy Claude,' as he was identified, thought of himself as a consummate violinist and felt obliged to share his talent with the Scholastics and faculty of De La Salle College. For this contribution he was also termed 'Jimmy the Fiddler.' In truth, Jimmy Claude may have had multiple talents, but they were not in the realm of violin recitals. That didn't deter the young monks, for whenever Jimmy Claude entered upon the stage a whistling, stomping, clapping audience greeted him exuberantly. He was happy to acknowledge the outstanding ovation with his dead pan face and speak in his unique French Canadian accent. Jimmy Claude seemed to accent the wrong syllable of words and his slow speech almost made one conclude he was translating into English from another language. This attribute only led to what we interpreted as a comedic pause. After one particularly enthusiastic welcome, Jimmy Claude raised his violin and bow and produced a screech somewhere between the howling of an alley cat and the dissonant sound of chalk scraping on a blackboard. Despite this inauspicious beginning, he then continued his recital until he abruptly stopped. While his audience remained spellbound, Jimmy the Fiddler intoned in his peculiar style, "I cannot go on. I broke my G String." I doubt the entertainer knew why such an announcement induced a degree of hilarity rarely heard in the halls of academia.

As far as I can ascertain, Brother Leo didn't reserve any high spot in the pantheon of Christian Brother paragons for Jimmy Claude. I recall one of his comments uttered to no one in particular. Apparently, Jimmy the Fiddler was in charge of the mail that entered the Scholasticate. His job was sorting and distributing the mail which, by the way had to be read by the Director first. After one contretemps in the Director's office, he was heard to comment in his very idiosyncratic style, "You do the Institute a favor, and what do you get?—a kick in the ass." Evidently, Jimmy the Fiddler had a minor stash of coins and when one envelope arrived with postage due, he paid the minor pittance from his illicit patrimony. He then approached Brother Leo and insisted upon repayment. Leo gave him a sermon on the vow of poverty and the ban on private funds and refused to replenish the small sum Jimmy Claude had invested in expediting mail. That led to his muttering about a "kick in the ass."

While we were in our senior year, Jimmy the Fiddler was honored with a Golden Jubilee dinner catered by *Avignon Freres*, a fancy food purveyor that enhanced celebrations like graduations and particularly eventful commemorations. As the main honoree, Jimmy the Fiddler was offered the opportunity to comment on his vocation and devotion to the Brothers. Again his peculiar accent and impeccable timing enriched his monologue. Jimmy began by notifying all that he was forced to leave the Institute when he was a young Novice. There was some illness in his family, and he was summoned home to help out somewhere in the hills of New England. In Jimmy's succinct presentation he proclaimed in very terse statements. "So I left. So I did not drink. I did not smoke. I did not go out with girls. So I came back!" The Fiddler had summarized his fifty years in twenty-three monosyllabic words in the time frame that an ordinary speaker might have read Lincoln's *Gettysburg Address*. Unlike the Dean, Jimmy Claude rarely indulged the Scholastics with his presence on section walks after meals.

One of the more interesting facets about De La Salle College was its magnetism for international representatives from around a world in revolution or development. One Brother arrived unannounced unexpectedly with only the clothes on his back. He had taught in a Brother's school in Cuba, and since Fidel Castro's successful ouster of Batista and his cronies in 1958, the revolution brought to completion by Fidel had definitely taken a turn leftward. It was clear to most that the future of Cuba now would be as a Communist society. This Brother fled along with multitudes of refugees and somehow ended in Miami as so many did. How he traveled north to Washington, I don't know. I do know he arrived in the Scholasticate with no baggage, no identification other than an intimate thorough knowledge of the Brothers. He was offered shelter and food under those circumstances. Within a few days, he began to receive cryptic telephone calls, always prefaced by his self-effacing, "Who would want to speak with me?" While we didn't eavesdrop, his telephone conversations in Spanish would assume a frenetic pace and tone for some time. Later we deduced that he may have been involved in the Bay of Pigs, but that is only supposition. At the end of the year he was assigned to La Salle Second Street where the mysterious telephone calls continued, or so I am informed.

While Cuba clearly had a dictator leading it into the Communist bloc, the central African states had a more unpredictable fate. French Equatorial Africa and the Belgian Congo sent emissaries to our Scholasticate. One, a Belgian chemistry teacher from the University of Leopoldville, spoke at length to us about the revolution, Patrice Lumumba, and the newly formed Kinsasha and Zaire. He claimed that he had been stopped at a roadblock by one faction or another. He was ordered out of a car and stood up against a wall to be shot immediately. Fortunately for him, one of the riflemen was a former student of his, and he intervened and saved his life. In his description of Zaire and the confusion of revolution and counter-revolution, he spoke only highly of the Belgians who were civilized while everyone else was somewhere below the chain of being. I never heard such a racist description before or since, and I suspect that the revolutionaries had had enough evidence of colonialism to harbor great resentments toward him.

A group of College students from French Equatorial Africa accompanied by a Brother also visited our Scholasticate. The six students entertained us with a selection of native songs and French standards, and then joined us in celebrating the Feast Day of John Baptist De La Salle. While their singing was first rate, their knowledge of American cuisine was somewhat lagging. I observed one of the singers helping himself to a generous dollop or two of straight mayonnaise. For dessert, several options of ice cream were served in their original containers. Seeing many of the Scholastics scoop portions of vanilla ice cream into bowls, he attempted to do the same, but he confused the mayonnaise condiment with the dessert. My conscience plagued me on whether I should alert him, but my cowardice won out. I did note that he consumed the mayonnaise without hesitation and probably thought its taste was unique, but typical of American food. The presence of these singers reinforced the notion that the Christian Brothers had a world wide presence, even in some unexpected places. Revolutions and insurrections, nationalism and colonialism collided right in our refectory and commonroom.

Perhaps an even greater example of international intrigue lay in the personality of Brother Tom Tai who was teaching in Hanoi at the beginning of American involvement in Vietnam. Tom Tai was a very pleasant, round faced, gregarious individual whose English was quite good. He spoke of his escape from North Vietnam. His family was imprisoned by Ho Chin Minh's men, and he was ordered to give a series of lectures to the villages throughout Vietnam. He had some pictures of his family, and I particularly remember a portrait of a beautiful young girl wearing the traditional *ao dai*. She was Tom Tai's sister and one of the guarantees that he would do the bidding of the communist government. Tom maintained he continued to preach the company line until he reached an area near South Vietnam controlled by President Ngu. Tom defected across the border where he presumably came into contact with CIA agents who had him sent to America. Periodically, a huge limousine would approach the driveway to the Scholasticate, and Tom Tai was whisked away for a conference with Robert Kennedy, we were to learn later. I believe Tom knew of the plot to kill President Diem Nhu before he was killed, but I don't know that for sure. The assassinated man's wife, Ngo Dinh Nhu, called 'The Dragon Lady' in the American press, claimed that "With friends like the United States, one didn't need enemies." I believe Tom wasn't a revolutionary, but was an honest man trying to make head or tail of an incomprehensible system which later became the quagmire of American politics and military strategy called the Vietnamese War.

Another character that came to the Scholasticate and remained for a long period was named Brother Flavian. He claimed that he had also lost his documentation and identification papers when he left a country then called Ceylon. Although it was said later that he was actually an imposter, he was honored with the name Brother Flavian when he was in Washington. He was a spellbinding speaker in an eerie way. Brother Flavian spoke of his participation in several exorcisms when he was in Ceylon where he characterized evil as more personal and physical than in the west. At these exorcisms he was generally a participant who offered his strength to restrain the victim of possession of the devil. Flavian had a hypnotic manner in describing how the principals could speak in tongues and languages unknown to the exorcist or himself. His huge, black eyes were orbs of terror as he mentioned their incomprehensible strength. I suppose his verbal climax was his description of sudden rain squalls and lightning strikes to prove that the demon had been dispossessed. His earnest demeanor and obvious reticence to discuss these events added to his credibility and our gullibility. He also narrated tales with morals to them. One referred to the individual who sought a dispensation from the Brothers, and with the papers clutched in hand, he was killed by a taxi immediately outside the Brothers' residence. I don't confess to know my confreres' judgment, but Flavian convinced me of his sincerity if not of the physical evidence of evil.

We played host to at least two South Americans. Brother Mariano came from Colombia. I was asked to drive him downtown and help him select an appropriate wardrobe, not exactly my forte, but Mariano needed little sartorial advice. Mariano had sufficient funds which I believe were the result of some educational grant. For a man who confessed ignorance about our monetary system, clothing styles, fashions and so forth, Mariano didn't need any advice from me. He was way ahead of me. I don't recall what he was studying, but he was constantly on the move from De La Salle to places unknown. The other man from South America was not a Brother at all. The only name I knew him by was Jaime from Araquippa, Peru. He was a member of the Third Order of St. Francis and practiced poverty to an exemplary degree. His simplicity and straightforward honesty were admirable. I think he was like the apostles of old, sent out on a mission with just the sandals on their feet. Despite knowing little about Jaime, I was impressed with his character, his humble demeanor, and his sincerity.

Occasionally, we had visitors from Australia, England, Ireland or another of the many countries where the Brothers had foundations. We used to refer to The Canadian Club who were Brothers that came from Canadian schools to enhance their educations in the United States. Most spoke French Canadian and were quite well off financially. I understand that the government pays teachers in Canada and the stipend offered the Brothers was significantly higher than any income American Brothers had. The term 'Canadian Club' also referred to their recreational preferences, for the beer budget of American monks couldn't compete with the whiskey options for our visitors from the north.

In the near future we would hear more about Africa as the monks started to staff schools in Haile Selassie's Ethiopia in Asmara and Addis Ababa. The Brothers learned about Kenya, and Tanzania where more mission schools were established. In a few years some of the current Scholastics would journey to these countries and provide services of many kinds. One of my classmates, Jimmy Jordan, remains to this day serving as headmaster at St. Mary's School in Kenya.

One country where the Brothers had been established with an American connection for many years was the Philippines. Dating back to the American involvement after the Spanish American War and the battles against Aquinaldo's rebels, American Brothers had staffed De La Salle College in Manila. One of the Brothers from New York had been bayoneted and left for dead in the college chapel when the Japanese evacuated Manila under the onslaught of Mac Arthur's promise, "I shall return." Besides the university in Manila, the Brothers conducted a school in Bacolod. Two young Filipino Brothers came to Washington to continue their studies. Brother Alvario Sixto was a short, bespectacled man who had a great love of baseball. He was also what some Scholastics called an 'operator,' a person who manipulated assignments and opportunities to his advantage. Joe O'Brien nicknamed Brother Sixto 'Five-0' for his speedy operations. Sixto apparently came from a very well-to-do family in Manila. Their kindness and Brother Leo's sense of hospitality provided an opportunity unique in our Scholastic experience. Sixto's family sent a number of cases of San Miguel, a popular Filipino beer, to help us celebrate Christmas. Alcohol, whether beer, wine, or hard spirits, was never served to the 'young Brothers,' and I had the impression that the faculty didn't see much of it either. For this occasion, however, we were rationed a bottle of the suds which most pronounced very delicious. At the time I didn't drink any spirits at all, so I can give no evaluation about the beer's finer points.

Another individual who made an outstanding impression upon the Scholastics was Brother Andrew Benjamin Gonzalez. His affable personality was clearly discernible on his round smiling face with a perpetual grin beneath curious eyes in a head resting upon a rotund body. Brother Benjamin was a gentle, unassuming young man whose talents were not so evident, for his pleasant visage concealed an absolutely brilliant mind and generous heart. He seldom seemed busy with his own pursuit of a graduate degree in English. In fact, one could deduce that he had no academic responsibilities by merely observing the assistance he offered everyone else in demand for his skills. One of his outstanding gifts was a world class typing ability. His flying digits inerrantly flew across the keyboard of the typewriters available to the Scholastics in a special typing classroom. Benjamin would often offer his skill to assist one of us delayed in completing a paper or thesis. I don't know, but I doubt whether he made any corrections upon the text, but his speed was renowned and his accuracy unchallenged. He earned the awesome respect of those of us who witnessed him typing his master's thesis directly from his brilliant mind to the keyboard without consulting any notes or taking any respite. While many of the Brothers were gifted intellectually, I can't think of another who could duplicate this feat. At the service of so many others while cruising through his own responsibilities, Andrew Benjamin gave little hint of what he was to become. In recent months, I read his untimely obituary from an esteemed newspaper published in Manila. Andrew Benjamin had become a major contributor to the educational world of the Philippines. This child of humble origin with his magnificent talents had become a national hero for his work at De La Salle College in Manila and his achievements for the national government's work in the entire country. Perhaps what the obituary couldn't cite were this man's humility, charity, and generosity that earned him the admiration of those of us who knew him in Washington in his youth.

Supplementing the international flavor of De La Salle College, we had the bicoastal perspective of some Scholastics from California. Brother Ulbertian Bertin was a short, taciturn, bespectacled English major who had attended St. Mary's College in Maraga, California. He came east and brought with him some of the aura of the Golden West. Bertin went about his business in a quiet, unobtrusive way despite the fame that came with this distant youth. A more gregarious individual who measured six feet ten inches tall from his toes to the tip of his blond crew cut, Brother Nathaniel Martin came from Maraga. While members of the college basketball team salivated at the prospect of his playing for the Scholasticate against perennial foes like the candidates from Xaverian College, the 'Gypsies' from the Salesians and the seminarians from Trinity College and the Paulists, Nat seemed disinterested in most sports. What captured his interest was music. He was a very talented drummer who played the real thing as well as imaginary sets during most of his waking moments. His love for music was probably the most outstanding feature of this pleasant man. His conversation and preoccupation with all things rhythmic characterized the time he spent with us, but he nonetheless managed to make many friends and add an entertainment feature into our class.

Our class celebrated the arrival of some new blood. From the Novitiate we received the contemplative, budding intellectual called Brother Jasper or Ray Smith, a physics major who had begun at Manhattan College. Ray changed his major to English literature and was frequently in quest of 'the eternal verities.' When challenged to defend some of his untenable opinions about writers or even politics, he sought refuge in his statement, "Don't you believe in the eternal verities?" After he left the monks, he emigrated to Australia where he taught in college and became somewhat of a noted published poet, giving credence to his claim to poetic genius. Having shared some classes with the budding philosopher, I was very pleased to note his great success 'down under.' Coming from Yonkers, he had a great interest in sports, especially basketball. As the president of the Jock and Sneaker Club, I often welcomed him in friendly games on the courts of De La Salle College.

We had our numbers augmented by a few Brothers who came from the Novitiate group one year before us. Jimmy Zmich, the gifted saxophonist, switched into majoring in biology and had to spend an additional year in acquiring the necessary credits. He had company in the person of Mike McCausland, a fellow graduate of Incarnation and an 'original' from the Juniorate. Mike and I shared German class. His intellectual acumen was somewhat camouflaged by the Washington Heights accent he seemed to possess in greater amounts than I did. Mike's height made him practically the equivalent of a redshirted basketball player, for the team enjoyed his prowess one more year than it might have anticipated. After graduating with his biology degree, he pursued his doctorate in Clinical Psychology and taught at Manhattan College, first as a Brother, and then as a layman after he left and married. Another member of that prior Novitiate group joined us when Brother Alfred Bernardine, Neil Walsh, switched and entered American history. Neil worked in the garage for a number of years and was a fine example of what La Salle Troy could send to the monks. He had a great sense of humor, but often demonstrated it to the greatest degree when we used to tease him about a number of things.

Most of the course work for a degree from Catholic University was demanding, but not exorbitantly so. Organization and a modicum of persistent study generally satisfied whatever preparation I needed for my classes—a great contrast to the frustrating experience I had with chemistry in Troy. Maybe because I was concentrating on material I enjoyed, I found the courses generally informative and productive toward my goal of becoming a teacher myself. One of the disciplines I didn't fall in love with was philosophy. In my sophomore year we took logic and epistemology taught by Brother Celestine Paul Wilson. I had the sense that he brought little preparation to his classes and relied on his impressive array of minutiae and information rather than organization, even in such a structured discipline as logic.

Many of his classes ultimately ended up as descriptions of the head cases he dealt with in his practicum in St. Elizabeth's mental hospital. One of his field trips, however, marked an experience that I appreciated and carried with me throughout my life. After urging us to keep a door between us and any inmate, and reminding us that the clients had poor sanitary habits, he advised us to wash our hands frequently. He wisely cautioned us about getting into any prolonged conversations with clients since we might say something that triggered a psychotic response.

One of his first interviews was with an idiot savant who could memorize the numbers on a full train of box cars. When asked to give a description of his current residence, he launched into a minute, detailed outline of the windows. He accounted for the number of window panes, their dimensions and placement and several other statistics that a normal person either wouldn't know or wouldn't care to divulge. Apparently, this individual knew he wasn't mentally balanced, but in order to appear so, he cited so many details that only demonstrated his imbalance. After this recital, we were treated to another inmate who described how to clean a car. He advised the use of a brick to rub the dirt (and the paint, incidentally) off the car. He would become violent when any individual whose car he had selected for this treatment objected. He vehemently claimed his mail and letters to John F. Kennedy were stolen and never delivered. He harbored the hope that if Kennedy only knew of his incarceration, he would insist this man be released immediately. A paranoia about this maltreatment became evident when he began a tirade against those who were persecuting him unjustly.

One of the quietest individual's interviewed was a young woman who claimed to have been raped by Nelson Rockefeller nine years ago. She awaited the delivery of his child ever since. According to her mood, she would respond to an impetus sent to her by her mother. The mother insisted on sending her a common candy at the time called Chocolate Babies, a small, sugary confection shaped like a gingerbread man. When she was calm, she would wrap the candies in tiny blue blankets and croon to them as if they were the offspring she so long anticipated. This was in her catatonic state. At other times, when agitated, she would bite the heads off the chocolate babies and toss them out a window and attempt to join them in a suicide leap. We didn't witness her in her aggressive, suicidal stage, but her virtually inaudible responses and faraway stare gave evidence and credibility to Brother Paul's description.

We heard a man with genius IQ who only agreed to speak to us because we were college students. Assured we had some intellectual credential, he opted to enlighten us about the intricacies of escutcheons and symbolism of nobility and their respective Coats of Arms. He gave us a stimulating lecture on heraldry and the First Families of Virginia. His lecture was fascinating but ended abruptly when queried why he was in St. Elizabeth's. He too was a paranoid, but his enemy was the common man who resented his nobility and genteel background as one of the descendants of the great families of Virginia. At one point, Brother Paul looked ready to abandon the room and lead us to safety. Apparently his surge of rage subsided as quickly as it had arisen.

There was another client who had delusions of grandeur. He claimed to have had a series of visions in which Mary, the mother of Jesus, had appeared to him. Many mystics may have had the same boast, but this man's were pornographic, since Mary allegedly entered his body through every orifice he could cite and describe in detail. She had ordered him to convert the world and this is what he was attempting to do with us, his audience. When Brother Paul deemed his graphic description enough evidence, he requested the mystic to change the topic. The man rose to his full six foot five height and announced in menacing tones, "You're interrupting my mission." Paul wisely suggested the man continue until he relaxed, sat back and continued his preaching.

What all this had to do with logic, I can't say, but it was one of the most impressive episodes of my educational career. In epistemology,

or the philosophical exploration of our ability to know, I remem.
Paul demonstrating how our senses, through which we apparently
learn everything, could be deluded. He mentioned the common
event of watching a boiling pot and then touching the individual
with ice. Our visual sense overrides our sense of touch. He spoke
of placing an orange under one's nose and feeding the test object
a slice of pear instead. The sense of smell seemed to overcome the
sense of taste. He spoke of specialized glasses in which everything was
rotated to its opposite position. Up was down and left was right. After
wearing these unusual glasses, the mind turned everything around to
a rational position. When the glasses were removed, the mind had to
readjust to reality. I suppose the real challenge to epistemology was
to understand how a physical object could become a mental image
in a generic sense and then be translated by the brain into a specific
object. For example, he mentioned that the senses perceive a piece
of furniture, determine its essence, and then by the application
of Aristotelian accidentals determine not only the essence of the
image, but its specific definition. One perceives an object, analyzes
it rather quickly, decides its essence is desk and then defines it as
an end table.

When I went to the University, I took a class in Thomistic
Metaphysics taught by a rapid speaking professor called Father
Whipple. Frankly, if Paul Wilson made little sense of epistemology and
logic, Father Whipple's only contribution to me had something to
do with existence limited by essence, substance by accident, potency
by act. Perhaps that may be summarized, at least in my recollection
that as long as something was pure existence or pure potency, it
could be anything. Once it became something with accidents or
essence it was limited. For example, once a tree was a tree, it could
no longer be a rock. My next course at the University was much more
interesting. I took a course in the history of philosophy, which I could
describe as a survey course of all philosophy. I enjoyed this course,
and it made more sense to me than the more ethereal philosophical
explorations.

One of the special delights of this class was the appearance of
students from the Speech and Drama Department. For the S and D
majors, every entrance into a class was an exercise in self-indulgent
preening. I truly suspect that the girls especially deliberately waited
for the class to begin. They would then throw open the door

and sashay into the classroom with an affected greeting for the accumulated fans. I can't speak for the professor, but I found their grand, histrionic entrances delightful entertainment.

In my first year attending classes at Catholic University, Dr. John Farrell, one of the pre-eminent professors in American history was awarded a sabbatical in the second semester. In the first semester he presided over what was called Reading List, a carefully culled topical exploration into a number of debatable issues in American history. The one I remember most was the causes of the Civil War. I was especially taken with the notion that our nation, almost one hundred years into its existence was comprised of two incompatible cultures, generally described as the Cavaliers in the South and the Roundheads in the North. On more than one level this was a rational and tenable explanation that secondarily viewed slavery, the tariff, expansion into the west, economic determinism, as well as a vacuum of leadership as contributory causes. Accustomed to dealing with history as a repository of facts and data rather than debatable points, I was totally agog about the possibilities in reading.

'Bo' Farrell, as we called him, was very knowledgeable and guided our reading carefully. He assigned a major term paper, and I got involved in a study of the Impeachment of Andrew Johnson. I investigated as many sources as I could conceivably find in the Mullen Library, and discovered one of the nasty facts of research. As soon as one completes his research, someone else publishes another point of view and argues for a different interpretation. Despite my wish to continue reading *ad infinitum*, time and happenstance demanded that I call a halt to reading and start writing. Techniques that Ray Weitekamp taught us in the previous year were invaluable in organizing the text and footnotes. I was ready to write a book about the colorful characters that had even peripheral roles in the impeachment trial. Federal generals smitten by Vinnie Ream, a sculptress working in the Capitol, greedy Northern politicians, opportunistic Congressmen from the West, negotiating to admit additional states to the Union, unproven allegations of sexual and economic misconduct as well as Johnson's ill-advised gulp of Schnapps before addressing Congress, and psychological ploys to prevent Senators from voting on impeachment all contributed to what would make an excellent epic movie if not an endless television series. In addition 'Bo' Farrell taught us a course in American

Colonial history. It was interesting and thorough as most of his courses would prove to be.

In the second semester when he went on Sabbatical, a retired professor from Yale replaced him. Dr. A.B. Darling had written a book entitled **Our Rising Empire**, a complete and interesting exposition on colonial America. I remember his personal quirks too. Dr. Darling never taught so many religious garbed individuals in Yale, and he seemed hypnotized by the fact that we had studied for one year in Troy. The American history class was probably eighty per cent Christian Brothers with a few Xaverian Brothers supplementing the black robed presence. Among his students were only two women named Galloway and Kilheiffer. Approximately one or two lay men and a few graduate students completed the roster. Dr. Darling would preface his lectures with "Men of Troy . . . . and Miss Galloway," omitting Judy Kilheiffer. Then he would invite us to sit on the Potomac or the Mississippi or Cape Fear or wherever he was lecturing about. He seemed to love to run off the names of Indian tribes like 'Cherokee, Chickasaw, Choctaw, and Creek." I suppose he omitted the Seminoles for the Floridas weren't part of the thirteen colonies at the time. His lectures were always stimulating, and I determined that my decision to become an American history major was the right thing for me.

In the second semester, Bo's reading class was taken over by a young, beautiful, newly minted doctorate from the University of Maryland. Her name was Dr. Welter, and she too was an inspiring teacher. Dr. Welter seemed confused as to how she should address these mostly young religious, with two laymen, one Bob Gill and the other a somewhat dishevel person who was trying to maintain a job, acquire a BA, and support a family simultaneously. This class had only one female, the girl from North Carolina named Judy Kilheiffer. Judy had become engaged to a graduated senior who was in the Air Force and always felt comfortable among those of us sworn to be chaste. Nonetheless, we did kid Vinny Callahan when he insisted on moving up closer to Dr. Welter's desk so he could hear better. Most of us suspected Vinny's eyesight was challenged by the beautiful gams crossed and uncrossed by the professor, and he needed a clearer view. For her part, Dr. Welter asked Tom Mamara, Brother Andrew Urban, how she should address him. She said, "Do I call you Andrew, or can I be real friendly and call you Urbsie." His response was more blushing and embarrassment than vocal.

Our beautiful, young Reading List professor was replaced the following year by another woman who probably was her antithesis. Sister Marie Carolyn Klinkhammer, OP, was a middle aged, brilliant but an obstinate, opinionated tyrant. Despite her dazzling grasp of American history and encyclopedic knowledge, her major contribution to our class seemed to be in the realm of language. The placid demeanor one may associate with a nun was readily shattered by an intemperate use of idiom that evoked the wrath of a demigod who used her podium to launch a belittling, deriding attack on the poor miscreant. If someone confused the correct usage of the verbs 'may' and 'can,' a tirade of epic proportions could be expected. Worst still, if a Brother used the conversational pronoun 'you' where an impersonal 'one' was preferred, Sister Gothica, as I liked to think of her, would assail the offender far beyond reason. Her ridicule and scorn would leave the errant one in a state of gross embarrassment. Perhaps her greatest display of righteous indignation and outright fury was reserved for the person who uttered the idiomatic phrase, "I tend to think." Sister Gothica would start her diatribe on a lower tone and work herself into a maniacal display of rage. She would loudly exclaim that one can think or not think, but that it was impossible to 'tend to think.'

In one of her seminar sessions, I rashly, but earnestly, inquired whether the Southern accent was primarily a result of the African influence upon the slaveholders or whether the aristocratic southerners had evolved from the speech patterns evident throughout the other American colonies. Sister Klinkhammer quickly stifled my intellectual curiosity by accusing me of attempting to roil the waters of her celestial, cerebral, idyllic vision of academia by descending into a farce associated with the nether world. While the students may claim to have learned American history and being very careful about expressing themselves verbally in her class, Sister Klinkhammer ultimately suppressed any enthusiastic response or intellectual curiosity. That didn't seem to upset her in any way, because she still had autocratic control over the seminar. The timid refused to question the expert, and that was fine with her.

In fulfilling my requirement to take two years of German, I found myself separated from most of my fellow classmates. Typically, when lay students dominated the class roster, someone would despairingly cry out at the sight of a Brother entering for the first session. Their

jeremiad, "Arrgh! Black robed Curve raisers!" was actually a mid̶d̶
accolade to the reputation of the Christian Brothers as solid students.
In my first year of German, I attended a class with Mike McCausland.
Our teacher was a Mrs. Melnor who had a pronounced German
accent and obviously little experience in teaching the language. She
summarized the highpoints of German grammar by insisting that
"The wowel hoops in the wehicle" explained it all. Translated that
meant that the verb *"einkommen"* would evolve into *"Kommen sie ein."*
My only recollection of the class was when a fellow student named
Rita Downy engaged me in conversation while Mrs. Melnor called
the roll. When she got to my name, I was preoccupied and didn't
respond. Mike was shouting, "He's here. I know he's here," when I
finally came to my senses. Although the course was taught according
to the audio-lingual approach popular at the time, I missed the
grammatical style I knew from French and German. The lab work
only induced snores when I listened to the tapes.

In my second year of German, John Hannaway was in my class,
and we had a new professor, Herr Schacher. On his first day in class
Herr Schacher looked the epitome of the Germanic master race. He
looked well over six feet with blue eyes and blond hair and erect,
aristocratic carriage. His accent was clipped and precise which also
added to his image. Upon closer view, his six feet shrank to about
five foot nine. John and I grew to enjoy his classes, and he accepted
John's invitation to join us for some festivity at De La Salle College.
Herr Schacher was not German at all but from the German speaking
canton of Switzerland.

Part of my joyful selection of courses involved participation
in English classes knowing that I didn't have to take English
comprehensives at the end of my senior year. I chose a course
in Romantic Poets taught by one of the legends of the English
department. Giovanni Giovanini had the posture of nobility and the
air of aristocracy. He was very slender and always impeccably dressed.
Above his tailored suits, his head seemed larger in proportion to his
thin torso, and atop his head he had a lush growth of white hair.
His appearance and mien earned him the designation of 'Duck on
a Broomstick.' He was reputed to have entrusted his son to some
tutoring by Xaverian Brothers until he found a **MAD** comic on a table
in a waiting room at Xavierian College. He immediately withdrew his
son from such influences despite the well deserved reputation for

scholarship that the Xaverians had warranted. He was incidentally, an excellent teacher who measured every word and considered his classroom somewhere in the ivory tower of academia. One of the by-products of the course in Romantic Poets was the presence of a number of Speech and Drama students. As usual, their dramatic readings and classroom performances added to the splendor of the class. Oral tradition maintains that Jon Voight and Jason Patric may have been in the class in their pre-celebrity days. At the time they were unknowns, and I didn't pay much attention to names. On the other hand, everyone knew Jackie Gleason's daughter Linda was a participant in the class.

Dr. Giovanini (many uniformed thought his name was Joe Vanini) seldom told jokes or engaged in frivolous chat. Those occasions where he did attempt to introduce humor seem to be evident only to himself for the class seemed not to share the incongruity pointed out by the professor. Humor in the classroom of 'The Duck on a Broomstick' instead would have to come from the students or the interplay between professor and class. On a specific occasion while discussing Keats's line about the oxymoronic "beauty is truth and truth is beauty," Dr Giovanini asked what kind of philosophy was embodied in that expression. Most of us were reticent to take the plunge into the mind of the professor, but Jasper Smith blithely announced that the expression was a perfect example of Cracker Barrel Philosophy. Poor Giovanini's facial expression and body language indicated a total collapse in the face of this contribution. He stammered, "No, no, I was thinking of Neo-Platonic!" The contrast between Jasper's contribution and the correct response was one of the hilarious episodes I recall from that class. If Giovanini were not so stiff and formal, the humor would only be more pronounced when the professor got flustered. I thoroughly enjoyed his class however and enjoyed the notion that I didn't have to learn all the recondite minutiae he demanded from English majors, especially about the authors' views on literary criticism.

I enjoyed another English class in American literature. It was taught by a balding man with a southern accent. Dr. Foley had merited the title 'Betty' Foley from previous monks because of some of his effeminate ways. His classes were far from the severe lectures of Giovanini, but just as enjoyable. The class may have been a requirement for engineers whom Dr. Foley insisted he would have spelling their names correctly by the end of the course. The engineers took the course lightly and injected a unique perspective in interpreting some of the works of American literature.

Although I didn't have them, two professors from the philosophy department were quite popular among the Brothers. One was a cosmology professor called A. B. Foley. He was a priest who apparently rewarded any Brother who took his class, wore a robe, and attended class with an A or a B grade, hence his name. Those seeking a higher index or perhaps an easier course often selected Father Foley. Unlike 'Betty' Foley, there was another teacher who was called 'Dapper Dick' Nolan because of his sartorial excellence. His apparel was always top notch and earned him that appellation. Again his course was quite popular among the Brothers.

Latin majors had Dr. Sieffert who was notorious for his demands and attention to detail. English majors had to deal with a woman Shakespeare professor called Dr. Bates and a Father Rooney who proselytized for the wonders of the works of T. S. Eliot. The many who were bounced from Chemistry in Hillside found a very popular professor of biology in Dr. Braungart. His interesting classes led a number to become biologists in high school classrooms. Barney Quigley was the only student who had to deal with the world renowned Dr. Herzfeld who was immediately hired by Harvard when he retired from Catholic University. For my part, I had little to do with these professors other than hearing about them second hand.

As a minor in British history, however, I had the pleasure of taking a few of Dr. Zender's classes. His knowledge and fascinating lectures on the perfidies of the English monarchy and the machinations of the parliamentarians always caught my attention. I think he had confused me with Paul Murphy, however. Like me, Paul was an American history major minoring in British history. Unlike me, he asked a host of intelligent perceptive questions during class. I didn't mind if Dr. Zender had us confused for I figure I benefited from the comparison.

In my years at Catholic University, I learned a great deal, observed some excellent professors, acquired a thirst for greater knowledge and thoroughly enjoyed myself. Upon graduation I was recognized as worthy of *cum laude* honors and membership in several honor societies. The most prestigious was *Phi Beta Kappa*, the one objective I pursued during my collegiate career. I was also elected to *Phi Alpha*

Theta and *Pi Gamma Mu*. The Brothers paid for my *Phi Beta Kappa* key which I gave to my mother. After her death, I received the key from my brother and gave to my wife. It was stolen in a burglary, but I had it replaced. It is probably the one achievement academically for which I am proudest. Many of the Brothers worked much harder than I did, but few enjoyed the process of education more than I.

Aside from the academic preparation for teaching, De La Salle College offered several other activities that were related to the profession. Perhaps the most proximate preparation for a career in a classroom was offered by Boys Village. Boys Village was a vestige of a previous age in the segregated south. It was an entirely Black institution headed by a Black man named Mr. Vesey whose entire staff was Black, as were the boys who were assigned to the reformatory. Most of the students came from the streets of Baltimore. Our contribution to the integration as well as to the education of the institution was weekly religion lessons. Organized by the Benilde Club of De La Salle, volunteers would drive to Upper Marlboro, Maryland to present catechism classes to the youths.

The students were respectful and cooperative toward the Brothers, and I know of no incidents opposed to that judgment. One of the boys, however, was particularly known for his creative devilment. Davy Graham had become a minor legend to those of us who made the trip to Boys Village. I always enjoyed the opportunity to participate, and it even became more interesting when Maryland decided to desegregate the reformatory. Selecting some White hard core cases to pioneer the demands of 'deliberate speed' from the Supreme Court, the few White kids viewed us as deliverers from their 'cruel and unusual' punishment. At first they numbered only a few, and life in the institution may have been very difficult for them. At least that is what they claimed as they prayed we would expedite their deliverance. I suppose what is noteworthy is the fact that such institutional racism still persisted into the sixties. Now it may sound like ancient history, but we were experiencing the changing of the South. Mr. Vesey used to come to De La Salle College and make a presentation at least once a year. In return over the duration of my three years in Washington, I often traveled to Boys Village.

Segregation or integration was also having some impact in our very back yard. It seems every White kid who played on our fields attended Catholic schools in the area. Some went to St. John's which was run by the Christian Brothers. Others attended John Carroll High School where the basketball coach John Thompson later became very famous. The brightest high school kids seem to attend a Jesuit high school called Gonzaga and the most athletic went to DeMatha taught by the Trinitarians. Most of the high school kids who played on our basketball courts and fields also played for their respective school teams so they weren't often with us. Some we knew by name, but most were anonymous. That was not so with the grammar school kids, all of whom went to the local Catholic school, called John Baptist De La Salle, taught by the Sisters of Charity of Cincinnati.

Since I spent part of almost everyday on our ball fields, I got to know many of these youngsters quite well. There were several Brant brothers named Pat, Dennis, and Mike who all enrolled in St. John's for their high school education. Another fellow I recall was Tim Nugent whom I tabbed the 'Cynic.' Tim was a funny lad who announced proudly that he was the smartest boy in his eighth grade class. He of course was ranked seventeenth because sixteen girls were ahead of him. Tim enjoyed repartee more than sports. His classmate, a red head who later attended Gonzaga, was called Paul Wilkinson. He claimed to be a descendant of a man with that name who was involved in the Burr conspiracy in New Orleans in the infant days of our Republic. A fine young athlete named Ray O'Brien frequently played in our backyard and he later attended St. John's too. The finest athlete, a gifted kid who probably was one of the best athletes I ever knew, was called Steve Garrett. Steve had a very strong arm that belied his relatively small stature. In choosing up games, I often would select him over college age kids because he could run, catch, and especially throw a football with great aplomb. Steve later starred in high school football and basketball at DeMatha, a nationally noted athletic powerhouse, and then he went to the University of North Carolina at Chapel Hill where he played quarterback. I used to get a letter from him occasionally. I did hear later that his collegiate career stalled when he married and dropped out of college.

All of these kids had one plea. They wanted the Brothers to ask the Black kids who came from the DC side of our property to leave. The unique geographical placement of our grounds had one side of the property abutting Washington, DC which apparently was entirely

Black. Another side of our property adjoined Avondale, Maryland and was completely White. No Black kid attended any school other than the public institutions and what is quite telling in retrospect, I cannot recall a single Black kid's name. Perhaps that may be because they came in a group and generally played full court basketball by themselves. There never were any brawls, but the segregation of our guests was notable, at least to me. Despite this evidence, nonetheless, I never challenged the *status quo* or gave any serious thought to the situation. I suppose the racial sensitivity of later years was safely ensconced in my shell of indifference and apathy.

The Scholasticate was neighbor to two large institutions run by other religious orders. On one side of our property near the ball fields, the Carmelites whom we called 'The Big Sisters of the Rich' conducted a senior citizen assisted living program called Carroll Manor. This kind of arrangement whereby elderly folks were sheltered in a supervised living environment was an alien concept to those of us who grew up with grandparents living at home. I recall the facilities were very modern and perhaps even classy. I have no idea how much residency cost, but the care was tender and loving. The title Big Sisters of the Rich merely described the luxury of the manor and not the lifestyle of those nuns. Their circumstance contrasted greatly with the Little Sisters of the Poor in downtown Washington who periodically benefited from our largesse as we did from theirs. They would call occasionally and announce a superabundance of some perishable item and invite us to collect some for our consumption. On our part, we did some manual labor and minor repairs for their institution.

In my last year in the Scholasticate, work was begun on another segment of our property line. After a while we discovered it was to become a home for expectant mothers who could deliver their babies safely and far from busybodies who might make their lives uncomfortable. We could see the mothers-to-be sometimes walking around the grounds but they actually were seldom observed. The Brothers were called upon during the winter break between semesters to clean the completed structure, set up furniture, and prepare the building for the staff and patients. When it was finally dedicated, Cardinal Cushing from Boston delivered the dedication address. Ironically, and amusingly to us, he chose as his theme "The Wolf at the Door."

Sometimes longer trips were scheduled to break up the traditional horarium of the Scholasticate. One of these trips was to a Trappist monastery in Berryville, Virginia. Of course the grounds were well kept, and the monks appeared properly recollected and in prayerful thought. I do admit, however, that I did come upon some monks having a conversation whose topic I didn't know. Believing that they were vowed to perpetual silence, I guess I was disedified although they may have had good reason to break silence.

Once I was asked to drive a bus to the Williamsburg restoration with another Brother. Our passengers were the faculty of St. John Baptist De La Salle School. One of the local nuns was Black and our first stop was at a Howard Johnson's in Virginia. As clear as a Push or Pull sign can be, a decal stated that No Colored Were Allowed. The nuns ignored the insult, and all breakfasted at HoJo's, including us. I remember driving southward over the rolling hills of Virginia with rich red soil on either side of the road. It was early in the morning and the mist in the valleys between hills would cover the windshield. Every dip in the road demanded working windshields that seemed to operate contingent on the power from the engine. Downhill was fine, but uphill the wipers wouldn't necessarily work efficiently. My companion and I enjoyed the restoration, and the nuns were on their own. I was impressed when I discovered the tavern where Thomas Jefferson and some fellow students at William and Mary founded the original *Phi Beta Kappa*. The signs of house rules indicating that guests should remove boots before joining the eight or nine others who would share the same bed too stand out in my mind. Our return trek was agonizing for some. I was asked to stop at the nearest commode for some of the sisters. Every potential stop was closed until we saw a sign for Stuckey's only ten miles beyond. The poor nuns did their agonizing best to hold their bladders while we hurried to Stuckeys. That anticipation led to the aphorism "Stuck at Stuckey's" for it too was closed. The resolution of the dilemma has left no trace in my memory except for the compassion I had for the victims of Stuckeys.

An occasional picnic trip was organized to either Gambrill State Park or Cunningham Falls, both in the Catoctin Mountains near Camp David. The description offered by John Greenleaf Whittier presents an ideal image of the road to these parks. In Frederick,

Maryland, the home of Barbara Frietchie, one readily recognizes the town depicted by the poet so aptly over a century earlier:

> Up from the meadows rich with corn,
> Clear in the cool September morn,

> The clustered spires of Frederick stand
> Green-walled by the hills of Maryland.

> Round about them orchards sweep,
> Apple and peach tree fruited deep,

> Fair as the garden of the Lord
> To the eyes of the famished rebel horde.

On the road northward toward Gettysburg in southern Pennsylvania, one passes the entrances to the Maryland State Parks. Consecrated by the blood of fallen Union and Confederate troops and hallowed by the heroism of the old lady who urged Stonewall Jackson's troops to "shoot if you must this old gray head, but spare your country's flag she said," the parks became the scene of one of the bitter hallmarks of segregation. On our last trip to Gambrill State Park, the Scholastics shared the facilities with a group of altar boys from some parish in Baltimore. Among the youngsters was one Black boy who was denied admission to the large swimming pool. Most of the Brothers took little notice of the bigotry, but the ostracized boy was invited to share whatever picnic foods we had on this trip. Some suggested we boycott the pool in protest, but their arguments were readily ignored. Again, as citizens of the early 1960's most of us were oblivious to the racism surrounding us and ingrained in some of us.

At some point in my early years in Washington, I was invited to visit the Junior Novitiate for the Baltimore district. It was located in Ammendale, Maryland, near the University of Maryland. Unknown to me, I was to become a feature attraction for a trait I didn't know I possessed. Apparently, my Washington Heights accent was so pronounced that it stood out from the rest of New Yorkers. When I spoke to the Junior Novices, they couldn't contain themselves for the laughter my voice induced. Most of those boys came from Baltimore or Pittsburgh, and I suppose they were unaccustomed to

New Yorkese. I didn't mind providing the amusement, but I had no idea about my hidden skill.

At Christmas time, the Baltimore Novitiate at Ammendale offered us a place to celebrate the annual 'Holly Hunt.' In theory, the seniors would gather holly and its berries from the many trees on the property and bring them back for an authentic display of yuletide atmosphere. By the way, I don't think anyone was searching for mistletoe. Actually, it was an opportunity for the senior class to have a special outing while the rest of the Scholasticate performed the pedestrian tasks of cleaning and decorating for Christmas. In my junior year, I was given the responsibility of assuring that the house was totally cleaned and that decorations were adorning the walls and corridors in a safe but appealing array. My experience during that supervisory role convinced me that I wanted little to do with administration or overseeing my peers.

I had enjoyed the opportunity to supervise manual labor in the Juniorate at Barrytown, but I was inept in Washington. After negotiating with the powers that were to provide some snacks in the scullery, I discovered that some of the work force had found a home away from labor. Despite my attempts to get Jim Nerney back on track, he remained affixed to the snack table and enjoyed meeting the individuals who took a temporary break from their labors. After about an hour of futility in asking Jim to get back to work, I approached Brother Steve Rusyn and asked him to try to induce Jim to return to his assignment. Steve got very angry and lectured me on failure to have the courage to address the recalcitrant myself. Now I had alienated two groupies, Jim Nerney and Steve Rusyn. I decided I didn't need this kind of aggravation and salted it away for future reference.

Christmas time in Washington provided another diversion for those of us seeking something different. On the rather extensive grounds of the Scholasticate a large number of evergreen Christmas trees grew abundantly and lavishly. At some time before we arrived, some neighbors had helped themselves to prime samples of Christmas trees for their homes, so a Christmas tree patrol was organized. On the cold nights, in groups of twos for a shift of about an hour, some Brothers volunteered to patrol the grounds to assure the safety of the trees. Brian Schwall and I represented one such deterrent. Bill Simon decided to test our vigilance. He snuck out of the building and armed with a club, he began banging on a tree. Brian and I knew it was Simon, but we decided to teach him a lesson. Brian made a lot of noise approaching the selected tree while I circled around and waited in ambush for the felon. Bill fled from Schwall right into my tackle. By the time Brian and I finished pummeling him, pretending we didn't know who he was, Bill was protesting loudly. I suppose any distraction was welcome. In our last Christmas in Washington, I remember a group of us singing a parody of *Hark the Herald Angels Sing*. Our lyrics were similar but an authentic message from the heart-

Hark the Herald Angels Shout
Six more months and we'll be out!

On two special occasions I was selected for an unusual trip to the New York metropolitan area. Cardinal Hayes High School on the Grand Concourse in the Bronx was having a vocational instruction day. For whatever his reasons, Kirby selected Joe Troy, Joe O'Brien and me to represent our Scholasticate. We were allowed to stay at home the night before the presentation, and the late hour took its toll on me under the klieg lights of the high school stage. I thought I was going to fall asleep, or possibly even pass out. I survived the ordeal and in fact thrived in the classroom presentation. Each of us was assigned to one or two groups. In one of my groups, a young lad named Dave O'Connor came forward and requested additional information. I continued to write to him, and he ultimately went to the Juniorate in Barrytown. Evidently he was an extremely bright student and a wonderful, if temporary addition to the candidates. I was delighted that I played a minor role in his recruitment. On the way back to Washington, I thought Joe O'Brien was going to have us heaven bound sooner than we expected. As a new, inexperienced driver, Joe annoyed a truck driver with his irregular movements, and when honked at, Joe displayed his displeasure and the trucker insisted on prolonging his tailgating. Finally, we convinced Joe to let well enough alone.

On another occasion a Brother died and was being buried from Oakdale, Long Island. Kirby selected pretty much the same group to attend the funeral and burial with him. Typically, we were awakened at 2am to make the drive to New York. Naturally, we had no money or maps. While Kirby presided over a rosary, mental prayer, or morning prayer, Joe Troy was my navigator in the dark. We missed a vital turn off the Baltimore Washington Expressway and found ourselves somewhere on a godforsaken stretch of road in the Delmarva Peninsula. While Joe and I tried to resolve our location without alerting Kirby, we had only a place mat from a diner to direct us. We ended up following signs to the Delaware Memorial Bridge and ultimately found the correct approach. In the meantime, we were barreling along the lonely road, for we had to be at Oakdale on time for the funeral. A little white spot in the road turned out to be the stripe on a skunk. The intersection of rubber and polecat produced an instant stench. Disrupting meditation, Kirby soon said, "Say Brothers, what is that stink?" We confessed to having run over the skunk, and the Director's response was, "We can't go to a funeral smelling like this." Our prayers must have been answered for after a hundred miles the obnoxious scent to our vehicle dissipated and we were able to attend the memorial service. Immediately after the ceremonies, we headed back to Washington.

With an interest in alternate scheduling, Dermot O'Sullivan and I formed a breakfast cooking team that specialized in fried eggs, pancakes, and French toast. I was always in awe at the devotion Dermot brought to the grill. Each egg, every pancake, or piece of toast was lovingly shaped, flipped and deposited upon the platters for service to the hungry community of about one hundred and fifty monks. Immediately after the major production, we would drive to the National Shrine of the Immaculate Conception where we attended Mass in the crypt. There were always a dozen Masses being said simultaneously at the dozen altars. We might serve Mass for a guest priest, or we could hear Mass from a series of benches facing the main altar in the shrine crypt.

The dedication of the National Shrine coincided with our time in Washington. There were some who found the blue dome with stars on it rather gaudy, and they described the Shrine as the Easter egg. Some versed in art also claimed the huge, colorful mosaic at the back of the main altar was bizarre. The image of a huge Christ bedecked in red robe, some hinted, was traditionally associated with homosexuality. Christ's good looks and handsome visage led some to refer to the mosaic as Tyrone Power. Despite criticism and architectural discussions, the Shrine was the seat of many special ceremonies. At some, the choir of the Brothers would perform. At others, a choir composed of members from many Orders would sing. For the first time, I heard violins and trumpets in church and found their contributions significantly prayerful. Occasionally a noteworthy preacher or teacher would speak from the pulpit. I was impressed by the diversity of religious orders present for some of the ceremonies. Perhaps the most noteworthy was a group of blue clad nuns in very simple habit and sandals. They were called the Sisters of the Jakes, for their apostolate supposedly was cleaning the bathroom facilities at Shrines of the Blessed Mother. I believe they had been founded by John De Foucault. Their evident poverty and threadbare garments and discalced sandals set them apart in other ways from many of the more winter ready Orders.

Whenever a prominent speaker addressed a group at Catholic University, we were invited to sign a list and hop on the bus for the lecture. We were usually invited to musical performances. I remember being hypnotized by a performance of Handel's *Messiah*. Another feature embedded in memory is a concert by the talented Leontyne Price. While cultural events were generally authorized, I don't think permission was granted to attend any athletic events. On the other hand, we attended many featured dramatic and comedic plays staged by a very talented Speech and Drama department led by a Dominican named Father Hartke.

One occasion which we were encouraged to attend was the blood donation day. During this event, I had the learning experience to note an incongruity in our national law. I volunteered to donate a pint of blood and waited in line for a half hour before reaching the doctor. He rejected my offer because I was only nineteen and legally a minor. He mentioned that I needed written permission from my parents. When I notified him that the request was virtually impossible, he settled for my guardian's signature. I had to wait while one of the Brothers returned to De La Salle, told Brother Leo of my need, and then brought the autograph back to the college gym on the return bus trip to the campus. At least the doctor brought me immediately to the head of the line. He began to explain that if he took my blood without written permission, he could be convicted of felonious assault. When I assured him I had no intention of doing that, he cautioned me on the need to avoid believing people. At first, he told me about an auto accident where a cabby insisted he would lose his job if he was in an accident. Feeling sorry for the man, the doctor didn't file an accident report and found himself sued for leaving the scene of an accident. He then scanned the gym and reassured that he could confide in me, he related the following story. In his practice a very reliable nurse worked for him for several decades. She asked him if he would write a recommendation for her niece although he didn't know her. Confident in her trust, he wrote a recommendation for the woman. His voice rose as he rhetorically asked, "Do you know what she did with my recommendation? Do you know what she did with my recommendation?" Before I could hazard a guess, he announced that she had been the object of a morals squad raid. She had opened a whore house and placed his seal of approval on her cleanliness and proficiency. He had a difficult time convincing the police of his innocence. I enjoyed his confidence and felt comfortable with his reticence upon insisting on written permission. On the other hand, I contrasted what was felonious assault upon a nineteen year old male for donating blood, with the incongruous example of a ten year old female who could secure an abortion without parent notification or permission.

The three years in the Scholasticate in Washington are pleasant memories for the most part. I enjoyed the manual labor, even the opportunity to clean up after meals. Perhaps that is attributable to Clay Hollinger in some part. Clay was always a practical joker and enjoyed picking on me. While I was bent over the scullery sinks scouring pots and pans, Clay pretended to stifle a sneeze. Finally a resounding 'achoo' echoed in my ears as what I thought was mucous sprayed along the back of my neck. Clay began wiping what was the result of water from his hand from the back of my neck. My hackles rose, but my innate knowledge that I could never catch him no matter how hard I tried restored my composure. When I saw him perform the same joke on someone else, I felt more comfortable. He did the same thing when the kitchen crew was cleaning turkeys. He must have had three pounds of turkey viscera which he cast on a table after a Homeric sneeze. I only observed his performance and found it hilarious. On another occasion, Clay and I pretended to exchange punches. A few phantom punches, some scuffling foot work, and an occasional shove characterized our pretend fight. Poor Paul Wilson, the Brother overseeing the kitchen at the time, didn't know what to do. We had a good laugh at his embarrassed expense and the apparent confusion of our noted psychologist. Clay seemed to enjoy these periodic sorties into frivolity that recalled our pleasant, playful days in the Novitiate.

There were two annual events that were social engagements hosting guests. The first celebration was the Orphans' Picnic. I don't recall where the orphans came from or what religious Order ran the operation, but most of the kids were elementary school age. They came to our campus and were treated like royalty, likely a contrast to their usual treatment. Each child was granted every whim as far as a game was concerned, and he was feted with the typical fare of a family picnic. I do recall that Rich McKay officiated over a games competition for them. One of the games featured a race in which the contestant had to eat several Uneeda Crackers and then whistle a tune. The crackers dried the mouth and prevented any whistle from emerging for several moments. Another competition against time concerned tying the wrists of two boys with interlooping circles. They would then attempt to writhe and contort their way out of the interlocking circles. After a while someone would deduce that no matter how they twisted or turned, they remained entwined. Finally but surreptitiously, usually two of the Brothers would then demonstrate that the feat could be accomplished. After minutes of frustrating gyrations, the solution was presented by slipping the twine in a loop over one's wrist and the interlocking circles were separated without any movement. What appeared to be impossible actually took a little analysis and intelligence. The boys seemed to enjoy the challenge however and even uttered premature shouts of joy when they thought they had wriggled free by physical feats.

Another annual event was Nuns' Day. Every Nun in the DC area was invited to attend a picnic afternoon concluded by a first run movie. Sometimes the local movie theatre would show a production for free on a Saturday morning. I remember seeing *The Nun's Story* with Audrey Hepburn and *The Wreck of the Mary Deere* starring Charleton Heston under those circumstances. The Brothers would try to compete with a satisfactory movie. As usual, the title of the feature was leaked before the picnic. For this occasion, our movie gurus had selected *The Hustler*, a film about a pool shark played by Paul Newman. When the beloved Sister Klinkhammer heard about the selection, she immediately protested to Brother Leo, claiming that it was an insult to the integrity of Sisterhood to present such a film about a lowlife. Trying ever to please the Nuns, Brother Leo followed Sister Gothica's criticism and cancelled the film. When that news got out, a number of Sisters felt offended by the paternalism they believed was behind the abortive attempt to shield them from reality. Every Scholastic was enthralled with the thought of how Leo Kirby could resolve this dilemma. One of his positive attributes seemed to be the ability to resolve dilemmas like this to the satisfaction of all. To his credit, he found an appropriate solution. He would offer two films and the final film would be *The Hustler*. Those whose sensibilities were offended could graciously leave at intermission. Those who wanted to see the feature were welcomed to stay late. Almost all the Nuns stayed for both presentations, even the critic Klinkhammer. She probably wanted to note what was so offensive about the picture. The picnic food and atmosphere was always joyful, and I think the Brothers anticipated the event as much as the several hundred Nuns who would attend.

One of our predictable entertainments was a movie about once a month. Brother Andrew Kevin Giolla was in charge of selections in my sophomore year. He had ordered *The Brothers Karamazov*, starring Maria Schell. I was sitting near Kevin when the film opened with her licking the toes of someone and then beginning an erotic dance. Kevin was heard muttering, "Please stop. Please stop!" I suppose selecting movies was a dangerous enterprise when so many critics and reviewers were on hand. Later Brother Michael Sevastakis, ironically called Mike the Greek because of his diminutive stature, headed the selection committee. He was heavy into drama and intellectual fare with Hitchcockian overtones. Finally, he selected a lighter presentation when we were treated to *Pollyanna* with Hayley Mills. I readily confess I enjoyed the light concoction after heavy doses of foreign films, *film noire*, arty presentations of brutal crimes and so forth.

As usual, Brother Cornelius Luke had arranged for his yearly visitation and few viewed the expected guest with any degree of comfort. In a reddition session with Brother Leo, he asked me what I thought of 'Flookie' Luke's impending inspection. I pondered the question carefully for I realized that to say anything offensive about Luke would incur the wrath of Brother Leo Kirby. Finally, I came up with a comment that did my evasive answer credit, or so I thought. I told him that Luke must be like St. Paul, a comparison that my Director seemed to like. I then commented that from his epistles, Paul appeared to be a man who indicted whomever he visited for their offenses or lapses whether that was eating flesh offered to the

pagan gods, celebrating pagan holidays, or a host of peccadilloes
that plague the ordinary mortal. Brother Leo liked the comparison
so much that he urged me to tell Luke when I had to see him in
reddition. Like the coward I truly was, I chose to keep my mouth
shut for a change and try to escape from the presence of the Visitor
General. I always believed the best coping mechanism for reddition
with Luke was discreet silence and mute agreement.

At graduation time the families of the graduates were feted with
a catered meal presented by *Avignon Freres*. It was funny to see the
Black workers unloading dishes, tables, chairs, linens and so forth
after announcing in French "Nous sommes Avignon Freres." Their
final product was something that we were very proud of, and our
families felt like celebrities. Tables were dispersed throughout the
property under trees to take advantage of the shade from the hot
May sun. Someone took pictures of every different family and later
those pictures were offered as a slide presentation. When a picture
of my brothers and me appeared, Rich McKay shouted, "Look! The
Flintstones." His comment brought peals of laughter to the audience
and I concluded that no response was adequate to the allegation.
The three of us were muscular and perhaps intimidating to some,
but in no way did we resemble cavemen.

At the conclusion of my senior year, I pronounced another set of
triennial vows after our usual retreat. I had no hesitation in doing
so for I was sure that I would persevere and frankly enjoy teaching.
Brother Leo had issued a handbook to each of the seniors which
contained information and procedures for operating an efficient
classroom. He wrote personal notes about our strengths and
weaknesses, and frankly I was pleased with the comments he wrote
in mine. He asked our preference for teaching as well. I wanted to
teach in an elementary school more so than any high school because
of my recollection of the Brothers who taught me in Incarnation.
I liked the concept of supervising after school activities too. As a
history major, my services were not essential in a high school so I
received my preference. I was delighted to discover that I would be
assigned to a parish across the Harlem River from Incarnation. My
first class assignment was to Sacred Heart, a parish at that time that
was quite similar to what I knew in Washington Heights. At the end
of retreat we were sent on a vacation with a request to bring back

any donations we were offered because we would need that money for living expenses in Troy later in the summer.

That appeal for funds was generously met by family and relatives, and when we arrived in Troy we were well heeled. Brother Thomas Kelly was our director, and he was looking forward to a carefree summer of golf and no hassle. We, on the other hand, were to take our teaching practicum in La Salle High School in ancient Troy. I had excellent fortune in the assignment of my mentor. Brother Christian Edward was very much like Brother Peter Mannion from the Juniorate. He never uttered an extraneous word in the classroom, and every gesture contributed to a serious, academic lesson. Tom Lynch and I both practiced under his guidance and thrived from the experience. I enjoyed teaching and believed I did a fine job planning game strategies and motivational tools to capture the attention of the summer school attendees. Some of our fellow graduates had mentors who were not so effective.

The bankroll that we brought with us to Troy was spent like drunken sailors on leave. Those who planned picnics would order filet mignon and other such prime cuts instead of hamburgers and hot dogs. Our recreational activities also were profligate. I recall going horseback riding with a few Brothers, but the one whom I remember most was Greg Simon. While he and some others rode the ponies, I took pity on the horse and stayed on foot. I had learned that I wasn't born to the stable on a family vacation when a horse took off with me as a reluctant passenger. The runaway mount almost trampled a young girl tossing a softball in the air. Finally, I managed to rein in the horse and slide out of the saddle without further complications. Never considering the career of jockey, I determined that dressage or other equestrian activities were not in my future.

Other Brothers attended movie theaters with regularity dipping into the funds that seemed inexhaustible. A local pool with some flirtatious maidens attracted some of the graduates too. On a picnic to Lake George, some Brothers rented a speed boat to try their skill at water skiing. I suppose I would have made a very cheap director, for I thought such an expenditure was extravagant. My observations and deductions do not necessarily reflect what my peers believed, at least for that summer when we had more money than we could legitimately spend. For the most part, Sam Schaeffer and I continued our fast ball contests in the backyard. I did not do so out of a sense of poverty, but out of an entire joy for the game. I believe Sam was the same way. I don't set myself up as a paragon of poverty, but I imagine my personality lent itself to cheap entertainment.

We sometimes took trips to recreational facilities. One notable trip was the picnic at Barrytown where we played baseball against either the Novices or the Juniorate. After a full day's play and dining, we boarded the bus for the return trip to Troy. Depending on each Brother to take care of himself, we arrived back in Troy without two of our number. Tom Kelly had been replaced by Mike Harrington who had been assured that the assignment was a sinecure and that all he had to do was officiate at prayers and play golf. Instead, Mike was burdened with two AWOL Brothers. Neil Walsh and Stinchcombe had celebrated their graduation with a custom of wrestling whenever possible. At Barrytown, they headed into the field near the pump house and were so busy pummeling each other, they lost track of time. When they returned to the bus, it was gone. They reported to the local Brothers' community and were driven to the train station in Rhinebeck. Meanwhile, Mike Harrington had directed me to take the community truck down to Barrytown and pick up the errant wrestlers. When I got to Barrytown, I was told they took the train to Albany. As I headed north on route 9, I noticed that I was almost out of gas, but I had no money or credit card. I observed that Hudson, New York was quite a vestigial remnant of the wide open towns along the old Erie Canal. Prostitutes with young children in hand tried to wave me down and negotiate for services.

When I arrived at the train station in Albany, I couldn't find anyone so I used the last of my gas fumes to drive back to Hillside Hall. After two hours sleep, I was at mental prayer and noticed that our AWOL brethren were deep in prayer. Mike Harrington called me to the back of the chapel and asked where I found them. I told him my trek was totally unsuccessful. Later, Neil and Stinchcombe explained that they had changed their idea of taking the train and decided to hitch. They were picked up by some teenagers joy riding in a car owned by the driver's unaware father. The kids drove them directly back to Hillside Hall. Mike Harrington also had to deal with a collision between the bus driven by John Kullberg and our back garage. Nothing untoward was noticed while Kelly was in charge, but plenty happened after he left.

At the end of summer school session, many of my classmates were assigned to Lincroft, New Jersey where Christian Brothers Academy was opening a new facility. These Brothers were asked to unload furniture and help set up the brand new school. I was not among them and I preferred to go rather than stay in Troy. Brother Eulogius Austin had trained me to be his Econome Assistant, and I was to replace him while he went on vacation and retreat. The task seemed well within my grasp, and he had alerted me to a stash of money if I encountered any monetary difficulties. A few days later, Mike Harrington asked me to direct him to the money for some need or other. The pile I previously saw with Eulogius had evaporated. Brother Gene Miller appeared looking for the funds, for they contained some NSF grant money he needed. The case of the purloined pile remained unsolved on the surface.

When we graduated from Catholic University, we numbered about forty. Those numbers have dwindled significantly over the years. I have pondered whether the defections from the Institute were the result of a flawed training process or some other cause. I considered whether the Community forsook the individuals or the individuals forsook the Community. Yet almost to a man, everyone retains an admiration for the Institute and a deep abiding affection for their confreres. Frequent reunions and mutual contacts are the general rule for those who have left or for those in the vast minority who have remained faithful to their vows.

St. La Salle was perspicacious when he chose the spirit of faith as the characteristic of the Christian Brothers. Faith is a gift that needs nourishing through prayer and sacrifice, but when it contradicts reason, it is opposed by a formidable presence, especially among those as highly educated as the Brothers are. Our theology teachers used to emphasize "faith seeking understanding," but after Vatican II the Church seemed to convulse into confusion, lack of focus, incomprehensible chaos, and a secularization that contrasted with the faith in which we were nurtured. Furthermore, community life is very demanding in charity and generosity. The aftermath of the General Council seemed to promote individuality and self-assertion. As Black Bart once described the situation, "The Christian Brothers had become a repository for everyone from astronauts to zookeepers." Instead of charitable communities, many Brothers experienced a hotel kind of existence where bed and board were supplied while they plied their personal interests. Where there is little encouragement or sacrifice to a united cause, one is easily swayed by the fulfillment found in a personal relationship rather than community involvement. So many Brothers left not so much because of something within the Institute, but toward a life where their individuality and self satisfaction might be found in the personal relationship with a woman. Intangible faith and zeal are unfair competitors for self-satisfaction and sexual gratification.

Our formation prepared us for a community existence that was to morph into some unknown form or unfamiliar identity. I am sure each former Brother may contest my interpretation, and I certainly invite him to do so. A self-evident fact is that most Brothers left after Vatican II, and the attempts of the Institute to reinterpret the rules and community life within the context of broader change. In essence, the defections among Christian Brothers were typical of a larger phenomenon within the Catholic Church. Priests and religious abandoned their commitment by thousands. The boom times of the fifties and early sixties led to the bust of the late sixties and seventies. This silent revolution seemed to be led by the young, and gradually the movement filtered into the ranks of older, more mature religious. Maybe the Holy Spirit took a sabbatical at that time, or maybe the belief that God's ways are not our ways makes the most sense of the situation. Whatever one concludes today, it is apparent that our formation had little defense against the blandishments of a world celebrating the individual and his perceived self-fulfillment.

Chapter Seven

Graduate Studies

For every Brother entering the classroom for the first year, expectations were plain and simple. He was supposed to focus on his teaching, supervisory and school related activities. After his exposure to one year of teaching, he was expected to enroll in a master's degree program. For those of us who were assigned to the metropolitan area of New York, our first degree was automatically determined to come from Manhattan College unless that esteemed institution did not offer a Master's in our field of concentration. After one had acquired a master's degree in his major field, he could then pursue other studies at other institutions. I suppose a rationale for this arrangement was simply economics, but New York State also wanted its permanently certified teachers to earn a master's in his subject area within a time span of five years. Consequently every Saturday morning around 9:00am Brothers and some lay folk from around New York would gather in the classrooms by the Quadrangle of the campus.

My pursuit of a master's degree in Modern European history from Manhattan was a search for more than knowledge and accreditation. I appreciated how seriously the Brothers took learning and how rigid they could be in determining that no compromises would occur in the pursuit of completing prerequisites. I got to know some sterling role models for college teachers. My first course was taught by the then chairman of the history department, Brother Casmir Gabriel Costello, a tall, white haired distinguished, soft spoken individual. 'Cas Gabe,' as he was called, was well versed in his subject and relished his lecturing on the French Revolution. His classes were always interesting and his required reading assignments pertinent. 'Cas Gabe' expected his students to apply themselves seriously and attend all lectures and complete assignments within allotted time. While lectures were his standard occupational procedure, he also required occasional presentations to the class or oral reports. All were to be satisfied in a dignified, professional manner.

Brother Basil Leo Lee was a teacher of another sort. He savored tales of the insignificant but instructive aspects of history. His course was in American Constitutional history. I had heard that his doctoral thesis was on Bishop Hughes and the Draft Riots of 1863. Supposedly the thesis was acceptable for the scholars, but not for the clerics of the Archdiocese. His work was impounded and accessible only with special permission. Knowing something about the Draft riots from my personal reading, I can surmise that he found fault with the Bishop for not putting a stop to the rioting before so many were killed. Anyway, Brother Leo was a fine instructor, although one of my memories might contradict his in-depth knowledge of the subject area. I only conclude that the episode in mind indicates that as thorough as one knows American history, there can also be gaps.

Assigned to give class presentations, each Brother could select some issue in Constitutional history and make an oral explanation and submit an outline with bibliography. Most took this demand with the respect it deserved. One of the class members did not. A Brother noted for his *ad lib* performances and peculiar ideas, more or less made a parody of his delivery. Brother Kevin 'Cu' Cullan was a brilliant, yet eccentric individual. 'Cu,' nicknamed no doubt to honor the legendary figure from Irish mythology, delivered a lecture on the Church of the Latter Day Saints. 'Cu's hierarchy of sainted figures, both human and angelic, was a virtuoso display of minutiae unknown to all without access to his fecund imagination and creativity. He had created a theology premised on his own creations and populated it with figures from the **Book of Moroney.** While most of the class knew he was spouting names, ideas, theological explanations and historical events that never occurred, Brother Leo either let him rave on or chose to ignore a confrontation. No one knew what grade 'Cu' was given, but the lecture was outstanding, if fictional. He completed his 'coup' by grabbing notes that Jack Farrell had prepared for his presentation and distributed them as having come from his labors. When Jack went to give his presentation, he could only claim that 'Cu' had covered most of the material and that the papers we had received previously were actually his. I suppose an intricate knowledge of the

Church of the Latter Day Saints might have exposed this performance about the LDS, but it remained unchallenged and 'Cu' reclaimed his reputation as someone who was brilliant, but suspicious.

The curriculum in the history program at Manhattan was weighed more in European history than American. I enjoyed a great, incisive view of Russian history in a class taught by a former embassy official from Czechoslovakia. I had a fascinating class in twentieth century European history. For this class I had submitted a paper on *The Concept of Aggressive Warfare as Evolved in the Nuremberg Trials*. It was interesting to read how the victors determined the morality of submarine warfare, or war crimes of the defeated. This was one of the papers I used to complete my requirements for the master's degree. Both of these classes were taught by laymen faculty teachers of Manhattan, and they were outstanding too.

After he graduated from the Scholasticate, Brother Patrick McGarry had replaced Gabe Costello as chairman of the history department. Pat's doctorate from Columbia University buttressed the credentials of the small history department staff. One of his first developments was to change the requirements for the master's degree. Now, instead of a thesis, three major approved papers were considered adequate. Comprehensive examinations over nine hours testing were still requirements, however. I have found that comprehensive examinations are an excellent format for tying together the knowledge of numerous courses taken over several years. The requisite study pays dividends. Besides chairing the department, Pat McGarry taught a class in Nineteenth Century European history. As usual, his class was demanding, cerebral, and comprehensive in approach.

The change in requirements for the master's degree led me to another facet of the Brothers' education at Manhattan. Brother Tom Reilly, called 'Monk' by most, was a year ahead of me. Both of us had started at Manhattan when courses were awarding two credits instead of three. McGarry made each course now worth three credits. The change left me one credit shy of the thirty I needed. Monk mentioned that he was able to get an undergraduate course at Catholic University worth three credits, changed to two graduate credits in transferring to Manhattan. He claimed this was expedited because he was beginning the theology program at Manhattan later that year. Armed with that tidbit of information, I asked for an interview with

Brother Alban Dooley, the keeper of integrity at Manhattan graduate division. Brother Alban was known as a stickler for detail and as a non-compromiser under any circumstance. Encouraged, however, by the example of Tom Reilly who had taken the identical course at CU along with me, I entreated Brother Alban to grant me the same concession. Several of the courses at Catholic University straddled both undergraduate and graduate credits. Undergraduates had a third session added on Fridays designed to discuss the content of the two previous lectures. Graduate students were excused from that session, but they received two graduate credits while the undergraduates received three. I thought I could convince Brother Alban that I could easily surrender these three undergraduate credits on my transcript for two graduate credits at Manhattan.

Brother Alban listened attentively and graciously as I described my work in the Bronx. Teaching, coaching, teenage activities, parish leadership, involvement in the CYO and Catholic School Athletic League administration were all laid out for Brother Alban's appraisal. After I finished my saga of preoccupations, he said to me, "You know, Brother Kevin, you sound very busy. Perhaps you should quit graduate school." I could wheedle no compromise from such a man of integrity, nor did I follow his advice since I was only a credit shy of my course requirements at Manhattan.

Tom Reilly caused me some grief of another kind. On one of the Saturday mornings when class was held, the eighth graders in northern Manhattan and the northwest Bronx were taking the Cooperative Entrance Exam for Catholic High Schools. The test was administered in Smith Hall across from our classroom. Tom invited me over to see the test. Thinking little of it, I accompanied him during a ten minute break from the class. Unknown to me, Tom and some Brothers at Good Shepherd had written a letter critical of how the staff of Manhattan Prep had controlled the testing time. When we appeared in the back of the auditorium, Brother Celsus John 'the Bear,' immediately intercepted us. Known for his great sense of humor, I experienced another facet of his personality when John grabbed me by the chest and heaved me out the door. Tom Reilly was smart enough to evacuate without physical escort. Later John wanted to know why I was there, and I described my appearance as mere curiosity. He then lambasted the Brothers from Good Shepherd and just assumed I was one of them.

My final course at Manhattan was taught by a Canadian monk from Toronto. His name was Brother Bonaventure. Again, he epitomized the stringency associated with Brothers teaching Brothers. His class took place in the summer so it was abbreviated in time but not in substance. He taught a course in the Protestant Reformation. Actually, it was very well taught, and he was very demanding in the required readings and other incidentals. One of Brother Bonaventure's signature demands was summarized by the popular song at that time by Helen Reddy. "Downtown" was our class theme, for among our daily assignments he had us searching out information that could only be found in the Columbia University Library or perhaps in the Fordham Library. Manhattan's library was inadequate for our purposes. It dawned on us that our meager summer funds were being depleted on subway fares to complete our tasks. While some of our confreres in other disciplines organized car trips to Jones' Beach or the Rockaways, we expended our small funds on public transportation to libraries. The paper I had to submit was *Reginald Pecock, Precursor of the Reformation*. Bishop Pecock of Chichester was an individual who insisted on translating the Bible into English and simplifying the liturgy. Many of his ideas paralleled those of John Huss, a more notable Protestant precursor. As in so many classes, each individual was assigned a topic to lecture the larger group about. Brother Bonaventure seemed to give any nun in our class a free pass. His comments were usually plaudits for a job well done. When a Brother made a presentation, he was severely critical about the style of presentation or the content. Few escaped his unfavorable review and caustic remarks. I think a number of Brothers decided on different majors after exposure to this man, but his class was very informational and challenging. Whenever I hear the song "Downtown," I am reminded of this man who insisted on granting no quarter to any Brother, but relished polishing his students into careful, eloquent lecturers and conscientious researchers.

Without any help from Brother Alban, I completed my course work in 1966, submitted the requisite papers, and prepared for comprehensives while I remained at St. Augustine's in the Bronx. I actually only spent one summer at Manhattan where I roomed with Greg Simon in Jasper Hall. Greg didn't tell me he snored like a full fledged typhoon, but we operated on different schedules anyway. In the afternoons I often played a variety of basketball/rugby games in the college gym with Aquinas McNiff, Kevin Gilhooley, Mike Dwyer, and a few other hardy souls. The lack of mobility was a major factor in choosing to stay at Augustine rather than Manhattan College. I was, moreover, able to enjoy the night time teenage supervised activities organized by Greg Flynn in our backyard.

When I had finished satisfying the faculty on the comprehensives, I was urged by Brother Leo Kirby to think in terms of a doctoral degree. By October 1967, however, I was approached by Brother Augustine Loes, Visitor of the New York District at the time, with an option to study and teach our Scholastics in Washington. Since I addressed this situation elsewhere, suffice it to say that I accepted the offer at first and then changed my mind for compelling reasons, at least in my opinion. Gus graciously accepted my plea to remain at Augustine and continue the work I had been doing there while I attended graduate doctoral studies at New York University in the Waverly Building near the site of the tragic Triangle Shirtwaist fire near Washington Square.

At that time, I was sent to the National Social Studies Convention in Seattle. The inspector of elementary schools in the Archdiocese of New York was Brother Christopher Victor Dardis. Vic organized an itinerary to the west coast that brought me first to Los Angeles for a few days where I enjoyed the hospitality of the brother of my Director Brother Matty Kissane. My host who lived in Redondo Beach took me on a tour to Tijuana, Mexico and made sure I made the plane to San Francisco. Tijuana, especially the racetrack *Caliente* and the bodies and goods for sale or rent convinced me that Mexico and I were incompatible. In San Francisco, I met up with Brother Robert Lynch from the LINE District. He had attended conventions before, so he was my guide in Baghdad by the Bay. I enjoyed the presentations in Seattle, marveled at the brevity of the monorail, learned the origin of 'skid row,' and absorbed the latest thinking in social studies education. Upon my return to New York, I found my father and brother Ray waiting for me at the airport terminal. My mother had had a stroke at Thanksgiving dinner and wasn't expected to survive. That information quickly stifled my joy about the convention and affected my plans to accept the assignment to Washington.

Attending the convention in Seattle bore with it several commitments. For example, I was invited by Brother Dardis as well as Sister Helen O'Neill, SC, to address some sessions of social studies seminars at the yearly Archdiocesan Teacher's Institute. Moreover, I was asked to present a series of six after school workshops for teachers offered in as many centers or schools as enrollment dictated. Each workshop had perhaps about two dozen attendees. I introduced some of the concepts I had learned in Seattle. A new style of teaching, for example, incorporated a discovery method. Using primary sources or available artifacts, one was supposed to surmise some conclusions about a particular event. Dates and names and events seemed secondary to the process. Actually, most of the students enjoyed the process, learned the major names and events, and for the most part comprehended the time sequence. Another aspect of the new system involved game simulation and creative lessons in planning.

Outlining an Ideal Town introduced concepts about zoning, regulations, services, and of course the required economic funding. Debates about the value of some professions were generally animated. Rating professions usually was identified by the value placed upon their projected salaries. Rarely did a teacher deserve the same income as a policeman or a firefighter. One of the lessons I learned was that the most outspoken were generally acknowledged as leaders. In one particular episode, democracy was used only to ridicule an individual. Tom Merritt, one of the most imaginative and enthusiastic participants in the project, earned the group's disdain by his election to garbage collector. Tom immediately demonstrated the emotional trauma that the stigmatized feel. He stopped participating and withdrew from the group. When I pointed this out to the class, they compensated for their mistake by electing him to a more prestigious position, and Tom returned to his former self. In a precursor to the television series, we had simulated lessons in survival on a deserted island. The game simulation energized the class even if it occupied segments of time generally reserved for more traditional pursuits in the classroom.

Sister Helen O'Neill contracted with me to design, create, and distribute a questionnaire on social studies in the Archdiocese. A new phase in the development had to do with the assessment of Black history and texts that could demonstrate some information in that neglected field. For my questionnaire from which I was then to correlate and draw conclusions, as well as for the workshops, I received a modest stipend for my endeavors. Some of these funds I shared with my students who accompanied or helped me with the workshops or paperwork connected to the questionnaire. Some I donated to an open classroom operation that my confrere Ed Phelan was developing.

My presentations and workshops earned me the opportunity to appear on Instructional Television run by the Archdiocese up in the seminary at Dunwoodie. Taking six of my students and some elementary tools, we demonstrated some of the techniques for the television cameras. I participated in an interview with the guru hired by the Archdiocese to review textbooks. His name was Alweis, and he had a proprietary interest in pushing his own textbook. I believed that the interview went reasonably well, was assured that it had, and stopped at a restaurant on the way back to the Bronx. After feeding my assistants, I looked forward to speaking about the experience to my community members. Unfortunately, my arrival coincided with the television show *Laugh In,* so I was quickly shushed until the show had ended. I contrasted that welcome with the joyous encouragement that Mr. Alweis had gotten from his doting bride, and community life came off as a very poor second to marital bliss.

Instead of working for my doctorate in Washington, DC, I was determined to do so in the metropolitan area. New York University sounded as good as any other step toward that goal. I interviewed with Professor David Reimers and spoke of my incongruous interest in Black history. He assured me that NYU could meet that need, but over my tenure there, I discovered that wasn't exactly so. In my very first seminar with Reimers, I learned the technique of NYU and found it paled in comparison to the demands of Manhattan College or Catholic University. In the School of Arts and Sciences at NYU, many of the students were part-timers. Some seem to arrive at the Washington Square Waverly Building with the intent of playing hippie or observing the Greenwich Village scene. Rather than devote their efforts to serious work or even completing assignments, many of the seminar students chose to ignore assignments and instead boast of their prior achievements under some notable professor in American history at a prestigious school. Integrity seemed overwhelmed by self-aggrandizement in some of my fellow seminar participants.

I wondered why Dr. Reimers never challenged these contributors when they prefaced their remarks with, "Rather than concentrate on the assigned reading, I would like to comment on what Professor Eric Goldman, or Ray Billington, or Richard Hofstadter, or some other such luminary, concluded about the topic." Oftentimes, the topic was far off the theme we were supposed to explore. Frankly I was appalled by the lack of seriousness or professionalism in my fellow students. Their casual approach toward our various themes did not prevent them from criticizing others, especially members of religious orders who were depicted as leeches upon their parishes. After hearing too much, I determined to present my minor biography as a 'leech' in the South Bronx. As soon as I described the lifestyle and contributions of the Brothers in St. Augustine's, the climate in the class instantaneously changed to outright adulation. Although I didn't wear my clerical suit to class, I remained a mystery to my seminar mates until I extolled the work of my confreres. I also concluded that I was studying with a group of students more interested in wine and cheese parties with faculty members than they were in any form of scholarship. I scorned their superficiality, especially when they seem to commute from wealthy suburbs for an adventure in role playing as hippies or intellectuals or beatniks from Greenwich Village. Although I never got to know them as individuals, their 'performances' in class were enough to make me a skeptic about either their scholarship or their honesty.

Despite my negative impression of the people in the seminar, I found the class very productive since I did the assigned readings and wrote a research paper that influenced me a great deal. I chose for my topic "*Levels of Racial Sensitivity on Public Carriers in Virginia from 1890 to 1900.*" The topic may sound dry and uninteresting, but my research provided some interesting insights into racial prejudice. For example, when asked to rate or estimate what Black people wanted according to their most insistent demand, Whites in Virginia presented an inverse image of the same results evoked from Black people. According to the Black sequence, their order of preference was first and foremost, job employment in a competitive market. Their second choice was equal opportunity and wages for employment. In third place was clean, safe housing. Social equality was ranked fourth, but confined to public carriers and then public service providers. In last place was intermarriage with White people. When Whites were selecting what they thought Blacks demanded, the first was an insistence upon marrying one's sister. The respective choices were directly opposite to what the other race actually desired.

I discovered that racist segregation in the south wasn't actually institutionalized until the 1880's when laws segregating public carriers and public restaurants and service facilities, parks and restrooms entered into law. Those laws set the stage for *Plessy v Ferguson* in the 1896 Supreme Court decision. I found it fascinating that the law actually empowered conductors on streetcars and trains to be experts in determining racial composition. If a conductor said an individual was Black, he became so *ipso facto*. Even more incredible were the laws that gave the conductor a gun to enforce his judgments.

Another course gave me a poor opinion of my fellow students in the history department of the School of Arts and Sciences at NYU. Perhaps the most exciting class I had at NYU was six credits over two semesters in American Intellectual history taught by Professor Baker. In the first semester approximately seventy students enlisted in the course. By the beginning of the second semester of a class that I found intellectually stimulating as well as demanding, the class registered about a dozen students. The rest grew weary of Professor Baker's insistence on attendance and participation as well as the intense reading requirements. They then withdrew for a safer, less challenging pursuit of credit. If the class had been a bomb or poorly organized or monotonously presented, I might sympathize with the abandoned, but I surmised the prime reasons were laziness and disinterest in demanding work.

In another class, I found Professor Dinnerstein an interesting character who specialized in Ethnic Minorities. His classes were good and his assigned readings were eclectic and specific. Professor Dinnerstein boasted of being Jewish as his Yarmulke and full facial beard seemed to indicate. He asserted in a pronounced Jewish accent that all he had to do was change his name and he would be welcomed into the American mainstream. I believed that there were a few characteristics that he had to address first since I was a strong believer in the presence of the Puritan Ethic and the power of WASPS. As his class was nearing an end, the political upheaval of the time cancelled all classes at NYU. The students in the Greenwich Village vicinity protested the Cambodian Incursion and effectively shut down the University. Prior to this, I enjoyed reading the graffiti and commentary that were written on paper sheets that lined the Waverly halls each week. No doubt the papers shielded the walls from needing new paint jobs every day, and the protestors felt their opinions were publicized.

To satisfy the completion of Ethnic Minorities, I wrote a paper on the role of the Irish in the election of 1916. I thought that the

Easter Uprising might have generated some response among the many Irish immigrants in Boston, and they might insist on a plank in the democratic platform. According to my research, their efforts backfired when Woodrow Wilson, an avowed Anglophile, and Charles Evan Hughes agreed that no 'hyphenated' American issues were to taint the election in 1916. In essence the Republican Hughes spurned the notion of allowing any Irish voter to affect his campaign on American soil. Irish American efforts to introduce the issue of Irish independence had little influence in the election and most Irish democrats continued to vote the democratic ticket leading to Wilson's re-election.

The professors at NYU were an interesting cast to say the least. I took six credits in Economic history from Professor Irwin Ungar and enjoyed his reading list more than his lectures. One of the professors was a descendant of a British prime minister, or so he claimed. Professor North Callahan maintained he was named after Lord North, the man who prompted much of the rebellious attitude toward British taxation after the French and Indian War. His classroom style was very easy on himself, but he had an encyclopedic knowledge of the subject of the American Revolution. Professor North used to plop at his desk and invite any questions that might strike any student. If none was forthcoming, he would start at the head of the alphabetical roll. While I wasn't impressed with his class preparation, I was overwhelmed with his ability to supply knowledge on demand. I asked him what role Aaron Burr played in the Revolution. I was aware what most of our early fathers contributed to the cause of freedom, but I didn't know much about Aaron Burr. His immediate reply indicated that Aaron Burr, like his nemesis Alexander Hamilton, was on George Washington's staff, but he spent most of his time consorting with an Indian maiden that he named 'Princess of the Golden Thigh.' That seemed consistent with his rakish reputation.

Dr. Reimers alerted me that the definition that NYU calculated for credit in Modern European history started with the French Revolution. Since I had three credits from a Protestant Reformation Course, they couldn't be transferred. He accepted my French language accreditation, and I seemed on my way to successfully completing NYU's doctoral demands. Penury, however, interfered. I had left the Brothers and my departure seemed to coincide with acceleration in tuition fees. Moreover, I now had two children and some distraction aside from my full time job. I then discovered that the university charged me $150 for every semester I stayed home. I wrote a letter pleading my case and my accumulated bills were generously dissolved. Now I had only to complete one course, satisfy a second language demand, take comprehensives and write a dissertation. Upon my readmission with waived expenses, I took another course taught by an interesting Professor.

Professor Richard Scally was a new man on campus. He taught a class in Nineteenth Century British history. As soon as I enrolled in the class, I also sat for a second language test. In choosing between Latin and German, I opted for the former and translated one of Suetonius's writings apparently sufficiently competent to satisfy the second language demand. Dr. Scally's class was another story. He had very hypnotic lectures that entertained me a great deal. One of his interpretations was about the British nineteenth century attitude for birth control. He alleged that unwanted children were in a sense sublet to a wet nurse, and two months later the parent would return to inter the infant's corpse in an unmarked grave. The wet nurse actually was supposed to starve her charge. This was an effective, legal method for eliminating or disposing bastard children born of British nobles and susceptible servants. He claimed that infant mortality was so high in Britain, that few even had the courage to name a baby until it was two or three years old. That way the infant had survived most of the fatal infant diseases that medicine couldn't control. I read about this phenomenon of omitting names for at risk babies occurring among the desperately poor in the ghettos of Rio de Janeiro.

The *coup de grace* to my career at NYU actually coincided with the arrival of my third child and an assignment to jury duty in Rockland County. Maureen was born on November 28, 1976, our celebration of our nation's bicentennial. To say the least, she was a difficult baby for her first ten months. Unfortunately for me, I had promised my wife Mary that I would tend to Maureen during the night time since she had to chase Brendan and Katherine during the daylight hours. Maureen proved to be a cat-napper who cried for my help every two hours. A month later I was summoned to jury duty instead of my classes in BOCES. I had a research paper to write on the *Emergence of Sinn Fein* for Dr. Scally who incidentally had a great interest in Irish history. I have seen him interviewed on several occasions when the topic was Ireland or the Irish in America. I pillaged the stacks of the new library with the red sandstone exterior across from Washington Square of every book I could find about the rise of Sinn Fein. With a dozen books of every quality on hand, I retreated to the jury room on a daily basis where I hoped to satisfy the research demands offered by secondary sources. To complicate matters, every individual in my family was suffering from shoe filling diarrhea attacks of the flu. Mary at least could take care of herself. My ministrations, cleansings, and class work proved incompatible. When I had a rough copy of my paper written, I undertook its typing. My product was so poor that I decided to Xerox the original in the hope of shielding some of the typos and their corrections. Finally, I submitted the paper with great reluctance.

When Professor Scally returned my paper he asked to meet with me in his office. He planned to award me with a C for the course on the basis of my poorly written and presented paper. He actually thought I had taken the title page from someone else and submitted an entirely plagiarized paper. I explained the circumstances to him, and he generously promised to give me an Incomplete until I submitted a paper following up on some of the sources he recommended to me. I spent the time re-editing the paper when I should have been reading for my impending comprehensives. I appreciated the second chance and hold Professor Scally in that pantheon of dedicated teachers who also are humanitarians.

When I received a written reading list, I made a startling discovery. Many of the Professors I had had at NYU had moved on, retired, or were excessed through budgetary cuts. Their replacements had an entirely different set of standards and reading material for my mastery. Many were Marxist historians or economic determinists whose reading recommendations didn't parallel the books I had already consumed. If I were to sit for comprehensives, I would have to read an entirely different set of preliminary books and develop a perspective that actually didn't suit my convictions. With those thoughts in mind, I told my wife that I had better reassess my pursuit of graduate school and focus instead on the joys of family life, as well as selling our house and moving to another location. Although she was hard to convince, I believe that Mary recognized the quandary I was in especially since there was a time consideration for completion of the doctorate. My formal classes therefore came to an abrupt end in 1977.

Before I concluded my personal educational hegira, I had the opportunity to attend a class for a single semester at Columbia's Teacher's College. I found the assignments in that prestigious school ridiculously undemanding. About fifteen or twenty students, many of them college professors in teacher training courses took the class. Few expectations were expressed, and our grades would be either pass or fail. The grading system was designed to thwart any government effort to draft scholars out of school if they were not progressing admirably. The bland pass/fail, incidentally, seemed to punish those ambitious scholars while it encouraged the less enthusiastic. Most seemed very content with that acquisition of credit for salary increment without too much work. During the course, at least everyone showed up for every class, and no one boasted about the teachers or mentors with whom they worked. No paper was required, but we were assigned a demonstration lesson. Fortunately, my demonstration had a superlative effect. I was able to show how a positive personal image could enhance student work. A young Black girl from the neighborhood around Columbia was my project. At first she seemed very shy and uninterested, but with some encouragement and praise for racial achievements, she not only completed her assignment but insisted upon doing two more *Haiku* poems. For many of the class I then became the resident expert even though most were older than I and even teaching college courses. For the next several months, I used to receive telephone calls from my classmates asking my opinion on diverse topics and approaches. While I was flattered by the attention, I didn't extol the wisdom of the class.

Aside from teachers' workshops, I didn't pursue any more history courses, but I would like to cite an experience of another nature. As a new teacher in elementary school, my initiation coincided with the appearance of new math. Pedagogues had determined that the math manipulations we had committed to memory and the calculations we could readily perform in our minds were no longer the subject of much attention. The New Math advocates would argue for greater conceptual knowledge evidenced through a thorough facility in comprehending different bases, employing abaci, manipulating chisanbop, the Asian finger calculations, deriving answers to division and multiplication problems through estimates, or solving spatial maneuvers. Brother James Cusack, one of my painting guides from Oakdale, was selected as master teacher in the field. I enjoyed the class, but felt that something was missing from the old calculations requiring mastery of multiplication tables and other rudimentary facts.

When I left the Brothers, I was still attending NYU in the history department. During my interview for my job with BOCES, I insisted on my right to complete the history degree, and I resolved not to enter any special education classes until I had finished my doctoral studies. Strange to say, that arrangement didn't bother Dr. Hansen who probably believed that I would leave BOCES a lot sooner than the twenty-nine years I stayed. During that time, I received permanent New York State certification in special education for those with learning disabilities. Since I had been doing the job despite the absence of any real training in the field, I was grandfathered in. Other courses were offered by BOCES, and one in particular deserves special mention. An extraordinary teacher named Jim Morgan presented the case for using the Madeleine Hunter design for teaching. He was a born teacher and an inspirational man who employed all the techniques he spoke about during his demonstrations. He easily won my respect for his expertise and management procedures in the classroom.

For the rest of my career, my professional development seemed far greater in my independent reading from history than from anywhere else. I have always enjoyed reading and thought I might even make a decent college teacher. I did have that opportunity as an adjunct at Bergen Community College and at the School of New Resources at the College of New Rochelle, but full time employment found me mired in a virtually immobile job market for many years. Unless one wanted a career in administration, lateral moves seemed almost improbable.

In my graduate career, I found many institutions demanding, challenging and some merely functional. As a general rule, I deduced that the more prestigious a school, the less challenging its curriculum. Perhaps there was an element of conviction that we have the best minds so we just let them do their own thing. My experience put Manhattan College at the top of the heap for requiring solid academic performance. My next demanding institution was The Catholic University of America. Perhaps the demand for comprehensives made these two institutions more exacting than the mere accrual of credits. A great distance behind came New York University, and that was even trailed by Columbia's Teacher's College. I am proud of the education the Brothers offered me, and I am confident that

I can match most of the institutions in the country for a solid well founded education.

During the course of my graduate learning, I witnessed what I considered ridiculous procedures for teachers. In some graduate schools the curriculum and course requirements were so minute that I could only find disdain for them. Occasionally, I had the opportunity to help some of my confreres when they were writing an essay or preparing a take home examination. The requirements were almost juvenile, thereby tainting the Institutions with the notion of selling credits for salary increment. Some of my confreres were excused from writing anything because they knew the professor. Even worse, in my opinion, were the options of attending workshops in places like Disney World to develop skills in basket weaving or cartoon drawing or some such nonsense where recreation superceded school work. Secretly, I harbored the pride that my degrees and credits were hard earned and valuable, not avenues for cash increments. My satisfaction with my graduate education is mostly personal. My reading and courses have made me a successful crossword solver or *Jeopardy* observer. Rarely have I found my graduate knowledge a benefit in my classroom other than those times when I have had the opportunity to teach on the undergraduate level.

Chapter Eight

A Dream Fulfilled

From the time I was in the sixth grade and observed the example of Brother Christopher Lucian Callahan, I dreamed of the day when I could be just like him in front of a class, supervising extracurricular activities, and offering a positive influence to a group of young lads. In pursuit of that dream, I noticed the techniques and strengths of the various individuals, Brothers and otherwise, who had the burden of educating me. Some, primarily in the elementary school at Incarnation, punctuated their lessons with the rod of learning. Not one of them ever transgressed beyond the reasonable, nor did I envision any brutality, sadism, or other perversion associated with corporal punishment. Rather, like most of my peers, I believed that the educational process involved an occasional nudge from the pointer or the hand of the instructor. Such application indicated zeal in making me what I could potentially become, and I harbored no resentments at all.

For the seven years of my actual formation, I continued my dream and observations of generally outstanding educators. The rod of instruction had been retired, but the interest in my progress and development was evident in other ways, like interpersonal encouragement and counsel. Conscientious monitoring of my submitted work was a given. Humor in instruction seemed as important as content. Order and discipline, in the classroom as well as in the individual, were the '*sine qua non*' for a successful student. The proof, as they say, is in the pudding, and I thought I had acquired an excellent education that prepared me to be an outstanding teacher.

During my college preparation I had taken several methodology courses, a few psychology classes, and even the history of education. In all this exposure, there was no mention of corporal punishment.

Vaguely perking up in my memory is some allusion to a 'ferrule' in references to the **Classroom Management of the Christian Brothers.** Even St. La Salle may have advocated a judicious use of the 'ferrule,' but that advice was as applicable as the use of an hour glass or water clock in the classroom.

At no time in my official formation was the issue of corporal punishment addressed. It wasn't like the five hundred pound gorilla, but it was an issue that apparently didn't rate commentary. There was neither advocating nor condemnation of it, nor did I ponder long stretches of time in considering my attitude toward a traditional approach to elementary education. In more recent times, I have recognized the paradox of a Christian educator who should embody Christ's love and compassion be remembered more for his physical brutality, sadism, or punishments. Such thoughts came to me after reading postings on the Manhattan Board on the internet. Some students were protective of many of the Brothers I knew personally as good men, but others enthusiastically condemned some of the men who taught them. The lessons of corporal punishment seemed more lasting in memory rather than accelerants for learning. I would have my own adventure in that area to weigh and assess after my first years of teaching. Suffice it to say, that as I embarked upon my teaching career, I had made no resolution to draw upon 'ferrule,' or to exclude its use from the classroom.

In my three score years and some, I have witnessed several of our 'eternal verities' assume new definitions. These former self-evident truisms transitioned, redefined, or refined themselves into virtually new meaning. For years we believed our government always told the truth, and our foreign policy was altruistic. Our enemies envied us, rather than hated us. Our clergymen were holy men of God, and all religions were humanitarian in theory and in act. Our food was safe; our water pure; and our very air unpolluted. Mother Nature was very resilient and could recover from whatever abuse we heaped upon her. Good food was enhanced by tobacco. Driving and telephoning were licit and compatible. Morality was immutable, and marriage was a sacred institution. And let me add, education and corporal punishment were inextricably entwined. Like so many of these aphorisms, each has demanded re-evaluation in recent thought. To change, one must know there is a problem before the problem may be addressed.

When I graduated in May, 1962 I was particularly pleased that my projected assignment was to Sacred Heart in Highbridge of the Bronx. Sacred Heart and Incarnation were competitive neighbors separated by the Harlem River but connected through the Washington Bridge on 181st Street and the original footbridge that contained a main aquaduct for Manhattan. Both neighborhoods had similar populations, generally Irish Americans or immigrants who worked blue color jobs or civil service. They had little pretense and shared an intense appreciation for the work of the Christian Brothers. Proof of this admiration was evident in the number of candidates who annually applied for admission to the Christian Brothers or to Cathedral, the high school preparation program for the Archdiocesan priests. Rich in vocations, fecund in upwardly striving families, disciplined to respect religious, and motivated to search for a better life for themselves and their families, the parishioners of Incarnation and Sacred Heart seemed poised to make my initial efforts at teaching an unmitigated success. A good teacher wasn't even essential for tapping the rich pool of talent that populated each class.

The Brothers who taught in the elementary schools in New York were generally young, and after a few years experience they moved into high schools or administration. There were several old-timers, however, who were principals and Directors of some of the elementary schools. Brother Clement Patrick Gardner, a former vocation recruiter, was the prime leader of St. John's in Kingsbridge. Brother George Burke held a similar position at St. Raymond's in Parkchester. Brother Burchard Kevin O'Neill, my former eighth grader teacher and a personal inspiration to me, was the 'Mentor' of a challenging school in Harlem called St. Thomas the Apostle. Brother Arthur Philip Braniff ran Sacred Heart, and the dean of the entire grammar school circuit had to be Brother Conan of Jesus Holmes at Ascension. Each may be described as 'old school' professionals who were pretty set in their convictions. Brother Conan may have been an 'ancient school' professional, for he was quite elderly and had little direction over the operation of the school. Generally, the school was run by unofficial younger talent like Brother Stephen O'Neill, Brother Cassian John Burke, and my buddy and groupie, Brother Andrew Urban or Tom Mamara. Brother Conan didn't quite understand the economics of community life. He would give his teachers one way car fare on the Seventh Avenue subway to Manhattan College for

Saturday classes. How they returned was their problem. Funding for school projects and expenses generally arose from the imaginative plans of the younger leaders and tapped without Conan's knowledge for daily expenses, tuition to graduate school, athletic competitions, or general recreational activities. Each Brother realized that survival depended on having funds at his disposal despite the prohibition of such assets according to the vow of poverty.

On one occasion, Joe Troy, Joe O'Brien, Tom Mamara and I were the invited guests of a former classmate of us all who owned a restaurant on 161st Street near the Yankee Stadium. Nat Racine knew three of us from Manhattan Prep, and Tom was his classmate in Immaculate Conception on 151st Street, the Hub of the Bronx. As his guests, Nat promised us no bill, but somehow we were presented with a tab that we couldn't meet. Thanks to Tom and to Conan's fiscal policies, he was able to cover the tab and bail us out without washing dishes when Nat was called away from the table just prior to the waiter delivering our bill.

A younger tier of Directors and Principals operated within the grammar schools. Holy Name had a man who had to close the long, productive association of the Brothers with St. Jerome's when there was no longer any safe housing for them. Now Brother Ray Leech was at Holy Name and under suspicion by the parish pastor of being a 'hatchet man' who closed schools for the Brothers. Brother Thomas Kelly officiated at Incarnation, Brother Anthony Griffin who later went to the African missions, led Good Shepherd, and Brother Charles Patrick, better known as Joe Hosey was the principal of Immaculate Conception. Brother Sylvester Cottrell was the principal and eighth grade teacher at St. Augustine's on 168th Street and Franklin Avenue in Morrisania.

Aside from Brother Philip Braniff, my initial community at Sacred Heart reflected the youthful status of the Brothers in the grammar schools. Three Brothers taught the eighth graders; three taught the seventh; one was assigned to the sixth grade and Brother Philip was the Principal. As grammar schools went, Sacred Heart was among the largest in pupil enrollment. Over all the grammar schools, an Inspector of Elementary Schools presided with efficiency and professionalism. Brother Bernard Peter Maye was an impeccably dressed religious man of irreproachable integrity and energy. His reputation for expertise in the field was virtually unchallenged by even the most experienced Brothers in the grammar schools. At least twice a year, he observed the teachers and offered comments, usually of an encouraging manner. His carefully chosen words and general demeanor demanded respect and compliance. Brother Peter supervised spelling, speech, writing, mental arithmetic, and penmanship contests.

In conjunction with the academic requirements of his position, he supervised the Catholic School Athletic League. He was notorious for his development and use of a measuring machine which determined the legitimacy of athletes who competed among the Brothers' Schools. At one time, eligibility for the different levels of competition was determined by body weight, but as usual some abuses about starving kids to make certain weights changed the criteria. Now, midget competitors had to be less than four foot eight and juniors beneath five feet two. Seniors were all above that height. A student could come from any grade as long as he satisfied the height requirement. Some Brothers coached the kids to sag at the knees, so Brother Peter devised a board that he could trigger to force the contestant to stand up straight. While some mistakes could be made, most of the contestants were valid. Of course those who grew after the measurement could well become the most valuable.

In the eighth grade at Sacred Heart, a trio of Brothers who had been teaching about five years functioned as experienced educators. Brother Mark Di Pietro was the oldest and therefore the most experienced. He had absolutely no interest in competitive or intramural sports so he functioned as Sub Director of the community and Econome who purchased food and essentials for the Brothers. Many used to pique his interest in becoming a principal. From many rumor sources, Mark would learn about possible changes and immediately visit his prospective domain. In fact most of his spare time seemed consumed in eye balling potential posts. Brother Benedict Humbel came from Detroit and specialized in math. He was a particularly conscientious teacher who related in a very friendly manner with the students. He enjoyed the responsibility of coaching the midgets in track. He had reduced every event to a science and drilled the youngsters down at Macomb's Dam Park next to the House that Ruth Built. Brother Christian Donald Smith was casual as well as competent in his approach to teaching Social Studies. He enjoyed coaching the senior division in basketball and track.

When I was in my first year of teaching, I observed the techniques of Brother Donald as coach of the basketball team. He was blessed with two outstanding players. One whose last name was Henry was an affable Black kid who just was huge but seemed to be laughing during most of the games he played. He didn't appear competitive except that his size demanded respect. The other was a tall, lanky kid named Tommy Owens. Tommy had a fine jump shot and had the competitive spirit that marks a potentially outstanding athlete. Tommy was very highly ranked academically within his class. At the end of the year, he had won a scholarship, either academic or athletic, to La Salle Academy where he played varsity basketball under the legendary coach Dan Buckley. Tom grew to about seven feet tall and was granted a scholarship to the University of South Carolina where he developed finer skills under the tutelage of Frank Maguire, the individual who essentially created a pipeline for talented basketball players from New York to compete for the Universities of North and South Carolina. When Tommy graduated from college, he began a professional career that spanned at least twelve years. He started in the American Basketball Association but completed it with the NBA Portland Trailblazers.

In the sixth grade my groupie, Brother Andrew Raymond Buck or 'Bucky,' taught with two experienced lay people. Mrs. Furey was an outstanding, imaginative teacher who often devised pranks or games to play on the rest of the staff. She had the assistance of Bob Baisley who had been a year ahead of me at Manhattan Prep. Bob was a fine teacher too, and he ultimately became an administrator at Cardinal Spellman High School in the Upper Bronx. This trio of educators seldom had any problems, at least that I knew of.

I was assigned to a seventh grade class to teach English and Language Arts to about one hundred and twenty-five boys. 'Big Klu,' Brother Michael Klusman from Detroit, was one and the same as the guy who beat me pillar to post in high school football. He still presented a formidable figure as he taught math to the same students. Big Klu had a bizarre sense of humor in some ways. He particularly enjoyed falling flat on his face from a standing position. I don't know how he didn't hurt himself, but it was an impressive, voluntary collapse. He helped coach the junior track team. Brother Columban Michael Dwyer chose to become my guru or mentor, and that was fine with me. He taught the Social Studies segment of our classes which were heterogeneous and not grouped according to ability. While I deeply appreciated Mike's interest and advice, he bequeathed one legacy to me that I wish I didn't follow.

I never had trouble maintaining class discipline, but I was concerned that some students didn't appear to be making much of an effort. I thought they could be so much better. Part of the mentality of the teaching Brother is a conviction that he is responsible for more than the curriculum. He is expected to prod his students into character development and maturity. Good academic skills are essential, but good study habits, integrity, honesty, and accountability are important too. With that in mind, Mike Dwyer advised me to use a paddle to prod the reluctant students along the path of learning. What I didn't calculate was the disparity between a fully developed adult male, six feet tall and weighing almost two hundred pounds at the time, and the adolescent boys who were my charges. I started to use corporal punishment as an incentive to learning. Rarely did I use it for disciplinary purposes, for frankly, I don't recall any. However, missed homework, failure to memorize assignments or other such minor offenses now merited a swat from the strong right arm of the teacher upon the rear of the young adolescent. I readily admit now that I was totally wrong, but that recognition came only a few years later. I would protest vociferously if anyone were to predicate a sense of sadism, perversion, or pleasure was my motivation. I suppose it might be described as a minor imitation of 'conversion by the sword.' From a perspective of many years, however, I have the sense that individual students may well remember the punishments more than the incentives, the painful embarrassment rather than the inexperienced approach of a young teacher who thought he was doing an essential service.

It was clear that such behavior seemed appreciated by at least some of the parents who entrusted their sons to our care. One flighty fellow in my class was named Roy Regan. Roy's mother was concerned that her son wasn't serious enough and advancing up the tree of knowledge. She urged me to beat him with a paint brush whose bristles had stiffened from poor cleaning. Aside from the preparation such discipline required, I protested that Roy would eventually be fine. I made a prodigious mistake in commenting to a widowed mother of two. Her son Matthew was more or less the class clown, and when Mrs. Ryan asked me to be more demanding of him, I imprudently replied, "Mrs. Ryan, frankly I find Matthew very funny." Her response taught me never to say such a thing to a parent. "I don't send my son to school to amuse the teacher," she exclaimed to my embarrassment. At least I had the prudence to ignore the parent who advised me that her son's 99 IQ left him one point short of genius. Perhaps I was forewarned by her resemblance to Gravel Gertie from the Dick Tracy comics. That episode brought to mind an anecdote that Kirby described from his early teaching career. He evidently had a student in his class whose clothing seldom saw the washing machine and whose body was unfamiliar with soap and water. He told the boy's father as gently as he could that the boy's body odor was causing a great deal of ridicule and abuse from his peers. Despite Kirby's good intentions, the father's reply was a classic. "I send my son to school to be taught, not for the teacher to smell him."

My daily lesson plans and preparation were generated in a small common room in the Brothers' house on Nelson Avenue. The house was ancient and quite narrow, but relatively tall. At the top of the three story house was a television antenna which made an impression on me early in the academic year. On the lowest level, the Brothers had a recreation room featuring a television and some chrome and vinyl furniture. During an ominous thunderstorm over the Bronx, lightning apparently hit our antenna, traveled down the wire, and hopped onto the chrome frame of a two seater chair. At the time, no one was sitting in the chair, but the electric charge ran down the arm of the chair and burned a hole in our tile floor. I suppose if it were not for the chrome our television would have been destroyed. No one ever felt comfortable sitting in that chair whenever it rained despite the adage that lightning never strikes twice in the same place.

The old house had been a former convent for the Sisters of Mercy who now had a brand new convent around the corner. Despite the ancient plumbing and other evidence of age, the house was comfortable and efficient for our purposes. We had an Irish lady who was our usual cook. Somewhere along the line she failed her culinary arts classes, and some thought her hygienic customs were inadequate. Each morning a Brother was supposed to make the coffee before Mass. When it came to my turn, I proved the adage that a little learning is a dangerous thing. As a Scholastic, I noticed that the coffee grounds in Washington used to have egg shells in them. Someone told me that the shells cut the bitter edge off coffee. I determined that when my turn came, I would serve excellent coffee. I didn't know that the grounds contained only shells, for I reasoned that the eggs must be in there too. I vigorously mixed two eggs and added them to the shells in the coffee. The percolator did the rest. When my ravenous confreres arrived after Mass for their morning cup of coffee, a strange precipitate lolled in the liquid. The boiling water had cooked the eggs, and they seeped through the container into the body of coffee. Most couldn't stomach the concoction, and I was willing to strain the product for my own consumption. My best intentions led to the disaster of epic proportions for those whose bodies needed the caffeine kick in the morning.

In October of 1962 the world seemed on the brink of nuclear war. President Kennedy and Khrushchev of Russia got into a confrontational situation known familiarly as the 'Cuban Missile Crisis.' Kennedy, citing the Monroe Doctrine and national security, ordered a blockade of Castro's Cuba. Russian ships were headed toward Cuba carrying what spy planes interpreted as missiles capable easily of striking along the east coast. With a nuclear threat ninety miles off the coast of Miami, Kennedy activated our military. My brother Bernard, for example, was a navigator on a KC97, a refueler for B47 bombers in SAC, one of our major deterrents during the cold war. His wing was ordered under top secret and put on high alert. While the world waited for someone to blink, America stood poised for nuclear war. The Russians finally recognized the threat and retreated back with the missiles, thus averting the nuclear confrontation that seemed so imminent at the time.

Later that year, Bernard organized an inspection of Maguire Air Force Base in central New Jersey where he was stationed. He used to rotate to the 'idiot shack' in Goose Bay Labrador and wait for a red alert. They practiced their drills constantly and never knew when the threat was real or a drill until they were recalled in mid air. A group of his fellow officers agreed to host my class on a trip on Armed Forces Day in the spring. With several buses we rode to rendezvous with Lieutenant 'X' at the airbase. During our tour we were introduced to the behemoth B52 which was to become the replacement for the B47. As I inspected the plane, I mused that it had the same chance of flying as an apartment house. We were invited into the war room where locations of units throughout the world were noted. An armed guard demonstrated the telecommunications they had among the bases. He sent out a message to all bases and invited comments back welcoming the distinguished visitors. In a matter of seconds, the teletype began spitting out messages from throughout the entire world. The class as well as I was very impressed. We enjoyed the day immensely, and I believe the military enjoyed the respect and interest my students displayed. As for Lieutenant 'X,' he generally became recognized as my brother, and his name tag exposed my last name too.

One of the reasons I wanted an assignment to grammar school was the probability of coaching the youngsters. I looked forward to intramural sports. Perhaps the most popular intramural program was softball played either in the empty parking lots of Yankee Stadium when the team was away, or in Mullaly Park which is destined to be the home now of a new Yankee Stadium. The boys were quite good in baseball and softball, but far from proficient in our intramural basketball program. They played a rough style of game devoid of any finesse. I surmised that few would follow in the footsteps of Tommy Owens. Sacred Heart had a rather large gym, however, and many weekends were spent in choose up basketball games.

I was thrilled to be given responsibility for the boys CYO junior basketball team. The team was measured for height restrictions by Mr. Curran, the CYO Coordinator, somewhere in the Bathgate area. I began practices in the hopes of producing a winning season. There were two eighth graders on the team. Peter Falco viewed himself somewhat as a prima donna whose ego never needed a massage. He was selfish with the ball and anxious to gun from anywhere on the court. He played with enthusiasm, but the concept of team still eluded him. He was somewhat disillusioned when I imposed my concept of team play and his need to share the ball and follow team strategy. After a few pine sessions, he became more docile. The other eighth grader was called Arthur Lichte. He actually was not so talented as a basketball player, but he worked hard and fought for every rebound. He was a consummate team member and avid to set picks and send passes to the rest of the team. I suppose he might be considered a player with a penchant for doing the dirty unheralded work that every team requires. I was not surprised to read about him in a recent edition of the **Manhattan College Magazine**. Arthur attended Manhattan College after high school and in order to assist his family in college expenses, he joined the ROTC. Upon graduation, he became a pilot in the Air Force, and ultimately was promoted to three star general. Among his assignments was the responsibility for taking care of Air Force One and its staff. His rise in the air force could be predicted from the leadership and determination he displayed on the basketball courts of Sacred Heart. If I hadn't read the article, I would never have known about his great success.

The rest of the starting five was comprised of seventh graders of varying degree of talent, but not desire. Perhaps the most combative of the trio was an angel faced demon named Jimmy Dilloughery. I describe him in such contradictory terms in no way to be derogatory. He was a frenetic player who played intense defense and was willing to take a charge with some additional dramatics if such a ploy would help the team. His innocent visage camouflaged an internal drive that made him an unrelenting presence on the court. He too was a generous player who used his talents to the maximum for team benefit. Kevin O'Connor, probably one of the smartest kids in the seventh grade, also started. His intelligence seemed to outweigh his instinct for the ball and the necessary moves a good basketball player practices intuitively. Kevin probably thought too much instead of reacting instinctively. Perhaps he became a better ball player as he grew in experience, but as a seventh grader, he could be counted on to follow plays and coach's directions literally. He was actually one of my favorite students, and I was pleased years later to discover that he had earned a doctorate in Spanish and had garnered a teaching position in a college in California. I met him when he visited his sister who was a neighbor of mine in Stony Point. The young shy lad had grown into a self-confident, tall intellectual. I hope I had contributed something to his self-esteem. The fifth member of the squad was a hyper, nose-for-the-ball dynamo named Joe Gorman. Joe hadn't honed any shot or mastered dribbling or other finesse points of the game, but if there was a loose ball on the floor or an errant pass, somehow his body was surrendered to its acquisition. Joe played as hard a game as anyone I had ever met. I think his real love, however, was football. I at least had the option of coaching a zealous, self-sacrificing individual.

In the process I learned a lot about the realities of CYO basketball as featured in the Bronx. Many of the teams had nuns in charge who generally delegated the coaching, refereeing, book keeping and timing to avid volunteers of questionable integrity. The home team was responsible for supplying referees that might come from an objective pool of paid individuals, or more likely, volunteers with a vested interest in the outcome of the games. If this story sounds familiar, just recall the recent Little League World Series champs from the Bronx who were exposed for invalid birth certificates, creative addresses and other forms of chicanery. Often the referees could be intimidated by local crowds as well. The team that didn't send a representative to the scorers' table to make sure every basket was credited or the number of personal fouls didn't escalate or evaporate through clerical error made an egregious mistake. A key observer was generally required to coach and advise the time keeper when to start and stop the clock.

Home court advantage had some architectural aspects that the local team could use to their benefit. For example, St. John's in Kingsbridge played in a surface below a surrounding set of stands from which all kinds of debris and paper clips could be traced to hostile spectators. In St. Luke's gym, there were poles in the middle of the floor and one end of the gym had a staircase which could be used as an additional defensive presence. Some gyms had very low ceilings which prompted line drive shooting rather than arcs. Perhaps the clearest summary of what it was like to play in this league where the visiting team had to be at least fifteen points better than the home club occurred at St. John Chrysostom School. The neighborhood was very much a crime scene, and the parish curate was known as the 'Hoodlum Priest.' When we observed him referee our game, we came to understand why. As one of his protégés dribbled down the length of the court at least five feet out of bounds, I politely brought it to the attention of the 'Hoodlum priest.' His kind remark was, "If you don't like it, leave."

Many of the teams Sacred Heart played were poorly prepared and barely competitive. As coach, I didn't believe in demoralizing our opponents by running up scores or embarrassing the competition. It was easy enough to permit the second team or substitutes to get some playing time, but the objective was to win. Dealing with the Shysters, however, was another matter. Our team, though determined, lacked the real skills of intuitive ball handlers or accurate shooters. Maybe one of the reasons why Sacred Heart seldom produced basketball players like St. Jerome's or St. Raymond's did was the custom in Highbridge of playing multiple sports instead of concentrating on one. The kids were fine baseball players as were the boys from Incarnation. Sacred Heart held little interest in roller hockey, although the opportunities for playing near the stadium were obvious. Football was also very popular and so were various street games. Maybe the steep hillsides and irregular terrain of Highbridge precluded some games, and the kids preferred to stay closer to home than to descend toward the Stadium or Mullaly Park.

On one of my excursions with the basketball team, I exposed my geographical ignorance of the Bronx and the inexperience of a young teacher and coach. We had an away game somewhere in the Pelham Bay or White Plains Road area of the borough. I knew how to get there by subway after securing directions from one of my confreres. My difficulty arose when a train broke down somewhere in the South Bronx. I thought I was near Immaculate Conception and estimated a short walk home via the Yankee Stadium. It was in the dead of winter and the mercury measured somewhere in the vicinity of zero. Although the subway was willing to offer transfers to buses, I had no clue as to what bus to take where. I dreaded looking so dumb in front of the team, so pride played a major role in my *faux pas*. With that ignorance as my armor, I decided to march like the Mormons across country. Although the neighborhood was unfamiliar and contained elements that might indicate rumbles or brawls, the temperature had driven most of the potential brawlers or rioters indoors. We were not so smart. I began walking with my dozen charges westward toward the Harlem River. After quite a while, I recognized Immaculate Conception Church and knew that Cardinal Hayes was several more blocks westward. My charges began to grumble and shiver from the cold, but I herded them safely along until we heard the welcomed roar of sixty-thousand fans attending the Giant game in the Yankee Stadium. That roar was tantamount to the apparition of an oasis in the desert. Another ten blocks north and then we scaled the Heights of Highbridge, very tired, very cold, and for me at least, very relieved.

Our team was respectable but no better, and our record was probably around five hundred. The kids enjoyed the season, and so too did I. I learned a few invaluable lessons. One of our opponents was a team comprised of youngsters from St. John's in Kingsbridge, a parish at which the Brothers taught. My observation led me to note that they were better ball players than mine, but they were out of control. The Brother who coached them spent more time trying to get the team's attention or the practice balls back from those who continued to shoot above his upraised hands and shrieking voice. I recognized that this team might be better individuals, but not disciplined enough to be called a team. I would like to boast that our cooperation and discipline won the game, but I don't remember the conclusion. I do recall that I resolved never to commit the errors compounded by my confrere who was older and more experienced than I. It was a matter of pine time or floor time, depending on how you responded to my coaching.

The future of my basketball players illustrates some practical conclusions after my first year teaching. Generally, I lost touch with almost all my students and do not know what happened to them. One of them was John Scanlan, the brother of Brother Thomas Scanlan, President of Manhattan College. When I asked about John, Tom told me that he had a fine job and was a happily married man. What more could a former teacher ask for his students? I also met an Irishman who was a productive coach in the North Rockland Soccer Association League. Our conversation produced information that he had lived on 162nd Street when he first came from Ireland. He stayed at his brother's home and his nephew John Tobin was in my original class. Like Scanlan, Tobin had achieved the same goals and equanimity in life. Aside from Kevin O'Connor, I don't know what happened to another single individual from the one hundred and twenty-five I had that first year.

Shortly after I left Sacred Heart in Highbridge, the neighborhood underwent the same despoliation as much of the Bronx. In my first class there were representatives from parishes farther south or east who had become wastelands thanks to government disinterest and arsonists. Just a few years later, the Irish population evacuated along with residual German and Italians. Those who moved in were racial minorities almost exclusively, and destitute as well. Sacred Heart became a school with an entirely different texture and color. Unfortunately, its decline coincided with the defections from the Brothers and the Order was forced to surrender its role in the parish under siege. It became a missionary outlet for the priests of the Holy Cross. The famed Fort Apache had become the Little House on the Prairie and the 44th precinct where my father had been a sergeant, became the busiest, most crime ridden district in the city, as well as a target for a rocket attack from some radical Black Panthers. Over time, Highbridge has emerged to a finer, more selective neighborhood, but it still has its moments. There have been a number of housing rehabilitations and citizens groups that have demanded appropriate city response. I am very proud to say that one of the major contributors to this rehabilitation is my very dear friend Brother Ed Phelan who has been the executive director of the Highbridge Community Life Center. His story is a tale for another place.

With the Diaspora of the White population of Highbridge, there are few exiles who have concentrated in a single place. Like those of Incarnation, they are scattered over the suburbs of New York in Westchester, Putnam, and Rockland Counties. Some have relocated to other sections of the Bronx or to Long Island. I occasionally scan the Bronx board to read any messages from former students, but so far I have uncovered only one message written by Richard Tucker. If my first class rates me as a success or failure, I have no clue. In either case, I recognize I could have done better if I were wiser.

I readily identify my major flaw in my first year teaching as misguided zeal in the pursuit of perfecting the Christian character of my students. That zeal led me to adopt what today might be viewed as cruel and unusual punishments, and it may have played a major role in my next assignment. Toward the end of the school year, I was assisting in coaching the junior track team, that is, those competitors under five foot two. The head coach was Mike Dwyer, and Big Klu and I were his assistants. I followed Mike's directions on training kids for the high jump or potato race, but I didn't understand the finer nuances of track at this point. We did enter the CSAL relay carnival held at Van Cortlandt Park near Manhattan College. In my first year I didn't understand the strategies and planning that went into relay carnivals, but I did have a chance in my next assignment.

After returning from the relay carnival, I was called aside by Brother Philip who had not accompanied us to the relays. I'll try to recount our conversation as carefully and accurately as I can, for over the years I have had much occasion to re-examine that conversation and its consequences, and I still don't have any grasp of the facts. Brother Philip told me that an irate father had come to the Brother's House to beat me up, for I had swatted his son too strongly on the rear.

The youngster had a bruised bottom, and the father only discovered so when the kid didn't sit down. The victim was essentially a fine young lad, perhaps reluctant to complete homework assignments. Our relationship was actually warm and cordial, and I recall his joining in a circle of students for many conversations. Brother Philip assured the parent that I would be informed and corrected about the brutal mistake on my part. I accepted that as only the second bit of advice Phil had given me during that entire first year. Phil said that he had defused the father's anger and told me to forget about it.

I readily did forget about it although I'd like to think I altered my approach with a paddle, at least somewhat. The victim and I continued our cordial conversations, and I saw no reason to resent his complaints to his father since I had been the villain. I would have thought nothing more about this except perhaps three weeks later, I was approached by Brother Philip and notified that I would be reassigned to St. Augustine's, a mile or two east of Sacred Heart. Phil described the transfer as a positive thing and proof that I had been an effective teacher in my first assignment. Traditionally, Sacred Heart had sent a number of Brothers eastward, so it didn't seem unusual. In no way was my transfer described as punitive or as the result of the contretemps with the complaining parent. The path from Sacred Heart to Augustine was almost like a modern day 'underground railroad' where White educators were shuttled into a ghetto neighborhood after some experience had been acquired. Before my assignment, I knew that Mike Harrington, Louie Rommell, Louie Ruch and Greg Flynn had traveled this route so I didn't hear it described as anything but complimentary for my quick development of teaching expertise. Within a few years Don Smith and Ray Buck would take the same 35 Cross-town Bus to Augustine too.

Brother Philip told me that Louie Ruch had volunteered for an assignment in Ethiopia creating a need for a seventh grade teacher in his absence. I absorbed all this information with a possible naiveté that only was questioned several years later. My replacement at Sacred Heart was an individual known among the grammar school Brothers as 'Savage JJ the Jungle Fighter.' He allegedly caused some disruption in St. John's for his frequent use of corporal punishment and was transferred to Sacred Heart. It occurred to me that one problem-me—was being replaced by another—him. I also had some other conflicting evidence in front of me.

During his visit to Sacred Heart, Brother Anthony John Halpin, the New York District Visitor, met with each of the Brothers. In our conversation I thought he perseverated upon the need for each young Brother to work with the students in activities after school. He decried the practice of taking an afternoon snooze. I wondered why he was telling me these things, but I attributed them to his poor knowledge of the younger Brothers in the New York District. I had always been involved in afternoon activities and worked with the students at virtually every opportunity presented. I thought little more of it until it dawned on me that he had confused me with my confrere, Ray Buck, the 'Phantom,' who would disappear into his bed sheets every afternoon. He was even known to confiscate a ball to stifle noise from students playing too close to his window after classes. I then wondered if Brother Anthony John had actually thought he was sending Ray Buck to Augustine. I spoke about this scenario later with my good friend Greg Flynn who wondered whether he had been confused with Don Smith when he was reassigned to Augustine. I suppose God and the administration can act in inscrutable ways.

I always hesitated to confront Phil Braniff for the truth. I don't know if my motivation was cowardice or blasé indifference. Later when Don Smith joined me at Augustine, he quoted Braniff as threatening my replacement with the same exile, if he didn't stop brutalizing kids. That is the one and only time I ever heard such allegations about my transfer. In retrospect, sending me to Augustine was the greatest thing that happened to me in the Brothers.

I had learned much during my year at Sacred Heart. One thing I learned was one should be very careful before one works at a Spelling Bee. Brother Philip asked me, the youth of the staff, to read the spelling words at a contest held at Immaculate Conception on 151st Street near Cortlandt Avenue and Melrose. I had the personal confidence and bravado that led me to believe that this was a piece of cake. The cake was there, but I messed up the coffee. One of the spelling words was 'percolator,' but in my finest Washington Heights accent I pronounced it 'perculator.' Asked to repeat the word, I repeated the error. The contestant spelled the word the way I had pronounced it, and his teacher stormed up to the scoring table with a protest. Fortunately for me, that table was supervised by Mrs. Conrad, our Sacred Heart secretary. The nun protested loudly exclaiming that she didn't want to cause any trouble. Mrs. Conrad prudently advised the complainant to overlook my incompetence, so the protest did not remain an issue. At least now I know how to pronounce the word. Brother Philip told an anecdote about another young Brother who was reading words for a contest. One read the word, used it in the sentence, and then repeated it. Brother Dave Van Hollenbeck read the word 'bizarre,' but when he was putting it into a sentence he stammered, "She wore a bizarre, a bizarre, ... ah, ah . . . hat." The audience got a kick out of the performance and correction uttered in haste.

There were plenty of lessons for a first year teaching Brother to learn, if he knew where to look. One of the clearest impressions I received was the respect and admiration some of the parishioners of Sacred Heart had for the Christian Brothers. Some entrusted not only their sons to the Brothers, but even offered an automobile when convenient. Perhaps the most generous and frequent donor of a unique car was Mr. Marrin. His son Jim was a groupie whose younger brother Bob had joined the Brothers too. The Marrin family possessed what might casually be described as a 'Mafiosomobile.' It may have been a limousine in some past glorious history like the decade of Prohibition, but for the early sixties, it appeared to warrant historical plates. Its major advantage aside from its reliability and availability on very short notice was seating space for eight or nine men. The entire community could fit comfortably in the car and often did when the Brothers celebrated an occasional event with a dinner out or attended a district meeting. Ben Humbel was always the intermediary who acquired the use of the car and thereby the responsibility of driving it with utmost caution. Mrs. Conrad, the school secretary, also had a car that she often lent to the Brothers, but it didn't have the seating capacity of the 'Mafiosomobile.'

Sometimes the Brothers borrowed cars for Friday night basketball games against other communities in the city. After what some might describe as a melee rather than a basketball game, the combatants would retire to the host community, shower, and enjoy an evening of conversation, pizza, and camaraderie. Some enjoyed playing poker for small stakes. A few became known as 'chip monks' for the avidity and joy with which they risked a few pennies for a winning hand. Some carried a huge jar of pennies just for the opportunity to play a few hands. I imagine a whole night's gambling might amount to

$1.50 gain or loss. I always found cards and games like monopoly very boring so I seldom got involved.

One of the greatest impressions I received in my first year of teaching was exposure to a unique apostolate many monks had assumed. At Christmas time and Easter, the neophyte Brothers would be assigned to either Lincoln Hall or La Salle Community in Albany. Geography was often the determining factor with proximity to the 'Coop' in Albany clearly a factor. Since the Hall was closer to New York City, I joined many of my confreres there. My initial response was similar to an adage uttered by some of the old hands who worked at the child welfare institution for years. Some grizzled veterans used to comment, "This would be a great place, if it weren't for the kids." Their callousness hid a love for the delinquents assigned to their care and shielded the outstanding devotion they exhibited toward a difficult clientele.

Lincoln Hall used to be part of the Old Catholic Protectory near Parkchester in the Bronx. When the Parkchester development was built, the Protectory had run its course of dealing with court assigned felons or orphans or "PINS,' persons in need of supervision. From the days when special train loads of orphans carried street urchins westward to work on farms or ranches run by folks in desperate need of cheap labor, New York and other metropolitan centers throughout the state had eliminated that contract labor arrangement and provided better social services. The Protectory had a farm annex, however, in northern Westchester near Katonah, and the residents of the old reform school found a new home. About a dozen cottages, each mostly self-contained except for school, chapel, dining, and gymnasia, dotted the rolling hills of the bucolic setting. Classes were conducted in a centralized building where there was a cafeteria. Each cottage held sleeping accommodations for about two dozen boys who were segregated according to age. In the cottage there were also two prefect rooms for night time sleeping or the modicum of privacy such an arrangement provided. The head prefect was generally a Brother of some experience, and he was assisted by a second prefect who as often as not was another Brother. Their job was to supervise the boys, monitor their behavior, and shepherd them to class and cafeteria and gym. These responsibilities impacted the community life that each Brother was accustomed to. On the positive side, each cottage had a car that was consigned to the 1ˢᵗ Prefect according to his whim.

In Christmas week, 1962 I found myself replacing the prefects of the Briar Cottage, each prefect for a brief time when he could escape for a few days vacation. The same was true at Easter Time. The head prefect of the Briar was a modest man whose demeanor hid some extraordinary talents. He was kind, observant, and informed. Many things that the kids could pull on the 2ⁿᵈ prefect who was a retired New York City Detective, didn't escape the investigations conducted by Brother Edward Nelson, called by many 'Captain Eddie.' If our clients could deceive a retired detective, imagine what they could do to a neophyte teacher. When Captain Eddie would return and we reported that all went well in his absence, he would uncover more scams and plots, and bullying that we didn't see. He was stern but fair and seemed to enjoy the affection of these disaffected kids. Later I discovered that after his stint at Lincoln Hall, Ed had acquired a doctorate in Physics and was teaching at some Midwestern University. Perhaps he was as clever at deceiving me as the kids were, for I had no clue about the intelligence and secret ambitions of this generous man. I had plenty of time to observe, for I was assigned to Lincoln Hall for the summer of 1963.

In all my time there, I heard many threats uttered, but I never witnessed corporal punishment. The primary punishment seemed to be withdrawal of smoking privileges. Since there were no walls or fences surrounding this beautiful acreage, an occasional kid would 'mope' or run away. Often, it was said, that a kid who was doing very well in the institution would prefer to have additional sentencing to going home. Here they were assured of some form of love, decent meals, warm housing and friendship—all factors sometimes absent from their homes and neighborhoods. One of the Brothers who made a substantial impression on me was a monk with the language of an aged salt but a heart of gold. Brother Ed Maguire later left the Brothers and entered the priesthood. So too did another man, Brother Luke McCann, assigned there during my tenure, join the ranks of the ordained.

Ed Maguire supervised the administration and coordination of cottage life. One young lad from one of the senior cottages had moped three times in one week. Generally, the State Police would notice an escapee who traveled predictable routes along the parkways to New

York City. Upon his return to Lincoln Hall, the boy would be placed in a cell with walls that couldn't permit him to hurt himself. Perhaps one of the maddening features of this cell was a door that appeared to need one good shove and it would collapse. I don't think anyone was placed in the cell for more than twenty-four hours. Upon release, the former escapee would be given his 'Linky Boots' from which the laces were removed before he was placed in the cell. In his 'Linkies' and pajama attire, the subject usually dismissed any hope of moping again for awhile. Besides he had often taken his frustration and anger out on the door that appeared about to collapse imminently.

One of these kids, however, had attempted several times to escape within a short period. Now his grandmother was coming to visit him on the weekend. Brother Ed Maguire's threats and words promised a dire result if the kid disappointed the loving grandmother. Ed told the kid, "If you try to mope again, I'm cutting off your balls, and your grandmother will have the finest pair of earrings she ever owned." He promised $5 to any monk who witnessed a mother hugging or kissing her son. If such activity occurred, Ed explained, "It came from the grandmothers." They seemed to have a special spot in his heart. At a celebration for him, Brother Augustine Loes, who had spent many years at Lincoln Hall, said his prayer for Ed Maguire was, "that his language would become less scatological and more theological." Ed Maguire was truly a giant for the monks at Lincoln Hall, but he wasn't a soloist. In fact his natural brother also worked at the Hall, and both would sometimes retreat for a quiet weekend to the apartment around the corner from the Brother's House on Franklin Avenue. From time to time, both would drop in the Brother's House for a social visit.

One of the most colorful characters who comprised part of the staff at Lincoln Hall was a burly redhead named Brother Rob Wagner. At some point he had been honored with membership of a chaplaincy with the State Police. Somehow, somewhere he had acquired a complete uniform, pseudo badges and a shotgun that gave him the appearance of a *bona fide* officer. Rob was not above donning the uniform and banging on the door of some delinquent or other, demanding their return to the Hall. The mother of three children I taught at St. Augustine described her first marriage. Her husband to be was brought down from the Hall under armed escort of Bob who may or may not have been best man. After the ceremony which brought legitimacy to the impending child of the couple, Rob hustled him into a waiting car and returned him to his cottage at Lincoln Hall.

While I had some proximity to the services performed by Captain Eddie, Ed Maguire, and Rob Wagner, many other staff members at the Hall rated my admiration. Some had placed their future careers on hold while they performed an invaluable service to an undeniably deserving population. Others seemed to have discovered a life long niche, like Dan Goeddeke from the farm crew. At some of the cottages, the prefects found an effective method of raising funds. They began to operate kennels for purebred dogs. At first the dogs were perceived as an impetus to help new admissions adapt more comfortably. Many experienced prefects noted that newcomers often related most affectionately and least suspiciously with a likeable canine. Later, these same canines were also contributors to the economic well being of their respective cottages. Each cottage specialized in a cherished or often unfamiliar breed. While some immediately thought of Beagles, others ended up with Rhodesian Ridgebacks, Irish Setters, Weimeraners, Golden Retrievers, and so forth. The breeding and rearing of the puppies often produced funds for the cottage which enabled the kids to acquire special non-budgetary items. These might run the gamut from extra basketball courts near the cottage or additional recreational equipment, even power boats for water skiing.

Community life in the welfare institutions differed greatly from the school scenes. Often prayers, Mass, and meals were offered in shifts to accommodate those who were on duty at regular meal time or were supervising activities that conflicted with communal obligations. Supervision was definitely a 24/7 responsibility. The admiration I felt for the staff at Lincoln Hall was also directed toward the Brothers who staffed the 'Coop.' The 'Cooper Keepers,' as some termed them, were cut from the same cloth. My admiration and respect, nevertheless, did not transcend into the realm of imitation. The majority of Brothers curtailed any graduate work since their obligations were incompatible with a predictable schedule. For some of the Brothers, a life in 'Linkies,' old dungarees and flannel shirts, was more prevalent than the rabatta and robe or clerical garb. I admired how so many generous Brothers could perform demanding duties whose efforts largely met an unappreciative recipient of their labors.

I remember one of the frustrations I experienced while working as a substitute prefect. I suppose the general game plan of each summer day was to exhaust the kids with games and athletic contests, so that they appreciated seeing their beds every night. An exhausted body and soul were attributes of a reforming personality. With that in mind, I was asked to supervise a softball game. The kids weren't interested in that at all. The pitcher rolled the ball toward home plate, and the batter swatted a bug well over his head. The catcher claimed he couldn't catch the ball, and after retrieving the sphere from the rear of the backstop, he threw it back to the pitcher. The flight of the ball sailed into center field where the defender might or might not redirect it by his foot toward the pitcher. To complicate matters more, some of the kids actually wanted to play, and they were as frustrated as I. I think the resolute obstinacy of the recalcitrant won the battle of wills, and I sought an alternate method of exhausting the players.

The clients of Lincoln Hall were a breed of student I hadn't met before. The nicest kid in the Briar was named Dillworth, and he was diagnosed with leukemia over the summer. He died in the fall. The only symptom of his serious illness was a desire to rest on his bed at every opportunity. Otherwise, he joked and participated in every activity. The most innocent looking kid in the group was one of the toughest and nastiest. The boy with the consummate political skills turned out to be a below the surface wheeler dealer who was running all kinds of scams until Captain Eddie returned and straightened him out. He was charming and occasionally offered helpful advice to the experienced second prefect as well as to me. Usually this advice or comment indicated the negative behaviors of others. When Captain Eddie returned and questioned the individual, he learned that most of the negative information was generally a subterfuge to shed suspicion upon his own illicit activities. I can't identify any one of the kids as potentially violent or headed inevitably toward a life of crime, but then again the Briar housed the youngest and therefore the least committed to a felonious future. At a future date I was asked to transfer to Lincoln Hall, and I declined the invitation on the grounds that I was very involved in where I was then currently assigned. I believe I was sincere in my appeal and relieved that my assignment was rescinded.

Some of my groupies made impressions on me that summer also. In an informal survey and casual observation, I concluded that those who were initially assigned to high schools drank more alcohol than those of us who went to elementary schools. They seemed to have more complaints about their communities. One quoted an outstanding example of the all-time bitches I ever heard, "Even the electricity in this community shits." Another maintained that he actually heard his notoriously cheap director assert, "I'd buy peanuts, but the Brothers would only eat them." Our high school contingent oftentimes was more interested in the golfing opportunities afforded by the neighboring courses which permitted the monks to golf free. Some even had personal clubs and golf club carts. My golfing career lasted about the length of my drives off the tee. I discovered that I could hit ground balls along the hard packed clay farther than airborne missiles from my driver.

The high school first year veterans were more interested in using community cars for night time excursions into the fleshpots of Mount Kisco, Katonah, Pleasantville, Mahopac, or Yorktown. These fleshpots were mostly movie theaters and ice cream parlors. I don't recall any trips to bistros or bars. It was interesting, nonetheless, to absorb some of the comments of my peers. One particularly pessimistic wish about a relationship with one's director was, "I think I'll buy a saddle when I return in September. It'll be more comfortable for both of us."

In a spontaneous competition, Joe Troy won the ineptitude championship through no fault of his own, by the way. His entire Cherry Cottage charges moped on their way to meals as a formal protest for something the head prefect had imposed on them. Although totally innocent of any wrongdoing, Joe Troy absorbed the mockery of his confreres as was our general custom, and did so with humor.

I am sure each of us learned many things during our exposure to this new type of student. In one sense, it prepared me for my impending transition to another school. It provided the opportunity for my director, Brother Philip Braniff, to educate me about one of the facets of community life that wasn't covered in any of our prior conversations. At the Hall, my group and I had the chance to reacquaint ourselves with ice hockey, and our reintroduction after a few years uncovered some aches and pains that our generally well conditioned bodies were unfamiliar with. I returned after one of these sessions to an empty community house on Nelson Avenue on New Year's Eve. Bill Simon and I decided to meet at the Coliseum on 181st to attend the movie *Gypsy*, since neither of us met or heard from any community members after our arrival. When I returned at the end of the showing, Phil was anxious to let me know that an unwritten tradition among the communities was that every Brother was supposed to stay within the community after 8:00pm on New Year's Eve. Perhaps it was his educational style, but that was about the only suggestion I got from him for the entire year. Phil waited until a transgression occurred before addressing the issue with the generally uninformed younger Brother.

I did have the opportunity to tap Brother Philip's vast experience in elementary schools at one time however. On Saturday mornings when most of the Brothers went to graduate school, I determined to offer some classes in topics uncovered by the curriculum. The most popular was a series of science experiments with rudimentary equipment. Phil suggested some interesting demonstrations about air pressure. With a milk bottle and a soft boiled egg, he showed me how to get the egg intact into the bottle once the outer shell was removed. The quickest way was by igniting a small pile of paper at the bottom of the bottle. When the unshelled egg was placed at the mouth of the bottle, the fire would get quenched and the burnt oxygen would lead to a decrease in air pressure resulting in the partial vacuum sucking the pliant egg into the bottle. To reverse the process, he suggested I invert the bottle with the egg at the inside neck. Then, by running hot water over the sides of the inverted bottle, the heated air inside pushed the egg back out. I had never seen the experiment before, but the class was duly impressed with the demonstration. We played with dyed water and siphons to indicate air pressure and gravity. Another phenomenon we observed concerned pendulums and oscillations. The students were fascinated that Leonardo Da Vinci had done the same experiment using a swaying lamp in church and timing the process with his pulse. I should cite my gratitude to Phil for helping make these voluntary extra classes popularly attended.

On a few weekends I reprised adventuresome hikes similar to the ones I recalled from my elementary school days at Incarnation. One of those excursions stands out in my mind for my timing was abominable. I chose a very clear but frigid day to take a hike across the 181st Street Bridge, cross Washington Heights, and head down to the eastern bank of the Hudson River near the famed little red lighthouse. As usual, my pertinacity outweighed my perspicacity. Our trail followed the railroad tracks outside a fence that ran along the river to Dykeman Street. The path was about three feet wide, but the bank of the river was piled high with ice floes from a previous thaw farther north. The footing was treacherous and I should add perilous, but I didn't realize how bad it was until we had moved about half a mile toward Inwood. Slipping and sliding on the gelid route, we stumbled north, fortunately without losing any personnel to the tides of the Hudson.

Upon reaching Inwood, we crossed Dykeman and scaled the 'Snake Hill' near Fort George and George Washington High School. Most of my two dozen companions now had frozen feet, cramping muscles, and empty stomachs, but we continued down Amsterdam Avenue and retraced our steps to Highbridge. The following day was a Monday and a discernible number of absentees were veterans of the march that resembled the legendary retreat of the marines from the Chosin Reservoir in North Korea. If brains and prudence had been implemented, a different route and shorter distance might have been feasible, but I had to learn through my mistakes. Unfortunately, my students suffered from my stupidity on more than one occasion.

One of the incidental perks of assignment to Sacred Heart was the periodic chance to observe the Yankees or the football Giants at the Stadium. My father sometimes supervised a police detail for important games. He could slip me in through a guarded gate but my seating depended upon ingenuity or desperation. Usually seats could be found among some reserved for servicemen who had passes issued through the USO. I could easily walk to my parents' new home on Wadsworth Avenue and 191st Street. Usually I could borrow my father's car and drop him off at Bathgate Avenue's 48th precinct and switch roles at the end of the day. My brother Ray sometimes provided wheels of a sort too. I forget what the occasion was, but he promised to pick me up at a certain time. As I waited in front of the Brother's house, a dry cleaning truck pulled up, and Ray invited me to share the racks of suits in the back of the truck. I think I would have preferred to ride the bus.

Many times the Brothers walked over to the Heights to see a movie at the Coliseum. We might leave the house with four, but we often arrived at our destination with three. At Amsterdam Avenue, Bucky would suddenly take a right without saying anything. His ability to disappear earned him the sobriquet, 'The Phantom.' He continued to master this skill when he was assigned to join me a few years later at St. Augustine Brothers' house.

While I taught in the school, Sacred Heart had a pastor named Monsignor Humphrey. He had presided over the parish for what appeared to be several decades, but now he was more a rumor than a presence. Nonetheless, once a year the entire community decked out in their habits had to appear in his bedroom where a huge dog seemed to be the dominating presence. Monsignor Humphrey would count the number of Black robes in front of him and determine whether he had been shortchanged or not. Once satisfied that the number of Brothers was consistent with his preconception, we were ushered out of his presence. For the most part, the parish was directed by Monsignor Devlin who seldom had any complaints or suggestions relative to the monks. Father Reisig and another priest completed the staff. Our unnamed priest was called Father HA for 'Horse's Ass' because of his pompous ways.

After my year at Sacred Heart I would have volunteered for another, if given the option. Rather than belabor the motivation for my transfer any longer, let me just claim that whether it arose from punitive or political motivation, I preferred to use the term Providential, for it incidentally led to what I termed the "Golden Age" of my teaching experience. Although my pride smarts at the impugning of my character, if I warranted exile for rash punishment, I am more disappointed from this perspective that it was useless in developing me as a teacher. It ignored any lessons I might have learned about the efficacy of a swat on the behind leading to an expansion of brain power. In my new assignment I would recognize the incongruity of a vowed religious seeking God's blessing through dedication to education and character building, but whose legacy in the mind of his students may have been warped punishments. In Sacred Heart the overwhelming majority of students succeeded easily in standardized tests, Archdiocesan examinations, and teacher prepared tests. It was relatively tempting to take credit for their success, but I was soon to discover what kind of teacher I actually was.

Chapter Nine

From Armageddon to Eden

From the very beginning of my tenure at St. Augustine, calamity seemed predicted during my very first weekend in the community. Our Brothers' House was the finest structure on the block, although it was said that one of the brownstones north of the school had belonged to Jacob Rupert, the beer baron who bought the Yankees and brought Babe Ruth from Boston. Since the previous Brothers' house had collapsed from age, a new residence for eight Brothers was erected adjoining the school. Three of those Brothers taught and commuted to Immaculate Conception on 151st Street. Both parishes had contributed to the construction of the modern two story brick building. In Immaculate, Brother Charles Lewis Rommel was the principal, and he had a reputation for thoroughness and exactitude refined during his tenure at Sacred Heart. The seventh grade teacher was Brother Celestine Robert Keeley who was meticulous and omnivorous in mastering detail. One of the monks claimed he even memorized the serial numbers on the bathroom bowls in Immaculate. The third member was Brother Kenneth Christopher, or Bernie O'Neill who began his teaching career assisted by these professionals.

Before school began, the entire community decided that a trip to Breezy Point where the Flynn family owned a bungalow would be a fine start to the academic year. I was designated to ride a delivery bike down to Webster Avenue to buy some bags of ice for cooling beverages. I rode the unwieldy bike with the huge basket in front easily enough to Webster Avenue. It was all downhill and easy pedaling. The return trip up several blocks was another story. About midway up the hill, Park Avenue paralleled the New York Central train tracks open to the air, but about fifteen feet below the road surface. At street level a green train station house shielded the view of the eastern side of Park Avenue whose name conjured wealth in Manhattan, but trash in the Bronx. As I built up momentum for the additional two or three blocks of hill on 168th Street, the light changed. Unseen by me, a delivery truck was taking advantage of the green light just as I frantically pedaled my way up the long stretch of incline. When I realized I was going to be bisected by the truck, I awkwardly turned southward to escape the speeding vehicle. I managed to turn enough to avoid a direct crash, but my handle bars scraped a five foot gash in the body of the truck before the bike and I fell to the ground. Fortunately, both fell away from the back wheels of the truck, and most of the ice cubes cooled the hot, Belgian blocks of the road.

The driver stopped and approached me as I rose from the ground. He questioned me about the extent of my injuries, but all I could see was the five foot gash in his truck. I assured him I was all right, for I was convinced I was at fault and wanted to escape as quickly as possible. He took my name, and I returned to the Brothers' house minus most of my cargo but suffering some bruises that required explanation. I thought no more about the episode until two weeks later. An insurance agent entered the school yard looking for a small kid named Richie O'Prey. He wanted a signed declaration from me stating that I was not suffering from minor scrapes, scratches, and nervous disorders. Joe Hosey offered to introduce him to the 'small kid who was hit by the truck.'

The insurance company asked me to sign a paper excusing them of any responsibility for the accident and waiving my right to sue. I was glad to do so, and the agent exhaled a breath of relief. He claimed that when the report arrived on his desk, and he saw the site of the accident, he was afraid that a lawyer would convince me to sue the truck owner's company for leaving the scene of the accident. I was just happy not to be asked to reimburse them for cutting a huge slice in their truck. I reflected that had I fallen to my left, I would have been run over by the truck and most likely killed. Maybe there was someone looking over me, but my initial adventure in my new community left me emotionally shaken. The misadventure did little to assuage any suspicions my community members may have had about the wisdom of my new assignment.

Perhaps with only a nod toward hyperbole, I liken my transfer to St. Augustine's School on Franklin Avenue to an ordeal of epic proportions. In tranquility, I think of my transition as some sort of Armageddon. The Four Horsemen of the Apocalypse, familiarly recognized as War, Famine, Pestilence and Disease, are replaced by more personal defects. I relate to my flaws as Ignorance, Presumption, Prejudice, and Pride. My personal acclimatization to an environment so unlike any I had known before left me bewildered, defensive, and almost powerless to adapt to the strange atmosphere in which I found myself. In later years, I would recognize the same phenomenon when I attempted to function in Japan and China amid a society where my language and communications skills were useless. The struggle in Morrisania in the Bronx took place over two or three years, and thanks to my protagonists, I entered an idyllic educational scene where I found fulfillment and joy. When I arrived Black America valued the conk process as fashion plates for men. By the time I left, the Afro and the Dashiki were commonplace and symbolic of the huge shift in racial pride. Before bliss, however, I had to endure some purgation, illumination, and union similar to the works of Rodriguez in my spiritual readings from the Novitiate.

My transition for that period was almost like a purgatory where I had to adjust my thinking and some of my values. I identify my change as mostly Providential, for it refined me in many ways. My personal purgation brought me from prejudice to understanding. Along the path the price was steep. My confidence moved toward consternation. My convictions led to confusion. My comfort transformed into contrition. Complacency yielded to complexity. Concern replaced comparison, and composure submitted to compassion. The primary agents for my personal transfiguration were the students who comprised my first and second year classes at St. Augustine. Those in my first class presented an image that confounded me deeply. My recollection of class records indicated that at least a half dozen had scored fifty-five on administered IQ tests. Like many classes, however, the majority of students were avid to learn, cooperative, and malleable to intelligent leadership. Their names are familiar and recalled with a gratitude for their endurance and understanding that their teacher hadn't exhibited yet.

John Daley perhaps symbolizes many of these students. He worked hard, suffered the injustices of inappropriate penances for others, and aspired to a productive role in society. I was very pleased to be invited to his high school graduation from Rice, and maybe a little proud in the role I played in his college education. I encouraged John, Randy Punter, and Peter Witter to join the SEBCON program offered by Manhattan College. All three entered Manhattan, graduated, and have established fine reputations in their chosen careers. As I understand it, Randy has become a teacher. Peter has begun a career as an officer in the United States Air Force after graduating from the ROTC program at Manhattan, and John was offered a job recruiting students for Manhattan. He accepted that job, but fulfilled his ambition of joining New York's Finest.

These three representatives of the majority of my initial class of thirty-four prove that even an incompetent teacher using poor techniques can achieve success in spite of himself. Many others like Stephen Hayes, Cecil McIntyre, James Parker, James Ford, Angelo Rollo, Dennis Toscano and Kevin Bell have disappeared into society with varying degrees of financial and social success. I appreciate their patience with me, and I confess only that I believed I did what I thought right.

I don't want to make this read like a confession, but I acknowledge that I had to learn a lot before I was able to help these students. Perhaps the biggest adjustment I had to make was in comprehending the differences between a White society and a Black society. In the White community, I knew from my youth the appropriate responses and behaviors that carried acceptance. In the Black community, I had to understand that certain behaviors were residual responses to coping with a prejudicial society that administered justice unevenly, that assigned guilt without cause, and that often punished vigorously for minor offenses that may or may not be the results of behavior of the individual. As a relative of mine in Northern Ireland maintained, Catholic crime or offense against a Protestant demanded retribution whether the charged individual were guilty or not. The reverse situation didn't necessarily demand any response, however. I am reminded of Tom Robinson's conviction in **To Kill a Mockingbird** as an example of what I mean. Guilt was assessed although evidence was nebulous, or even exculpatory.

After decades of coping with such preconceptions as Black testimony was suspect in court, that particularly Black males were inveterate liars and thieves, unreliable and sexually insatiable, even young Black males developed coping mechanisms that increased the odds of survival. One of these effective tools had to do with truth. Truth was power. Truth was objective. Truth was attainable in my exposure to society. Truth was an unassailable underpinning of society. At St. Augustine, truth became more elusive. When confronted with a question, a boy was inclined to give the answer he thought the interrogator sought, not actually what happened. Denial was essential, even if the evidence appeared overwhelming. Ignorance often seemed the safest refuge in time of trouble. That ignorance could reach enormous proportions when it imitated the movie roles of Steppnfetchit. Some of the suspicious students played dumb perfectly. Some could try delaying action by the shuffling routine and deferring any response by any means possible. In my mind, lying was lying, in the sense I used to know. In the Bronx it was more of a coping mechanism often designed to evade responsibility for one's acts or to divert suspicion elsewhere.

Racism had exacted a very heavy toll upon some of the individuals in my first class. No one had been lynched or anything like that, but many experienced the bigotry and antipathy of Whites in those few occasions where the races intersected. Having grown up in New York City, I certainly had heard and uttered my share of racial slurs, but I didn't believe there was any institutional prejudice. In traveling with my class through the transit system, I encountered suspicion and fear that I never recognized before. I had the same right to ride on a subway car or bus as anyone else in New York, but I didn't necessarily receive equal service. For instance, when I took some kids shopping for athletic equipment or games for a teen center, I encountered aloof sales personnel and ubiquitous store detectives, and perhaps in the most tragic day of my life, I had to hear a New York City policeman mutter derogatory remarks about my class and one of its members who had just lost his life. A casual walk through Morrisania was evidence of civic neglect and deprivation of public service. Sirens and klaxons told of police and fire protection, but the garbage and sanitary services left much to be desired.

Some of these factors, common knowledge among my students, took me a period of time to recognize. Should I have wondered if they didn't adjust to my demands as quickly as I anticipated? Unaware of exactly what kind of person I was, they suspected me and examined me in many subtle ways. On my part, my suspicions and examinations were far from subtle. With a lifetime of easy achievement, I undertook my new assignment with a presumption of immediate success. Success was far from immediate, and the path to it was littered with the casualties I inflicted along the way. My own education would change me extensively in the long run when I decided that my purgation had led me to the Elysian Fields. The assignment to St. Augustine was absolutely one of the greatest things that happened to me in the Brothers. I have my class and my fellow community mates to thank for that evolution.

St. Augustine School stood facing Franklin Avenue between 167th and 168th Street. For traffic the street was one way south, but unlike Incarnation, it never warranted playground status. On the street directly south of the school stood an armory where the National Guard used to train on the weekends and for two weeks at Camp Drum in the summer. Later it would house the homeless too. The school had several stories of classrooms and the Brothers were settled on the top floor which could be reached by a decrepit, wooden staircase that actually summited above the top floor. Our classrooms faced the backyard while the Sisters of Charity taught in rooms that faced the rectory across the street. A small office and bathroom were also conveniently located on the top floor. The walls were two-toned with the bottom section painted a very drab, dark brown. Each classroom still contained the capped gas lines from when the building had been illuminated by gas fixtures at the turn of the twentieth century. There was also a large auditorium on the ground floor situated above a lunch room and large bathrooms in the basement.

As a poverty neighborhood, St. Augustine was eligible for federal lunch assistance. Everyday, lunch would be served by a staff of ladies. Mrs. Scollard was in charge as she had been for about a score of years. She used to send some surplus lunch items over to the Brothers' house. Often the menu included hot dogs, peanut butter with raisin bread, or some such cold item. My particular favorite meal was what I termed 'prison soup.' The convicts at Riker's Island had a farm and made a soup for the schools. The soup was a heavy mixture of fresh vegetables with lots of substance. Almost all the students were eligible for free lunch which sometimes betrayed their lack of confidence in their benefactors. They eyed with suspicion, for example, any raisin bread sandwich. They swore that the raisins were actually roaches baked in the bread and therefore wouldn't eat the sandwich. Although quite old by Archdiocesan standards, the school had adequate visual aids and other paraphernalia of then modern education thanks to the poverty programs sponsored by the federal government. Constant maintenance of the school structure, however, was required, but it far surpassed the condition of the Church.

Some called the church 'the Cathedral of the Bronx.' It had stood atop the hill above the Third Avenue El for many years and was among the oldest churches in the Bronx. It had two wooden towers that tempted gravity and endurance. In the movie **Fort Apache,** the church can be seen in the background when Paul Newman contemplates the death of a suspect who jumped or was pushed from a roof top. The interior of the church had at one time been very decorative in the way of prevalent Rococo taste in art, but age and water damage had impacted the walls more than one might appreciate. I imagine the massive interior with its high vaulted ceiling was virtually impossible to heat, so the daily Masses were held in the downstairs church. By the time I arrived in the parish, the pastors were fighting a losing battle with balancing budgets and ledgers, so the church and its school relied heavily on Archdiocesan subsidies. Few priests saw a glorious future in dealing with the challenges of the parish, and there were few volunteers for the staffing requirements of such a church.

I recently read a book that brought to mind some of my impressions and frustrations upon my introduction to a culture that seemed so different from my own. In Pat Conroy's, **The Water is Wide**, he writes of his initial confusion upon teaching on one of the Sea Islands near Beaufort, South Carolina. Some of Conroy's experiences parallel my own, but his were described on a more literate scale, just as his creativity and adaptation in the classroom were more inspirational than my own. His struggles with bureaucracy and intransigent racism were absent from my experience, but some of the baffling behaviors of the students were similar.

When I was transferred to St. Augustine, the faculty of that school had just undergone a major reconfiguration. The former principal, Ken Cottrell or Brother Sylvester, was reassigned to become the principal of St. Mary's School in Yonkers. Brother Louie Ruch had volunteered for the missions of Ethiopia, and the fifth grade teacher, Brother James Curwood, had been sent to teach Latin at La Salle High School in Troy, New York. That left only one experienced member of the staff, Brother Gregory Flynn. The new principal,

Brother Charles Patrick or Joe Hosey, had shifted from Immaculate Conception along with a groupie of mine named Brother Patrick Omar, or Sean O'Keeffe. As the most experienced veteran, Greg Flynn brought some extraordinary talents to the job. He had been operating programs after school and on weekends among the alumni and had a loyal coterie of followers. His casual demeanor and easy going style also set a silent example of grace under pressure. Nothing seemed to faze this man. He accepted any challenge graciously and responded with good humor and wit. He loved working with the kids, and in many ways became a paragon of what I wanted to achieve if I only had his personality. His good looks which resembled James Garner rated gasps from some of the females, but Greg seemed oblivious of any adulation. He was as even tempered and modest as a paragon for the impetuous and impatient.

Joe Hosey was quite experienced and well organized, and well prepared for his role of principal. Joe had taught for several years at Good Shepherd and had been the teacher of a combined seventh and eighth grade class at St. Bernard's on 14th Street. He was accustomed to the challenging role of teacher administrator after working at Immaculate, so his new responsibilities at Augustine were old hat to him. Joe was a demon for learning. After earning his master's in history from Manhattan, he set about acquiring a doctorate in education at New York University. Exposed to the latest thought in education and honed by the versatility demanded in his prior assignments, Joe was innovative and confident that his faculty could run a fine school. His enthusiasm and obvious joy in teaching were infectious and made teaching under his direction quite easy and productive. The faculty readily emulated their leader and enjoyed doing so.

Future years would prove what excellent community mates I had for helping me adjust to my alien environment. After three additional years at Augustine, Greg spent some time at the 'Coop' in Albany and volunteered to follow Louie Ruch to Ethiopia. In the time subsequent to that, he has spent almost all his life in the service of the poverty stricken people of Addis Ababa, Asmara and Eritrea. While combating the infamous famine in Ethiopia, Greg was captured by rebels who resented famine relief being distributed in bags tagged with the sign of the Ethiopian government. In a battle in which four hundred men lost their lives, Greg was captured, but he presented a dilemma to his captors. They feared he was a CIA operative since he was the only White man in four hundred square miles. They thought they might incur the wrath and vengeance of the United States if he were harmed.

Instead they marched him on a tour of the horrible conditions of Eritrea and finally released him in the Sudan. Greg had subsisted on a single can of tuna fish a day, rations that he said were better than those of the rebel soldiers. This ordeal pared almost seventy pounds off Greg's sculpted physique which had merited the nickname 'Flex Flynn' in younger days. He also almost died from malaria and dysentery. After returning to the States to restore his health, he traveled back to Ethiopia and has continued to work among the poor. His latest venture has to do with educating the very young children of Addis Ababa's street people. I implored him to stay in the States, but Greg was determined to return, and I believe will only settle for the missionary life in Africa. While he worked with me in Augustine, I had an exemplary paragon of what a teacher in the Bronx ought to be. Greg never second guessed his actions, but then again, he may never have had too. His patience and understanding were generally impeccable, and his dealings with graduates were relationships meriting trustworthy confidence. His shoes would be very difficult to fill.

Joe Hosey left Augustine after three years in order to be the founder and director of an experimental elementary school for the gifted and talented poor boys of the inner city. A more qualified candidate would be harder to find, and a more competent administrator who allowed his staff freedom to experiment with new ideas was a rarity indeed. After settling Monsignor Kelly School safely on an established path with an experimental curriculum, Joe was then assigned to teach in the education department at Manhattan College. I think the collegiate life was quite tame after the challenges Joe faced in the elementary circuit. With doctorate in hand, he decided to leave the Brothers and then began teaching in the City University. Like Greg Flynn, Joe has remained a close friend and confidante over the years. My wife and I were introduced by his wife Dorothy who is godmother to our older daughter Kathy. Joe honored us by being godfather to our younger daughter Maureen. Finer people couldn't be found than Joe and Dorothy.

Both Joe and Greg, despite their different destinies, played a vital role in helping me adjust to the demands of my unpredicted assignment. One of Joe's attributes and one of the incidentals of joining a smaller faculty was exposing his staff to greater responsibilities. What eight Brothers did at Sacred Heart, four did at St. Augustine's. Aside from the teaching and coaching, alumni activities, and teenage supervisions, as well as involvement with parents marked a more demanding role for each of the Brothers. Joe's confidence and encouragement enabled me to develop talents that were either dormant or secondary at Sacred Heart. My maturation as a Christian Brother became all that more accelerated. When Greg moved to the Coop, I inherited much of the organizations and alumni activities that he had created. In short time, I was organizing Communion Breakfasts for the Alumni and supervising the dances and social activities that Greg initiated during his tenure at Augustine.

Since I credit Joe and Greg with being so helpful, I also realize that I had offered almost a 'tabula rasa' for them to work with. Most of their lessons were examples or behaviors rather than lectures or words. Both men earned my deepest respect and heartiest appreciation. As for Sean O'Keeffe, he may have been on the same learning program as I was, but he was reassigned to Holy Name on 96th Street. Sean's living at the Brother's house on Franklin Avenue while he taught at Immaculate may have eased his transition to our students, since he heard the tales and adventures recounted on a daily basis by the previously assigned faculty of Augustine.

Early in our tenure at Augustine, the country suffered the great loss of President John F. Kennedy. We had learned about his assassination in Dallas during classes on a gorgeous November afternoon. The school went directly to the church to pray for the President's survival, but shortly after returning to the classroom, we learned that Kennedy was pronounced dead. Sean's sixth grade class had difficulty reconciling this information, until he took the picture of the president that he had hung in the classroom and turned it around to face the wall. By so doing, the class understood that the political leader and a hero of many of the Black community had died. With that gesture several days of intense sorrow and mourning began. Sean himself almost fell into a depression like many others in our nation. I still recall the constant dirges played on the radio and the live coverage of JFK's funeral and interment. The only major depressing event comparable to the assassination of Kennedy was the tragedy of September 11, 2001 when hijacked planes crashed into the Twin Towers, the Pentagon, and a field in western Pennsylvania.

Although I had the magnificent example of Greg and Joe, I must acknowledge another source of my education and adjustment to the atmosphere of St. Augustine's. It came from a very unlikely source. Unlike them, this influence was one of my least productive students and a candidate for least likely to influence his teacher. I write of a 'talkative moron,' a certified 55 IQ, and a lad who had the most atrocious grammar and speech patterns of anyone I knew. As his lessons for me might indicate, Michael Roberts was a most unusual boy, but I think his conversation and style indicated a much quicker mind and intellect than any standardized test might measure. As I mentioned earlier, I believe that racism had provoked a certain coping mechanism that led the unsuspected to exhibit unusual behaviors.

Mike had rated a bottom line IQ of 55, not so much because it represented his learning acumen, but rather it reflected his attitude toward such tests. When I was officiating over a standardized test, I was explaining how to fill out the computerized answer sheet. I instructed the students to fill one letter of their name in each empty box above the alphabet arrayed in a vertical row. When they had spelled out their last name, they were to spell their first name employing the same technique. As I directed the students to find the first series of boxes that started with A and led to Z, I told them to descend the column until they found the letter they had inserted in the first box. As he was penciling in the circles, I heard Michael say,

"Oh. It's sorta like a game."

I was convinced Mike had randomly filled in boxes simply to keep previous administrators happy. Whether they spelled his name or not was irrelevant. After checking his paper, I asked Michael if his name were Robert or Roberts. He responded with the same reverence he had for objective truth,

"Sometimes I spells it with an S . . . . , and then again . . . . , sometimes I don't."

Over the next seven years, Michael and I would have many conversations. He seemed to enjoy entertaining the strange White man who listened to him intently. He had to be putting me on, but I was thoroughly enjoying it. One never knew what Michael would say at any time. In the era of compulsory class Mass attendance on Sunday, I noticed that Mike was not among the worshipers. In one of our first confabs, I asked Mike why he wasn't at Mass with the class the previous Sunday. His response was broader than the words he expressed. He said,

"Because I smells."

"You smells?"

"Yeah, Brother Kelvin (he never did quite master my name, and whatever he called you first, he always called you), *I smells."*

"What do you mean, you smells?"

"Well you see, Brother Kelvin, there ain't no water in my buildings, so's I have to wash up at the Johnny Pumps on the street. You don't want me nekkid in the street, do you?"

I couldn't argue with his reasoning, but I also got a glimpse of the conditions under which he lived. He repeated the same kind of logic when he told me about the rigors of his Lenten fast. Mike was as concerned with accuracy as much as he worried about what constituted meat during Lent. As I elaborated on the rules for fasting and abstaining from meat in the years, prior to Vatican II, Mike boasted that he would follow the church's rules about fasting and abstaining. I wouldn't be so bold as to predict what Michael thought about fish, but he was determined to follow the orthodox regimen of Lent. At the time meat was banned during the entire Lent, and Mike assured me he was going to follow the rules.

"I's givin up meat for Lent. I's only gwoin to eat roast biff."

"Mike, roast beef is meat."

"Okay, then I's just gwoin to eat chicken."

"That's meat too, Mike."

"Okay, Brother Kelvin, I'll just eat 'poke."

At that point, our verbal exchange abruptly ended, and I suspect that he just retained his idiosyncratic definition of meat and believed he was following the Lenten regulations conscientiously. For my part, I saw little advantage in prolonging this conversation, for I am sure Mike would swear he gave up air for Lent if he thought that's what I wanted to hear.

Whenever this master of conversation engaged me, I couldn't tell what the topic was or where it was going. A prime example of this occurred when he announced he loved to play the drums. Egging him on, I said, "Why do you play the drums, Mike?"

"I plays the drums. I don't wanna play no trumpet."

"What's the matter with the trumpet?"

"I don't wanna play the trumpet. I don't like the trumpet. I like girls."

Despite that *non sequitur* which should have warned me, I repeated,

"What's wrong with the trumpet? Why don't you like the trumpet?"

"Brother Kelvin, yuh see, girls and trumpets is different. You can blow a trumpet but you can't blow a girl."

Only the rash could tell where a conversation might conclude. He summarized his opposition finally with characteristic brevity and incisiveness by muttering after an extended exhalation of air,

"It takes my breff away."

One of my longest dialogues with Michael occurred when I found him stalled on the stairs just outside my classroom.

"You're late, Michael. Why are you late?"

"I's thinking, Brother Kelvin."

"What are you thinking about, Michael?"

"I's thinking about squats."

"Squats? What's squats?"

"You know, squats when you hit us. I don't want no squats."

I still hadn't learned about the futility of expecting pressure to the buttocks to produce intelligent responses. Then Michael unexpectedly shifted the focus of the conversation by explaining the reason for his arriving late to school.

"Monday's muh day in courts. The judge say I'm a nice boy."

"In court? What are you doing in court?"

"The judge say I'm a nice boy."

"What did you do?"

If I hadn't heard his response, I would swear it had to be a fictitious reply.

"The judge say I'm a nice boy. I beat up my ole lady's ole man with the hind leg of my dead dawg."

I asked him to repeat what I swore I couldn't have heard correctly. Mike's reply was a verbatim repetition of his initial response. I asked him to explain at greater length, so Mike offered the following narrative:

"When my big dawg, Killer, died, me and my brudder Steven, we cut off his big hind leg in case we needed a club. Muh ole lady-that's my mother—got her welfare check for my baby sister Hattie. Then muh ole lady's ole man, dat's her boyfriend, he come round looking for the check. He started beating on muh mom, so me and Steven beat him up with the hind leg of muh daid dawg. The judge say we're nice boys."

After such a story who could find the strength to reward him by swatting his behind?

The boy who could keep me enthralled with his stories didn't demonstrate much physical mobility. A prime example of Michael's physical exertions occurred when my previous class from Sacred Heart played my current group in Augustine in a softball game contested in the parking lot of Yankee Stadium. My previous class, now under the tutelage of Ben Humbel, had a number of good baseball or softball players. I had few who were remotely interested in the game. Around the corner from the school sat Morris High School where concrete fields were available, but they usually catered to the ghetto craze for basketball. I doubt I ever saw a softball game in progress there. When we squared off for the soft pitch game, Augustine won the 'mean look' contest, but after that all went downhill. Sacred Heart blasted the ball all over the field. Michael was playing right field, and after one prodigiously huge shot sailed far above his head, he shouted to me on the pitcher's mound,

"Brother Kelvin, get another ball, I'll get that one later," as the hitter triumphantly trotted around the bases. Despite his lack of exercise, Michael was a strong runner in the 220 yard dash, but he must have rationed his efforts so that he could remain focused on his strength.

When Michael graduated from St. Augustine, he enrolled in Taft High School on Morris Avenue about ten blocks northwest of Augustine. He wasn't very happy there, for he claimed that the teachers made fun of him and laughed at him. They weren't like his teachers in Augustine, although I would have to confess that he had often entertained me. Mike viewed our treatment as almost one of a peer counseling program. Michael informed us about the peculiarities of the neighborhood, and we listened intently. He also knew the Brothers genuinely liked him and wished him well. He dropped out of high school and came by to explain his life plan to me.

I invited him to join me on a trip to visit my family down in Long Beach, Long Island. He was pleased to accompany me. At my Aunt Helen Clancy's house, he met her husband Joe and my brother Bernard. He started to explain his future plans.

"If I joins the army, they make me a cook! What I gonna tell my children what I did in the army-cook for four hundred men? I aint gonna join no army. If I joins the navy, the sharps get me.

289

"Pardon me, Michael, the sharps?"

"Yeah, you know the sharps, those fish that eat you. I don't join no navy for I don't want to be eat by any fish. If I joins the air force, they send me up in planes. I don't wanna die in no plane crash, so I'm goin to join the Marines. The Marines know how to fight. They not like Keef who got shot up there in Vietnam. The Marines know how to fight. I join the Marines.

In his statement about the service, Mike underscored that Black ghetto kids were enlisting in large numbers to volunteer for the more dangerous outfits in America's fighting forces. Special Forces, air borne, and the Marines were especially appealing to the young kids who often had a choice of military life or drugs in the ghetto. My uncle and brother queried Michael a bit more, and then he asked what they did.

Joe Clancy admitted that he had been a paratrooper who had dropped out of planes many times in World War II. In fact, Joe had dropped with the 82nd on D-Day and had been listed as MIA and presumed dead for three weeks. He also fought in Belgium, Holland, and in the Bulge when his unit was sent to *St. Vith* to assist in the support of the 'Battered Bastards of Bastogne of the 101st.' Despite these dangers, Joe was very proud of his service and respected the troops in Vietnam. Bernie on active duty with the air force mentioned that he currently flew in airplanes as a navigator. Bernie had flown many flights in and out of *Tan Son Hut* airbase in his 141 cargo plane. He also had spent a full year in MACV headquarters in Saigon. Michael seemed to ponder on their war experiences, but he said little. When we were heading home later, I mentioned to Michael how funny my relatives had found him. Michael's response was as lucid as usual.

"One of dem flies in planes and the other one jumps out of 'em, and dey think I'm funny!"

In Michael's reference to Keith Lundy, one of his closest friends from the class, he alluded to a situation that reflected the turmoil of the sixties. Keith's family dissolved, and he moved out of the Bronx to Philadelphia. He was a quiet, polite kid who always was cooperative, and like many in his class, he excelled in track, especially at the high jump. When I wrote to the administrators of West Catholic in Philadelphia, the Brothers there readily admitted Keith on that recommendation. Unfortunately, Keith's adopted family broke up within a few months, and at the age of fifteen he was inducted into the army by a not too scrupulous recruiting sergeant who was having trouble filling his quota. Keith actually loved basic training, and probably because of his youth and fine physical conditioning, he found the harassment and physical punishments more games than anything. He smiled all through training and occasionally wrote a letter saying how happy he was. In a short period however, before his sixteenth birthday, Keith found himself guarding the streets of Washington, D.C. in the aftermath of the Martin Luther King assassination riots. A short time later, he sent a photo of himself with the 101st Airborne somewhere near the DMZ. He had been there only a brief time when he was severely injured in the chest and mustered out with seventy per cent disability. Keith, like many kids from the ghetto, sought admission into the most dangerous and demanding roles in the military, and Mike found his treasure in the Marine Corps.

After Mike finished his basic training in the Corps, he returned for a visit bedecked in his dress blues and a modest array of medals on his chest. He explained to me that in the Marines, the non coms had names for ethnic groups.

"*Dere was the Splibs, the Chucks, and the Poke Chops. The splibs was the Puerto Ricans. You was a chuck, and I am a poke chop.*"—if my memory is accurate on that long passed conversation. He had an interesting tale to tell about the Vietnam casualties, too.

"*Charlie ain't killin our soldiers. No sir, Brother Kelvin. Dey's dyin of the Black Syph.*"

By this time in our relationship, I determined that it was senseless to explore the 'black syph' any deeper, nor to cross-examine Michael about his military career. He made it to Vietnam and back home again without getting wounded. Miguelito, another kid from the class behind him had been wounded seriously in 'Nam, and sent to Japan for rehabilitation. Within a short time, Miguelito was sent back to 'Nam so he went AWOL and wasn't heard from again. During his time 'in country' Mike wrote a number of letters to me offering me praise for being a good friend and confidante. Although he was reticent to write assignments during his elementary school career, he was quite competent in expressing himself in the letters he wrote to me. Naturally, I made a special effort to respond to all his notes. Upon his return, our dialogues continued.

As I sat on the Brothers' house steps, I saw this dapper young man bedecked in a lime green beaver hat and cashmere sweater bopping down the street. It was none other than my favorite story teller. Now he began to regale me about his adventure on Southern Boulevard.

"Me and Steven were walkin down Suffrin Boulevard, and we saw these fly girls. Brother Kelvin, they was nines at least. I rates them with five for figure and five for face. Well you know how it is, Brother Kelvin, I walks up to them and you know I sorta put my hands on them. Brother, dey wasn't girls.

Another lesson from my educator in the mores of the neighborhood! Michael generally used the front stoop of the Brothers' house to educate the strange teacher who found his conversation so entertaining.

Michael and I shared a mutual love that engendered a symbiotic relationship. I learned so much from him, and doubt I taught him as much. He needed the friendship and a sympathetic male ear, for he seldom sought advice, since he had already made up his mind. His dream in adulthood was to be a James Bond type with plenty of girls, and drinks, and action. When I injected a note about responsibility and maturity, Mike more or less looked at me as if to say,

"What you ravin about, Brother Kelvin?"

Since my days in the Bronx, I have scouted news articles about what may have happened to some of the kids I taught. About ten years ago, I found a piece that wrote of a man of the same name, neighborhood and age who murdered his girlfriend when she refused to let him back in her house. I believe I was reading about the one and the same individual who educated me years earlier. Although I wouldn't predict that fate for him, I don't find it beyond either my comprehension or his potential.

While Michael represented one form of passive resistance to authority, another exemplar of the practice took the form of a young lad I named after an imaginary Greek God named 'Inertius.' Alphonso Blackwood Dingbell had the build of an Adonis. Michelangelo could have chosen him for his model for the famed statue of David in Florence. Alphonso's sculpted upper torso would be the envy of any body builder or weight lifter. What I couldn't fathom, was how he ever got in that condition. 'Phonso' seemed to have two gears in the classroom—stop and reverse. When he uttered my name, he would moan, "Bro . . . ." and then he would have to stop and catch his breath. Alphonso also had mastered the enigmatic grin similar to the smile Fess Parker's Davy Crockett used in the old TV series to cajole a bear down from a tree. It was an inane procrastination that led nowhere, but occupied time. Evoking a simple yes or no answer from Alphonso was probably a five minute investment in teaching time. I remember saying to him on one especially exasperating time in the dead of winter when the heat was blasting, "Alphonso, do me a favor, and go sit on the radiator. That will give you a clue as to what you are doing to me." In contrast to his behavior in class and around academic responsibility, his performance in sports and intramural activities indicated a speed and endurance that many athletes might cherish.

The manner in which the students behaved in the classroom was quite different from their participation in sports and after school activities. Most of the students were fine athletes who competed hard and were determined to win. Their self confidence on the field of sport contrasted with the self-consciousness in the classroom. Cooperation and enthusiasm replaced passivity. The boys were then extremely friendly, joking with the Brothers and following their coaching directions carefully. The evident affection and camaraderie after class were obvious to any casual observer. There were no threats uttered, no punishments other than pine time meted out, but the students seemed perfectly comfortable with the arrangement. I wasn't astute enough to recognize that the boys weren't schizophrenic, but were employing coping mechanisms for the different expectations and demands. Clearly they were prouder of their athletic prowess than their intellectual potential. If they harbored any resentment that carried over from the classroom to the ball field, they kept them quite under control.

Some of the boys undoubtedly had serious learning disabilities, perhaps even including the lack of intellectual acumen. After some introduction to these individuals, I manufactured one of my aphorisms, "The initial encounter with sheer stupidity is an awesome experience." I had requested an identification sentence about the Ku Klux Klan, and the response was creative if inaccurate. Melvin said the Ku Klux Klan was the name of the first Chinaman to come to America. I recall one case where I asked a young gentleman his name. He was totally bamboozled by the request and seemed unable to process the appeal in his head despite my repetitions. Only later did I understand that I probably had intimidated him so badly that he thought it was a trick question. I also dealt with a young Hispanic boy who was considerably limited, almost as extensively as my comprehension and ability to understand his limitations. Fortunately, he was admitted into a special education program that was located in part of the Immaculate Conception School complex. His evident happiness and relaxation in the new environment were lessons to me in particular. I struggled with his mother's advice to talk to him about "Choggie." Totally unable to make sense of the request, his mother kept insisting I talk to him about his hero, "Choggie Berra of the Chankees." This poor man in a foreign environment had a great deal to learn. Another withdrawn individual who seemed completely adrift was diagnosed with tuberculosis during one of the periodic health inspections. His problem was a new one among many for me.

My role as religious educator carried with it the obligation to develop a sense of honesty and a reverence for the truth. In my early days at Augustine, that responsibility was severely challenged by even the simplest cases of petty larceny. Since most of the students had little money for replacing essential items like pens, the theft of a pen or pad seemed more serious than its economic value. The victim often brought his plight to the teacher's attention. One such case involving an amateur petty thief, sticks clearly in my mind. Henry Sumpter had lost one of those pens with replenishable cartridges so cherished at that time. In my organized search, 'Fudgie,' so named because of his jet Black skin, told me he saw it on the floor, and it was picked up by Calvin. Calvin was a huge seventh grader over six foot and two hundred twenty pounds. He loved the animals at the Bronx Zoo and aspired to shovel 'zoo doo' from the elephant and lion's cages for the rest of his life. To fulfill that ambition actually made him happy as a 'pig in his environment.' With 'Fudgie's' information, a minor search of Calvin's desk uncovered the lost item. When I inquired of him how it got there, Calvin used the time honored alibi of the hardened criminal.

"It been planted," he replied. After returning the pen to its rightful owner, I asked Calvin to write a one hundred word essay speculating on how the pen ended up in his possession. His first effort was a fabrication about a conspiracy to get him in trouble. I advised him to try another explanation. On his second essay, Calvin went on about how he knew he was innocent, God knew he was innocent, and no individual like me, could get him to confess to a crime he hadn't committed. After

contemplating a third assignment, I finally asked 'Fudgie' to repeat what he saw Calvin do. When he described the finding and relocation of the pen, Calvin suddenly had an epiphany.

"Oh yeah, now I remember."

I think I learned more in that episode than he did.

One of my very first encounters with retrieving stolen goods led to an introduction to a diminutive fifth grader with a flexible conscience. Ellsworth Johnson had a guilty look all the time because of his shifty eyes and his predilection for evasion. Cecil had lost a blue, clear vinyl pencil case with a few writing implements and erasers enclosed. After a minor investigation, I recalled that Ellsworth had sat in that desk during a reading class. As he was preparing to go home, I stopped him, and I asked if he had seen a blue pencil case.

"I aint seen no blue pencil case. I did see a red one."

"Would you mind opening your school bag, Ellsworth?" He readily complied, and when the hot goods were evident he shouted,

"It been planted!"

I tried to encourage a more rational response by stating that it certainly looked suspicious. That evoked a sermon and character reference from Ellsworth that I remember verbatim to this day.

"Now listen, Brother. I don't lie, and I don't steal, and I don't like to be accused of something I didn't do."

I supposed I chalked up the experience to a new concept of truth and merely reclaimed the stolen item, returned it to its owner, and marked Ellsworth as worthy of considerable attention in the future. True to my foresight, I had plenty of interaction with the gentleman with the vocal response several times over the next few years.

Ellsworth's family was quite poor, even by the neighborhood standards. When Brother Ed Phelan visited the house, he noted the walls and kitchen desperately needed a paint job. Being the kind of man he was, he offered to paint their kitchen with his paint and sweat *gratis*. He also recruited Brother Hughie Stringer to help him. I was in my distant mode at the time and felt no temptation to enlist in their charitable work of supererogation. After the two Brothers arrived at the apartment and started painting, an irate neighbor banged on the door. He indicated an army of roaches was escaping through the kitchen window and marching up the outer wall and infesting his clean apartment. Ed stationed two of Ellsworth's siblings at the window armed with shoes instructed to obliterate any of the

Bronx pests that tried to escape to greater heights. At the end of the day, the experience had turned Hughie's stomach and induced nightmares for a while. For Ed, it was all in a day's work.

A year or two later, I was checking homework books of my class, and detected a penetrating stench. Although it took sometime to narrow down the source, I decided it was emanating from the homework book of Ellsworth Johnson. I sent Ellsworth to the principal at that time, Brother Matty Kissane. An accompanying note carried the message,

"Does he, or doesn't he, and if so, what is it?"

Matty returned with Ellsworth and admitted that a noticeable stench was present. As we mused about its source, I remembered the connection with the homework book, so I extracted the offender's book from its pile and could almost visualize the fumes rising from its pages. Matty and I tried to conceal our mirth, but we were unable and Ellsworth notified us,

"*I know what you're laughin at. I know what you're laughin at. The cat pissed all over my homework book.*"

His admission did little to sterilize my hands, but it did stimulate my funny bone. As impoverished as his family was, it was a no brainer to replace the reeking homework book with a 'freebie' from our stationery stock.

One of my favorite slow learners was a lad named Monroe St. James Madison. Monroe was a talented song and dance man with a repertoire that permitted his own interpretation of songs like, *If I Had a Hammer* or *Blowing in the Wind.* Greg Flynn had my class the previous year, and true to his own concept of culture, had introduced the class to Irish music. He taught them to sing *Brennan on the Moor* and *Roddy McCawley,* supplementing some traditional Black songs like *Cotton Fields Back Home.* Monroe was able to add riffs to every song and take off on a talented tangent. He had plenty of experience for in my first year at Augustine when my frustration hit the wall, I would take time out for a songfest. Joe Hosey used to say, "I guess O'Prey's had it again!" I was so impressed by my class' singing and riffs that I tape recorded them and held the result for many years. We also starred in an auditorium performance for the rest of the school.

Some of my adaptation to my new assignment had little to do with classroom instruction. I also had to learn about some cultural differences. Perhaps the clearest indication of my curriculum concerned Kendall. As I walked around the classroom checking homework, I stopped at his desk and complimented him on a job well done. I underscored my praise with a gesture of reassurance. I patted him on the head and quickly learned why he was called 'Crisco.' In the dead of winter Kendall used to grease up his head with an insulating patina of Crisco, the cooking lard. It kept his head warm and body heat in at the top of his skull. As for me, my hand now had an uncomfortable layer of the substance which I attempted to cleanse with as much discretion as I could muster under the circumstances.

Early one morning I was distracted by a noise in the corridor outside my classroom. The mother of one of my basketball players was outside another classroom stripping her son of all his clothes. Guy nonchalantly stood in less than essential garb while his mother went through his pockets and otherwise patted him down. As soon as she discovered that her rent money was missing, she had rushed to the school in the belief that her son had taken the essential cash. A quick word with Guy's teacher and the mother soon was engaged in the frantic search. Finally reaching the bottom of his feet, she discovered the stash in the sole of his sock. She immediately took the rent money to pay her debt and left Guy standing in the altogether. The expression on his face was one of indifference. He wasn't beaten, chided or berated, but merely discovered. I suppose Guy resolved to find a better hiding place next time he uncovered his mother's hiding place.

Another lesson I was soon to learn was the reverence West Indians had for learning. They didn't accept laziness or low performance, and sometimes their high standards caused some resentment among native American Blacks. A distraught mother of an indifferent student approached me with a recommendation on how to deal with the reluctance of her son to exert what she perceived as a serious academic effort. She exhorted me to fill a vat with ice cold water, strip her son naked, and beat him with a baseball bat. At the end of the treatment, I was advised to throw him in the cold water. I thought about this approach in terms of a lesson plan. Imagine gathering the necessary materials. First, find a large galvanized tub and a twenty to fifty foot water hose. Two, connect hose to faucet in utility room and extend to classroom. Three, provide clothing rack for stripped clothing and keep baseball bat at the ready. Finally, after filling the tub and stripping the lad, after a generous portion of whacks with the bat, I should throw him in. I wondered what the rest of the class would be doing as I administered this punishment. Perhaps even more so, how was I to clean up the subsequent splashing and move a heavy vat filled with cold water. Fortunately, the son hearing his mother's suggestion decided that he might make a superior effort without the punishment inflicted. Sometimes when I consider some of my egregious physical punishments, I recall those that I failed to administer.

Part of the seventh grade religion series was preparation for the sacrament of Confirmation. I was supposed to teach my students about the seven gifts of the Holy Spirit, or the Cardinal virtues, and so forth. A bishop would select a few students and quiz them before Confirmation. To prepare for that Father Harry Sullivan, the curate, visited the classroom and had the poor sense to choose Monroe for a question. He asked him who the Holy Ghost was. After innumerable hints, our budding theologian finally shouted in exultation,

"*Oh! Dat's de Bird.*"

Father Sullivan advised me to hide him from the bishop, or else we both would lose our jobs.

Monroe lived on Fulton Avenue north of the school near Crotona Park. He was, like so many others, a better athlete than scholar. In fact, a group of basketball players mastered playing the game on unicycles, and Monroe was one of their stars. They were noticed by someone who got them involved with a traveling circus like Ringling Brothers, Barnum and Bailey. Our circus entertainer traveled throughout the country playing on his unicycle. He brings to mind an episode when he was running track for Augustine. Like many of his peers, our unicyclist wore a pair of long johns since winter seemed to linger longer in that part of the Bronx. We had reserved a spot on a relay team for Monroe, but he wouldn't compete with his long johns. Joe Hosey went to our modest supply store and found a jock strap. He tossed it to the embarrassed competitor and said, "Here, wear this." Monroe opened the box and recoiled in horror.

"*I ain't runnin round in dat.*"

Joe assured him that he wore a pair of track shorts over the jock, and Monroe simply said,

"*Oh.*"

Another first place medal was our reward, and our pupil learned a little more about male athletic wear.

Although a talented athlete and an affable individual with musical skills, Monroe was short on some of the very basic knowledge known to most people. He had a younger brother who was much more astute but nowhere near as friendly and personable as he was. Perhaps, Monroe's ignorance wasn't totally his fault, for I must confess I enjoyed keeping him guessing. A parishioner from Immaculate Conception had given the Brothers an old vehicle that defied some of the basic principles of physics and mechanics. It often broke down, and on one occasion rolled down off the Whitestone Bridge as far as the toll plaza. Joe Hosey and I drove a borrowed car to collect the antiquated Renault. Using the time honored Bronx poor man's towing vehicle, we had a strong dumbwaiter rope that we tied to both cars. As Joe pulled the Renault down Fulton Avenue, Monroe jogged along side and the following conversation took place:

"*Whatcha doin, Brother?*"

"Monroe, do you see that car in front of me?"

"*Yeah!*"

"Do you see that rope?"

"*Yeah!*"

"Well, I'm pushing that car with this rope."

Without batting an eye, the startled eyewitness exclaimed,

"*I never seen dat before!*"

At the end of the block, he offered a cheerful good bye and left jogging back up the street.

One of the survival techniques we evolved seemed to keep the kids off balance with imagined responses to ordinary questions. At lunchtime, the younger students particularly used to let off a lot of steam running around. One fellow, Pierre Francois, used to run himself ragged and declare when he was winded that he was suffering a heart attack. Greg would comfort him by telling Pierre not to worry for he was only experiencing a coronary thrombosis. The fancy words meant nothing to the boy, but he always felt reassured by the diagnosis until the repartee practically became a daily occurrence.

The Renault mentioned in the above episode was a welcomed gift, but it carried with it some unexpected adventures on the road. Returning from a meeting at Manhattan College, the car suddenly swerved across two lanes of traffic on the Henry Hudson Bridge. Greg Flynn was driving, and the car took that side trip without any adjustment to the steering wheel. Nor did the recalcitrant steering system respond to Greg's frantic efforts to avert the steel fence that separated us from the Hudson River several hundred feet below. Somehow the car decided that our thrill was ended and stayed in the slow lane for the rest of the trip. Every morning Joe Hosey went out to start the car for the three Brothers who were getting ready for the commute to 149th Street. On particularly cold days, Joe used to spray ether into the ignition to encourage its start. At other times, a standard starter was sufficient, but it also had an old fashioned cranking device in the front of the radiator if all else failed.

One particularly frigid morning Joe asked me to start the car, and my mechanical expertise demonstrated that my ignorance in certain matters might match Monroe's. It was bitter cold, so I took an aerosol can with the word ignition written on it. Certain I had the right tool, I sprayed it into the carburetor and then discovered that the mist was not ether but ignition wire sealant. I had gunked up the carburetor to the point where it wouldn't start for two weeks. After a discreet amount of time, I approached the car again. This time I had a labor force of a number of kids who would push the vehicle while I exhausted my expertise with cars and popped the clutch in an effort to get the sputtering car to start. The boys pushed the car back and forth in the schoolyard for forty-five minutes with no success. I suspected there was another problem by this time and then a quick scan proved that I had committed another major omission. I had never turned the key in the ignition. When I discovered that, I implored my propulsion unit to try once more, and I surreptitiously turned the key this time. The car started immediately, but I didn't dare tell my students that they had labored so hard, so futilely, because of my stupidity. The car served us more or less faithfully for a number of months until we somehow acquired a nice, new station wagon that belonged to Bernie O'Neill's brother. I suspect his brother bought the car and then discovered that monthly payments were too demanding, but I don't know that as fact. In any case, our 'Classic' Renault was replaced by a modern station wagon.

With a nice, reliable Chevy Station Wagon that stayed in the correct lane and responded to steering directions, we took excursions farther afield. Greg, Bernie and I decided to take a trip to Harriman Park and enjoy the outdoors. Our plans were disrupted by a flat tire on the Palisades Interstate Parkway. Again, the three of us failed the basic car maintenance course. We couldn't get the jack to work. A police car passed us a few times, but didn't stop because he believed that three men should be able to change a tire. Finally, I was dispatched to walk to the nearest telephone and call Hosey for the solution to the jack. Joe had no suggestions, but he said he had used the jack last week, and it was fine. As I returned to the car, I could see the raised wheel and a police car. When I spoke to the policeman, I thanked him for lending us his jack. He said it wasn't his and that we had used the original jack. Apparently, gravity would keep the jack in place as the weight of the car transferred onto the jack. The cop finally said, "What do you guys do for a living anyway?" We confessed that we were teachers. His laconic response aptly described his amazement at our ineptitude,

"Well I was damned sure you weren't mechanics."

Greg Flynn had contributed to my adaptation to Augustine in very many ways. His laid back style and easy going manner weren't in my repertoire, but I could benefit from his verbal advice. Since he had taught my first class in the sixth grade, he knew them very well. He mentioned to me that if I really wanted to know who did what, or what was happening, I should blame a specific individual. Jean Bernard Romano was a tall Haitian who reserved a scowl and menacing look for most occasions. In truth, 'Jumbernard,' as he was called, was like the cowardly lion from *The Wizard of Oz*. If I accused him of a petty theft of a pen, Jumbernard was quick to say,

"I didn't take it, but Andre did."

I shouldn't be proud of my next procedure, but I was desperate to know what I was often dealing with. I would approach Jumbernard and say,

"Jumbernard, why am I upset at you?"

"Is it because me and Andre stole Kendall's lunch money?"

"No."

"Is it because I left the schoolyard at lunch time and swiped some candy in the store at the corner?"

"No."

"Is it because I copied Angelo's homework?"

"No, not exactly."

"Is it because me and Andre went up Linda's house and you know . . . ?"

"No."

"Is it because me and Tyrone were smoking in the bathroom?"

"No."

"Is it because I swiped Calvin's pens?"

"No."

Jumbernard would recite his peccadilloes like a litany in rapid singsong fashion, and I would add an amen to his confession to bring it to a halt. He never tried evasion when I confronted him with a generic accusation, and as Greg indicated, Jumbernard would recite his shortcomings apologetically. Most of his offenses were totally unknown to me.

After sneaking out of the schoolyard on two consecutive days and being caught by me upon his return, I finally said to him,

"Jumbernard, I have tried speaking to you in English, but you apparently didn't understand. Now I am going to try another language."

Since I was still in the swinging mode to instill morals and lessons, Jumbernard anticipated some physical pain. In the meantime, the class had a decade of the rosary to recite after lunch. As the class recited the ten Hail Mary's, he could be heard above the prayerful din as he moaned and whined and wept in the back of the classroom. When the prayer had ended, I called this six foot whimpering specimen to the front of the class. I told him I tried speaking to him in peaceful terms, but he ignored my advice. So now I was going to hit him. Although he was cowering and recoiling, I caught his cheeks between my two hands with a resounding smack. Jumbernard leaped backwards over a desk and thrashed about on the floor emitting a wailing cry amid long flailing arms and legs,

"Muh tongue! Muh tongue! You chopped out muh tongue."

"Jumbernard, you stick out your tongue, and everyone in the class who can see your tongue will raise his hand."

He extended his tongue, and everyone in the class raised his hand in affirmation that his tongue was still in his head. Then Jumbernard said, *"Den what's dat in muh hand?"*

He pointed to a small piece of flesh that looked like a speck of dandruff. I assured him that no permanent damage had been done, and he managed to gain control of himself and promised not to skip out of the schoolyard again. Like many of the students, Jumbernard didn't excel in the classroom, nor did he particularly sparkle in sports as many did. Despite his size, his greatest attribute may have been intimidation, for he offered little else on the field of competition. I suppose one reason may be that he had a peculiar gait when he ran. His six foot frame seemed to be locked in one position from knee cap to head, preventing him from playing basketball efficiently or running quickly. He did have a great sense of music and enjoyed singing.

One of my fondest memories of him focuses on a subway ride to St. Patrick's Cathedral for a ceremony called the novena for the Archconfraternity of the Divine Child. In the overcrowded subway car, I could hear Jumbernard start singing a song popularized by *The Dixie Cups*. The words, *"Goin to the Chapel, gonna get married"* sounded almost liturgical in that car. He also enjoyed singing *"The Name Game,"* and some ditty *"Three, Six, Nine, the Goose drank wine, the monkey chew tobacco on the street car line,"* about a baby doll character who kissed a soldier and her mother wouldn't buy her a rubber dolly. Outside class, Jumbernard was also friendly like the rest of the boys, but he was usually suspicious that he was under investigation for something or other. With a heaving sigh of relief, Jumbernard was happy to see his graduation day, and he seldom appeared thereafter.

In my early days at St. Augustine, Greg Flynn organized a basketball game for the high school kids against an assortment of what might be termed all star Brothers. The Brothers had size, width and no stamina compared to the lithe, athletic individuals who showed up in the Morris High School gym. Eddie Archibald played for Rice; Foster Davis started at Cardinal Hayes; and Gregory Jenkins was a bright light for De Witt Clinton. Others were no longer in school, but every one of the Brothers' adversaries was stellar. They had honed their game against the likes of Lennie Elmore of Maryland and Kareem Abdul Jabbar of Power, UCLA and the Lakers, Charley Yelverton of Fordham and the Trailblazers, Nate Archibald, the NBA legend out of Clinton, and Dean Menninger who starred at Rice, Marquette, and the New York Knicks. Davis would play for Tennessee and Jenkins dabbled with his career at Paul Smith and the NBA tryouts. The rest of the team like Michael Nunez, recently discharged from the military, could sky, dunk, and run forever. The Brothers were at a clear disadvantage.

I was the referee in this game and all I remember was trying to make the game a contest by calling frequent time outs for the Brothers to regroup their wind and preserve their health. My other impression of the game was the image of sneaker laces at my eye level. Those kids were jumping so high that I got a good glimpse of the athletic footwear which in those early days of designer sneakers was Converse All-Stars. Without my intervention, the game was no contest, for the kids controlled the backboards on the rare occasion when their shots didn't drop. By the end of the game the Brothers were dragging tail while the kids were ready for another double header. They enjoyed ripping the Brothers, but were good sports and attributed their success to a better than average night. The defeated knew better.

That game was a harbinger of the kind of experience I would encounter while coaching the basketball team. I entered a Five Foot Four inch Junior Varsity team comprised of elementary school kids into the Bronx CYO. The team featured an easy going jump shooting expert called the 'Jolly Green Giant.' He didn't seem to break a sweat as he drained shot after shot from the right side of the key. Later he would play at De Witt Clinton before transferring to Laurinburg Prep in North Carolina. There he would star for the team, even playing ahead of Charlie Scott who had a number of successful years with North Carolina and the Celtics of the NBA. The 'Jolly Green Giant' in the meantime, like so many budding ghetto stars, developed a taste for heroin and became one of the famed junkies who could have been somebody except for a predilection for the drug.

The 5'4" team had a group of Hispanics who also played very well under my direction. All I had to do was control an impulse for showboating and urge team play. The players responded with pride and excellent performance. Joe Fagundo supplemented the 'Jolly Green Giant,' and Edwin Cruz and 'Papo' Godreau formed an excellent back court. A muscular Jose Hernandez monitored any rebounds that occasionally caromed off the backboard.

I discovered that Bronx CYO basketball was quite unpredictable, and I formulated a principle that a fifteen point differential was essential for a road win. My team could score quickly and often, and the defense was impressive. Our problem occurred when St. Rita's used a ringer who had to be in his late teens. On their court, he actually throttled my players by the throat and punched and shoved them with no regard to fouls. We would have a record that year of 26 and 1, with our only loss coming from the massacre at St. Rita's where the loss was a foregone conclusion. Despite the unsportsmanlike behavior, we had lost by only two or three points, and when they played us in the public school gym on 163rd Street which we used as home court, we beat them since the referees monitored his mayhem more carefully.

We would meet St. Rita's in the Bronx Championship game at Cardinal Hayes. By this time I believe Mr. Curran, the head of the Bronx CYO, had uncovered some altered birth certificate, but he let the individual play. The objective zebras fouled out the intimidator in the first quarter, and we went on to win the Bronx crown and walk through the competition to garner the Archdiocesan championship. One of the principles I believed in was never embarrassing our opponents. When we had a comfortable lead, I would substitute young, inexperienced players who would carry the team in the future. We remained very competitive for some time.

In another league conducted by the Brothers, we also competed with a height restriction of 5'2". Most of these players were seventh graders, and the starting five sounded like immigrants from the Auld Sod. I had an all Irish five with names like Daley, Daniels, Brady, Bell, and McIntyre. They too played very well, and Augustine warranted a reputation as a basketball force to be reckoned with. Brother Jerome Lippert claimed that he had a 'tall' 5'2" team, and he wanted to scrimmage us before the season. I suppose Jerry had discovered a flaw in the administration of the measuring machine manipulated by Brother Bernard Peter, for they were taller than one might anticipate. We beat them anyway.

Some other individuals from these teams stand out for one reason or another. One was a bundle of energy and athleticism that enabled him to leap, smash into walls, and make him impervious to pain. Bernard Miller was somewhat of a space man. His dalliances in a world unrecognized by the rest of us left him with a series of injuries that tested the "credulity of a rational man," as Howard Cosell used to say. Before an important game, Bernard once walked into a fire hydrant and almost ruptured himself. There it was, but he didn't see it. On another occasion, Bernard caught his penis in his zipper, and we had a dilemma as to what to do. His mother was a nurse, however, and he was finally released from his self imposed prison. On both occasions, he played a stellar game being high scorer and best rebounder. In his later years, Bernard startled some of the newly arrived Brothers because he believed in blasting his ghetto box as he washed his car in his backyard across from the Brothers' house. That may not sound so unusual, but this cleansing process took place between 3:00 and 4:00am.

Bernard wasn't the only outstanding player among stellar performers on a team where height wasn't necessarily an advantage.

One of the most peculiar was a boy the kids called 'Tugboat Kenny,' (AKA 'Chug-a-mug'). 'Tugboat' was built like a bowling ball and probably could be the paradigm for a great NFL running back. His compact torso and muscular build probably weighed about 180 pounds on a 5'2" frame. 'Tugboat' could run faster than anyone and had the resilience of a bouncing cannon ball. His vertical leap defied the vision of any onlooker. He had an outstanding jump shot, could drive with authority, and his broad shoulders made rebounding his province too. As long as I permitted him to apply cream to his 'ashy' legs and arms, Tugboat was ready to produce win after win.

One of the embarrassing scourges of our track and basketball players was a condition known as 'ashy skin.' Dried skin gave the athlete the appearance of an outer crust of dirt unless a cream or lubricant was applied, leaving a sleek, glowing exterior. None of our contestants would compete unless the requisite application took place shortly before the game began. Today, one might think of steroid creams, but in that era it was strictly cosmetic.

The importance of every game, however, could be assessed by the number of ace bandages 'Tugboat' applied to his limbs. When he arrived for pre-game warm up with a bandage around his biceps, another binding his thigh, and a third wrapped around his calf, I finally had to provide some leadership. I issued a dictum that proclaimed anyone who had to wear an ace bandage was "*ipso facto,*" too injured to play. That was the end of 'Tugboat's' personal injuries. Somehow he usually muddled through a stellar performance minus the accompanying bandages.

In addition to his athletic prowess, Kenny provided one of the most entertaining explanations for a forgery that I ever encountered. His athletic achievements far exceeded his grades, and occasionally he found himself with a failing assessment on our weekly report cards in the classroom. After one such episode, he returned to school with a report card that clearly had been tampered with. His explanation was a classic in originality as well as performance. When confronted with a smeared grade of 75 when my record book indicated a 64, Kenny launched into what he perceived as a perfectly logical exposition.

"Kenny, this report card appears strange to me."

"*Brother, I can explain that. You know when I bring home a failing grade muh father gets very upset, and he chases me around the apartment and hits me with a baseball bat.*"

"Gee, Kenny, that sounds painful."

"Yeah, so I wait until muh father goes to take a baff. When he's in the tub, he can't be chasing me around the apartment beating me over the head with a baseball bat."

"Sounds reasonable to me, Kenny."

"So I waits until he's soakin in the tub, and I hand him muh report card. You know, Brother, when you're in the tub, your hands are wet and he grab that card and he smudged up the 64."

"And then what happened, Kenny?"

"I took the smudged up report card and placed it on muh mother's dresser so it would dry out, and my baby brother came along and changed it to a 75."

"That sounds very hard to believe."

"It's duh troof, I swear it's duh troof. I swear on the bible, it's duh troof."

"You'd swear on the bible, Kenny," as I reached for the good book and took it from a shelf nearby. I told Kenny to raise his right hand and place his left on the bible. As I started to recite the famous court oath, Kenny's left hand kept jumping off the bible. I decided that I didn't want him to think he was committing perjury, so I said to forget about the bible.

"Kenny, I want you to take your story to the rest of the Brothers. Tell them exactly what happened, and let me know how many believe you."

We used to send cases like this around among us as a source of rare entertainment. One Brother, for instance, specialized in sending a messenger with a six foot window pole, who would say,

"Brother Matthew told me to tell you, you know what you can do with this pole."

About ten minutes later a very forlorn looking student returned with his head downcast and his step considerably slower than his track performance.

"Well, Kenny, how did you make out? How many of the Brothers believed your tale of woe?"

"No one believed me, but it's the troof."

After a considerable delay, Kenny then confessed that he himself had been the culprit. I think I was so pleased that I had finally evoked a simple straightforward reply after such a preposterous explanation that I merely thanked him for his honesty and requested no further tales of parental abuse, exciting chases, and precocious activity on the part of his baby brother.

While 'Tugboat' was a name that I thought was an apt description of an excellent player, another team member didn't quite share the glory of a positive sobriquet. Michael wasn't as strong as 'Tugboat,' nor could he drive and rebound like this prototype small player, but he was a good shooter and a superb passer. Unfortunately Michael had a rather severe acne problem which led to his less flattering nickname. Despite my efforts to extirpate the name, the team insisted on calling him 'Pusshead.' Michael was quite shy aside from basketball, and he accepted this negative description with panache. Opponents were intimidated by the cries of support for 'Pusshead,' and any effort I made to alter the appellation was met with indifference and neglect. When we would play some tournament games at high schools, the observers would cringe when they heard the cheers for 'Pusshead,' and maybe it helped the defense give him some extra room for maneuvering on offense.

Coaching the team was a great pleasure for me since most of the players stored their egos for another time and place. They generally played team ball and passed with becoming frequency. Almost all of our games were unseen by parents or neighborhood adults, so there was absolutely no interference about substitutions, playing time, or strategy. Coaches never had to deal with unsolicited advice unless it came from another Brother who discreetly made some helpful suggestions. If there was any concentration on shooting, it generally came from the tendency to feed those most likely to score. Showboating meant instant pine time, and the team knew it. If anyone belittled the opposition, benching was an immediate repercussion. I wasn't a great coach, maybe not even a knowledgeable one, but I had the ear of the players and the confidence to lead.

No less a commentator than Ray Buck hit the nail on the head when he declared that winning primarily was a question of "having the horses." All my coaching demanded was reining in the horses from time to time and sharing opportunities evenly. The kids responded enthusiastically. Once, two of my starting five decided to assert their star status and failed to travel with the team to Tolentine for an away game. They arrived just before game time and were greeted by cheers from the team who now recognized our chances of winning had just escalated. I didn't reprove them, but I left them on the bench the entire game. We lost that game by a few points and the chance to win the Bronx championship, but I thought the lesson for the individuals was greater than any trophy.

While I focused on the 'junior varsity' level, Greg Flynn coached the varsity which played in several tournaments at Spellman, Hayes, and Mount St. Michael's. These teams had unlimited size eligibility, but there were age limitations. Thanks to the generosity of the Athletic Director at La Salle Second Street, our team was outfitted with classy uniforms. When the varsity at 2nd Street got new uniforms, the old ones were donated to St. Augustine. Our new regalia pleased our players immensely, but it brought into question among some of our opponents whether we were also using high school players on the elementary school teams. Generally Greg's teams did quite well, unless they came up against St. Thomas the Apostle from Harlem. If a team beat St. Tom's in one tournament, the opposition could anticipate an entirely different roster at the next tournament. St. Tom's had an American Indian who was very tall, very well built, and possibly overage. Their coaching staff seemed to have more flexibility with the rules than we had.

After Greg was transferred to the Coop, I inherited the Varsity and concentrated on that level. That introduced me to the playing style of one of my most memorable players. I had Russell Cameron in my class my second year, but his potential as a basketball player made him a substitute on our championship team as a sixth grader. Russell brought an element of unpredictability whenever he played. At one game against Our Lady of Mount Carmel near the Italian community on Arthur Avenue, he made a slew of side bets that we would win. We lost, and Russell urged me to get the team immediately on the Third Avenue El. As we entered the El stairs, a hostile crowd of disgruntled opponents had gathered to collect in injury the defaulted money Russell had incurred. Fortunately, we managed to get aboard the southbound train before greater damage could occur. When I confronted Russell for an explanation as to why we were under Mafia threat, he was very honest and straightforward, a characteristic he often displayed when confessing his faults. He would continue to educate me on the seamier side of life in Morrisania.

Russell was somewhat of a con man always in pursuit of a buck. Even as a seventh grader, he had written a composition that indicated what he cherished most in life was money. He argued,

"People say money isn't everything, but I'd like a million dollars to find out for myself."

He hustled by betting, thieving, mugging, robbing, and hard work. Along the path, he kept me informed. At one point, we were gathered on Boston Road to meet Mayor Lindsey at the Community Progress Center around the block directly behind our school. Russell approached me and described the man representing the community in greeting the Mayor.

"Do you see that man in the gray suit standing at the microphone? That is Mr. Somebody or Other who controls the drugs and numbers in the neighborhood. I want to be just like him, for he has money, power and respect."

I had no argument to refute Russell's analysis of the situation. Few experienced Brothers would argue about raising the 'God question,' or 'witnessing for Christianity' where power had its own standards.

After graduating from St. Augustine, Russell attended Rice High School and played on the freshmen basketball team. After a few weeks, he was expelled from the school for punching his coach. In due time, he approached me for help. He claimed that if he stayed in Morris High School, he would never get a diploma and wouldn't win a scholarship to college. He asked if I could get him out of the neighborhood where temptation abounded. On his behalf, I contacted some Brothers at La Salle Military Academy with the offer to supply a scholarship project. I was totally candid about Russell's brushes with the law and involvement with drug dealers. The Brothers at Oakdale promised to discuss admitting him on a hardship scholarship since there was no way he could pay for boarding school. After serious consideration, the Brothers at Oakdale decided admitting him would be tantamount to letting the fox into the chicken coop. Most of the students at La Salle were wealthy and given to temptation which Russell could easily satisfy. Convinced that the military academy wasn't an option, I tried St. Raymond's High School.

Brother Andy O'Gara was the principal of the school, and he had distinguished himself in my eyes for his policy toward minorities from the South Bronx. He offered to interview Russell, so I sent him to the school. A few hours later, Andy said that this huge Black kid who filled his doorway arrived for the interview. Before he even saw him, Andy resolved to give the kid who punched his coach another chance. When he saw the tall, massive frame of Russell in the doorway, he had no idea that he had just improved St. Raymond's basketball team significantly. Russell managed to survive in the school for around two years, but with three months until graduation, he was expelled for violating the school drug policy. The day after his expulsion, he was at the school trying to sell shoes to his former teachers. Work didn't intimidate Russell if all else failed.

One summer he joined a group of college age kids peddling magazine subscriptions door to door. Of course he maintained he was ambitious and intent on raising tuition money. At the end of the summer, he was one of the highest salesmen and eligible for a special dinner where he could order anything he wanted from the menu of a decent restaurant. Russell told me how he pored over the options and finally settled on a Salisbury steak since it sounded so tasty and classy. His summary, uttered in disgust was, *"Brother, you know what they brought out to me? A hamburger, a damn hamburger."*

The curriculum in Augustine didn't cover menu scrutiny.

It wasn't long before Russell was back at the Brothers' House door. After his expulsion from St. Raymond's, he managed to acquire sufficient credits in his final semester of his high school senior year, and was awarded a diploma. He was offered a scholarship to North Carolina A&T, if he could forward his transcript from St. Raymond's. Unfortunately, Russell owed them about $400 in back tuition, and the school refused to release his transcript until the money was forthcoming. I didn't have the heart or the courage to ask Andy for another favor, but I had been given some stipend for delivering several teachers' workshops in social studies. It was rapidly transferred into the Russell Cameron account, and he was off to college.

As a teacher at St. Augustine, I learned how easy it was to be misquoted no matter how carefully one might express himself. When he was a student at St. Augustine, Russell quoted me as saying,

"A woman is like a valuable asset, but it is advisable to carry a spare, as one does in a car."

I never remember that lesson, but I suppose he heard what he wanted to hear. He had a girlfriend who was the sister of a good friend and together they had a baby when both were about eighteen. In the meantime, Russell decided to make some quick money by engineering a few jewelry store stick-ups. In three attempts, he and his partner were thwarted, and in each case his co-conspirator was shot or arrested. Russell continued to live a charmed life, it seemed. After a few months in North Carolina A&T, he was expelled for harboring another woman in his dorm. I think he was too embarrassed to try to hit me up for some more income, for I didn't hear from him for awhile. A few years later, I received a package in the mail. It contained the graduation program from an institution aptly named in Russell's case, Philander Smith in Little Rock, Arkansas. There, among the graduates, was the name of Russell Cameron who graduated *Magna Cum Laude*, ironically with a major in Criminal Justice. In a brief note, he also added that he had gotten a scholarship for a Masters Degree Program at Washington University in St. Louis, but he first had to pursue a tryout with the Detroit Pistons. When he didn't make the NBA, he worked on his degree and is now somewhat of a success, I hope. He used to call me on New Year's Eve and occasionally throughout the year. His last call, a desperate plea for plane fare money to fly to Boys Town in Nebraska for a job interview fell upon the deaf ears of a man who now had to provide for his own growing family.

Russell was a lovable rogue in a way. Despite his poor record in stick-ups, he decided to try another field of criminal activity. He resolved to try his imposing, intimidating presence as an asset in mugging. He also defied all odds of probability while mugging people on Boston Road. At 6'6" with another four to six inches of wild Afro, Russell was pretty identifiable. Add a green beaver hat and a long green overcoat, and it isn't hard to identify such a felon on the streets of Morrisania. Russell had mugged somebody, and his description was broadcast to the anti-crime unit patrolling the area. Of course they spotted him almost immediately and took him in cuffs to the Bathgate Avenue Station house across from St. Joseph's. Since my father was a sergeant there, I was well familiar with the place.

Russell's mother called me complaining that neighbors saw Russell cuffed and brought into a police car, but when she called the station house, nobody apparently knew anything about the young man. Ever suspicious of New York's Finest, as were most of the adults in Morrisania, she called me and asked if I would inquire about him. As I was getting ready to head to Bathgate, Russell rang the door bell. Apparently, the arresting anti-crime detective was the father of a fellow basketball player at St. Raymond's. They reclaimed the stolen goods and told Russell to just sit still in the office and say nothing. When the shift changed, he could walk out the door without any problem. That was why no report was filed, and no one could give Mrs. Cameron information about her son Russell. The good luck of the rascal continued to defy credulity.

As one might expect, Russell and I had many conversations over the years. He was genuinely fond of the Brothers and of the school. He appreciated whatever was done for him. He cautioned us about walking around the neighborhood. Guys like him would mug us for twenty-five cents, he asserted. Somewhere I hope Russell is successful, modestly wealthy, and enjoying a good life. There will always be an element of the larcenous or avaricious in his character. Yet his honesty and candor were also part of that personality. I cherish his candor and his confidence more so than any of the substantial athletic contributions he made to the school teams. He remains one of the most unforgettable individuals I encountered on my path from Armageddon to Eden.

Russell had a younger brother Craig who lacked his size but may have been a better ball handler. His career was short-circuited, however, when he was caught conducting fundraising activities at gunpoint on the 35 Cross Town Bus. Russell always stated that he couldn't handle Riker's Island like his brother did. Craig too has a special spot in my heart for a kindness that caught me totally off guard. I had kept him after school in the quest for a completed homework assignment when Sgt O'Keeffe from the 48th Bathgate precinct rang the Brothers' house bell. Sgt. O'Keeffe informed me that my father had been found dead at home in Piermont. I excused Craig and headed straight to my father's house. During my father's wake, one of the mourners who arrived by himself in the midst of a blizzard was Craig Cameron. The funeral parlor was extremely hot, and I advised him to remove his overcoat. He said that was impossible and opened it enough to expose a shoulder holster and pistol. I told him to give me the gun, and I would take care of it. That night Craig was unable to get home because of the intensive snowfall, so he stayed with me and the community of Brothers at Good Shepherd. I called his mother and mentioned the gun. She told me to return it to him. I did so, and it was that weapon that won him the trip to Rikers.

Craig epitomizes many different levels of the relationships between student and teacher at Augustine. He was bright and hopefully his first prison term was his last. His personal perspectives were warped by an environment that ridiculed law and preached versatility in accumulating wealth by any means. Role models were those who made money, garnered community approval, and ran *sub rosa* undercover operations. Bribery, numbers, narcotics, arson, violent crime, and abortion mills were a way of life. Yet there was evident goodness in many of these misguided individuals. How grateful I am that I could see a part of them that was redeeming, laudable, and forgiving. These qualities presented hope that things might change in the future, if only the kids could survive their youth and didn't get caught in the meantime.

While my experiences and coaching in basketball supplemented my introduction to relationships with the students, another sport where I learned a great deal about human nature and strategy was in track. In the spring, we would go 'tracking' to Macombs Dam Park, next to the Yankee Stadium where they now intend to erect the new stadium. Each of the Brothers would start the trek down what we termed 'Shit hill,' for its incline contained an unending amount of dog droppings. Once the slide had been safely traversed, we would then head across 165th Street for about one mile. Some kids would walk with us, but most traveled directly from their homes throughout Morrisania. Once at the track we would organize some stretching and practice techniques.

Many times the examples of the high school and college athletes who also used the oval were prime demonstrations of what the kids should do to master passing batons, doing the high jump, or what was then termed the broad jump. There was also a finesse race involving placing about six blocks within a circle after retrieving each at a different distance. It was called the potato race and some of our athletes liked it very much. The danger was in fouling out by missing the circle in haste. It was often too risky to invest our most skilled racers in that competition. The natural talents of our athletes far outweighed the instructional aspects of the respective competitions. Perhaps the most important contribution of the coach was in appropriate registrations for the various contests. Whether one should stock relay races with the most talented on a single unit or whether the best runners should be spread throughout the various teams often determined the number of medals or points that might lead to a team trophy rather than individual fame. Typically, judicious assignments usually led to the best team scores

St. Augustine was a comparatively small school since it had only one class of a maximum of forty boys per grade level. Since most schools had at least two classes or perhaps three, we were at a disadvantage numerically. Two factors accounted for the great success the school had over the years. One was the prudent entry of competitors according to an intelligent strategy. Sometimes one sized up the opposition and determined where our relative strengths lay. The other advantage followed the maxim of Ray Buck, "You gotta have the horses!" Our students were avid devotees of track, placing it second only to basketball. Many of the athletes from both sports were our major 'horses.'

As valuable as 'Tugboat Kenny' was as a basketball player, he was an even better competitor in track. Given a fair chance, we could always anticipate 'Tugboat' winning the 110 yard dash and anchoring a victorious 440 relay. At one of our competitions, I asked 'Tugboat' why they didn't call his name for the finals of the 110 dash. He regaled me with a conversation that occurred during his trial heat. He said that one of his opponents told him to move aside, and Kenny repeated the request to the same individual. Kenny said he was shoved, so he shoved back. For 100 yards of the race the two individuals argued, pushed and shoved each other, leading to disqualifications. I could only conclude that they were justified.

Most of the time, the CSAL, or Catholic School Athletic League, was in a class by itself for integrity, organization and honesty. Forty-eight hours before the competition, each school submitted the names and events to Brother Bernard Peter who had already measured all the contestants pretty accurately. Twenty-four hours before the competition, only four changes were permitted, and then everything was finalized. That is where strategy entered, for the coach had to guess what events the opponents loaded and what events they skimmed on. On the day of the competition, every runner was stamped and classified, and the heats and the finals were generally conducted with competent officials. In one race, however, Bernard Miller defied the judge's attention in the 660 relay. He had taken the baton in third place and was hemmed in by the opponents from two schools. Ever resourceful and determined, he stepped onto the infield track and left them in the dust before he reentered the race track. We noticed it from the stands, but whoever was the judge on that leg must have been looking elsewhere. In any case, thanks to Bernard's innocent innovation, we were awarded the gold medal in the event.

All the training and coaching in the world wasn't enough for some. An excellent runner named Ollie Jones was speedy, strong, and a neophyte when it came to techniques. Despite many practice sessions, his zeal and ability cost us a race. Unsure whether Ollie might take the baton from the wrong person, the coach assigned him to run the first leg of a 440. True to his skill, he had about a ten yard lead on the opposition after about forty yards. As the second man had been trained to do, he moved to the inside lane as was his privilege since Ollie clearly had the advantage. Ollie, on the other hand, never moved to the inside, but ran the leg in the third lane. When it came time to pass the baton, our runner was in lane one and Good Shepherd was in lane three. Ollie came in with a full head of steam and ran right over the poor, unsuspecting athlete from Good Shepherd. Our team never did pass the baton, and we were disqualified for disrupting another team.

While the CSAL seemed to be run by virtual professionals, the same wasn't true for the dad's clubs who ran some tournaments sponsored by the CYO or Mount St. Michael's for example. At the CYO meet, with no definite rosters and no prearranged heats, contestants from high schools, hungry for a cheap trophy, roamed the stands offering their services. Of course we always turned them down, but one could witness their pleas had been answered by other schools or parishes. In the midget division we had an excellent 110 yard relay team, which featured two swift runners, Willie Rawlins and Donnie McKissick. They won their heats in a breeze and appeared the overwhelming favorites in the finals. As the teams lined up with Willie Rawlins leading off, the starter shouted, "Ready, Set . . . ." and the competition broke in a false start. While those who jumped the gun ran, Willie congratulated himself on his restraint. The starter then fired his gun and said,

"You should have jumped too."

Second place was about the best the team could garner because of the late start.

A major advantage to my assignment to St. Augustine was the need to accept broader responsibility sooner than I might have at Sacred Heart. I welcomed the challenge and enjoyed opportunities that I might not have had elsewhere. Because of our deep involvement in basketball and track with the CSAL, I was asked to play a minor administrative role in organizing and supervising the sports. That responsibility left me as on site authority for the varsity basketball tournament. The games were held in St. Raymond's School, and most went according to plan. As usual, St Tom's had a team favored to make the finals. On this specific day, however, they failed to show up for the game on time. The coach from Good Shepherd, a long shot winner at best, requested a forfeit. Brother Richard Calley, their coach, impressed me immensely during that episode. I asked him to wait another fifteen minutes, and then I granted his team the incongruous victory over the heavy favorite. At that point St. Tom's arrived and pleaded that they had been waiting at the wrong gym all this time.

Their coach had a reputation as the 'father of lies,' but I refused to believe he would misrepresent his case before the game. I asked Brother Calley if he would play the game in case St. Tom's appeal was upheld and another game would mess up the schedule for the following week. Calley agreed under protest, since I had originally declared the forfeit. Predictably, St. Tom's walloped Good Shepherd, but a committee met on the following Thursday and upheld the original forfeit. Brother Richard exuded nothing but class, and I grew in respect for him and for his professionalism, patience, and understanding of my dilemma. I prefer not to comment further on the chicanery of St. Tom's.

Besides a vibrant interschool competition, the Brothers also supplied competitive games on an intramural level. Greg's father had erected a basketball backboard to create a full length basketball court with an east to west orientation. For a while, we also tried roller hockey intramurals, but that sport didn't appeal to the citizens of Morrisania. On an east to west orientation, the school yard offered a decent touch football venue and directly behind the Brothers' house, other games like punch ball or kick the ball could be offered. By far, however, the favorite intramural sport was basketball at the gym at PS 110. Bob Duball was the head custodian at the school and his interests coincided with our own. Evidently, the public school system reimbursed the custodian a flat amount of money to cover the cleaning, supervising, and maintenance of the gym. Mr. Duball used to cover our fees knowing that we would supervise its use and maintain order and keep it clean. For those responsibilities we had the use of the gym every afternoon from 3:00pm to 5:30pm, as well as two sessions a week in the evenings from 7:30pm to 10:00pm. We were happy to have the gym, and he was able to pocket the differential in what it cost to maintain the gym.

Duball used to tell us about stashed textbooks in the garbage. It was illegal for him to give us anything obsolete, but many times the trash contained unused books, furniture, desks, and so forth—a treasure trove to our impoverished school budget. We could pillage the garbage but not select anything before hand. There were significant scams abounding in the custodial staffs of some Bronx schools, but at least PS 110 kept honest books. My father used to have the responsibility of cruising around the 48th precinct to check on broken windows in school buildings. Apparently, some custodians reported broken glass; claimed they were repaired; and then billed a second time for replacement although none had been done. We were pleased to share the largesse of the public school budget despite our constraints.

Our high school kids used the gym on the two evenings a week according to the schedule Greg had worked out with Duball, and I merely resumed the procedures after Greg's departure. PS 110 was an elementary school and the gym was a little shorter than customary, but it surely beat out the ragged outdoor courts of the neighborhood. The whole arrangement was indicative of the kind of service the Brothers offered the parish. Each Brother would certainly claim that our primary concern was in educating the elementary age boys of St. Augustine. The reality, however, demonstrated that our roles went far beyond school. No one felt overworked, but each was challenged to offer whatever talents he could and no one was found wanting.

Aside from athletics, the Brothers offered a number of social activities to our graduates and their friends. The program touched only a fraction of those for whom it was intended, but it offered an alternative to hanging out and testing the current drug of choice. A definite cadre of teenagers did make very good use of our customary Saturday night sessions where dancing, games, and socialization took place under circumstances generally well-supervised. Despite our strong efforts, we had to remember that some of our teenagers were subject to severe temptations, and our supervision was a damper on whatever more risky opportunities may be present elsewhere.

The members of our teen club organized a few dances that offered unbelievable chances for mistakes. Few of our graduates would arrive at the door under the influence of drugs or alcohol, but many of their friends did. We tried to redirect them home. With a neighborhood where scams were rampant, we also tried to present an honest return for the modest admission fee. Some took us for fools, and some of our members preferred larceny to hospitality. One area of difficulty we encountered was in the coat checking process. We had receipts for coats and racks upon which to hang them. Theoretically the process was efficient and foolproof. Practically, it was likely to cause problems. Our guests for these cheap dances, where records played and no bands performed live, enticed patrons from all over the Bronx and Harlem in modest numbers. To some of our guests we appeared almost like the proverbial country mouse in city mouse territory. Sometimes the roles were reversed. Many guests wore expensive leather coats during the cold winter, and one of our club members decided to toss a few out the window to co-conspirators waiting below. At the end of the night, we were short two or three expensive leather coats. Calling aside the teenage leader of our group, we argued that our reputation was at stake, and he was entrusted with getting the stolen coats back. Vincent Baker uncovered the offending cabal and pressured them to return the coats with no questions asked. While our reputation remained intact, it didn't deter others from trying additional scams upon those 'ignorant' country mice from the Bronx.

A guest from Harlem who thought those from the Bronx were naive to scams currently conducted within the Black community tried to swindle our club out of money. He checked a modest hat, got a receipt, and enjoyed the dance. At the end of the night, the cheap hat had morphed into an expensive, rare vicuna coat. No one remembered checking a vicuna coat, but the victim insisted he had done so. Finally, someone noticed the lonely lid sitting unclaimed on the top of the coat rack. When the number matched the receipt in the claimant's hand, the case was solved. The offended party who made much of his loss was willing to take the entire gate of the affair as compensation for the loss of his imaginary coat.

If anyone arrived at the door high or with alcohol on his breath, he would be turned away. The primary villains, however, were girls who carried booze or reefer in their pocketbooks for their boyfriends. I remember a close trio of lads showed up willing to pay admission. The fellow in the center was so blitzed, however, that it took the two book ends to keep him standing up. We didn't always succeed in eliminating alcohol, and we got an emergency call to rescue a passed out imbiber who was nose deep in the urinals in the basement. One of our priorities was to keep the rectory ignorant of such miscues, so he and a few friends were ushered out the door at the back of the school. We were always concerned that the pastor would cancel any future dances if untoward behavior was detected.

Not all problems arose from the teenagers. Our graduates had the smarts to either follow the rules or to stay away. Others, friends or high school classmates of our kids, were generally the offenders. Jim Nolan, a twenty year veteran of the submarine service played an important role in our early warning system. Jim retired as a Chief Petty Officer, and I suppose had witnessed many aberrations during his career. He also was licensed to carry a gun since he worked for the Federal Reserve. He discreetly carried it as he helped monitor our entrance requirements. One night, a White man showed up and claimed to be a boiler repair man, and he brusquely brushed past Jim. Jim believed that no White boiler man ever arrived for repairs in the ghetto at eleven o'clock at night, and he was ready to pursue the intruder. I went down to check on the man who turned out to be a NYPD detective. Unknown to us, the rectory had authorized the police to have a wire tap for a telephone line to a nearby building. The suspect was running an abortion mill, at that time illegal in New York. The detective had to retrieve the tapes and replace the used ones with a new one. Jim wouldn't relent until we told him the true identity of the impolite intruder, but we didn't announce what they were searching for.

There was no escaping the fact, nevertheless, that St. Augustine Parish was located in a high crime area. Visitors to the Brothers' house often commented on the noise of the fire engines and police cars, but the community members had grown accustomed to such background distractions and barely heard the commotion. The community was spared the rioting that followed Harlem, the murder of Martin Luther King, and the blackouts caused by electrical failures. Most storekeepers locked down their stores and pulled down the iron gates, euphemistically termed 'Harlem curtains.' Besides, there weren't too many large stores in Morrisania worth pillaging. My friend Russell mentioned that he went in search of a five finger discount, but his arrival coincided with the fortuitous arrival of several bus loads of the Tactical Police Force. The shelves with the meager selections in our local convenience stores were salvaged and safely secured from pillaging. That wasn't so on 149th Street or the Fordham Road area.

On the first major blackout when the entire city lost power, an eerie silence overtook the general hum of the neighborhood. My first inking of trouble was the sound of the fire box on the corner. I suppose it had a back up battery, but the clanging of the pulled alarm was the solitary indication of some disruption. As I walked to the firebox, I could see the elevated Third Avenue subway slow to a stop short of the 166th Street station. The evening sky was beautiful as sunset was imminent, and the cloudless sky moved to twilight. No other noise was obvious since vehicles didn't travel Franklin Avenue that much. The Brothers were celebrating Jim Corcoran's birthday, and some friends had been invited. I guess we could boast that few of us had candlelit dinners on our birthday. Many other Brothers' communities throughout the city had more harrowing experiences as later tales emerged. For instance, the monks at St. Bernard's on 14th Street and the west side performed valiantly as impromptu traffic directors with only their courage and flashlights to direct the huge tie-ups that resulted from inoperable street and traffic lights.

Early one morning the Brothers were fast asleep when a pounding on the front door awoke all in the house. Joe Hosey answered the front door and encountered a young, barely clad woman with a toddler in hand. Her slip was torn and bloodied. By happenstance, that evening we had a six foot ten guest named Artie Walsh from the 'Coop' who also was a registered nurse. Hosey summoned Artie to take care of the wounded woman. Artie thought he had been called to minister to the little tot who at most needed a band aid. The woman, however, had a severe gash in her hand. As the story unfolded, our midnight intruder claimed her psychotic brother had murdered their mother in Harlem and was coming to murder her. When she heard him at her door in the building overlooking our school yard, she tried to elude him by fleeing down the fire escape. In typical ghetto fashion, she had nailed the window shut in order to repel burglars herself, so she had to smash the windows with her bare hand, thereby inflicting a serious wound. The police were called, and Hosey lent her his overcoat as a shield for modesty and against the cold. She left with the police who found the maniac trashing her apartment in his attempt to wreak vengeance upon his family. A day or two later, Hosey noticed that his beloved, albeit bedraggled overcoat, was now nailed to the broken window frame to keep out the cold. Sometimes, charity, it might seem, leads to greater sacrifice than what appears initially.

In my earliest introductory days to life in Morrisania, I was aware that crime and violence were often not far away. A few days before my arrival, a recent graduate had been stabbed in the abdomen and was in critical condition. I used to check with his friend and neighbor every so often, and I would get the odds of his survival. When queried about the condition of the victim, Danny used to say,

"The odds are eighty to twenty, he gonna die."

After about two weeks, the odds had changed to fifty-fifty. Later, they would improve even more. I asked Danny what had happened. Danny informed me,

"They gave him de operation."

I naturally asked,

"What operation?"

His response was direct and simple, but I don't know about its accuracy. *"They gave him de operation, you know, Brother. "They cut off his balls, Brother."*

The patient did survive but I never learned exactly how.

My medical informant was one of the few students who enjoyed roller hockey. He never did master the nomenclature, for he persisted in calling the puck, *"de pluck."* Danny also was an excellent runner and avid basketball player. He contributed many points in track and added a positive dimension to our basketball team. What he couldn't do was read. While we were traveling northward on the Pelham Bay Line to Spellman for a basketball tournament, Danny was engrossed in the **Daily News.** Unfortunately it was all a pretense, for he was holding the paper upside down and only pretending to read. Meanwhile, his half brother was starring for Cardinal Hayes and his full brothers, 'Foo' and 'Doo,' were performing well in school. Yet Danny had his academic limitations and speech mannerism that a linguist might enjoy reading. One of his favorite singers was *"Areeffa Franklin,"* and he actually uttered the sentence, *"Come Souff wiff me."* His mother, meantime, worked in the Brothers' house as housekeeper.

Toward the end of my time in St. Augustine, I had another encounter that was indicative of the violence and omnipresence of drugs and an ethic that I didn't understand. A graduate White boy, probably the end of his kind in the neighborhood, used to drop around and chat from time to time. He had played basketball for the school and his race didn't inhibit him from total acceptance among his peers. He had adopted the *lingua franca* and *patois* of the neighborhood to the point where only audible exposure would lead one to suspect he was Black. His pale, white complexion and slightly red hair, in reality, pointed to his Irish heritage. Late one night he came to the Brothers' House with a desperate plea. According to his explanation, the cops rousted one of his friends suspected of dealing heroin. The suspect had handed off his supply to Jim Howard who sauntered away as the cops patted down his friend. Jim then claimed some guys saw the shift in heroin and robbed him of the stash at the end of the block. When the suspect returned and asked for his heroin, Jim was given the ultimatum of returning the dope or paying its value. He had two days to come up with either. After talking with him, I checked with some street savvy individuals who claimed Jimmy had better pay up or skip town. Going to the police would be a death warrant. I didn't have any money to give Jimmy, so he skipped town rather than visit the morgue. His appeal also represented a dilemma we often faced about the credulity of some of the requests. Upon investigation, however, usually the narrator was close to truth. I had never been approached by Jim before, but I couldn't vouch for his drug activities or involvement, only that he associated with a suspicious crowd.

The Brothers used to walk all over the neighborhood without any incident, however. Since we had no gym or facility for weekend sports activities, we would venture east to Southern Boulevard and west to Jerome Avenue. From the hub on 149th Street in the south to Fordham Road in the north, we traversed what could have been dangerous territory. Some claimed potential muggers knew who we were and had little to tempt them. Others thought we were plainclothes cops and didn't want to mess with us. Whatever was the truth, we never encountered any hassle, menace or threat, even passing the notorious 'Sportsman Bar,' affectionately labeled 'the bucket of blood' or the 'Bar Nunn' whose very name indicated the class of clientele that frequented it.

The school and the Brothers' House were not granted any such immunity. Burglars often hit the school in the hope of getting the televisions, slide projectors and hi-fi's or tape recorders that were supplied by federal anti-poverty programs in title nine. The thieves generally knew exactly where to go. Ed Phelan set up his own alarm system which rang in his bedroom, and he was instrumental in finally catching our habitual burglars. One memorable occasion taught me that not all the thieving was caused by the thugs. After breaking into the school, we were assessing the moderate damage which amounted to a few broken locks when the parish curate said,

"Look what the burglars did," as he toppled an eight foot statue of the Blessed Mother. In thousands of pieces, I suppose it helped balance the ledger that month. This same curate was conversing with police who had come to collect an overdosed man from the bottom church. As they exchanged pleasantries, he said,

"The man has been drinking. I can smell alcohol."

The jaded cop of many years experience merely informed the prelate,

"No, that's my partner."

This same prelate was known to 'age' diplomas and certificates in the rectory oven so that the forgeries might look more genuine in the hands of job seekers.

As the Vietnam conflict escalated so too did the crime rate in Morrisania. The price of copper made any such sizable amount of the desired metal jeopardized. The school had a heavy brass banister leading up the front stairs. In the middle of the night, some entrepreneurs dismantled it from its moorings and made off with the treasure. One might think that we should have learned from that, but the thieves were so confident that we slept the sleep of the just that they returned to rip off the copper drain pipes and downspouts from the Brothers' house. The thieves were right, for not one of us heard the clamor that should have accompanied the theft. Incredibly, eight intelligent men sleep peacefully while the very rain spouts and gutters directly outside their windows were ripped from their position. When all evident sources of copper were extracted, the thieves literally mined the copper telephone wires buried underground. Ma Bell's men were kept occupied in replacing the stolen cables for some time.

Aside from a stolen car battery belonging to a visiting community vehicle, we seldom had any personal property taken. Maybe the vow of poverty had its reward in offering little temptation to offenders. We were able to park the cars we had in the schoolyard and lock the gate so no car was ever stolen. None of the Brothers who had been in Augustine for any length of time ever felt unsafe or unwanted, even when we crossed paths with the 'Five Percenters' or the 'Nation of Islam.' The presence of such associations was obvious, but never more so than when police came to examine the school records of a boy who had been in our care in the fifth grade. At that time, I felt he was one of the meanest individuals I had ever seen. Despite having his broken ankle in a cast, he, without any emotion or motivation, managed to kick one of his classmates when he fell down in the schoolyard. The detective who came to the school claimed that Nathan was wanted for eleven murders. He allegedly belonged to an initiating team of Five Percenters who demanded the murder of a non-Black as an entry requirement. Nathan had participated in murdering ten Hispanics and one Chinese man. The tragedy of the situation and the reason why the police examined his records was the suspect had so many aliases and identification papers and birth certificates, they couldn't prove his age. Nathan was only fifteen years old and therefore would face trial in Juvenile Court, and the severest penalty might be eighteen months in a reformatory. Our records indicated that he indeed was only fifteen years old.

Sometimes our interaction with certain individuals was humorous, if not scary. One of our sixth graders, Leo Rooder, was an intellectually limited child with an inane smile and a penchant for thievery and devilment. His mother was a huge, opinionated lady who insisted on consulting with the rather diminutive Barry Luna frequently. On one of her consultations, she arrived on a very hot afternoon, and Barry had difficulty opening the window in our front room. Mrs. Rooder immediately told him to sit down while she took care of the stuck window. After a powerful yank the window problem was solved. Then Mrs. Rooder began her commentary. She claimed that Leo had just returned from that exclusive boarding school in Westchester called Lincoln Hall. Barry knew it as the welfare institution operated by the Brothers. Then she began a tirade that included the revelation that the United States had actually lost World War II to the Nazis. She said that most people didn't realize this because the Nazis changed their uniform and now masqueraded as New York City cops. She seemed to work herself into a lather, and soon Barry was looking for an opportunity to close this avenue of personal learning. In the future Barry made sure windows operated properly and that an appropriate personal escape route as well as exit strategy were in place before her next conference.

Although the late sixties were definitely an era when 'Charlie Fever,' or suspicions about Whites was rampant, the parents of our students rarely cited this as an aspect in the relationship between student and teacher. Their attitude, on the contrary, was almost always deep appreciation and respect. Whatever the Brothers suggested for their children carried the force of law and sincere efforts were made to comply. In return, their confidence engendered a desire to what was best for each student and made the teacher's job so much easier.

After two or three years at Augustine, I underwent my own transformation. I'd like to think of it as similar to Saul getting knocked from his horse and blinded on the road to Damascus. No such immediate conversion was mine, for it was definitely evolutionary and gradual. As my tenure in the school increased so too did my value and understanding. I can't point to any single event, but I know I became a changed man. The school changed and the neighborhood changed too, and I am sure they all conspired to make me a better individual. What began as a war of wills evanesced into the most meaningful experience I had in my teaching career. Armageddon had become Eden, and I had entered the Golden Age of my educational career much to the relief of my students.

Chapter Ten

From Eden to Emigre

In the switch from Highbridge to Morrisania, only about one mile eastward in the Bronx, I underwent a personal transition that consumed several years. Familiar with Sacred Heart but ignorant of much of what Morrisania contained, I spent at least two or three years making the adaptations to my new environment. I can't recall any overnight conversion or instant recognition of the responsibilities of my new assignment. Yet there was a great contrast between the two parishes and their respective schools. Illustrative of the difference between the two areas might simply be the Carmelite Convent on the hillside overlooking the footbridge between Manhattan and the Bronx. The cloistered Carmelite nuns used to contact St. Augustine, not Sacred Heart, whenever they had surplus supplies of day old bread, pastries, pies, and so forth. Even cloistered nuns recognized the economic and social differences of the two neighborhoods. At Augustine, we used to collect the surplus food in our battered Renault and then distribute it from the Brothers' house door to deserving families within the parish. At Sacred Heart, there was never a call from the nuns who perceived little need within their own parish boundaries.

During my tenure at Augustine, I learned far more than I taught. Somehow the milieu of Augustine underwent a significant, even palpable change too. Trying to resolve in my mind what I had experienced has led me to several factors that I identify as contributable to my evolutionary development. After three years the characters and the behaviors that struck me so intensely and described in the previous chapter seemed to evaporate or disappear into thin air. The forces of history and social change were heavy in the land. The impressions I associated with my early days at Augustine were reflected in Kenneth Stamp's **The Peculiar Institution,** a fine general study of slavery in the south. Since outright rebellion was inimical to one's health, and disobedience brought the lash upon oneself, more subtle forms of resistance and contempt were employed. Indolence, feigned stupidity, carelessness for tools, unreliability, disregard for truth, and so forth were forms of coping with the oppression of an uneven relationship between master and slave. I contend it was applicable also in the interplay between White teacher and Black student in the classroom.

I also found the classic study of the roots of racism in Winthrop Jordan's **White Over Black** very informative as the author traced the introduction of Europeans to the 'Dark Continent.' From the Age of Exploration to the Age of Elizabeth and Shakespeare, Jordan underscores the psychological, sociological as well as theological interpretations that led especially the English speaking world to identify itself as far superior to the Black race. The impact of social custom, literary heritage, theological explanation, and a sociology based on the conviction that White was an ideal imprinted an attitude that affected White Europeans. Whatever traits deviated from that paragon therefore were inferior. This attitude was pervasive, permeating the minds of White Europeans and their progeny in the New World.

There were a significant number of factors that seemed to make this form of relationship obsolete in the early 1960's. In that period there was a demographic shift within the neighborhood of Morrisania, for instance. Arsonists and squatters had destroyed much of the apartment houses on Washington Avenue, and its residents were relocated into the Webster Avenue Projects, or the modern housing on Tinton Avenue. I often recall the message of one parent who claimed that every night when her family slept in an apartment on Washington Avenue, she anticipated a conflagration started either by a junkie by accident or an arsonist seeking insurance settlements for absentee landlords. Only when the family was finally resettled in the Webster Projects did a restful night's sleep and a sense of safety ensue. Many also moved northward in the Bronx, or farther eastward toward Soundview Avenue. A few even managed to be early denizens of Co-op City, but most of these families continued to send their children to the School on Franklin Avenue. Shifting population, however, isn't an adequate explanation for the substantial change in the behavior of the students.

I don't believe my own adaptations are sufficient reasons for the marked alteration in student behavior either. My demands weren't that outrageous, nor were my relationships that acrimonious. In fact, I identify the relationship between myself and my students as respectful, even friendly. While I appreciate the growth factor within myself, I believe the improvement within the students was even greater. The early 1960's were a period of unprecedented improvement in the self-image and self-confidence of the Black students under our charge. I recall the commentary and mockery they uttered when we viewed the opening of the World's Fair in Flushing Meadows in 1964. CORE had organized a demonstration in an attempt to block traffic and access to the Fairgrounds. As they strived to prevent visitors from approaching the grounds, many arrests were made and the event was carried live on television. The verbal assessment of my observing class was simply, "Those crazy niggers!"

Only once in my time supervising the schoolyard at lunch time had I overheard such a derogatory statement. Lenny Wilson chided Russell Cameron for horsing around by acidly remarking, "Act your age, not your color." No matter how often I recall and examine that statement, I am stymied by its message and intent. I don't know whether Lenny was being satirical or exhibiting a form of self-loathing about his race. He and Russell were good friends although they had different interests, and Russell was far superior in strength and athleticism. The message was delivered in a gentle admonitory tone and didn't quite fit the profile of the game in which the students exchanged verbal insults about one's mother or family. Shortly after it was uttered, the advice would have seemed totally out of place. In very short time, like the comment of those watching the demonstrators, that assessment changed radically.

Black literature had begun to develop a sense of pride in one's heritage, and the poems of Langston Hughes, Claude McKay, and Amiri Baraka brought a feeling of empathy along with their perusal. Toni Morrison and Maya Angelou offered themes and scenes quite familiar to a Black reading audience. Ralph Ellison's **Invisible Man** was assuming a face through the books of Richard Wright and James Baldwin. References to the Harlem Renaissance and the options available at the Schomberg Library presented evidence of a collection of Black oriented literature that was unknown to most. On a more cerebral level, academics wrote of the achievements of such notables as W.E. B. Dubois, the author of a seminal book on Black pride called **The Souls of Black Folks.** Among other achievements, Dubois, the founder of the NAACP, expounded the theory of a talented tenth of the Black race, a group in which the limited resources of Blacks should be invested. He believed that that elite group would leaven the mass of the Black race and lead the people to ultimate equality with Whites. His approach differed significantly from the more menial track presented by Booker T. Washington who suggested that more modest careers would ultimately enrich the race and encourage an alliance with White people.

Black historians like John Hope Franklin, the author of **Before the Mayflower,** wrote extensively of the role of Blacks in American history. C. Carter Woodson and Benjamin Quarles focused on **The Negro in the American Revolution.** The highly respected James McPherson added an extensive study of the **Negro in the Civil War.** Few students read any of their works, but their pioneering efforts led to the inclusion of Black contributions to American history. Stories about figures like Frederick Douglass, Benjamin Banneker, Harriet Tubman, Sojourner Truth, Nat Turner, Denmark Vesey, Gabriel Prosser, Marcus Garvey, the Buffalo Soldiers of the Ninth and Tenth Cavalry, and George Washington Carver etched a human dimension in textbooks that was non-existent before. Racial pride grew substantially along with knowledge of what some Blacks had achieved in prior years.

On a more popular level, some students read books about the Black Panthers of Bobby Seale, **Soul on Ice** by Eldridge Cleaver, or the quite accurate portrayal of a Black youth in the ghetto as described by Claude Brown in **Manchild in the Promised Land.** James Farmer's CORE and the non-violent advocacy of Martin Luther King were well received among Black adults. More militant youth heeded the calls of H. Rap Brown, Stokley Carmichael, and James Baldwin. By far, however, the most influential book and inspiration for self-esteem and racial pride came from the thoughts, speeches, writings, and **Autobiography of Malcolm X.** Malcolm X extolled the physical characteristics that identified Blacks. Many previously sought White features associated with the nose and lips, or straight hair, but Malcolm preached the beauty of blackness. The broad nose, dark skin, thick lips, and thick hair of the typical Black were features that should be promoted, not adapted to a White standard according to the words of Malcolm X. The movement with the motto "Black is Beautiful" gained momentum and popularity daily.

Black heritage, moreover, was something to be cherished and nurtured, not neglected and ignored. While few of my students changed their names or religion at that point in their lives, I suspected many would do so later in life. The Muslim religion extrapolated from the association of their White slave masters or White oppressors. Africanisms, such as names and attire, proliferated with the speed of popularity of the Afro and its affiliated pick. Black, red and green colors appeared more frequently as signs of Black pride. Huge Afros sprouted among the students, and an occasional dashiki appeared amid one's wardrobe. As Black pride swelled, so too did academic aspirations and ambitions. Some students enjoyed the African rhythms of the songs of Miriam Makeba, and others developed an intense interest in African dance troupes that supplemented the ever popular preoccupation with Karate and the martial arts.

Even the mass media seemed caught up in the frenzy of Black joy. The typical movie roles of the past like Butterfly McQueen and StepnFetchit were replaced with genuine human figures of heroic stature, played primarily by Sidney Poitier in *Lilies of the Fields* or *To Sir With Love*. Harry Belafonte, David Parks, and Ossie Davis even produced films for a Black audience that also appealed to Whites. On radio and television I used to enjoy the humor of *Amos and Andy* and misguidedly believed that the portrayal of the main characters and the Kingfish were accurate images of Black males. Now Black youth could catch the acerbic humor of Dick Gregory or Richard Pryor, but most were impressed with the wit and image projected by Bill Cosby. Blacks were no longer invisible from television advertisements too. Their economic purchasing power was courted extensively. For the James Bond types, one could counter with S*haft* or *Superfly*. These shows paved the way for Black marketable actors like Will Smith, Denzel Washington, and Morgan Freeman in our current day.

Music, of course, had always been extensively mined by a White population who enjoyed the skills of jazz and blues. Duke Ellington, Ella Fitzgerald, and Lionel Hampton had a broader audience, it seemed, than Dinah Washington or Billie Holliday. Some claimed that Elvis Presley was such a great success because he was a White performer who mastered a Black sound. Groups like the Inkspots were replaced by performers who appealed to a White audience, as well as its traditional Black admirers. One of the first groups of the Rock and Roll era was Tony Williams and the Platters. As a matter of interest, Tony Williams' nephew was in my second class at St. Augustine. Other popular performers were the Temptations and the Fifth Dimension, and Sly and the Family Stone. Whites supported such groups as fans, as did my students, but in Morrisania there was little reciprocity for the performances of such White artists as Bob Dylan, Joan Baez, Simon Garfunkel, folk singers like the Kingston Trio, Peter, Paul and Mary, or protest songs. If I had to select the most popular artists according to my informal mental survey, I would have to nominate James Brown, the Godfather of Soul and Aretha Franklin, the Queen of Soul. In fact, Aretha's most popular song which I identify as illustrative of the mood of the audience was *Respect*. James Brown's, "Say it loud. I'm Black and I'm proud," was almost the anthem of the youths I taught.

Black teenagers could easily identify with the music that permeated their lives. Much has been written about the British invasion in the early sixties, and how Beatlemania, the Stones and innumerable British recording artists dominated the charts of popular music. In my estimate, the invasion barely penetrated the Bronx, or at least Morrisania. With the notable exception of one young lady who was totally overwhelmed by Paul McCartney, the Beatles were a non-factor or entomological pests. Our students listened exclusively to Black radio stations which rarely featured any White artists at all. Since our music tastes often reflected what the students played rather than the stations Whites might prefer, most of the faculty were indifferent to the onslaught of English performers.

Another source of Black pride was the emergence of the professional Black athlete. Jackie Robinson was indeed a folk hero, as well as an outstanding athlete, but the sixties also brought forth a plethora of athletes in football and especially basketball. The running of Jim Brown and the line play of Rosie Greer were well known to the kids who had yet to see a Black quarterback on a major college team or professional football club. That was not so with basketball, by far the most popular sport in the Bronx. Black basketball models abounded, and it was no accident that one of the most respected was the man who changed his name from Lew Alcindor to Kareem Abdul Jabbar. Did his conversion from Catholicism to Islam presage a mass development among Black youth, and did his name change epitomize the evolution of Black pride? I think so, just as I recognize that the other outstanding athlete who elevated the aspirations of Bronx youth was the world renowned Cassius Clay who became Muhammed Ali, probably the single most admired athlete in the country.

The confluence of these many factors led my students to greater self-esteem, higher personal aspirations, intellectual curiosity, academic pride, and a healthy sense that there was a worthy place for them in society. Sister Regina Lowe, SC, a woman who dedicated her entire educational career to teaching Black youth in the Bronx and in the Bahamas, recently confided to me that one could not overestimate the value of enhanced self-esteem among Black students. Without a doubt, the period during my tenure at St. Augustine was marked by an unusually effective growth in our student's self-concept and ambitions.

Sensitive to these developments in their early stages, Brother Charles Patrick Hosey invoked several strategies to increase the growth of pride and achievement among our boys. First and foremost, Joe proposed that the role of corporal punishment be virtually abolished. Traditional use of paddles, or rulers, or pointers was eliminated since they seldom had any positive effects other than alienation and resentment. The faculty responded to Joe's request, and the students' reaction wasn't tangible but psychological. Before Joe's policy could be tested extensively, the Christian Brothers noted his talents and tapped him to found a new school for gifted boys from the inner city. As such, Joe was reassigned to Msgr. Kelly School, located in Holy Trinity School on the Westside of Manhattan. We helped him administer an entrance examination that screened applicants and identified through test and interview those who might benefit most from acceptance in the innovative program. In the next few years, St. Augustine sent a few candidates to Msgr. Kelly, but few of our applicants could meet the criteria when it was opened to the entire inner city population of New York. One of our former students, however, Kevin Allen graduated from Msgr. Kelly and is now a medical doctor alongside his talented sister Barbara.

With Greg Flynn reassigned to the Coop and Hosey at Msgr. Kelly, our faculty had significant changes, but those assignments didn't seem to explain the improvement in student behavior or achievement. Barry Luna was a fine sixth grade teacher, and Hughie Stringer added something different to the style of teaching. Brother

John McManus brought a dedication and devotion to his teaching and preparation that were admirable. Brother Matthew Kissane provided leadership that encouraged the faculty and officiated over a realignment of responsibilities that had a major impact upon learning in the venerable school. Matty's finest achievement, however, may have been his openhanded policy in enabling each faculty member to pursue his personal concept on how to approach student, curriculum, and behavior. With that in mind, perhaps Matty's biggest challenge came from an unexpected source.

One of the newly assigned community members was Brother Edward Phelan. From the beginning he was so successful that I almost suspected that he had sold his soul, like Jabez Stone in **The Devil and Daniel Webster.** No matter how preposterous or daunting Ed's plans were, they all magically succeeded with results that were far from predictable. In his first year, Ed resolved to acquire a new source of funding for our annual sports night event in Morris High School. Despite the skepticism of his community mates, Ed managed to sell ads for a magazine that he ran off on the old mimeograph machine and folded inside a free Coca Cola cover. While the final product didn't look professional, it was awesome to the local merchants who had purchased advertising space in the newest journal to hit Franklin Avenue. Ed's imagination stimulated an ambitious science program that involved a mobile science lab on a cart rolling from classroom to classroom. In the meantime, this indefatigable teacher was also completing his master's degree at NYU and then enrolling at Fordham University where he would merit a doctoral degree in Urban Education.

Some of Ed's plans rattled the psyche of Matty Kissane, but every program proved to be an outstanding hit with the students. When Matty went on a ninety day retreat to Sangre De Cristo, which we called the 'Snake Pit,' his replacement was Barney Cullen, an old hand with years of elementary school experience. Barney was duly impressed with the changes that had been wrought over the years, and he continued his supportive collaboration on all the school's activities. Although he was only an interim replacement, he encouraged no disruption of our typical procedures. I think he also learned to appreciate the effort and creativity of the Brothers who staffed the school in an era that held some familiar and some new fangled approaches to elementary education.

In assessing the faculty and any changes that may have occurred during my tenure, I cannot candidly identify significant contributions that may have generated the substantial change I witnessed among the students. Although I cannot write enough about the energy and direction that Ed Phelan brought to the school, I must consign greater influence to an administrative development that made progress more measurable and captured the interest of the students. That administrative alteration was the work of Sister Genevieve Brown, SC and Matty Kissane, FSC, representatives of religious orders that had staffed the school since the first decade of the twentieth century. Sister Genevieve was a veteran administrator and educator who had spent a number of years on the Sisters of Charity missions in the Bahamas. She was soft-spoken and kind, rarely given to emotional outbursts of any sort. Her persona was attractive to young children who could detect her kindness and concern through her demeanor rather than her words. In the new arrangement, she would become the principal of the first four grades, leaving Matty Kissane to handle the top four classes of boys and girls. Teaching girls for the first time took some adjustments in voice as well as approach.

Within this hierarchy, I joined a team teaching, developmental staff that was highly trained and extremely motivated. The best arrangement seemed to be dividing the boys and girls homogenously into two groups that we labeled Advanced and Regular. Sister Joseph Mackin, SC was a devoted, experienced teacher who excelled in Math. She taught two levels in the eighth grade and two in the seventh. Her demands were high, but her returns matched her expectations. Her focus on mathematics spurred many of the boys to achieve much more than one might anticipate. Sister Regina Lowe, SC concentrated on English for the seventh and eighth graders, and Ed Phelan wheeled his science cart between the same groups. That left me with the responsibility of teaching social studies. We also determined that one could be assigned to only two subjects or four, but if someone had a knack for a particular subject, he had to compliment another. The matching subjects generally were Math and Science and English and social studies.

In my approach to teaching seventh and eighth grade girls, I rapidly discovered that the least offensive word could repel a female student for months. While boys didn't appear to hold grudges or have sensitive psyches, the girls were another story. Even a kind word could trigger a negative reaction, if it were timed poorly. In my attempt to adjust to the sensitivities of the young ladies, the boys benefited greatly. One had to be fair and avoid the glib remarks that sometimes accompanied my sarcastic commentary. Under a softer, kinder approach, the boys seemed to flourish and rather than acceding to the girls, contributing more to classroom discussion. Both seemed to enjoy the innovations and new approaches advocated by the National Social Studies Teachers Association which seemed more viable under homogeneous grouping and departmentalization. With specific time allotment for each subject, the four major areas were covered daily. Other subjects like religion, current events, handwriting, spelling and so forth were covered beyond the four allotted periods and home room. All seemed to benefit from the new arrangement. The students enjoyed exposure to four teachers rather than one. The teachers relished the concentration for a specific period of time, and the opportunity for mutual consultation with peers led to a more objective understanding of each pupil.

While the girls of St. Augustine had always outperformed the boys academically, the boys closed the gap somewhat. At the end of one year, two even won scholarships to Regis High School, a tuition free institution run by the Jesuits for gifted males. Ferdinand Braaf, an immigrant from Curacao, and John Tam, a Chinese immigrant from Hong Kong, won the scholarships especially because of their expertise developed in the math classes conducted by Sister Joseph Mackin. John Tam, especially, seemed unable to make a mistake or when so doing, seemed incredulous that he had done so.

A phenomenon that accompanied the improvement in the school was the growth of requests for admission. Some Nuns in the South Bronx who recognized the talent of their male students, but thought they might benefit from a male teacher, recommended individuals who excelled in our program. Domingo Echevarria had been problematic in his former school, but his behavior and performance in Augustine were outstanding. Jose Texeidor was a brilliant student who seemed mired in indifference until his arrival in our program. He rapidly asserted his right to top spot among boys and was a treasure in our classes. Kurtis Harris and his sister Kandi enhanced the rolls of their respective classes. Kurtis became an excellent orator and won several oratory contests. His natural good looks and personality made his presentation on the stage all that more impressive.

Not all our students were successful. In the fifth grade, a youngster named Herbie Gomez was very unhappy in the school. His displeasure often spilled over into resentment, and his inability to control his response was often a challenge to those who tried to help him. On one specific occasion, Brother Barry Luna was trying to get Herbie to complete a necessary assignment. He was kept after school while he groused about life in general. Sister Susan Doonan, who taught the first grade and was especially soft and kind with all students, approached Herbie and inquired how she could help him. Herbie's reply was, "Get the fuck out of my face. I hate you and I hate this school." After a few episodes like this, Herbie's wish to leave was honored when a neighboring school offered a straight player deal. We could place Herbie who wanted the 'trade,' but we had to take three members of a single family in return. We were delighted to do so. Twins Avery and Aaron Brown apparently had driven their teacher to distraction, but in Augustine, both performed well. Avery was a comedian of sorts, and Aaron enjoyed sports. Both worked well in class, and their behavior was never problematic. Along with them came their older sister, Dijon Brown. Initially she seemed suspicious of these new teachers, but she soon settled down and became productive too.

Another addition to the school proved to be invaluable, not so much for himself, but for what he brought with him. William Smith was a very pleasant, easy going individual who couldn't get too excited about schoolwork. His parents knew the benefits of a fine education and were determined to see their son succeed. They decided that Augustine offered the best opportunity to fulfill that goal. William's father was a highly educated, articulate Black man who had an excellent knowledge of Black history as well as the reality of American society. Thanks to his efforts, the parish offered Black history classes to adults who loved his contributions. After awhile, the volunteers in this seminar rotated the responsibility of informing the others about a specific aspect of the study. Mr. Smith deserves commendations for his help which was his response to our accepting his son into the school.

I would also be remiss, if I did not cite another factor in the improvement in the school. Thanks to the organization and determination of Sister Helen Jarzinski, SC and Mrs. Gray, a series of anti-poverty funds from the Lyndon Johnson War on Poverty enabled

St. Augustine to provide a twelve month learning center for the neighborhood. Sister Helen had always been creative and searching for new avenues to follow in the pursuit of service to the poor. She found a very capable assistant in Mrs. Gray who had some political ties to the local democratic powers and who also had two children in the school. Wilbert and Nannette, a year apart in St. Augustine, had an older sister who had graduated a few years earlier. Attending meetings, filling out forms, filing applications, and impressing folks in interviews, Sister and Mrs. Gray were rewarded with grants of over one hundred thousand dollars a year. Out of this funding arose the Happy Holidays Day Camp, more often called 'The Double H.' Most of its activities occurred during the summer, but its role and staff contracted during the winter months while school was in session.

During the summers, moreover, the grant provided for an executive director, a few teachers, some older teen trainees, a secretarial staff and an unpaid Board of Directors. This staff was also supplemented by Job Corps workers from the neighborhood. Sister Helen and Mrs. Gray nominated excellent Executive Directors from among the parents of our students. Each of these lay folk had fine people skills, organizational talent, and a determination to run a cost effective program that operated efficiently and honestly, unlike many of the anti-poverty programs in the neighborhood. Helena McCallum, a sixth grade teacher during the school year was the first of a number of excellent supervisors. She was followed by Janet Banks, the mother of two of our students, and Denise Dixon who also taught the sixth grade in Augustine. Each provided an excellent program that offered a summer service second to none. Aided by an involved Board of Directors, the leaders selected fine, experienced subordinates who leavened the Job Corps members and guaranteed that the one hundred and fifty campers were properly supervised and instructed. The string of success, however, was broken when the executive chair was offered to a young, talented, glib immigrant from St. Thomas in the Virgin Islands. Michael Arthur Dickens had much talent, but he succumbed to the venality that seemed to permeate some of the programs surrounding ours. Mildred Johnson, a board member, became suspicious about some financial receipts that seemed inaccurate, so she began her own investigation.

Mildred uncovered about two thousand dollars of doctored receipts, and she summoned the Board and Mr. Dickens to render an account of his stewardship. Arthur readily confessed that he had embezzled about two thousand dollars and offered to sign a confession and go to the police station immediately. The Board wanted neither a signed confession nor an arrest. Instead, they insisted on restitution and resignation. Both were forthcoming. A week later, Mr. Dickens received a job within the poverty programs that offered even greater temptation for fiscal chicanery. At least the reputation of Double H remained intact. I suppose the price of success for our vibrant program was the tolerance for incompetence and inefficiency elsewhere.

During July and August, on a daily basis, each camper arrived at 9:00am and attended two or three classes in reading, math, and science taught by the Scholastics from Washington or one of the college students from the parish. One of the major reasons for the success of the academic part of the program was the presence of young Brothers who volunteered to spend their summers working at Augustine. One or two of them would receive a stipend from the camp that enabled the rest to support themselves in the Brothers' house. In the course of my time there, about a dozen volunteers served admirably. Names like Dennis Davin, Bob Ginard, Jim Bassett, Steve Touhy, George and Michael from Detroit taught the classes and then supervised and accompanied the campers and their keepers on recreational trips in the afternoon. George Stevens and Bill Fecteau were also impressed with the operation, and in fact they came to teach permanently at the school. Bill is still working with the people of the Bronx at the Highbridge Community Life Center as a member of Ed Phelan's staff.

After a few years of teaching in St. Augustine, George left the Institute and married a parishioner. Without the substantial help of these generous, conscientious volunteers, the program would not have been the success it was. The presence of these young Brothers and the great cooperative relationship we had with the Sisters of Charity led to my most embarrassing moment of my life. Just before the Brothers were to depart at the end of the summer, the Sisters invited us to an evening of games in the convent. One of the games was rifling through magazines to spot an advertisement or illustration that contained a specific item. Each of us had a pair of scissors to cut out the image when it had been located. That summer, I had been particularly despondent since I had just left the Brothers, but I soon got into the spirit of the game. As Mike from Detroit was searching through a magazine, I reached up and snipped the belt loop on his pants. I confess it was stupid, inappropriate, and totally beyond my typical *modus operandi*. Mike's reaction was more like I had tried to castrate him or something. When he discovered what I had done, he went ballistic, yelling, screaming at me, and then the *coup de grace*—he slapped me across my face three or four times. I can only surmise that he must have suppressed a great deal of resentment against me for something I know nothing about. I suppose all my time in religious life had prepared me for this moment, for I had never let anyone attempt doing that to me before. I apologized to the infuriated man, and as quickly and discreetly as I could, I excused myself and went back to the Brothers' house to regain my composure. George Stevens later joined me and mentioned that he thought he was going to witness a massacre of the striker. The following morning, I offered Mike my year's vacation money to buy a new pair of trousers, believing that he couldn't actually take the entire sum. He gratefully accepted my apology and my cash, and in return, I have erased his named totally from my memory.

Aside from the Brothers who assisted in the program, it also had about thirty Job Corps workers. Most of these were graduates of the school and very comfortable working with the young campers who were between the ages of seven and thirteen. Each Corps member worked for thirty-two hours a week. Their exclusive responsibility was to guarantee the safety of the kids in their care. They assisted in the classroom, but while traveling in the subways they shepherded their charges carefully, and we never misplaced or lost a child. In the meantime, the members were also learning job skills like punctuality, appropriate dress, interpersonal relationships, vigilance, and responsibility. They well earned their meager pay while their counterparts in a program just around the corner were given the same money for no show jobs, no supervision, no work, and the only responsibility was coming to the payment center on Fridays near West Farms to collect their unearned salaries.

A select few older teens were given the task of supervising the Job Corps personnel and guaranteeing that they performed the guidance required on trips in the afternoons to various parks, pools, museums, and other attractions throughout the city. Safety on the subways and Els was paramount, and frequent head counting required of all members. In my own role in Double H, I was more or less the Executive Assistant with a non-paying position. I assigned the groups and their supervisors. I selected the spots where I thought a specific age group might enjoy, and I oversaw the classroom instruction. The whole operation ran very smoothly, even on rainy days since the grant also provided audio-visuals, athletic equipment, games and puzzles. Each day I tried to disperse the various groups, so that we didn't concentrate too heavily on one activity or place. Given the variety of tasks, I can only maintain that the only problematic concern I experienced was some of the Job Corps kids who hadn't attended the school, and who envied the idle group around the corner. Fortunately, they were few, and after a brief period, often imitated the excellent examples of our conscientious staff members.

In the summers during the evenings, the day camp was supplemented by an evening program where the Brothers supervised the various activities, like dancing, games, and music. The teenage club had purchased a Coke machine, and charging minimum price, the machine produced enough money to afford occasional bus trips to far destinations on Saturdays. Some of the kids used to say, "Pay the extra dollar and see the world." Our longest trip was to Barrytown where the pool and the old house close by were the chief attractions as well as the two gyms in the Juniorate. Barrytown seemed to absorb and entertain its inner city visitors while the heat of the summer probably contributed to the exhaustion of the group by the end of the day.

Perhaps our most memorable trip, however, was a three busload caravan to La Salle Military Academy at Oakdale. Our trip to the Mecca on the Great South Bay with its sports facilities and beautiful grounds wasn't quite the same after our visit. After hearing about the Barrytown trip, almost all of the Job Corps kids who hadn't attended St. Augustine's School must have resolved to make this excursion. Since we didn't know them as well as the usual kids, they presented some challenges that we didn't anticipate. For instance, about midmorning, I received a frantic message that a young lady had had a heart attack at the boat house. Rushing to her assistance, I met her friend who informed me that the victim had a weak heart wall that could collapse at any time. Sister Regina and I, with the apparent heart victim, hurried to a doctor who served as medical consultant for the Academy and met us at his office. For most of the time, the victim was babbling incoherently, a factor that only raised our anxiety. After the doctor examined the patient, he reassured us with the news that her heart was fine, but that her brain was totally fried with alcohol. While that was somewhat of a relief, we also got the doctor's counsel on not bringing this type of inner city kid out to the suburbs. Sister Regina's chagrin was matched only by her relief about the relatively minor diagnosis.

After our return to the grounds, we got a complaint about another rather large young lady who was misbehaving in the rowboats. Upon further investigation, we determined that she had been trying to urinate over the gunwale of the boat. I began to wish for the return of the buses and a peaceful retreat to the Bronx. Sadly, one of the buses got a flat tire, and the driver had to call back to the Bronx for a replacement. Then it wouldn't start at all, and they had to send an entirely different bus back. We were determined to keep in a three bus convoy, so we delayed leaving. The wind picked up, and now the chilly breeze off the Bay drove most of our kids inside the boathouse. Around midnight the rescue bus finally arrived, and we restocked the buses and headed home. Meanwhile, a crowd of anxious parents had gathered at the school giving the scene some similarity to relatives waiting for the survivors of the Titanic or Andrea Doria.

When we finally arrived on Franklin Avenue, many sighed in relief, myself being one of the majors. As we relaxed for a few moments in the rec room in the basement of the Brothers' house, we received the telephone call. Matty Kissane got exasperated taking bus attendance, so he declared all present and accounted for, thereby authorizing our departure in convoy. The phone call was from Oakdale. About an hour after our departure, William Rogers sauntered into the Brothers' house on the grounds and inquired about the rest of us. He claimed he had climbed a tree to escape the chilly wind and had fallen asleep shielded within its foliage. One of the Brothers at Oakdale promised to drive him to the city later in the day for it was now about 2:00am. His family didn't appear either upset or surprised at this adventure. I resolutely promised never to bother Oakdale again as a host for our teenagers.

The vast majority of memories of those summers are quite pleasant and sources of pride at what we accomplished. Our graduates earned a decent wage that permitted them to pay for clothes, sneakers, records, radios and special electronics. In return for their pay, we got overwhelmingly positive performances which increased our kids' marketable skills. Many of the full time faculty of Augustine also participated in volunteer roles. Sister Susan Doonan, SC, Sister Eileen Hance, SC, and Sister Carole Liberti, SC provided additional expertise among our youngest campers, and all benefited from the contributions of everyone. I suppose the best commentary about the summer Double H experience was the fact that many reapplied for positions year after year. It kept our alumni in contact with the school and provided additional equipment during the winter months. Actually, the best analysis also presents an enhanced image of a dedicated group serving the community while fulfilling a desperate need competently. How could the school and parish suffer from those conclusions?

During the academic year of the later sixties, the Scholasticate was undergoing several changes. The Scholastics were moving into smaller communities and no longer enrolling at The Catholic University of America. They also had the opportunity to test the apostolate of the Brothers for short term visits. Our judgment upon that process is rather mixed. One of the Brothers who appeared to be somewhat effeminate arrived at Augustine intent on helping out. The students couldn't believe what they observed. One said that the Brothers sent to Augustine were either "big and strong or small and mean." This fellow was neither, and his mincing steps and lisping voice alerted the kids that he was not to their liking. One boy, Milton Laurents, remarked to me as he watched the individual amble to the gym after school, "We know why he's a Brother." Perhaps the superiors could have been more circumspect in assigning those seeking a taste of our apostolate.

Believing that Joe Hosey needed additional help, a young Brother experiencing some academic troubles in Washington was sent to help our staff. He certainly meant well, but he soon alienated all the students. Joe left him to cover his class while he attended some district council conference, and we had a full scale revolution on our hands. I don't know what this man did, but the mildest, generally most cooperative students had to be restrained from striking him. At the time Joe returned, we apprised him of the situation, and how we had to virtually isolate the incompetent for his own safety. Our assistant proved the maxim that the robe didn't make the Brother.

Not every placement was a disaster. Brother Mark Liotta was sent to enrich the music program, and he did an outstanding job. Not only was the classroom instruction more vital, but the liturgy and school ceremonies became more impressive under his guidance. The Brothers at Manhattan Prep used to send a number of catechists down to assist us during release time instruction. Despite the obvious challenge of teaching the students dismissed from classes in the public school to get an hour's worth of instruction once a week, the young high school students generally performed well.

Altogether, St. Augustine had improved immensely during my time there. I'd like to take some credit for that progress, but I realize that many individuals and factors must be accredited with the development. At best I can think of myself as a contributor to the cause abetted by many creative, dedicated Brothers, Sisters, and lay teachers. Perhaps those who warrant the greatest praise are the students themselves.

As a young White male growing up in New York City, I had made many assumptions that a young Black male might not have. For example, I believed that the complex transportation system involving buses and subways was an equal opportunity system. I realized that no one had to sit in the back of a bus or surrender a seat to a White person, but I didn't recognize the pernicious effects of profiling. Whenever Black teens traveled in any kind of numbers they became suspected felons. I discovered this early in my days at Augustine. We had taken the kids to the World's Fair, and after an exhausting day of visiting attractions, we boarded the subway for the long ride home. The car was quite empty for rush hour had ended. As usual, I took up a standing position by the doors so I could keep an eye on my class. As they sprawled on the seats, a White man about my age, sidled up to me and said, "If those Niggers make a move, I'm right behind you." A few years later, Bernie Goetz would put a face on this hostile, suspicious attitude toward Black teenagers when he shot several who were harassing some subway passengers. In my incident, I assured him that he was safe as were all the other passengers on board. He wanted to know how I could be so sure. I told him who they were, and that I was their teacher, a Christian Brother. He then extended his hand to me in friendship and exclaimed, "Pleased to meet you. I'm a Fordham University graduate myself."

If anything, when the kids traveled under our supervision, they attracted attention only by their good behavior, harmonious singing, or verbal quiz games. Many, nonetheless, chose to leave the cars whenever the kids entered. With some, their very fears were palpable.

As a White kid in Washington Heights, I assumed that I could rent or buy anywhere I chose or could afford. That wasn't so for a Black counterpart in Morrisania. There were several families that wanted to move, could afford to relocate, had sufficient credit history, but they couldn't find a neighborhood where they would be welcomed. After many years in the school, I often taught multiple siblings from the same family. The women seldom told stories, but the men occasionally would relate their frustration. One man in particular who worked very hard and supported his eight children, six of whom I taught, spoke candidly to me one afternoon. He expressed his wish to own a modest house in a decent neighborhood where he could take a Sunday stroll with his family without passing 'Harlem curtains,' boarded up stores, empty buildings, garbage strewn lots, winos, and whatnots, but he argued that he didn't want to live in a neighborhood where his neighbors resented his presence and offered hostility rather than hospitality.

The father of Dougie Harrison described his dilemma upon discharge from the army in 1946 in somewhat similar terms. He returned to his home in Jacksonville, Florida where he was accosted by a carload of drunken White men. They insisted he take them to the nearest bordello, arguing that every Black man knew where to find such a facility. His insistence that he just returned from a tour of duty in Japan did no good, so he directed them to a building he prayed was empty. He then went directly to the bus station as quickly as he could and bought a ticket to New York. He didn't know what might happen to him if the disappointed swains came in search of him. Upon arriving in New York, a friend encouraged him to enroll in mortuary school and join him in founding a Black funeral parlor in Mount Vernon. He passed up the opportunity of a lifetime, for segregation made Black undertakers very rich. Instead, he took a steady job as a janitor in Morris High School. His tale wasn't a lament, just a window into the strange twists a Black life could take.

A very impressive Black man also instructed me about his adventures at NYU under the GI Bill where White coeds constantly tried to prove their liberal views by bedding him. Whether it was his moral sense, which I estimated to be quite high, or his view of the hostility of the male students whose anger he might arouse, were his prime deterrent, he concluded that his best, safest approach was to boycott the wine and cheese parties, the beer blasts, and other collegiate celebrations. That way he was safe from the flirters or their self-appointed protectors while he studied for his degree.

I got to know another gentleman quite well too. He had been visiting his relatives in North Carolina and had his young family in tow. Unknown generally to White men, a Black man runs the risk of insult and rejection even upon the most basic requirements of road travel. When he stopped for gas and his young daughter asked to go to the bathroom, she was denied access since the station lacked 'colored accommodations.' Rather than retreat, the man ordered his daughter, too young to be embarrassed, to relieve herself right by the gas pump. Whether a father was simply buying gas, or entering a store, or seeking a meal, he could encounter embarrassing treatment, especially mortifying in front of his family. By the way, I experienced the same kind of indifferent treatment when I took some kids to Albany. We stopped to eat at a diner and were virtually ignored. Finally someone approached after many who had entered after us were served. Most of the requested items were no longer available, we were told, but we did receive reluctant service after an undue amount of time. Equal service at equal cost and equal respect were still in the far distant future, even for the New York State Thruway.

Although no father who spoke to me ever talked of encounters with Klansmen, night riders, or of muggings, lynching, or other abuses, each echoed the belief that fear of embarrassment, belittlement, or inequality was a predominant theme within their family lives. Each wistfully hoped only for a level playing field, a society that treated them fairly and justly, an economic world that gave them the chance to advance, and to create a safe haven for their families in a neighborhood where they could anticipate acceptance.

As a White youth in Washington Heights, I presumed that the police were friendly and anxious to protect me from harm. That may not have been a clear assumption among Black youth in the Bronx. The worst treatment I can cite from my youth may be the occasional policeman who went beyond the perfunctory to swipe a stickball bat during one of our street games. Because of my father's influence, I viewed the police as protectors of the innocent and objective in their administration of justice. When I got to St. Augustine, those impressions were sometimes sorely tested. In an effort to improve police/community relations, I invited the Black Commander of the Forty-Second Precinct on 162nd and Third Avenue to address our graduates at our annual Communion Breakfast. Captain Johnson projected the correct image of what a competent commander ought to be, and as such was perceived as a role model by our alumni. Some other episodes would not be so positive.

I often gathered a few kids from the neighborhood when I took a recreational tour of Harriman Park, or went to visit my brother Ray and his family who lived in Nyack and later moved to Piermont. On Veteran's Day in 1969, I had a few graduates in my car as I drove eastward on Route 59. I recall on that date, many cars had headlights on to signify support for the war in Vietnam. By that time, my support for the war had faltered significantly. As I drove, a police car pulled in behind me, and I commented to my passengers that a new driver might become rattled by the sudden appearance of a patrol car, but I had nothing to worry about for I had committed no violation. About a mile later, the cop flashed his lights and signaled me to pull over to the side of the road. The kids thought this was a wonderful experience to witness their former teacher stopped by the police. As I attempted to exit the car, I was told via bullhorn to stay behind the wheel, and the officer approached. He asked me for license and registration and the identification papers of the only female in the car. He took the papers and disappeared into his patrol car. After about half an hour, he returned the documents courteously and inquired why I was in the area. I mentioned that I had purchased something at the Nanuet Mall. He then claimed I had switched lanes without signaling, an offense I seriously doubted I had committed, and to this point, I thought perhaps he was zealously searching for a runaway teenage girl. He issued me a written warning, and then added his personal advice, "In the future, do your shopping in the Bronx!"

I had heard enough tales of policemen manufacturing traffic offenses, so I merely said nothing. Later I wrote a letter to the head of the Clarkstown Police Department offering my commendation if the officer had indeed been searching for a specific teenager, but I found his unsolicited advice about where I should shop reprehensible. My letter went unanswered, and I never heard back from him.

The father of two of my students had an encounter with my brother Ray when he was a policeman in Harlem. Apparently, Ray and his partner stopped a car that was driving erratically. The passenger launched into an oration, spewing names and places to impress the officers. At one point, the man uttered, "I'm Dynamite Albright, and I don't take no shit from no turkey." He then asserted his deaconship in St. Augustine's on Franklin Avenue. Although we had no such figures, he rambled on about how tight he was with Father Kane, the Pastor. My brother inquired whether he knew a Brother Kevin, and Dynamite responded that he was a coach with me for his son Gregory's basketball team. Of course, the only truth in that was his son's athletic status. Then he started raving about his success with me. Ray smiled and told him about our relationship. Dynamite screamed, "We've got it made in the shade," and Ray's partner was totally befuddled by this time. Dynamite escaped any ticket, and at least the police had helped him in one situation.

Incidentally, Dynamite had a brilliant, artistic, talented daughter Linda who sang and danced at The High School of Music and Art, made famous through the TV show *Fame.* This beautiful girl was learning to drive when her instructor stopped for cigarettes. He left her behind the wheel with the engine running. A strange man jumped into the car and ordered her to drive. Three plainclothes detectives were in hot pursuit and blasted the unwelcomed passenger, but also shot Linda in the arm. Her future came to a decrescendo when she lost the use of her arm for the rest of her life. I suppose the police were justified in shooting the intruder, who was a Peruvian hit man totally unknown to Linda, the victim of being in the wrong place at the wrong time. Catastrophe was never buried too deeply under the surface in the Bronx.

The absolute nadir of my experience with the police occurred on the most tragic day of my life to date. I had promised to take my class on a picnic as a reward for some achievement or another, and I only had a day or two to select from, for the school year was rapidly coming to an end in 1968. I decided to take about twenty-four boys down to the Hudson River by the Little Red Lighthouse where we could play ball on the fields I had often used as a child, and they could fish in the Hudson. After taking the 35 Cross-town bus, we walked across Manhattan from Amsterdam to Riverside Drive, and then meandered down to the lighthouse. I had offered fifty cents to the first boy to catch a fish, and then I started to light a cooking fire in the grill on the south side of the George Washington Bridge. The fishermen were casting on the rocks on the north side where I had played so often in the past. Just as the fire for the hotdogs began to catch, Seaton Adams sidled up to me and said, "Joe Vidal told me to tell you that Michael Gourdine fell in the river." Seaton replied to my query that Michael was all right since he got out of the water. I started to check on the kids when I noticed a group of White kids staring at what I thought was my class. I started to run believing I was interrupting a potential brawl.

As I got to the rocks, I asked about Michael Gourdine since I didn't see him anywhere. The kids pointed into the placid waters of the river and said, "He's still in there." As the full story emerged, Jose Hernandez had caught a fish and Michael Gourdine had run out on the rocks to see the fish. Jose lost his footing and Michael attempted to help him back ashore. Michael slipped in too. Joe Vidal jumped in to get Hernandez, and someone extended a fishing line to Gourdine. He caught the line, said, "I'm saved," but then the twine snapped, and Michael went under. He wasn't seen again until his body surfaced three days later after a severe June thunderstorm. I couldn't tell where he might be under the surface of the water, but I dispatched some kids to find the police. They found a patrol car parked under the tunnel of the West Side Highway. and the car was on the scene in what appeared to be seconds. One policeman said to me, "Get the rest of the kids off the rocks before you lose another." I told the survivors to sit on a huge rock across from the Lighthouse. The police told me that they had to take the two boys who were in the river to Medical Center to be checked out. I said I would go with them and told the class to head back to Morrisania by the same route we had taken. The boys started to cry and one of the cops exclaimed, "That's the trouble with Niggers. They just can't take it!" I couldn't believe what I heard, and my temper rose but I also was in shock over the loss of Michael.

I called Matty Kissane from the hospital, and he drove over and picked up Jose and Joe and me. As soon as I could, I put on my clerical suit and went to the Gourdine household where a number of neighbors had come to support them. The family was remarkably kind to me and perhaps even understanding. They took solace in that Michael had drowned trying to help someone else. That evening I was devastated probably more so than I realized. One of my memories of that day was the unexpected arrival of Mrs. Daley. I had taught her children, John, Joan, Keith, Mark, and Glen, and I often spoke with their older children Earl and Joanne. Mrs. Daley said the kids were at home and feeling sympathetic toward me, and she decided to come to the Brother's house to offer whatever kindness she could. She told me that with all her children, she recognized that she could never guarantee that anyone of them might not meet a disastrous accident, no matter how vigilant she was. Her words and presence were remarkably comforting to me. That evening Joe Hosey and some Brothers from Msgr. Kelly School also came to help express their support.

After Michael's body surfaced, a funeral was held, and a burial cortege drove all the way to a Shinnecock Indian burial ground on Eastern Long Island. The Gourdines remained very understanding, but later a lawyer convinced them to sue the Archdiocese for their loss. I had to give a deposition about that day. Joe Vidal had come to me and mentioned that a lawyer was snooping around, and he wanted to ask me what to say. I told Joe to tell the truth as he saw it. In the deposition, two allegations were made. The lawyers maintained that the location was inherently dangerous, but it was a public park with fireplaces and benches for picnics. Secondly, there was insufficient supervision. There is merit in that, but the subway system allowed one adult to supervise forty students. As I awaited my deposition, I recall falling asleep, not from fatigue, but I suppose from the unconscious wish to be elsewhere.

I continued to teach two of Michael's younger sisters and always had a pleasant relationship with the family. I felt their loss, and when an out of court settlement against the Archdiocese was made, I thought it was poor compensation for the loss of a son. That loss has haunted me the rest of my life. I often speculate whether I ironically will be called upon to make the sacrifice the Gourdines did. It has made me hyper-vigilant whenever water is involved, and if I can avoid it, I will. The most distressing aspect of the day, aside from the tragic death of the fourteen year old Michael, was the gratuitous remark of an insensitive policeman.

As a White youth in Manhattan, I learned that one had to be circumspect, even wary, about parks in different neighborhoods. I would no more think of traveling to Harlem to play on their basketball courts as I would of invading Little Italy's baseball fields. Different ethnic and racial groups congregated on personal turf so to speak. I did not presume that any of the large city parks, however, were part of that equation. The Sheep's Meadow in Central Park, for example, seemed available to anyone on a first come basis. On Ascension Thursday, 1969 my education would be retooled for correction. On that day, I took my class on a picnic trip to Van Cortland Park. We took the Jerome Avenue el north to the last stop and walked along Woodlawn-Jerome Cemetery's perimeter. Just north of the golf course there are some parking lots and ball fields adjacent to the Major Deegan. This was our destination where we hoped to play some soft ball and enjoy some sandwiches and soda which we carried with us. After several hours of this activity, a problem arose. One of my students, George Michaels, decided to take a stroll in the woods where he discovered a score of White, drunken eighteen year olds who were imbibing freely and making out with their girl friends. George, a boy who never could pass up a remark, made some comment or other that enraged the drunks.

In the past, George had accused me of being a closet member of the Ku Klux Klan because I made him do so much academic work. I defended myself by reminding George that the last thing the Klan wanted was an educated Black, but if he truly believed his allegation, he should demand that his parents withdraw him from the school to preserve him from such racism. Naturally George rethought his statement, even though he sought the comfort of his best friend Harold's agreement. I mention this because he was prone to making immature, obnoxious statements that he didn't really believe. In any case, the drunks were outraged and determined to extract vengeance from his body. When George told me that a bunch of White kids wanted to beat him up, I advised him not to worry since we had about thirty kids of our own to defend them. As the drunks emerged from the woods, it was evident, nonetheless, that they were not in a conciliatory mood, nor were their rational faculties intact.

When I saw about ten White drunks in the distance, I believed they would see our numbers and fade away. Not to be. As they got closer, I noticed they were at least four years older than my kids and armed with sticks, clubs, knives and other instruments of pain. My thirty man army quickly retreated to a safe distance as I approached the indignant youths intending to restore some rationality to the scene. Only about four or five of my class remained at my side. The first words I heard from the adversaries were, "Kill the Nigger loving Motherfucker who brought the Niggers into our park." George was nowhere to be found, but Michael Devonish took a tree branch to the top of his head. By this time, one of my assailants had a garrison belt wrapped around his fist and poised over my skull. Another had a switchblade opened and pressing against my Adam's apple. I urged the tipsy kids that no one should get hurt because of one boy's big mouth. They reiterated their comment about my demise. I assessed one of the group to be close to sober, so I directed my remarks to him. I told him I was a Christian Brother and that these boys were my class. I saw no need for anyone to get seriously injured because of intemperate remarks of one individual.

Upon hearing that I was a religious, one of my confronters advised the others not to curse in front of the Brother. The incongruity between threatening my White life and not muttering profanities in front of a religious didn't strike any of them as ironic. Nonetheless, the soberest individual told the boy to remove the garrison belt hovering above my brain and the boy holding the knife to my throat to back off. I told the kids that we were about to leave the park soon and urged them to return to their girlfriends in the woods. Shortly thereafter, I was happy to leave the park in one piece and mobile enough to walk to the el-shaken, but not stirred. The incident was taken in stride by my class who only kidded Devonish by referring to him as 'Steel Skull.' Michael didn't shed any blood from the blow nor tears at the description.

When I was speaking about the event the next day in the Brothers' house, we had a guest for lunch. The fifth grade teacher, Mr. Fields, was a Black Fordham graduate whose commitment to education would last only as long as his deferment from the army. He blustered about what he would have done, and how he would have dispelled the drunks who probably would have left at least his body in the park and perhaps those of some of the students. I was reminded of the heroic marine guarding the general's car at Pearl Harbor and what he would have done had he been on Iwo Jima. Mr. Fields, however, reflected a reality of what the Vietnam War was doing. Many males took refuge in education since it offered a deferment from service in the military. As soon as he was assured he wouldn't be drafted, Mr. Fields took a cushy, state job through some personal, political connections. I suppose in the meantime, he represented a good role model and image to his impressionable charges.

Some of Matty Kissane's hirings left me quite confused, but they mirrored the tenor of the times. One of his hired teachers was a medical doctor who fled Castro's Cuba. Unfortunately, despite her advanced education and certification, the Cuban government would not allow any proof to be mailed to America. Thus, she had to take any job offered at any reduced salary. She was a very nice lady, but she barely spoke English to her class. Matty also thought that a crazy Italian revolutionary might enhance the faculty, so Enzo was hired. With his bushy blond beard and broken English, he confused his class too. He blamed his daily tardiness for school on the erratic running of the Third Avenue El, a situation that Benito Mussolini would never tolerate. He too was hiding from the military to avoid being drafted and shipped to Vietnam. The only time I saw him get excited was after the National Guard shot the students at Kent State. The avowed Communist and Atheist insisted on organizing a prayer service for the victims.

Matty, however, was more successful in hiring a young man from Good Shepherd who had graduated from St. Leo's in Florida. Hal Hiller was an outstanding teacher whose interest in the kids transcended the classroom. He spent many hours assisting in coaching and attending other programs. One of his greatest assets was a sense of humor that entertained the faculty. I enjoyed his company a great deal, and to him I owe another embarrassing behavioral reaction. Hal advised me that he heard I was getting married in the summer of 1970 just after I left the Brothers. He heard it from the intended bride's mouth. I assured him that if I did get married, it would be a result of the Stockholm Syndrome where the kidnapped individuals become enamored with their captors. With the information I had, I made sure to avoid the subject of the marriage and avoided the young lady conscientiously, but I never directly addressed the issue. In my immaturity and inexperience, I knew of no other approach than evasion.

Vietnam became an omnipresent factor in so many things in the 1960's. **Muhammed Speaks**, the organ of the Fruit of Islam, would picture Cardinal Spellman blessing purple heart medals and place a caption that indicated medals for murderers. For any of the graduates, the eventuality of joining the military was a reality. Most wanted to get involved with the more dangerous units, like the air borne, green berets, or rangers. In one sad case, a mother approached me about the wisdom of approving her son's early enlistment. She said he had begun to dabble in heroin and would soon be destroyed by the neighborhood. I suggested he might be better off in the military than hanging around Boston Road. Upon his enlistment at the age of seventeen, he volunteered for the 101st Airborne. Two years later, his broken body returned for a funeral. I was teaching his brother Osmond, at the time, and I recall catching his attention and asking him to stop playing with the distraction on his desk. When I asked him what he was fiddling with, he said "These are my dead brother's medals." After that experience, I wrote to President Nixon who claimed that minority youth were flocking to the military where they would find opportunity for advancement and equality. I remarked that the youth were not flocking to the military as much as escaping from the ghetto.

The Vietnam War was very instrumental in improving St. Augustine's image and that of its students in a sort of convoluted way. Raymond Johnson was a graduate of Cardinal Hayes where he excelled in track and oratory. He was a handsome, imposing young man who might have considered an acting career were he so inclined. Either he couldn't afford college, or he had little interest in furthering his education at this stage of his life. Although I never taught him, I did have his two half brothers in my class. Raymond was determined not to be drafted into the army although he was prime material for the military. He had amassed a considerable folder indicating reasons why he should not be drafted and according to him, his local draft board now took up the challenge of getting him in uniform. Approaching me with his new plan for avoiding conscription, Raymond suggested that he acquire quasi teacher status by training young orators from the school. He would coach and train them, and all I had to do was describe his performance in a letter which he would present to his draft board.

Raymond's service to his local community seemed a greater contribution than he might reluctantly offer the military, so I acceded. Two or three times a week, he met with a few volunteers and created an excellent trio of interpretive orators. Using speeches he had heard in the national finals when he himself appeared, he trained a series of speakers to the point where they were almost invincible in competition. Michael Devonish and John Dudley especially were outstanding in their delivery of *God is Dead and You have killed Him*. They won virtually every contest hosted by every high school within the next few years. Antonio Joseph and Kurtis Harris had great success with Spartacus' *Speech to the Gladiators* as well. The third selection was Atticus Finch's speech in defense of Tom Robinson from the book **To Kill a Mockingbird**. When the upper grades consolidated, classes became departmentalized and girls were in the classes, he did a superlative job training Michele Evans and Stephanie Johnson. These orators did so well that some of the competition suggested that we should give them a sporting chance and refuse to compete.

I can't recall how many contests in which we won individual and team trophies, but it became repetitious. The orators developed great self-esteem and confidence which I hope served them well in the future. I know John Dudley has sparkled as a community leader, and Michele Evans is an Oncologist associated with Johns Hopkins. I know nothing of the others, but their experience enriched their lives and promoted a positive image for our students as well as a reputation among the other schools of the Archdiocese. As for Raymond, he convinced some reporter from **The Daily News** to print an article with accompanying picture of the orators and himself. I don't know what the draft board did about his status, but he stalled long enough to acquire a safe number when the selective service went to a lottery system. The special orators, as well as I, have a great debt to this talented young man. Some might quibble about his motivation, but no one could speak against the effort and the result of his working with these kids. Besides, the Vietnam War enticed many males into the generally female occupation of teaching. In the ghetto these positive images and examples were especially important.

Since I had been in the parish for seven years, I had established a reputation, for good or bad, among the kids and their parents. I certainly felt honored and treasured by them, and my own self-esteem was well rewarded. My relationship with the parents was especially heartwarming. In a neighborhood where many families were run by a single mother, male presence was something valued. One mother used to refer to her son Milton as my son. She would telephone a few times a year with a plea, "Your son won't get out of bed this morning. I want you to talk to him." I would talk to Milton and he would struggle into school a little late, but content to be there. After he graduated from Rice, I attended his wedding, and his mother insisted I sit among the front rows with his family.

Another student joined our seventh grade after attending school in Powhattan, Virginia. His mother was especially grateful to have him enrolled in our school. When she returned to Virginia for a short visit, she left her car in my care. I suppose she recognized that the schoolyard was a safer parking spot than the alternate side parking of the Bronx, but she also encouraged me to use her car whenever, wherever, and however I chose. I enjoyed the generous loan, and she felt her car was in good hands.

Even after I left the Brothers, I continued to hear from some parents of my former students. Linda was an especially brilliant girl who had intelligent sensitivity and insight into many issues of the day. While she was at Cardinal Spellman High School, several classmates were discussing interracial dating. When queried whether she would date a Black boy, she replied, "I suppose I would because I am Black myself." Perhaps she could pass for White, but she was proud to be Black. She was the kind of kid who journeyed through many different phases, and her mother got fed up with her 'grunge' period. She called me since she believed I had a special influence over her daughter, explained that Linda refused to care for her gorgeous, lustrous black hair, or even bathe as often as she should have. When she asked me to speak with her, I was glad to do so. Whether Linda was embarrassed that her mother had called about such a delicate matter or not, I couldn't confess, but I convinced her to alter her ways and re-enter a broader path of society.

I can only recall two episodes of negative parental involvement. Neither was directed toward me, but they were reactions to the judgments of Matty Kissane. One involved an eighth grader in my class who had brought graphic pornography to school where it was confiscated. The previous year Matty had humorously threatened to make the offender the first Black to integrate the moon. Anyway, Matty determined that the offense was diametrically opposed to the Christian values we espoused, so he expelled Freddie. His mother threatened Matty with a demonstration from the NAACP and other agencies, but nothing ever transpired. The second episode concerned an absolutely gorgeous, young girl from the fifth grade. She was habitually late, even on a daily basis. I had taught two of her older brothers, and the family was held together by an elderly grandmother. The kids' father was in jail, and the mother was a junkie. Although every faculty member urged Matty to cut Lola slack, he was adamant insisting that Lola's popularity had nothing to do with his decision. The grandmother came to the school and in a passionate plea for her daughter met an unmoved administrator. Whether she ultimately cursed the principal literally, if not in language but in dire prediction, she was devastated. I know these decisions weighed heavily upon Matty, but he insisted he had to do what he had to do. Matt had a reputation as easy going, but when he was insistent there was no surrender of principle. Whenever one of the community members made a request that Matt judged unworthy, he used to respond in a voice that oozed with sarcasm, "In your Easter Bonnet!" Obviously, none of the Brothers took the message literally.

Sometimes involvement with graduates and their parents transcended the ordinary and found me in court with them. A very dear lady who had been so kind to me approached me with a request. Her son had admitted using heroin and was intent on getting out of the neighborhood. He was even amenable to going to Lincoln Hall as a Person in Need of Supervision. It was Brother Mike Kennedy, I believe, who had also been a great inspiration for me when he was the principal at Cardinal Spellman, who assured me that the Hall could have a spot for Michael. He would, of course, have to undergo a psychological test, but he didn't anticipate any problems. I agreed to go to Children's Court near the Grand Concourse with Michael and his mother. In a hearing before the judge, a court appointed public defender sounded very officious, but was interested in my comment about Lincoln Hall. He boasted that he could have Michael remanded there, as if his brilliant legal mind had breached the walls of injustice. Michael had the bravado of youth as we stood before the judge. The judge inquired who I was, and what I had to offer. I mentioned that the Director of Lincoln Hall virtually assured me that Michael would be accepted there, if the court consigned him. The judge muttered something about 'virtual' and then mentioned that if Michael wasn't psychologically accepted, he would end up in Spofford, the notorious juvenile hall. Finally, the judge remanded Michael on the condition of passing the psychological, and if not, he was to reappear in court for further adjudication. He then addressed Mike's mother and requested whether she wanted to be responsible for Michael until that time, or would she insist he be sent to Spofford. Upon wobbly knees, Michael's bravado rapidly dissipated as he awaited his mother's reply.

Fortunately, Michael was acceptable to Lincoln Hall, and he fell under the guidance of my old buddy, Brother Faber or T.A. Murphy, from our painting days in the Scholasticate. Over the next eighteen months, I occasionally visited Michael and gave his family a lift to the Hall. I believe Mike bravely endured his confinement, and at the end, I offered to let him share my apartment on McLean Avenue in Yonkers. His mother was much wiser than I and declared no way. I never considered the full responsibility of a mature teenager living with me and what signals that might send to others. Moreover, fully employed, I had little opportunity to supervise Michael, but all I could do was trust him. Michael stayed at home and became a success story in an improbable scenario. He is now the pastor of a small church in the Bronx and enjoys his family and the esteem of his congregation.

Although I never taught Foster, I had seen him play basketball at Cardinal Hayes and knew he was talented enough to warrant a scholarship in round ball to Tennessee. I did teach three of his siblings, however. His mother asked me to testify on behalf of Foster at a trial in Bronx Criminal Court. My education in the ghetto glimpsed another aspect of life. According to the testimony of the arresting undercover cop who was observing two suspicious individuals from the steps of St. Augustine Church, Foster and his friend had been peddling marijuana. When questioned why the police had focused on Foster, the detective replied that Foster and his buddy were dressed outlandishly like drug dealers with a garish array of colors under broad brimmed hats. As they ran up to cuff the culprits, they allegedly tossed the contraband under a car, and nothing was found in their possession. I was called as a character witness for Foster. After swearing in, I mentioned that I knew Foster for six years, that I had taught three of his brothers, and that in that time none of the boys had ever been in trouble. The prosecutor asked if I had ever taught Foster. In truth I hadn't, so he terminated the cross examination as a waste of court time. It at least reassured Foster's mother.

As we waited after testimony had been completed, the court appointed public defender, who had been police commissioner at one time, approached Foster's mother. He said that for four hundred dollars on the spot, the case could be dismissed. I have no idea if the cash was for the judge, the lawyer, or court fees, but the money was ponied up; the charges were dropped, and Foster returned home. The whole process had a stench to it that permanently left me with a jaundiced view of justice in the Bronx.

Orlando Gonzalez was one of the brighter boys I had taught in my earlier years at Augustine. When he was about seventeen, he was arrested for robbing a jewelry store. Orlando's mother asked me to accompany her to the court because she didn't have a good command of English and would like to have me serve as moral support as well as interpreter. As we waited for the trial to begin, I learned that Orlando and a friend had pulled a knife on a jeweler. The jeweler struggled with the thieves, and in the course of wrestling over the knife, Orlando bit the man on the nose. The man suffered a heart attack and was hospitalized. Word came as we waited in Bronx Criminal Court on 161st and Third Avenue that the man had subsequently died, and the trial had been rescheduled for Bronx Supreme Court a few blocks west on the Concourse. Orlando now was charged with murder in the course of committing a felony. In his later trial, I believe a settlement was reached, but Orlando was sentenced to two to five years in prison.

In some sense our Christian mission of peace and love, forgiveness and neighborly appreciation ran counter to another current in culture. In Morrisania there was an embedded notion of violence that was part of the influence on all our students. A code of honor and vengeance also demanded retribution for even the slightest offense. One of our paragons of what we intended our students to be, enlightened me once in a classroom discussion. After forty years I distinctly remember the vehemence and fervor in which Lionel responded to a question about forgiveness and turning the other cheek. Lionel said, "*If anyone insults me or disses me, I'll go into my bag and take out whatever it takes to lay him out!*" His sense of outrage at the prospect of forgiving convinced me he meant every word of it.

Lionel's summary of neighborhood attitude might be attributable to another class member. Gregory was a modest, shy individual who often stuttered, but always sought the background in classes and in the schoolyard. He epitomized a quiet, respectful lad who was cooperative and perhaps docile. I was stunned when I read in later years that he had gone to his home and murdered his wife and two children for some reason unfathomable to most of society. I certainly would not have selected that future for him.

Many of the students, innocent and optimistic in the latter stages of elementary school, adapted an attitude that one could identify as vengeful, prone to violence, and perhaps irrational. In the course of my seven years at Augustine, I taught at least a dozen future murderers that I know of. Few had given evidence in their youth that they would follow that path. Graduates and their families came to call upon me often for support in their times of trouble. These former students were not evil individuals in elementary school with the exception of the mass executioner for the Five Percenters. Most fell victim to the plague of drugs, or the allure of a fast buck. Some exhibited little self restraint, and their anger spilled over into violence and rage. If I were asked to predict who those dozen might have been when they were in school, I probably might accurately predict only two or three. The neighborhood presented temptations and models of criminality that spoke louder than respectability. Yet the vast majority of the former students became solid citizens whose achievements and lifestyle didn't appeal to the tabloids that covered the violent criminal activities.

Violence wasn't the only anti-Christian force operating upon our students. One fellow, Timothy, was into Satanism and devil worship. He had founded his own religion he said and offered me a bishopric if I wanted it. His theology involved satanic worship, formulaic incantations and arcane ceremonies culminating with White female virginal sacrifice on the autumnal equinox. The combination of his fascination with evil and his sexual fantasies resulted in a traumatic experience for him. As he was involved in his fantasies in his basement apartment, lightning struck and electricity went out. His mother claimed Timothy was so frightened that he then had an asthmatic attack and had to be hospitalized. At least the episode cancelled his interest in his bizarre religion for a period.

I mention these episodes for they encompass much more than instructing a class in elementary school. In conjunction with my role as educator, I also assisted in some parish sponsored fundraising. Each year, the auditorium and lower lunchroom would be surrendered to a bazaar with the accompanying booths and games. The parents of the kids would volunteer to supervise a variety of games. I was asked to participate in a giant money wheel game that attracted many strangers seeking a big payoff. Each bettor placed a quarter on a particular number, and it was my responsibility to make sure the quarter stayed on the same number as the wheel spun. Many contestants would attempt to shift the money as the wheel rotated. My job was not to watch the wheel, but the playing board. Then when the winner was announced, it was imperative to collect the loser's money before it would be considered the next bet. All of this required vigilance and tact. One couldn't accuse an individual of cheating, but careful observation precluded that possibility.

The parish attempted another fundraiser by sponsoring horse racing. It didn't take much equipment other than distinctive paper and a movie projector. The film was of a race from somewhere in the past. The names of the horses were far from famous, and the odds were determined by where the money was placed. Rudimentary math was required after every race. The total of the bets would represent the pool from which forty per cent went to the house, or in this case, the parish. The sixty per cent remaining funds would be divided according to the amount bet on each nag. If, for example, four individuals bet on horse number 6, we would divide the sixty per cent four ways. If eight bettors selected horse number two, then the sixty per cent would be divided eight ways. The house would win on every race. Although some profit was made, attendance remained small, and the races were cancelled.

Funds were always paltry at St. Augustine, and it took its toll on the pastor. Father Kane was a kindly man who struggled for years to maintain the buildings and church. He died from a bleeding stomach ulcer. When the Archdiocese was pondering his successor, some Brothers and Sisters tried to assist the Powerhouse, as downtown Cathedral was called. We generated a petition and circulated it among the parishioners. The demands or criteria were broad and simple. Those who signed the petition sought a pastor who wanted to be among them; who had some understanding of minorities; and who would be willing to work with the people in determining liturgical schedules and policies. When we had amassed a number of these signatures, we asked for an appointment with the Cardinal. In the meantime, I learned through Sister Helen O'Neill, the Superintendent of Elementary Schools, that we had acquired a rabid reputation. Sister Helen had appointed me to give several workshops and to create a social studies questionnaire. In that capacity we had occasional contact. She said that the rumor downtown was that a bunch of radical, rebellious religious and lay people were trying to establish a parish coup. That description is ironic for the leaders were far from the image. When we asked for the meeting, we then were referred to Msgr. Schultheiss of St. Raymond's who was Vicar of the

Bronx. He would bring the petitions to St. Patrick's. We presented a rather improbable facsimile of a rebellious rabble. Two of our number were Sisters of Charity, each with a score of years dedicated service in the mission fields of the Bahamas. The two Christian Brothers numbered myself and Ed Phelan who has clocked forty years of heroic service to the Bronx. One of our members was a twenty year retired Chief Petty Officer named Jim Nolan. Mrs. Gray, the community liaison person substantially instrumental in bringing The Double H Day Camp to St. Augustine, was another contributor, but the ultimate irony of our rebel status has to be 'Ma' Gaynor. 'Ma' Gaynor was an elderly Jamaican parishioner noted for her generous donation of time and expertise to the kitchen functions of Augustine. 'Ma' Gaynor enjoyed dictatorial powers, when it came to preparing food for alumni dinners or Communion Breakfasts. Her preparations reflected her Jamaican roots. Every piece of chicken to be cooked was handwashed with lye soap before being thoroughly rinsed. There would be no salmonella or bacterial infections coming from her kitchen, although one might fart bubbles for a week afterward. 'Ma' Gaynor's agenda consisted of insuring the restoration of her beloved weekly novena which had been cancelled because of an increase of crime in the neighborhood. Labeled revolutionaries by factotums in the Cathedral, we actually were more like victims of the hysterical allegations of the notorious Titus Oates whose resume read like the summary of the Al Sharpton—Tawana Brawley fiasco of several years ago. Instead, we apparently were treated like the Gunpowder Plotters of Guy Fawkes' Day.

When Msgr Schultheiss deigned to see us in his rectory, he treated us politely but officiously. He complained that his school was losing a few Christian Brothers in the consolidation required by fewer religious. That comment evoked a loud, passionate prayer from 'Ma' Gaynor, "Lordie! Lordie! Do anything, but don't take our Brothers away." Poor Msgr. Schultheiss was confused, but he insisted he would give our petitions to the Cardinal when he met him in person on Friday. We left, believing that we had made some progress, but we had underestimated the political machinations of the clergy. The next day, a new pastor was named. Father Fleming, about whom we knew nothing, was our new pastor. Radicals that we were, we believed that it would be unfair to prejudge him, so we determined to accept him graciously. All Schultheiss had done was spare the Cardinal the inconvenience of receiving our petitions. He evidently knew that the appointment was a done deal and that he had stalled long enough to make our efforts meaningless.

Perhaps one may notice that I have said very little about our parish clergy during this essay. Essentially, they did their thing and allowed us to operate independently. On only a very few occasions did they even enter the school or attempt to interfere in its running. During my time at Augustine, we were just as happy to have the clergy occupied elsewhere. Toward the end of the 1960's, we did encounter a priest who lived in the neighborhood. Father Vic Butler was from Martinique, and for some personal reason, he was on a leave of absence and living with his sister on Boston Road. He may have belonged to the Josephite Fathers. He and I became quite friendly, and he often said Mass on the weekends in the Brothers' house. Periodically, he would also drop in for dinner after his work shift with United Parcel. He was pleasant company and had an anecdote he shared about his introduction to American racism. Having been born in Martinique, he was fluent in French. On his first visit to the states, he toured New Orleans and tried to hail a cab from the front of the hotel at which he was staying. The cabbie told him, "No niggers allowed in my cab." Vic feigned ignorance and began speaking in French. *"Pardonez-moi. Je ne comprends pas. "* The cabbie declared him an appropriate foreigner and therefore eligible for riding in his taxi. Later Vic returned to the Josephites, and I believe he was appointed an auxiliary bishop in Camden, New Jersey.

After I had left the Brothers' house a priest, attending classes focused on the theology of Lonergan, the Jesuit theologian, took up residence with the Brothers. Father Gene Ahner was from Chicago and was a very positive asset to the Brothers. Later, Gene would officiate at my wedding across the street in St. Augustine's Church with the blessing and urging of the pastor, Father Fleming. Another priest also resided in the Brothers' house for a while. Father Mike Reiss came from Ohio, and he too was studying at Fordham, just a few el stops north of Augustine. He lent me his hatchback when my car was totaled coming home from classes at NYU. He worried so much about it, however, I quickly returned the gift.

The regular parish priests assigned by the Archdiocese to Augustine were a disparate lot. Father Bob Arce, who is currently a pastor of a Spanish parish in the Bronx, was very friendly and scored heavily in

RICHARD JOSEPH O'PREY

my ledger by offering my father's funeral Mass amid a blizzard and its aftermath. He was an avid restorer of trolley cars in the museum in New Haven and invited all of us to tour his hobby restoration. Father Jeffers was a priest who actually exhausted his boundless energy in serving the people of the parish. We also had a priest from Spain named Marcos who spoke faltering English and rarely associated with the parish staff. Father Dan Keane aspired to higher things, but he exercised his imagination in serving the parishioners. He later became pastor somewhere else in the Bronx. Father De Lucca moved south to St. Luke's where he continued to work among the Spanish, and another priest left after my first year in the school. A few visiting Canadians also helped out while they pursued their studies at Fordham. For the most part, however, the clergy and the Brothers seemed to operate in different spheres. All recognized that any future volunteers from either group would be few and far between.

During all my time at Augustine, I pursued my education. I had been offered the chance to earn a doctorate in the Washington area, and I initially accepted that. When I changed my mind, I met with Brother Augustine Loes and outlined my reasons for staying at Augustine. I argued that I sincerely believed I was doing essential work in the parish, and that I was making a positive contribution on many fronts. Gus told me that I could stay there, but in June, 1968, I was assigned to Lincoln Hall. I was distraught and Matty Kissane mentioned that Gus had said if I had a problem with my new assignment, I should go immediately to 330 Riverside Drive. Since Matty reached me at my father's house in Piermont, it took me a while to get to the Provincialate. I presented my arguments from early January and persisted in my wish to continue at Augustine. Gus was very gracious although my insistence created some conflicts for him. In the meantime, I continued to take graduate courses toward my doctorate in American Social History at NYU. The class work was interesting and the professors informative, but the most outstanding recollection I have is the school shutting down over the Cambodian incursion. I would continue to take those courses over the next several years. I remained at Augustine, but the events of the rest of that year were to change my convictions and lead me to enter voluntary exile from the work I loved so much.

Like the Tet Offensive of 1968 altering the perception of our military forces in Vietnam, that same year provided several factors and forces that altered my feelings about religious life. A series of family tragedies began the year, when my mother succumbed to debilitated state and died on March 4th. She was waked in Connors on 207th Street, but Msgr. Watterson presided over a solemn high funeral at Incarnation Church. He refused to accept any stipend for the Mass because I was a Christian Brother. My mother's death was expected, but nonetheless I lost a loving confidante and a serious supporter of whatever I chose to do. Her death was not so acceptable to my father. After seven years of sobriety, he began to drink again. On the night my mother was interred at Calvary, my father got ill. I presumed his complaints about kidney pain and failure to urinate had something to do with his drinking and associating similarities with one of my mother's bouts with kidney failure. I refused to take him to the emergency room until first thing in the morning.

When we arrived at Nyack hospital at 6:00am, my father was diagnosed with a prostate condition that required surgery as soon as possible. He was hospitalized and operated upon almost immediately. He survived the procedure, but lost a great deal of weight, something that he could ill afford. The doctor had told him that he couldn't drink, so his imbibing wasn't problematic. My brother Ray, however, almost was killed in an auto accident on the Palisades Parkway on the night after Martin Luther King's assassination in Memphis. His precinct in Harlem was under siege and rioting was rampant. For the second time in his police career, he felt like an enemy soldier occupying a foreign land. After the riot was quelled some of the officers had a few drinks, and Ray did his share. As he drove home on a very foggy night along the Palisades Parkway, he was apparently lured off the road by an abandoned car on the shoulder. His Beatle plummeted down a ravine, but fortunately he was observed by a Black minister of a church in Nyack who was following his lead. The police found Ray virtually unhurt except for a broken ankle and severe leg wound. His car was totaled, and the parkway police found his shield and gun. He was taken to Englewood Hospital, and my father was contacted by the police. We visited Ray in the hospital and picked up his gun, shield, and the commentary that he had been drinking heavily, and should have been killed in the accident. In fact, without the eyewitness seeing the accident, Ray might not have been discovered for some time.

Probably the most traumatic episode of my life took place in mid June of 1968. The drowning of Michael Gourdine on a class picnic would haunt me for some time. I didn't blame myself for his death, nor did I believe that I could have done much to avert the tragedy. If dragging the river for three days and searching the very vicinity from helicopters were futile, there wasn't much I could have done. I was told that Michael's body had been wedged under a rocky shelf not far from where he entered the water. There were also some abandoned bedsprings that may have added to the perils of the depths. In the aftermath of the tragedy, many folks were very supportive and sympathetic. Michael's family was extremely kind to me and I heard many encouraging words, especially from my students and their parents. Some Brothers also were compassionate, but most of the support came from beyond my community. I continued to be affected by the recurring memory of what happened that day, and what the policeman had said. Little did I suspect how deeply and emotionally that event affected me.

On one of our 'pay a dollar and see the world' tours to Barrytown in mid August, I received a telephone call that my grandmother had passed away. She had lived with my family for my entire youth. She protected my father from the bigotry of Northern Ireland when they were virtually homeless while my grandfather worked in mines in Utah and Montana. Nanny, as we called her, never wanted to leave Ireland, but she would follow her only son to the end of the earth. In her later years, she would become a heavy burden for my father. Over the summer she tried staying with my Aunt Helen's family in Long Beach, but Nanny was never one to keep a discreet silence about anything she observed. In the sixties the Clancy kids were enjoying some of the new found joys of adulthood, and of course, Nanny had to put in her opinions and reviews. That practically tore apart my aunt's family, so she returned to my father's house in Piermont.

There, she began to bombard the police and fire departments with imaginary problems, and my father felt compelled to place her in a home. At this turn of events, Nanny was very despondent, and in fact, seemed to will herself to die by refusing to live. She couldn't understand why her daughter-in-law had died before she did. All this activity exacted a heavy toll on my father. Her death at the age of eighty-two, in a sense, was the resolution of an unsolvable problem, but that solution offered little condolence to my grieving father. Nanny had Bernie, my brother, for her last visitor. He inquired whether she would like to see a priest and arranged for that. After the priest left, my grandmother turned her face to the wall and simply passed on.

As 1968 progressed, so too did my father's drinking. Every time the telephone rang in the Brothers' house, I anticipated hearing some bad news or other. My peace and tranquility came strictly from the families and students I had at Augustine. Complicating the problem was my father's opportunity for retirement. He had worked so many long hours because of a Papal visit and some other events that his pension increased beyond expectations. Economically, he had to retire from the job that he loved and kept him sober. He put in his papers and accepted vacation time and terminal leave. Unfortunately, his drinking then continued. I urged him to return to AA, but he bridled at that. Finally, my last ultimatum to him was not to call me until he had decided to attend a meeting, and I would go with him.

On the evening of February 6, 1969 I answered the doorbell at 1168 Franklin Avenue, and Sgt. O'Keefe from the 48th precinct told me he had bad news about my father. His body had been found by a delivery boy. According to the circumstances, it appeared that my father suffered his first and final heart attack in his bedroom as he reached for some medication. The coroner believed he was dead before he hit the floor. Another funeral was arranged, but Mother Nature interfered with the Mass. On the last day of the wake at Connors, a severe blizzard struck New York, paralyzing the city transit system. Only the subways remained open for all the streets and bus routes were clogged with abandoned cars or heavy snow banks. My father's funeral was scheduled for Incarnation, but the hearse couldn't emerge from its garage. A plan to have the Mass in Good Shepherd fell through when my brother accused the undertaker of peddling a cheap coffin that might collapse on the steps of the church.

Finally, the Mass was offered within the funeral parlor, and only a few could attend. Father Bob Arce from Augustine said the Mass, and the faculty had accompanied some of the students to the funeral parlor by taking the train south to 96th Street and then switching to the Seventh Avenue IRT north to 207th Street. Their presence was comforting. After the funeral, my father's body was brought to cold storage downstairs in Connor's for a trip to Calvary was entirely out of the question. The family gathered at Mrs. O'Dwyer's apartment on Arden Street, and we then went our separate ways. I walked all the way back to Franklin Avenue which was so clogged with snow that Ed Phelan had organized an army of kids to clear the street using food trays for shovels. Ever media wise, Ed had television record the school kids attempting to clear a path for a fuel delivery that could enable the opening of school. It wasn't until St. Patrick's Day, however, that we were able to bring my father's body to Calvary.

Again, the people who supported my exorbitant emotional needs at this time were friends, graduates, students, and parents. For entirely different reasons, the community of Brothers who used to play such a vital role in my motivation and self-satisfaction were undergoing some severe changes themselves. After Vatican II, the Brothers began a re-evaluation of their apostolate and community life. A general chapter and a regional chapter had established principles to guide the Brothers in this new Church. The New York District also held its own chapter, and I was elected a delegate. I really didn't want to serve, but felt obligated to be both honest and candid, although I was now seriously considering leaving the religious life. I fulfilled my objectives, but left a sense of rancor among some Brothers who didn't like what I had to say. As with this work, if one uses candor and honesty, generally misunderstanding, misinterpretation, and hurt feelings can occur

One of the conclusions of the New York Chapter was the justification of each apostolate. The elementary schools were asked to write a rationale for their existence, and I was selected to do so. I also indicted some of my confreres of the same racism I confessed to in my earlier years before my exposure to its insidious effects at St. Augustine. Indeed, aside from my life threatening position in the park at Van Cortland, I experienced few harrowing episodes of prejudice. Rather, I felt the tilted playing field of inequality that so many spoke of. I experienced the anticipated embarrassment of rejection or rudeness while traveling with my students. In the summer of 1970 after I had just left the Brothers, I took a cousin visiting from Ireland on a tour of the nation's capital and of Williamsburg. I invited a Black girl from Augustine to accompany us and provide a companion for my cousin. I recall feeling the isolation and concern when I stopped for gas at a remote station in Salisbury, Maryland on the Delmarva Peninsula. Nothing happened, but the fear was present nonetheless.

With support from lay people, I must also cite the circumstances whereby my own community didn't fulfill that need. It seemed to me that each Brother was heavily involved in good works that precluded much attention to community matters. Some of these preoccupations warranted late hours and compensatory sleeping time instead of participating in traditional prayers and Mass as a community. Dinner time often was a catch as catch can operation, and attendance was also erratic. Our director, Matty Kissane said that this was the wave of the future. My response was, "Then you'll be surfing without me." Matty was involved in some ponderous decision making as well as I was. Jimmy the Plug, the principal of Immaculate and regional coordinator of School District Seven was extremely busy. His presence, serving the elementary schools in the South Bronx often took him away from community activities. At one point, he asked for an honest appraisal of his job. In this era of dialogue, I was brutally honest and mentioned that I felt he was a lackey for the clergy. The next day, although he protested he could take whatever was said, he was going to change communities. I felt particularly responsible for his discouragement and what I could best describe as future estrangement from me. My main support within the community was the ever loyal, sympathetic, empathetic person of Ed Phelan. To this day, I am especially grateful to what he meant to me in those trying months.

After my allegations of racism at the District Chapter, I was invited to address several convocations of Brothers in smaller groups. Ed accompanied me and thank God, reinterpreted much of what I said. He had a knack of understanding what I wanted to say, more than what I had actually said. Joining us was Helena McCallum who offered a Black perspective on what White religious could do. I still felt hypocritical since I now had asked for a dispensation and didn't want to sound like a disappointed reformer. The individuality and disparity of careers instead of educational staffing of schools would make a fatal impact upon the elementary schools in particular. Brothers would choose communities and schools where they would feel most comfortable, among friends, or among students they were used to teaching. That would leave very few to fill the ranks of places like Augustine. That was my primary regret when I chose to leave. I felt like I was abandoning the very people who had been so kind and patient with me. I only assuaged that fear when I learned that Ken Cottrell, the former Brother Sylvester, had offered to return to the school as eighth grade teacher. It was also reassuring to note that George Stevens and Bill Fecteau, two summer volunteers, would join the faculty too.

Lost in the verbiage is another factor that should be address. I realize that my emotional needs were extraordinary at this time. I also accept that the religious community that I had relied on successfully for years had evolved into an organism that was undergoing rapid and substantial change. What I also came to believe was that my future happiness and satisfaction could only be accomplished with the support of a woman. Many females had unconsciously forged the conviction in my mind that my future required the support of a wife, not a religious community. If I were to recite all the females who unwittingly reinforced this notion, I would reach significant numbers, and many of those had no clue that they had that effect upon me. The comforting words of some of the mothers I spoke with, the genuine affection and concern of some of my female students, the repartee among graduates and even the solicitude of the nuns and faculty members of the school reinforced my conviction that my self-satisfaction and esteem lay within marriage, not a celibate community of men. The only way I could meet that conviction was to resign from Augustine and hope that Providence and nature would enable me to find my goal.

Leaving the parish took longer than one might expect. After I officially received my dispensation, I returned often. I attended the board meetings of the Double H Day Camp and continued to participate in the Black history adult seminars. I stayed in touch with many of my former students. I came to realize that I had left Augustine a changed man, as far as some aspects were concerned. They were entirely for the better. I also came to comprehend that I left as a fifteen year old teenage boy, inept in dealing with the opposite sex. I left not so much from something, as toward something, and that continued to be vague and elusive until I met my future wife in October, 1971. I left with the sense that I had shared a marvelous adventure in the South Bronx; that I had witnessed a dynamic era in the period of Black pride; that I had learned so much more than I had taught. As the years progressed, I came to think of my time at Augustine as the Golden Age of my educational career. If my fondness for the people I shared that adventure with isn't evident in this chapter, then I do them a gross disservice. Occasionally I will ponder whether I would have remained among the Brothers if I hadn't been so personally needy at the time of my departure. That speculation isn't productive, for my life as a husband and a father has been totally satisfying. I would never again, however, experience the respect, admiration, cooperation, and inspiration that the people of Augustine offered me. I also remain proud of my tenure among the Brothers who I believe are the finest bunch of men I have had the privilege to meet over my lifetime.

Chapter Eleven

Into A Shadowy Realm

In a place not far remote from here
In a time more recent than the past,
*There existed a **Band Of** Courageous Educational **Sages**.*
Their code of conduct was simple but rare.
They faced ignorance with intelligence; hypocrisy with honesty.
They arrayed persistence against apathy and devotion against
incompetence.
They confronted hostility and animosity, suspicion and antipathy
With equanimity and serenity.
They sought neither the acclaim of society
Nor the approval of their peers.
Rather, they dealt with those whom others had rejected.
They taught some who needed the skills of a trade or the
Discipline of the workplace.
Some developed the muscles and flexibility of those
limited by physical disabilities.
*Others of the **BOCES** nurtured those whose intellectual challenges limited*
The traditional educational success.
Still more attempted to quell the psychological disorders
That prevented normal progress in schools unwilling to deal
With the unusual and atypical.
They sought not the recognition accorded those who educate
Gifted minds or even ordinary students.
They disregarded the comments of their peers nor sought the
Gratitude of those whom they served.
But the forces arrayed against them were formidable.
Some bosses preferred to count beans rather than brains.
Some chose to harass rather than assist.

Some elected to see negatives where positives existed.
Was this the epic battle between forces of good versus the powers of evil?
Or was this a minor skirmish between conflicting opinions or techniques?
The BOCES remembered the injunction of the biblical psalm
That gave them plaudits beyond this world.
"Qui ad justitiam erudiunt multos
Quasi stellas in aeternum!"
They that instruct others unto justice sake
Shall shine as stars for all eternity.

You be the judge of their sincerity and motivation.

When I sought secular employment in education, I had much to learn. Later years would lead me to conclude that the best avenue to gainful employment was through personal contacts, not talent. In my quest for a job in education, I underestimated the degree of difficulty finding employment suitable to my talents and interests. Initially, I thought I would have little difficulty finding a position in one of the lesser City Colleges, like Hostos Community College. A colleague had mentioned that he knew someone who was seeking a history teacher in this rather insignificant educational institution on the Grand Concourse. By the time I applied, I learned that my contact had been replaced, and his successor was hiring only Puerto Rican Marxists, qualifications I clearly didn't possess. I also rashly rejected a job offer at Westchester Community College because I believed I would be cheating the students. The position was teaching basic psychology and sociology, although I was a history major. My potential employer mentioned that the courses were only temporary until an opening would occur in history, but my personal sense of honor compelled me to pass up this opportunity. I would not be so quick to do the same today.

As the summer of 1970 wore on, I still wasn't too concerned about finding a job in a school system. By August, that disinterest had accelerated into a preoccupation. In that mood I encountered an unknown organization that was like the Central Intelligence Agency. It was nowhere, and it was everywhere. Its tentacles extended into many branches of academia, and its functions were nebulous and vague. For twenty-nine years, I served as a member of this parallel educational structure. None of them was as satisfactory or rewarding as my eight years as a Christian Brother. I found little appreciation for my talents. I encountered suspicion rather than confidence. I often experienced ridicule, rather than respect. Even among my supervisors and supportive staff, my impressions were as varied as the individuals. Some impressed me profoundly while others consciously or unconsciously offended me deeply.

I had never heard of The Board of Cooperative Educational Services (BOCES), until I was actually hired by them. Only later did I learn that BOCES was extensive and pervasive throughout the region of Southern Westchester. Almost like governmental pork barrel legislation, it took upon itself a life of its own. According to the philosophy of the organization, it was responsible for filling the needs of twenty-three school districts within the region of Southern Westchester. These districts ranged from the affluent, like Byram Hills and Bronxville, to the less endowed districts like Yonkers, Elmsford, and Greenburgh. BOCES was committed to providing the services that no one district could offer its special needs students.

Like a downwardly spiraling helical caduceus, that mission extended deeper and deeper into the depths of psychological and physical demands. Like the young girl Alice, I felt like I was descending into another world that paralleled the one I knew. As the years built up, I descended farther and deeper into that chasm as New York State redefined the demands of its special needs students. As a mystery organization, BOCES offered services that few recognized. For example, BOCES was responsible for organizing interschool leagues, athletic schedules, classroom programming and appointing officials for judging varsity sports. It also offered report card options and teacher training programs. An extensive audio-visual library was indeed at the service of component districts, as well as individual teachers. It moreover served as a search engine for high level administrators for the component districts. Without delving deep into the convolutions of educational programming and subsidiary options, one could barely discern a fraction of the cooperative opportunities offered by The Board of Cooperative Educational Services of Southern Westchester. As unknown as its contributions were, its personnel was often as mysterious and arcane as the legendary Enigma Code of World War II fame.

With administrative offices and officials housed in an imposing Georgian mansion with spectacular columns lining its façade, the building represented a combination of class and expense. The most obvious face of BOCES, however, was the most impressive flagship organization of BOCES. That was an imposing campus, comprised of several modern state of the art buildings that formed the nucleus of the Occupational Education unit. Even that aspect contained different levels of targeted students. In evening classes, building engineers could receive training in Boiler certification and other esoterica demanded of public maintenance individuals. It also offered nursing programs and English as a Second Language, as well as citizenship courses for immigrants. These generally were conducted in well maintained modern buildings during the evenings, although there were many satellite campuses throughout the region. More likely than not, the individual who repaired your boiler, fixed your plumbing, rewired your electronics, installed electrical items, provided nursing assistance, or built structures with wood, cement or brick, had received his license from courses taken at this shadowy organization.

Perhaps the best known and visible reflection of the largely vague BOCES Empire was the Occupational Education alternative offered to high school students. Among the elite programs presented in this curriculum were impressive courses in computer repair, cosmetology, data processing, auto mechanics, air conditioning, culinary arts, horticulture, building trades, and electrical training, printing, and office skills. Most of these programs were demanding and maintained a high level of expectation in proportion to the rewards at the end of the program. Nurses were awarded degrees in Licensed Practical Nursing, and some of the artisans were quick to hire the best students. Cosmetology was far from a snap course, and it demanded knowledge far beyond cutting or styling hair. In judging the Occupational Education image, I am reminded of a vivid scene from the **Caine Mutiny.** Fred MacMurray, and Van Johnson had arranged to meet the admiral of their battle fleet. They boarded an attack carrier and were so overwhelmed with the organization and efficiency of the crew that MacMurray says, "This is the real Navy. The Caine is something else not in this class." As Occupational Education represented the elite of BOCES, it had far murkier, shadowy programs that seldom matched the image of the flagship.

Throughout Southern Westchester, in strip malls, industrial parks, church basements, storefronts and district schools, BOCES maintained programs that had a less distinguished façade. The audio-visual library and teacher training program were located in the same industrial park that offered The Westchester Dinner Theatre operation. A lower level Occupational Education program, called Basic Occupational Education, was centered in a remote structure called Fairview Park off route 119 in Greenburgh, before it was relocated to the rear of another industrial park that featured a huge Coca Cola distribution center. BOE, as the more rudimentary program was called, was a preparation for the real Occupational Education campus demands next to the Westchester Community College Campus. Now that complex is called the Dr. Lehrer Center in honor of the man who was superintendent of BOCES for most of my tenure. The BOE program offered more simplistic courses, no degrees, and little training beyond the most fundamental skills in various trades. Most of the students who attended BOE were limited in aptitude, attitude, and application, but it supplemented academic classes for a very needy population from BOCES itself and the more challenging students from the component districts.

In addition to the beautiful campus abutting Westchester Community College, BOCES also had a large Special Education complex called Rye Lake Campus located on a former Nike Missile Base in North White Plains quite near Westchester Airport. Built in 1970, an impressive structure called the Rectangle dominated the elevated portion of the campus. This building was generally used for middle school aged children. At the foot of the sweeping hill, an artistic brick building called the Decagon was for the younger population. Also within the compound were a number of former army barrack huts that held classrooms for the most restrictive environment for high school emotionally challenged students. The communication control office of the transportation coordinating center occupied one of the buildings and the grounds also provided overnight parking for the huge fleet of buses required for the smooth operation of the various programs.

Perhaps it is Rye Lake Campus that may reflect the diversity and nebulously vague qualities of the Special Education aspect of BOCES. Clearly, the most outstanding program was designed for the physically handicapped, the most severely limited population. I could only praise the dedication of those who applied themselves on a daily basis to this group of students. Exulting when their charges hadn't choked on a meal or had been able to arise from their wheel chairs, or hadn't soiled their diapers before they were placed on a commode, these tender hearted individuals cared deeply for their charges and learned to accept little recognition for what they had done for the kids who were in the program until they aged out at twenty-one. I certainly could not have dealt with this population, but I could respect those who did. Hearing them rejoice at what was the simplest accomplishment for a three year old, I envied their patience, their solicitude, and their humanity. It is in praise of such as these that I write of BOCES as a positive influence among a very challenging population that local school districts had no finances, expertise, or interest in servicing.

As a truly shadowy program that was nowhere and was everywhere, the Special Education component offered educational opportunities to the learning disabled and educable mentally retarded and physically handicapped students that school districts found difficult to service. This population might be addressed in a classroom within a district school, a storefront, a church basement, or a strip mall. The broad array of disabilities made the students maneuver through a gamut of programs designed to meet their specific needs. Obviously, some children gave evidence of limited educational ability. Often they had visual, audio, or mental capacities that made their curriculum quite evident. An alphabet of disabilities offered a host of conditions that ran from ADD (Attention Deficit Disorder) to ADHD (Attention Deficit Hyperactivity Disorder), to NI (Neurologically Impaired), to PH (Physically Handicapped), to ED (Emotionally Disturbed), to EMR (Educable Mentally Retarded), to a generic LD (Learning Disabled), for those who eluded ready classification. In order to be in Special Education, each student had to have at least one of these designations which changed as language evolved to conceal any negative images that might detract from enhanced self-image. A whole lexicography was required to keep up with the current nomenclature acceptable to the academic community.

Those who were relatively identifiable as mentally retarded seemed the easiest to deal with. They were entitled to remain in school at taxpayer expense until they were twenty-one and eligible for a sheltered workshop or supervised employment at some repetitive task. With that classification, they were not entitled to a high school diploma, but would be awarded a certificate of attendance asserting that they had attended school for the requisite number of years. In my experience, this certificate was named in honor of my friend Pat Murphy who dealt with this population through most of his educational career. A "Murphy Diploma" was his legacy. It may not be the Dr Lehrer Center for Occupational Education, but it was an honor bestowed upon Pat by his peers for his contributions to this segment of BOCES for many years.

My experience in BOCES was among a more vague, ill defined class of students which reflected the current policy of descending deeper into the institutions and residential placements that used to deal with emotional problems. In the beginning of my career, such a descent wasn't quite as evident. I was hired by BOCES to conduct an entirely different kind of program from the one to which I was ultimately assigned. My good friend Pat Murphy heard through Ray Weitekamp, our history teacher in Washington, that I was still in search of a job. Pat contacted me and alerted Dr. Noel Rios, assistant director of BOCES, that I might be a good candidate for an unusual role. Noel had planned a new approach to dealing with academically disaffected youth among an 'at-risk' population. He envisioned a program that combined academic exercises with a monetary reward for employment. Initially, IBM seemed very interested when he pitched the plan to lower level minions. I joined him in presenting his ideas to the company. He had hoped that IBM would provide some kind of elementary level positions with modest salary or monetary inducements which would encourage the students to stay in school and acquire a high school diploma. I was the designated coordinator for BOCES, and our projected housing was in Fairview Park in Greenburgh.

As our presentation rose up into the ranks of expensive suits, it soon became apparent that those in a decision making capacity who controlled purse strings deduced that the program itself was a high risk effort with little chance of success. While all the employees on lower levels exuded confidence and interest, when we entered the realm of keepers of the coin or budgeters, we were rejected, or at least postponed. Over the next two or three years Noel would invite me to join him in another attempt to entice IBM to fund the project. Obviously, we were never successful. In the meantime BOCES had offered me a teacher's contract which I had signed, so I ended up in a standard middle school district location class assignment that was just opening. Since I had few options this late in the summer, I gladly accepted the position, intending to move on after a year.

My middle school class, numbering about ten students, most of whom were from Valhalla and Greenburgh, was assigned to supplementary space in the back of the high school classroom in Westlake of Mount Pleasant School District in Thornwood, New York. My class had no personal space, no typical educational texts, no materials to work with, and no direction other than what the high school teacher offered us. Fortunately, the high school teacher in Westlake was a unique character who introduced me to the BOCES way through his somewhat filtered view of the organization. Ted Aronson was a talented teacher, a generous man, and a gregarious individual. I appreciated all that he did for me, while I conducted class using his materials, texts, books and so forth in the back recesses of his classroom. Without him, I would have been totally lost, and my appreciation for his contributions to me permeated my association with BOCES until Ted retired in disgust many years later.

Ted certainly had a skewered point of view. He had aligned himself closely with the faculty of Westlake, particularly the athletic and coaching staff. His humor and style made him popular with the faculty and eased their assessment of me when I joined him. Ted was on an unrelated quest that he was glad to share with anyone who would listen. He was determined to bed every female member of the Westlake faculty, and according to his assessment, he was quite successful. He also targeted the young female teachers who entered BOCES. Ted wasn't quite as successful there because he claimed a high official in the program unfairly used his private plane as a seduction instrument. I could only attest that I was never invited for private flying lessons myself, but Ted was well informed about the various relationships he knew about in BOCES. Apparently, I had left a community of celibates and now associated with a company of satyrs.

At an early conference in which our superintendent was urging the staff to promote the different programs within BOCES, I suggested that our publicity would be better served, if we had someone who distributed information and pictures to the media, such as I had noticed in my newspaper in Rockland County. Ted was frantically signaling me to shut my mouth. When I finally detected his gestures, I discovered that the current superintendent whom I was addressing had appointed his mistress to precisely that kind of position. No criticism would fall on fertile soil, so I was better off keeping my mouth shut. That lesson was the first in the intricacies of our far fetched empire.

Most of the BOCES employees in the Special Education branch were assigned to outposts in various locations within Southern Westchester. As outposts went, mine was commodious, especially when the construction of the middle school was complete, and I was redirected to a pleasant classroom in the middle school. At first I was in a room with a full glass wall that opened every movement in the corridor to our scrutiny. It also exposed whatever was taking place within our classroom. Someone decided that a more private venue might be better, and I was relocated around the corner to a spacious, typical classroom. Our prior accommodation was then turned into a faculty room where individuals could type, run off materials, or just relax with a cup of coffee, or in those days, even enjoy a cigarette.

Ted exercised a great deal of insight into his explanation of how BOCES operated. He evidently had a jaundiced view of authority, but he recognized that some of our administrators were excellent people. Although he spoke of supervisors wallpapering the Holiday Inn on route 119 on company time, he dealt with them because he liked them. Others secured his distrust and his refusal to deal with them. Although he would seldom say why, he cautioned me about trusting some of the individuals. Generally speaking, his distilled views were affecting my own opinions. He would remain a close confidante of mine, until he was more or less forced into retirement, a standard practice within BOCES. Retirement often became preferable to appointment to an impossible educational mission or to a location that offered nothing but headaches and neglect.

My first class was a more or less homogeneous grouping of learning disabled students. They carried the designation of LD or Learning Disabled accurately. One student had an evident physical problem, for she was legally blind, a result of German measles during her mother's pregnancy. She was usually cooperative, but every now and then she would get obstinate. If I let her stand on one foot and twirl in a circle while singing *Raindrops keep falling on my head*, she would relax and return to her usual placid self. She also had the additional assistance of a tutorial itinerant visual handicapped instructor. One of my boys always complained about unfair treatment by his stepfather. Joel maintained that his adoptive father beat his brother with a stickball bat when he was sixteen, but he had started pounding him when he was only fourteen. Joel was a pleasant, playful kid who later founded a sound studio which was featured in a magazine article.

My favorite student was a young man named Duncan who had recently lost his father. Duncan was an avid student, and he only exhibited one overt problem. Whenever a female teacher entered the classroom, Duncan would scream out, "You stink! Get out!" Evidently his olfactory nerves were highly sensitive to perfume. Many of the female members, especially an itinerant art teacher, would get very embarrassed. I never quite succeeded in eliminating Duncan's outbursts, but it was a small price to pay for such a nice kid. One young lady from Valhalla was the shining light of the intellectual achievements in the class. She was quite capable, and I can only assume she upset the wrong person in her school, for she certainly could have succeeded in regular classes. Debbie was extensively mainstreamed in Westlake, and that seemed to placate her as well as induce a superior attitude toward the rest of the class. Probably the most unsettling individual in the class was a boy named Ricky. He had a strange look in his eyes that indicated he may not be on the same page as most others. Whenever I disturbed him in even a minor way, he would whip out a sheet of paper and start writing a letter to Joe Namath. Ricky thought there could be no greater ignominy than a negative report from him to the quarterback of the New York Jets. I suppose that was a minor punishment compared to his future transgressions when he arrived in high school. He developed a compulsion to hang live cats or set them afire. Perhaps our finest emissary was a young lad from Tarrytown whose charm, personality, and conscientiousness made one wonder why he was ever admitted into BOCES in the first place. He was mainstreamed and seemed to represent our class as a goodwill ambassador to the faculty and the rest of the student body.

My first class was more an aggregate of learning disabled, rather than those with emotional problems or substance abuse issues. Sometimes each student required praise and support to complete an assignment or additional instruction in a one to one situation. Outbursts and temper tantrums were seldom evident, and as the semester wore on, additional students were placed in the classroom. With a designation of LD, New York State permitted about fourteen students as the maximum roster, and numbers in that first year were never a problem. As designated labels became more particular, and New York believed that students should be assigned to the "least restrictive environment" possible, greater challenges emerged. Students who had been placed in institutions were mainstreamed into our district locations and often exhibited the symptoms that indicated why they had been in more restrictive places. Emotional outbursts and oppositional behaviors became more prevalent.

Unlike my experience in parochial school, I had the assistance of several professionals. Ann De Paso was a part time aide and a full time source of encouragement. I also had the benefit of a classy social worker who had no time for delay, no patience for boasters, and no interest in pursuing chimerical dreams. Dottie Carter was an ideal partner in supplying information and support for me, especially as related to Greenburgh students. Dottie seemed to know every family, every administrator, every peculiarity of Greenburgh 7, and she wasted no time explaining herself. Perhaps more so than any staff member I encountered in BOCES, Dottie was a familiar presence like the educators I knew in the Brothers. She was a supreme supporter for the teacher. At one conference where I was being chided for something or other, Dottie interrupted the berater to advise her that she was fortunate that her son had such an excellent teacher as Mr. O'Prey. She described me as a cross between John Dewey and Horace Mann, and the biggest possible tragedy would be her son being reassigned. Once the parent was placated in such fashion and the conference ended, Dottie then took me aside for a discussion on the facts of life and parental involvement in BOCES. Essentially, she suggested that I never do whatever I did again. Her style, her honesty, her candid advice, and her suggestions made me a great fan of hers. I admired Dottie Carter as an individual who spoke her mind, was interested in the students, and cared for the professionals. She was able to balance the needs of each with a straightforward, no nonsense performance time after time. Dottie's contributions to my adaptation to BOCES were welcomed, and I missed her role when she retired to work full time for Greenburgh shortly after I had the pleasure of her expertise.

Another individual from my initial exposure to the style of BOCES was a class clinician, or psychologist. Doris Yudin was a number of years older than I, but she seemed to take a benign interest in my association in BOCES. On one occasion, she inquired how I had made out on my first written evaluation. Frankly, my supervisor, Bob Thomas, had trashed me, at least statistically. I was only 28% satisfactory, and everything else needed improvement. Doris was incensed, since she believed I was doing a fine job, so she urged me to contest the accuracy of the review. I did so by writing a note to Dr. Hansen, the Director of Special Ed. I mentioned that if this evaluation were true, I would feel professionally obligated to resign. If he believed it were accurate, then he should relocate me to some innocuous position where I could do least damage, instead of consistently increasing my class size. Bob Thomas explained that the general procedure was to be harsh on my initial analysis, so that I could show improvement in the future. That probably would reflect on his management skills more than my competence. I was learning about the BOCES way, I suppose.

The crux of my first evaluation seemed to be my absence of special education credentials. When I was hired for the project that never got off the ground, I suppose it made little difference. I mentioned to Noel Rios and to Bob Hansen that I intended to continue working toward my doctorate in American Social History at NYU, instead of shifting gears into special education. That information didn't seem to startle them or cause them to reconsider my employment. Much of the evaluation form centered on courses one was taking in special education, so that was the genesis of my deficiencies. It also highlighted the fact that I never quite felt at ease in BOCES or totally committed to the program. Typically, I never heard from Hansen about my letter, and I also became a good friend of Bob Thomas. He arranged a fellowship to attend a course entitled 'Designing and Assessing Tools for the Classroom.' I would reap about six credits from Teachers' College at Columbia as a reward for my deficient credentials.

The last time I met Doris, I found her weeping at the exit doors from Ardsley Middle School, where the administrative offices were then located. Without much provocation, Doris told me her tearful account of what had happened to her. Her beloved husband had recently died, and that tragic loss seemed to trigger a terrible response from BOCES administrators. Her contributions immediately became suspect, and her expertise over many years was no longer valid. Instead of solace or solicitude upon her loss, she was treated with disrespect, disregard, outright hostility, and harassment. Frankly, I was dumbfounded on what to say to the woman who had been so kind to me in my early years in BOCES. After we parted, I resolved to send her a condolence card on the loss of her husband, but I was completely unable to defend the treatment she had gotten from administration. I did remember her experience and her implicit advice to trust few of those entrusted with our supervision.

If I had never witnessed the same treatment directed toward others, I might have found some credence in the approach of our lower administrators. Instead, I witnessed a similar episode with another veteran teacher named Jack, a talented musician. Jack's daughter had been found murdered in New York City, and that seemed to be the signal for harassment that would drive Jack into a retirement he wasn't ready for yet. After years of producing perfectly acceptable written reports and Phase One and Phase Two of Individual Education Plans or IEP's, Jack's now became 'unacceptable.' Since our reports were not computerized at the time, that meant that everything had to be typed or written out in long hand, a long and tedious process, no matter how one looked at it. Jack rewrote his reports, and without more than a cursory look, they were returned to him for rewriting. He showed them to me and asked what was wrong with them. I could find no significant deficiency in anything he wrote. His personal evaluations now pictured a man who wasn't competent in even the simplest responsibilities of a classroom teacher. After the personal abuse, insults about his lack of dedication, continual rejection of his written reports, Jack told me he had had enough and planned to retire. If he were so incompetent, one must wonder why he was allowed to substitute teach within our program from time to time. Actually, Jack was happy with that, for it brought needed income, and he no longer had to placate his tormentors about his writing or teaching skills.

The issue of reports and written Phase Ones was something I had further knowledge about. I knew that some teachers had special virtual secretaries who wrote their Phase Ones and other reports. These individuals had difficulty putting together three consecutive syntactically correct sentences, and their spelling might make a reader weep with shame at the state of education. For considerations other than composition skills, they were exonerated of the tedious tasks that the rest of us were assigned. I didn't find it difficult to compose these reports, especially when we developed computerized forms. My difficulty arose, however, when in the interest of speed, I didn't use caps and standard print. I wrote all in caps, and I had also learned never to submit the reports early, for they only encouraged my boss, the 'Mole,' who was a micromanager, to go over them with a fine tooth comb. If they came in at the end of the deadline, they apparently were more acceptable. The 'Mole,' whom I won't honor with an official name, insisted I retype my reports, for I had used all caps. I asked him to show me in the directions we received, where it indicated otherwise. When he could find no citation, he listened to his assistant and permitted my blaring typing to be acceptable. In the future, nevertheless, I did use caps only where appropriate. I wasn't trying to harass him or to challenge him, but I didn't want to be pushed around by this minor nabob who savored whatever power he had. Not many of us would volunteer to have his hemorrhoid operation featured on the Learning Channel on TV. Even fewer of us would urge their staff to witness their starring role. Perhaps this minor incident may reflect the ultimate in self confidence he exuded, or the conviction that he was right in his dogmatic interpretation of his offspring—the Therapeutic Support Program.

Although no one could fault him for his energy and devotion to duty, one might criticize his insistence upon adherence to his flagship's demonstration at Hastings High School. For years, I had enjoyed an independence based upon respect for the written reports I submitted, and the classroom management skills I exhibited. Under the supervision of the 'Mole,' I began to feel insulted, and perhaps even maligned. I refuse to use his name for the same reason I choose to cite my other nemesis, the 'Troll.' I called my supervisor the 'Mole,' for I believe he chose to be blind to some blatant, errant practices among some staff members. He chose not to see several derelictions of duty, nor to challenge some of members who had a very tenuous association with truth. The 'Mole' knew they were lying, but he preferred to vest his trust in them rather than in my point of view. Maybe my ego has interfered with reality, but I always enjoyed the confidence and support of previous BOCES administrators as well as the officials and staff members at Westlake High School. Now I came to believe that my opinions were solicited simply for the joy of ignoring them.

Ted Aronson had warned me never to trust the man I called the 'Troll' either. Ted was among other things a sound judge of character. The 'Troll,' actually a homunculus in presence, had a cheesy way of ingratiating himself into a group and a smarmy way of pronouncing the word 'kids,' but I believe most of the negative things that happened to BOCES employees seemed to be with his knowledge and back stage connivance. Between the 'Troll' and the 'Mole,' my last years in BOCES were very unpleasant, unlike the introduction I had to the organization years before. A tandem team many times, they resembled physically the cartoon duo of Mutt and Jeff in several ways. I began to suspect that this combination was conspiring to make my days in BOCES more onerous than they had to be.

Part of the change I observed had to do with the shift in leadership as well as in population. BOCES had a number of component group homes that provided a challenging array of problems. Children's Village, Pleasantville Cottage School, Graeham School, Hawthorne Cedar Knolls, Leake and Watts, St. Mary's in the Fields, group homes, and Jennie Clarkson often sent us students who may have been the cream of their residential programs, but they usually packed a set of behavioral problems that could make every year unique and memorable. Usually, however, the placements from these institutions had group home parents, supervisors and social workers who could assist in dealing with the individuals. In some ways, these children were more manageable than those from private, often negligent homes where alcohol and drugs were often issues.

For twenty-nine years, I really felt like an outsider. For most of my career, I preferred assignment to district locations where I could relate with the standard faculty members, and saw my peers only at meetings, or when supervisors came to my classroom. In fact, one of the symptoms of that alienation occurred about twenty-five years after my first class. In a gathering of staff prior to the school year, I was chatting with Pat Murphy, Greg Gates, and Ted Aronson. Our superintendent, Dr. Richard Lehrer, came over to say hello. He greeted each of my confreres by name, and then introduced himself to me, and asked my name. I was so embedded in what I thought was anonymity that it took the organization a full additional year to realize that it had failed to acknowledge my twenty-fifth anniversary with them. Part of the explanation lies in the vague, disparate programs spread throughout Southern Westchester, but a substantial part may be attributed to my own style of avoiding central administration whenever possible.

I also learned an invaluable lesson early in my BOCES career. As part of his legacy, Noel Rios planned an educational trip to Boston for middle school kids. I volunteered to go and also intervened in the case of one of my students from Tarrytown. Randy didn't have sufficient funds, or so he said, and I got Dr. Rios to let him ride free. When we arrived at Boston University, Randy had plenty of money, and then drove me crazy. There were only three male teachers and perhaps seven females. However, the group numbered about forty boys and five girls. We divided up the boys among the three male teachers but we knew nothing about most of the kids. That was to be a major deterrent to law and order. I finally cornered Randy in his room after pursuing him through several dorm floors. Content that he was now at least confined to a safe space, I was dismayed to discover him emerging from another area several rooms away. Randy had climbed out the window of the eleventh floor of the dormitory and edged along the ledge to the first open window. After that display of bravado, I declared myself defeated, and like my two male counterparts, retreated to my own room. That lesson impressed on me the need to avoid any overnight excursions with BOCES students in the future. I kept that resolution, especially when the Therapeutic Support Program hosted overnight camping expeditions or survival training programs. I always declined the invitation, and at least my wishes met with approval. I didn't want to be responsible for anyone that was not in a controlled environment.

At the conclusion of my first year in BOCES, I was willing to continue for another round while I took my doctoral courses. The nature of the commitment changed, however. At the end of the year, virtually all the first year teachers were reassigned to a new program in a new building at Rye Lake Campus. I was one of the unlucky ones. Most of us had no idea what was in store for us. Instead of having my independence and personal responsibility for a class, I would have to be part of a five or six person team teaching adventure in frustration.

Many times I felt a closer relationship with the administration of Mt. Pleasant District than I did with BOCES. I particularly enjoyed my relationship with Jim Mullen, the principal of Westlake High School. He sought out my opinion on our mutual problems and listened to my analysis carefully. He always treated me as if I was an intelligent professional. That was not necessarily the way I felt treated by BOCES administrators, who I believed barely knew me. Dr. Rios was certainly an exception, for he remained interested in my teaching at BOCES until his resignation. At one point, in my second year, he approached me at Rye Lake Campus, and in conspiratorial tones, asked me to request a transfer to Scarsdale High School. BOCES was opening a class there, and he had confidence that I could start the program off successfully. He mentioned that since I had just been reassigned to the Open Classroom Program at Rye Lake Campus, his recruitment could be construed as tampering, but if I initiated the request, he would readily approve it. After consulting with my fellow team members, Lois Baldwin insisted I would be abandoning the team if I left at this juncture. Therefore I never followed up on that offer. I learned to regret my loyalty, for Rye Lake Campus was so much more than I anticipated. BOCES went ahead and hired a new man for the job at Scarsdale, and I embarked on a year of terror.

We might as well have planned a doctoral seminar for the Primates at the Bronx Zoo, as design a program for the students who introduced the rectangle to an all out year long assault. Our open classroom structure provided twenty-three exits from the teaching centers, and every one of them was used at one time or another. In the interest of community and coziness, we were addressed by the students by our first name. Mine must have been 'Fat Fuck' for that was the appellation I merited most of the time. By Thanksgiving Nancy Brown had surrendered her hopes for a viable open classroom curriculum, and we were issued keys to be tied around our necks, as we opened and locked doors behind us. We had evolved from open classes to lock down jails. Mike Feldman and I were more like designated gorillas than teachers. Lois was about the only individual who was able to instruct a few interested students, if Mike and I could keep the destructive at bay.

One of my vivid memories of that year involves a young man from Pelham who intended to get even with me by putting his head through a glass window. As the boy shrieked obscenities and unintelligible animal roars, Mike enveloped him in a bear hug and sedated him, until he quieted down. A year later this same individual murdered an elderly lady who used to send him on errands. He beat her to death in the hopes of generating some hidden income information.

Our daily exercises began with the worst of conditions. We used to try to conduct a group meeting to discuss the plans of the day. That generally led to total chaos. In the middle of a primeval fight in the room with two dozen boys, four teachers, and an aide, a particularly spaced out beautiful young girl who could sit in an imaginary chair, a skill none of us ever mastered, strolled through the flailing bodies and admired the fish tank with the swimming fish. She muttered, "Be kind to the animals." Before the day was over she had eaten every fish in the tank. One of our more sadistic gentlemen determined that hamsters could sing. All they needed was a rotating phonograph with the needle embedded in their heads. Hamsters went the way of all fish, and in fact no animals were allowed to be part of the program from that moment on. Before that could be totally implemented, however, one of our boys, Billy, was caught smashing a kitten in the face with wire mesh. Of necessity our curriculum had to include first aid and respect for living creatures, be they animal or vegetable.

Part of the décor of our program was the incomplete finishing touches to the brand new building. Workers continued to fine tune the internal lines, pipes and phones that accompanied the effort to complete the Rectangle. One of the electricians was running wires behind the plasterboard when our most engaging youngster watched him snake the wire within the wall and then move a number of feet away to withdraw it into an outlet. As the worker looked on, Guy yanked the wire out of the wall. The electrician then evaluated the program as accurately as any professional. He told me he was a veteran of World War II and had the responsibility of guarding hundreds of German prisoners of war. None of them, he exclaimed, were anything close to the troubles our middle school subjects presented. He editorialized somewhat when he wistfully told me that I probably was highly educated, and in fact probably had graduate degrees. He then said he would never switch places with me for any amount of money.

Not everything about Rye Lake Campus was bad, however. Having a group of teachers who worked together to resolve our problems was one of the pluses. Another was the presence of an excellent educator who was also our supervisor. Joanne Mrstyk was an attractive, energetic, creative leader, who tried to help us as much as she could. Joanne loved her work, but she recognized the futility under which we operated and seemed to appreciate our feelings of impotence. When I told her my frank opinion, she thanked me for it and encouraged me to express my honest thoughts. She also promised to do whatever she could to have me relocated to a district class. Not only was my evaluation perfect, but she succeeded in having me return to Westlake Middle School, no small favor, believe me.

In returning to Westlake Middle School, in a way I felt like I was coming home. I believed that concentrating so many children with so many disparate problems in one place was counterproductive. The aggressives had targets in the meek, and the physically handicapped were especially vulnerable. An unspoken advantage to a district location was the fact that BOCES had less influence philosophically over the classroom. The building principal was an individual who had to understand our needs, and we had to accept his need to maintain decorum within the school. Violence, loud disruptions, thievery, vandalism, contempt for the faculty were all under the aegis of an administrator who wasn't hampered by a philosophy of toleration. In the middle school I had the pleasure of working with Jim Riendeau, Nate Romano, and Margaret Hussar, all of whom demonstrated a respect for our program and an appreciation of our special skills. We were always invited to participate in any school activities, and often our better students could enjoy the fruits of mainstreaming in academic classes or learning skills in music, shop, culinary arts, and gym. Flexibility, camaraderie, and communication with the teachers seemed to be the linchpins of success, and they were present in the Middle School. Although not under the Mount Pleasant administration and responsible to BOCES, I appreciated the help and understanding I received while at Westlake.

After ten rather pleasant years in the Middle School, one man's misfortune became my opportunity. Ted Aronson had solidified the reputation of BOCES among the high school staff. He was acknowledged a character, a generous man, and as sociable as one could be. Every Yuletide, Ted sponsored a seasonal party where his invited guests came from peers within BOCES and fellow staff from the high school. He also had a special relationship with the gym teachers and coaches. Ted was the athletic guru who knew the latest scores, trades, betting lines, and whatever else the athletically addicted talk about. As a graduate of Michigan, he had a very special interest in their football and basketball teams. He could converse about the most arcane data and opinions that he had garnered in his daily reading of all kinds of newspapers and magazines. Ted also coached Boys' soccer and girls' tennis teams. All of these qualities had enhanced BOCES in the eyes of the Westlake High School faculty. All this would come tumbling down in a tragic domino effect.

The superintendent's son was a talented soccer player on Ted's team. He also was suspected of some illegal sales within the school grounds. Jim Mullen's predecessor would lose his contract when he brought drug sniffing dogs into the school, and they located a stash in the aforementioned player's locker. The previous week, Ted had refused to start the boy in a soccer game, for he appeared at the field intoxicated. To protect the boy from embarrassment, Ted kept him on the sidelines. Apparently, the superintendent used some kind of convoluted logic which led him to conclude that Ted's benching and snubbing had actually driven his son to drugs. The superintendent insisted that Ted be reassigned from the high school. The entire faculty knew of the circumstances, as did I. I asked Ted if he would mind if I applied to replace him in the high school. Ted acceded immediately, for he knew there was no chance of appealing his transfer. In that way, I got to spend the next nineteen years in the high school unit of special education.

I enjoyed the high school much more than the Middle School. I liked the earlier start to the school day and the subsequent earlier dismissal in the afternoon permitted me to take care of my children. This schedule permitted many of the students to spend half a day taking academic classes and then going to the Occupational Education component for the other half. I also enjoyed the relative maturity of the students, and I got to know the high school faculty well. Ted had already established a respect for special education teachers; so in essence, I inherited the benefits of what he had achieved. When I first started in BOCES, our teachers made about twelve hundred dollars more than the Mount Pleasant staff with comparable credentials. There was no jealousy, however, for they respected the challenges of our job. After a number of years, nonetheless, the pay scales were reversed, when the union at Mount Pleasant presented greater demands than ours could. Each year at our BOCES orientation, we would be told how exciting the year was going to be, and how lucky we were that we still had jobs. Some districts had begun to assess our contributions to their extraordinary students as too expensive, and enrollment declined.

Perhaps, it sounds extraneous to state that the BOCES staff members were treated respectfully and honorably by Westlake, but I found that not to be so, when I was transferred for two years to Sleepy Hollow. Frankly, I found that faculty xenophobic and practitioners of a pyramidal structure that was as close to a caste system as one can imagine. The science teachers spoke to the math department, and

English teachers consorted with social science teachers. None spoke with shop personnel or special needs teachers, and at the bottom of the heap was the gym staff that was just a notch above BOCES. As special ed teachers, we were presumed stupid and incapable of mastering the curriculum of typical classes. Some of the faculty was actually stupefied when they observed me solving the daily crossword puzzle from the **New York Times** within fifteen minutes.

If we professionals rated little respect or appreciation, our students fared even worse. The Sleepy Hollow faculty was quite intolerant of any misbehavior by the BOCES Students. I must make a clear exception for the gym staff, for they were always friendly and sociable. Perhaps they could relate to the outcast mentality. One of my students was an exceptional basketball player from Dobbs Ferry. He was actually the star of the varsity basketball team. He got into some kind of difficulty and chased his adversary within the corridors of the school. As he ran after his quarry, a hall monitor extended her arm hoping to stop him. The boy brushed her arm aside. No major trouble resulted from my student, but I spoke with the hall monitor about ten minutes after the event. She had no complaints and no injuries. By the end of the school day, the faculty had convinced her that she had been physically assaulted, and the perpetrator should not only be expelled from the school, he should be arrested. That night a complaint was filed with the Tarrytown police, and my student was arrested and spent a night in jail for aggravated assault. The issue was so contrived, that the charges were dropped, but the individual had been taken from his home while his mother worked the night shift at some hospital.

The office administration wielded justice with a biased interpretation too. If any of our students were involved in any problems, they were suspended quickly. Tarrytown was not so quick to resolve its own problems. One of my students was a young career criminal from Tarrytown who had just been released on parole. He quickly took up the sales of desired but illicit commodities. I saw him dealing in the parking lot and reported him to the office in the hope that his trafficking would stop. They ignored my alarm, and the kid continued to deal openly. Apparently, everyone knew of his criminal activities, but as a native son, no one would confront him. If he had been from another town, he probably would have been arrested for grand theft auto and drug dealing.

One or two other adventures awaited me in my years at Sleepy Hollow. My first supervisor was Joe Schwarzberg, but he was too preoccupied with his pursuit of his fabled job as Director of Occupational Education. Joe arrived with an agenda that startled me. Since the class at Sleepy Hollow was newly created, he seemed to believe we had a very small population. When he came one day, four of my class had been suspended through the OC ED program, and I only had a skeleton representation present. Instead of noting that two gym teachers stopped by to inquire about my students' absence, he preferred to deprive me of the help of a classroom aide. Despite his few visits and preoccupation with a promotion, he wanted to slash the budget by removing my aide, an efficient, highly intelligent woman named Jane Herz. Jane was not only a certified teacher, but she also was very connected to the group home in Thornwood. She took special interest in the two group home students from that class, and I credit her with teaching Freddie how to read. By the end of the year, Jane had secured a teaching position at Ossining, and she was replaced by a young woman who was frightened of the students and possibly misplaced among a high school population. Whenever I was away on a sick day, she would take several days to recover. In the meantime, she was also completing her practicum from Marymount using my class as her experience, and she earned a degree which enabled her to take a position among a younger population.

With Joe Schwarzberg winning the coveted position of Director of Occupational Education, I received a new supervisor, a short, rather attractive young woman named Sandy. Unlike Joe Schwarzberg, she was visiting on site often and intrusively. She plagued me with questions about my intentions, my objectives, my rationale, my assignments, my approaches, and so forth. She didn't belittle them, nor assail their credibility, nor their effectiveness, but she just wanted to know, or so she claimed. I felt like I was subjected to frequent cross-examination in a courtroom about the most miniscule matters. She offered no commentary, nor did she make any judgments. She just pestered me for interpretations. Finally, I was relieved of this nuisance when she ran off with a clinician from Pleasantville. Her final legacy to BOCES was a mega lawsuit involving physical abuse of a minor in another program. She restrained the child of an eminent psychiatrist by sitting upon the student to restrict her to the classroom. The psychiatrist was livid and delivered a legal brief that was a virtuoso exhibit of the trauma such an action caused upon the psyche of his child. Naturally, such an egregious offense warranted millions of dollars in compensation. I never did hear how the lawsuit evolved, but I was relieved of the pestering from Sandy. I guess my inconvenience was minor compared to the impact she had upon the other two locations.

My students in Sleepy Hollow were a mixed group at first, and then slowly additional candidates were admitted without much consideration for their impact. One of the friendliest kids I encountered in BOCES was Marty, a hallucinatory kid from Eastchester. Marty told many wild stories and especially enjoyed his sessions with my clinician Wilma Gilbert. Through Marty, I learned about a new form of theft. One afternoon, he returned all disheveled from lunch with an incredible account of his mugging in one of the corridors of the school. Marty claimed that the bullies wanted his sneakers. His earnest description as well as the testimony of the hall monitor who broke up the brouhaha led me to identify a new kind of crime-sneaker theft. Soon it was rampant, and often described in the newspapers. Marty was a favorite of the gym teachers. He often created key chains or identification stubs using metal and plastics from his shop at Basic Occupational Education. I still use some of his products to this day.

An individual who had a considerable negative impact upon the Sleepy Hollow staff was the preposterously dressed Alphie. Alphie always wore a coonskin cap and enough gold around his neck to pass for a descendent of King Tutankamen. Alfie maintained a very low profile in the classroom and appeared to be interested in his work. He asked few questions and might have passed for statuary if he didn't move too often. Outside the classroom, he was something else. He could disappear in seconds. He also convinced a gullible clinician that he had a work/study job that enabled him to leave at half day. By the time the clinician got to investigate Alfie's progress in the work/study program, the boss hadn't seen Alfie in six months. Whenever Alfie was absent from school, a conglomerate of undesirables would stop at the classroom door inquiring about his presence and return to school. Obviously, Alfie was conducting the sale of illicit goods which supported his love for the golden neck chains. Alfie also was arrested for a burglary he committed at his best friend's house. After casing the place, he doubled back and pillaged whatever he estimated to be of value. When he told me about his alibi, I advised him to think it through before the police questioned him. The county jail was his next venue of learning.

Alfie was a hero to a rather small lad, a wanna-be gangster from Greenburgh. Andre was the first one I encountered in my BOCES career who carried a box cutter more conscientiously than he did any pen or pencil. Just recently, I read that this aspiring thief was released from state prison and shortly thereafter robbed his local deli, murdered the two shopkeepers, and pegged shots at the bystanders. I suppose he's back in prison now, perhaps as a lifer for he had been there for three different charges within the last few years.

Not every student had thievery on his mind. I had a tall youngster who fancied himself a professional of sorts. On his slender six foot six black frame, he always wore a business suit with shirt and tie. His accompanying brief case only added to his image. His attire and accoutrements could lead one to conclude he was a junior banker or stock broker in training. If one left him alone or offered assistance in a polite way, Fred returned in kind, but naturally he was an easy target for those students in BOCES or from Sleepy Hollow to tease and ridicule. Once angry, Fred was also very difficult to sedate.

A final change to my clinical support was the arrival of the 'Tiger.' Like the 'Troll' and the 'Mole,' he doesn't rate a name because of my scorn. At first, I enjoyed his tales of his life among the privileged. He claimed to be a scion of one of the First Families of Virginia. He had attended prep school in New England and was admitted to a prestigious 'eating club' at one of the most selective Ivy League institutions. He summered among the glitterati at the Hamptons and moved readily among that plateau of society that I could only read about. After a while, I recognized a few quirks, however, that led me to reassess my new clinician.

I jokingly asked him one day during the uproar created by the Mayflower Madam scandal, whether he knew the young madam or not. The 'Tiger' replied, "Well to tell the truth, I did date her a few times. You know she's not only a Biddles, but she's also a Barrows." The gulf between our youthful years was perhaps unbreachable as time went by. The 'Tiger' made a name for himself by establishing a national reputation for dealing with the issue of bullying in schools. He appeared on television and in the printed media. No doubt he heaped reflected glory upon BOCES, but I learned to distrust him intensely for a number of reasons.

The 'Tiger,' told me that he had my current clinician transferred for her incompetence in dealing with high school students. She purportedly lacked his expertise in dealing with the kind of students we had. I had always been appreciative of her skills, presence, punctuality, and adherence to a schedule. These were attributes that I discovered would become rarities with the 'Tiger' himself. In the course of our dealings, I would hear allegations about staff members from him that were downright insulting. Not only was the clinician I respected declared incompetent, but the 'Tiger' also described in lurid detail the sex life of an administrator I admired. To the number of character defamations, I should add his condemnation of two teachers. One he diagnosed as clinically depressed and should be removed from the classroom. The other was said to be too stupid for him to work with. While I listened to these stories, I found his motivation too transparent to any rational mind, and I believed no one would heed him. I did not find that analysis to be true. He seemed to enjoy the confidence of the 'Mole' and the 'Troll' who acted upon his suggestions.

Only too late did I come to question the stories he was passing along about me. In due time, I believe this rumormonger convinced BOCES administrators that I had two major defects. The first was contempt for authority based on the practice I had of ignoring retirement dinners for our administrators. Personally, I had family matters that were priorities for my time and money. The 'Tiger' also sold the concept that I could not relate to clinical staff, making me impossible to work with. Many of his assessments seem to bear fruit, for the depressed individual was relocated and harassed daily in an unworkable situation. The clinician was reassigned elsewhere, as was the dense teacher. Since he didn't have a game plan for the administrator, the savaging of her reputation only fell upon my deaf ears. My optimism that any rational mind could find the 'Tiger's appraisals so transparent was based more on providence than on reality. When I shared some of my concerns with Greg Gates, our union president and paragon of what a special education teacher ought to be, he told me he flat out refused to work with him. I didn't have that power, I thought. I credit my clinician with adding me to his list of reconstruction projects for upper administration intervention.

I realize my words carry a vitriolic venom or poison that I reserve for few individuals, but my contempt for the 'Tiger' and my respect for BOCES have restrained me from speaking my piece for years. During the course of my relationship with him as my clinician, we had several differences of opinions. I had many among other clinicians, but I never accused one of them of being duplicitous, cowardly, and vindictive. Let me illustrate some of my associations with this pre-eminently acclaimed figure. I don't question his credentials nor his national fame. I do despise his performance among my students. The 'Tiger,' after a while, seldom even met with my students. He would interview me about their academic and emotional progress and then write up summaries that made them appear as the result of his weekly sessions. He disappeared for extensive periods of time, leaving neither explanations to us underlings nor places where he could be found. The rumors abounded about his wooing a Cher look-alike in Pleasantville High School however.

When the 'Tiger' did interview some students, he only spread chaos. I had a delightful, compliant, gentle giant who was driven to the point of attacking the good doctor in his office in the middle school. I received a frantic telephone call for emergency assistance. Upon arriving at the door, I saw the clinician cowering in a corner with the massive bulk of Alvin wagging a finger in his face and advising him to "mind his own business." Alvin seemed ready to bench press the clinician into oblivion. Alvin quickly responded to my presence, and we left the doctor in his office. I never asked what drove Alvin to the brink, nor did the doctor ever account for the episodic outburst.

Once again the 'Tiger' summoned immediate help in dealing with one of Pat Murphy's female students. Priscilla had maneuvered in such a way that she was able to lock the doctor out of his office, and she had the keys. A panicky call was made to Murphy, but he couldn't respond immediately because his aide was away from the class momentarily dealing with a group of students. By the time Pat got to the office, his reward for his rescue efforts was a public thorough chiding about his tardiness in responding to the emergency. Fortunately, Pat had a sense of humor and thick skin bred by the proletarian, plebian background in Washington Heights. I got along with Priscilla simply by teaching her to spell 'Washington.' Whenever she appeared to be losing her temper, I would ask her to spell the word, and the distraction permitted her to regain her composure. Such a simple procedure would have worked for the clinician, if he cared to learn from some of his social inferiors.

Two more examples perhaps explain why I reserve almost exclusive disdain for this individual. The greatest, most destructive challenge in my Westlake tenure occurred rather strangely. One of my students, Michael by name, was an aficionado of weight lifting and body building. He seemed almost the model for neurological impaired, for he gave an adequate impression of total ignorance, and then a few moments later accurate information would spew forth in a spate of facts. Michael also may have been in the vanguard of steroid abusers before they became prevalent. He was on the football team and related quite well with students in our class as well as those from Westlake. In gym one afternoon, an Albanian playfully jumped on Mike, who then threw him on the ground and pinned him-all in fun, or so thought Michael. At the end of gym class, his assailant's younger brother casually ambled into my classroom, approached Michael and slapped him across his face. Michael was so dumbfounded, he froze trying to comprehend the nature and extent of the insult. In the meantime, the fellow who slapped Michael dashed out of the classroom and thereby exposed the plot. Apparently, the leader of the Albanian faction was insulted by Michael's toss and wanted revenge. His younger brother was the means to sucker Michael into an ambush of at least a half dozen Albanians who planned to stomp him. Michael's delayed reaction confused their plans, but by then Michael realized what had happened and wanted to retaliate. A trip to the principal's office and a promise to investigate the affront placated Michael somewhat, but all underestimated the need for Albanian revenge.

On Monday, Michael asked his huge gentle friend Alvin to cover his back during lunch. As Alvin descended the stairs, he was sucker-punched in the eye, kicked in the face, and lapsed into unconsciousness. Alvin had to be taken to Westchester Medical on a gurney, after he was administered to in the nurse's office. When Michael saw what had happened to Alvin, he went berserk. As I tried to restrain a boy stronger than I, I searched for my clinician. The 'Tiger' had retreated to the telephone line to call the police, and he then had to leave Westlake immediately for another designated haven. That turned out to be the typical response to violence or threat-immediate evacuation. In fact, like a fire truck hurtling to a blaze, the 'Tiger' could be observed rushing pell mell in the opposite direction of any conflict. Without the help of the 'Tiger,' Jim Mullen and I, the assistant principal, and the head of guidance, dealt with the enraged Michael. Alvin spent several days in the hospital and almost lost his eye. He wisely resolved never to return to Westlake.

Michael was just as determined that he wouldn't wimp out again. I was given the assignment to shadow Michael from the moment he arrived in school until he left. If nothing else, I could attest to any attack. In the meantime one of the principals among the Albanians was advised that jail awaited him, if he violated parole in any assault. Michael resented my shadowing, since he believed it questioned his heart. When I followed him into a bathroom, he physically picked me up and moved me out of his way. Although Michael could have injured me, he had no intention of doing so, nor was that his style. Nonetheless, he was forthwith reassigned to Greg Gates' class and flourished there until his graduation. The 'Tiger' remained in his lair somewhere hidden from peril.

Perhaps another example may indicate that the 'Tiger's reaction to crisis was repetitious. During lunch period, one of Murphy's students had climbed a ladder up to the Middle School roof and threatened to jump. Another harried call came into the high school, although our intrepid clinician was yards away from the potential disaster. Since the telephone rang in both classrooms simultaneously, we used to pick it up and 'eavesdrop' until we knew the intended party. Doing this, I learned of the potential suicide at the same time as Pat. We both hurried down to the Middle School, only to be passed by the psychological expert hustling in the opposite direction to an undisclosed location. The 'Tiger' was an effective indicator of trouble, as inerrant as a weather vane that indicates wind direction. When one intercepted him, one knew trouble was in the direction from which he fled. Pat climbed the ladder to the roof, and I followed him. It took only a little cajolery for Pat to convince the student to come back down with him. One might think that a psychological expert was indispensable in this situation, but one practical, thoughtful teacher with a good relationship with the student was enough.

The straw that finally broke my back in dealing with the 'Tiger' was several years in coming. I accepted him for what I interpreted him to be. As long as he didn't bother me, I could tolerate him and his peculiarities. On a day when Westlake had an administrative delayed opening, I drove my own kids to school and then arrived in Westlake at least thirty minutes before the designated time. I had little concept of what had transpired in my brief, legitimate absence. The 'Tiger,' who did not know of the delayed opening because he had disappeared to unknown places during the previous days, had arrived to find my classroom empty. He called BOCES administration and the attendance office to ascertain whether I had taken a sick day. Then he called central administration to report me AWOL, and finally frightened my wife with a call announcing I had failed to show up at work. When I made little of my legitimate late arrival, he uttered from his perch on Mount Olympus, "That's not good enough!" I then learned about his series of calls and lost my temper at his officious behavior. I was accused of doing what he did on a daily basis, and then he demanded a rendering of my account.

Unfortunately, my regular supervisor at the time, Lois Baldwin, had been injured in a plane crash, and she was temporarily replaced by the 'Mole.' I have no certainty what transpired between my two support personnel, but I let the 'Mole' know I didn't want to deal with the 'Tiger' again. For the first time in my BOCES career, I had complained about a fellow staff member. If this scenario sounds like a zoo, perhaps it also illustrates some of the zany problems that could arise in BOCES. At one time, an administrator from Westlake High School asked me, "Who the hell is he, and just exactly what does he do?" For all my years in BOCES I tried to represent the organization honestly and honorably, but when I pondered that question, I could only rhetorically ask myself, "How does one explain the inexplicable? How does one defend the indefensible?"

At the end of my time at Sleepy Hollow, I suppose I had been declared a failure for embedding a Counsel Support class, and I was reassigned without explanation to Westlake. If BOCES were to succeed in Tarrytown, its best chances lay with its best teacher. Although I was quite happy to return to Westlake, I felt like I hadn't been able to crack the veneer of the entrenched faculty of Sleepy Hollow. My replacement was the deservedly hotshot of the Special Education department. I have nothing but praise for Greg Gates, a man of intelligence, tact, experience, 'savoir faire' as well as a host of other positive assets. If there were anything such as a paragon of what Special Ed should be, it was the embodiment of Greg Gates, an intelligent, thoughtful, professional who met the standards of both BOCES and the composite districts. He enjoyed the respect and even the admiration of his peers. He demanded the compliance of administration, and even represented our Teachers' Union with honesty, sincerity, and integrity. I have only great homage to offer this man who embodied much of what every special educator might aspire to be.

Greg was a true friend, a noble peer and a respected exemplar of what each of us should be. He asked me to serve as editor of **The Connecting Link,** the printed journal of the BOCES Teachers Association. For several years I served under his leadership as editor of the union newspaper. Actually, I was never fired, but my meager stipend stopped, and I discovered another individual had assumed the responsibilities of editorship. I had advised Greg that I could handle the written work, but I couldn't afford the time to attend meetings and discussions. At least that was acceptable for two or three years. After a year or two at Sleepy Hollow, even this paragon of excellence failed in maintaining a BOCES Counsel Support class, an especially telling deficit grade for what that District thought of imported students.

Over the course of twenty-nine years in BOCES, some meetings retain a vivid image of the organization and the complexity of its mission. My introduction to this phenomenon occurred when I was in Westlake Middle School. On the very last day of school, I was summoned to a major meeting with one of the parents of a child whose safety and health I protected from extermination on a daily basis. He was an irritating 'nudnik,' but I felt sorry for him for his father had just died in a motorcycle accident. Without knowing any particulars, I joined the widow, her pastor, and John Walsh, our social worker and miracle worker combined. John had been commissioned by Dr. Hansen to replace him at the meeting, so he was in a sense like Charlesmagne's Paladin, or representative on the far frontiers of Special Education. I had no clue as to the agenda of the meeting, nor did I know whether John had any information either. As the meeting progressed, however, it became evident that it was incumbent upon me to prove my sanity to the reverend. What his credentials for psychoanalysis might have been were as murky as the indictment.

I was accused of being insane, for I demonstrated the same behavior pattern as the departed father of my student. He used to resent when Richard played with the food on his father's plate, and the irate man would storm out of the house. I apparently exhibited those symptoms when I stopped Richard from plucking jelly beans from my shirt pocket. Thinking I was there merely to report on Richard's performance in class, I appallingly realized I was supposed to prove that I was sane in the face of frivolous charges. No wonder Dr. Hansen was too busy to participate. After the boy's mother likened me to her dead husband, the pastor looked somewhat askance. Later he told me that I had been found certifiably sane, and that he would write a letter declaring so to Dr. Hansen. I don't recall John Walsh saying anything. Perhaps he was as dumbfounded as I, or was afraid his sanity was next in question. By the way, John Walsh, a social worker in the mold of Dottie Carter, was as conscientious, supportive, and informative, as any clinician I worked with. When he retired, I wrote a commentary of him, identifying him as 'Emeritus' and the living archives of BOCES itself. 'JW' exemplified what BOCES could be when utilized appropriately. As I left the meeting, the anomaly of proving my contact with reality to a woman I didn't really know, for a reverend I didn't know, in circumstances over purloined jelly beans, I found incredibly at variance with my notion of professionalism.

The sanity session made about as much sense to me as the insistence from the 'Mole' that I cook breakfast for the mother of one of my students later in the Therapeutic Support Program. Because I hesitated to do so, he harassed me incessantly, while the mother, a toothless, former Biker-chick from Texas, got along fine with me. Then the 'Mole' used to joke about my romantic relationship with the mother. At least I took his comments to be in jest, a side of him I seldom observed.

In another conference in the Middle School, I was the audience rather than the main character in an unusual BOCES parent conference. Mitch Schwarz was a very competent, professional supervisor who worked industriously and conscientiously, but he found himself over his head in a meeting he was chairing. One of my students, a gullible young lady, fell in love with one of Pat Murphy's educable retarded students. Timmy was from Graeham School and arrived at Westlake daily with every item he possessed from underwear to silverware. Tim argued that if he left anything back at the home, it would be stolen. Far from a paragon of hygiene, he also had a surplus supply of adult diapers, if an accident should occur. Despite frequent reminders, he failed to brush his teeth or his hair and in general looked unkempt. Tim began his courtship in school, but he carried it over to the telephone in the evening. The damsel's father, a blue collar ethnic who had already paid for his son to complete medical school, knew that his daughter was intellectually limited, so he was especially protective. He called Mitch and requested a parent conference to discuss the romance.

During our conversation, the father made it clear that he didn't want his daughter having anything to do with Tim. Mitch of course gave him his personal guarantee. At the completion of this meeting, the parent asked to speak with Tim, and Mitch determined that as long as he was present, everything should go smoothly. When Tim appeared in his disheveled manner and was Black besides, the father approached Tim, and uttered a caution. "Tim," he said, "no doubt you are a nice boy, but if you ever appear with my daughter again or telephone my house, I'll personally find you and cut your fucking balls off." "Do you understand me?" Tim nodded and Mitch gulped. I didn't laugh, but found the embarrassment and the new direction to the professional conference enlightening. One never knew how a conference might conclude.

At a team meeting, I found the same kind of agenda present. What was on the table was not often the main idea. After I complained about the 'Tiger,' I was assigned another clinician the following year. Glenn counseled the kids, was present every day or alerted me as to his whereabouts. He was faithful to his schedule and in general was many things his predecessor lacked. Unknown to me, the 'Troll' and the 'Mole' planned to fire him and make me an accessory. Imagine a meeting with the four of us discussing class problems. The 'Mole' took notes about Glenn, and the 'Troll' took notes about the 'Mole' taking notes. Glenn and I went about our business in our customary fashion. Typically, we agreed about most tactics, but differed on a minor approach. I thought little of it until later in the year. When the 'Mole' asked me about Glenn, I endorsed him in general. Virtually anyone would be an improvement on the 'Tiger.' Later when Glenn wasn't given tenure, he was told that his failure to get along with me was crucial. He had argued with me in our conference and acted improperly, both characteristics unrecognized by me. I told Glenn that I had not urged his firing, and frankly if I had, it would be the first time the 'Mole' ever listened to me. The fate of my clinician had been predetermined the previous year, and I was the selected patsy for the implementation.

In my final year in BOCES, I had run into the 'Troll' after he had been hired by another school district. He mentioned an aside that I had always had difficulties with clinicians. I mused about that comment many times, and I found it to be quite false. Most of the clinicians I encountered during my career in BOCES were fine people, competent and reliable. That is not to say that I didn't have any debates with them about appropriate actions or plans for some of the students. Wherever they occurred, a mutual respect and polite disagreement characterized our relationship. Often at root of the problem may have been the undeclared relationship between teacher and clinician. I always thought that the bond was between equals, but some may have come to view their role as taking precedence over the classroom teacher or exercising some authority. That dichotomy was never addressed or resolved officially, but in practice, time proved that the clinicians had more influence than teachers.

Until I met the 'Tiger,' every clinician seemed polite and willing to work together with the teacher. I know that the 'Tiger' altered grades on students without consulting me and seemed enthralled with his own agenda. After a number of years together, I found his officiousness intolerable and his function unsatisfactory. Since the parting of our ways, I had a series of clinicians from Ken Mann, an excellent soft spoken individual, to Rachelle Kritzer, extremely reliable and competent. Our TSP program was not so fortunate when Rachelle had to take several maternity leaves. The saga of her temporary replacements might rate some explanation, however.

In retrospect, I found the downward spiral into the Therapeutic Support Program (TSP) the genesis of my dissatisfaction with BOCES. For twenty years I had enjoyed a healthy, respectful relationship with the faculty, guidance office, and administration of Westlake. I believe there was mutual trust and professional courtesy. My association with Westlake would prove to be a negative upon my entrance into the TSP. My supervisor believed that the paragon, the flagship of the Therapeutic Support Program, resided in Hastings. Its staff, its principles, its function were ideals, for it embodied the notion of the 'Mole's creation. Frankly, I didn't admire it so much.

In trying to duplicate the model program from Hastings, my Westlake experience proved detrimental. My convictions, my relationships, my ideals and my advice ran counter to the paradigm, so I basically was ignored. Whatever I advised, whatever I urged, was totally disregarded, and the program only increased my dissatisfaction when a second class was added, just like the model in Hastings. When Rachelle became our counselor, I recall losing my temper, not at her, but at the flagship staff that had transferred arsonists, weapon carriers, and druggies into Westlake in the guise of providing a better environment for the students. I thought Hastings had taken advantage of the new clinician, and I said so vehemently. Perhaps Rachelle thought I was angry at her, but that wasn't so. I thought our working relationship was fine, but when she had to go on several maternity leaves, the teacher/clinician combination didn't operate as smoothly.

A series of unfortunate replacements might give credence to my inability to co-exist with clinicians. Rather, I believe my experience underscores the ill-advised hiring practices of our administration. Rachelle's first replacement was a nice lady who followed the trend of the "Mole.' She disregarded my advice and chose to follow the counsel of my counterpart, a teacher new to Westlake. She rated only derision and mockery for her judgment, especially for her reaction to the sexual advances and fantasies of one of my students. My fellow staff members for the most part ignored the timid lady's complaints.

Rachelle's second replacement was an older woman whose zeal included an attack upon Ted Aronson. When she started to justify the aberrant behavior of one of our students who was disrespectful to Ted, I walked out on her. She parroted the litany of complaints about him, and I told her I refuse to listen to such tripe. While I expressed my feelings, I continued to deal with her, but the rest of the team virtually ignored her. In fact, when one of our students became pregnant by another student, they didn't even inform her.

When we were exiled from Westlake, we were fortunate to find available space on the beautiful campus at Manhattanville College. The college offered the downstairs of a three story dorm awaiting renovation. That space was subdivided into three classrooms, a counseling center, and two bathrooms, and a full service kitchen. Part of our curriculum now was the implementation of creative cooking and nutritional development planned by the students and supervised by some teachers and aides like Carole Hager. No doubt our food budget superceded any other item except for rent. The one drawback to the arrangement was an ineffective heating system which enabled frigid temperatures to create a panic mode in the dead of winter. At Manhattanville, as at Westlake, I enjoyed the sage advice, the calculated wisdom, and the practical advice of Carole Hager. More than most aides, Carole had the experience and know-how that made her my major asset at our new location.

Perhaps the worst experience I had after Rachelle's final maternity leave was the hiring of a very forceful woman. At first, I thought we had lucked out at Manhattanville, for we had been summarily dismissed from Westlake for requiring too much administrative attention. In a short while, this clinician created a dichotomy between the teaching staff and the students. We were perceived more as enemies instead of people who intended to help the students. Rather, all help and all intercession would come by way of the clinician. I wasn't too swift to notice this, but some of the staff did. Carole Hager and Freda Maus, two of our aides, noticed the pernicious effect this clinician had upon our program. What I did note was the 'Mole's attention to her dicta. After discussing the principles we wished to incorporate in the unique campus of Manhattanville and some of the rules required for their implementation, all our hours of conferences and planning went to naught, for only her decisions counted. This insidious counselor seemed to hold a hypnotic influence over our supervisor, for he followed only her directions and ignored all others. I had started to compile a written rationale for the TSP at Manhattanville since I was declared team leader by default. I even advised my supervisor to appoint my aide, since he had no regard for my talents or opinions. I was leader in stipend only, and I discovered this early in the fall. Playing her role as savior and intercessor, she changed all our discussions and conclusions about the use of students' automobiles with a fiat worthy of a dictator. Frankly, I was so incensed that I raged at her and left for the afternoon. All our plans, all our principles, all our conclusions, all our intentions were at the mercy of her opinion, the only one the 'Mole' generally considered.

By Thanksgiving, I was counting the days until Rachelle would return, when a new program evolved. The clinician began a smear campaign against Rachelle and a carefully crafted procedure for maintaining her position as our clinician for the rest of the year. This came to a head in a public lynching chaired by the 'Mole.' For the first ten minutes, we listened to programmed input from the students that exalted the achievements of the maternity replacement. After ten minutes of praise, the comments turned into slanderous, character assassination directed against Rachelle. Despite the warning that Manhattanville classes would look like the opening hanging scene of the thanes from *Braveheart* if our clinician couldn't continue, that scenario didn't play out. I couldn't sit through the calumny and ridicule permitted by the 'Mole', so I declared my position in no ambiguous terms and left the meeting. The rest of the staff for the most part had already left, apparently more interested in preparing a lunch than listening to the orchestration. Later my supervisor chided me for my behavior, claiming that he had everything under control and that in time he would bring the participants around to his way of thinking. I sincerely doubted that then, and I still do. Despite the contretemps, Rachelle returned to claim her rightful position as clinician. Her replacement was only the second individual I officially complained about in my twenty-nine years in BOCES, but again, my opinion and that of other staff members was inadmissible for some obscure reason.

I thought the transfer to Manhattanville was the best possible solution to the team approach that I abhorred at Westlake. Eventually, I would determine that my future in BOCES would take a terrible toll on me, when we were advised to seek new locations for the coming year. I had stayed in BOCES until my three children graduated from college, and my income would be more in keeping with my outgo. Ironically, my stipend as team leader helped my retirement pension. Although I was the only one to retire without an incentive within a five year span, I had received the disrespectful incentive. Having accrued a total of one hundred and ninety-three sick days, I neglected to cull that potential minefield, and surrendered them to my best intentions for BOCES. In truth, if I had calculated all my accumulated sick time, I probably would have amassed over five hundred days. Since we could only amass two hundred at most, I lost most of my time, a tribute to my dedication and unacknowledged loyalty to BOCES.

I thought my personal morals were incompatible with some of the behaviors permitted in the classrooms. Lying coupled on the classroom floor, or perched on laps during counseling sessions or team meetings, heterosexual hugging and kissing were evidently ignored by much of the staff. I also privately questioned the propriety of some of the Japanese cartoons and violent videos that were showed on a daily basis in another classroom. I resolved to apply my usual rules in my own classroom, but few students opted to come when they had more enticing alternatives in the other classrooms. Finally, when we introduced proselytizing lesbians, demanding the same recognition of their sexual proclivities, our forbearance was justifiably questioned. I think the 'Mole' thought my convictions were medieval or at least Victorian. My concept of school behavior was a far cry from what was otherwise tolerated. I also had difficulty determining whether we were running a school or a mental hospital.

Counseling certainly was a necessary component to our program, but some individuals made it an exclusive endeavor. They might enter the counseling and skip three or four classes several days a week. That was compounded by frequent absence, or more likely, daily tardiness, for they were allowed to drive to Manhattanville and might arrive at ten or even twelve o'clock. I kept a daily grade book, wherein no one was penalized for counseling sessions, but absences were recorded. Grades were assigned for class participation and written work. Students were absolutely forbidden to sleep during my class sessions too. When I alerted my supervisor that several students, one in particular, had missed so many classes that she couldn't pass, he thanked me for the information. On the last day of school he told me to change her grade and pass her nonetheless. I refused to do so and advised him he could alter the grade if he chose, but I asked him to indicate that the grade came from him and not from me. That was my *bon voyage* message from BOCES. I presume he altered the grade anyhow, for I read the name of the student in question listed as a graduate in my local papers.

I write this vitriolic review of my final years in BOCES in a state of mind that is unsettling to me. For my twenty-nine years I attempted to be a loyal employee, often covering for some of the failings of the organization. I also tried to be a contributing teacher and even team member given my convictions. I hope I have insulted few of my peers for that is not my intent. So many of the people I worked with were consummate professionals. Few were scoundrels, and maybe a few were misguided. It's possible that I was such an enigmatic figure that few understood my sense of humor, my devotion to sincerity, or my private opinions. Actually, I enjoyed listening to some of my peers who had an incredible gift. They could emit two note flatulence and refer to it as comparable to Ludwig Van Beethoven's *Ode to Joy*. A few confreres didn't acknowledge or accept the honorific term teacher, for they identified themselves as program directors. They didn't teach math, or language arts; they ran programs. Generally their speech betrayed them. Using words like 'rubrics, gestalt, Madeleine Hunter, anticipatory set, etc.' they pronounced themselves as the vanguard of education and their students as excellent achievers. Sometimes their dicta were couched in language that couldn't combine three syntactically correct sentences consecutively, or their misspellings on the blackboard were evidence of their personal foibles if not their teaching style. Yet some might be praised as models to the rest of us.

Incidentally, please do not construe this criticism in any way directed toward an individual who probably was the finest teacher I witnessed professionally. Jim Morgan was an exemplar and a person who knew what he was teaching and used the techniques of Madeleine Hunter in his presentation. I complimented him and uttered my total praise. He seemed to be surprised, but I was sincere and proud our organization had such a professional representing us. I also told his co-presenter, a woman in her fifties named Ruth. My praise evoked a response that I find incomprehensible to this day. Ruth said upon hearing my praise, "The first time I laid eyes on you, I knew you were trouble." I'm sure Jim Morgan would find that reaction wasn't dignifying my response according to the principles of Madeleine Hunter.

After almost three decades of BOCES, some students stand out in my mind more than others. Some are comical, and some are tragic. Perhaps the most tragic was a youngster I had in Westlake. He had been adopted, but his parents found him more or less than they bargained for. If there was ever any argument that homosexuality is genetic, I could cite no finer example than Bill. Most of the time he acted like a typical boy, but then his body seemed to contort, as if he were struggling with an inner self. After a number of tics or jerks, his speech would lisp, and his wrist would go limp. He seemed to fail in stifling this side of his personality. His parents wanted to return him, but were unable to do so. When he was in his second year in high school, he ran away to Greenwich Village and supported himself as a chicken hawk, or sold himself to older men. In a few short years, he died of AIDS.

One family was especially notorious in my early years at Westlake. The Bird brothers were like an outlaw mob that terrorized the neighborhood. They came from the Armonk district of Byram Hills and led me to believe that there might be some chemicals in the water there that encouraged rage. David, the older boy, was very quiet, even withdrawn, unless he became upset. His younger brother Greg was gregarious, friendly, and unpredictable. When the assistant principal at Westlake told Greg that his motorcycle wasn't permitted on school grounds, Greg chased him on his bike, until the harried man took refuge by climbing a tree. The principal once intervened when Greg was leaving the school without permission. Greg picked up a large fire extinguisher and advised Jim Mullen, "Either get out of the way or I'll throw this extinguisher through the glass door and leave that way. Jim decided to step aside.

When Greg finally was eligible for graduation, he was determined to celebrate his achievement in style. He and several hundred fellow students from Armonk had a huge beer bust and bon fire. The fire department was summoned to douse the conflagration, and Greg ordered them to leave. They summoned the police who arrested the demonstrator, who then urged his fellow celebrants to besiege the police station. State police and officers from adjacent departments were drafted for reinforcements. One of the officers controlling the canine corps was bitten by his own dog during the melee.

In Westlake Middle School, I shared a classroom with several outstanding teachers, including Liz Rice and Pat Powell. One of our students was a young girl from Jennie Clarkson. A later investigation uncovered that she deliberately threw herself down a flight of stairs and pretended to be unconscious. The police and an ambulance arrived. The young lass was strapped on a gurney and taken to the ambulance. As the policeman was closing up the gurney, he crushed his testicles in the device. Now he too went to the hospital in agony. Our aide accompanied the convoy to Westchester Medical, and her description of the officer stripped to his shorts, but still wearing his gun belt, evoked quite a bit of laughter.

Two Irish American lads were the challenging members of one of my classes in the Counsel Support Program. Scott was fifty per cent of a twin combination. He was nicknamed 'Destroy,' as the complement to his twin who was called 'Search.' The mother of the twins spent her time making novenas to God in hope of peace, but Scott's temper was a force to reckon with. He used to threaten the lunch staff at Westlake about their selection of his preferred hamburger. Usually, he saved his menacing behavior for Basic Occupational Education, but he also had to mail in his assignments to complete his eligibility for graduation. In mid June, he had smashed a beer bottle over the head of someone who crossed his path in Pelham Park, and the police were waiting to arrest him if he appeared in school. In the class he was joined by a tall, lanky fellow from Hastings named, Mike. Together they enjoyed each day thoroughly and managed to complete their high school education.

Denise was a fairly pretty young Black girl from White Plains or Valhalla. One day she brought a stack of studio photos to school featuring her poses in black leather and dominatrix equipment. Fortunately, I had the diplomacy and experience of John Walsh to help explain that perhaps the photographer may not have her best interest in mind. Denise later was arrested for trying to kidnap a baby from the hospital. I guess her naiveté was one of the factors that we never adequately addressed during her time with us.

Two characters from Yonkers introduced me to the difficulties of the Therapeutic Support Program before a second class was added. During their trip up the Saw Mill River Parkway on the Yonker's Special Ed bus, they actually were dismantling a wheelchair with another student confined to it. As they loosened nuts, bolts, removable parts, they tossed them out the window at passing cars. One target was so irate that he tried to get the bus to pull over, but the driver ignored him, and the passengers taunted him from the safety of the van. Determined to get to the end of this farce, he followed the van to Westlake and confronted the boys again. He was threatened further, so he took his complaints to the main office, and he was directed up to my classroom. He was absolutely furious. He said he was the son-in-law of the county executive, and that if he were not satisfied that something would be done to the vandals, he would request a county wide investigation of BOCES busing. Although the carrier was Yonkers and not BOCES, I called the 'Mole' who assessed the problem as demanding instant attention. The target was placated, when he learned that the offenders would be punished to the legal extent of the law.

Rob, one of the mechanical dismantlers, was often in trouble despite the best efforts of his mother, the toothless, biker-chick from Texas. When he was suspended, she used to remove the TV and edibles from a room and lock him inside with a port-a-potty. Despite her extreme measures, Rob was incorrigible. His compatriot was called Elgin, a favorite of the 'Mole.' Elgin really was quite bright, but had little interest in standard education. He confronted Mr. Mullen, told him that he wanted to be transferred back to Rye Lake Campus, or he would start destroying the school building. Jim Mullen decided that the switch was in everyone's best interest, and the next day an instant IEP change took place. Rob was declared 'no program, but he managed to get himself transferred back into Yonkers High, until he was arrested for Grand Theft Auto.

One of the more difficult characters I had to deal with was called Lamont, as in The Batman. Lamont was the only kid I ever heard threaten his probation officer. He also was a good athlete who played running back for Westlake. At one of the football parties, he boasted of having oral sex with the team captain's girlfriend, while locked in the bathroom. Of course all misbehavior was denied by the young damsel. This team captain was the Vice President of the student council. He came into my classroom in search of vengeance, but he was rational, and accepted my advice to take this to the school administration. I was so impressed with this young man for the polite and docile approach he took despite his anger. At the end of the school year, Lamont decided he wanted to play football at Hastings, and he was switched by the 'Mole.' The following September, the clinician at Hastings accused me of dumping my garbage onto her program, an accusation that had some validity when predicated of her. The transfer was totally the instigation and inspiration of our supervisor.

Sometimes I wonder exactly how disturbed some of our population actually was. In a way, I believe I underestimated the degree of emotional disturbance that many of our students exhibited. After graduation BOCES and staff members usually lost contact with the individuals unless the newspapers contained articles about some miscreant or other. Perusing the papers led to the news that several of our graduates had rage outbursts that led to murder, and one case underscored the degree of depression we sometimes had to deal with. One boy whose final image at Westlake was struggling with the assistant principal and me over some issue, later committed suicide by jumping off the roof of the projects in White Plains. Many students now had a bi-polar disorder that made dealing with them unpredictable.

Perhaps, the most notorious was a beautiful blonde, Geena Davis look-a-like. Vicky had been in the Hastings program, but she was reassigned to us for academic 'enrichment,' or so we were told. Her beautiful visage and serene, angelic appearance masked a violent temper beneath the surface. Her greatest boast seemed to be the number of police cars she could summon to her personally generated riots. When her mother asked us not to permit the use of our telephone, she took her anger out on me. She hurled a full can of Pepsi at me, but it harmlessly whistled by my ear. Her next missile was a four foot orange tree that had been grown from seed. As a faculty member, I was fair game for her destructive tendencies, but when she threatened the life and health of another girl in the program, she finally was returned to district as needing a different environment. The target of her attack never returned to Manhattanville, so we actually lost two students for the price of one.

Eric was a foul-mouthed sexist who failed to utter any sentence without an obscenity or profanity. He invariably made inappropriate remarks to the girls in the program. Somehow, he and I managed to co-exist without too much animosity, but his remarks to female staff members led to his dismissal. He had been given permission to drive to class, and his lateness, absence, and occasional snoozing in his automobile led to the unlikelihood of a timely graduation. The group believed he should be returned to White Plains and placed on homebound instruction to complete the modest credits he needed for graduation. If he stayed with us, his attendance and misbehavior would most likely interfere with his graduation. Since he was in my home room, I was asked to present our case to his Committee on Special Education. I was accompanied by our clinician who was the messianic replacement for Rachelle. At the session, Eric disagreed with the plan and claimed he was the target of discrimination. I was able to explain the situation to him and to the committee in a rational, sensible way. At the end of the meeting, the clinician was overwhelmingly effusive in her praise on how I handled the issue. I listened to her exuberant eulogy and thought to myself, "You have no idea who I am, or what I can do. You have consistently dismissed my capabilities and talents and relied exclusively on the estimate of the Mole." That thought permeated my perception of where I fit into the scheme of things in the Therapeutic Support Program. At one point in Westlake, one of the teachers and I were having a soul searching, intense, professional conversation. She concluded that I was the biggest waste of talent in the entire school. I didn't know whether she intended the comment as a compliment or a condemnation, but I did realize that so few knew what talents I possessed.

A triad of individuals from Dobbs Ferry and Hastings added a special flavor to our program. One, a boy named Nick, had been severely mugged and beaten over the head with a lead pipe. In his first year, Nick was warehoused at Westlake, for he did no work and participated in no classes. I agitated for his return to district, since we were doing nothing for him. The next year, Nick demonstrated that the vagaries of performance were very unpredictable, for he settled down and became a fine student. In his final year, however, he had met a Jamaican woman who moved in with him and her allure distracted him from coming to school. His attendance became very erratic, although when present, he worked well. Nonetheless, when he amassed about seventy day's absence, I questioned whether he could graduate. The following year, I included a variable determining grades that addressed the attendance issue. Nick went on to a junior college somewhere near Rochester where he seemed to major in cow-tipping.

Steve was a clown, easy going and ready to laugh and enjoy life. When I spoke with his mother upon his entrance into the program, I advised her that we could not provide a Cadillac or BMW equivalent of an education, since we lacked foreign language or even science lab facilities. I assured her, however, that we could provide the educational equivalent of a serviceable Ford or Chevy. Steve instead insisted on a Yugo. He very accurately estimated the minimal amount of work he would have to do in order to pass. He was uncanny in his ability to zero in on minimal expectations. Finally, he did get his Yugo, and I understand he was hired to work for BOCES.

Gerry was probably the most unpredictable personality I ran into in the TSP. He had no respect for school rules or procedures, and mostly contempt for those who attempted to teach him. He was, however, quite bright when he focused on academics. That focus was rare, for he excelled in other ways of demonstrating his individuality. One of his favorite exercises was pulling his heavy winter coat over his head and playing teepee. He would light a cigarette and smoke it in the classroom and expel smoke signals through the opening atop his head. On several occasions, I found him lying on the floor in the back of the classroom. He had strewn multiple complimentary copies of **USA Today** in a pile and would extend a hand cadging money. He claimed he was training for his future as a homeless vagabond. Dobbs

Ferry concluded they were wasting tax payers' money on Gerry, so he was withdrawn from program after a year. Shortly thereafter, he was a guest of the penal system in Westchester County.

Despite the serious efforts to evaluate candidates for our program, we occasionally were hoodwinked. One particularly charming individual from Ossining led us to believe that he had been mistreated and misjudged, but he had seen the error of his ways, and was ready to address his education seriously. Actually, I believe he was anxious to find a market for his drugs. Anyway, we accepted Darnell and discovered that we had more than we bargained for. He had intimidated most of the students in the program and established a reputation as a genuine thug. His personality, however, was quite congenial, and he managed to get along with those he thought essential to his business. Unknown to us for some time, he also carried a gun to school everyday. Finally, Jim Mullen insisted he be reassigned, so he was sent back to Ossining where he was arrested for firing his weapon at police officers who came to his house.

One of our students might indicate some of the difficulties BOCES had in its admission problems. For some districts, the more devastating description of behavior guaranteed a quicker resolution to their placement request. The student might not resemble the character described in his application, or he might have been the victim of a particular individual's ire. This student was the converse. He was described as docile and cooperative generally. When he arrived, he acted appropriately most of the time, but when he was upset or felt insulted, he could not be placated. He would physically attack his perceived tormentor. What his application failed to mention was the fact that his actual reason for expulsion was bringing a gun to school to exact revenge on an individual. Despite my many conversations with him, John who wore his dead grandparents' rosaries around his neck, insisted that no one could insult him and remain untouched. The rosaries, by the way, were the only things his grandparents did for him or so he said. When he demanded revenge for an imagined slight, he was identified as "no program" and placed on homebound instruction. Later we learned that the school district social worker while dealing with John's incident married his mother and sanitized the application. Despite his unique speech pattern, he decided to stick up his local deli store behind a mask that did little to shield or disguise his idiosyncratic voice. The shopkeeper identified him without trouble. He became another guest of Westchester jail shortly after leaving us

A major stumbling block to progress seems to be the slow reaction to a serious problem within BOCES. We were advised that meetings were required for the reassignment within BOCES or any program change. In reality, it was much simpler, when politics were involved. Pat Murphy had a depressed student who wandered the halls of the high school listening to his portable radio. As often as Pat asked for assistance, he was denied or put off until Jimmy decided to occupy the polling booth during a budget vote at Westlake. John Whearty, the superintendent, caught sight of this forlorn creature and demanded an instant IEP removing him from the school. Pat and I used to jest about adjusting handicapping conditions to suit the needs of the class. A bizarre sense of humor or dark side helped us cope with some of the daily travails. We actually enjoyed putting on the 'Tiger' when we would discuss some of our plans.

Sometimes, in reading the background of those applying for admission to the program, one could detect serious problems and at other times, it seemed the individual had scratched the wrong person, be that a particular teacher, an administrator, or some important person. Some accounts were also bowdlerized to hide the truth. Sometimes an individual had a special advocate, especially if that person was a private psychologist or social worker, or had done individualized testing for the person. One such case concerned a huge boy who entered our program with a history of violence. At Manhattanville, we used to have a full Thanksgiving dinner, and on this day, the huge fellow knocked over a student who literally soiled his pants as a result. I was confined to a room with the aggressor and watched his 'non-violent' persona in action. He tore telephones out of the wall, yanked fire extinguishers, and cleared desks of paperwork, and finally threatened our teaching assistant. I had established myself as the block to the exiting door which he was able to dislodge fairly easily. Finally, the teaching assistant threatened him, and said the issue wasn't over yet. The kid went berserk again, but I urged our staff member to leave the room while we dealt with the enraged student.

A full scale investigation resulted. The 'Mole' wanted to know what happened, but really didn't. I told him I was too busy surviving to notice all that was occurring. About a month later, a superintendent's hearing was scheduled with testimony and cross examination from lawyers. I told the 'Mole' that if I were placed under oath, I would have to admit that I heard the kid threatened, and that indeed, the assistant had waved a finger in his face and said, "This is not over." I was notified that it probably wouldn't come to that, but we had to go to Berkeley Drive anyway. At the last moment, the hearing was cancelled.

Maybe, I never could commit myself wholeheartedly to the organization, and my biases are unjustified. Yet I recall the positives from the years prior to my TSP experience. I have remained in contact with few of my confreres ever since my retirement. The joy I always had in teaching was seldom fueled by my BOCES experiences. Instead, I thoroughly enjoyed my adjunct work at The School of New Resources of the College of New Rochelle and at Bergen Community College. I even relished the teaching of merit badge certification among cub scouts and boy scouts. I savored the opportunity to coach girls' basketball teams for my parish and invested some time in teaching religion. Teaching was what I did, and what I enjoyed. Sometimes my BOCES life didn't permit much of that. Still I have to recall some of the occasional students who stand out for one reason or another. Since I know of few who were successful, I suppose most will be of a negative style. I probably could summarize my synopsis by recalling a statement of a nineteen year old applicant who invited us to, "Call me Mayhem." Sometimes I think that he encapsulated so much of what occurred. The men and women who executed the program demands have almost exclusively won my admiration. Most of the clinicians and supportive staff have my respect. Administrators who remained chained to their central offices may not have known what actually took place, and toward the end of my time in BOCES, most of them were fleeing the organization as quickly as possible. Even our last superintendent, Dr. Beni, left for a more lucrative position. I had known him as a teacher in Westlake Middle School, and I thought he was the most talented and capable potential administrator I encountered. He had the personality, the ambition, and the skills to relate to staff and student alike. When he sought an administrative position, I even gave him two leads which led to nowhere. I was delighted to learn he was our superintendent, but my delight turned to disappointment. The last message I recall hearing from him was that we were too expensive for many districts. I realized that our rating on pay scale had descended significantly from when I first entered BOCES. I thought our new motto ought to be, "Give us the students you don't want or can't handle, and we'll deal with them for less than what you pay your teachers."

For almost three decades, I earned a decent salary that enabled me to raise and educate my family. I had to find emotional satisfaction elsewhere, however. In summarizing my days at BOCES, I thank God for the many wonderful individuals I met. I pray that I was helpful to most of those entrusted to my care, and I justify my pay by realizing I gave what I thought was the best I could do under the circumstances. In honesty, nonetheless, I must confess that those twenty-nine years were mostly a means to an end rather than an end in itself. During that time, one of my chief apparently unrecognized achievements was the assistance in developing at least five of my aides into certified Special Education teachers. Perhaps I did better with aides than I did with students, but no one knows much about the future of our graduates. Upon my retirement, I think little of my days as a BOCES teacher. I have fond memories of most, but my experiences pale when I compare what I experienced when I taught as a Brother in the Bronx.

Chapter Twelve

Recollections

During the fall of 1970, I was adrift, but not irrational. When I left the community of anchorites to unite forces with the traditional sybarite culture of the revolutions of the sixties, I did not succumb to the mentality of what was supposedly happening. Swinging singles bars were not my style, and I never considered myself an Adonis or God's gift to women. If truth be told, I wasn't too different from the mid teen who entered religious life, but now I was determined to find my life's soul mate as soon as possible. My fifteen years in the religious life had been exceedingly meaningful, but they also had left me socially inept and unprepared for a world that was quite alien to my usual 'modus operandi.' Fortunately, there were many who had preceded me into the social whirl and were anxious to help me. Believe me; I needed all the help I could get.

My approach to dating was quite simplistic but rational. I didn't want to waste time chasing women who were indifferent, or perhaps even hostile to my religious background. I resolved that the best tactic in my quest for a lifetime companion was to concentrate on those who had similar experiences, such as former nuns. Several friends abetted my search by arranging meetings with women who had spent years in the convent and had decided recently to leave, like myself. Some candidates stand out in my recollection, but not all impressed me with the qualities I avidly sought. One former nun spent an evening singing paeans to pot. That hardly impressed me, for I envisioned years of reefer rot down the road. Another nominee raved about a Jesuit community associated with Union Theological Seminary, and I determined rapidly that time with her was ill-spent. A young woman who came from outside my designated target group showed the difference that existed between the standard mores of that period and me. She suggested a romantic weekend in Miami. I don't know whether the prospect of the exorbitant expense, or the accompanying romantic implications threatened my moral fiber more. I did go out with her several times although the weekend never occurred, but our relationship ended abruptly with a telephone call. She told me that an ex-boyfriend had proposed marriage, and she didn't know what to say. My curt advice was neither helpful nor intended to be spiteful. I merely said, "When you make up your mind, let me know." That was the last time I heard from her, and I know she ended up accepting the wedding proposal. Could I claim to be a pawn in their gamesmanship?

I can't say that I had no candidates who were interested in me. My failure to respond to their overtures was more the result of ineptitude than intentional insult. When threatened, I retreated. Finally, however, the process of meeting a soul mate came to an excellent conclusion on October 24, 1971. Even that relationship exposed my maladroit approach to romance.

From the end of June, 1971, Joe and Dorothy Hosey had been telling me about a young lady who had left the Blauvelt Dominicans at the conclusion of the school year. Both indicated that she and I shared many common traits and would make an excellent couple. With a recommendation of that magnitude, it was certainly worth my personal scrutiny as soon as possible. Nonetheless, I procrastinated or deferred for several reasons. Primarily, I was busy taking a course at NYU in American Economic History Since the Civil War, and the proposed candidate was teaching in a summer camp somewhere in the lower Catskills. I had also programmed a cross country camping trip with Ed Phelan, Don Smith, and Brian O'Neill from St. Augustine's.

After my course at NYU ended, we embarked on our venture 'West of the Hudson." When I complained to Ed that I thought our vehicle, a two door Volvo, was heavily laden with a huge roof rack containing luggage and camping gear, and the back trunk was jammed with accoutrements of all sorts, Ed promised to lighten the load. He removed an extra roll of toilet paper and asserted that the car was now ready for transcontinental duty. The camping expedition held many interesting stopovers. We battled floods in Mammoth Cave, Kentucky, bears in the Blue Ridge Mountains, snakes in Lake Talladega, Alabama, scorpions in Carlsbad Caverns,

New Mexico, drought in the Grand Canyon, spaced out druggies and motorcyclists in Big Sur, and car trouble near Truth or Consequences, New Mexico. We broke a fan belt twenty miles from the nearest town. An elderly pecan farmer happened by in a pickup truck that he might have bought as a teenager. He also was accompanied by a gigantic German shepherd. Like the rules of the sea, I suppose, desert etiquette required him to inquire whether we needed help. Either that, or Ed Phelan's Guardian Angel was working overtime. The codger said, "Ain't picked up nobody in twenty years. Don't know why I stopped for you." He added that locals didn't especially appreciate bearded hippies out of New York causing trouble in the vicinity. When we assured him we were indeed teachers and not drug addled revolutionaries, he invited Ed and me to join him in a trip to Hatch, New Mexico. He drove us to a gas station where we bought a replacement and left a deposit on a huge wrench which would enable us to adjust the belt in the Volvo engine. Then he added, "I best drive you back out to your car, 'cause ain't nobody going to pick you two up." First he had to stop at his home to explain his delayed schedule to his wife, and then we reversed the trip with the hound panting heavily upon our necks. When we arrived at the car, he refused any money for his kindness and wished us luck. We replaced the fan belt, tightened it properly with the wrench, and then returned it to the gas station to reclaim the twenty dollars deposit. His charity was one of the pleasant recollections of our jaunt.

One of my reasons for the cross country trek was to serve as godfather for my brother's as yet unborn baby. Shortly before we arrived at Travis Air Base, Noreen was born, and I performed magnificently in the ceremony with Evelyn's sister Kathy acting as proxy for her older sister Mary Joe who was with the Madames of the Sacred Heart in Rome. Despite the distractions of a newborn, Evelyn was a considerate hostess although she described our sleeping accommodations as 'the goat room' because of the residual odors from two weeks on the road. Although we would stay at an occasional Brothers' house or school along the way, most of the lodging was at campgrounds. We did enjoy our unannounced arrivals at the facilities of Brothers in Columbus, Ohio, Covington, Louisiana, San Antonio, Texas, Sangre De Cristo in New Mexico and Pasadena, California. On our return trip we included stops among the Brothers at Detroit, Michigan and Syracuse, New York.

Bernie and Evelyn insisted on a special trip to an unforgettable restaurant. *Juanita's* belonged to a former madam from Sausalito who had been run out of that up and coming community. She relocated to somewhere near Sonoma, California, where she purchased a huge farm house. Her restaurant was unique insofar as chickens, ducks, dogs, cats and other fauna like foxes, enjoyed the freedom to roam throughout the dining area. Perhaps, the décor might be described as "*Nouveau Animaux.*" We all ordered the house specialty, which were prodigious portions of prime rib that may have been waved once or twice over a low flame. First, we had the selection of many options from a self-service salad bar where the items and dressings were stored in former hospital bed pans, identified immediately by Kathy McAdams using her expertise as a registered nurse. That didn't whet the appetite, nor did the huge portions of raw meat. At the end of the meal, the waitress wrapped the leftovers in doggie bags that were designed to look like roosters. The grand finale of the dining experience at *Juanita's* was meeting with the proprietress who laid sprawled in a king size bed with an enormous mongrel for company. When we went to pay the bill, she selected Ed Phelan for unusual attention. As Ed stood at the foot of her bed holding his doggie bag, she uttered the immoral challenge to a man who probably wasn't addressed quite the same way at anytime in his holy life. Juanita asked why he was standing there with his cock in his hand. Ed knew better than get involved in repartee with this veteran of many such encounters.

Despite Bernard's determination that we sample every vintage known to the Napa Valley oenophile, and examine the Air Force's newest behemoth, the C5A, and inspect its 'green meatball' navigation system, we had to leave shortly. After the Christening, we headed eastward through Lake Tahoe to Salt Lake City. After a long drive through the Nevada desert to the mountains east of Salt Lake City, we discovered our projected campground had closed to the public. We were advised to head to the top of the mountain where there was a large meadow suitable for camping. When we arrived at the summit, we encountered scores of Latter Day Saint teenagers engaged in revelry and conduct unbecoming the followers of Joseph Smith and Brigham Young. Rather than pitch a tent under those circumstances, we drove halfway down the mountain to a picnic ground. Ed and Don decided to sleep in the reclining seats of the Volvo, and Brian and I resolved to risk foraging beasts by sleeping on picnic tables. In the morning, both Don and Ed emerged in pain, each expressing the belief that he had not slept a wink because of the movements or snoring of the other. Don actually implored us to drive him to the nearest airport, which we reluctantly did.

The morning after dropping Don at the Salt Lake City Airport, we headed north toward Pocatello, Idaho and the Snake River. We followed the river until we stopped at Jackson Hole in the shadow of the Grand Tetons. The view was gorgeous, but just a harbinger of what was to come. Yellowstone National Park was clearly the most impressive view of pristine America that we observed during our expedition. The cliff dwellings of Bandolier National Park, the huge Caverns at Carlsbad, the shoreline of Monterrey, the sheer beauty of Tahoe, and even the deserts made no impression comparable to the boiling cauldrons and explosive geysers of the thermal springs surrounded by mountains, waterfalls, rivers, lakes and forests. As we encountered bison, wapiti, bears, moose, antelopes, and deer, the wonder of the natural setting was only enhanced. We stayed as long as we could, but the journey through the Little Big Horn, Wyoming, and South Dakota was hot and enervating so much that we sprang for a motel in Rapid City. There, we treated ourselves at a Woolworth's counter to the finest breakfast of the trip.

After Yellowstone, the trip was anti-climactic and even prosaic. Ten thousand miles, four flats, one fractured fan belt, one desperate evacuee in Utah, a plea for me to start smoking again in New Orleans, old and new friends, gorgeous scenery, propositions in Las Vegas, intimate and intimidations with nature—all within a month, and we were still on speaking terms. Now, however, each of us had responsibilities to fulfill. I would begin a horrendous year at Rye Lake Campus in BOCES, but that was more than compensated for by my introduction to the woman of my dreams.

After so many laudatory comments about Mary Burke, I still postponed meeting her, until I had enrolled for my American Intellectual History course and had begun my purgatory in BOCES. In my own self-inflicted 'rules of engagement,' I also had to fulfill my promises to those who had offered to introduce me to people they thought I ought to get to know better. Finally, I met Mary in the Hosey household. My initial reaction was awe. Here was a vision of Celtic beauty—tall, slender, dark haired, deep hazel eyes, with facial features and complexion enhanced by generations of heather scented breezes, and the soft mist of an Irish day. She was clad in a comfortable blue denim pants suit that bespoke comfort and ease. I was immediately smitten, and I determined to marry this woman I barely knew. Her conversation exposed an intelligence and wit accompanying an ironic sense of humor, and most extraordinarily, an understanding of the peculiarities of my own style.

As Mary spoke, I visualized the many parallels between our lives. For just about as long as I had taught as a Christian Brother, Mary had done the same as a Blauvelt Dominican nun. Her ministry had taken her to St. Pius in the South Bronx, to several schools in Florida, and finally to Holy Cross on the Westside in Midtown Manhattan. Most of her time had been dedicated to the poor and needy, except in Florida where she taught the children of space age engineers associated with NASA. She also was actively pursuing her doctorate in Biology at Fordham University. In fact, she had a subsistence wage as a Lab Assistant in Fordham that supplemented her income as a research scientist studying the marine biology of a lake in Armonk, as well as the Hudson River fisheries. Aside from her graduate studies and employment, she also was a weekly teacher in a school on 14th Street. Certainly very busy and barely ably to pay her rent, she exhibited the ambition and determination that I so admired. Impressed with her work schedule and future plans, I hoped to be part of both.

As our conversations broadened, I also uncovered parallels in cultural and religious backgrounds. Like my father, her father had left Ireland in search of a better life. Born in Balnamona Cottage in Shanballymore, County Cork, Tom Burke sought modest success in America. Like his brothers, Mike and Paul in Chicago, and his older brother Dick in New York, Tom hoped to find employment and a future that included greater economic security in America. He had found both with Con Edison, for whom he worked for forty-four years. In Cork, Tom had little time for the recreation of the wealthy, which included the introduction of the steeplechase race. Shanballymore lay between the church steeples of Doneraile and Buttevant where the first steeplechase race occurred. Instead, America beckoned most of the older male children of the family while Tom's sisters married several local farmers, and his brother Johnny, the youngest, become the sole occupant of Balnamona Cottage in later years.

Around the corner from St. Augustine's Church, at a rooming house offering accommodations by Jack O'Leary's mother to newly arrived Irish immigrants on Boston Road, Tom met a fellow boarder named Kathleen Durkin who would become his bride. Kathleen shared many similarities with my own mother too. She was born at the foot of the Ox Mountains about six miles east of Ballina in County Mayo. About twenty miles northwest of that spot, my mother was born and raised in Ballygarry near Kilcummin Head where Killala Bay and the river Moy empty into the Atlantic. When Kathleen learned that an older farmer had offered a huge dowry to claim her as his bride, she wrote immediately to her own father working in America. Kathleen requested passage to America instead of a marriage she didn't want. Her father had been born in Philadelphia, but his family returned to Bonniconlon in Mayo, and he raised a large family there despite his employment on a coastal packet boat on the east coast of the United States. His job on board ship provided money for his family, and many of his neighbors found a sympathetic source when they were hard pressed for cash.

Kathleen in her later years enjoyed telling the tale of her trip to America. Her father had sent her a first class ticket on an Atlantic steamer, but she was so unfamiliar with the menu choices that she subsisted on tea and toast, until she arrived in New York. After a brief tenure in Waterbury, Connecticut, she returned to New York where she stayed at the boarding house of her cousin, Mrs. Margaret O'Leary on Boston Road. Kathleen began working for Bell Telephone as an operator, and she remained there for many years, retiring only to take a similar position with National Distillers.

With a family from a similar background to my own, I realized that Mary and I were products of an environment that cherished the Catholic Church and Irish culture. Assured that she was the object of my quest, I resolved to marry this wonderful woman as soon as possible. Nonetheless, my highly undeveloped sense of romanticism played second fiddle to my convictions that I had to keep my word in the self-imposed 'rules of engagement.' Before I could secure my quest, I had to fulfill my obligations to those I promised to see. Ignoring the possibility that I might lose out on the grand prize, I pursued some other candidates, only in perfunctory satisfaction of my promise. It wasn't until about six weeks later, near Thanksgiving, that I got around to calling Mary and asking for a date. Despite her busy schedule and mine, we managed to agree on a day or two after Thanksgiving.

Again, my notion of romanticism needed a common sense boost which it didn't have. Instead of attempting to impress the woman I was determined to marry, I selected a rather pedestrian Italian, neighborhood restaurant frequented by the Brothers, but with no other major advantages to boast of. With hundreds of world renowned restaurants in New York City, I selected one with the ambiance of kitsch, with cheap wall paper featuring either Neapolitan or Venetian scenes. There was little danger of interrupting Jackie O or Henry Kissinger, or one of the beautiful people in this small eatery on Mount Eden Avenue in the Bronx where the food may have been plentiful, but hardly of the gourmet type. During the meal, I outlined my marital plans to Mary and explained that I wasn't interested in wasting time if she were uninterested in me. She noted that she had left the Dominican nuns barely five months earlier, and she believed any commitment might be impetuous, but she didn't dismiss the possibility. As I sat back and savored the wisdom of her comment as well as the possibility of success, the ambiance of the eatery came to the fore. Passing within inches of our table, a kitchen worker dragged a swill pail across the floor and into the back exit. Fortunately none of the slippery, slime slopped onto our table, probably the result of Providence rather than care. Of such romantic influences are memories recorded. Mary and I laughed at the intrusion, but thought it was symptomatic of my sense of romance-from the sublime to the ridiculous in seconds, or so it seemed.

For the next several weeks, we continued to see each other, while we explored neighborhood cinemas and beaneries. I thought nothing of introducing Mary to movie theaters that had seen better days. Comfortable in the South Bronx, I took her to see several films at the 167th Crosstown and Luxor Theaters on 170th near the Concourse. I suppose the apex of my romantic spots was the Loew's Paradise near Fordham Road. While we got to know each other a little better, I recognized that Mary had great potential for income, but that the reality was more like food stamps. Calling upon her one evening, I saw the undissected shark in her kitchen that she had brought home to prepare for a lab experiment at Fordham University. Her apartment ceiling on Creston Avenue collapsed onto the floor when she wasn't home, and she drove a Dodge 'bomb,' a virtual wreck that a friend had given to her. She was on a first name basis with every AAA tow truck driver in the Bronx, for her car generally needed a jump start on any cold morning. As I drove it one day, I banged my knee on the dashboard and the entire instrument panel fell in my lap.

I also suffered the demise of my beloved Volvo that had served us faithfully on our cross country travels. One evening in early December, as I drove home from class at NYU, a man in a Cadillac bisected the front of my car totaling the miserable wretch. I had to replace it with a new car, and I selected a Camaro. It did little to enhance my romantic image, however. When I first drove up to Creston Avenue to collect Mary for a dining experience that was forgettable, I parked, and then returned with her shortly thereafter. I fumbled with the keys and was unable to open the door, until Mary notified me that I had selected the wrong Camaro. She heard me describe the car as silver while I was attempting to enter a white one. Once I found the correct car nearby, the fiasco continued. An essential cotter pin in the brand new vehicle had been dislodged, and I couldn't shift the gears. I had to open the hood, push or pull levers as Mary maneuvered the car out of a tight parking space. Finally, with the two of us operating in tandem, we got on the road as I muttered something about new cars.

Our dating continued, however, and on December 10th I had invited her to accompany me to Ted Aronson's holiday party on Riverdale Avenue. Every Christmas season, Ted hosted a party for the Westlake faculty and selected members of BOCES. We enjoyed the party, and afterwards, I repeated my wish to get married. Catching me off guard, Mary agreed this time, so we officially became engaged in the early hours of December 11, 1971. As yet, we had not introduced each other to our families, and few knew about our plans. Indeed, when Mary told her mother she was engaged, the information seemed to slip right over her head until 2:30am when she called and asked Mary to clarify exactly what she had said.

On my part, I introduced Mary to my family, which pretty much by this time in New York was reduced to my brother Ray and his family. Ray actually knew Mary's brother John and they had several mutual acquaintances from Tolentine days. When Kathleen Burke invited us to meet her, we had a pleasant dinner. I foolishly asked Tom permission to marry his daughter, and the laconic man said something like I was going to do what I wished any way, so don't bother him. I suppose I did little to impress my future father-in-law. At one point in our conversation when Ray called me "a horse's ass," Tom said that was one point with which he agreed. Either my skin was thick enough from the parrying thrusts of community life, or I was so elated over the future prospects of my marriage, Tom's commentary had little impact upon me.

Tom was a very distinguished man given to formality in most of his interaction with people. Taciturn and very personal, he rarely showed much emotion. Although evidently intelligent, he never spoke of his formal education so he could have had only a rudimentary schooling or had attended Maynooth. As far as I could tell, he had little connection to sports, but he had an avid, all consuming interest in politics and the news, especially on the national level. His concern about sporting events only went so far as whether their schedule impacted *Sixty Minutes* or *Meet The Press*. He pored through magazines and newspapers to obtain his information and was a devotee of the evening news with Tom Brokaw. Missing the evening news was almost tantamount to skipping Mass on a Sunday. Despite his assimilation of so much political news, Tom seldom offered any opinions, and avoided discussions or exchange of points of view. Although his voting record was private, I doubt he ever voted any ticket but Democratic. Given his characteristics, it strikes me that Tom would have made an excellent talk show host eliciting responses from penetrating questions without any personal editorializing or commentary. Perhaps his residual Corkonian accent would have added a special dimension to round table discussions on television.

At six feet four inches, Tom had a sinewy build that hid enormous strength. Always energetic, he handled a sledge hammer in the destruction of a concrete slab with efficient short strokes that did three times the damage as my imitation of the legendary John Henry from songdom. He reputedly took the same approach in his constant cleaning, painting, and maintaining his apartment on Andrews Avenue near Fordham Road. To fuel this toiling machine, Tom ate prodigious meals served according to a pre-ordained schedule. With rake or shovel in hand, he seemed most relaxed whenever he visited our home. Always a creature of habit and routine, he usually kept in shape by long walks. In the years I knew him, I never heard him speak ill of anyone, nor did I hear anyone say anything negative about him.

On the other hand, Kathleen, my mother-in-law, sometimes seemed painfully aware of her brief exposure to formal education in Ireland. Unlike Tom, however, she engaged in social conversation enthusiastically, and displayed familiarity with the issues of the day. She would muse, however, that in the demands of a rural farm in Ireland, her chores and assistance in taking care of her younger siblings took precedence of 'nouns and pronouns.' She also focused proudly on the accomplishments of her children and demonstrated concern for the progress of her grandchildren. Kathleen seemed to enjoy doing the household chores that others found repugnant or time consuming. When she came to visit us, in a short time after an introductory chat about family, she could be found dusting lamp shades, cleaning Waterford crystal, or sewing delicate items in need of a 'stitch in time.' Unlike her husband, Kathleen kept her extended family in Ireland, England, and the States, informed about familial matters. She seemed to coordinate tales of the sick, the celebrations, the mourning, and the worries of all her relatives. Yet gossip wasn't her thing, for her role was more of the sympathetic ear than the nosy relative. Kathleen also had a number of religious devotions that she followed carefully, believing in the intervention of God in the affairs of mankind.

In a short time, I got to meet Mary's sister Fran and her husband Bill Hynes and their newly adopted son, John. They had just purchased a large house in Pelham, and they offered it as a potential site for our projected wedding and reception. I drove to Mary's brother John's house in Central Valley to pick up some Christmas decorations packed in an egg carton. To my embarrassment, I could barely find an area large enough in the interior of the Camaro to put the carton. The trunk had no space, and the back seat was quite small too. Fortunately, Mary saw humor in the situation, as did her brother who congratulated me with the sibling statement, "So you're the poor simpleton who's going to marry Mary."

Our Christmas season passed rapidly while we planned a June wedding. Since I had inherited a third of my father's insurance upon his death, I already had a sum of money that could be invested in a house. Thus, Mary and I decided a cheap date might incorporate some house hunting. Our impetuosity put a rapid end to that plan, for we became enamored with the very first house we inspected. It appealed to us because of its description. The realtors called it a 'splanch,' for it was actually a split level ranch. As we entered the foyer we were attracted by the spacious living room and recreation area about four steps below. The overriding impression was one of space. The kitchen and dining area were attractive, but what appealed most to us was actually a one car garage and a guaranteed parking slot in the driveway. Coming out of the Bronx, one could be most relieved that alternate side of the street parking and circling blocks could be a preoccupation of the past.

We went to dinner in Piermont and concluded that we should make a bid for the house. By the time we made that decision, another couple had made an offer, and it had been accepted even though ours was higher. The seller felt his word was important. We were encouraged to put in a contingency bid, which we did. A few days later, the original buyers retracted their bid, and we were offered the house. As Fifth Avenue reverberated to the strains of the Irish pipers on St. Patrick's Day, we closed on the house in the law office of Buzzy Ronan, a good friend of my brother's and the attorney who represented my father's estate.

With a house now, we decorated mostly with '*nouveau junque*,' and whatever castoffs were available. I moved out of McLean Avenue, but Mary retained her apartment on Creston Avenue. Weekends now were spent in painting and cleaning the house. Our wedding plans did not progress as smoothly as our house buying did. Fortunately, Father John Fleming offered St. Augustine's Church for our wedding site, for the prospects of a home wedding were out of the question, and the use of Fordham Chapel had too many strings attached for our taste. Father Eugene Ahner, a priest who was studying at Fordham but living among the Brothers in Augustine, agreed to be the celebrant. Since I dreaded dancing, I insisted that we have none at the wedding, and therefore we needed no band. The generosity of Fran and Bill Hynes in offering their new home in Pelham was deeply appreciated.

When I decided to rent a tuxedo for the wedding my lack of class surfaced again. I canvassed Fordham Road and found a shop where I selected a combination that was more appropriate for a mariachi player than a groom. My brother Ray was livid at my choice, so I blame that sartorial man of unquestionable taste, Brother Ed Phelan who had accompanied me to the tuxedo shop. My frilly blue shirt and white jacket with black piping apparently was *tres gauche*, but I didn't know any better. The week before our June 25, 1972 wedding featured hurricane rains and flooding throughout Westchester, but the rented tent in the Hynes' backyard proved impervious to the onslaught. On the wedding day itself, we had decent sunshine, making the age of St. Augustine Church a little less apparent. Many of our guests were former parishioners, so the venue lent another element to their return. A number of my former students and friends also made the wedding more colorful. My future father-in-law's fears about rooftop snipers proved unfounded.

At the reception everyone seemed to have a delightful time, enjoying the casual atmosphere and mobile seating arrangements. Some preferred the interior of the house, but most stayed close to the bar and the food. Mary and I enjoyed the reception very much, but I had little notion of how much expense and confusion had gone into this kind of reception, a novelty at its time. Kathleen and Tom Burke were very kind and generous, and Fran and Bill tolerated the Irish singing and carousing of the O'Prey guests. Mary and I finally left around ten pm, and to my embarrassment, I got lost on my way to our house now in West Nyack where we planned to spend our wedding night before heading off on an automobile tour of Canada and the Maritime Provinces.

Our itinerary was plain and open to change. We had a new 1972 Camaro, and our schedule led us wherever whimsy indicated the time and location. We visited Saratoga, Lake George, Lake Placid, Montreal, Quebec, and into the wilds of northern Maine when we decided to head through Moncton, New Brunswick and into the Maritime Provinces. A ferry brought us from Antigonish, Nova Scotia into Prince Edward Island. On our return trip we opted for a viewing of the John Cabot Trail, and then a ferry ride from Yarmouth, Nova Scotia to Portland, Maine. The day for the tour of the trail was a combination of heavy rain and fog, so we took a long central route to the ferry at Yarmouth. After considerable driving we arrived late in the evening and booked passage for the first morning ferry. Since we were quite tired from all the motoring, I, being a big sport, also booked a stateroom where we could recover during the eight hour crossing of the Bay of Fundy.

After a cursory nap in the tiered bunks, we decided to try our luck at the gambling options during the time the ship was in international waters. Like the gazelle from the scriptures one occasionally hears read about in weddings, I arose from the top bunk with élan and enthusiasm. In my zest, I pushed off the top bunk, banged my head upon the bulkhead and crashed backward against the iron bunk thoroughly bruising my right hamstring. I could barely move my leg. After drinking a gallon of water, I hobbled out of the berth and onto the gaming floor. As time passed, my mobility decreased so much that I couldn't move my leg at all. Mary had to drive the car off the ferry and complete the journey back to New York, while I moaned in pain the entire way. My macho image, if ever I had one, took a terrible hit from that experience. Fortunately, within a few days my leg had healed sufficiently for me to gimp around and even drive.

One person whom I never impressed in our early marriage was my beloved father-in-law. Tom Burke found me a total enigma, and he apparently harbored many misgivings about the wisdom his younger daughter exhibited in marrying me. Like many Irishmen of his generation, Tom had a minor thirst that could be quenched by a few boilermakers, a concoction of Ballantine or Schaefer Beer and a shot of Seagram's. I didn't share his enthusiasm for the drink, and thereby raised some concerns he had about my manhood or integrity. Despite his many invitations to join him for a few, I always made some silly excuse for not partaking. Tom didn't say much, but his mutterings began to take a toll upon his newest son-in-law. Finally, Tom's brother Mike visited on his way back from Ireland to Chicago, and Tom was vehemently insistent that I join him in at least one drink. I submitted, and he poured me a Texas jigger that could unhorse a committed alcoholic. As Tom was distracted, I deposited most of my drink into a nearby plant.

Later in the evening, Tom's celebration led to a minor accident when he fell and had to be taken by ambulance to Mount Vernon Hospital. Naturally, we accompanied him. While he was being examined, he had to go to the bathroom, and his least favorite in-law was ordered by the doctor to accompany him to the men's room. While Tom relieved himself, I supposed he wondered what kind of man I was, since I observed him closely and carried on a conversation with him. He refused treatment, and we returned to Pelham. In the morning, I was summoned to his room where the bruises and broken ribs felt quite sore. Tom said to me, "Kathleen says I owe you an apology. I don't know what I said or did, but I apologize." I assured him that everything was fine.

As time progressed, I believe Tom and I saw more eye to eye, and my stock rose considerably. The 'bearded weirdo' from the Bronx proved to be at least of average intelligence and good judgment most of the time. As far as I was concerned, Tom was one of the finest men I ever met, and as a father-in-law, he was unsurpassed. His wife Kathleen also was superb and never judgmental or offering a great deal of advice. Over the years I was grateful that my children had the opportunity to know at least their maternal grandparents, since my parents had died before I had even met Mary.

One of Tom's characteristics was a precision in dress that presented the image of a man far beyond his income. Tom believed that a midnight blue suit and a dapper hat matched his beautiful blue eyes, so all his clothes offered that combination. He is the only man I know who insisted on painting with an ironed white shirt and dress tie. Often he worked on my lawn in his suit and tie. When he helped me build a cement patio in West Nyack on a day when the thermometer passed 95 degrees, his concession to the heat was doffing his suit coat but continuing to mix cement in his trademark spotless shirt and tie and hat.

His wife Kathleen was also very meticulous in her style, as well as perfectly coifed in her hair. Kathleen was very generous believing "There won't be any money to argue over when she dies." Often she would slip Tom a twenty with instruction on how to distribute it. He followed directions carefully, generally enriching the piggy banks of his grandchildren. Since neither drove, I often picked them up and dropped them home in Bronxville after their visit. That kindness was more like a fundraiser than inconvenience, for I would invariably find a portrait of Andrew Jackson to subsidize the meager toll on the Tappan Zee Bridge. Their generosity was most apparent when Mary and I decided to sell our house in West Nyack and purchase a house to be built at Fawn Ridge in Stony Point.

Sig Jacobsen was an immigrant from Norway, and far from the traditional mode of contractors, he offered an excellent house at a modest price with fine workmanship guaranteed. When we selected one of the very last lots for sale, it was on the side of a hill at the end of a cul-de-sac. Tom loved the privacy and seclusion the site offered, although the driveway became problematic in the winter. Tom insisted our basement was useless without an outside door, and Kathleen believed that a porch would offer a comfortable spot for fresh air. Since Mary and I were concerned about the expense of the new house, they gladly paid for these two items, both of which ultimately added a great deal of pleasure to our future time in Stony Point.

We would often drive up to monitor the progress of the building, and Tom relished the chance to wander among the framing and wallboard, as well as the grounds while puffing on his beloved White Owl cigars. As soon as we closed on the property, Tom rebuilt a stout, stone wall from the debris that lay scattered after bulldozers and neglect had led to its destruction. He built the wall eight feet thick and perhaps four feet high. In the twenty-three years we occupied the house and owned the property, not one of his carefully laid stones moved a millimeter. I can't say the same for myself. I tried to build a retaining wall along our driveway, but the abundant rocks and boulders that gave Rockland County its name, never quite fit together as harmoniously or permanently as Tom's creation. Together, we also constructed a stairway from the top of the driveway down to street level to be used in time of snow or ice. Perhaps my expertise in stone construction may best be summarized by stating that I was starting to build from the bottom up when Tom politely suggested that we work from the top down. Naturally his suggestion proved very valid.

Tom enjoyed our half acre of forested land very much. Usually, he would light his cigar and inspect the shrubs and plants we had added. In time we planted almost thirty Colorado blue spruce trees that we bought in Orange County, but his pride and joy was a decorative Japanese maple that he surreptitiously planted when I was at work. He admired his handiwork and checked its progress every time he visited. The spruce trees grew close together along the edge of the driveway, until I had to cull one a year for a few Christmas celebrations. In time, the blue spruces grew tall enough to cast a shadow on my driveway and interfere with my solar drying power, but they also provided a shield from public view which brought delight to my fellow planter. The Japanese maple reached a point where every year several plants would emerge from the English ivy I planted with my daughter Maureen to obviate the need to mow the lawn on the side of the hill. I even have a descendant tree planted here in Massachusetts that came from the seeds of that maple.

Our house in West Nyack had offered many amenities that we enjoyed. We had space enough in the four bedrooms and adequate access to the bath and a half. What we lacked was the ability to work unobserved by our curious three children. The neighborhood also was virtually devoid of children when Brendan reached an age where peer companionship was essential. Dr. Medici, our pediatrician, suggested that we move to a younger neighborhood where Brendan might have greater freedom and companionship. One of the first things we checked when we inspected Fawn Ridge was the number of swing sets in the backyard.

Our five years on Foxwood Road held many lessons for us. We came to believe what we treasured most was our growing family. Mary and I didn't have much time alone, for we were joined by our firstborn, eleven months after our marriage. Brendan was a very cute baby, and he probably misled us into believing the ease with which new parents could adapt to their challenging roles. My greatest recollection was the awareness that marriage meant never leaving a car empty handed again. Brendan's birth also demonstrated that our time and energy were contingent upon his appetite. Sixteen months after his birth, he was joined by his sister Katherine. Katherine, unlike Brendan, seemed suspicious about the world she entered, and that every new face, every new experience had to be carefully analyzed before she offered reluctant acceptance. Unlike Brendan, she had some difficulties with digesting her formula and suffered colic for two months. Her sensitive skin and brilliant red hair set her apart for other precautions like sunshine and fabrics. In the meantime, Brendan had developed some orthopedic problem with his feet, and he required special shoes and a bar attached to the soles of his shoes when he slept at night.

While Mary and I anguished over the restriction the device seemed to impose on Brendan, he learned that his feet were ideal weapons for assaulting the ends and sides of his crib. He took great delight in smashing the heavy shoes against the wooden crib and raising a racket that amused him and assured us he wasn't wearing a torture device from some medieval chamber. After several months, when Brendan began walking, we were advised to provide him with special orthopedic but relatively normal shoes manufactured by Stride-rite and the orthopedic device became history before it destroyed the crib.

Within nine months of Katherine's birth, we decided to try a vacation in a seven by nine foot tent. Assuring Mary that campers were family oriented, we tried our first experiment at Calicoon, New York on the Delaware River. Our first meal proved disastrous. I overstocked charcoal and wrapped potatoes in aluminum foil, but I didn't calculate the temperature that our fire could generate. I also removed some frankfurters from our Coleman cooler so they could defrost. As we took a walk that induced hunger, especially for Brendan, we returned to discover that blue jays had invaded our thawed franks puncturing the plastic outer packaging and helping themselves to generous portions. Thinking that at least the potatoes were saved, I unwrapped the 'mickies' to bare a collection of ashes instead of sustenance. I suppose Brendan didn't mind the substitution of cookies instead of our planned menu.

That night I retired to our van in the company of nine month old Katherine while Mary, Brendan, and our very helpful babysitter, Maureen Conlon crowded into the miniscule tent. As soon as the sun set, however, the wild bacchanalia of college kids began. Challenged by the rapids of the Delaware River, they fortified their courage with beers and shouts until the wee hours. Our family atmosphere turned into a fraternity blast. Katherine didn't sleep much at all that night, and neither did I. In the morning our revelers were fast asleep, but we were all exhausted. I didn't expect Mary to be impressed by our experience and was ready to write off any further camping expeditions.

A few weeks later, Mary suggested we try again, and this time we explored the Catskill Mountains. We loaded up the van and headed north about seventy miles. This time Mother Nature would add a challenge to our sleeping in the small tent. Mary wasn't aware that anything touching a canvas tent leads to bleeding when it rains, so she piled many items against the sides of the tent, and we were soon inundated by a summer downpour. In the morning, she suggested we return to West Nyack and await more clement weather. We did that and were rewarded with fine weather suitable for a visit to the Catskill Game Farm. On the next day, we were supposed to head to Cooperstown for another session, but my van stubbornly refused to start or accept a jump start. A call to a towing company brought us limping into Tannersville where the trouble was diagnosed as a broken solenoid wire which was rapidly repaired, and we were on our way.

At Cooperstown we spread our soaked bedding and camping gear out in the sun and left for a tour of the area, especially the Farmer's Museum. Upon our return, we had another cloud burst, but kind, family-oriented campers had stashed our exposed gear inside the tent, and the hot dry wind of the day had dried everything out. Our experience was so positive, that we decided to extend our travels to the Thousand Islands where an international incident awaited us. When we inquired about a boat trip to Canada, we were assured that the trip would take thirty minutes, and the vessel had plenty of room for Katherine's carriage. What we weren't told was the trip back involved a circuitous tour of many islands and consumed well over two hours. The space for the carriage also was right above the engines and propellers which caused the deck to vibrate and reverberate with great noise. Katherine immediately registered her complaints about the circumstances, and Mary decided to take her below to a warmer cabin where she was almost content. The problem occurred when the boat returned to American shores, and Mary was ordered to navigate an iron staircase upon which she almost stumbled while holding our daughter. Mary refused to follow the captain's orders despite his insistence that the law demanded her compliance. Under her protest and his protestations, immigration officials were summoned in this special case. She explained her rationale, and the representatives of both the ship and immigration offered to take her to a doctor. Mary didn't want a doctor, just secure footing.

Despite that disagreement, our camping trip went smoothly, so we decided to extend it to Watkins Glen where we camped at a beautiful forested area. When we finally headed home after two weeks, our van decided to interrupt our contentment. Just east of Binghamton, New York, there is a long hill, and the van started to hiccup and belch as we began the ascent. We pulled off the road into a nearby station where a Don Knotts Barney Fife character promised to uncover the problem. He installed new points and plugs and sent us on our way. Almost immediately, the problem arose again. We decided to continue anyway and managed to eke a few more miles out of the recalcitrant engine. Later, when I took the van to our regular mechanic, he determined that our air filter was clogged from the dust and dirt of the campgrounds. Barnie Fife, or Don Knotts, became an unpleasant memory of an incompetent, but apparently honest mechanic.

We decided that our small tent would be replaced by a pop up Apache Trailer that weighed as much as our car. The van had no difficulty pulling the load, however, and we tried our success at Hershey, Pennsylvania, Lake George area, New London, Connecticut and Misquamacutt, Rhode Island. The camping served our vacation needs, until a greater opportunity arose. I proved as inept at backing a trailer, as I did in dealing with most things mechanical or electrical. I never did master the fine touch required for maneuvering the Apache. At the end of the summer I required the deft skill of a neighbor to back the trailer up our driveway in Stony Point. Artie Santangelo, with a host of neighborhood advisers, did the honors, but I was convinced that the days of hauling a trailer must come to a conclusion.

In West Nyack, the trailer wasn't a worrisome concern since our property was relatively flat, and I could pull the trailer through without any egregious mistakes. Our neighbors in West Nyack were also delightful people. Directly across from our front door, Mrs. Lawrence tended a garden that offered spectacular floral displays throughout all but winter time. She also monitored an essential drain that prevented flooding during heavy downpours. The Naclerio family moreover, had a unique arrangement for the suburbs. Louie and his wife Rosa had a modest farm where he raised chickens and had a sheep. Rosa, born in Naples and not too fluent in English, compensated by insisting on sharing the pastry and bread confections she created with the aplomb of a professional chef. She particularly loved feeding Brendan who became addicted to her cookies and treats.

The Naclerios had three daughters, Anna, Gina, and Laura. Perhaps because of her mother's difficulties with English, Laura didn't speak much, but Mary invited her to join a modest nursery school operation she ran for Brendan and Thomas Hynes. Fran would drive Thomas up to West Nyack and then spend quality time with the redhead who didn't want to be shortchanged. The Naclerios were very grateful and showed it in more ways than one. Louie became my personal consultant on any of the mechanical problems that might go wrong with the boiler, the hot water heater or any other appliance. Whenever I mentioned some problem, Louie would disappear only to reappear with appropriate tools in hand, and explain to the teacher what he was doing.

Another character from that neighborhood was Jim Conlon, a former paratrooper in the 82nd. Jim had a large family of older children, and he loved animals. He had an extensive corral where he kept a horse named Rio. Rio was a beast that wasn't above traveling across the road to munch on my grass or flowers. Jim said he wouldn't charge me for the consequent free manure. Jim had a taste for Manhattans and felt free to come down and try a few, generally finding my preparations inadequate since I didn't stock bitters. He, moreover, had a few guinea hens that made ungodly sounds and pillaged the excellent growth they discovered in Mrs. Lawrence's garden. She placed a bounty on the head of any guinea hen that might accidentally be crushed under the wheels of a vehicle. Among Jim's many children, Maureen Conlon turned out to be a delightful assistant. She was a babysitter who baked for her hosts and her trusts. She often stopped by the house when Katherine was born and asked to take Brendan for walks, even introducing him to trick or treating on Halloween. Poor Brendan staggered home with a face smeared with chocolate in his bear costume designed and created by Mary. When Maureen went to college, her brother Paul and sister Mary also satisfied our babysitting needs.

During our engagement, Mary demonstrated great income potential. After examining fish entrails from the Hudson River and scouring the local lakes for samples in the wee hours of cold mornings, Mary decided that she didn't want to invest the time and effort in continuing her doctoral work in biology at Fordham. She applied for seven school district jobs and was offered a position by each. Having taught from the primary grades through college, Mary related best to the primary grades, so she opted for a first grade class in Tarrytown. In contrast, my pursuit for a regular teaching job in social studies proved non productive on every level. A number of years later when I applied for a special education position at Clarkstown South, I was tentatively awarded a job, but I would have to surrender seventeen years of seniority, tenure, and take a pay cut of seventeen thousand dollars. My interviewer even had the nerve to exclaim, "If you were a football coach or taught band, we might do better—but a special ed teacher—no way." I thanked him for the interview and then commented that if I were to accept his offer, I would be aiding and abetting him and complicit in a crime called theft of service.

Mary only managed to remain at Tarrytown teaching for six months, since she didn't want to disrupt her class by leaving on maternity in the middle of a semester. In the meantime, I continued my classes at NYU toward a doctorate and enjoyed the opportunity to teach at Bergen Community College and the School of New Resources associated with the College of New Rochelle. My investment in

BOCES was primarily a monetary agreement where I would accept my salary for my services rendered, but I couldn't contemplate working throughout the summer with the same kind of students I dealt with during the school year.

Brendan's birth on May 14, 1973, followed by Katherine's on September 27, 1974 provided distraction from my education, and I temporarily postponed my classes at NYU. After arguing for reinstatement without financial penalties, I resumed classes and planned to prepare for comprehensives when we discovered that Maureen would join us on November 28, 1976. Her arrival changed many things. I determined that I couldn't continue school, work full time, sell our home in West Nyack and move to Stony Point. Moreover, unlike her siblings, Maureen had a difficult first year of life. She seemed allergic to many things, had a displastic hip that required her wearing an orthopedic device all the time, and slept intermittently. Despite my mother-in-law's insistence that Maureen's displasia must have come from O'Prey genes, the orthopedist claimed the defect was common among Northern Italians and East Europeans, neither of which were recognizable as ancestors.

Since she was chasing Brendan and Katherine throughout the days, I had promised my wife that I would look after Maureen during the nights. That arrangement seriously impacted my peace of mind and sanity. Exhaustion, weariness and the accompanying impatience taught us about the true price of parenthood. While her brother and sister seemed to enjoy the rhythmic movement of an automobile, riding in a car seemed to bring out the worst in Maureen's temperament. For Maureen's first ten months, she provided many challenges that neither of her siblings offered. Her movements were constricted by an orthopedic device that earned her the nickname 'the Turtle' by her less than understanding older brother and sister who enjoyed banging on her shell.

Thanks to our bicentennial child and her distracting behavior, we managed to buy a car we didn't want and tried to make arrangements for the extras in our house that was being built. Lesson one about buying cars and planning a new house seemed very basic, but it was beyond our capability at the time—don't bring along a squawking baby. A blond son, and a redheaded daughter, now were supplemented by a sister with dark eyes and hair. In later years, I used to joke that her impact upon us could have had a strong marketing affect upon birth control. After ten months, however, Maureen's personality markedly improved, once the orthopedic device was removed. She smiled and was soon walking and talking and demonstrating an even temper and fascination with life in general that made her an attraction to all. I sometimes wonder what Brendan and Katherine felt about this new addition to our household who changed so many things. Fortunately, the three kids grew close together and helpful to each other as far as I could determine.

While we still lived in West Nyack, Brendan was enrolled in a pre-school program at St. Thomas Aquinas College. To some extent Mary thought that Maureen's dislike of car travel may have arisen from the need to awaken her from her naps in order to drop Brendan at school or pick him up. It seemed every time she fell asleep, it was time to wake her up. Katherine was much more amenable to the travel arrangements since she was older. After moving to Stony Point, we found that nursery school admittance was more difficult than early admission to Harvard or one of the Ivy League schools. Attempts to place Brendan proved futile, until an old friend of Mary's, Annie Kilduff, offered to speak on Brendan's behalf to a group that ran a program called Crickettown. Through Annie's intervention, a spot was found for Brendan, and we began a dynastic presence at the nursery school. It was run by an ex-Peace Corps volunteer name Audrey Richeter. She was assisted by two very competent and concerned individuals named Phyllis Rabinowitz and Noelle Frank. Our three children enjoyed Crickettown immensely, learned many skills, and attended the summer camp for several years. While transporting the kids to the school, Mary also got to know many of our fellow Stony Pointers, a factor that played an essential role when Mary resolved to re-enter the workforce.

Within a year of moving northward to a climate that demanded a snow blower, a down jacket, and a chainsaw, Mary decided that she would return to work on a part time basis. Actually, she was enticed to do so by conversing with an employee of United Air Lines which had a reservation office in Rockleigh, New Jersey, quite close to where my brother Ray and his family lived. The positives in such a move were a modest increase in income, but a significant advantage in perks such as medical coverage and flight privileges. One could receive all by working only for a few hours a week. After her training, she worked the night shift because of my ability to help out with the kids immediately after school. An arrangement with a kind lady named Carole Sutherland gave us further flexibility since she agreed to collect Maureen from Crickettown or look after her whenever our schedules were incompatible. Carole's daughter was a little older than Maureen and proved to be a fine companion too.

Perhaps the greatest asset to Mary's new job was the opportunity to expand our horizons via airplane travel. The Apache trailer and its problems under my steerage paled in comparison to a world of adventure accessible through the airline. Our very first trip was to Paradise Island via Delta. Many of the different airlines provided mutual contracts for stand bys and we used many like Braniff, Eastern, Aer Lingus, TWA, Pan Am, Lufthansa, and BOAC. When the air traffic controllers went on strike and many airlines folded, one of the victims was the reciprocity among airlines for employees. Since we found flying so reasonable, our camper had become expendable. Soon Mary and I had flown to Acapulco, and the kids had the chance to visit Disneyland in Anaheim. On my fortieth birthday, Mary and I flew to Phoenix to attend a weekend at The Point. Our appetites were whetted, and we returned shortly thereafter to take the kids to see Grand Canyon, Old Tucson, Tombstone, and the Indian museums in Phoenix. While one may only stumble in describing the awesome grandeur of the Canyon, we also were impressed with the windblown rim of Crater National Monument, and the periodic ruins we encountered on a shortcut near Flagstaff. The remains of apartment house complexes made of adobe and red clay stood roadside with the snow topped mountains of Flagstaff in the background.

Tom and Kathleen were also invited along for a tour of California that began in Los Angeles and followed the *El Camino Real* or coastal road to San Francisco. I think Tom thought I was going to scrape his elbow along the Cliffside. He was especially anxious to visit San Simeon, the luxurious home of William Randolph Hearst, and he, of course, was delighted by a winery tour in Napa Valley. Most of our motoring was done to the music of our three singers attempting to pass time by repetitively singing "*Mamacita,*" a catchy tune they were learning in school. Frankly, I think they were also driving Kathleen to distraction.

When Mount St. Helens erupted in 1980, we decided to observe its effects first hand a few months later. We flew into Seattle, toured the space needle, and even crossed Puget Sound on a ferry. We had contemplated taking an inside passage boat to Vancouver, but the time and expense were overwhelming. In settling for a half hour crossing of Puget Sound, I did not realize how fortunate I was. During the entire 'cruise' I was beleaguered by incessant demands to stop and get off the ferry. When I considered what I would have paid to have this response for eleven hours and at hundreds of dollars, I realized there was a God who was looking after me. We couldn't get within five miles of the volcanic eruption, but the devastation was awesome, even from that distance. Huge trees were lodged in the upper branches of the trees still standing, but every trunk looked like it had been whitewashed to a height of twenty feet. Volcanic ash was everywhere, so we scooped up some on the slopes of Mount Rainier and later used them in a school science project about the effect of ash on growing vegetation. Unofficially, the effect seemed miniscule as the seeds sprouted and flourished in the test samples whether they contained twenty-five, fifty, or seventy-five percent ashes in the soil mixture. A special treat was meeting up with Dan Clancy who was working in the area on the construction of nuclear plants. When I had visited Seattle a few years earlier, I wondered why people raved about Mount Rainier, since I never saw it in the week I was there thanks to rain, mist and fog. When our family visited in August, the weather was clear, and the mountain loomed over the skyline with a vigilance and pervasiveness that gave credence to its presence and majesty in its appearance.

Mary's airline job made it practical to fly to Florida to visit Helen and Joe Clancy. We were impressed with their retirement environment and resolved to buy a house near them in Hudson, Florida. Shortly after that, we purchased a modest, three bedroom house and spent many summers down there. Often Tom and Kathleen would join us for a few weeks. When Mary had to return to Rockleigh for work, I was marooned with the three kids and my in-laws. Joe Clancy taught the kids about the pleasures of Weeki Wachee and the rope swings and tall slides. Usually, we would take a trip once during the summer to Disney World and the enticements of Orlando. Busch Gardens and Treasure Island also were occasional treats. Friends from Stony Point, like John Paul Gazzola, Jeannie Woods, and Patrice Kelleher, spent some time with us, as did my nephew Raymond and his sister Tricia, and John and Thomas Hynes.

I enjoyed puttering around on the lawn although I fought a losing battle against the dollar weed. An occasional snake frightened the life out of me, and I saw no alligators. After four to six weeks, I would drive my little diesel Rabbit the twelve hundred miles back to Stony Point. With my in-laws staying with us in Hudson, my children got to know their maternal grandparents quite well, and they also became familiar with my aunt Helen and her husband Joe, the elder statesmen on their paternal side. Floridian heat didn't seem much of an inconvenience. Perhaps the most phenomenal event occurred when Tom claimed he saw lightning approaching, and he outran it to the inside of the house. The man whose life began in Ireland apparently had inherited speed faster than light. For her part, my mother-in-law Kathleen, enjoyed an occasional luncheon date with my Aunt Helen where they exchanged stories of the times when they worked for 'Ma Bell.'

With travel privileges so enticing, we decided to try visiting Oahu in February, a season of crowded flights. Joining us again were Tom and Kathleen who not only shared our California and Florida experiences, but now they were headed to a place which Tom was sure was a foreign country. He was quite concerned about dietary differences, so he resolved to survive only on Bacon, Lettuce, and Tomato sandwiches no matter how hard we described the fiftieth state of the Union. Of course, he never doffed his midnight blue suit, starched white shirt, or stylish hat the entire time we were there.

Once on Waikiki Beach, our redhead, Kathy, was playing with pail and shovel at the edge of the water. As the water gently lapped at her toes, a contingent of Japanese tourists converged on her. Through gestures and indecipherable efforts to speak English, they indicated they would like to pose for pictures with her. Kathy indifferently continued shoveling sand and water, while at least forty Japanese slid into focus a few at a time. The Occidental with the red hair was a regular tourist attraction demanding permanent photographic evidence. Maureen's contribution to our first trip to Hawaii was the pain from a severe earache. My first stop in Hawaii was to a medical clinic where the doctor asked what the pediatrician generally prescribed and gave Maureen some amoxicillin.

After a week on the island visiting zoos, gardens, hula demonstrations and beaches, our most harrowing moment occurred at Hanauma Bay. Tom decided to walk along the perimeter of the bay which actually was the crest of an old volcanic eruption. While we fed the colorful fish in the calm waters off the shore, Tom hiked along the edge of the extinct volcano until his midnight blue suit and fashionable hat disappeared around the bend and out of sight. The tide turned, and waves now crashed with a menacing pace that threatened to close off Tom's escape route. Nonetheless, he nonchalantly strolled safely back to where we were. A trip to see trained dolphins and orcas was also a pleasant memory although Maureen's fidgeting led me to leave the demonstration early. At least when we went to visit Pearl Harbor, Kathleen minded her while the rest of us took the naval launch to observe the hallowed monument which appeared to bring evident glee to some of the Japanese tourists.

Upon arriving at Honolulu Airport for the return trip to New York and mentioning that we needed seven standby seats, the gate agent rolled her eyes and looked piteously at Mary for her bravery or her foolhardiness. By a stroke of good fortune or perhaps some divine intervention invoked by the consistent prayers of Kathleen, or even the guardian angel activity for our children, we found room on a return flight via Chicago and then onto Newark. The trip actually was an excellent experience and evidence of the rewards of Mary's employment.

Supplementing our domestic travel, we also had the opportunity to travel abroad. Mary and I took a four day all expenses included tour of Acapulco. While my friend, Pat Murphy, urged us to stay at the Princess Hotel on the shores of the Pacific Ocean, our package included a stay at *El Mirador*, a hotel that may have pioneered the popularity of Acapulco for vacationers. When we left the airport in a taxi, we also had two other couples sharing the distressing ride along cliff sides to the bay. I think the taxi stuck to the road because of centrifugal force and the unerring ability of the driver to dodge oncoming traffic. He arrived at the shore where a number of first rate hotels, like *Las Brisas,* lined a broad avenue across from the beach. That was not our destination, for as soon as our fellow passengers were deposited, the driver veered up an alley, driving under overhanging laundry and seedy looking houses. *El Mirador* was the reward for our sweating the probability of kidnapping. We only then discovered that the hotel was neat, clean, and presenting a totally Mexican motif, including few English speakers. We learned that on the ledges below our room the legendary cliff divers of Acapulco performed their athletic dives every afternoon. They had to time their take off to coincide with the arrival of an ocean swell or they would crash upon the rocks. Later, we visited The Princess Hotel and realized that we were in trouble when the luxurious poolside restaurant had a broad menu, but listed no prices. Our meager repast there cost more than our entire plane fare and accommodations at *El Mirador.*

The quest for more Spanish culture was still in our bones, for we also stood by for a quick flight to Madrid. I remember chomping at the bit while Mary's biological clock seemed to take more adjusting to the difference in time zones. My international *savoir faire* and knack for linguistic *faux pas* surfaced immediately upon our arrival at the Madrid Airport. When I approached a cab driver, I asked in my best English speaking imitation of the ugly American, "*Combien de lira?*" for our trip to the Cristoforo Colon Hotel. The cabbie stifled a laugh, no doubt, but he also doubled the fare I should have paid for the ride. Only once committed to the ride, did I realize that I had stammered my request, not in pesetas, but in lira, Italian money, using a bastardized version of French. Searching for a place for lunch after touring the Prado, I insisted we try a beanery called The Nebraskan. How more American could one get? I ordered a plate of fried eggs and sausage. My entrée turned out to be frankfurters and slithery eggs smothered in olive oil. Hungry, I devoured my meal and continued to taste the olive oil for two weeks. The custom of *tapas,* or late night hors d'oeuvres never quite captured our appetites, since we were generally too tired to stay up that late. We also took a bus tour to Toledo. The ride through the pretty countryside was pleasant, and when we arrived in Toledo, I was about to learn something about history and the city of El Greco.

One of the most imposing structures in the city was the Cathedral. Perhaps its most eye catching element was the collection of slavery chains that were hanging from the front façade. Apparently, during the crusades, when the Christians liberated some slaves from the Muslims, they placed their former chains like victory symbols for all to see. I also got a glimpse of the wealth and power of the former colonial exploiter of South America. The Cathedral had a display of the gold and silver monstrances, chalices, and other items that reflected the imperial status of a country that enriched itself from the mines of the western hemisphere and tempted the privateers and pirates of England to grow rich on their plunder.

While the Cathedral certainly was a highlight of Toledo, another building was more or less a tribute to its multi-cultural background.

The building was currently a Catholic convent, but decorating the walls were Jewish symbols like the Star of David, the shofar, the Ark of the Covenant and so forth, because it had been a synagogue before it was a convent. Even prior to its use as a house of worship for those Marisco Jews who refused conversion and were driven out into exile or into a grave, the structure was an Islamic mosque. The peculiar art style of Islam was evident throughout the house of worship. After the fall of Granada, the Moors and the Muslims were expelled, but each religion left its vestige upon this unique building in Toledo.

Typically, our trip to Europe was all too brief. At our hotel I discovered someone who identified me as coming from Washington Heights in New York City, after I simply invited him to join us on our elevator from the lobby. I am still confused at his expertise in the mode of Dr. Henry Higgins from **My Fair Lady.** Upon our return, we found ourselves involved in another historical movement. At the Madrid Airport where the police patrolled with machine guns, we discovered that a plane load of *Marielitos* had arrived in Spain on their way to the United States. Truly they were an unsightly group and unruly bunch. My sympathies for these émigrés from Castro's regime in Cuba were finely tuned despite my first impressions. At the time our President Carter appeared to be the humanitarian of the year, until America discovered that Castro emptied his jails of career criminals and his asylums of the mentally unbalanced.

My first encounter gave credibility to the later claim that Carter's generosity had been abused. One of the *Marielitos* approached me and uttered something in Spanish. I excused myself and apologized for my ignorance of Spanish. He repeated the message many times, and each time I excused myself. Finally, another passenger sidled up to me and whispered, "Ignore him. He is saying all Americans eat shit." I suppose that experience is proof that knowledge of the local language can be helpful. I then advised Mary that our trip back to New York might be quite an adventure if we didn't request first class. A polite inquiry led to placement in the upper seating of a 747 where we were spared the antics of our fellow passengers. I reflected that America would have trouble absorbing this small bunch, never mind the thousands that came to our country via other routes.

During the Falkland War, we traveled to Germany. After stopping on Lufthansa at Dusseldorf and Frankfort, we landed in Munich, accompanied by our neighbors Artie and Stephanie Santangelo.

Mary and Stephanie had taken a quick tour of the Rhine just a few months earlier, and they loved Germany. Since Stephanie also worked at United, she had the same flying privileges. We had reservations at a small B&B near Marienplatz where the people of Munich were celebrating *Weihnachtfest*, or Christmas festival. We tested the *bier* in several *ratskellers*, but Artie was desperate to go to a place called *Die Malthausen*. With secret information garnered through the grapevine of the New York Fire Department, Artie knew that a short trip down an alley led to a side entrance that permitted free entry to the *Biergarten*. What he didn't know was the entry was also an exit from the men's room. As clientele relieved themselves, the four of us headed in the opposite direction to a table where an oombah band was energetically performing. I was fascinated by our fellow revelers. At one table sat a gentleman who was reading a proclamation in the Hitlerian mode, and the only people paying attention to him were the waiter and me. At a nearby table, a woman stood up and leveled the man she accompanied with an effective roundhouse to the chops. At another table an inebriate was leading the band which basically ignored him. With two liter steins of beer costing about forty cents, and multiple choice of wursts and noodles, the meal was cheap and the entertainment priceless.

At our adjoining table, a distinguished tall man with ice blue eyes sat nursing his beer. Mary insisted I buy him a beer, since he looked quite like my father-in-law Tom. When I approached his table with my beer fueled fluency in German, more facile as time wore on, I offered to buy him a beer. By the time he returned from the bathroom, he understood my German and smiled as his wife kept saying, "*Nein, nein, ehr ist getrunken.*" When the waiter arrived, the distinguished gentleman responded to my temptation to show my children's pictures. He whipped out a selection of his own. In a photo dated 1943, he appeared with top hat, monocle and tuxedo. He explained that then he was the "*Uberburgermeister*" of Munich, a title roughly meaning 'mayor.' He also produced a photograph of his son who was in Brazil. At that time there was a great deal written about Nazis hiding in Brazil, and whether the remains of the butcher Mengele had been discovered. I realized I was in the presence of a former genuine Nazi from World War II. After he consumed his beer, he arose and approached Mary. After clicking his heels, he kissed her hand. Our visit to Malthausen was indicative of the enjoyment we got on our trip to Munich.

Since Artie was anxious to test the speed limits of the autobahn, we rented a car and headed to Dachau, Garmisch, and finally, Innsbruck and Salzburg in Austria. Dachau was very sobering and stark as we entered under the famed iron gates that read *Arbeit Macht Frei*. Only one of the barracks remained standing, although the others were outlined by their cement foundations. The museum claimed that Dachau was more a political concentration camp and itinerant stopover for those on the way to extinction. There were only two small ovens in evidence, and the museum claimed that only one person had been executed on the grounds, an RAF flier. Like much else in Germany, the Second World War wasn't publicized too much. We witnessed a photographic display of a cortege from 1943 in the church where we attended Mass. Far from fluent in German, I didn't understand why Stephanie was perturbed. She explained that the priest had blamed the Falkland war on the British and asked the congregation to pray for the Argentines.

Stephanie is a world class shopper who enjoys scouring stores for sales. She took Mary in hand while Artie and I toured the usual spots. We explored the museum in Munich which downplayed any American developments in science, and had German counterparts primarily featured. Despite the evident lead in space exploration which shifted from Russia to the United States, the Munich museum seemed to laud the milestones of a European coalition in space achievements. One amusing memory recurs often when I think of our trip. Our B&B was a single stop on the subway to Marienplatz where most of the action took place. In the *Untergrund* one went to a major menu board and selected the appropriate ticket. Naturally, Artie bought the cheapest one for the single station ride. Again, Stephanie was incensed, for Artie had inadvertently purchased a ticket for a dog. Evidently, in Munich, there are scales for many classes of individual rides, like senior citizens, students, children under a certain age, and finally for pets. Proof again that proficiency in the language helps. As a souvenir of our trip to Germany, we took two things home with us—a resolution to return someday and a complete Hummel Christmas manger set.

The first trip we took to Europe with the kids was compliments of Pan Am. We stayed at the hotel at Heathrow and took the tube into London to visit some of the features of the city. A death defying incident faced us instead. In her concern to help Maureen bridge the gap between the train and the platform at Victoria Station, Mary left her pocketbook on board. My efforts to stop the train as it pulled out of the station were futile, and I was directed down several levels of the massive station to tell my troubles to a station master, a West Indian, smoking 'funny' cigarettes, personally rolled. I thought my plane tickets and passports were traveling all over London while I was in the clutches of a 'ganja' fiend who was assuring me that the pocketbook would be returned. I panicked so much that the saliva in my mouth dried up, and I couldn't even speak coherently. Within half an hour, however, the telephone rang and the station master at Tower of London, responded to the APB bulletin. Thanks to a plethora of IRA bombing attacks, the tube was covered with bulletins advising passengers to report any abandoned packages, and that was what happened. Mary's pocketbook became a suspected bomb planted by the IRA and was almost immediately reported. It was returned intact, and I speculated that we wouldn't have been so fortunate in the New York subway system.

We finally got on the train to visit Mary's Aunt Annie and her husband Ted Hall who lived in the railroad stationmaster's house at Bearsted near Maidstone in Kent. Ted had been raised in a British orphanage and, typical of the options in front of him, like so many aged out orphans in England as well as America, he enlisted in the army when he was eighteen. That was just in time for his capture in Singapore when that stronghold fell to the Imperial Japanese Army. Ted spent the duration of the war in a prisoner of war camp. Rather than relate horror tales of the confinement, however, he delighted in telling that when the Japanese signed the unconditional surrender aboard the USS Missouri in Tokyo Bay, he played the "Star Spangled Banner" on his trumpet in the accompanying band since there was a paucity of American musicians available.

Our kids embarrassed Mary when they conscientiously removed the raisins or currents that Annie had baked in scones for the occasion. They did enjoy a trip to the local pub as Annie's guests, however. When we returned to Victoria Station, we were blissfully ignorant that the tube stopped running at midnight. As happenstance dictated, we got the last train to Heathrow and only discovered our luck as the janitors were cleaning and locking down the station at Heathrow.

At the risk of making this chapter read like a travelogue, I want to include a very special trip we took. We flew to Osaka and took a bus to Kyoto, and I lost all contact with my fellow linguists. Japan was a place where I felt like Gulliver among the Lilliputians. My bulk was more of the sumo wrestler style, and Mary's height was a phenomenon the Japanese were not accustomed to. Although Brendan hadn't grown to his full height of six foot five, the fact that he wore shorts distinguished him from most boys of his age. If Brendan were a phenomenon in shorts, Katherine was a spectacle with her fiery, red hair. Maureen was still rather diminutive, and her warm friendliness induced waves from batches of school groups visiting Nijo Castle. That was a preferable role to the criminal activity she inadvertently committed when she played Pachinko in an arcade. The proprietor started yelling at her and screaming at us. Apparently, Pachinko is more a gambling pastime than an arcade pin ball game, and Maureen was too young to gamble.

That episode was reminiscent of our first language encounter with the Japanese. I bought five bus tickets and was settling into what I hoped was the correct bus to Kyoto. The ticket salesmen called me out of the bus, yanked the tickets out of my hand, and gestured toward our youngest child. I had no idea what was wrong, until he handed me back four adult tickets and one child's. Japan was committed to following rules no matter what. Even as we were leaving on the bus to Narita Airport, Mary asked me where I had the passports. I told her they were in a suitcase in the baggage underneath. She insisted I retrieve them, so I asked Brendan to get the bags, and another incident occurred. The bus driver started yammering, and we deduced that no bag left the compartment without the corresponding ticket. When we produced the ticket, peace reigned again.

Frankly, I found the regimentation and obsequious obedience in Japan very hard to appreciate. With benign smiles on their visage, anyone I asked anything of gave me the New York salute—a nod of the head, a shrug of the shoulders, and palms extended upward to shoulder height. My lack of communication skills seriously impeded my appreciation of Japan. When we approached even the most narrow of virtually empty alleys, all pedestrians stopped, even if the traffic light was green. One had to wait for the music to start before crossing, and it was considered bad form to attempt to cross when the music ceased. For one honed on the fine art of jaywalking in the streets of New York, this seemed comical, even robotic, but we followed the dictum of "When in Rome, do as the Romans do."

Perhaps the greatest extreme of this custom was witnessing a utility crew which was working in the middle of a street. They would run out to the middle of the road as the music began, set up their barriers, and begin work until the music stopped. Then they gathered up their barriers, closed the manhole and retreated onto the side of the roadway, only to await the next legitimate opportunity.

One could not fault the service and attention to guests in the hotel. After encountering confusion over food outside the hotel, we determined to eat a brunch at considerable cost at the hotel every morning. Waiters and busboys stood attentively nearby, and immediately withdrew used plates or silverware. I contemplated how difficult it might be, if one wanted to pinch a souvenir from the table. When offered tips, room service and other personnel would bow and refuse any money offered. That would be a major contrast to the city of Hong Kong where we were heading next. Despite its organization, neatness, punctuality, and politeness, Japan just left me with a serious case of nerves, for I couldn't find anyone who spoke my language or could answer my questions. Any miscue seemed to risk a month's mortgage investment too.

After panicking in Tokyo Railroad Station and finally discovering the station for the bus to Narita, we were fortunate to get on a plane to Hong Kong. As the plane descended for its landing, I was able to watch the televisions in the nearby high rise buildings. When we took our first taxi, I discovered that Hong Kong could aptly be named the "City of the Open Palm." Everyone had his hand out, from drivers to bell hops, to the series of individuals who showed up with complimentary green tea. Exiting the hotel was like encountering a mass of hustlers, one of whom insisted that I needed a new suit, and he would make it for me. At the time of our visit, we were urged to shop in only government approved stores, because of all the scams incorporated by the mislabeling of the retailers, the improperly packaged sale items, and in general the shoddy workmanship of bargains. Yet the city was definitely alive, and probably the most beautiful setting I have ever witnessed. If one could survive the temptation of unbelievable bargains and shop cautiously, one could make great, reasonable purchases.

Besides a trip up a funicular to the top of Mount Victoria, we took a jaunty double decker bus ride to Stanley Market. What I recall most about the experience was the filth of the public facilities and the stifling heat of the day. Brendan saved us from both, when he located a side alley pizza shop with the unlikely name, *le Gato*. It not only had clean restrooms with western bowls, but it was also air conditioned. Maureen and Kathy revived sufficiently to make several outstanding buys in the hawkers' stands after that. For my part, I was surprised to learn that the Japanese had a prisoner of war camp at Stanley Market during World War II.

Our view of Hong Kong harbor from the upper floor room in the Shangri La luxury hotel in Kowloon was breathtaking. The huge harbor offered a vision of multiple boats from military warships to huge container merchants, from sampans to junks, from luxury liners to rusty tramp steamers. The busy waters even offered space for small fishing vessels that plied the nighttime fisheries. I never observed a busier harbor, a greater array of floating ships, or a more scenic setting than I did from our hotel room where we had draped washed underwear, socks and so forth for we each traveled with a single carry on bag apiece.

We had gotten visas to visit Red China before we left New York, for we planned to visit Beijing and the Great Wall. Serious unrest arose on the political scene and our state department advised staying out of Beijing. We contented ourselves with a hydrofoil ride up the Pearl River into Red China and a tour with a regular company. Our guide was quite articulate and informative although he didn't toe the company line. His one foible, except for his honesty about making money, was his linguistic inability to differentiate between L's and R's. At one point he told us we would visit a 'Flea' Market and my kids were excited at the prospect of poring over great knickknacks at a reasonable price. The 'Flea Market' turned out to be a 'Free Market' where local farmers brought their extra produce for sale, once they had met their quotas set by the government. Again, the heat produced visual emanations of foul aromas rising from the raw, unrefrigerated meats and poultry, as well as several large snapping turtles suspended on a clothesline.

Our stop at a decent hotel for lunch included a bucket of water which one could use to flush the toilets which weren't working. Along the road we witnessed that many of the citizens preferred TV antennas to indoor plumbing. I was astounded as our bus started and braked, dodging the cyclists and water buffalo that appeared deaf to his constant horn blowing. The meal offered us as part of the tour may have been delicious, but to this epicure it looked like an aggregate of shredded meats in gray, white, red, and unidentifiable. One familiar dish was an egg omelet which attracted the greatest attention of our tour group who preferred not to guess whether they were dining on chicken, beef, or pork. When we reboarded our bus, Maureen's offer of sharing a small stash of Ritz crackers we bought in Hong Kong was practically met with cheers, as volunteers offered to accept her largesse. After our day long bus tour and requisite visit to see the pandas in Canton, we returned to Kowloon via train with a great number of memories and impressions, most of which made us happy to be capitalistic Americans.

More adventures lay in store when we left for the airport at Hong Kong. Apparently, as the day and humidity in Hong Kong waxes, each planeload must get lighter, so standbys have the best chances early in the morning. We took a taxi to the airport while a brief monsoon drenched everything in sight. At the airport, I settled into reading **The Prince of Tides** by Pat Conroy and soon became oblivious of my surroundings. When I was interrupted by a polite, throat clearing sound, I found myself again bemused and befuddled by my language skills. A young lad about twelve, the most dauntless of a group of ten, stepped forward and said to me, "*Ahh, interwoowoo?*" As usual, I had no clue what he wanted even though contextual items should have alerted me immediately. He had paper and pencil, and a small hand held tape recorder which he extended to me and repeated, "*Ahh interwoowoo?*" Fortunately, Mary translated for me, and she advised me that he wanted to interview me. Once I got the message, I gladly put my book aside and consented. His first question, I handled honestly and politely for he asked "*Ahh, How you like Hong Kong?*" I was effervescent in my praise of its scenic beauty and bustling activity. He bravely went on and then added, "*Ahh, How you like the foot?*" Quizzically, I stared at my shoes, and he reiterated the question. Finally, Mary interpreted that he meant the food, not my foot. Frankly, I thought Hong Kong offered interesting cuisine, generally identifiable to this gourmand, and I could also find Western fast food outlets if I had to. My interviewer thanked me profusely, and I contemplated anew my inability to read contextual clues or struggle with the simplest communication problems beyond my own language.

We fortunately got on the plane and headed to the States, I know not where. By the time we returned to New York, we had consumed thirty-six hours and traveled on a dozen different aircraft, as we flew back home. I had had enough of the Orient and have no desire to return. I did enjoy most of the unexpected adventures once I learned to laugh at my personal ineptitude.

Of all our meanderings, I most enjoyed our trips to Ireland. After a hiatus of almost forty years, I returned to the Emerald Isle and visited at least a half score more times over the next twenty years. While I was deeply impressed with Ireland's treasures like Glendalough, the Rock of Cashel, the Dingle Peninsula, Kinsale and Cobh, Ceide Fields, Newgrange and Trim, and even the ruins of Moyne and Ross Abbeys in Mayo, my fondest recollection concerns the people. Without a doubt, reuniting with family descendants, whether in Mayo or County Down, Meath or Dublin presents the greatest impression of the Island. Over the twenty years, we have witnessed a vast change in Ireland's economy and standard of living. Membership in the European Common Market has brought a boom and many job opportunities that didn't exist previously. On my last visit, the construction and road improvement projects throughout the country were evidence that the past had truly passed.

I would no longer witness the challenge of 'Irish roulette,' a situation in which two vehicles, speeding on a narrow road on the opposite side to which I am accustomed, would be careening toward a head on collision, if one didn't pull to the side. What made it peculiarly Irish and especially challenging was the presence of a cyclist between the on rushing vehicles. The only constant in the formula was that the cyclist would continue on his serene way, while the drivers determined who would veer to the shoulder. Gone too, was the occasionally donkey, cow or sheep that made road traveling an unexpected journey. Roads were wider, interlopers fewer, and travel safer.

Evaporating too seemed to be the penchant for leisure and conversation. Irish youth were addicted to the cell phone, and many seemed drawn to the bigger cities. International travel, unheard of in my parents' day, now was a frequent pastime of many Irish. Even the strife in the North seemed to take a respite, although evidence of conflict always dogged our paths in County Down. The B&B's that added an element of Irish charm, now appeared to be repositories for transitional personnel from Eastern Europe, particularly Poland. The native Irish seemed avidly more interested in more lucrative pursuits than the hospitality havens that made their homeland so attractive.

Of all places in Ireland, my heart most belongs to the area of northwest Mayo called Kilcummin which retained the roots from which my mother came. The turbulent Atlantic always in sight and the more serene Moy River emptying into Killala Bay near the family burial site at Rathfran Abbey remain a vision of an Ireland recollected since my days there as an eight year old. Ballycastle, where my cousin Susan Tighe and her family enjoy a panoramic view of Dun Brista and Downpatrick Head, provided a haven and springboard to visit so many relatives. My Aunt Madeleine Boyd still lives in Carrowmore across the road from her daughter Mary Golden's family in Carrickanass. I enjoyed the conversations with my Uncle Bernie in his cottage in Ballycastle and the cheerful presence of so many young cousins. They still epitomize what I cherish most about Ireland. My cousin Brendan Boyd and his family have shared their home in Sligo overlooking the Lake Isle of Innisfree with my family.

Mary's cousins, Mary and Jim Vahey, have opened their house in Dublin to us many times. Like the descendants of the Duggans from Mayo, the Durkins have also visited us in America. Their kindnesses and help have blessed us on many occasions. It was Pat Vahey, God bless his soul, who introduced us to the passageway tombs and told the rollicking story of the evacuation of the losers after the Battle of the Boyne. Their ruins lie in splendor at Trim.

We also visited my father's relatives in County Down. Most are centered around Newcastle, Tullaree, Kilcoo and Castlewellan. We had first hand experience of the strife there, when the Orangemen firebombed eleven churches on the eve of our trip to the Giant's Causeway. We also felt the unnecessary expulsion from an Orange pub called Percy French, when they refused to serve us and advised my Aunt Helen to eat across the street. Helen had returned to the land of her birth after seventy years and enjoyed visiting the scenes of her childhood. She also witnessed the pride and arrogance of some of the inhabitants who painted the curbs of their towns red, white and blue if they were Protestants, and green, white, and gold if they were Catholic. We were advised to avoid stopping in any Protestant town if we could help it, but we had to get some money changed in Carrickfergus. The scorn of the parking lot attendant was offset by the kindness of other patrons there.

Our trip to the north was curtailed prematurely when our hosts, Marri Cowan and Martine Fulcher advised us to leave before the fever of the marching season intensified, or else to stay until it had spent its passion. When Mary and I returned in 2005, we listened to the television commentators describe our hosts and fellow neighbors as bandit country, or IRA sympathizers. When the newly established police force raided a house in Kilcoo to arrest a suspect in the largest bank robbery in Northern Ireland history, we happened to see the substantial display of firepower arrayed against a single individual. That display led to a counter demonstration where several cars were set afire, and the road to Newry blocked.

Marri Cowan and her husband Jim have only very recently been discovered to be blood relatives, they have always befriended us, and welcomed us into their house for any length of time. The Cowans provided a *Ceile,* or Irish entertainment, as a special delight. Like so many others throughout Ireland, our hosts provided warmth and welcome and often shelter. We visited my father-in-law's relatives in Cork, and I found myself stymied again by the peculiarities of the Cork accent. We happened upon a crowd of townsfolk lining the roadside in a rural part of the county and determined it was road bowling, a contest where winners attempt to hurl a stone from one town to another with fewer tosses than their opponents. When I attempted to confirm this judgment, my inquisition left me baffled. for I didn't understand a word the man uttered. Fortunately another individual used gestures that got the message across.

If the Celtic Tiger has been such a success in Ireland, one must be grateful. Yet those who cherish nostalgia and reverence for the past, must be somewhat rueful about the changes it also has wrought. Ireland has surrendered its diversified farming, and she has concentrated upon dairy, as the EU planned. Its countryside and byways are penetrated by huge machinery, and its youth find full remuneration in high tech industries. In essence, those qualities that made Ireland a vestige of another age are disappearing faster than the donkey. Yet it remains my favorite place.

In recent years, Mary and I have relied on planned tours, such as the one we took to Italy in 2000. I savored the blend of antiquity, Renaissance, and modernity that our Perillo tour offered. From exploring the remains of Pompeii, to walking in the Coliseum, to scrutinizing the Vatican Museum and the treasures of Florence, the trip was full of images and memories that left an indelible impression upon me. Unfortunately, it also led to a debilitating health problem, for I had seriously injured my back in Pompeii and had to have surgery to correct a spinal stenosis. With a notion of the simplicity of the surgery, I re-injured my back, and still find that my feet don't necessarily respond to the impulses my brain sends. More recently, my consequent cramping in the legs has abated, but it remains a difficulty. Despite that drawback, we followed a Collette Tour that traced the allied invasion of France and the path to Berlin.

Thanks, primarily to Mary's job at United Airlines, we traveled more extensively than most families. My children have wet their tootsies in the Atlantic Ocean from Cape Cod southward to St. Augustine's in Florida. They have waded in the Caribbean and sampled the waters of the Gulf of Mexico from many beaches along the west coast of Florida. They have cooled in the waters of the Pacific in California, Oahu, Maui, and even Stanley Market in Hong Kong. They visited attractions like Disneyland in Anaheim and Disney World in Orlando many times. They enjoyed tours of Universal Studios in California, and my son starred in a film presentation at MGM in Florida. Brendan was outfitted with an oceanic slicker while four hundred gallons of water were dumped on him, as he steered a fishing vessel in a tank. The subsequent depiction on video appeared very real. Several times they have visualized the wonders of Epcot and rode the roller coasters and attractions at Busch Gardens in Tampa. One would think they appreciated these adventures. Yet, our biggest *faux pas* was never taking them to the rides and beaches of the Jersey Shore, where most of their friends vacationed. As time evolves, I suspect that their opportunities may have been more memorable than those of so many peers and maturity may lead to that conclusion.

We have also spent considerable time in recent years in South Carolina where my daughter Maureen has relocated. Our daughters' peregrinations have led us to many destinations where we hadn't planned. When Kathy determined that Indianapolis wasn't a happening place and resolved to storm San Francisco, Mary flew to Indianapolis and together they drove to Baghdad by the Bay. Mary flew home and joined me in worrying how Kathy would find a place to stay, a job, and other essentials we consider important. With the good fortune of having several fellow alumni in the Bay area, she imposed on a group who were assisting in a rape victim's counseling center, and then she found a place of her own shortly before Christmas. When she discovered that her fellow roommates in this apartment were strippers and had an appropriate décor for their profession, she left and stayed with my niece Liz Walker near Palo Alto. Then she found a room with another Domer named Eric Hince, and finally Mary and I sighed some relief since she had also acquired an entry level job at American Arbitrators Association.

After several visits to her, some generated by mysterious health ailments, she found a studio, if one wished to use a generous term, in the Mission District down the street from St. Francis Church on Mission Street. Kathy later determined to get a graduate degree in City and Regional Planning, and when the University of North Carolina made her the best offer, she relocated to Chapel Hill. We became familiar with the Research Triangle, and then Kathy returned to a good job in Portola Valley near Palo Alto. She, of course, still had to live in San Francisco where many youths gave the city a special panache in reputation and reality. She remained in California until the infamous 9/11/01 and became so irate over the callousness of some fellow Californians that she wanted to come closer to family. Her first cousin, Tom Hynes, had been one of the thousands of victims in the collapse of the World Trade Center. The contrast of her affection and knowledge of Tom with the bitterness of folks who said the United States deserved the attack, induced her to come to Massachusetts.

Surprisingly, Kathy found several job options in Massachusetts, and has settled into a firm called Epsilon Associates. She enjoys her work, but several circumstances have led her to dislike the Bay State, and she has finally reached parity with the salary she earned in California.

Like her sister, Maureen also had a *Wanderlust* that led me to challenge her to cease her efforts to see the entire world before she turned twenty-one. When she enrolled in Stonehill, a small college in the Brockton/Easton area of Massachusetts, she set a series of events into play that made my life a little more nervous. First of all, she chose a band of students that reminded me of the casting call for *Deliverance*, but I was premature in my judgment. During the summers, Maureen managed to work at Yellowstone National Park which I found preferable to a fishing vessel off the Alaskan Coast. After one summer in Yellowstone, she also was admitted to Oxford University for a semester studying English. That of course, led to an impromptu visit to the intellectual center for Mary and me. In fact,

Mary began the emigration to California immediately upon returning from visiting the various colleges and attractions of Oxford. We even managed to connect with Jim and Mary Vahey who came over from Ireland to visit their daughter, and together we drove to Bearsted for a visit with Aunt Annie.

When Maureen returned to Stonehill, she obviously needed to live off campus, and that necessitated a car. After Mary and I visited her, we noted her bicycle trip to school and to the deli where she seemed to be majoring in Portuguese cuisine. We determined that more impressive wheels were imperative, especially during harsh winter conditions. Some of her friends, aside from the deliverance crowd, were rather unusual. One was a young Japanese lad named Akihito Kasuga. Aki, we later discovered, was a scion of the famous Mikimoto Pearl Company. His grandfather had developed the process of cultured pearls and had made millions. Rather than look like a millionaire, Aki resembled a destitute student. He also parked his car at our house in Stony Point for about six months. Another unusual individual was Nafissa Nasser who was reputedly a descendant of Mohammed and related to the ruling family of Jordan. After graduation, Nafissa invited Maureen and several classmates to her wedding in Amman, Jordan.

After flying standby to London and finding the city virtually empty while it mourned the first anniversary of Princess Diana's death, Maureen was lucky to find a hostel to stay overnight in preparation for an early morning flight to Amman. The group arrived at the airport in Amman in the early morning and found no one waiting. In true collegiate form, Nafissa had confused the arrival time and date. Once she was contacted, however, the airport personnel started offering the Americans coffee, doughnuts, and attention. Upon the reunion with Nafissa, the group was chauffeured to the royal enclosure where they were housed in a royal compound consisting of several houses on the shores of the Jordan River. A special chauffeur and housemaids were assigned to make sure the guests were welcomed in royal fashion. They attended three separate wedding occasions: a state wedding officiated by Hussein's brother, a women's wedding, and the official Muslim wedding.

The photographs brought back from Jordan attest to visits to the ruins of Petra, a camel ride in the desert, scuba diving in the Red Sea, and mud baths in the Dead Sea. House servants refused to let the guests as much as make their own coffee or pull up their beds. For two weeks the Americans were treated to a most unusual wedding celebration and the hospitality of their jovial classmate.

When Maureen returned, she began working as a waitress at Don Pablo's, a restaurant at the Palisades Mall which some locals have termed 'The Death Star Station' because of its unusual structure. Shortly after that, Maureen moved south to assist Kathy with a new dog, Lucinda, and she was employed at a day care nursery for yuppies in the Research Triangle. At the end of the year, the peripatetic Maureen followed her heart to be near the individual who had captured it. Maureen followed Nick Daily who would eventually be her husband. He was in Stephen F. Austin University in a dusty burg in East Texas called Nagadoches. There, she was employed as a bar manager in an unpretentious bistro called "The Flashback." Later she applied to work at an airline to acquire the flight privileges she remembered from her youth. That took her to Fort Worth and employment with American Air Lines. Typical of that time, she spent more time laid off than working, but she managed to get a transfer back to Raleigh/Durham to work in the lost baggage office. After facing one problem or another in a sequence of events, she applied to Duke University where she received sufficient scholarship aid to enable her to acquire a Masters in the Art of Teaching English. After one year teaching in Durham schools, she and Nick moved to Charleston where she has gotten a wonderful job at a school called Porter-Gaud.

While Kathy and Maureen traversed the country, Brendan remained in the New York area. His career at Manhattan College began inauspiciously, for he scheduled weekends home for the first month. After that, he imbibed the college spirit and entered wholeheartedly into the campus life. As a scholarship awardee, he was asked to represent the college at a series of public meetings or open houses. He earned additional income by manning the scoreboard at basketball games and some tutorial assignments. In the summer of his freshman and sophomore years, he became an expert at erecting huge party tents. Before he developed that unusual expertise, he started off by sounding a crucial all points bulletin for medical assistance. While Mary and I had taken a cruise from Los Angeles to Mexico, we received a frantic telephone call from several sources. Brendan had smashed his hand with a heavy hammer and Artie Santangelo, Fran and Bill Hynes, and anyone who would listen was summoned to assist him. Despite that problem, he enjoyed the physical labor the job offered. On his last vacation home, he decided he had enough labor when a blizzard struck Stony Point, and he and I shoveled our driveway for a combined thirty-seven hours. After that incident, he would find any opportunity to stay at Manhattan too enticing to resist. With pleasant, playful roommates, friendships with the math and computer faculty members, and dates with his future bride, Christine, Brendan provided little chance for us to put him to work at home. All was not wasted, for Brendan was selected as a second team Academic All American by **USA Today.** The newspaper honored him for his volunteer work and fine academic performance. He even tried his hand at treading the boards in an absolutely horrendous play production. His starring role permitted him to emote exuberantly but briefly since his sole line consisted of "Amen!"

Before he had graduated *Magna Cum Laude* from Manhattan, he was offered a job at Depository Trust, and he has remained there ever since. As soon as he had a job on Wall Street, he set about finding appropriate lodging, finally discovering a subterranean apartment in Edgewater, New Jersey. He remained there until his rent doubled, so he moved to the vicinity of Kingsbridge in the Bronx. While he has often second guessed his career choice since he abandoned his quest to teach, he has also wondered about the commitment in time his job demands. They in turn have rewarded him plenty for his ambivalence, and they also paid for much of his graduate studies. Every now and then he speaks of a doctorate, but family considerations have impeded his plans.

Most of my recollections concern my children. My assessment of their youthful days makes me proud of their academic achievements. Each has succeeded very well, some more easily than others. Each won scholarship assistance to college, and each attended the school of his or her choice. They attended Albertus Magnus high school by choice and excelled there too. My only reservation about their experience in the school was in the sports program. Frankly, my kids didn't seem to have what it took to excel on the sports teams they chose with my blessing. I didn't have the answer myself, for I believed they had the talent. My daughter Kathy excelled in basketball, but refused to surrender her time and convictions to the demands of the program. Instead, she turned to volleyball and was selected to All County twice and awarded a Scholar Athlete recognition worth

$1000. My son Brendan quit basketball when he grew tall enough and strong enough to be a factor. Although he had played on school teams from the sixth grade, he found the competition and rivalry too intense for his taste, and instead focused on the track team. His fellow members there encouraged each other and promoted a sense of team achievement. Maureen seemed to be vigilant, and observing what her older siblings encountered, she went directly to volleyball and enjoyed it a great deal.

All three found part-time jobs during their high school years that supplemented their athletic interests. Brendan held a part time job at Egghead during his high school years, and that job inspired his interest in computers and electronic gadgets of any kind. Kathy worked at Suncoast Videos in the Nanuet Mall and Highway Robbery, an unpretentious bargain outlet catering to Hispanics in White Plains. In the second year of college she also found employment at a Hertz rental claims unit headed by an old friend from Crickettown days named Sal Di Vincenzo. Sal used to claim Kathy not only could design and build a nuclear sub, but also command it. Maureen became a stalwart employee at Staples. She and Kathy also tested the challenges of working at Bear Mountain at the concession stand. Of course, the expense of these jobs and activities, like the Junior Olympic Volleyball program, demanded extensive transportation. It was no wonder that Brendan's winning essay that found Mary and me designated as the outstanding parents at Manhattan College during his senior year, began with the "Chug, Chug of the diesel engine," that signified our venerable Rabbits and Golfs that came equipped with adult chauffeurs.

In elementary school, Brendan and Kathy played soccer to no great acclaim. Maureen said she would only play because she wanted to drag her brother and sister to her practices, for she was exasperated having to travel to all their practices and games. Brendan's coach, Ken Collopy, was a nice man, and I offered to help him, although I knew little about soccer. I soon learned that the sport was like a psychological test for contestants. The meek and mild played defense; the self-assured and aggressive played forward. For the most part Brendan fell into the former category, and Kathy had a territorial sense about her participation. She protected a radius of fifteen feet. Otherwise, she might as well have stayed on the sidelines. At one point her coach ordered her into the goal where she was assailed by the opposite team. Not knowing about a goalie's privilege of touching the ball, she kept tapping it back to the enemy. Elvio Nardi, the man who almost single-handedly made North Rockland a soccer force to be reckoned with, blew the whistle, called time out, and berated me for allowing my daughter to be put in the goal without any training. He then approached 'Red' and gave her personal instructions on how to play the net. Elvio chided the coach and told him never to do that again.

Brendan got involved with Little League Baseball where the aggressive played infield, caught or pitched, generally without much evidence of special talent. The rest were consigned to the outfield or the bench. Some of his coaches were fair men and concerned parents. Others were too young or too involved in their own son's performances. The sport did little to enhance Brendan's self confidence.

An area where Brendan excelled was in scouting. Initially, he was in a troop from New City since he attended St. Augustine's School. When he switched to St. Gregory's, he might as well have asked to play with the Yankees. There was no room for him in the pack where his classmates were. Fortunately, a new pack was organized, comprised primarily of boys from Crickettown School, and Brendan found a home there. He enjoyed scouting a great deal, but he was forced to quit when an unsympathetic scout master wouldn't let him play basketball, and be a few minutes late for meetings. By the time that occurred, Brendan had amassed most of the badges and credits needed for Eagle Scout recognition. I, too, enjoyed his scouting, for I taught his fellow pack members the Civics and Religion courses required for merit badges in those categories. I also was invited to address two eagle scout ceremonies, sharing the podium with the then rising politician Governor Pataki.

A notable experience awaited us in our new home when I spent an overnight with the cub scouts. We were supposed to instruct the youngsters in fire safety and other such essential topics. Before we left for the camping adventure, Brendan decided to play a trick on his sister Kathy. He placed a plastic squirmee on the light bulb by her nightstand with the expectation that the light would project a spider's image on her ceiling. Instead of an image, the heat of the bulb was sufficient to melt the plastic, and it produced a horrible stench. Suspecting an electric fire, Mary and the girls evacuated the house, and about a dozen fire vehicles responded to the 911 call.

As the volunteers discussed which wall to tear down first in search of the fire, someone noticed the ash on the light bulb and applied some logic. Mary claimed the next morning she wanted to wear a bag on her head since she was so embarrassed. Perhaps, Brendan had a thing for electricity, for he also decided he wanted to see what would happen if he inserted a paper clip into the socket of his first grade classroom. The sparks and burn marks on the floor satisfied his curiosity and warned his teacher that she had better keep a better eye on the lad.

Mary had to switch schedules many times at United in order to maintain her job status, since the airlines were undergoing all kinds of deregulations and competition among themselves at cutting costs. As such, her tenure as the Brownie leader had to be sacrificed to her job, and I became her honorary replacement. Since I always enjoyed teaching, I did enjoy the experience of organizing and presenting material for our weekly Brownie sessions with Kathy and Maureen in attendance. Mary also volunteered me to be an administrator in the Don Bosco Basketball camp. The Salesians wouldn't allow Brother Thomas to run the program alone, so he had to find someone. Mary volunteered my services 'gratis.' For six weeks for two summers, I organized the league and the assignment of officials, timers, scorekeepers, and so forth during the scrimmage games. As usual, there was little burden to my job since it was a pleasant diversion from BOCES. I drafted Kathy and Maureen to serve as my aides, so their summer was pretty active too. The only embarrassing facet of the job was the necessity of filing an affidavit with New York State attesting that I had never been indicted nor convicted of any pervert activity.

I also enjoyed a three year tenure as basketball coach for the St. Gregory's girl's team. For the most part, we ran the gamut from competitive to pathetic, but our team motto was "Fun," when we were the latter. When we were good, I used to recite the words from Longfellow's *Maud Muller*, "Of all sad words of mouth or pen, the saddest of all are these; it might have been!" I was far from the most competent coach, but I believe most of the girls enjoyed the opportunity. My biggest regret was being unable to have each play equal time because of the competition from powerhouses like St. Augustine's and St. Anthony's who seemed to enjoy running up scores. One season when we were quite good, I received a telephone call from the teenage coach of Sacred Heart in Tappan. She wanted to forfeit a game that was postponed on account of snow. I asked her why, and she explained that her girls were so despondent over the overwhelming defeats they had endured, that they preferred not to play at all. I told her that my team had many levels of talent, and that we would attempt to win, but not by more than ten points. We played the game and won by six. My substitutes enjoyed the opportunity to play, although some of the starters wanted to enhance their stats.

I learned that each of our children developed an urgent need to remain on campus between their sophomore and junior years in college. Brendan claimed that he had the opportunity to work/study in preparing for incoming freshmen and hone his skills as the operator of the scoreboard for the basketball season. Not to be outdone, Kathy had to take a course, so that she could fulfill requirements necessitated by her switch from architecture into the Program of Liberal Studies. Maureen couldn't pass up the opportunity to prepare for her role as teacher's assistant for Professor Lancey. As the college bills mounted, so too did our use of the second mortgage on the house in Stony Point. Each child received an admirable education in the college of his or her choice. Each seemed to mature with the experience of meeting fellow collegians. It did seem that distance to college seemed directly proportional to the adventuresome spirit that each acquired. I suppose the bottom line should be the end result. All have earned masters' degrees and have found meaningful employment. Each has met a soul mate who has enriched his or her life with a love and a commitment that has nurtured small families. Each has brought honor and pleasure to the parents who worried too much about them.

Once all had graduated with honors from their respective schools, I could entertain the possibility of retiring from BOCES. Such a move would also entail selling our home and relocating, which we did in 2000. Mary and I chose to try Cape Cod as our new location. At best, we have some misgivings about that selection. One of our first impressions of Massachusetts contained the expression that we were literally 'wash ashores' who never quite fit in. Mary developed an interest in quilting and produced many highly skilled, artistic works. I preoccupied myself in amateur writing and mastering communications via e mail. Together we learned the intricacies of Cape Cod Hospital and the medical community of the Bay State.

Adding to my discomfort in our adopted home, I never could get accustomed to the driving peculiarities of the natives. It seemed to me that a driver education course contained such esoterica as how to interpret a yield sign as an encouragement to accelerate. If one doesn't speed up and ignore right of ways in rotaries or on major highways, one apparently is sent back for remediation until mastery of the forced entry is acquired. Another aspect of driving on Cape Cod has to be the assumption that there is never a dearth of space between cars, either by pulling in front of your vehicle, or cutting you off while on coming cars turn violently left across your path. I still don't know how my fellow drivers can control their shift cars as they maneuver into traffic while holding cell phones to one's ear with one hand and a cup of coffee and/or cigarette in the other. Driving instructors seem to have omitted any references to turn indicators. For the most part, they are non participatory elements in the car. When used, they are often employed as a feint or intent to mislead other drivers. To observe whatever a blinking light may indicate is to invite collisions. At least most motorists respect stop lights although stop signs enjoy only cursory recognition. No matter how fast I drive, I always find a Massachusetts driver who fancies himself an amateur automotive proctologist. I conclude that a driver's license in Massachusetts is also a certificate to practice proctology on the state's roads. Maybe I am too critical of our Bay State, but Mary and I plan to return to New York as soon as feasible.

Very few recollections are negative. Some are too personal to put to paper. Most, however, are the gems that delight my days of reminiscing. On a balance sheet, I can count my blessings rather than my scourges. My family, my neighbors, my acquaintances have left me with pleasant thoughts. I could find many more selections to add to this commentary, but I am sure I have noted far too many. God's blessings, man's acknowledgements, and my family's love have been the golden repository of my golden years.

Chapter Thirteen

Tranquility

I have no need to scale mountains, nor cruise oceans. I have little desire to travel to exotic locales or investigate foreign cultures. I feel no temptation to scour foreign climes and third world venues, or even explore the continents unvisited by me. If I never see Ayres Rock, Mount Kilimanjaro, the Galapagos Islands, Mayan ruins, Machu Picchu, or participate in an African safari, or observe penguins in Antarctica, I will not feel unfulfilled. My personal travels have left me with some ambivalence about the value of personal eye view rather than books or camera images. Some things can't be captured by a lens. Among such I number the Grand Canyon and Yellowstone National Park. The vistas presented by the majestic canyon to the human eye overwhelm any camera image conceivable. The interplay between light and shadow upon the buttes and crevices change every moment so that the image is more a motion picture than a photograph. In Yellowstone, the grandiose diversity of natural phenomena in juxtaposition to each other leaves one breathless. The canyons, waterfalls, cauldrons, hot springs and geysers, mountains, lakes, and fields inhabited by wildlife are so awesome that no camera does it justice. The beauty of Maui is like a professionally arranged floral display, but the munificence of nature on an epic scale at Yellowstone cries out for visual contact. While a camera might find poignant images of the disaster at Pompeii, only the human eye can measure the awful extent of the explosion of Vesuvius. The human cost of the Normandy Invasion is clearly evident in the almost antiseptic photographs of the neat, orderly crosses in the cemeteries of the American dead. A personal investigation leaves the same impression. The horror of war, however, is more deeply glimpsed by a personal inspection of the huge ossuary containing the innumerable bones of the victims in World War I tossed at all angles, witnessed through windows at Verdun.

Cameras do a better job using the professional artists' techniques in finding the maximum angle to highlight places like the Coliseum in Rome or the magnitude of the Giant's Causeway in North Ireland. The camera permits the viewer to imagine a huge expanse of unique geological formations while the naked eye perceives the wonder on a compact scale closer to reality. Although the personal visit to the Sistine Chapel is an awesome experience, the beauty of Michelangelo's Creation, Judgment and panels of biblical scenes demands a more serene, leisurely exploration and examination as in a perusal of pictorial replications rather than the cursory trip through the chapel. For the rest of my days, like John Keats, I shall recall a quote from his *On First Looking into Chapman's Homer.* Keats begins his ode with:

"Much have I travell'd in the realms of gold,
And many goodly states and kingdoms seen."

I find those words summarize my travels and my sense of fulfillment, and limit myself to the images and descriptions I find in books. I, too, like Emily Dickinson, have come to believe that "There is no frigate like a book." I am not driven to perfect my golf game or my tennis stroke, even if my back permitted such activities. Perhaps one might describe my attitude as complacency, but I prefer the nomenclature of contentment. I ask few things as I face retirement options.

First and foremost, I pray for good health. I have already realized that aging brings with it some compromises in return for extended time. My eyes now require bifocals and brighter lights. I have heard the threat of cataracts that haven't reached the point of medical intervention. Some of my family allege that my ears need some electronic enhancement, so that I can listen to television or follow a conversation without losing train of thought. My memory still retains vivid images and a multitude of data, but it just takes longer now to retrieve that information. I was accustomed to instant recollection, but I have reached a plateau or valley, depending on one's perception, where names, dates, events, or places take a circuitous route to my conscious mind.

On the other hand, my general health remains good. Thanks to genetics, I seem to be spared the problems associated with cholesterol, but I have inherited hypertension that must be medicated daily. My pains and aches are minor and generally associated with the spinal stenosis that compresses my sciatic nerve against some vertebrae. During one of my neurological examinations, I was fascinated to hear the brain waves generated by pinpricks, but they seemed to take a detour when it reached the affected part of my spine. I have been advised not to climb ladders, shovel snow, work with rakes, or carry heavy burdens. While I used to enjoy some of those past times, it is a small price to pay for a minor back ailment and occasional serious cramping in my right leg. When a doctor tests my responses with the famous hammer to the knee, he might as well be slamming my elbow, for usually there is little or no response to the stimulus. Again, I happily live with that situation and make adjustments like stooping over and using a claw, a metal extension of some kind to pick up dropped items, or buying foot gear that requires no lacing or tying. Good health generally leads to a better quality of life and that is my quest.

My greatest interest in my retirement remains my family. I also pray that my wife Mary's good health parallels my own. Together we have enjoyed a marriage that brought many blessings to both of us, and so far neither one has been burdened with the physical problems of each other. In that eventuality, we have a rather good long term health care policy to assist, if it is needed. We also have had no great financial needs. Our lives have been modest, perhaps frugal by some standards, but we have sufficient funds to enjoy a pleasant retirement together. If we do any traveling, it shall be on guided tours where someone else worries about meals, lodging, or transportation, unless we return to Ireland which actually feels like a second home to us.

I am also very proud of my three children. Their success in college and in graduate schools is demonstrable proof that our sacrifices and investments in education have fallen upon fertile soil. Their general lifestyle and ethical standards are also something we cherish. Their respect and appreciation toward us are gratifying and secretly pleasing although we think they may do too much worrying about us. Each of our children has opted for a different form of employment, a marriage partner they love, and a home they are trying to make as warm as possible.

Brendan has been working for the same company since the day he graduated from Manhattan with a degree in math and a minor in computer science. The interest that was sparked as a youngster working on our computers and his exposure to the co-workers at Egghead Computer Software engendered a great love of computers. He has wisely used that love and skill to achieve a lifestyle that is quite beyond anything I knew. Taking advantage of the encouragement he received from Depository Trust Corporation, he has studied graduate courses in computer science, information delivery systems and business at Stevens Institute, New York University, and Iona. His master's degree is from Iona, but he also has a smattering of credits from the other schools too.

At Manhattan, he met his future bride. Christine Jolly is a civil engineer who also found instant employment after graduation. She earned her master's degree in engineering from Rutgers and successfully passed all certification exams that have enabled her to work for the highway department of Rockland County. Her special interest is in water purification and sewage, not something I comprehend to any large extent. Yet one wonders if her true passion is actually medicine, for she has volunteered for the Emergency Medical Technician team wherever she lived. Maintaining certification as an EMT has remained a priority of hers for some time. She has all the paraphernalia required for her role. Radios, gear, jackets, and equipment are ready for instant use although her responsibilities as a mother of young children had made her temporarily take a leave of absence. Unlike Brendan, Christine also has an interest in carpentry, plumbing, electricity and other household skills generally unassociated with the distaff side. Brendan may be called upon, however, for his gross motor skills and heavy labor, for he has enjoyed the strength that comes from his height and weight.

Along with her interest in medicine, Christine has always demonstrated proficiency with martial arts. Without knowing exactly what she takes, I believe her expertise is in karate and Taekwondo. Brendan and Christian have taken classes together, and despite Christine's diminutive size, she has been known to toss her husband about playfully in simulated combat. I don't think Brendan is concerned, but he remains in awe over her ability to wield the mechanics and techniques that allow smaller folks to move what appear to be immovable objects.

On October 4, 1998, Brendan and Christine were married at St. Athanasius Chapel in Monroe, New York, close to where Christine was raised. Their reception took place at the Officers' Club at West Point. At the reception I discovered a new aspect to the roommates Brendan had at Manhattan. Each graduated *Summa Cum Laude*, and I thought of them as more bookworms than party animals. Derek Smith and John Sokolovic proved that their interest in books was sufficiently complemented by an intense participation in celebrations, dispelling any notion of one dimensional individuals. After the reception, highlighted by a full moon rising over the scenic early autumnal Hudson River, we carried on a post reception celebration which ironically was the grand finale at the Thayer Hotel on the grounds of the military academy. As the hotel prepared for renovation, we made sure its final party was memorable. True to our family custom, there was fine food, abundant drink, merry fellowship, stimulating conversation, and in the tradition of the O'Preys, an off-key songfest of Irish songs.

Brendan and Christine also provided great joy to Mary and me, when they presented us with our first grandson, Michael Thomas O'Prey on May 10, 2003. As a doting grandfather I could cite volumes of anecdotes about this wonderful lad, but I'll leave that to his parents. Michael is extremely photogenic and has a personality that instantly attracts attention. He has adopted his father's interest in computers and all kinds of games and electronics. When I have tried to take care of him, I must rely on his expertise to operate even their television. A special endearing quality of Michael's is his red hair, an inheritance, I presume from my father. Mary and I have enjoyed visiting Michael and his parents, and seeing him flourish into the personality he bears today. Most recently, he has begun pre-school, and I am assured performed admirably in a skit in which he sang "Itsy-bitsy spider."

On September 23, 2006, Michael was joined by a baby sister named Megan Andrea O'Prey. Like Michael, she has been a healthy baby, and do I dare say, very amenable. In time we hope to get to know her as well as we do her older brother, but her personality, even at an early age, indicates a child with many positive attributes. When one meets Megan, her smile lights up the room and her outgoing personality welcomes all. Her laugh is proof of an admirable sense of humor and an enjoyment of life. Megan demonstrates a love of music and rhythm that is very striking, especially when she plays with her many battery operated toys. She swings and sways to the music, and her head bobs up and down to the beat of the sounds. Many believe she looks more like Brendan than Christine but I reserve judgment on that. With Michael and Megan in New York, their presence has made our residence in Massachusetts less enjoyable, for we would like to live closer to our grandchildren and see them more often.

In 2002 Maureen announced that she would wed the 'mountain man' she discovered in the wilds of Yellowstone National Park. Nick Daily wasn't exactly a 'mountain man,' but Maureen claimed that she always wanted to marry one, and Nick was the closest she met in reality. Nick originally came from Iowa, but his family had to move to Fort Worth when Mike Daily, his father, was assigned there by Motorola. Nick's Texas roots have been fertile fodder for his future father-in-law's strange sense of humor, but Nick has always listened politely, if not attentively to my gibes. The New York chauvinist encountered the Texas patriot and bandying words have been the result. I claimed he was nurtured on a diet of road kill opossum and armadillo, mountain oysters, and rattlesnake.

Nick's palate actually is partial to the best hamburgers in the world, which come from Billy Miner's Saloon in Fort Worth, or so he claims. In truth, the restaurant presents a succulent hamburger with untold combinations of condiments to add according to one's whim, a judgment I can make with some authority since my son-in-law insisted we visit the emporium whose shirt he sports at every opportunity. Nick also favors any kind of barbecue embellished with Bush's Baked Beans in every variety. He so loves the beans, a consistent producer of what I term 'Texas ozone,' that he even accused me of stealing the last of his stash. Despite my protestations of innocence and virtually offering an affidavit of non-involvement, he has hesitated to offer me any credible evidence that my word is acceptable.

Despite my efforts to make the barefoot boy from Fort Worth, Texas comfortable in the Big Apple, Nick has decided that it's not his kind of fruit. On an occasion when I thought I would treat Maureen and him to Mc Donald's, Nick's uneasiness became only more pronounced. We dropped Mary off at her job at the Highbridge Community Life Center, and I headed off to a McDonald's on Southern Boulevard near the Bronx Zoo. On the way, I was stopped by the New York City Police, since unknown to me, one of my tail lights was not working. As I spoke to one officer, his partner crept along the passenger side of the van where the nervous Texan was seated. When the cop put his hand on his revolver, Nick thought he had lost every opportunity to die in a blaze of glory like the psychopaths at the gunfight at the O.K. Corral. Instead, he would die at the hands of a trigger happy member of New York's Finest. Immediately, his prodigious appetite fell victim to the stress of metropolitan living.

Explaining that I would fix the rear bulb at first opportunity, I was allowed to continue on my way. Little did I know that New York style McDonald's would virtually destroy what was left of Nick's hunger. As we approached the parking lot, the children's play yard looked more like a firebase from the Vietnam era, for it was surrounded by razor wire. Once inside, the ambiance did not improve, for Nick eavesdropped on a conversation at the next table. One patron was trying to purchase for a pittance, the bride of his table companion. Nick later said these kinds of things didn't happen in the Lone Star State. The cowpoke's alienation from Gotham only grew worse when he attended a Phish Concert on New Year's Eve at Madison Square Garden. After spending an afternoon trying to avoid the trampling herds of pedestrians, he and Maureen took refuge in Roy Roger's Restaurant across the street from the Garden. Upset by the constant reminders of the police to walk faster, he spent the rest of the afternoon counting taxis from the safety of the fast food eatery. That night, to make matters worse, he and Maureen got off the IRT in Kingsbridge and headed in the wrong direction. After a brief period of bewilderment, they realized their mistake in crossing the Major Deegan Highway and returned to find Brendan's apartment in the basement of a private house.

I think the lad from Fort Worth found New York City too intimidating, too crowded, too fast, and perhaps too confusing. I don't think he ever returned to the city again, nor has he ever verbalized a desire to do so. For my part, I continue to belittle Texas at every opportunity. I facetiously claim, for example, that the Texas archives are stored at Six Flags Amusement Park right next to the *Archie* and *Veronica* comic books which constitute the states literary treasures.

Occasionally, he will send a zinger in my direction too. Nick majored in forestry at Stephen F. Austin University in Nacogdoches, Texas. While I described his major as "Shrubs and Buds or Buds and Suds," I respected his work especially when he was doing medical research as well as forestry control. Recently, he resolved to stop cutting down trees and get a graduate degree in environmental coastal control, botanical medical research, or agricultural experimentation.

I told Nick that his descent from the trees was actually an evolutionary development few Texans experienced. Secretly, I was proud of his decision, applauded his initiative, and relieved that he would soon leave one of the most perilous jobs in our nation.

Sometimes my most intense efforts to make Nick feel at home went awry. On one Thanksgiving Dinner, I inquired whether Nick had ever heard of 'the Pope's Nose.' He denied any knowledge of such an item, so I informed him that it was the fatty section from which the turkey's tail feathers protruded. Nick mentioned that in Texas it was a special treat or honor to the person who carved the turkey, if he was given the 'Pope's Nose.' I said I would gladly accede to honor him, by giving him this virtually inedible part of the turkey's carcass. When I placed the fatty, grizzled tail on his plate, he smiled and said nothing. As the meal progressed, I noticed that the 'Pope's Nose' had been nibbled but not consumed. I discovered that what Nick was referring to were the two succulent cavities that contained delicious dark meat immediately preceding the tail. Our confusion over definitions led me to virtually insult Nick when I honestly intended to follow his family's traditional honor. Perhaps it also indicates my ignorance and myth about Texan eating habits.

While Nick was driving to North Carolina with my daughters and their house guest, Lucinda, a Bassett hound puppy, Nick was asked to make the ultimate sacrifice. When Lucinda got car sick, he offered his beloved Dale Earnhart Cap to contain her effluent. Only later did I grow to appreciate Nick's great love for the NASCAR driver and the sacrifice he made on behalf of a puppy that terrified him. As for Lucinda, we hosted her for about seven years until we had to place her with the New England Bassett Hound Rescue. Because of my back, our schedule, our increased need to move around to check on grandchildren, it was no longer feasible to retain this delightful dog. Lucinda, however, found a new home which she shared with a doting family, a fellow canine, and a house with a doggy door, and an enclosed backyard where she could do her laps in the famed Bassett five hundred tradition.

While I have cited several accounts of my gibes directed toward a son-in-law to be, I must credit Nick with clever, devious plans to disrupt my complacency. My comments last as long as sound waves, but Nick offers more permanent reminders of the glory of Texas. He has purchased a refrigerator magnet which reminds me, "Don't

Mess with Texas," or bears the Texas flag on another, but his finest performance concerned a souvenir he purchased for my enjoyment. He bought me a glass beer mug from the Stockyards in Fort Worth. Although I am not much of a beer drinker since it rapidly puts me to sleep, I appreciated the harmless appearing glass container shaped like a Texas boot. What I didn't know was that its design was meant to take the suds and slop it up one's nostrils if the glass wasn't handled just right. I never did master the technique and suffered the embarrassment of a nose wash compliments of my son-in-law.

On April 14, 2002 Maureen and Nick got married at Elizabeth Seton Church in North Falmouth. Their wedding plans incorporated only a modest display of dancing and music. The Daily's thought that meant a performance similar to *Riverdance,* but the couple were able to tailor their wedding to their particular tastes. Insisting on hiring a local trolley rather than limousines, the wedding party was chauffeured to and from the church in a vintage trolley. Most of the guests stayed across the street from the Coonamesset Inn where the reception was held. Before any wedding, however, I had to deal with some Texas idiosyncrasies. Apparently few folks in Texas use their given names. Sometimes a nickname or an alias seems as common as the armadillo. I encountered that problem when I was handed an ever growing list of guests Nick intended to invite to his wedding. I accused him of distributing wedding invitations to anyone who purchased a ham sandwich in the deli in Fort Worth where he was temporarily working. I kept getting additional guests after Nick assured me he had submitted his entire list. Perhaps an example may suffice to describe my coping with Texan names. I was told to send an invitation to a Teddy Shaeffer at a specific address. My careful calligraphy on the invitation was smeared with "addressee unknown," and I made further inquiries. Evidently, Teddy Schaefer had earned his name because he had a dog by the name of Teddy and his loyalty to a brand of beer had warranted a surname of the same. Teddy's actually name was Kyle Cushman. Many of the names were casual conversation addresses rather than the formal titles that invitations warranted according to my social gurus. I met a Sammy Sofa who turned out to be Samuel Davenport and a Gary Goober had another name too.

Most of our Texas guests, excluding the Daily family, were too young to rent a car in Massachusetts, so all kinds of lifts and arrangements were required. That did not stop the exuberant lads from dragging, reluctantly, my son-in-law now assures me, to one of the biggest dives on Cape Cod. I called it 'Nipples' for it was more a strip joint than anything else. Fortunately, the Texans and the local Wampanoags competed to a Mexican standoff in the potent potable contest. Upon returning to the motel, however, the youths thought that a 'Shivaree' was in order and disrupted fellow guests to the point of complaint to management. It was probably on an occasion like this when Nick won the honorific title of "Cold Molasses." He was awarded such a descriptive alias for his ability never to tip his hand in poker or expose the contents of his wallet. Yet he could amass an array of empty long necks comparable to the number of longhorn herds that plied the Old Chisholm Trail in the glory days of yesteryear. As to the truth to the rumors that he has more bank accounts than underwear, or that moths emerge when his wallet sees daylight, I cannot attest, for I have never glimpsed either.

On the next night after the reception, the fellows were relocated to a far corner of the complex, and indeed given a party room to commemorate the wedding at the Coonamesset Inn. Instead of a formal banquet, Maureen and Nick had opted for food stations and floating seating arrangements, and both features added to the enjoyment of the celebration. With unlimited multiple samplings at their disposal and a free bar for thirsty souls, conviviality was a notable element to the occasion.

On the morning after the wedding between the Catholic bride and the 'disparity of cult' groom, Mary and I hosted a brunch for those who had not left the vicinity. Over seventy guests arrived, and our extensive preparations looked like they would be unable to satisfy the appetites with the catered food, two spiral hams, a huge salmon, and special chicken dishes we offered. Brendan was sent out for more bagels and rolls, and we managed to assuage the hunger of our guests. Perhaps a sign of the party success of the affair lay in the personage of James Hanley, a fellow graduate of Stonehill, who had flown in from Portland, Oregon to join the celebration. James retired at night with a full beard, and somehow he awakened in the morning clean shaven and could offer no explanation for the alteration.

After Nick graduated, he and Maureen moved to Hillsborough, North Carolina where Nick got a job with Bartlett Tree Company. Maureen was struggling with permanent employment with American Airlines, but she submitted her resignation on the day she was selected as the 'face of the future of American Airlines.' Featured in an in-house publication, American Airlines took credit for Maureen's decision to work for a master's degree at Duke University in the Art of Teaching English. Upon the completion of her degree requirements, she and Nick decided that warmer climates than North Carolina's, summoned them so they moved to Charleston, South Carolina. Nick was able to switch locations at Bartlett, and Maureen found a wonderful position as English teacher at an expensive, private school called Porter-Gaud.

The newcomers to the Low Country quickly went house hunting. They found a modest three bedroom ranch within the confines of Charleston. Like Brendan and Christine, their newly purchased house needed some upgrades and a new paint job. Their most evident improvement, nonetheless, was in the grounds outside. Nick's skill and labor produced a much neater and cozier looking home in this eclectic neighborhood on James Island.

For the past few years, Mary and I have driven down to share the joys of winter in Charleston. We rented condos on Kiawah Island and Seabrook Island and got to visit Maureen and Nick often. Now the happily married beach lovers have added to their family with the arrival of Seamus Patrick Daily. On May 8, 2007 after a largely uneventful pregnancy, Maureen gave birth to a seven pound four ounce boy whose health and hearty appetite are testimonials to his Texas heritage. To a great extent, he also seems to have inherited his father's genes in appearance and temperament. Mary and I were advised to motor slowly southward after spending Michael's birthday in New York. We got as far as Luray, Virginia near Skyline Drive when we were abruptly awakened at 4:30am and advised to head directly to Charleston. Four hours later Seamus entered the world to the joy of all. Recently the entire clan of O'Prey's convened in Charleston to celebrate Seamus' christening. Thanks to his timely arrival, Mary and I had quadrupled our grandchildren within ten months. Nick also has been able to cut back on his perilous tree activity since The College of Charleston has awarded him several grants and a position as Research Assistant to cover the expenses of a newborn. Seamus has imposed his presence upon the Palmetto State offering a unique combination of Texas and New York attributes onto the cradle of the Confederacy.

After Kathy described herself in toasting the bride as the 'spinster' sister at Maureen's wedding, we should have anticipated a change in status in her life too. While finishing her degree at the University of North Carolina in Regional and City planning, Kathy lived above a garage in Carboro. To meet rent and living expenses, she also had worked at a local pub called *Yeats*, and in the city hall of Chapel Hill on some planning issues. She met a young man named Kaih Fuller through mutual friends. That meeting would blossom into love and eventually into marriage.

When they first met, Kaih was working as a *sous chef* in the kitchen of Michael Jordan's restaurant, Twenty-Three, named after his jersey number both while he starred at UNC and with the Bulls of the NBA. It was quite a classy restaurant, and Kaih assured us of VIP treatment, if we dined there. We did so, enjoying the largest prime rib seen outside Juanita's in California. This cut of delicious beef compared favorably, since it had been cooked to perfection and ostentatiously presented with the greatest care. As a special honor, Kaih asked the head chef to stop by our table and inquire whether everything was to our liking. Unfamiliar with the protocol of restaurants and head chefs, we learned that personal attention like this was reserved for Dean Smith, the legendary retired coach of the Tar heels and other such notables. Mary and I were impressed with the measures Kaih undertook to make us comfortable and honored. After that brief introduction to Kaih, I was to learn a great deal more about this unusual individual.

Kaih has an intense love and interest in local history, natural history, and nature. He reads extensively in these fields, and in fact is a voracious reader of many genres. Books, magazines, and articles are always strewn throughout his house attesting to the simultaneous consumption of knowledge about these areas of concentration. Focusing on the peculiarities of local history, Kaih often borrows books about the historical or unique features of the area in which he currently lives. I recall reading a few of his accumulated monographs on unusual monuments in New England, or an amalgam of odd facts about little known treasures most others know little or nothing about. In this fashion, I learned that Leominster was not only the home of Johnny Appleseed, but it also harbored the infant plastics industry. Chief products were the mundane hair comb and sunglasses of a by gone era, as well as the garish pink flamingoes that populate many suburban lawns. Supplementing the public library, Kaih also explores garage sales and other such outlets for unusual items.

Although not quite pleased with academia, he is bright and well informed through his broad reading. Besides his culinary interests which led to his perfection of cooking techniques, the appropriate tools of the trade, and a willingness to experiment with bland recipes to which I was addicted, he also is meticulous in many other ways. Recently, I discovered that he had separate cutting boards for meats, vegetables, bread and sundry other items. Each food representative was also stored in special places and warranted special knives, ladles, spoons, and so forth for their preparation. One of his hobbies was creating sauces and collecting samples of foreign products wherever he could find them. As the chief meal preparer in the household, Kaih offers a menu replete with palate pleasing entrees, marinades, and vegetables prepared with loving care.

Because of the intrusive, inconvenient hours demanded of restaurant staff, he took these same meticulous habits when he decided to pursue carpentry seriously. Since moving to Massachusetts, he has worked as a house framer and roofer, but his finest work seems to be the artistic creations he produces for gifts. He is truly a craftsman whose work is well done, and of course, well installed or hung upon walls. His patience and attention to detail show throughout his home. Every room he paints, every fixture he installs, every molding he adds, enhance the house he and Kathy purchased in Leominster. That same interest in décor has expanded to his front lawn, where he has added Buddha's statue and other paraphernalia that are appealing to the eye and the imagination. On Halloween, the little kid in Kaih emerges for he has decorated his house and lawn with an extensive array of tombstones, fog machines, and decorations that reflect the great fun he finds in the holiday. I am told that Halloween only takes second place to the devotion he exhibits to our nation's birthday on the Fourth of July.

Kaih approaches another of his hobbies with the same dedicated interest. He has a consuming fascination with photography. He has collected a number of images, generally viewed from an unusual perspective, and has decorated his home with his handiwork. Kaih also has considerable computer skills, and he exhibits the talents that reflect his painstaking attention to detail in so many other pursuits.

Kathy and Kaih selected a wedding venue near Stonington, Connecticut, where Kaih's family lived and where he spent his youth. They were married on October 12, 2003 in Sacred Heart Church in

Norwichtown, Connecticut. My former classmate, Tom McConaghy, who had left the Christian Brothers to become a priest, presided over their nuptials. I enjoyed meeting up with the Domers who were Kathy's classmates at Notre Dame. Many flew in for the occasion, and her friends Julie Wallman and Katrina Morris did some readings, while Kara Spaak was an usherette. A number of others joined in the celebration and the reception at the Seamen's Inn near the Seaport in Old Mystic, Connecticut. As usual, the fare was delicious, the camaraderie memorable, and the enjoyment contagious despite the inclement weather. Since we were not on home grounds, we partied afterwards at the hotel, and in the morning, I had a very pleasant breakfast in the company of my friends, the Schwalls, who had flown in from Denver for the occasion, and Ed Phelan, my perpetual tie to the Brothers.

After renting in Acton, the married couple bought a small ranch house in Leominster. In this former mill town situated between Boston and Worchester, Kathy and Kaih have taken advantage of the nearby mountains to indulge in another of Kaih's pastimes, hiking. On a recent trip to Ireland the outdoorsman insisted part of his introduction to the Emerald Isle had to be climbing to the summit of Slieve Donnard in County Down, as well as scaling Mount Carrauntuohil, the highest elevation in Ireland near Killarney in Kerry. Kaih has had to postpone his dream of following the Appalachian Trail from its northern terminus to its southern end because of family obligations. Since they bought the house which was in move-in condition for the most part, they have added a few features that reflect the skills of Kaih. Perhaps of even more importance, they had a baby girl whom they named Shannon Helen.

Shannon was actually born on the very same day, September 23, 2007, as her cousin Megan. One was born in Leominster, and the other born in Suffern a matter of hours apart. As Nick's mother Barbara Daily described them, "That makes them first cousin twins!" Like Megan, Shannon was a big baby, measuring almost twenty-three inches long and weighing eight pounds eleven ounces. She has continued to stretch, and often gets taken for an infant much older than she actually is. Like Kathy and Kaih, Mary and I are thrilled to welcome her into the family, and as Kathy remarked, "You have tripled your grandchildren in one day!" The past year has been deeply enriched by the platinum haired beauty and her 'twin' cousin.

Because the Leominster trio is quite isolated from family help, Mary and I shelved our plans to move back to New York. We are still one hundred and twenty miles from them, but that is only half the distance of traveling from New York. Every now and then, even if Kaih is working on the weekend, Kathy will drive down with Shannon for a day or two. Unfortunately, they have had to place her in nursery day care, but apparently that hasn't inhibited her at all. With a baby, however, Kathy has reconsidered her job which she enjoys but finds extremely time consuming. She is weighing the possibility of attending schools for nursing if she can squeeze that into her already imposing time commitments.

As I contemplate my future, I pray for two blessings: family and health. Mary and I can live on a budget comfortably, but not poshly. If we want to travel, we can make decisions as time and circumstance permit. Certainly we would like to revisit Ireland again. If we are to travel elsewhere, we probably will do so with a guided tour since our experience has been most positive. Unlike many who write out yearly resolutions or objectives, we have managed to live as the moment's needs dictate. We realize that family obligations, family occasions, especially where our grandchildren are concerned, are priorities that we hope we can address despite distance. There is little chance that our three children will somehow precipitate within short distance of each other. With Maureen, Nick and Seamus anchoring the southern extension and Kathy, Kaih and Shannon representing the northern reaches of our empire, Brendan, Christine, Michael, and Megan constitute our most likely targeted vicinity. The American way seems to embrace movement and extended families are vestiges of the past. We intend to enjoy the birthdays and celebrations of each grandchild whenever possible.

We hope to have the health that expedites our wishes. When I injured my back, I had little interest in travel, even of the shortest kind. Age has made us discriminating about sleeping accommodations. I used to be able to sleep on the hardest of surfaces. Now I must choose my sitting chairs carefully. We used to wonder why Tom and Kathleen Burke wanted to return to their own beds. Now we share that desire. Poor health can strike at any time, as we discovered on a trip to Ireland. Consequently, we appreciate the value of health and mobility.

I must confess that our hobbies are probably more sedentary than healthy. Mary thoroughly enjoys quilting, and indeed, has joined a very pleasant group of quilters every Monday morning. When she isn't quilting, she reads incessantly. For my part, I seem to fancy myself an author of sorts. I have undertaken this labor with some reservations. I am not sure I have done justice to my task. On the other hand, I feel a compulsion to write, whether I have an audience or not. Congratulations, if you have made it this far in this disparate narrative that some advisors claim should be at least three or four separate books. I don't threaten you with a further edition of my thoughts, but I don't rule out that possibility either.

As Alexander Pope so succinctly stated in his *Essay on Man*, "The child is father of the man." Many times I have reflected on that thought, and I find it particularly perceptive when analyzing my character convictions on morals, Almighty God relationships, and general personality traits. Yet I am convinced that St. Paul's 1st Epistle to the Corinthians adds a dimension that must not be overlooked. St. Paul famously wrote, "When I was a child, I spoke like a child. I understood as a child. I thought as a child. But when I became a man, I put away the things of a child." Maturity dismissed some childish beliefs. I suffered no trauma with the discovery of the myths of Santa Claus, the Easter Bunny, and the Tooth Fairy, but in the realm of thought and opinion, many of my premature assessments underwent serious reconsideration.

After a lifetime of freedom of expression and verbal custom, I have discovered that some of my conversation broaches the territory of the politically incorrect. My children have assumed the responsibility of re-educating me about some of my terminology that I had presumed to be objective, honest, and non-offensive. The neutral, ambiguous term 'sexual preference' is more acceptable than the descriptive 'homosexual,' for example. I have been informed that Asians are people, and that Orientals are carpets. Vocabulary from the past apparently carries many pejorative, judgmental connotations. Fortunately for me, no one has recorded my speech or comments uttered in years past, so I fear no skeletons in the closet of expression. Most ironically, many of the terms I used in conversation were certainly, at least in my mind, more acceptable than the nomenclature in common use in my youth. I suppose it all indicates that the English language is a living evolving organism, often changing faster than its speakers.

Aristide Briand is credited with the aphorism that states that anyone under thirty who is not a liberal, has no heart, and anyone over forty who isn't a conservative has no head. I believe there is much truth in what he says. Yet the terms 'liberal and conservative' are often polarizing and cited as mutually exclusive. I believe there is a considerable overlapping between the two, as well as areas where one doesn't contradict convictions, if one is part of each. Some may be fiscal conservatives, but social liberals, or political liberals and religious conservatives. I believe I have elements of all. The principles of one age often evolve into almost contradictory statements at a later date. One must be judged by one's current opinions.

Unlike the politician who has his nose in the wind sniffing for any change in public opinion that may jeopardize his re-election, the individual has the freedom to analyze any situation according to the principles that operate regardless of his age. Over the years my racial attitudes have changed. My toleration of once intolerable practices is an aspect I might not have abided years ago. My political convictions vary according to issues rather than dogmatic directives. My attitudes toward people and society have ameliorated considerably too. I cannot muster crusades to change a world that seems impervious to principle. The acceptance of the limitations of my power, the recognition of diversity of opinion, and respect for alternate assessments have all led to greater patience and tranquility on my part. My intellect and will are at peace in my quest for a niche in society. Musing on imponderables is just that. If there is any legacy I leave the world, it is in the family I nurtured, not in anything I achieved.

In conclusion, without Shakespeare's brilliance or even the irony of William Butler Yeats, I prematurely ponder my epitaph:

I began in innocence and grew in ignorance.
My faith, my life, and my reason taught me love and understanding.
A new generation left me with my one enduring legacy—my family.
I once was; but now I am a footnote in human lore.
You now are. Will you be more?

Printed in the United States
112806LV00008B/4-12/P

9 781436 305365